FUNDAMENTALS OF
LANGUAGE TEACHING

WHAT EVERY SPANISH TEACHER NEEDS TO KNOW

A METHODS BOOK
FOR TEACHERS OF SPANISH

BY

JAMES S. TAYLOR AND BLAIR BATEMAN

BRIGHAM YOUNG UNIVERSITY

ISBN 978-1-257-99425-0

CONTENTS

Preface v
Acknowledgments.. vi

CHAPTER 1   **WHAT MAKES A LANGUAGE TEACHER** 1
       IS THIS THE CAREER FOR YOU? 4
       PREPARATION FOR TEACHERS 6
       IDEAL TEACHER PREPARATION PROGRAMS 11
       GETTING THE MOST FROM THE TEACHING PRACTICUM 17
       REFERENCES AND SUGGESTIONS FOR FURTHER READING 19

CHAPTER 2   **ARE YOU CONVERTED?** 21
       ARE YOU "SOLD ON" FOREIGN LANGUAGE STUDY? 23
       FOREIGN LANGUAGE STUDY IN THE UNITED STATES 24
       RATIONALE AND ADVOCACY FOR FOREIGN LANGUAGE STUDY 25
       WHAT CAN WE DO? 27
       REFERENCES AND SUGGESTIONS FOR FURTHER READING 31

CHAPTER 3   **WHAT WE CAN LEARN FROM THE PAST AND THE PRESENT** 33
       THEORIES OF LANGUAGE LEARNING 35
       A HISTORICAL OVERVIEW OF LANGUAGE TEACHING METHODS 37
       PRESENT TRENDS: A COMMUNICATIVE APPROACH 43
       A "COMPREHENSIVE MODEL" FOR LANGUAGE TEACHING 44
       REFERENCES AND SUGGESTIONS FOR FURTHER READING 46

CHAPTER 4   **GETTING THINGS READY** 48
       SETTING COMMUNICATIVE GOALS AND OBJECTIVES 50
       NATIONAL *STANDARDS FOR FOREIGN LANGUAGE LEARNING* 52
       SELECTING A TEXTBOOK 55
       PLANNING 58
       PREPARING THE CLASSROOM 66
       PREPARING VISUAL AIDS 71
       REFERENCES AND SUGGESTIONS FOR FURTHER READING 75

CHAPTER 5   **STARTING, ORGANIZING, AND MANAGING** 77
       TEACHING YOUR CLASS IN THE TARGET LANGUAGE 79
       OTHER MANAGEMENT TECHNIQUES 85
       ADMINISTRATIVE PROCEDURES 90
       RECORD KEEPING 91
       MANAGING STUDENTS – CLASSROOM DISCIPLINE.................. 92
       LANGUAGE DECISIONS 93
       REFERENCES AND SUGGESTIONS FOR FURTHER READING 96

CHAPTER 6   **ARE YOU LISTENING?** 98
       THE NATURE OF LISTENING COMPREHENSION 101
       PRINCIPLES AND TECHNIQUES FOR TEACHING LISTENING SKILLS 105
       LISTENING AND VOCABULARY 107
       CLASS ACTIVITIES TO PROMOTE LISTENING.......................... 110
       BEYOND THE CLASSROOM 116
       REFERENCES AND SUGGESTIONS FOR FURTHER READING 118

CHAPTER 7   ¿HABLAS ESPAÑOL?...120
WHAT IS SPEAKING PROFICIENCY?...124
PRINCIPLES FOR DEVELOPING SPEAKING PROFICIENCY 126
TECHNIQUES FOR WORKING WITH BEGINNING STUDENTS 127
ACTIVITIES FOR PROFICIENCY 134
SIMULATIONS 141
INTERVIEWS...142
TASK PERFORMANCE ACTIVITIES 143
GAMES 145
ACTIVITIES IN PRESENTATIONAL MODE 150
SIMPLE TEACHING TECHNIQUES...151
PRONUNCIATION 156
REFERENCES AND SUGGESTIONS FOR FURTHER READING 159

CHAPTER 8   WHAT HAVE YOU READ LATELY? 161
READING AND THE *STANDARDS FOR FOREIGN LANGUAGE LEARNING* 164
WHAT IS READING FOR MEANING IN A FL COURSE?...........................164
DEVELOPING READING PROFICIENCY 168
USING THE "APT MAPS GUIDE" PRINCIPLE IN DEVELOPING READING.......174
TECHNIQUES FOR TEACHING READING AT DIFFERENT LEVELS 176
USING DICTIONARIES 182
REFERENCES AND SUGGESTIONS FOR FURTHER READING 184

CHAPTER 9   DON'T FORGET TO WRITE! 188
WHAT IS WRITING?...190
BEGINNING AND INTERMEDIATE WRITING OBJECTIVES 192
TEACHING WRITING AS A SUPPORT SKILL..196
TEACHING INTERPERSONAL WRITING 198
TEACHING PRESENTATIONAL WRITING 199
TEACHING WRITING BY HAND AND ON THE COMPUTER....................208
ASSESSING STUDENTS' WRITING 211
REFERENCES AND SUGGESTIONS FOR FURTHER READING 214

CHAPTER 10   WHAT SHALL I DO ABOUT GRAMMAR? 216
WHAT DOES GRAMMAR MEAN? 218
A COMPREHENSIVE APPROACH TO GRAMMAR INSTRUCTION....................221
USING VISUAL AIDS TO TEACH GRAMMAR 235
SOME TECHNIQUES FOR PRESENTING SPECIFIC GRAMMAR CONCEPTS ...238
REFERENCES AND SUGGESTIONS FOR FURTHER READING 239

CHAPTER 11   TEACH CULTURE? I ONLY HAVE TIME TO TEACH LANGUAGE! 241
WHAT DOES "CULTURE" INCLUDE?...244
WHY TEACH CULTURE? 245
WHAT CULTURAL CONTENT SHOULD I TEACH?....................................248
HISPANIC UNIVERSALS 252
WHERE CAN I FIND CULTURAL INFORMATION? 254
TECHNIQUES FOR CULTURE TEACHING AND LEARNING....................256
ASSESSING CULTURE LEARNING 270
REFERENCES AND SUGGESTIONS FOR FURTHER READING 271

CHAPTER 12   ASSESSMENT 274
TYPES OF FORMAL TESTS 277
FORMATS OF TEST ITEMS..279

TESTING THE FOUR SKILLS, GRAMMAR, VOCABULARY & CULTURE 279
ALTERNATIVE FORMS OF ASSESSMENT 290
PORTFOLIO ASSESSMENT...292
GRADING 296
REFERENCES AND SUGGESTIONS FOR FURTHER READING 298

CHAPTER 13 **CAN TECHNOLOGY HELP?**..301
THE ROLES OF TECHNOLOGY IN THE FOREIGN LANGUAGE CLASS............303
NATIONAL EDUCATIONAL TECHNOLOGY STANDARDS.....................304
TECHNOLOGY THAT HAS DIRECT APPPLICATION TO FL TEACHING 306
TEACHING STRATEGIES WITH VIDEOS..308
LANGUAGE LABORATORIES..310
USING COMPUTERS 313
THE INTERNET AND WEB 2.0 314
REFERENCES AND SUGGESTIONS FOR FURTHER READING 319

CHAPTER 14 **ADVANCED AND SPECIAL CLASSES**..324
WHY LONG SEQUENCES?..326
ARTICULATION 326
SPECIAL CLASSES 328
TEACHING LANGUAGES TO OLDER ADULTS 330
VARIED CLASS SCHEDULE CONFIGURATIONS 332
ADVANCED CLASSES AT THE HIGH SCHOOL LEVEL 333
TEACHING ADVANCED CLASSES 335
TEACHING LITERATURE 348
SPECIAL CLASSES FOR HERITAGE SPEAKERS OF SPANISH.............349
REFERENCES AND SUGGESTIONS FOR FURTHER READING 354

CHAPTER 15 **TEACHING FOREIGN LANGUAGES IN ELEMENTARY SCHOOLS** 356
FLES IN THE CURRICULUM 359
TYPES OF FLES PROGRAMS...361
SOME FUNDAMENTAL PRINCIPLES OF TEACHING
   LANGUAGES TO ELEMENTARY SCHOOL CHILDREN 368
TEACHING STRATEGIES FOR ELEMENTARY SCHOOLS 369
REFERENCES AND SUGGESTIONS FOR FURTHER READING 376

CHAPTER 16 **BEYOND THE CLASSROOM**..379
THE SPANISH CLUB 381
PENPALS / KEYPALS..389
INTENSIVE PROGRAMS AND LANGUAGE CAMPS 390
PARTNERSHIP PROGRAMS 391
GETTING HELP...391
GETTING YOUR STUDENTS TO FOREIGN COUNTRIES 393
REFERENCES AND SUGGESTIONS FOR FURTHER READING 394

CHAPTER 17 **EVALUATING AND IMPROVING YOUR PROGRAM**....................................397
EVALUATING YOUR TOTAL PROGRAM 399
EVALUATING YOUR SCHOOL'S INSTRUCTIONAL PROGRAM 400
ARTICULATION 403
HOW DO YOU GET HELP FOR YOUR PROGRAM?....................................404
BUILDING YOUR PROGRAM..412
REFERENCES AND SUGGESTIONS FOR FURTHER READING 419

CHAPTER 18 **EVALUATING AND IMPROVING YOURSELF AS A TEACHER** 423
EVALUATING AN INDIVIDUAL TEACHER 425
HOW DO WE GET HELP FOR PERSONAL IMPROVEMENT?............................427
PERSONAL IMPROVEMENT 430
YOUR RELATIONSHIP WITH YOUR STUDENTS 435
IMPROVING YOUR PERSONAL LANGUAGE PROFICIENCY 435
COMBATING STRESS AND "BURN-OUT" 439
REFERENCES AND SUGGESTIONS FOR FURTHER READING 441

APPENDICES
A. GUIDE FOR WORKING WITH ADMINISTRATORS 443
B. GUIDE FOR WORKING WITH COUNSELORS.................................448
C. OTHER BOOKS BY JAMES S. TAYLOR 450

PREFACE

This book is the product of many years of teaching foreign languages in the classroom. We put it together because of a long-perceived need for a book of this type. True, there are numerous "methods" books available, but some of them consist entirely of theoretical discussions about innovative approaches, while others are restricted to the narrow confines of just one theory or method. Even of the best methods books that have become available in recent years, few if any address the process and qualifications for becoming a language teacher, advocacy for foreign language programs, the needs of advanced and special classes, out-of-class activities, and professional development for teachers.

We have tried to make this a complete guide or handbook that covers all areas of language teaching and includes sound principles and successful techniques from all methods and approaches. We have seen many "new" approaches come and go and have seen much that is good in all of them. Rather than advocate a dogmatic adherence to one method or approach, we advocate a flexible position that allows for versatility and creativity on the part of each individual teacher. While we have included theoretical considerations here, we look at theory not as an end in itself, but how it can be applied practically in the classroom. Because we are convinced that what classroom language teachers and especially **prospective language teachers in their pre-service training** need is a solid arsenal of tried and proven principles and techniques which have had extensive use in actual, normal classroom situations and have been shown to bring success, our major emphasis will be on sound principles, practical ideas, and proven methods.

We envision this book as a handbook, a key to effective teaching. First, it will be useful to individual teachers, especially those who are beginning their teaching career. It will give them a solid base of reliable techniques that will allow them to teach in their novice years with confidence and purpose. Then later, they can explore the numerous theories and hypotheses and see them from a real-life perspective.

The book will also serve as a valuable resource to experienced teachers who are looking for fresh, vital, and exciting ideas to liven up their classes, to "recharge" those who are going through the doldrums of "burnout," or to help some perhaps discover why they are not succeeding in some areas of their teaching. After many years of experience with teacher committees working on district curriculum guides and state-level courses of study, we have found that even experienced teachers crave new ideas and approaches, with lots of practical help. We have found that seasoned teachers seldom, if ever, complain about over-simplification when they're collecting practical ideas. The book will also provide them a large selection of possible solutions to some of the problems they may be experiencing.

Finally, the book will be an ideal text for methods classes. Although students who are training to be teachers will eventually need to develop their own philosophy of teaching and their own teaching improvement plan, this book will get them well on their way. We guarantee that if they work conscientiously through these chapters, they will enter the classroom with confidence, even eagerness, to lead their students on the adventure of learning a foreign language.

Although this book has been specifically prepared for Spanish teachers, the underlying concepts, methods, and techniques we present can by used in teaching any language. Teachers of other languages need only adapt the materials to the unique needs of the language they teach and to focus our resources and suggestions on their specific language.

Acknowledgements

Our own teaching experience in the schools and colleges has been the primary source for the content of this book. For this reason we would like to thank our own language students for all they have taught us. The best preparation for teaching is in the practice itself.

The training of teachers has contributed much to our insights and to our repertoire of ideas and procedures for helping people get a second language inside them. Over the many years of experience as cooperating teachers and as college supervisors in student teaching programs, we have gained a great deal from the student teachers we have taught and observed. We express our gratitude to them and to the cooperating teachers and administrators who on occasions have taught us directly as well as indirectly. Closely akin to the experience with student teachers has been our experience in the training programs and supervision of teaching assistants or graduate instructors on the college level. These outstanding young people are especially creative and energetic and have added much to our own teaching.

Ideas from colleagues are often hard to pin down. We are a composite of all the associations and discussions we've had. We recognize that there are very few totally original ideas. Many of the ideas and tips contained in the book are our version or our personal refinement of techniques and procedures that have been around for decades (or perhaps, centuries); there is indeed "nothing new under the sun." We are constantly amazed at how many of our own truly original ideas get into other people's writings, a hazard of too long a time of putting off publishing our ideas.

Therefore, we dedicate this book to our own language students, the students we have trained in methods classes, and the practicing teachers we have worked with in schools and workshops. To all language teachers at all levels--our colleagues.

James S. Taylor
Paul F. Luckau
Brigham Young University, 1996

Comments on the Revised Edition

We have been gratified by the success this book has met with in the past 15 years. We knew at the time we completed the first edition that it would be soon outdated and would need many changes and additions. The untimely death of Professor Luckau, along with a myriad other activities and responsibilities have postponed that revision, but thanks to the urging of our colleagues from Brigham Young University, and Spanish teachers across the country, we have been motivated to revise, update, and add many new materials. We express sincere gratitude to Deanna Taylor, Teri Taylor Griffin and Kathy Taylor, without whom this revision would not have taken place. Many of the drawings in this book were done by them. Professors Nieves Pérez Knapp and Cherice Montgomery, of the BYU Department of Spanish and Portuguese, made significant contributions. The realities of life haven't changed; this new edition will soon need its own revision. That will have to be left to someone else.

James S. Taylor
Blair Bateman
Brigham Young University, 2011

CHAPTER ONE

WHAT MAKES A LANGUAGE TEACHER?

YOUR OBJECTIVES FOR THIS CHAPTER ARE TO:

1. IDENTIFY THE QUALITIES THAT SHOULD BE PRESENT IN SUCCESSFUL FOREIGN LANGUAGE TEACHERS.

2. SUMMARIZE GUIDELINES SET UP BY PROFESSIONAL ORGANIZATIONS FOR THE DEVELOPMENT OF FOREIGN LANGUAGE TEACHERS.

3. DESCRIBE IN DETAIL "IDEAL" FOREIGN LANGUAGE TEACHER DEVELOPMENT PROGRAMS AT THE ELEMENTARY AND SECONDARY LEVELS.

4. SUMMARIZE WAYS OF GETTING THE MOST OUT OF THE TEACHING PRACTICUM.

5. PREPARE YOURSELF FOR GETTING A JOB AS A LANGUAGE TEACHER.

6. ASSESS YOUR OWN MOTIVATIONS AND PREPARATION FOR BECOMING A LANGUAGE TEACHER.

Look Who's Teaching Spanish!

Mr. Downs stepped into the principal's office with a quizzical look on his face. "You wanted to talk to me, Mr. Dudley?" he asked.

"I'll come right to the point," the principal answered. "I know you lived in Mexico for a couple of years and that you speak some Spanish. Since Miss Gomez will be leaving us this spring, I would like you to teach some Spanish classes next fall."

Mr. Downs was flabbergasted. He was the football coach! Along with his P.E. classes he had taught some health classes, but that was his minor in college. He had absolutely no idea about how to teach a foreign language. It was true that he had spoken Spanish quite well at one time, but that was ten years ago, and he hadn't used it since he had returned to college. "I'm not sure I can do it, Mr. Dudley. I've never taught a language before, and my Spanish is pretty rusty."

"I don't think there will be any problem," replied Dudley. "If you can speak it, you can teach it. Mr. Larson, the other Spanish teacher, can help you with ideas. This way I won't have to hire another teacher, and we'll get someone to help in the drama department."

~~~~~

Miss Kyutee could hardly wait for school to start. Her first year of teaching had been a lot of work but she felt like it had been a success. One thing for sure was that fourth grade was right for her. This year, however, she had some things she wanted to change. She just needed to come up with more motivational type activities. That is why she was so excited about her plan to teach Spanish. She was positive that the students would love it and be as motivated as she had been during the two semesters she had studied Spanish at the University.

Miss K. had always intended to take more Spanish, and even visit a Spanish speaking country, but she had decided to finish college, teach a few years, and then take a trip south of the border. It was true that she still made a lot of errors when she tried to use the language and her vocabulary was quite limited, but she reminded herself that that wasn't too important at the elementary level. Besides, the students would never notice.

Emiliano Zapata was proud of his heritage. Although his parents had fled Cuba when he was a young boy, and he had been raised in Miami, he still considered himself a Cuban. He was especially proud of his use of the language. He had always spoken it with his family and friends and made sure that he read Spanish newspapers and magazines almost daily. When he enrolled at the local university, he had taken several Spanish literature courses and had always been the top student. He found that he could easily impress the professors since he could express himself much better than the poor "gringos" who still made millions of mistakes and had a very limited vocabulary.

Emiliano had been appalled when he visited the class of an American friend who had been hired as a teaching assistant. His friend's pronunciation was not good, and he made many mistakes as he taught. The students seemed to like him, and he was good at explaining grammar, but he still had a long way to go with the language.

As Emiliano made an appointment with the chairman of the Spanish Department, he mentally rehearsed what he was going to say. "What do I have to do to teach beginning classes here in the Spanish department? I can handle the language so much better than any of your T.A.'s, and my pronunciation is native. You need teachers who can speak the language."

~~~~

Virginia and Madeleine were ecstatic. Dr. Theo Rettich, the protégé of the greatest Spanish linguist in the country, had been hired by the university and would be teaching their linguistics class.

As the semester progressed, however, they became more and more disillusioned. Dr. Rettich would come to class, sit down at a desk and read his lecture notes. Seldom would he interact with the class, and it never occurred to him to illustrate anything on the chalkboard. Once during a lecture, as he was reading his notes, Dr. Rettich stopped, and muttered to himself, then went back over his notes trying to solve a problem which had suddenly become obvious to him. After several minutes of painful silence, he mumbled: "This is not correct," and stood up and left the class.

CHAPTER ONE

WHAT MAKES A LANGUAGE TEACHER

> **If to do were as easy as to know what were good to do, chapels had been churches, and poor men's cottages princes' palaces. It's a good divine that follows its own instruction. I would rather teach twenty what were good to be done than be one of the twenty to follow mine own teachings.**
>
> *The Merchant of Venice* —**William Shakespeare**

So you want to be a *foreign language teacher*? Why? Is it because that career sounds stimulating and "exotic" and conjures up visions of traveling to exciting new places, talking to important, fascinating people, and eating delicious new food? Is it because at some point in your life you learned a second language and liked it so much that you wanted others to have the same experience? Before you jump headlong into this profession, you had better give it a long hard look to see if it's really what you want to spend doing the rest of your life.

IS THIS CAREER FOR YOU?

First of all, you must decide if you really want to be a *teacher*. Teaching is often referred to as the "noblest" of professions, but it can also be frustrating in a number of ways. You must be resigned to the fact that most of your rewards will come from the satisfaction you get from the effect you will have in the lives of your students and not from monetary gains.

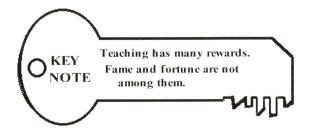

KEY NOTE — Teaching has many rewards. Fame and fortune are not among them.

You should know that teaching is not an eight to five kind of job that you can forget about in the evening when you return home. More often than not, teachers take assignments home at night to correct, and spend weekends and much of their own money on materials and visual aids.

Teachers cannot be mass produced as if they were machines coming off an assembly line. Each one is a unique individual who brings different qualities, talents, experiences, and attitudes to the task. It is vital that you never lose sight of the fact that the process of becoming a teacher is a partnership endeavor between *you* and the developing institution. They don't make you a teacher—you become a teacher. This means a concentrated, long-range effort on your part to develop the talents and skills that will make you successful. Since human behavior is not an exact science, it is extremely difficult to pinpoint what makes good teachers, but after years of study, research, and experience, we have a number of ideas about what features are present. However, the teacher–developing institution cannot simply imbed those qualities in you. It is necessary for you to be personally very active in the process. The ideas, helps, procedures, methods, approaches, techniques and strategies presented in your training need to be seized enthusiastically and adapted to develop your teaching style. That teaching style may have aspects of uniqueness and sameness that will be augmented by discussion with other prospective teachers.

A generalized accusation sometimes leveled at professional educators is that "those who *can make* it in the world of business, *do so*, those who *can't make it, teach*." The underlying implication is that only those of mediocre ability go into teaching. While it is true that some teachers should not be in the classroom, the accusation is very unjust to the hundreds of thousands of intelligent, well-prepared teachers who are very successful in a career they have chosen—not for material rewards, for they are few—but for the satisfaction of using their special skills to serve others.

Are there teachers in our colleges and schools who shouldn't be teaching foreign languages? Unfortunately there are—for a number of reasons. A myth that continues to persist is that anyone who can speak a language can teach it. This mistaken conception is one of the leading causes of poor language teaching at all levels. In schools across the country, native speakers who have never studied the structure of their mother tongue are frustrating students by the thousands.

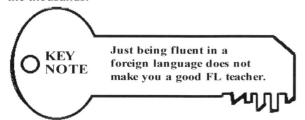

KEY NOTE — Just being fluent in a foreign language does not make you a good FL teacher.

At the other extreme, we find language teachers who can barely use the language. Teachers with limited mastery of the language often have limited success in teaching that language. This is most evident in elementary schools where teachers who can scarcely say *Buenos días* or *Guten Tag* are indelibly perpetuating their own errors in their students. At the university level, some PhD's with brilliant academic credentials, who have been assigned to teach beginning and intermediate classes are beating into the ground any hopes that their students had for proficiency, as they lecture in English on the historical development or the grammatical complexities of the language.

Sometimes a situation develops in a school that causes the principal to go to the coach, or the drama teacher, or the band teacher and ask one of them to teach foreign languages. More often than not these teachers are "drafted" because they had a couple of semesters of language study in college or because they lived for a period of time in a foreign country. Once in the classroom, many of these "draftees" just get the job done by focusing on grammar explanations because they

mistakenly believe that those are their objectives. After all, that's the way they were taught!

Are there language teachers in our colleges and schools who are good at their job? Fortunately there are, and the cases mentioned above should not diminish their successes. The examples of poor teaching we have described should not discourage us, because poor teaching can be changed. All language teachers, future or present, have the moral responsibility to examine themselves carefully to determine if they really are suited to teaching and if they have the proper skills and adequate training to teach the particular courses they are assigned to teach. If they are not, they should feel a strong obligation to take the steps to improve, or look for another career. In this chapter we will identify what goes into the making of a successful language teacher and will outline the steps which need to be taken to become one.

What Are the Essential Qualifications?

What kind of a person is a candidate to teach a foreign language? Certainly more than just someone who can speak or who knows something about the language. Obviously there are additional qualifications. National guidelines call for the following characteristics to be present in someone desiring to become a language teacher.

1. Intellectual capacity. Generally speaking, *any teacher* must be a bright, capable individual who is interested in people, things, and events—someone with an intellectual curiosity who enjoys helping others learn.

2. Desire to teach. Perhaps the most important factor that sustains a teacher through all the ups and downs of teaching is the *desire* to teach. This desire can be seen best in the teacher's enthusiasm. Enthusiasm is contagious, it converts and convinces, it combats burnout, and it keeps the teacher coming back in spite of disappointment and frustration.

3. Language mastery. Ideal language teachers must be at ease with the language. Their vocabulary should be broad enough that they rarely have to grope for words. Their pronunciation should be such that even though natives may recognize it as foreign, they have no difficulty understanding what they are saying. It should be free from a harsh and distracting American accent and should serve as a good model for their students to imitate. They should be able to understand the spoken language in most contexts, to read most texts with good comprehension, and to write with clarity and correctness.

4. Strong conviction of the value of language study. Since today's language teachers must constantly justify their existence, someone planning to teach a language must be personally committed to the position that *everyone* can gain from foreign language study, and that it should be an integral part of the "general education" we require in our schools and colleges. Candidates must be strongly committed to the teaching of languages.

5. Appreciation for the culture. Ideally, the teachers will have had residence in countries or areas where the foreign language is spoken and will have observed many of the cultural aspects first hand. They will have studied the civilization and way of life of the speakers of the language and will understand the differences between the target culture and their own. They will be able to explain culture to their students with a positive and accepting attitude.

6. Understanding of language and structure. In addition to their personal mastery of the language, the teachers must be able to present the structure and vocabulary of the language to the students in a logical and clear fashion. They need to evaluate their students' progress, diagnose their problems, and prescribe activities that will lead them to proficiency. Natives do not automatically qualify with these abilities.

7. Interest in and satisfaction with teaching. Ideal teachers understand the nature of teaching, know the objectives of education in their areas, and have a good grasp of the psychology of learning. They should be interested in working with people of all ages and enjoy teaching them—especially young people.

8. "Teaching Personality." We are referring to the special something that makes a teacher that seems innate. It involves those qualities that enable a person to establish rapport naturally, to

sense intuitively what the students need, to perceive ways to present ideas, to set up situations, to involve group participation, and to inspire the students to learn willingly, yes, enthusiastically. However, we change the hackneyed expression from *"teachers are born, not made!"* to *"teachers are born, and then made!"* Teacher development work is universally applicable, but the teachers must bring much with them.

Teachers of foreign languages must be well-rounded individuals. Not only must they be "practitioners" of the language; they must also be "experts" in other areas such as English, music, art, anthropology, current events, history, literature, sociolinguistics, psycholinguistics, education, geography and language in general. Teachers must also be role models, counselors, facilitators, motivators, often friends, sometimes special advisors, actors, party hosts, guards, even police, nurses, and the like, but these added jobs are part time, thank heavens!

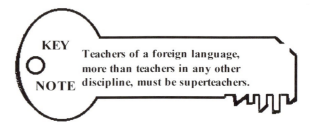

KEY NOTE — Teachers of a foreign language, more than teachers in any other discipline, must be superteachers.

PREPARATION FOR TEACHERS

With all that is expected of public school teachers, you may wonder who decides what teachers need to know and be able to do in order to fulfill their multiple responsibilities. There are at least three levels of organizations that make these decisions: (1) teacher preparation programs at colleges and universities; (2) professional associations and organizations in the field of education; and (3) state departments of education.

Teacher preparation programs at colleges and universities determine what courses education students are required to take. For foreign language teaching majors, these courses generally include classes in language, literature, and culture; one or more courses in language teaching methods; and education courses. (More will be said on teacher preparation programs later in this chapter.) In order to make their graduates more marketable as teachers, many institutions require foreign language teaching majors to have a teaching minor in another subject.

Teacher preparation institutions do not have complete freedom to set their own requirements for teaching majors; they are largely constrained by the standards developed by **professional associations and organizations.** One of the most important of these organizations is the Interstate Teacher Assessment and Support Consortium (InTASC). Created in 1987, InTASC is a partnership of state education agencies and national educational organizations dedicated to the preparation, licensing, and ongoing professional development of teachers. InTASC has developed a set of ten standards for teachers, which were revised in 2011, that serve as a model for many teacher preparation programs. You should become familiar with these standards, as you will probably hear them mentioned periodically in your education courses.

In the field of foreign language education, the professional organization for teachers is the American Council on the Teaching of Foreign Languages (ACTFL); this is an acronym that you should learn by heart. ACTFL has published a set of Program Standards for the Preparation of Foreign Language Teachers that supplement the more general InTASC standards in the accreditation of foreign language teacher preparation programs. These standards are listed on the following pages.

InTASC Model Core Teaching Standards

Standard #1: Learner Development. The teacher understands how learners grow and develop, recognizing that patterns of learning and development vary individually within and across the cognitive, linguistic, social, emotional, and physical areas, and designs and implements developmentally appropriate and challenging learning experiences.

Standard #2: Learning Differences. The teacher uses understanding of individual differences and diverse cultures and communities to ensure inclusive learning environments that enable each learner to meet high standards.

Standard #3: Learning Environments. The teacher works with others to create environments that support individual and collaborative learning, and that encourage positive social interaction, active engagement in learning, and self motivation.

Standard #4: Content Knowledge. The teacher understands the central concepts, tools of inquiry, and structures of the discipline(s) he or she teaches and creates learning experiences that make the discipline accessible and meaningful for learners to assure mastery of the content.

Standard #5: Application of Content. The teacher understands how to connect concepts and use differing perspectives to engage learners in critical thinking, creativity, and collaborative problem solving related to authentic local and global issues.

Standard #6: Assessment. The teacher understands and uses multiple methods of assessment to engage learners in their own growth, to monitor learner progress, and to guide the teacher's and learner's decision making.

Standard #7: Planning for Instruction. The teacher plans instruction that supports every student in meeting rigorous learning goals by drawing upon knowledge of content areas, curriculum, cross-disciplinary skills, and pedagogy, as well as knowledge of learners and the community context.

Standard #8: Instructional Strategies. The teacher understands and uses a variety of instructional strategies to encourage learners to develop deep understanding of content areas and their connections, and to build skills to apply knowledge in meaningful ways.

Standard #9: Professional Learning and Ethical Practice. The teacher engages in ongoing professional learning and uses evidence to continually evaluate his/her practice, particularly the effects of his/her choices and actions on others (learners, families, other professionals, and the community), and adapts practice to meet the needs of each learner.

Standard #10: Leadership and Collaboration. The teacher seeks appropriate leadership roles and opportunities to take responsibility for student learning, to collaborate with learners, families, colleagues, other school professionals, and community members to ensure learner growth, and to advance the profession.

ACTFL Program Standards for the Preparation of Foreign Language Teachers

STANDARD 1: Language, Linguistics, Comparisons

Standard 1.a. Demonstrating Language Proficiency. Candidates demonstrate a high level of proficiency in the target language, and they seek opportunities to strengthen their proficiency.

Standard 1.b. Understanding Linguistics. Candidates know the linguistic elements of the target language system, recognize the changing nature of language, and accommodate for gaps in their own knowledge of the target language system by learning on their own.

Standard 1.c. Identifying Language Comparisons. Candidates know the similarities and differences between the target language and other languages, identify the key differences in varieties of the target language, and seek opportunities to learn about varieties of the target language on their own.

STANDARD 2: Cultures, Literatures, Cross-Disciplinary Concepts

Standard 2.a. Demonstrating Cultural Understandings. Candidates demonstrate that they understand the connections among the perspectives of a culture and its practices and products, and they integrate the cultural framework for foreign language standards into their instructional practices.

Standard 2.b. Demonstrating Understanding of Literary and Cultural Texts and Traditions. Candidates recognize the value and role of literary and cultural texts and use them to interpret and reflect upon the perspectives of the target cultures over time.

Standard 2.c. Integrating Other Disciplines in Instruction. Candidates integrate knowledge of other disciplines into foreign language instruction and identify distinctive viewpoints accessible only through the target language.

STANDARD 3: Language Acquisition Theories and Instructional Practices

Standard 3.a. Understanding Language Acquisition and Creating a Supportive Classroom. Candidates demonstrate an understanding of language acquisition at various developmental levels and use this knowledge to create a supportive classroom learning environment that includes target language input and opportunities for negotiation of meaning and meaningful interaction.

Standard 3.b. Developing Instructional Practices That Reflect Language Outcomes and Learner Diversity. Candidates develop a variety of instructional practices that reflect language outcomes and articulated program models and address the needs of diverse language learners.

STANDARD 4: Integration of Standards Into Curriculum and Instruction

Standard 4.a. Understanding and Integrating Standards in Planning. Candidates demonstrate an understanding of the goal areas and standards of the *Standards for Foreign Language Learning* and their state standards, and they integrate these frameworks into curricular planning.

Standard 4.b. Integrating Standards in Instruction. Candidates integrate the *Standards for Foreign Language Learning* and their state standards into language instruction.

Standard 4.c. Selecting and Designing Instructional Materials. Candidates use standards and curricular goals to evaluate, select, design, and adapt instructional resources.

STANDARD 5: Assessment of Languages and Cultures

Standard 5.a. Knowing assessment models and using them appropriately. Candidates believe that assessment is ongoing, and they demonstrate knowledge of multiple ways of assessment that are age- and level-appropriate by implementing purposeful measures.

Standard 5.b. Reflecting on assessment. Candidates reflect on the results of student assessments, adjust instruction accordingly, analyze the results of assessments, and use success and failure to determine the direction of instruction.

Standard 5.c. Reporting assessment results. Candidates interpret and report the results of student performances to all stakeholders and provide opportunity for discussion.

STANDARD 6: Professionalism

Standard 6.a. Engaging in Professional Development. Candidates engage in professional development opportunities that strengthen their own linguistic and cultural competence and promote reflection on practice.

Standard 6.b. Knowing the Value of Foreign Language Learning. Candidates know the value of foreign language learning to the overall success of all students and understand that they will need to become advocates with students, colleagues, and members of the community to promote the field.

The ultimate authority that grants teaching licenses is the **state department or office of education**. In most states, the department of education grants licenses more or less automatically to students who have graduated from and been recommended by an accredited teacher preparation institution. However, states usually have additional testing requirements that teacher candidates must meet in order to satisfy the federal government, which, since the passage of the No Child Left Behind Act in 2001, has demanded that teachers be "highly qualified" in the subjects they teach. For foreign languages, this usually means that teacher candidates must pass an ACTFL Oral Proficiency Interview at a specified level, usually either Advanced Low or Intermediate High (see Chapter 7 for more information on these levels). In addition, many states require teacher candidates to pass a "Praxis II" content test for the language they will be teaching. The Praxis tests are designed by the company Educational Testing Services (ETS); more information on the tests is available at the ETS website. Each state sets its own cutoff score for the Praxis that is considered a "passing" level. Some states require other tests. For information on the requirements in specific states, check the website of the state's department or office of education.

Obtaining a Teaching License

It is important to understand that the licenses granted by state departments of education are not simply as a "Spanish (or French or German) teacher"; rather, they are general licenses to teach at a specific level, either the elementary or the secondary level. In Utah, an elementary license allows teachers to teach grades K-8; a secondary license, grades 6-12. (This means that middle-school classes may be taught by someone with either an elementary or a secondary license.) Along with a license, teachers must have an **endorsement** to teach one or more specific subjects. For example, a candidate who graduates from a secondary education program with a Spanish teaching major and a geography teaching minor would likely get a secondary license with an endorsement in Spanish and an endorsement in geography. You may have heard of licensed teachers going back to school to earn an endorsement in another subject; this simply means that they plan to continue teaching at the same level (high school, middle school, etc.), but they want to be qualified to teach another subject in addition to the one(s) they already teach.

In most states, teachers who have been teaching for several years can qualify a promotion or higher-level license by fulfilling

10

additional requirements. In some states there are several levels of licenses, each of which is associated with a successive pay increase. An increasing number of states are requiring National Board certification (see Chapter 18) for their highest level of license.

An additional requirement for obtaining a teaching license in most states is to pass a criminal background check. To complete the background check, applicants must submit fingerprints for review by the Federal Bureau of Investigation and/or the state bureau of criminal identification.

Alternative Routes to Licensure

In response to teacher shortages, most states have now made provisions for candidates to obtain a teaching license through routes other than traditional teacher preparation programs at colleges and universities. These routes are known as **alternative routes to licensure** (ARL). There different alternative routes. Most often, teacher candidates in ARL programs are college graduates or professionals in other fields who decide to enter the teaching profession but do not want to return to college to complete a four-year education degree. Other ARLs are sponsored by nationwide programs such as Troops to Teachers and Teach for America.

It is difficult to make generalizations about ARL programs because they vary enormously in their requirements. Some states, including Utah, have fairly rigorous ARL programs. In order to qualify for a license under Utah's ARL program, candidates must have a bachelor's degree or higher with a major in the subject they plan to teach. Participants in Utah's ARL program complete coursework determined by a transcript review, take required content knowledge tests, teach for a minimum of one year and a maximum of three years in a licensed position, successfully pass evaluations of classroom performance skills by the principal and, upon program completion, are recommended for licensure by the principal and ARL advisor. In order to obtain a world language endorsement in Utah, ARL candidates must pass the Praxis II content test and an Oral Proficiency Interview in their language and complete a course in language teaching methods.

Although ARL programs can streamline the path to licensure for non-traditional teacher candidates, these programs have certain drawbacks. Depending on their requirements, they may or may not prepare teacher candidates with the same broad base in adolescent development, multicultural and exceptional education, and classroom management that they would receive in a traditional teacher education program. Even in rigorous ARL programs, candidates generally receive much less mentoring than they would in a traditional teacher preparation program. Whereas candidates in traditional programs student teach in the classroom of an experienced mentor teacher, under the guidance of a university supervisor, ARL candidates are largely on their own. Even if an ARL candidate is assigned a mentor teacher, the mentor generally does not work in the same classroom, and is therefore unable to provide the same quantity or quality of feedback as a mentor teacher in a traditional student teaching experience. For these reasons, we strongly recommend that college and university students complete a traditional teacher education program rather than opt for an alternate route to licensure after they graduate.

Teaching in a Different State

What happens if you obtain a teaching license in the state where you graduated from college but plan to teach in a different state? Most states have reciprocity agreements with other states whereby they allow teachers to begin teaching with another state's license, provided that they meet certain licensure requirements specific to their own state within a reasonable period of time. These agreements are facilitated under the NASDTEC Interstate Agreement, which is actually a collection of over 50 individual agreements by states and Canadian provinces. Each individual "agreement" is a statement by that state outlining which other states' licenses will be accepted, and on what terms. For more information on reciprocity agreements between specific states, check with the state department or office of education in the state where you plan to teach.

IDEAL TEACHER PREPARATION PROGRAMS

Every year over 3,500 language teachers graduate from over 800 different teacher training institutions and find employment in the nation's schools. With few exceptions, all states require, by law, an approved teaching certificate before allowing anyone to teach in the public schools. As previously mentioned, this certificate is usually granted automatically by the state upon the recommendation of any approved teacher training institution located in the state.

Ultimately, the nitty-gritty of education for certified teachers is in the hands of the *training institutions*, that is, the colleges and universities that actually set up the curriculum, teach the courses, supervise the teaching practicum, and make the final evaluation of the candidates. What we will do here is postulate an "ideal training program" for the levels where languages are taught.

Secondary School Teachers

The large bulk of language teachers in the nation (currently more than 80,000) are at the secondary schools. What should go into the training of a successful secondary school teacher?

Candidates. In our discussion of the characteristics expected of secondary school teachers of languages, we mentioned that they needed to understand and enjoy working with young people, be capable classroom managers, and be convinced of the importance of language study in the public schools. Notice that these characteristics closely relate to the *personality* of the individual. The adage that some people are "born teachers" contains a great deal of truth. There are others, however, who no matter how hard they try can't develop a "feel" for teaching. Whether these qualities are innate or are developed as individuals form their personality is not certain, but it is clear that a *teaching personality* is necessary.

The curriculum. Typically, the training program for a secondary school language teacher consists of work in six areas, as illustrated in the following chart:

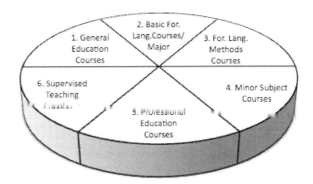

Let's look with greater attention to detail at what the content and organization of these courses should be.

1. General education courses. Most of the educational institutions that train teachers have a "general education" or "liberal arts" component that must be completed by *all* graduates. Rightly so—a college graduate should be a well-rounded individual with a broad academic background, not someone whose studies have been limited to a narrow area of specialization.

This broad liberal arts emphasis is especially desirable in a training program for language teachers. It should include the humanities, social and behavioral sciences, natural sciences, mathematics, and the arts.

Some specific general education courses are especially relevant to language teachers. Among these are: general philosophy, social/cultural anthropology, cultural geography, comparative world cultures, and history of civilization.

If this liberal arts component is not a universal requirement of the *institution*, it should at least be an integral part of the *teacher training curriculum*.

2. Basic courses in the foreign language (major). The ideal foreign language education program would consist of at least 30 semester hours of courses in the foreign language. They would include advanced grammar, conversation, reading and writing, culture, literature, and phonetics. These courses should be proficiency oriented, not just a theoretical or academic review of the grammar of the language. They should be taught in the foreign language, with ample opportunities for individual practice. The students should finish these courses with an ability to use the language for communication. Actual proficiency tests should be given often to determine if the student is reaching minimal levels of functional use and remedial work should be prescribed if necessary.

When native speakers of the language take advanced grammar classes, they should study the language structure sufficiently to prepare them to explain matters clearly to their students, who need something more than just an offhand "that's the way you say it." Too often natives can pass these classes because they speak fluently and correctly, but they really don't understand the underlying grammatical concepts.

In a phonetics course, teacher candidates should not only study the sound system of the language in a formal way, but also work at improving their personal pronunciation until it is acceptable and can serve as a model to their students. They should also learn how to teach pronunciation.

The literature courses should be taught in a way that will permit continued personal development in all four skills. They should not be totally lecture oriented, and should require other assignments such as discussions, brainstorming, oral reports, and written papers.

The civilization and culture classes should go beyond the usual history/fine-arts emphasis ("Big C" Culture) and should include geography, study of contemporary patterns of life, values, and behavior. But prospective teachers must be prepared to teach more than folksongs, food, and festivals. They will also be teaching about the politics, economy, and social problems of the countries where the target language is spoken. Some introduction to sociolinguistics should also be included.

It is essential that the language competence of the teacher candidates be evaluated in terms of actual performance in the language, not just the successful completion of a specified number of courses. This presupposes that some type of evaluation instrument, such as the ACTFL Language Testing International tests, be administered and that the students reach a minimal level of proficiency before being certified. The responsibility of providing activities both in and out of the classroom that will bring the students to this level lies with the training institution. It is also that institution's responsibility to administer the tests and to certify the student's proficiency. These tests should not be left until the final semester before graduation or certification—there must be time for additional

work if needed. Most professional education groups currently recommend that teacher candidates reach a rating of Advanced or higher on the **ACTFL/ETS** speaking proficiency or an equivalent test.

3. The language methods courses. The program should include at least one, preferably two, methods courses—perhaps one to be taken before student teaching and the other during or after. The pre-service courses would prepare the students with basic techniques for teaching the major skills (speaking, listening comprehension, reading, and writing), managing the classroom, teaching culture, preparing audio-visual aids, evaluating and adapting texts, and adapting and using technology. The in-service or post-service course could explore more in depth the various theories of language acquisition and implications for teaching strategies.

These courses should not be taught by a "generalist" who has little training, interest, or experience in teaching the foreign language. Ideally, they would be taught in the language department by a specialist who is proficient in the foreign language and has had extensive personal experience in the foreign language classroom. Whenever possible they should be taught in the foreign language. The courses must not be limited to discussions of methodologies, but must include numerous opportunities for practice that allow the student to develop basic skills. These practice sessions would obviously be in the foreign language. They should not be limited to one particular approach or theory, but should acquaint the future teachers with a wide range of methods and approaches.

Nine of the most important skills to be learned in these courses are:

1. Conducting classroom activities exclusively in the language.
2. Using authentic activities and exercises that develop student mastery of the structure of the target language.
3. Directing activities that guide students toward free, personalized communication in the language.
4. Providing numerous opportunities that develop listening and reading comprehension, as well as writing skills.
5. Using a variety of learning situations that bring the reality of the culture closer to the

student in natural ways so it can be appreciated and assimilated.

6. Developing, encouraging and promoting student participation in events in the contemporary ways of life in the culture.
7. Using modern technology, such as computers and videos, to reinforce students' acquisition of the language.
8. Practicing the use of visual aids and electronic equipment to enhance classroom presentations.
9. Developing the ability to determine students' learning styles and adapting instruction to meet those learning styles.

Ideally these courses would include numerous presentations made by the students that are videotaped and critiqued by the specialist. Latitude should be present which allows teachers to adopt the teaching style that best suits their personality and preparation.

4. Basic courses in the minor subject. Most secondary school teachers prepare themselves to teach in a second area. It is very likely that their teaching assignment will require them to teach something besides their major. The core of minimum preparation for a teaching minor is also set up by the college or university. Foreign language majors should not neglect their preparation in their minor area just because of the heavy demands of their major. They should prepare themselves well in the minor subject, take the methods course if there is one, and student teach at least one class in that subject.

But what about prospective teachers who are *minoring* in the foreign language and whose major is English, math, social sciences, music, or some other subject area? Only rarely do state and professional organizations provide guidelines for these minors. It is natural that these teachers be primarily concerned about their major area, but it is quite common (between 30 and 50%) for them to be assigned to teach the same classes that a language major would teach. In an ideal program, the language preparation of a minor would be the same as that of the major. The only difference might be the taking of fewer literature and civilization courses and focusing more on language competence.

Essential among the requirements for the minors must be the foreign language methods classes. A methods class in English or math will not give them the skills to teach Spanish or Japanese. While it may be true that these teachers might never teach advanced language classes, their mastery of the language should not be much different from that of a major. Similarly, the student teaching experience should include teaching at least one class in the foreign language.

5. Supervised teaching practicum. Prospective teachers should have a lengthy period of practice teaching—at the very least from eight to ten weeks—supervised by expert, experienced teachers and working with actual language learners. For students preparing to teach in the public schools, this will be the "student teaching" experience. The importance of this activity cannot be overemphasized. Student teaching influences perhaps more than anything else the way the teacher candidate will eventually teach. To the consternation of methods course professors, many student teachers seem to suffer a total lapse of memory as they student teach, forgetting all of the principles and techniques they practiced in the methods class. It is far easier for them to follow the example of their mentor teacher.

The mentor teacher is thus vital to the training program. This person should be selected with great care, preferably by trained FL specialists who can recognize good language teachers when they see them. These "master teachers" should be the type who can best help the student teacher learn. Some teachers are good models, but not good mentor teachers because they cannot yield their classes into the hands of someone learning to teach.

The university must go to great lengths to prepare this mentor teacher to be effective. There should be a training program and some specific guidelines that the mentor teacher is to follow. Some universities even give these teachers the status of ***adjunct professor*** and give recognition to the importance they play in the teacher education program. In addition to the recognition, other benefits can be included such as free classes at the university, special library and activities privileges, etc. These types of remuneration can be more important than a token honorarium.

The student teaching experience must be more than just observation. Eventually the teacher candidate should completely take over the classes and be responsible for the preparation of lesson plans, presentation of lessons, giving and scoring of tests, preparation of materials and visual aids, use of electronic aids, and all the other tasks expected of the regular teacher.

During the student teaching, frequent observation by, and consultation with, the mentor teacher and the specialist college supervisor should take place. Both are expert language teachers themselves. In a positive, supportive way these supervisors should critique the practicing teacher and offer specific suggestions for improvement. These supervisors will write comprehensive evaluations that will be the principal basis for hiring the individual.

6. Professional education courses. It is highly desirable for teacher development programs to start with some kind of "exploration of education" course. This course should come at the very beginning of the students' program, in most cases, during the Freshman or Sophomore year, the earlier the better. This course sends the students out into the schools to observe a variety of programs and levels, and permits the students to decide if they really do want careers in education. In a real sense these courses allow students to "deselect" themselves if they decide that teaching is not for them. It is very unfair to the students to wait until they have finished most of the coursework before sending them out into the schools. If at that time they decide against teaching, they have misspent several semesters of work in the teacher development program.

Having confirmed their desire to be a teacher, the students would then take some "foundations of education" courses that introduce them to some general principles of teaching. Among other topics, these courses would treat different philosophies of education, explore effective approaches to teaching, present principles of classroom management, practice development and use of visual aids, address ways of meeting the needs of students from diverse backgrounds and with diverse learning needs, and explore uses of technology in education.

Elementary School Language Teachers

The acronym **FLES**, **F**oreign **L**anguages in the **E**lementary **S**chools, is commonly used to refer to language teaching to children. Typically, university students who have decided to teach at the elementary school level must complete a major in elementary education. Sometimes, but not always, a minor or area of specialization is also required. Elementary teachers are required to be able to teach a much broader curriculum than specialized secondary school teachers, and generally speaking work harder at relationships with their students. Chapter 15 discusses in detail the types of language programs found in elementary schools.

Candidates. In addition to the characteristics discussed at the beginning of this chapter, elementary school teachers need to:

1. Understand and enjoy working with children.
2. Be capable, patient classroom managers.
3. Know the elementary curriculum.
4. Be convinced that foreign languages have a necessary place in the total perspective of elementary education.

Generally speaking, elementary school teachers who work with a typical "sequential FLES" program do not need to be extremely fluent in the foreign language, but they must have a level of mastery which will allow them to be confident in teaching the class in the language and to be a good model to the children. We do not recommend programs that allow non Spanish-speaking teachers to try to teach the language. Although these programs build on children's natural enthusiasm for learning a language and give them a positive attitude about language learning, the children usually develop poor pronunciation, learn many incorrect patterns, and soon become bored with the constant repetition of what they hear on a tape or see and hear in a video. Teachers desiring to teach in immersion programs should have near-native fluency and native speakers can find alternative routes to licensure. (See Chapter 15.)

The Curriculum. Training of elementary school teachers usually consists of courses and practice in five areas as follows:

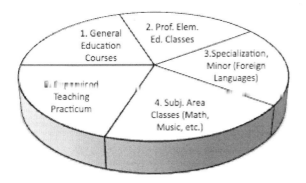

Let's look at each of these areas in greater detail.

1. General education courses. It is just as desirable for elementary school teachers as it is for secondary school teachers to get the general liberal arts education that is required of all university graduates. In the elementary school the teachers' expertise extends across several disciplines and the teachers must be well rounded in their outlook on life.

2. Professional education courses. As with the secondary program, the elementary program should begin with an exploratory course that will take prospective teachers out into the schools and allow them to decide at an early point if they have chosen the correct career. A high level of teaching skill is expected of the elementary school teacher. These skills are developed in the professional education courses that all candidates must take. They would examine philosophies of education, organization and financing of school systems, ethics, elementary school curriculum, and so on.

3. Specialty areas or minor. Most programs allow students to specialize in areas of interest such as: early childhood education, special education, and music. It is in one or more of these areas that future elementary teachers would make their preparation with a foreign language. Although non-immersion FLES teachers are at a much lower level of language use than junior and senior high school teachers, these students should take an advanced grammar course, conversation, a pronunciation and phonetics course, a civilization and culture course, and at least an introduction to literature course. In addition to these basic language courses, they should take at least one methods class in language teaching. If possible, a course in children's literature of the

language they will be teaching would be very valuable. The content and structure of the methods courses would be basically the same as outlined for the secondary program.

4. Subject area methods courses. Since the elementary school teachers are normally expected to teach all the curriculum subjects of a grade, they must prepare by taking methods classes in several areas such as: teaching math, teaching science, teaching language arts, teaching reading, and teaching social studies. In addition they usually take courses in art, music, children's literature, and physical education.

5. Supervised teaching practicum. The student teaching experience has been mentioned as being highly critical in the teacher training process. The candidate must be able to put into practice all the concepts and skills he or she has been practicing in all the other courses. He or she also needs the constructive criticism and help of both an experienced cooperation teacher and a college supervisor. In the case of teachers who will have a minor or specialty in foreign languages, the student teaching should provide opportunities to teach the foreign language, and have the help and guidance of supervisors who are also experienced language teachers. It is essential that mentor teachers be selected with great care and they should be given training and guidelines on how to work effectively with student teachers.

Teachers in Immersion Programs. What was said above about lower language competency expectations does not apply to teachers in immersion programs. (See Chapter 15 for a description of immersion programs.) The need for language fluency in teachers in this type of program is even greater than that of secondary school teachers. The state of Utah, for example, requires immersion teachers to have Advanced Mid levproficiency (as opposed to Advanced Low for non-immersion teachers). Ideally, these teachers are native or near-native speakers of the target language who handle the language with ease and are able to comfortably present the regular curriculum of the grade they are teaching.

Prospective immersion teachers need to complete the same preparation as regular elementary school teachers; they may be assigned to a normal program and must be prepared for that. In addition, they should have at least three additional courses: 1) a methods class in teaching foreign languages; 2), a foundations course in immersion education, which would focus on research and practice related to immersion programs; and 3) a course on content-based instruction, which would focus on teaching and assesssing the curriculum of subject areas, such as social sciences, math, physical sciences, and art in the foreign language.

Although immersion programs have been around for decades, specific training programs for immersion teachers are still few and far between. The University of Minnesota's Dual Language/Immersion Certificate program was the first in the nation to offer a coherent set of courses designed specifically for immersion teachers. More recently, Utah has become the first state to require a specific endorsement for teachers in immersion programs. This endorsement entails course work in foundations of immersion education; second language literacy development, content-based second language curriculum, instruction, and assessment; language acquisition; and student teaching or a practicum. (More on qualifications for immersion teachers in Chapter 15.)

If the candidates are not native speakers of the language, they should have some special training in the specialized vocabulary of the classroom. Students who attended elementary school in the target language will have learned this vocabulary. Candidates to teach in immersion programs should complete a practicum or at least part of their student teaching in an immersion program.

GETTING THE MOST FROM THE TEACHING PRACTICUM

Every responsible training program has a "practicum," an experience where the candidates "practice" their newly-learned skills. For those preparing to teach in the public schools, this will be *student teaching*. For students preparing to teach on a university level, this will be the *teaching assistantship*. Whatever your area may be, the practicum usually involves working with an experienced teacher, and you will be observed and evaluated by a supervisor. The following suggestions can be of great help:

1. Preparing to student teach. The teaching practicum will be a very demanding experience.

It is different from regular teaching in that student teachers will probably be teaching someone else's students, and they cannot draw on past expertise because this will probably be their first teaching experience. It is wise to prepare as much as possible beforehand; much can be done before the experience begins. You can spend a considerable amount of time preparing visual aids (flash cards, pictures, clock, conversation transparencies); remember, you will not have the files which all experienced teachers build over the years as they teach. You will need to "over prepare" as you develop your lesson plans. It will be extremely helpful for you to have a copy of the text being used in the classes you will teach, which will allow you to focus your visual aids and planning preparation on lessons which will be assigned to you.

2. Relating to your mentor teacher. Obviously, it is important to relate well to the mentor teacher(s). Remember, you cannot totally fill their shoes. You are not expected to be as effective; you don't have their experience. They know the system, the students, the textbook, the program, the school, the community, the administration, and the parents. Your goal is not to imitate them, but to use any ideas or suggestions they give to be as effective as possible with your own qualities and limitations and with your own teaching style.

Some mentor teachers are better models, some are better facilitators. You will need to adjust to the personality of your assigned partner (or assigned mentor teachers), and you will need to accept the role which they want you to follow. Ask for advice and suggestions about your teaching and volunteer to help and cooperate however you can. Be careful never to criticize any colleague, especially in front of the students.

3. Relating to your university supervisor. Somehow you have to consider your supervisor as your partner and ally. Don't forget that he or she is on your team and is there to help you become a good teacher. Ask for suggestions and always react to them in a positive way. While it is true that she/he or he will evaluate your teaching, you must accept the evaluations in a spirit of humility. If you become defensive and try to excuse your mistakes you will make little growth. Remember, this is a learning situation; try to remain teachable.

4. Teaching someone else's classes. It is difficult even in the best of situations to step into someone's classes and take over. The students will not treat you with the same respect given to the regular teacher. Sometimes they will test you to see what they can get away with. If you radically change things, they will resist. You may have to disguise your intents with a "challenge" approach, saying "I have been so impressed with your ability to use the language, I'll bet you can go half the class period without using any English." Most mentor or partner teachers give full support to the student teacher by making it clear to the students that you are an "associate" teacher and that you have equal authority and will both be responsible for the grades.

If it appears hard for you to implement some of the ideas and techniques you have learned in the methods class, don't make the excuse, "they don't do that in this school." Try anyway! You might be able to make some very valuable contributions to the program. Many mentor teachers indicate that they learn a great deal from their student teachers, and get many new ideas that they include in their own teaching.

Sometimes, you may just have to be content with doing what the mentor teacher does, and say to yourself, "My turn will come. When I get my own classes I'll teach them differently."

5. Becoming a "doer and a collector." After you have learned the routine, procedures might become boring and there is a tendency to just sit back and let the mentor teachers do most of the work. Don't just sit in class observing. Find out as much as you can. Have other texts been tried and discontinued? Why? Is there a language lab? Learn how to operate it with ease. Have you inventoried the mentor teacher's files and materials collection? Visit other language teachers in the school. Volunteer to work with other areas in the school, such as working in the attendance office, taking tickets at sports events, and helping with the school newspaper or play.

CONCLUSION

Language teachers must be a "special breed." They must begin with an intellectual curiosity. They must be competent in the language and several other areas. They must enjoy teaching. We see that the initial development of a foreign language teacher can be a rigorous process that really never stops. Those teachers who have been "drafted" into a new position of foreign language teacher may find that they have to go back and do some remedial work; the above ideas and procedures should be very valuable to "draftees." Those whose language skills are not completely adequate can always find ways to bring them up to par. Those whose teaching is not interesting or motivating will have to find ways to change that situation. But all of us can improve, and we should all be constantly working, experimenting, getting involved in workshops and conferences, and searching for ways to reach our goals more effectively. The above suggestions can help immensely to solve the developmental problems of beginning teachers at all levels. Although our development as a teacher begins with a rush in our college years as we take the courses, complete the student teaching, and perfect our language skills, it goes on after we get a job and get our own classrooms with our own students. In actuality, it should continue on through the rest of our careers as teachers. Current in the professional literature is the expression ***lifelong process***, applied to teaching careers or to commitment or to teacher development. The idea that teaching is a *forever* dedication is a good note to use in the finale of this chapter.

REFERENCES AND SUGGESTIONS FOR FURTHER READING

American Association of Teachers of Spanish and Portuguese. (1990). AATSP Program Guidelines for the Education and Training of Teachers of Spanish and Portuguese. *Hispania, 73,* 785-794.

American Council on the Teaching of Foreign Languages. (1999). *ACTFL Proficiency Guidelines – Speaking* (1999 revision). Alexandria, VA: Author. Available at www.actfl.org.
These guidelines were developed by ACTFL as an academic analog to the government language proficiency level descriptions, originally developed by the Foreign Service Institute (FSI) and currently revised and used by the various language schools participating in the Interagency Language Roundtable (ILR).

Carnegie Forum on Education and the Economy. (1986). *A nation prepared: Teachers for the twenty-first century* (report of the Task Force on Teaching as a Profession). New York, NY: Author. Retrieved from ERIC database. (ED268120)

Guntermann, G. (Ed.). (1993). *Developing language teachers for a changing world* (ACTFL Foreign Language Education Series). Lincolnwood, IL: National Textbook.

Holmes Group. (1995). *Tomorrow's teachers: A report of the Holmes Group.* East Lansing, MI: Author. Retrieved from ERIC database. (ED399220)

Interstate Teacher Assessment and Support Consortium. (2011). *InTASC Model Core Teaching Standards.* Available at:
http://www.ccsso.org/resources/programs/interstate_teacher_assessment_consortium_%28intasc%29.html

Language Testing International. http://www.languagetesting.com/
The website of a licensee of ACTFL that describes the speaking proficiency tests developed by ACTFL, and gives instructions about how to take them.

Image Credits

p. 7: Teaching. (n.d.). *Public Domain Clip Art.* Retrieved June 27, 2011 from http://www.pdclipart.org/albums/Education/teaching.png. Public domain.

ACTIVITIES FOR METHODS CLASSES

1. Summarize the characteristics listed in this chapter for "candidates" for your own particular level and make a checklist. Do you qualify? What are the areas you need to work on? What courses could you take to improve your preparation? Set up a specific plan for personal improvement and work on it during the upcoming semesters. Coordinate this plan with your methods instructor and make periodic reports.

2. Evaluate the teacher training program you are currently in. Compare the requirements and features of that program with the guidelines suggested in this chapter. What areas of preparation are not required? Are they important? Could and should they be included in your program? Discuss this in class with your instructor and peers and make some specific recommendations.

3. Interview some experienced language teachers. Ask them what training they received and find out how they feel about that training. What additional courses or experiences would have been helpful to them? Were there some parts of the training that they feel were of no value? Discuss your findings in class. Submit a report of the interview to your methods instructor.

4. The methods instructor can assign students to different groups and have each group research some aspect of foreign language teacher training, such as elementary school teachers, college courses, education department courses, and others. Form panels and present your findings in discussions in class.

5. Spend some time thinking about where you would like to get a job teaching. Write a résumé and begin setting up a job placement file. Decide which professors or administrators know you best and could write the most accurate letters of recommendation. Consult with the university placement service.

6. Make it a point to become acquainted with the foreign language specialist in your state and in a nearby school district. Discuss their foreign language programs and specifically talk about how they feel about teacher development.

7. Get acquainted with the professional organizations that help us set standards for language teacher training. Go to the library and find issues of their journals. Look through the journals to find articles about teacher qualifications and preparation. Report your reading to your instructor.

8. Obtain a list of the required courses for education majors at your university. For each course, determine which of the InTASC Standards and ACTFL Program Standards it addresses. Are all of the standards addressed in the required courses? Discuss this in class with your instructor and peers.

CHAPTER TWO

ARE YOU CONVERTED?

YOUR OBJECTIVES FOR THIS CHAPTER ARE TO:

1. BE PERSONALLY CONVINCED OF THE VALUE OF LEARNING A FOREIGN LANGUAGE.

2. MAKE STRONG ARGUMENTS IN FAVOR OF FOREIGN LANGUAGE STUDY AND BE ABLE TO ANSWER OBJECTIONS THAT MAY BE RAISED BY OTHERS.

3. HAVE A CLEAR PERSPECTIVE OF THE PLACE OF FOREIGN LANGUAGES IN THE BASIC CURRICULUM OF OUR SCHOOLS.

4. CULTIVATE A "CRUSADING SPIRIT" ABOUT INVOLVING OTHERS IN FOREIGN LANGUAGE STUDY.

5. LOCATE MATERIALS AND INFORMATION ABOUT THE IMPORTANCE OF FOREIGN LANGUAGE STUDY.

6. DEVELOP THE ATTITUDE THAT THE FOREIGN LANGUAGE EXPERIENCE FOR YOUR STUDENTS WILL BE MOTIVATING, FUN, AND WELL WORTH IT.

7. RECOGNIZE IMPORTANT DILEMMAS CONFRONTING SUPPORTERS OF FOREIGN LANGUAGE STUDY AND PREPARE TO RESOLVE THEM.

8. DEVELOP A RATIONALE FILE FOR TEACHING AND LEARNING SPANISH, AS WELL AS FOREIGN LANGUAGES IN GENERAL.

Miss Ortega was understandably nervous as she was shown into the principal's office. The enrollment in her Spanish classes had dropped off this year, and she was sure Mr. Bud Jetcutt would ask her to justify her second year classes that had only 15 students each in them. Mr. Jettcut came right to the point and it was worse than Miss Ortega had supposed.

Miss Ortega, I'm sure you are aware we are operating with a reduced budget this year, and this is causing us to reevaluate all our programs, especially our "non-solid, frill" classes such as Spanish. We are seriously considering dropping the Spanish program. We think it would better for the students to wait until high school to study foreign languages. Would you like to give us some input?

It was 7:15 a.m. as Mr. I. Commute stepped into his '76 Chevy and backed into the street. As he started down the street toward the high school where he taught Spanish, he switched on the radio. It was one of those talk shows where people call in and express their opinions. Mr. C. only half listened as some housewife complained about taxes, but the next call caught his full attention.

I would like to complain about the new requirement of two years of foreign language study for admission to the state university. I think it is a big waste of time. I took two years of French in high school and never used it. Last summer I went to Eastern Canada on a vacation and was hoping to use my French, but everyone spoke English. My neighbor who just returned from a two-month tour of Europe says it's the same there. Everyone speaks English. I think we would be better off if we required more math classes or something practical like finance or computers.

Jim Scott watched the frown spread over the face of professor Frump. An icy fear gripped his stomach and he felt the sweat begin to bead on his forehead. Had he been too dogmatic in expressing his convictions about language learning? The middle of a Ph.D. oral exam was no place to alienate or antagonize a renowned scholar. Jim had worked too hard and sacrificed too much to see it all lost now by an "unsupported" opinion in response to the simple question, "What should be the place of foreign language study in our public schools?" He held his breath and tried to compose his thoughts as Dr. Frump intoned:

Let me get this right, Mr. Scott. Do you really believe that foreign language study should be a required subject and taught to every child in every school in this country?

The high school auditorium was almost filled to capacity with students and parents. "You have to give the counseling staff credit," thought Mrs. Valenzuela. "Their suggestion to have everyone come to a special meeting prior to registering for classes will give the teachers all a chance to tell about our classes and what their value is. Now if I can just remember all the points I want to make, and especially how I can state them in such a way that these parents and students will be convinced that Spanish is very important." It seemed that scarcely a few minutes had passed when she heard Mr. Principale say:

We are fortunate to have Mrs. Valenzuela, our Spanish teacher, back with us this year. She will take a few minutes to tell us what she is trying to do in her Spanish classes and which students will profit most from them.

As the bell ending the Spanish class sounded, Jason moved up to Mister Hansen's desk and waited until all the other students had left the room. In addition to being his next-door neighbor and good friend, he was the best teacher Jason had ever had. Besides, Jason really enjoyed Spanish and was doing very well in the class. He was sure Mr. Hansen could help him find a solution to his problem.

Mr. Hansen, I need some advice. Tomorrow we have to register for classes for next Fall and I have a problem. As you know, I play the cello in the orchestra so I will have to sign up for orchestra. My parents want me to sign up for computer science, and my dad thinks I should take keyboarding, because it will help me in college. I have to take math, English and American history. That doesn't leave me any time for Spanish, but I want to take it because I enjoy it so much. What should I do?

CHAPTER TWO

ARE YOU CONVERTED?

> **He who knows no foreign language
> never really learned his own.**
> **--Goethe**

Perhaps nothing is as painful as sales people who have to sell a product that they themselves aren't really sold on. They find it very difficult to generate enthusiasm both in themselves and in their customers. Their sales pitches just don't ring true. It is so hard to convince others to buy something they wouldn't buy for themselves. This is true for water softeners, used cars, insurance, political positions, or a subject in school. Yes, even teachers, in a very real sense, are selling a product, and success will seldom come to the teachers who aren't convinced of the worth of what they are "selling."

ARE YOU "SOLD ON" FOREIGN LANGUAGE STUDY?

Before you can reach any measure of success as a teacher of Spanish you must be personally convinced of its value. Just as a car dealer can praise the virtues of a certain model car if he drives one himself, you will have to spend some time assessing the enrichment that has come into your own life from having learned a foreign language. You must be ready to give personal testimony of how your horizon has been broadened, your perspective more balanced, and your tolerance and appreciation of other cultures increased. You've got to be ready with account after account of how knowing Spanish has helped you out of difficulty, permitted you to meet some special persons, helped you save money, assisted you in your work, and so on. If you can't answer affirmatively to most of the items on the following checklist perhaps you should consider teaching some other subject.

Take some time now and work this matter through your own heart. In giving it careful thought, the questions you want to answer are:

Has having learned a foreign language . . .

- given you a better understanding of English?
- increased your ability to use English more correctly?
- increased your English vocabulary?
- given you a wider view of the world?
- broadened your intellectual horizons?
- made you more tolerant toward people of other cultures?
- given you more insight into why other people behave differently?
- increased your enjoyment of literature?
- helped you make new friends?
- given you insight to some historical event or name?
- helped you in a difficult situation?
- helped you to save money, save a life, help someone?
- allowed you to see more and learn more on a trip?
- permitted you to communicate with someone?
- helped you get a job, make a sale, perform a task?
- made you feel as if you were educated, not provincial?
- allowed you to see there is more than one way to express ideas?
- helped you eliminate stereotypes of foreign cultures?
- brought you to a better understanding of the world?
- helped you be more empathetic and understanding of someone learning English as a foreign language?
- eliminated stereotypes of Spanish culture?
- helped you understand and know this hemisphere better?

How many more benefits can you name that learning a foreign language has given you personally? Can you honestly say that you use it as much as some math or science skills you learned in school? Can you sincerely state that it has enriched your life as much as art or music?

Is Your "Product" of Value to Others?

Do you really believe that your own personal enrichment is not just something that has been unique to you, but would be of equal value to anyone else who learns the language? Can you with good conscience tell your "prospective buyers" that Spanish is something they really need? Will learning it give them something more than just a handy tool–is there something that will enrich their lives even if they never go to a Spanish-speaking country? It is true that knowing the language will make traveling in a Spanish-speaking country infinitely more rewarding and easier and can probably help people in any number of professions. But don't just emphasize the "practical" uses that can be made—not everyone will have the opportunity to travel. Remember that there are some "intrinsic" values in learning a language that can be rewarding, even if the learners never ventures beyond their hometown. In this regard, we borrow a very appropriate comment from professor Genelle Morain of the University of Georgia for our keynote:

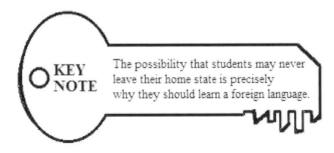

KEY NOTE

The possibility that students may never leave their home state is precisely why they should learn a foreign language.

Some teachers object to this "sales approach," stating: "It's not my job to sell, just to teach." In today's world where so many things compete for our time and attention, if you don't do a good job of selling, you probably won't have any students to teach.

FOREIGN LANGUAGE STUDY IN THE UNITED STATES

Foreign language education in the United States is a national embarrassment. Fewer than one half of American school children study foreign languages, and those who do typically stop after one or two years. Only a handful of states require it be included in the core curriculum, the others have relegated it to the category of "support" or "enrichment" subjects. And in not a few schools it is considered a "frill," of value only to the college-bound student or to the student who is doing so well in English (B+ or higher) that he hardly needs to be motivated or enriched.

In many areas in the world the necessity of knowing a foreign language is clearly apparent and it has been integrated into the core curriculum of the educational system. This has been the case for years in Europe where all children start learning a foreign language in elementary school and continue studying it until the end of their academic experience. Areas here in the United States where there are large ethnic minorities also see the importance daily of being able to communicate with their neighbors and friends.

What Should Be the Place of Foreign Language Study in American Education?

We are firmly convinced that foreign language study **is essential to every American child.** Granted, reading, writing, and basic math are ***absolute*** necessities, without which a person cannot function in our modern society, but beyond those we are talking about levels of importance, and the study of a foreign language is just as important as history, literature, and world geography, and is just as practical as science, advanced math, or shop. To quote the *Standards for Foreign Language Learning*: "Language and communication are at the heart of the human experience. The United States must educate students who are equipped linguistically and culturally to communicate successfully in a pluralistic American society and abroad. This imperative envisions a future in which ALL students will develop and maintain proficiency in English and at least one other language." (*Standards,* 2006, p. 7).

Many of our schools are not prepared to include foreign language study in their curriculum, but they should begin to make that inclusion, even if it takes a "mandate" passed by state legislatures such as has been done in New York, Virginia, Arizona, and other states. The argument that not everyone can learn languages is simply false. *All* students are language learners and can benefit from acquaintance with other cultures. Quoting again from the standards: "all students can be successful language and culture learners, and they must have access to language and culture study that is integrated into the entire school experience, benefit from the development and maintenance of proficiency in more than one language...language and culture education is part of the *core curriculum.*"

In a larger sense, we are educating children to be citizens of our nation who can defend and further its interests in dealings with foreign countries. We cannot ignore the fact that we share this globe with other peoples and cultures and must learn how to interact with them. Monolinguals who have never ventured away ... poorly ... people ... insist ..., "then

RATIONALE FOR ADVOCACY FOR FOREIGN LANGUAGE STUDY

As you prepare yourself to advocate for foreign language study, you will want to be well armed with carefully thought out arguments, strongly supported with reliable facts. Quotes from important people will lend credence, as will results from numerous studies that demonstrate the value of learning a foreign language. Start by beginning a file of materials, then put your ideas down on paper so you will have it close at hand when you need it.

There are a number of places you can go to get help in your campaign: your local foreign language association, the State Foreign or World Language Coordinator/Specialist, and a number of national organizations. These organizations regularly publish materials that summarize the value of foreign languages, and they can be passed on to the people mentioned above. A fruitful source is the **Discover Languages**® campaign developed by the American Council on

the Teaching of Foreign Languages (ACTFL) to raise awareness about the benefits of language study. The program has many, many ideas and materials to use in making people aware of the importance of studying languages. Among those materials are videos, quotes and brochures available on the ACTFL website (http://www.actfl.org). ACTFL also publishes a magazine, *The Language Educator*, which regularly features information about advocacy for foreign language study.

Another example is the pamphlet prepared by the Modern Language Association (MLA) entitled *Knowing Other Languages Brings Opportunities*, which you can order for distribution to parents, students and school administrators. They are free of charge.

Other sources you can go to for information are the report of the President's Commission on Foreign Languages and International Studies. You should arm yourselves with quotes of important and influential people, both past and present, such as Johann Wolfgang von Goethe (German poet-supreme–19th Century), Wilhelm von Humboldt (scholar and statesman–1767-1835), or Paul Simon (former Congressman and Senator from Illinois–presidential aspirant 1988), Senator Daniel Akaka from Hawaii, or even President Barack Obama who declared himself in favor of language study. Depending on your audience, you might want to quote religious leaders or even passages of scriptures that urge the study of foreign languages and cultures.

The World Language sections in State Curriculum Guides usually are an excellent source for rationale statements. The **New York State Syllabus** for foreign languages, *Modern Languages for Communication* emphasizes these reasons for foreign language acquisition: "In addition to the practical application of communication skills, the benefits derived from the study of a second language are many and contribute to the attainment of the Regents' goals for elementary and secondary education. Empirical findings indicate that second language study:

- Fosters a sense of humanity and friendship
- Increases students' adaptability to different environments and modes of acting and thinking
- Furnishes the key to thinking patterns, cultures, and social institutions of other peoples
- Provides insights into the human mind and language itself
- Prepares students for a world in which nations and peoples are increasingly interdependent
- Develops the skills and habits essential to the learning process, creative inquiry, and critical thinking
- Helps students to increase their sensitivity to and understanding of the language, values, customs, and traditions of others
- Leads students to discover and examine their own personal values and civic responsibilities
- Provides insights into America's values and an appreciation of national responsibilities in the world community is an additional asset to many careers and to professional advancement.

Wisconsin's *A Guide to Curriculum Planning in Foreign Language* list the following benefits:

Immediate Benefits
- Attaining greater academic achievement in other areas of study, including reading, social studies, and mathematics
- Developing a clearer understanding of the English language and greater sensitivity to structure, vocabulary, and syntax
- Earning higher SAT and ACT scores, especially in verbal areas
- Gaining a greater awareness and deeper understanding of other cultures and developing a more positive interaction with persons from other nations
- Gaining advantageous qualifications for student exchange programs

- Developing a global attitude
- Improving knowledge of geography
- Exploring career opportunities involving foreign language
- Earning college credits while in high school and/or fulfilling a requirement for college entrance or graduation

Long-Range Benefits
- Facilitating the learning of additional foreign languages
- Acquiring an indispensable skill in a global world
- Preparing for travel for business, education, or pleasure
- Performing research abroad
- Qualifying for foreign scholarships and fellowships
- Qualifying for foreign-study programs
- Student exchanges
- Junior year abroad in college
- Summer courses abroad
- Business internships abroad
- Exchanging professional ideas and information in commerce, science, law, education, arts
- Enhancing career opportunities
- Employment abroad in business, education, or government
- Employment in the U.S. by foreign companies
- Employment in the U.S. by United States export companies
- Employment in industries dealing with foreign tourists
- Employment in social services, hospitals, law enforcement
- Appreciating the aesthetics of literature, music, art, folklore
- Developing more flexibility in thinking processes through problem solving, conceptualizing, and reasoning
- Enjoying the satisfaction of achieving a personal goal–learning another language.

The following statement of Foreign Language Philosophy comes from **Indiana's** guide to proficiency-based instruction "The purpose . . . of foreign language education is to prepare young people to become culturally sensitive and communicatively competent travelers, students, and/or workers in other societies and cultures in the world, to interact positively and more effectively with the native speakers they meet and work with in this country, and to evolve more of those capabilities for productive citizenship in Indiana, the United States and the world."

Preparation for Confrontation. Foreign language teachers have to be realistic and face the fact that there are enemies of different sorts and intensities who have cases against foreign language study and who are even against programs which would further foreign language proficiency and cultural appreciation. Various kinds of people express a variety of arguments. There are no pat answers. There are difficult consequences for almost every course of action.

[handwritten note: Why learn a FL? — sense of humanity + friendship]

...nguage ...uments ...to start ...ed it is ...rather ...gument ...se and ...though ...nguage

...should ...ready ...nge as ...que to ...em in ...rselves ...efense ...emmas may come up in local areas—perhaps in a neighborhood (school) or in a city (school district) or in a state (districts in regions) or in the whole nation (especially in professional organizations or in government subsidy-programs). Even a local rural school board may confront and reject even the most reasonable or the most plausible arguments for foreign language study.

WHAT CAN WE DO?

You can begin your advocacy by working with those around you. The following people can be of great help in persuading students that it is important for them to study a foreign language: students, parents, PTA officers, school counselors, and administrators. Let's look at each of these groups with some detail.

Students. The students themselves are, of course, our primary target. Although greatly influenced by parents and peers, they are ultimately the ones who make the decision as to what they will learn. Too often they are guided by strictly practical considerations. "Will I ever use the language?" is a question they typically ask, and it is, of course, a pertinent one, but they must be told that there are other values besides the practical ones. "Isn't learning a language difficult?" is another common question. They need to understand that although they start at point zero, they can succeed if they give it enough time and if they work at it. While it is true that some people have greater aptitude for language learning, everyone can learn another tongue, and all will profit from the experience. And once they have begun you must instill in them the concept that language learning is not just a "one shot" experience of one or two years or one or two semesters–it is a long process that must be sustained over a period of several years.

As you counsel with your students you may want to remind them that some of the most prestigious colleges and universities require foreign language study as a condition for admission and this is also true of many state universities. Others require foreign language study for graduation and if students don't begin in Secondary School they have to take time to complete that requirement while in college.

Parents. Perhaps no one has a greater influence over what children study in school than the parents. Enlightened parents who recognize the importance of language study are often the force behind successful language programs, as they have gone to administrators and insisted that language programs be strengthened or, in many cases, initiated. Parents can often draw on their own experiences that have shown the value of language learning, and even when the students may not show interest, the parents can persuade them to study a language.

However, many parents have some very distorted or bigoted opinions about language learning. It is reported that when one parent was asked why her child wasn't studying a modern language, she replied that it was because of religious conviction. She regularly read the Bible and knew that Jesus Christ spoke English and "If it was good enough for our Savior, it is good enough for my son." This statement reflects the ignorance about language learning that is found in many adults in the U.S. A French teacher once told a mother in a parent-teacher conference: "The way things are going, Johnny will never learn French." "Well," she replied, "isn't it fortunate that he wasn't born in France?" In many cases we have to educate some adults along with their children. There has recently been a movement across the country to have English legally declared to be the official language of the state. Xenophobia seems be raising its ugly head once again.

PTA Officers. The cooperation between parents and teachers (sometimes even students are included in the organization–PTSA) is very important to the school-community, but also crucial to FL programs. Often the parents can be involved in starting valuable FL innovations and in stopping shortsighted curtailment or undue procrastination. Letters of concern may be the only recourse that professional teacher organizations have to combat FL program cuts or even total discontinuance; however the parents have strong influence with principals and other administrators, and they can go to great lengths to **demonstrate** not only disapproval, but also impatience for immediate redress. FL teachers should affiliate with PTA's and should cultivate friendship with the presidents and other officers. Of course, much good is done in working for the basic goals of this organization, but in the process care can be exercised to further the special needs of foreign languages.

"Back-to-School Nights/Days." A great deal of planning should put into these endeavors to show what is being done in the schools and in the individual courses. You should try every public relations idea possible to further the cause of foreign languages. This is especially necessary for the benefit of the cause and, of course, for the basic reason for these back-to-school activities.

School counselors. In our schools great reliance is placed on the advice given by counselors who help students plan their careers and decide what courses to take. Unfortunately many of them are not oriented to the importance of language study. You need to cultivate a positive relationship with

these persons and make sure they are aware of the advantages of foreign language study. Make it a point to cut out newspaper articles favorable to language study and pass them on to them. Make sure they are aware of foreign language entrance and graduation requirements at colleges and universities. Discuss with them the concept that foreign language study is not just "college prep," it is "life prep." They need to understand that foreign language study requires long sequences and students should start early so they will have time to become fluent. We need to dispel the notion that you "only need to take a couple of years, and then you have the requirement out of the way."

Administrators. Much of the shaping of our educational system is based purely on budgetary considerations. Administrators have to make decisions about where they are going to put their limited resources; it is only natural that they base those decisions on what they have come to see as priorities. We need to help them realize that foreign language study is not just an enrichment or "frill" subject, but rather a part of basic education. Administrators also need to learn that because of the nature of language study, classes often need to be smaller to permit more personal practice and correction. They need to be more concerned about qualifications and preparation as they hire language teachers, and should resist assigning someone to teach language classes who is not fluent in the language or has not been trained to teach languages. Just as they understand the need for a lab and supplies for the chemistry class, they need to be encouraged to give financial support to the special needs of language learning, such as media and computer equipment. You need to cultivate such a relationship that you can draw them away from the position they usually take, that "Languages are great, and it would be nice to have a strong program, but there is no money."

A marvelous source for help in your work with academic advisors and school administrators is Smart Briefs (you can sign up for them at http://www.smartbrief.com/actfl/). This is a service provided by the American Council on the Teaching of Foreign Languages (ACTFL) in which their staff gleans articles and information supportive and pertinent to foreign language instruction from newspapers and journals around the world, and makes it available to language educators free of charge. You need only sign up to receive this service via e-mail. It is free of charge. Here is a sample taken from a recent "brief" in April, 2011 (used by permission from ACTFL).

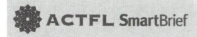

More U.S. students learn Chinese, though most study Spanish. The number of American students learning Mandarin Chinese is on the rise, while Spanish remains the most-studied language in U.S. schools, 2007-08 data from the American Council on the Teaching of Foreign Languages show. A slight increase from 2004-05 can be seen in K-12 students involved in foreign language learning, but that number still amounts to fewer than one in five students -- far below the numbers in other countries. ACTFL officials welcomed recent encouragement by President Barack Obama for U.S. students to learn foreign languages but questioned whether Obama's comments will translate to policy changes. Education Week/Curriculum Matters blog

Research: Bilingualism strengthens the brain. Some researchers say bilingualism has advantages far beyond the ability to communicate in two languages, and they refute concerns by some that growing up speaking two languages causes children to fall behind. Psychologist Ellen Bialystok says different languages in bilingual individuals are always active, but speakers are able to keep them separate, which leads to a stronger executive control system in the brain. "They can get a little extra mileage from these cognitive networks because they have been enhanced throughout life," she says. NPR.org

Calif. recognizes students who speak more than one language. A California district is the latest to sign on to a statewide program that awards bilingual and multilingual students with a special diploma. The state's Seal of Biliteracy recognizes students who maintain academic standards in English and demonstrate mastery in another language through

standardized tests, district exams or two years of language study. "It's so important to be trilingual, biliterate. It really helps you. It gives you a bigger chance of getting a job," said senior Fatima Barron, who speaks three languages. The Monterey County Herald (Calif.)

A very effective technique you should use often is to make numerous "spot commercials" in your classes during the year. This consists of occasionally inserting strong arguments in favor of language study into your regular class activities, just as commercials are inserted in TV programs.

Enjoy Your Product with Your Students

You may have seen the old Volkswagen 'bugs' or 'beetles' that were once very popular. They fun to e used er one. yment ith our guages l be a oughts hance al and f their h high ey can ou can

---

⊙ **KEY NOTE**   **The most important person in getting students interested and motivated is the TEACHER.**

CONCLUSION

Many people have not had the mind-opening experience of leaving a monolingual world and becoming bilingual. Many are still apprehensive about learning another language, and avoid people from other cultures. You as a foreign language teacher must help them see what a great step forward foreign language study provides in interpreting life, in preparing even for aptitude tests, in improving one's humanistic and aesthetic experiences, in becoming more cosmopolitan, and among many additional possibilities to become more communicatively competent and much more sensitive culturally. Prepare yourself now to convince others to study foreign languages. You have many helps to counter opposition and you can prepare to meet that opposition with cogent arguments. The big consideration is to collect ideas and techniques to further FL study in general and in Spanish in particular. The mission for the rest of your life is to be concerned and diligent in developing your rationale file. As Friedrich Rückert said (our translation): *With every language that you learn, you free a spirit, which up to that point was buried within you.*

| REFERENCES AND SUGGESTIONS FOR FURTHER READING |

(Many of these are explained in the chapter)

Alatis, J. (1976). Teaching foreign languages—why? A new look at an old question. *Foreign Language Annals, 9,* 447-458. DOI: 10.1111/j.1944-9720.1976.tb02669.x

American Council on the Teaching of Foreign Languages. (n.d.). *Important facts about the benefits of learning a language* (pamphlet, sold in packets of 25). Available for purchase at http://myactfl.actfl.org/ACTFL_iMISPublic/Core/Orders/product.aspx?catid=5&prodid=241

Committee for Economic Development. (2006). *Education for global leadership: The importance of international studies and foreign language education for U.S. economic and national security.* Washington, DC: Author. Retrieved from ERIC database. (ED502294)

Erickson, J., Haney, D., Semmer, M., & Thiesen, T. (2008, November). You don't have to be an experienced lobbyist to make a difference. *The Language Educator, 3*(6), 57-59. Available at http://www.actfl.org/files/advocacy/TLE_Nov08_MakeADifference.pdf

Gardner, D. P. (Ed.). (1983). *A nation at risk: The imperative for educational reform.* Washington, DC: U.S. Department of Education. Available at http://www2.ed.gov/pubs/NatAtRisk/index.html

Jarvis, G. A. (1975). We think we are *Evening in Paris,* but we're really *Chanel. Foreign Language Annals, 8,* 104-110. DOI: 10.1111/j.1944-9720.1975.tb01527.x

Marcos, K. M. (1998, Fall). Second language learning: Everyone can benefit. *The ERIC Review, 6*(1), 2-5. Available at http://www.cal.org/earlylang/benefits/marcos.html

Modern Language Association. (n.d.). *Knowing other languages brings opportunities* (online brochure). Available at http://www.adfl.org/resources/lang_brochure.pdf

National Advisory Board on International Education Programs. (1983). *Critical needs in international education - Recommendations for action: A report to the Secretary of Education.* Washington, DC: U.S. Department of Education. Retrieved from ERIC database. (ED247201)

National Standards in Foreign Language Education Project. (2006). *Standards for foreign language learning in the 21st century* (3rd ed.). Alexandria, VA: ACTFL.

President's Commission on Foreign Languages and International Studies. (1979). *Strength through wisdom: A critique of U.S. capability.* Reprinted in *Modern Language Journal, 64,* 9-57. DOI: 10.2307/324753

Simon, P. (1980). *The tongue-tied American. Confronting the foreign language crisis.* New York, NY: Continuum.

Image Credits

p. 25: American Council on the Teaching of Foreign Languages. (n.d.). *The Language Educator.* Retrieved July 4, 2011 from http://www.actfl.org/i4a/pages/index.cfm?pageid=4114. Used by permission.

p. 29: American Council on the Teaching of Foreign Languages. (n.d.). *ACTFL Smart Brief.* Retrieved July 4, 2011 from http://alquemie.smartbrief.com/alquemie/servlet/encodeServlet?issueid=054614C5-959B-4164-BA7D-DBCC7390F9F9&lmid=sample . Used by permission.

ACTIVITIES FOR METHODS CLASSES

1. Start a rationale file on the teaching of foreign languages. Choose a plan for organization of findings: Notebook/card file/file folders/key sort cards/folder on your personal computer/some combination of the foregoing.

2. Collect ideas, quotations, facts, arguments, and viewpoints from books, periodicals, and people (college and public school teachers, administrators). Google will give you many, many leads, including a link to a video of Barack Obama "singing our song." Use search terms like "importance of foreign language study" or "value of bilingualism."

3. Write a paper defending the value of foreign language study. Include your personal arguments and quotes from important people, scriptures, and studies.

4. Interview church leaders, government leaders, college and department administrators, representatives of various disciplines, students, and people in other walks of life and find out how they feel about foreign language study. Summarize your findings, and prepare responses to arguments against FL study.

5. Prepare a talk you would give at a PTA meeting or "Back-to-School Night."

6. Collect articles and materials in favor of language study that you can give to the counselors in your school.

7. Design and prepare a bulletin board which presents the value of foreign language study.

8. Prepare a series of "spot commercials" on the value of continuing language study that you can use throughout the year in your language classes.

9. Role play some of the following situations in your methods class:
   a. You are teaching Spanish in a junior high school and you are told thedistrict administration is thinking of cutting out FL study in the junior high schools of the district to emphasize FLs in the high schools only.
   b. You teach a Spanish in a large high school and are trying to build a stronger program. You have arranged to take a special program to the "feeder" junior high schools just before they register for high school.
   c. This week is "Back-to-School Night." What special handouts could you prepare? What would you say to the parents
   d. You are given the opportunity to talk to the people in a local church. Are there religious reasons for teaching and learning a foreign language?
   e. Your college is preparing a "Career Night." What could you tell the students about career opportunities in foreign languages?

10. If you are preparing to teach in an elementary school, write up a rationale for teaching foreign languages to children. Talk about the advantages and values of beginning that study early. You may want to refer to Chapter 15 for ideas. Show your file to the instructor.

CHAPTER THREE

WHAT WE CAN LEARN AND USE FROM THE PAST AND THE PRESENT

YOUR OBJECTIVES FOR THIS CHAPTER ARE TO:

1. SUMMARIZE THE ROLE OF INPUT, OUTPUT, AND INTERACTION IN LANGUAGE LEARNING.

2. DESCRIBE HISTORICAL LANGUAGE TEACHING METHODOLOGIES AND DISCUSS HOW THOSE TRADITIONS HAVE SHIFTED OVER THE YEARS.

3. IDENTIFY THE ADVANTAGES AND DISADVANTAGES OF VARIOUS METHODOLOGIES AND UTILIZE THE INFORMATION GAINED FROM PAST SUCCSSES AND FAILURES.

4. RESOLVE TO USE THE "ENDURING" PRINCIPLES OF A "COMPREHENSIVE MODEL" THAT HAVE CONSISTENTLY WITHSTOOD THE TEST OF TIME.

5. BUILD YOUR PHILOSOPHY AND OWN STYLE OF TEACHING WITH A SOLID FOUNDATION BASED ON A COMMUNICATIVE APPROACH.

6. DEVELOP A CAUTIOUS ATTITUDE ABOUT THE ALLURING ILLUSIONS OF CLAIMS OF MIRACULOUS "NEW" METHODS OF LEARNING LANGUAGES.

Dr. I. Vry Tower, a professor at State University had taught beginning and intermediate Spanish classes for 20 years. Although he was a literature specialist, he had accepted the fact that he was needed to teach language classes also. He had taken the responsibility very seriously and had worked hard with those classes. Through experience and preparation he had developed a "feel" for what worked and what didn't. He was convinced that students needed to work with grammar concepts, especially verb forms, and so he always used a traditional grammar-oriented textbook. He had developed a number of handouts that allowed the students grammar practice in addition to the exercises in the textbook. He knew that fluency came through practical use and besides using the language in the classroom (except for grammatical explanations) he included a variety of communication activities in the class. Dr. Tower was comfortable with his 20 years of teaching. He felt that those who left his classes fluent in the language (and some did) got there by hard work and natural ability. Those who didn't (and most didn't) "just didn't apply themselves or didn't have a lot of aptitude."

The thorn in Professor Tower's side was his colleague, Dr. Onn D. Bandwagon, who was proud of being up-to-date in the latest innovations in language teaching. Whenever a new theory or "oddball" method appeared on the horizon, Professor Bandwagon was there, ready to embrace it with heart and soul. With great gushes of enthusiasm and expectation, he would show up in Dr. Tower's office to report the marvelous results others reported getting and to affirm that this wonderful new approach was going to revolutionize language teaching. He never said it openly, but nevertheless the implication was always there, that Tower was hopelessly bogged down with antiquated methods, and unless he "got with it" he would be left far behind the success of others. Although his enthusiasm with each latest trend soon faded, Bandwagon was not troubled, because by then he had usually espoused a new cause and was beating a new drum.

Although they never really compared results, each professor was sure that his students could easily outperform those of his colleague.

Veri Bright had attended a workshop on "Super-Learning" during the summer and had carefully learned the principles and practiced the techniques. Now she was ready to try them out in her Spanish class. The workshop leader had claimed that if she used this revolutionary new approach, her students would learn to speak like natives, with far less effort and in half the time they had been spending with the traditional approach. While it seemed too good to be true, she was sure it would be worth the try.

After several weeks of mind-relaxing activities, playing of Baroque music, and performing dynamic reading, Miss Bright's expectations were considerably dampened. She found that she was intuitively reverting back to the old techniques that had always worked before, such as having the students role-play different identities, act out situations, practice in pairs and groups, and make oral presentations, and she could see that those activities were what was giving her students fluency in the language. The Baroque music and the mystic meditation didn't seem to be making any difference.

Veri wondered what would happen if she eliminated the music, the mental gymnastics, and the dramatic reading, which seemed to be the only aspects which were truly unique. So she left them out and, not surprisingly, it made no difference. Now she had more time for other activities with her students.

"Well," she reflected ruefully, "I should have known better than to believe those exaggerated claims. I already knew that learning a language only comes through hard work and lots of practice, and that a 'miraculous method' is just an illusion."

CHAPTER THREE

WHAT WE CAN LEARN AND USE FROM THE PAST AND THE PRESENT

> **The true past departs not; no truth or goodness realized by man ever dies or can die; but all is still here, and, recognized or not, lives and works through endless changes.**
> **--Carlyle**

Can anything be gained from looking backward? Yes, because often we are able to detect patterns which explain how we got to where we are now, and which give us some clues as to where we are heading. Failures and successes stand out more clearly in the perspective of time.

A wise man once said "There is nothing new under the sun." This is confirmed as we review what language teachers before us have done. Perhaps the most graphic description one could make would be that of "a boat on a shifting sea, tossed about by changing winds of doctrine." What at one time were considered to be sound and successful techniques were abandoned for more "enlightened" approaches, only to be "rediscovered" at a later date and hailed as modern "innovations."

From time immemorial, language learners and language teachers alike have been obsessed with the dream that some day, someone would discover the method which would produce miraculous fluency in a very short time with very little outlay of time and effort. Evidence that this dream is still alive is all around us in the form of advertisements on the radio and television and in newspapers and magazines that beg you to "Learn Spanish in just 21 days with our amazing new electronic system!" or guarantee you that "You too can speak like a native in just 5 easy lessons based on our revolutionary 'MOTHER METHOD' which utilizes the very same steps in which children learn their mother tongue!" and so on ad ridiculum.

Language educators are very much like a people, who, groping for a perfect society,

stumble from monarchy to anarchy, from autocracy to democracy, from socialism to communism, hoping some day to find their utopia.

Why does this dream of utopia persist? Perhaps because some people do learn languages quickly and with little obvious effort. We see this happen and tend to credit the results to the method, whatever it was. Others lay the blame for this false hope at the feet of past methods, which at first were hailed as miraculous shortcuts to fluency, which were described with grandiose claims of spectacular results, but whose "research," when examined more closely, turned out to be purely anecdotal and grossly over-exaggerated. Whatever the reasons, language teachers must all ultimately face the harsh reality that language learning (or "acquisition" if you will) takes time and effort, and competency comes only after many, many hours of practice and work. Disappointing as it may be, there is no "royal road" to mastery of a foreign language.

THEORIES OF LANGUAGE LEARNING

Before delving into specific language teaching methodologies, it may be helpful to review several current theories of language learning. An understanding of theory can provide us with a framework with which to evaluate the many teaching methodologies that have been used through the years. We will briefly review theories related to three aspects of language learning: input, output, and interaction.

35

The Role of Input: Krashen's Monitor Model

Stephen Krashen, an applied linguist at the University of Southern California, developed what has become known as the "Monitor Model" of language learning. Krashen's model claims that there are two different ways of developing competence in a foreign language: learning, which is the conscious and deliberate study of the language, and acquisition, which is a natural process similar to the way children learn their native language. Krashen believes that acquisition, not learning, is responsible for language proficiency, and that conscious learning functions as a monitor of the correctness of learners' speech, coming into play only when the focus is on grammatical accuracy.

Krashen further asserts that language acquisition occurs when learners are exposed to spoken or written input in the language that is slightly above their current level of proficiency, but is comprehensible due to contextual clues. Thus, comprehensible input plays a key role in language acquisition. Input can only be absorbed by students, however, when they have a low affective filter – that is, when negative affect or emotions such as nervousness and anxiety don't get in the way, filtering out the necessary input.

Although many experts disagree with Krashen's downplaying of the importance of conscious language study, his theory has influenced teachers to provide students with lots of input by speaking in the target language, playing audio and video recordings, and reading authentic texts, while using visuals, gestures, and examples to make the input comprehensible. This focus on comprehensible input has helped make our classrooms a richer environment for language acquisition.

The Role of Output: Swain's Output Hypothesis

In contrast to Krashen, who claims that input is all that is needed for language acquisition, Merrill Swain affirms that output is also necessary. In other words, students need many opportunities to speak and write in the language. Swain developed her "Output Hypothesis" after observing French immersion students in Canada who had excellent listening comprehension but made many grammatical and sociolinguistic errors when speaking. If input

were all that was necessary, these students ought to have spoken near-perfect French, since they had been exposed to thousands of hours of input.

According to Swain (1993), "pushing" students to produce output serves four functions: (1) it gives learners a chance to practice language principles, leading to automaticity in their use; (2) it forces learners to recognize what they do not yet know or know only partially; (3) it gives learners a chance to try out different ways of saying things to see if they work; and (4) it can generate responses from speakers of the language that give learners feedback on the comprehensibility and accuracy of their language use. Swain's hypothesis has been instrumental in encouraging teachers to provide many opportunities for students to produce output in language, and specifically, output where attention is given to linguistic correctness.

The Role of Interaction: Long's Interactional Hypothesis

Input and output theories both look at language learning as it goes on inside students' heads. A separate line of research has examined the role of interaction with others in the language learning process, and specifically the negotiation of meaning. This term refers to the process in which learners modify their speech in order to make it more understandable to their conversational partner. In conversations between students and native speakers, teachers, or other students, one or both partners may need to ask for clarification or check to be sure they understand or have been understood, which may lead them to adjust their speech to make it more comprehensible. Long's Interactional Hypothesis (1980, 1996) claims that these conversational adjustments facilitate language learning because they help connect input and output, as well as helping learners focus on particular aspects of language that they need to learn. A growing body of research has supported this theory, suggesting that students need frequent opportunities to interact with others in the language.

In summary, input, output, and interaction all seem to play an important role in language learning. Later in this chapter we will introduce an instructional model that takes these three factors into account.

A HISTORICAL OVERVIEW OF LANGUAGE TEACHING METHODS

Having examined some current theories of language learning, we now turn to a brief examination of language teaching methods through the years. What is there in the past that can help us? To what extent to past methodologies support what we currently know and believe about how languages are learned? Will a review of previous teaching, innovations, actions, and reactions give us any kind of foundation to build on? We think it can. We can search for "firm ground"– methods and procedures that have been proven successful. We can see the weakness and false assumptions of ill-conceived strategies through the perspective of hindsight. As we look at new approaches, we can resist the temptation to "throw the baby out with the bath," i.e., discard some sound and successful techniques just because a particular methodology has fallen out of favor.

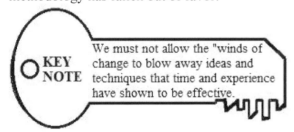

KEY NOTE   We must not allow the "winds of change to blow away ideas and techniques that time and experience have shown to be effective.

Focus on form vs. focus on meaning. For centuries, language teachers have expressed philosophical disagreements about how languages should be taught and learned. Much of this disagreement has centered on the debate between a *focus on form* and a *focus on meaning*. Those who advocate a focus on form (FOF) believe that language is a set of structures for encoding meaning, and that language learning consists of mastering these structures. FOF advocates believe in a "bottom-up" approach to teaching, where grammar and vocabulary are taught explicitly as the building blocks for language. Advocates of a focus on meaning (FOM), on the other hand, view language as a tool for communication, and believe that languages are best learned by actually using them to communicate. They favor a "top-down" approach where students are exposed to language in meaningful chunks rather than isolated words and sentences.

A related debate is whether or not people learn a second language (L2) in the same way that children acquire their first language (L1). FOM advocates point out that children learn their L1 by focusing on meaning, not form, and suggest that L2 learning occurs in a similar way. FOF fans counter that L2 learning is different from L1 acquisition, pointing out that adolescents and adults have developed cognitive skills that children don't have, including the ability to read and write and to recognize and analyze linguistic patterns.

As we will see, the pendulum has swung back and forth through the years. Some methods have given attention to form while neglecting meaning and vice-versa, while a few methods have attempted to strike a balance between the two.

The Grammar-Translation Method

During the first hundred years of our country's history, the main foreign languages taught in schools were Latin and Classical Greek. As these languages had ceased to be spoken, a different justification had to be found for teaching them. Scholars claimed that Latin and ancient Greek were still worth studying because the mastery of their complex grammar developed mental discipline and gave students access to great classical literature. Textbooks consisted of explanation of grammar rules, vocabulary lists, and sentences for translation. The teacher's role was mainly to lecture on the material in the textbook and assign translation homework. As "modern" languages such as French and German began to be taught in the United States in the late 1800s, they were taught using this same method in order to lend them the prestige that Classical languages enjoyed. (Spanish was not widely taught in the U.S. until well into the 20th century.)

At its best, the Grammar-Translation method did equip students to read or decode foreign language texts, but it did not teach them to speak the language, as emphasis on oral skills was limited to the reading aloud of passages of text and sentences that students had translated. The Grammar-Translation method continues to be used today in some Latin and Classical Greek classes, as well as in some other settings where the focus is on developing reading and decoding skills in the language.

What can we learn from this method? Perhaps the principle of most worth is that students learn what they are taught. If our goal is just to develop reading or decoding skills, Grammar-Translation techniques may be effective. If we want students to learn to oral skills, however, they need practice with listening and speaking.

The Reform Movement and the Direct Method

As language study shifted from ancient to modern languages, it became recognized that new methods were needed to develop speaking skills. Obviously there was value in gaining oral skill in French, German, or Spanish, since there were millions speakers of those languages, in contrast to the long-gone speakers of Latin and Classical Greek. To address this need, a number of reformers in the late 1800s and early 1900s developed what became known as "natural methods," claiming that second languages could be learned in the same way as we learn our mother tongue. The most well known of these methods was the Direct Method, which was developed in Europe and adopted in the United States by the Berlitz private school chain.

The Direct Method was based on the idea that languages can be taught without translation or use of the L1 if meaning is conveyed through context; thus, students learn "directly" in the target language. Lessons focused on everyday vocabulary such as classroom objects, simple actions, and words that could be depicted in pictures, which were taught through question-and-answer exchanges between teacher and students. Correct pronunciation was emphasized, but grammar was generally not taught explicitly. All instruction was in the target language. Although the Direct Method was successful in private schools, it never gained widespread use in public school classrooms. The method relied on teachers' skills rather than on a textbook, and many teachers didn't have sufficient pedagogical or linguistic skills to make it work. The Direct Method has also been criticized for not giving enough attention to grammatical accuracy.

What can we learn from these methods? Many basic principles of the Direct Method and other "natural" methods still hold true today. Oral competency seems to come more through natural, meaningful use than through formal analysis and conscious translation. The development of good pronunciation is also important. Most of the currently popular communicative approaches have roots in the "natural" methods of the late 1800s

The Reading Approach

With the advent of World War I, Americans developed a decidedly "anti-foreign" attitude. Enrollment in foreign language classes, especially German, declined dramatically, and most of the remaining foreign language programs were reduced to two years of instruction. A study begun in 1923 and published as the Coleman Report (1925) concluded that since two years of study was insufficient for oral mastery, a more reasonable goal for foreign language programs was the development of reading ability. Foreign language classes began to be structured around the reading and analysis of texts, either simple texts written for students and published in books known as "readers," or excerpts from great "masterworks." Some classes used the explication de texte technique where a short segment of text became the focus of an entire class hour as the structure, etymology of the words, and idiomatic expressions were discussed in great detail. Speaking and listening skills received little or no emphasis. The reading approach became the main method for teaching foreign languages in the U.S. through World War II and into the 1950s.

What can we learn from this approach? There are at least two lessons to be learned here. One is that although reading skills are important, an exclusive emphasis on reading does not teach students to communicate orally, which is what most of them expect to learn in our classes. The other lesson has to do with *what* our students read and *why* they read it. Currently, the best teachers and textbooks use a variety of *authentic texts* written for native speakers, including not only great masterworks of literature, but also newspaper articles, advertisements, comics, and even blogs. In addition to exposing students to everyday vocabulary and grammar, these texts allow students to read for understanding, information, pleasure, and other real-life purposes.

The Audiolingual Method

The Audiolingual Method evolved out of the Army Specialized Training Program, a program that the U.S. government developed to teach foreign languages quickly to military personnel during World War II when it found that foreign language graduates from U.S. universities who were taught using the Grammar-Translation Method or the Reading Approach had insufficient speaking skills. American schools and universities, however, continued to use these methods until 1957, when Russia launched the first artificial satellite, Sputnik. Concerned about Americans' isolation from scientific advances in foreign countries due to their lack of foreign language skills, Congress appropriated funds for developing new teaching materials and methods. The method adopted was named the Audiolingual Method because of its emphasis on oral skills. It was based on the Army method, as well as on a prominent psychological theory of the time, B. F. Skinner's Behaviorism, which claimed that all learning is a result of habit formation as humans respond to external stimuli and their response is either rewarded as correct or punished as incorrect.

A typical audiolingual lesson begins with a dialogue, which is presented either from a recording or verbally by the teacher, often accompanied by drawings to illustrate the meaning.Lines from the dialogue are memorized one by one, with students repeating each line in chorus. When the dialogue has been memorized, the teacher leads students in adapting it to their own situation or interests by substituting words or phrases. Sentences containing key linguistic structures are then extracted from the dialogue to form the basis for *pattern drills*, such as substituting new words or grammatical structures, negating affirmative sentences, or changing singular to plural, according to the teacher's cues. Any grammatical or pronunciation errors are corrected immediately by the teacher. Some grammatical explanation may be provided, but it is generally kept to a minimum, since the goal is not necessarily to understand language rules but rather to form correct habits in using them.

The Audiolingual Method was widely adopted in the U.S. and Canada and served as the main teaching method in the 1960s, enjoying almost evangelistic fervor among its proponents, who called it the "New Key" to language learning. The method's decline in the late 1960s and early 1970s was due to two factors. First, linguist Noam Chomsky (1959) pointed out that humans constantly use language to say new things, a process that cannot be explained by Skinner's behavioristic theories. Second, some language teachers and students experienced frustration with the method's avoidance of grammar explanations, its heavy emphasis on rote memorization and drilling, and its failure to teach students to carry on conversations outside of memorized dialogues.

What can we learn from this method? Perhaps the most important lesson here is that real communicative ability cannot be developed if students are limited to working with memorized materials and drills; they need opportunities to *create with language*, putting together words and structures to express their own ideas in meaningful communicative contexts. Despite its rejection by the language teaching profession, however, the Audiolingual Method does offer some useful techniques. Dialogues are natural examples of everyday language, and they can serve as a beginning point for communication and a basis for generalizations of structural patterns. (Many textbooks today still base their lessons around dialogues.) Memorization can be a valuable technique for acquiring vocabulary, provided that students then use the words in meaningful contexts. These Audio-Lingual techniques are usable in any foreign language course today.

The Cognitive Code Approach

By the 1970s, the Behaviorist theory of the Audiolingual Method had largely been replaced with the theories of cognitive psychology. A "cognitive code" approach emphasizes helping learners understand language rules and relate them to what they already know. Although cognitive theories were never formally refined into a "method," they do suggest certain learning activities and principles, among which are the following:

• All learning must be meaningful to the learner. When presenting grammar concepts, for example, the teacher should give explicit grammar explanations accompanied by examples to help students understand.

- In order to develop automaticity in language use, students need extensive practice using language skills. Often this practice is sequenced so as to progress from structured to more open-ended activities.
- New material should be presented in such a way that it can be integrated with students' previous knowledge. It should also be reviewed periodically.
- Students can benefit from instruction in language learning strategies, including metacognitive strategies that help them plan, organize, and monitor their learning.

What can we learn from this approach? In contrast to Behaviorism, cognitive principles remind us that language students need to understand what they are learning. In addition, they need to actually "learn how to learn," and they need meaningful practice using what they have learned. These principles have been widely incorporated in foreign language classrooms and textbooks since the 1970s.

"Humanistic" Methods

In addition to the adoption of the principles of cognitive psychology, the 1970s saw the creation of various "humanistic" language teaching methods that had their roots in psychotherapy. These methods were concerned with meeting both the cognitive and affective (emotional) needs of individuals. The most well known of these methods are Community Language Learning, the Silent Way, and Suggestopedia.

Community Language Learning, also called *Counseling-Learning*, was developed by Charles Curran (1976) based on psychological counseling techniques. The teacher's role is as a "knower/counselor" who merely provides the language necessary for students to express themselves. In part of a typical lesson, the students may sit close together in a circle. One student makes a statement that he or she wants to express to another student, and the teacher whispers in the student's ear the target language equivalent of the student's statement, which he or she then repeats aloud. Another student responds, and the process is repeated. The whole conversation is tape recorded and transcribed for later discussion of the language principles that arose in the course of the lesson.

The Silent Way, introduced by Caleb Gattegno (1972), has the goal of developing learner independence, autonomy, and responsibility. True to its name, the method instructs the teacher to remain silent most of the time, giving minimal input in order to give students time to think about the language. One tool used by the teacher is a set of colored rods called Cuisenaire rods. A typical lesson might consist of the teacher picking up different sizes, colors, and numbers of rods, saying "rod," "green rod," "two rods," "two green rods," and leaving students to rely on their own mental resources and each other to figure out how the language works.

Suggestopedia was introduced by a Bulgarian psychotherapist, Georgi Lozanov (1978), and is based on the claim that languages can be learned quickly by tapping into learners' subconscious mental resources. Lessons are based around long dialogues accompanied by vocabulary lists and grammar explanations. After studying these materials in a somewhat traditional way, the lesson proceeds to the "séance" phase, involving relaxation, rhythmic breathing, and Baroque music, interspersed with the teacher reading the dialogue repeatedly with varied volume and intonation. Lozanov claims that these techniques activate the subconscious mind and accelerate the language learning process.

Although Community Language Learning, the Silent Way, and Suggestopedia have received considerable attention, these methods have never achieved widespread use in public school classrooms due to their unconventional nature and the high level of specialized training that they require of teachers. Another drawback of the methods is that they pose challenges in *program articulation*, or the sequencing of foreign language classes so as to offer courses from beginning through advanced levels, where the content taught in Level 1 prepares students for Level 2 and so forth, even if each course is taught by a different teacher. Spanish 2 teachers, for example, might have difficulty determining exactly what concepts their students learned in Spanish 1 if they were taught exclusively with one of these methods.

What can we learn from these methods? The "humanistic" methods remind us of the importance of attending to students' cognitive and affective needs, tapping their mental strengths, and helping them become independent learners. They also remind us, however, that the methods we use must fit into a school curriculum and be practical for use in a traditional classroom setting.

Modern Adaptations of the Direct Method

Since the 1960s, a number of methods have been developed based largely on the principles used in the "natural" methods of the late 1800s and early 1900s. Among these are the Natural Approach, Total Physical Response (TPR), and TPR Storytelling. All three of these methods have been widely used in foreign language classrooms in the United States.

The Natural Approach was introduced in 1977 by Tracy Terrell, a Spanish teacher. Terrell later collaborated with Stephen Krashen to write a book on the approach (1983), which was based on Krashen's Monitor Model and incorporated techniques from the earlier Direct Method and other "natural" methods. Like the Direct Method, all instruction is done in the target language, and the input is made comprehensible by the use of pictures, objects, and questions. One key difference between the Direct Method and the Natural Approach is that the latter allows for a "silent stage" in which students are not expected to speak. This is done in order to simulate the process by which children learn their first language, as well as to lower the affective filter by creating a low-anxiety environment. Topics covered in beginning classes may include identifying and describing oneself; recreation and leisure activities; family, friends, and daily activities; eating; travel and transportation; and shopping and buying.

Total Physical Response (TPR) was developed in the 1960s by James Asher, a professor of psychology at San Jose State College. Asher discovered with the aid of a Japanese graduate student that he was quickly able to learn Japanese by physically responding to commands in the language such as *stand up, sit down,* and *walk,* and he developed a language teaching method based on this type of command. He reasoned that commands constitute a large part of the input that children hear in their L1,

and that physically responding to these commands activates the right hemisphere of the brain, reinforcing language learning. Other TPR commands that a teacher might give to students include *touch the chair, walk to the door,* and *point to the table.* Like the Natural Approach, TPR delays the introduction of speaking for six months to a year.

TPR Storytelling (TPRS) was developed in 1990 by Blaine Ray, a Spanish teacher in California. Ray had experienced success with Total Physical Response, but wanted to help his students move beyond TPR commands to more narrative and descriptive uses of language. He hit upon the technique of having students use actions to respond to stories that he made up based on their interests. A TPRS lesson begins with the teacher presenting key vocabulary words that will be used in the story, along with their English translation, and asking personalized questions using the words. The teacher then introduces the story, calling student actors to the front of the class to act out each event as it occurs. The teacher is encouraged to make the story "bizarre, exaggerated, and personalized" so that it will be interesting and memorable. As each new sentence is introduced, the teacher asks multiple questions in order to give repeated exposure to the new vocabulary. Finally, students are given a printed version of the story, which they first translate back to English and then retell in the target language.

TPRS differs markedly from TPR and the Natural Approach in that it makes the input comprehensible by translating to the students' L1 rather than by using visual or contextual clues. TPRS teachers are urged to avoid using words that have not been explicitly translated to the students' native language.

What can we learn from these methods? The above methods are currently quite popular in some foreign language classrooms, and many teachers swear by them. These methods emphasize the value of providing input in meaningful contexts and making the input comprehensible. They also remind us of the importance of making the classroom a low-anxiety environment. The methods have sometimes been criticized, however, for neglecting the teaching of speaking, grammar, or culture, reminding us that even popular methods have limitations. Other challenges posed by these methods are the specialized training required of teachers, and the articulation among different levels (Spanish 1, Spanish 2, etc.) when no textbook is used.

Summary

As we have seen, the pendulum has swung back and forth through the years between a focus on form and a focus on meaning. The Grammar-Translation method emphasized grammatical form, with little attention to meaning except in the decoding of ancient texts. The Direct Method, in contrast, emphasized meaning at the expense of form. Other methods have usually emphasized either form or meaning, but have rarely given equal attention to both.

Most language teachers nowadays recognize the need for focusing on both form and meaning. Students can hardly achieve fluency in the language if they only focus on grammar and vocabulary and never have an opportunity to use the language in meaningful contexts. On the other hand, research has shown that students who are plunged into communicative situations without attention to accuracy often develop "fossilized" patterns of errors that are nearly impossible to overcome, which prevent them from reaching high levels of language proficiency. *Both* form and meaning are integral parts of language learning.

Historical Summary of Language Teaching Methods

Method/Goals	How is language believed to be learned?	What is the syllabus organized around?	What do classroom activities consist of?
Grammar-Translation Method Learn grammar and vocabulary; read great literature; develop mental discipline	Through mental effort, memorization of rules and vocabulary, translating sentences	Linguistic structures (grammar) and vocabulary	Memorizing vocabulary and rules; translating sentences; reading classical texts
Direct Method Develop communicative ability; think directly in L2	Through direct association of words with objects and actions; large amounts of listening; speaking	Everyday classroom objects and situations; later, common situations	Presentation of vocabulary with visuals and questions; practice of speaking and reading
Reading Method Develop reading ability in L2	Through reading and analyzing texts (reading was the only skill emphasized)	Simple texts written for students, or excerpts from great literary masterworks	Analysis of grammar, vocabulary, and idioms in written texts
Audio-Lingual Method Develop native-like mastery of structure and sounds; learn to use language automatically	Through stimulus-response conditioning that forms correct habits in language use	Linguistic structures (phonology, morphology, syntax)	Dialogue memorization, structural drills
Cognitive-Code Approach Master rules to be able to create with language in new situations	Through conscious understanding of rules, repeated practice, and meaningful language use	Usually grammatical topics	Study rules and practice them to develop automaticity; use them in meaningful contexts
Community Language Learning Near-native proficiency; engagement of whole self	Through a social interaction process ("Language is persons in contact")	Students' comments and feelings	Translation, recording, transcription, group work, reflection

The Silent Way Practical knowledge of grammar; correct pronunciation	Through discovery learning and problem solving	Structures and related vocabulary	Cuisinaire rods, phoneme charts; repetition
Suggestopedia Learn everyday language at an accelerated pace	Through suggestion, by tapping subconscious resources	Dialogues, graded by grammar and vocabulary	Soft lights, Baroque music, comfortable seating; listening to dramatic readings; role plays
Natural Approach Help beginners become intermediates in basic communicative skills	Through exposure to comprehensible input (similar to L1 acquisition)	Basic oral and written communicative skills – situations, functions, topics	Activities involving input (use of visuals to introduce vocabulary, TPR, etc.)
Total Physical Response Teach oral proficiency at a beginning level	Through listening and responding to commands; active physical participation	Sentences, selected on the basis of grammar and vocabulary and on ease of classroom use	Respond to teacher's commands; later, games, skits, and stories
TPR Storytelling Develop speaking and reading proficiency	By hearing it repeatedly in meaningful contexts	Stories invented by teacher and students or taken from TPRS booklets	Listening to, translating, and retelling stories; "pop-up" grammar explanations
Communicative Approach Develop communicative and cultural competence in all language modalities	By using it in meaningful communication	Wide variety of syllabus types (functional-notional; task-based; theme-based)	Task-based activities; games; role plays; pair, group work

Similarly, the input, output, and interactional aspects of language learning have been unevenly emphasized by different methods. TPR and the Natural Approach, for example, are heavy on input but neglect output, at least in the early stages of learning. Community Language Learning emphasizes interaction, but input is limited to the teacher's translations of sentences that students want to say. Again, research and experience have shown that all three aspects---input, output, and interaction---are important parts of language learning.

In the last part of this chapter we will discuss the current trend in foreign language teaching – a communicative approach – and suggest a simple model for language teaching that we think fits well with this type of approach.

PRESENT TRENDS: A COMMUNICATIVE APPROACH

Like the Cognitive Code Approach, the Communicative Approach is not really a "method," but rather a set of principles that evolved beginning

in the 1970s and are still in use today. In the United States, these principles were partly influenced by the work of American Council on the Teaching of Foreign Languages (ACTFL). In 1986 the *ACTFL Proficiency Guidelines* were released, describing what learners can do at various levels of proficiency. These guidelines have encouraged teachers to think about what their students can currently do with the language, and what they need to be able to do in order to progress to the next level. During the ensuing decade, ACTFL collaborated with other language teaching organizations to produce the *Standards for Foreign Language Learning* (1996), which outline what learners should know and be able to do in five goal areas: Communication, Cultures, Comparisons, Connections, and Communities. The *Standards* remind us that a communicative approach is comprehensive in nature, helping students develop interpersonal, interpretive, and presentational communicative skills, as well as cultural understanding. (The *Standards for Foreign Language Learning* and the *ACTFL Proficiency*

Guidelines will be discussed further in Chapters 4 and 7, respectively.)

A communicative approach is based on the idea that language is a tool for communication, and students learn language by actually using it to communicate. Rather than outlining specific teaching techniques, a communicative approach focuses on *learning outcomes*–that is, what students know and can do with the language and culture. Teachers are free to use whatever methods or techniques they feel will best lead to these outcomes. Commonly used activities include information gap activities, jigsaw activities, role plays, task-based activities, and paired interviews.

A "COMPREHENSIVE MODEL" FOR LANGUAGE TEACHING

We now recommend what we will refer to as the Comprehensive Model. We think this model fits well with a communicative approach to language teaching, as it is based on principles that experience has shown to be successful in teaching communicative skills. The model is shown in the following graphic.

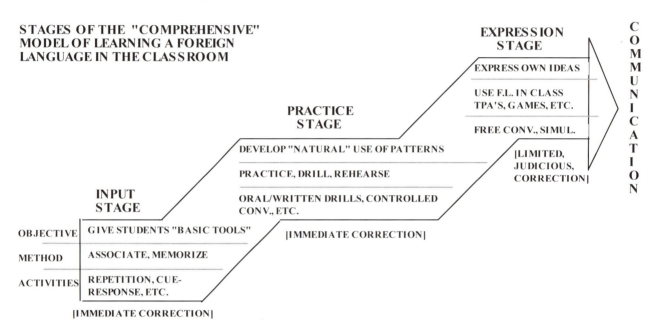

STAGES OF THE "COMPREHENSIVE" MODEL OF LEARNING A FOREIGN LANGUAGE IN THE CLASSROOM

The Comprehensive Model is not a "method" in that it does not prescribe specific teaching techniques. Rather, it is a framework that can help you select and sequence instructional techniques and learning activities. Years of language teaching have proven that there must be an *input stage*. We cannot start from nothing. We must have the basic tools to begin; and there are many different activities we can use to present these tools. Experience has also shown that we cannot start immediately at the *expression stage*. The students stumble and strain, become enmeshed in trying to express ideas with the structure of their native language, and lack the vocabulary to communicate what they want to say. There must be an intermediate, *practice stage*, which gives them ease and fluent use of the idioms and structure of the target language.

Again, we have numerous activities and techniques that we can utilize in this stage. Soon we arrive at the point where the teacher fades into the background and the students express their feelings and ideas, using the vocabulary we gave them in the *input stage* and the structures they mastered in the *practice stage*. Now our efforts are focused on providing situations that are as near as possible to "real life" and the students are using the language meaningfully and naturally.

We hope you can see how the Comprehensive Model gives attention to both form and meaning, as well as to input, output, and interaction. The input stage of the model can include either form-focused grammatical input or meaning-focused communicative input. The practice stage gives students a chance to produce output where the focus is still on getting the forms

44

right. And in the expression stage, students produce output in meaning-focused communicative contexts, including interaction with others in the language. In subsequent chapters, we will discuss how the Comprehensive Model can be applied to the teaching of specific language skills and grammar.

What method? It is our conviction that the answer to the question, "What method should I use?" is simply a matter of adopting a communicative approach that addresses all language modalities as well as culture. Within this approach, the framework of the Comprehensive Model can help you select and sequence whatever methods or techniques you feel are appropriate. Those who teach several language classes day after day must use an approach based on the realities of the classroom and discover what works with each class. We are convinced that there are good ideas in almost any method. Try them and keep that which succeeds for you. In the long run this "eclectic" approach, coupled with careful preparation and good teaching, will most often give you satisfying results.

Every teacher brings a different set of skills to the classroom. The goals of individual teachers are not the same; indeed, they may be different for different classes taught by the same teacher. As you gain experience in teaching, you will develop a "feel" for which methods and techniques work best. Be careful about jumping on bandwagons, but keep up to date with the latest thinking and evaluate all the approaches you can. Then simply use what helps you realize your goals.

CONCLUSION

Our principal goal with this chapter has been to answer the question "What can I learn from the past and the present?" Hopefully you will conclude with us that the past teaches that there is no "magical formula" for learning a language quickly and effortlessly, and that the present teaches that the frantic scurrying around by many teachers still trying to find a language learner's paradise through some marvelous new "super learning" method may give them a spurt of success—mainly because of their enthusiasm in their newfound utopia—but a more sensible plan will be to adopt a communicative approach that draws upon different methods and techniques, based on the desired learning outcomes and the unique characteristics of the students. Our Comprehensive Model can provide a framework for selecting and sequencing these instructional techniques and activities.

You should also be convinced that true language proficiency comes only through years of study and practice, aided by the insightful guidance of a dedicated teacher, not through some "miracle" method. Throughout this book, we will come back again and again to how important the teacher is. In this chapter we have taken you through a very quick journey of past and present approaches, methods, and trends. Teachers must do more than adopt whole approaches "willy-nilly," or in the same way, turn to a potpourri or hodgepodge of ideas. There needs to be a unifying principle of organization that comes primarily from the experienced teacher in concert with other experienced teachers.

REFERENCES AND SUGGESTIONS FOR FURTHER READING

Asher, J. J. (2011). *Learning another language through actions* (7th ed.). Los Gatos, CA: Sky Oaks Publications.

Bateman, B., & Lago, B. (2011). *Methods of language teaching* (instructional DVD). London, England: Routledge. *A DVD featuring textual descriptions of ten well-known language teaching methodologies, accompanied by video demonstrations of actual classroom lessons using each method.*

Blair, R. W. (Ed.). (1982). *Innovative approaches to language teaching.* Boston. MA: Heinle & Heinle.

Chomsky, N. (1959). A review of B. F. Skinner's *Verbal Behavior. Language, 35*(1), 26-58.

Chomsky, N. (1965). *Aspects of the theory of syntax.* Cambridge, MA: MIT Press.

Coleman, A. (1925). *The teaching of modern foreign languages in the United States.* Chicago: University of Chicago Press. (The "Coleman Report")

Curran, C. (1976). *Counseling-learning in second languages.* Apple River, IL: Apple River Press.

Gattegno, C. (1972). *Teaching foreign languages in schools: The Silent Way* (2nd ed.). New York. NY: Educational Solutions.

Grittner, F. M. (1977). *Teaching Foreign Languages.* New York, NY: Harper & Row. (Chapter 1: The Historical Roots of Foreign Language Teaching in America.)

Hadley, A. O. (2001). *Teaching language in context* (3rd ed.). Boston, MA: Heinle & Heinle. (Chapter 2: Methodology in Transition.)

Krashen, S. (1982). *Principles and practice in second language acquisition.* New York, NY: Pergamon Press.

Krashen, S. D., & Terrell, T. D. (1983). *The natural approach: Language acquisition in the classroom.* Oxford, England: Pergamon Press.

Long, M. H. (1980). *Input, interaction, and second language acquisition.* (Doctoral dissertation, University of California at Los Angeles.) (AAT 8111249)

Long, M. H. (1996). The role of the linguistic environment in second language acquisition. In W. C. Ritchie & T. K. Bhatia (Eds.), *Handbook of second language acquisition* (pp. 413-468). San Diego, CA: Academic Press.

Lozanov, G. (1978). *Suggestology and outlines of Suggestopedy.* New York, NY: Gordon & Breach.

Ray, B., & Seely, C. (1998). *Fluency through TPR Storytelling.* Berkeley, CA: Command Performance Language Institute.

Oller, J. W. Jr. (1993). *Methods that work: Ideas for literacy and language teachers* (2nd ed.). Boston, MA: Heinle & Heinle.

Richards, J. C., & Rodgers, T. S. (2001). *Approaches and methods in language teaching* (2nd ed.). Cambridge, England: Cambridge University Press.

Skinner, B. F. (1957). *Verbal behavior*. New York, NY: Appleton-Century-Crofts.

Swain, M. (1993). The output hypothesis: Just speaking and writing aren't enough. *Canadian Modern Language Review, 50,* 158-164.

Terrell, T. D. (1977). A natural approach to second language acquisition and learning. *Modern Language Journal, 61,* 325-337. DOI: 10.2307/324551

ACTIVITIES FOR METHODS CLASSES

1. Examine each of the methods described in this chapter in terms of its focus on form and/or meaning, as well as its attention to input, output, and interaction. For each method, write a brief summary of its strengths and weaknesses in relation to these criteria.

2. Study the *Standards for Foreign Language Learning* in Chapter 4 of this book, and then analyze each of the methods described in this chapter in terms of its attention to the five goal areas of Communication, Cultures, Comparisons, Connections, and Communities.

3. Find out if there are any intensive training programs in your area, such as the Foreign Service Institute, Defense Language Institute, Peace Corps Training Program, Missionary Training Center, or a university intensive program. Visit some of the language classes. Analyze the methods used by the teacher. Do they follow one specific method, or do they use an "eclectic" approach? Write a report to hand in to your instructor.

4. Visit beginning French, German and Spanish classes taught at your university. Analyze the methods. Are they using a specific approach? Do different languages use different approaches, or are they all using the same approach? Are they using the concepts outlined in the "Comprehensive Model?" Hand in a report to your methods instructor.

5. Visit beginning classes in some less commonly-taught language such as Chinese, Hebrew, Japanese, etc. Compare the approaches used by the teachers in those classes with those in the more commonly languages. How are they different? The same? Do they use any of the principles of the "Comprehensive Model?" What unique problems do those languages present, such as different writing systems? Write a report.

6. Visit language classes in some nearby public schools. What methods were used? How are they different from the university classes you have visited. Do the teachers communicate in English or the FL? Write a report.

7. Choose one of the methods described in this chapter that interests you. Read a book on that method from the reference list above and write a summary of the method in terms of its (a) historical background, (b) theory of language learning, and (c) typical classroom activities.

8. Spend some time working with the DVD *Methods of Language Teaching* by Bateman and Lago (ask your methods instructor if your university has online access to the DVD). Choose one or more methods from the DVD, read the textual description of the method(s), and watch the accompanying video(s). Write a summary of what you learned.

CHAPTER FOUR
GETTING THINGS READY

YOUR OBJECTIVES FOR THIS CHAPTER ARE TO:

1. IDENTIFY THE VARIOUS SOURCES OF SUPPORT YOU WILL USE AS YOU ESTABLISH GOALS AND PRIORITIES FOR YOUR CLASSES.

2. SUMMARIZE THE GOALS OF THE NATIONAL *STANDARDS FOR FOREIGN LANGUAGE LEARNING* AND PREPARE TO USE THEM IN YOUR PROGRAM.

3. WRITE EFFECTIVE LEARNING OBJECTIVES AND USE AN EFFICIENT APPROACH TO PLANNING PROGRAMS, COURSES, UNITS, AND DAILY LESSONS.

4. OUTLINE CRITERIA AND CONSIDERATIONS FOR EVALUATING AND ADOPTING OR ADAPTING A TEXTBOOK.

5. EMBARK ON A CONTINUING PROGRAM FOR GATHERING MATERIALS FOR YOUR CLASSES, INCLUDING AN EXTENSIVE COLLECTION OF VISUAL AIDS.

6. EXPLAIN HOW TO ACQUIRE AND USE MODERN MEDIA EQUIPMENT TO USE IN YOUR CLASSES.

7. DESCRIBE WAYS OF TRANSFORMING YOUR CLASSROOM INTO A PRODUCTIVE LEARNING ENVIRONMENT (A "CULTURAL ISLAND"), WITH ATTRACTIVE AND INFORMATIVE DECORATION.

8. IDENTIFY A VARIETY OF SEATING ARRANGEMENTS APPROPRIATE FOR DIFFERENT ACTIVITIES IN A FOREIGN LANGUAGE CLASS.

Whenever anyone visited Podunk High School and asked to be shown around the school, they were taken to Miss Moreno's class. It was truly the talk of the school and a wonder to behold. Passing through the doorway under the enormous "BIENVENIDOS" sign, the visitor was immediately struck with a colorful panorama of wall-to-wall displays of scenes from Hispanic countries, pictures from every Spanish-speaking country around the world, a variety of objects from dolls to *sombreros*, and in the front, flags from ten different countries. Students who had graduated always came back year after year to see what marvel Miss Moreno had acquired while they were gone. "Where do you get all these things, and how do you pay for them?" were the questions all would ask. "Oh, I get them from all over," she would reply, "I travel to Hispanic countries whenever I can and always look for things I can bring back to share with my students. I use my own money for those things. We also have some fund-raisers every year and I use the money to order things like books, CDs, slides, videos, and posters from catalogs."

Teachers were always quick to notice that she had a very nice CD player with large speakers, a DVD player with a large monitor, an LCD projector and several personal computers in the classroom. "Where do you get the money for all this equipment?" they would ask, green with envy. "Well," she would answer with a wink, "I happen to think I couldn't be a good teacher without this equipment, and I can always find ways to work extra hours with the principal or the audio visual coordinator. I got the money for the computers through a special enrichment grant I applied for. You can always find ways to get money if you are really convinced you really need something."

Perhaps most impressive was Miss Moreno's visual aid collection. She had several file cabinets full of pictures and transparencies, racks of maps and charts, and innumerable boxes full of toys, games, flash cards and clocks. "These are the fruits of years of collecting," she would remark, "I keep my eyes open wherever I go for things I can use as visual aids in my classes."

Needless to say, one always felt like he or she was in a different world in her classroom. Apparently, that was what she wanted.

~~~

Professor Solares was a respected professor of Spanish literature. He was a renowned authority on Spanish American drama and had published several books and numerous articles. He was, however, a somewhat dull teacher. He prepared himself well for his classes and was very methodical in his coverage of the subject matter. Nevertheless, his students were heard to comment (beyond his hearing, of course) that they sometimes found it difficult to stay awake.

Then one fall, the professor enrolled in a seminar on teaching improvement which the university offered, in which they discussed the concept presented by Robert Mager, that teachers should enter the classroom, not focusing so much on what THEY were going to do, but on what they wanted THE STUDENTS TO BE ABLE TO DO at the end of the class.

The seminar changed Dr. Solares' entire style of teaching. As he later remarked to a colleague, "I was looking at my classes completely wrong. I was always asking 'What should I do in class today?' Now I ask, 'What do I want my students to be able to do at the end of class, and how will I know if they can do it?' and then all my planning goes into strategies to get those outcomes. I really look forward to my classes now, and I'm sure my students enjoy them more."

CHAPTER FOUR

GETTING THINGS READY

> **The man without a purpose is like a ship without a rudder – a waif, a nothing, a no man. Have a purpose in life and, having it, throw such strength of mind and muscle into your work as God has given you.**
> **--Carlyle**

Preparing to teach is much like preparing to go on a long trip. You spend a great deal of time thinking about what your needs will be and what things you will have to get to take with you. Many new teachers are apprehensive about going into the classroom; they are afraid they will not be able to handle the students, they have doubts about their control of the language, they are not sure how to present certain concepts, and so on. That is why it is so important to get ready. If you are prepared you will not be afraid; it is more likely that you will be eager and anxious to get into the classroom, meet your students, and get started.

Just as road maps are vital to the success of any trip, so plans are essential to your teaching success. You must learn to make effective use of planning. You must also spend a lot of time preparing and collecting the materials you will be using and getting your classroom ready.

SETTING COMMUNICATIVE GOALS AND OBJECTIVES

Before beginning the planning process, you will need to spend some time setting your goals and priorities. Learning a foreign language can involve many possible outcomes. At one extreme there is communication in full, that is, in all four major skills and with all of the cultural overtones. At the other extreme there may be some very limited, specific skills such as: reading for an advanced degree requirement, deciphering old documents and letters for genealogical research, typing business letters as a secretary, listening to or monitoring foreign radio broadcasts (in the military). Some people need to become almost equivalent to well-informed native speakers.

Others may be happy to be able to talk to relatives, just barely getting the meaning across. Others learn enough language to use as a tourist. As teachers we must strive to accommodate as many of the goals of our students as we can.

Ideally, we would like to reach some degree of communicative proficiency for each possible purpose for language learning. This goal divides into four important aspects:

1. Task or function—why we want to say, understand, read, write, and/or appreciate a Spanish message.
2. Message or content—what we want to understand, say, read, write, and/or appreciate in Spanish.
3. Circumstance, situation, or context—where we want to use Spanish.
4. Correctness or accuracy—how well we need to use Spanish.

The American Council on the Teaching of Foreign Languages (**ACTFL**) Proficiency Guidelines describes the desired proficiency skills at several levels and can be an invaluable guide for you. They are found in their entirety in the appendix of this text. We will look at each skill separately in detail in Chapters 5 through 9. In this text, when we use the word *learning*, we include both implicit learning and explicit learning. We will use the word *communicative proficiency* and the word *communicative competency* synonymously even though for some they may have special meanings.

The following outline shows how proficiency **levels** indicate goals and priorities—*each one is only a sample of the many goals at each level*—(reserve full attention for later in the chapter):

1. A *novice-mid* speaker of Spanish
    Task (or Why?)—Basic socializing
    Content (or What?)—Greetings, leave-taking
    Context (or Where?)—Classroom, simulated home
    Correctness (or How well?)—Memorized high-frequency expressions (non-memorized language not understood)

2. An *intermediate-mid* speaker of Spanish
    Task (or Why?)—Ask and answer questions (about travel)
    Content (or What?)—Travel needs (Leisure time)
    Context (or Where?)—Simulated train station
    Correctness (or How well?)—Generally understood by a sympathetic person used to talking with non-Spanish speakers

3. An *advanced* speaker of Spanish
    Task (or function)—Narrate and describe past events
    Content (or situation)—Home and family life and daily routines
    Context (or circumstance)—Simulated home-stay with a Spanish family (first or second day)
    Correctness (or accuracy) – Understood without difficulty by native people not necessarily used to dealing with non-Spanish speakers

Sources of Support

There are several sources of support that we can use as we set goals and priorities: national professional organizations, state and local school agencies, textbook programs, and even university methods courses. Let's discuss each of those sources in detail.

National professional organizations. As we mentioned previously, the American Council on the Teaching of Foreign Languages (ACTFL), in collaboration with the American Association of Teachers of Spanish and Portuguese (AATSP), the American Association of Teachers of German, and the American Association of Teachers of French, produced a document intended to be a "beacon for effective [foreign language] programs into the next century."

This document, *Standards for Foreign Language Learning: Preparing for the 21st Century*, "defines **content standards** in foreign language education. These standards are intended to serve as a gauge for excellence, as states and local districts carry out their responsibilities for curriculum in the schools." These professional organizations determined what foreign language education should prepare students to do. They identified the broad goals of the discipline. Within each of these areas, they then identified the essential skills and knowledge students would need to acquire by the time they left the 12th grade. It is these essential skills and knowledge that comprise the standards. The Standards are listed on the following page.

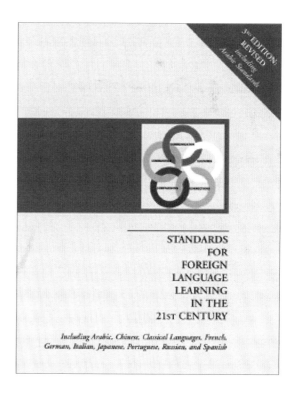

Standards for Foreign Language Learning

COMMUNICATION
  Communicate in Languages Other Than English

Standard 1.1: Students engage in conversations, provide and obtain information, express feelings and emotions, and exchange opinions.

Standard 1.2: Students understand and interpret written and spoken language on a variety of topics.

Standard 1.3: Students present information, concepts, and ideas to an audience of listeners or readers on a variety of topics.

CULTURES
  Gain Knowledge and Understanding of Other Cultures

Standard 2.1: Students demonstrate an understanding of the relationship between the practices and perspectives of the culture studied.

Standard 2.2: Students demonstrate an understanding of the relationship between the products and perspectives of the culture studied.

CONNECTIONS
  Connect with Other Disciplines and Acquire Information

Standard 3.1: Students reinforce and further their knowledge of other disciplines through the foreign language

Standard 3.2: Students acquire information and recognize the distinctive viewpoints that are only available through the foreign language and its cultures.

COMPARISONS
  Develop Insight into the Nature of Language and Culture

Standard 4.1: Students demonstrate understanding of the nature of language through comparisons of the language studied and their own.

Standard 4.2: Students demonstrate understanding of the concept of culture through comparisons of the cultures studied and their own.

COMMUNITIES
  Participate in Multilingual Communities at Home and Around the World

Standard 5.1: Students use the language both within and beyond the school setting.

Standard 5.2: Students show evidence of becoming life-long learners by using the language for personal enjoyment and enrichment.

The *Standards* are articulated in a very broad format. State versions of the goals and standards typically break each one of them down into a much more practical format which the teacher can use in curriculum planning. Following is an example of how one of these goals and standards could be adapted in more specific detail for classroom application:

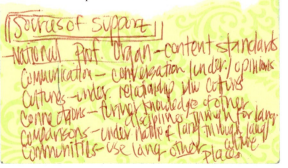

GOAL AREA ONE: COMMUNICATE IN LANGUAGES OTHER THAN ENGLISH

Standard 1.1   Students engage in conversations, provide and obtain information, express feelings and emotions, and exchange opinions.

Level	Progress Indicator	Classroom Example
Beginning:	Express basic needs.	Ask a classmate to lend a forgotten article, (money, pencil, paper).
Developing:	Elaborate on needs.	Explain why an increase in allowance is needed (need later curfew, extension on project).
	Interact in basic survival situations.	Ask directions to find the way to the hotel.
Expanding:	Manage unforeseen circumstances and complicated situations.	Role play strategies to deal with travel mishaps, e.g., lost luggage, lost passport, flight cancellation, car breakdown.

Perhaps the preceding information has been a little intimidating, but it is not as difficult as it may seem here. Remember, you will have an entire state or district guide at your disposition as you plan your curriculum, and it will include explanations of each of the goals and standards and will provide many suggestions for classroom activities that will help you meet those goals and standards.

State and local school agencies. In the public schools the *state school office* under the direction of the *state board of education* (these terms are generic, specific names may differ in the various states but the categories remain) has the mandate to be responsible for public education, and local (district) boards of education share that responsibility under the curricular framework provided by the state. The state school office publishes a **state version of the national standards**, a state **curriculum guide,** or a **course of study** usually in a framework form to be a guide for districts in making their plans for the education of students and the management of teacher activities. Goals are set up for both students and teachers. States are also responsible for **textbook-adoption** policies. Spanish is one curriculum area to receive this kind of attention. Spanish teachers should use the state and district guidelines in their planning for various levels: beginning, intermediate, or advanced, to achieve the goals and proficiency mentioned. It's a good

idea for Spanish teachers to get on committees on these foreign language curriculum guides. Find out who the specialists are in the state school office and the district offices and find out who the officers are in the local and state professional organizations and become involved in the professional activities. (More about this in Chapter 17.)

Within each goal area there are various ... th the ... brings ... ls, and ... anning ... n the ... th the ... as the ... classroom and in the school. **Counselors and administrators** also play an important role in planning, as do school language department chairpersons or leaders, if they exist. Schools with large language departments usually appoint a veteran teacher to act as department chair. A local district **specialist** may sometimes form committees of classroom teachers, school counselors, and even school administrators to participate in planning meetings to update and upgrade the courses of study and also determine ways to show accountability including evaluation and accreditation activities (see Chapter 17).

International sources such as the *European International Baccalaureate*, the *Council of*

Europe, the *Cervantes Institute*, the *Goethe Institutes*, and other international agencies also provide curriculum guides and tests that can assist the state and local committees to provide goals and priorities.

Accountability and assessment.. We have found that assessing all the major skills periodically—especially at the end of semesters—is extremely necessary to determine the success of our goals and priorities and that some kind of state or, even better, national testing gives teachers a chance to evaluate their progress in meeting the goals and priorities. Another type of evaluation is seen in the materials accompanying an accreditation appraisal of the total school program. (See Chapter 17.) The school Spanish programs also can use tests from the Spanish department of a local university, especially if the school Spanish teacher has a good working relationship with professors in the Spanish department (especially the **methods** teacher). This effort for accountability can keep all Spanish teachers on their toes and avoid the difficulties found in solitary planning and evaluation.

Textbook goals and priorities. Most teachers use a text program as a source for content and materials that they will use throughout the course. While the text should not be "driving force" of your classes, they can, however, provide you with a great deal of help. Today's texts are usually in line with the stated goals of the profession and will be designed to help you meet those goals. Study the priorities and goals stated in your textbook and adjust and adapt them to those that your have selected.

Putting It All Together

Don't leave home without your road map. In his book, *Preparing Instructional Objectives*, Robert Mager tells a story about a seahorse that didn't know where he was going and was finally swallowed up by a shark. Mager emphasizes the importance of preparing objectives that can be evaluated in terms of student performance. To get where you are going without getting swallowed up, you must define your goals and then set up plans that will help you reach them. Let's consider some sensible and practical approaches to deciding where we are going.

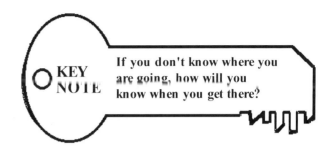

KEY NOTE — If you don't know where you are going, how will you know when you get there?

A language teaching colleague of ours in the public secondary schools told us how he made sure he planned creatively each year. He wanted to avoid the pitfall of the teacher who has one year's experience repeated thirty times. "I want to be a teacher with thirty years of exciting, creative teaching experience," he said. He went on, "In order to have a different experience each year, I throw away all my files and plans. I keep books and other printed materials that I have purchased or the school has purchased, but discard those aids and plans I have made for groups of students in a particular year. I want to plan afresh for each new year. Actually each class has a unique personality."

Compare that experience with the college English professor who was a creative writer, who kept all his notes and files. He maintained that creativity grows out of chaos and that one must have ideas and materials and notes surrounding him literally and figuratively, to engender the creative experience. Somewhere between these extremes is the circumstance allowing the best teaching in **your** life. There is no doubt, however, that we all must plan the teaching/learning experience. Early in our teaching we should write out our plans in detail; later we can take short cuts, perhaps use "telegrammic" style—or outline form.

Although there are teachers who teach without lesson plans, most of the good teachers of our acquaintance all write out daily plans from a general plan. Even after years of years of teaching, they recognize the need to "think" the lesson through ahead of time.

Content-Based Instruction

Many adults who have studied foreign languages recall memorizing lists of vocabulary words, studying grammar rules, and then plugging the words into the grammatical patterns, with little regard for the meaning of the sentences they were producing. Over the past few decades the language teaching profession has been moving away from this grammar-driven model toward a more communicative approach. This movement is based on the idea that language is a tool for communication, and is therefore best learned by using it to interpret and convey real information in the target language.

If students are to use language for real communication, it follows that language learning must involve meaningful content. If students are to listen, read, speak and write in the language, they must listen to, read, speak and write about *something*. This need for meaningful content has given rise to **content-based instruction (CBI).**

In content-based instruction, students learn language by using it as a tool to study subject matter. The best known content-based model is *immersion education*, in which students (usually at the elementary school level) study math, science, and other subjects in another language. A more common model in middle and high school foreign language classes is *theme-based instruction*. Nearly all major foreign language textbooks are now structured around specific themes; for example, one chapter or unit may deal with food, while others may deal with family, sports, music, art, travel, or other themes. In a theme-based unit on music, for example, the teacher might adopt the attitude "We're going to learn about Latin American music styles and musical instruments, and we're going to learn Spanish while we do it."

Research has shown that CBI can increase students' language proficiency at the same time as they increase their knowledge of subject matter and of the target culture. In addition, content-based models are inherently motivating for students, especially when the theme is one of interest to them.

Although most textbooks now follow a theme-based model, they differ in the extent to which the themes or content actually drive instruction. Some textbooks continue to focus mainly on grammar, with just a nod to the "theme" by including a topical vocabulary list, a couple of textual "blurbs" related to the theme, and a few pictures. The best textbooks include authentic reading selections related to the theme, videos and audio recordings from the target culture, and similar materials. In the following section we will propose some criteria for teachers to use in selecting a theme-based, communication-driven textbook.

SELECTING A TEXTBOOK

You will not be going into the classroom empty-handed. In the past the textbook was nearly all the teacher used and it was the basis of almost everything done in the course. Nowadays we are armed with many additional materials such as teacher manuals, student workbooks, audio practice materials, lab manuals, prepared tests, visual aids, DVDs and videos, computer software, and Internet practices, tests and resources. Today's language teachers don't just buy a textbook, they adopt a total "package." This package can greatly ease the burden of the teacher. It does, however, require planning to coordinate the use of the different materials. When and how will you use the videos? When will the students use the lab materials? Can you use the tests prepared by the textbook company, or will you have to prepare others? These and many other questions have to be answered before you start teaching.

Most recent textbook "packages" now include a teacher's manual or teacher's annotated edition, which greatly facilitates the teacher's task. The teacher's edition usually includes the authors' philosophy on language teaching and the suggested approach to using the text, complete long range and short range lesson plans, suggestions on teaching activities, and answer keys to exercises and activities. These teachers' editions often include chapter and review tests, or if not, the "package" may include a test manual.

Do you control the text or does the text control you? How many times have you heard a teacher complain along these lines, "I would like to spend more time on conversational activities, but I have so much material in the text to 'cover' that I just don't have time." In some situations it is necessary for a certain amount of work from a textbook to be completed within a year or semester, but most teachers are free to determine how much work they will do from the text. Unfortunately, many of these teachers feel that they have to confine class activities to what is presented in the text. After a year or two of teaching you should become less and less tied to the textbook, and become more flexible in designing your own activities, using the textbook mainly as a resource, and supplementing a great deal with other materials.

What should you look for in adopting a text? Happy are the teachers who are able to select their own textbooks. More usual is a situation where you inherit a text chosen by someone else and are told by the administration that because of budget limitations you must continue with it "for at least three more years." Whatever the case, you should start your plans immediately for finding the text which will best fit your own objectives and style of teaching.

There is another important consideration, however, *which must come first*. If you are teaching students who fit into some type of sequential program that involves more than one school, it is essential that you select the text in close cooperation with the other teachers who are involved. If, for example, you teach in a junior high school and you are encouraging your students to continue their study of the language in the high school, it is vitally important for you to meet with the high school language teacher to decide what text you can both live with, and to decide how much will be taught in the junior high classes so that the high school teacher can carry on with the same approach and at the point the students left off in junior high.

There are a couple of strategies that you will find helpful in your attempts to adopt the text you want. First, get yourself appointed to the text selection committee. Unless you can have strong input in the decision-making, you are doomed to working with texts that other teachers select.

Second, you should go to the websites of various textbook companies and request that they send you examination (complimentary) copies of texts that they publish. This is a common practice, and the companies will be glad to send you one free copy of their text in the hope that you will adopt it and they will sell hundreds in the process. As you begin to receive the examination copies, you will find the guidelines on the following page helpful in evaluating the textbooks that are sent to you.

Adapting a textbook. What do you do if you are unable to get the text you want to use, and are "stuck" with one you dislike very much? Financial considerations might be such that you will have to continue using the text you have, but you *can* take steps to adapt it. First, give up the idea that you "have to teach" what is in the text. Teachers generally have the latitude to add to or to modify what material is presented in their basic text.

After a year or two of experience you can look at a chapter of any text, determine what the basic objectives are, and then use other approaches or materials to reach those objectives. If the book lacks authentic texts, supplement it with readings and videos from the Internet. If the practice exercises are all mechanical grammar drills, then rewrite them in a more communicative context, practicing the same grammatical concept. Develop dynamic activities that will allow a more motivating, natural use of the grammar point.

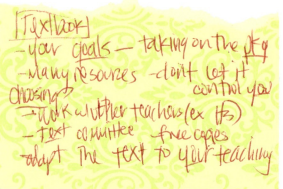

MODEL FOR TEXTBOOK SELECTION

1. **TYPE OF TEXT.** Is this a general textbook for teaching all aspects of the language, or is it specialized for teaching reading, listening comprehension, writing, conversation, vocabulary, or grammar? Is it intended to be the basic textbook of a course or a supplement to the basic text? Is it a part of a series? What does the series include?

2. **LEVEL OF TEXT.** Toward what ages and school level is the book intended? University, older adults, junior/high school, middle/elementary school, bilingual or special programs, etc.?

3. **LENGTH OF USE.** For what length of time is the book intended to be used? One or two semesters, one or two years, etc.? How many chapters are there? Does it have more content than you can possibly finish in the time available?

4. **FEATURES OF CONTENT.** What are the features of the book? Does it have attractive illustrations, preliminary lessons, review chapters, verb charts, an index, vocabulary reference pages, color pictures, interesting/motivating content, a pronunciation section, a grammar summary at the end, an end dictionary, reading selections, maps, diversions, games, songs, etc.?

5. **ACTIVITIES IN INTERPERSONAL MODE.** Does the book provide opportunities for students to use the language in a variety of real-life, meaningful contexts? Do the activities allow students to personalize their responses and express their own meaning in the language?

6. **ACTIVITIES IN INTERPRETIVE MODE.** Does the book include a variety of authentic texts from the target culture, including printed texts, audio and video? Are they accompanied by pre- and post-reading/listening activities? Are strategies for reading and listening comprehension taught?

7. **ACTIVITIES IN PRESENTATIONAL MODE.** Does the book provide a variety of writing assignments of different types? Does it teach writing strategies? Does it give suggestions for projects or oral presentations by students?

8. **GRAMMATICAL CONTENT.** Is the coverage of grammar topics appropriate for the level of the book? Are grammar concepts explained clearly, with sufficient examples and practice activities? Are they presented in contexts that illustrate their use in real-life situations? Is there a review built in for previously-learned grammar concepts?

9. **CULTURAL CONTENT.** What does the text include to teach culture? Culturally oriented dialogs, cultural reading selections, pictures with cultural explanations, cultural notes, etc.? Does it focus on the culture of only one area or does it present a variety of areas? Does it encourage students to think about cultural perspectives as well as proc[...] opportunities for students to compare the target culture wit[...]

10. **SUPPLEMENTARY MATERIALS.** What other materia[...] online practice program, computer software, testing progra[...] textbook without them? Is there a teacher's manual or editi[...] an "annotated" version of the student's text? What does th[...] teaching suggestions, answer keys? Is there a testing progr[...] self-correcting? Is it interesting? Are there lab manuals fo[...] materials affordable? Are there online resources: activities[...] program?

PLANNING

You will probably find it easy to outline your total program, that is, the main units for the first and second year in the schools and also the possible the third and fourth year general guides. A syllabus from local universities for their first semester, second semester, and probably the third and fourth semesters would help, since a semester at the university level gives us a rough equivalent as to what we can expect in a year at the public school. There are some schools that have six or more years of Spanish.

Critical to these programs is the need for coordination (articulation) between middle school and high school teachers. If there is no coordination, students may be forced to start over again in beginning Spanish as they move from middle school to high school.

The textbook can give you strong support as you plan your total program. Almost all recent textbooks present **scope and sequence** charts, which are models distributing the content of the text over the years or semesters suggested to cover the material. These charts may present the material according to *tasks* or *functions*, the *content* or *topics*, the *context*, and the correctness or *accuracy*. It is difficult to find a perfect textbook that deals with the four aspects; so, once again, we emphasize the importance of the **teacher's** preparation of the basic syllabus that should run the course.

Long Term/Program Plan

Utilizing all the resources we have mentioned up to this point, you should be ready to plan the "Big Picture," that is, your total program. Following is a model that you may find useful.

MODEL FOR LONG TERM/PROGRAM PLAN

	FIRST SEMESTER		SECOND SEMESTER	
1ST YEAR	Sept.	Oct.	Jan.	Feb.
	Nov.	Dec.	Mar.	Apr.
2ND YEAR	Sept.	Oct.	Jan.	Feb.
	Nov.	Dec.	Mar.	Apr.

This first figure is just a framework to allow you to see how you can distribute the course over a two-year period. The second figure has been filled out for the first four months of a Spanish 2 class to allow you to see how you would fill in the framework. Many teachers plan in much greater detail.

The content here is based on the textbook *Aventuras*, published by Vista Higher Learning.

(We are not advocating one particular textbook over another; we have simply used this book to illustrate how a textbook may be used in planning.) Note the strategies for textbook use, plus the inclusion of supplementary materials. In addition, other activities that require advance scheduling and preparation are considered and included in the planning.

EXAMPLE OF COMPLETED LONG TERM/PROGRAM PLAN

FIRST SEMESTER	
September Students write Autobiografías Chap 9 of textbook: <u>Las celebraciones</u> (fiestas, familia, relaciones personales) Composition "Mi familia" 3rd week Spanish club "Welcome back party" Movie: "Valentina" 4th Week Back to school-night Exam. Chap 9 Oral test in pairs: Plan a party with a friend	**October** Chap 10 of textbook: <u>En el consultorio</u> (el cuerpo, la salud, enfermedades y síntomas) 3rd week Spanish club: Guest speaker, Dr. Ramos from Argentina (family doctor) – Project: Plan personal de salud Exam Chap. 10 Oral test: Visit to doctor's office Skit: "¿Dónde está el dinero?"
November Chap. 11 of textbook: <u>El carro y la tecnología</u> (la calle, partes del carro, Internet y la computadora) 3rd week Spanish club movie: Cantinflas: "Por mis pistolas" Activ: Eat at "Mi ranchito" Project: Mi carro ideal Exams Chap. 11 Oral test: Accidente de carro	**December** Chap. 12 of textbook: <u>Hogar, dulce hogar</u> (la casa, los muebles, los electrodomésticos) Project: Video tour of home 3rd week Christmas party – watch student videos Exam: Chap. 12 Oral test: Real estate agent finding a home for a client

Unit/Chapter Planning

Unit planning involves short-term periods of time—two weeks plus or minus in secondary schools. Unit or chapter planning involves selecting a unit or chapter from your total program (syllabus) plan and expanding it over the days or weeks you will be taking.

Learning objectives. The first step in planning a unit is to determine the learning objectives for the unit. Simply put, *objectives* are what you want your students to be able to do at the end of a unit or lesson. They typically start with "Students will be able to . . ." Many beginning teachers make the mistake of focusing on what they themselves are going to "go over" or "cover" during a unit or lesson rather than what they want their students to be able to do. This generally makes for teacher-centered lessons rather than learner-centered ones, with the result that the teacher "covers" the material but has little idea whether the students have learned anything.

One characteristic of well-written objectives is that they are stated in such a way that students' learning can be easily assessed at the end of the lesson or unit. Suppose, for example, that you plan to have your students listen to a series of recorded phone messages. If your objective is simply to "Practice listening comprehension," you may end up with no idea whether students have learned anything from the activity. In contrast, the objective "Students will be able to write down the caller's name and phone number from a series of recorded phone messages" can be easily assessed by simply checking how accurately the students were able to write down the messages.

Compare the following examples of effective and less-effective objectives. Which do you think would make for a better lesson? Why?

Less-effective objectives	Effective objectives
Learn the present tense of regular -ar verbs.	Students will be able to use the *yo* form of regular present tense -ar verbs to tell what they do in their free time.
Learn vocabulary for family members.	Students will be able to use family-related vocabulary to identify relationships on a family tree chart of the Spanish royal family.
Watch a video about *las posadas* in Mexico.	Students will be able to describe the tradition of *las posadas* in Mexico, using key vocabulary such as *peregrinos, posada, villancicos* and *piñata*.

Types of objectives. Learning objectives may be divided into various types. Among them are the following:

Communicative objectives. These are the linguistic tasks or functions that you want your students to master. Examples of communicative objective might be "Students will be able to order a meal in a restaurant" or "Students will be able to describe their morning routine as they prepare for school."

Linguistic objectives. Some people combine communicative and linguistic objectives in the same category since they often overlap, but we think it is helpful to consider separately the grammar concepts and vocabulary that we want students to learn. Examples might be "Students will be able to give affirmative and negative commands in the *tú* form" or "Students will be able to use the preterite and imperfect to relate a humorous experience" (notice that the latter objective overlaps with a communicative objective).

Content objectives. This category of objectives refers to the subject-matter content that we want students to learn. Remember that in content-based language teaching, the focus is on using language to study meaningful content. Examples of content objectives might be "Students will be able to locate the countries of Central America on a map" or "Students will be able to identify animals that live in the rain forest."

Culture objectives. These often overlap with content objectives, since the content of our units is often cultural in nature. Examples of culture objectives might be "Students will able to compare and contrast eating habits in Spain and the U.S." or "Students will be able to discuss the cultural perspectives associated with *Día de los muertos* in Mexico."

Your methods instructor will tell you what format he or she prefers you to use for your objectives, but we encourage you to consider all of the above types of objectives in your planning.

Planning how to assess learning objectives. After outlining the unit objectives, the next step is to plan how you will assess each objective. Assessment will be discussed in detail in Chapter 12; at this point you simply need to know that your assessments should align with your objectives – that is, you should plan one or more ways of assessing how well your students have achieved each of your learning objectives for a unit or chapter.

Assessments may be either formal or informal in nature. *Formal assessments* include chapter tests, quizzes, and rubrics used for grading projects or compositions. *Informal assessments* might consist of observing students during pair or small-group activities, having students turn in some product of their pair work, or awarding pesos for participating in class. For example, an informal assessment of the objective "Students will be able to order a meal in a restaurant" might be to observe students as they role play in pairs during class; a formal assessment of the same objective might consist of an oral test at the end of the chapter where the teacher plays the role of a waiter and the students order a meal from a printed menu, and points are assigned for grammar, vocabulary, pronunciation, and/or overall completion of the task.

Your daily lesson plans should include ways of assessing the lesson objectives, which will often be informal in nature. Unit plans, in contrast, will also include more formal assessments such as written and oral tests.

Example of a unit plan. Following is an example of a completed unit plan. The unit illustrates a theme-based approach, centered on the topic of housing.

Unit/Chapter: *Hogar, dulce hogar* (*Aventuras* Chapter 12)		Class: Spanish 2 Dates to be taught: Nov. 26-Dec. 20
Learning Objectives	***Communicative Activities***	***Assessments***
<u>Communicative Objectives</u> (tasks/functions/topics) Students will be able to . . . • Describe the rooms and furnishings in a house • Tell who does which chores • Give formal commands • Express desire for someone to do something	<u>Interpersonal Mode</u> • Discuss who does the chores in their home • Draw the floor plan of their house and describe it to someone else • Play the role of a real estate agent finding a house that suits various clients	• Homework handouts from student manual • Vocab quiz – *La casa y sus cuartos* • Video tour of home (assessed with rubric) • Oral test: Role play real estate agent asking a client about the type of house he/she wants • Chapter test:

<u>Content and Culture Objectives</u>
Students will be able to . . .
• Describe similarities and differences between Hispanic countries and the U.S. in terms of types of housing and typical layout of houses
• Discuss differences between housing in rural and urban areas in the U.S. and Hispanic countries
	<u>Interpretive Mode</u>
	(reading, listening, viewing)
	• *A escuchar – La casa*
	• Video from book: *Los estudiantes llegan a la casa donde van a vivir en Ibarra; la Sra. Vives les muestra la casa*
	• Reading from book: *Bienvenidos a la Casa Colorada!*
	• YouTube video: *Un tour de mi casa*
		○ Listening: Dialogue – identify who does which chores
		  ○ Vocabulary: Identify rooms, furniture, and appliances in a house
		  ○ Grammar: Formal commands; present subjunctive expressing volition
		  ○ Reading: Ad for apartment for rent
		  ○ Writing: Write an email message describing your home to a Mexican

<u>Linguistic Objectives – Grammar</u> Students will be able to . . . • Conjugate verbs in the imperative (*Ud., Uds.*), including verbs with stem changes • Conjugate verbs in the present subjunctive and use them in expressions of will and influence	<u>Presentational Mode</u> *(writing, presentations, projects)* • Prepare and present video tour of their home - *"Una visita a mi casa"*	
<u>Vocabulary</u> • la casa y los cuartos • los electrodomésticos • los quehaceres domésticos • los muebles	<u>Change of Pace</u> *(songs, games, etc.)* Songs: *Yo tengo una casita, El patio de mi casa, La casita (Pedro Infante), A Juan no le dan* Games: *El profesor exigente, Agua va, Canasta de frutas, Llena el espacio*	

Notice the following about this unit plan:

- The first column lists the learning objectives for the unit, which are divided into communicative objectives, content/culture objectives, and linguistic objectives (including grammar and vocabulary). The objectives in this example are based largely on the content of the textbook chapter.
- The second column outlines the main communicative activities planned for the unit, divided into the three communicative modes of the *Standards* – interpersonal, interpretive, and presentational. We have found this format helpful because it reminds us that we need to give attention to developing students' skills in different modes. Again, the activities listed here are taken partly from the textbook, but with the teacher's own creative additions such as a YouTube video and a related project in which students film themselves giving a tour of their own home in Spanish.
- The last column outlines the plan for asssessing the learning outcomes from the first column. Notice that each learning outcome is assessed by one or more of the various assessments (homework, quiz, project, oral test, chapter test). For example, the objective "Describe the rooms and furnishings in a house" is assessed by both the oral test and the video project. Notice also that the teacher has planned multiple ways of assessing students'

learning, not just a test at the end of the chapter.

- The bottom center square of the unit plan lists "change of pace" activities, including songs and games. These activities are generally not included in textbooks, so it is up to teachers to rely on their own collection of songs, games, and other activities. (See the books *Me gusta cantar* and *Me gusta jugar* listed in Appendix C for ideas on songs and games.)
- Some teachers also find it helpful to include a space for concepts to be reviewed from previous units. Because most textbooks now provide built-in review of previously-learned material, we have not included that information here.

Distributing the unit activities. Once you have planned the learning outcomes, assessments and activities for the unit, you need to make a tentative outline of which activities you plan to do on which days. Following is a framework to show how you can distribute the content of a unit or chapter over the number of days you have determined to spend with the unit. The first week of the unit has been filled out. This distribution is, of course, only tentative, since you cannot always estimate exactly how much you can do on any given day. The distribution will be adjusted as you teach each day. For that reason some teachers write this part of the plan in pencil to permit revisions as they progress through the unit.

Tentative Daily Distribution

Day 1	Day 2	Day 3	Day 4	Day 5
-Warmup: *partes del coche* (review) -Vocab: *la casa* p. 282 -*A conversar* p. 286 -Game: *Agua va*	-Warmup: vocab *los muebles* -Video: *Les va a encantar la casa!* -Mi casa p. 290 -Song: *A Juan no le dan*	-Warmup: vocab *los cuartos* - YouTube: *Un tour de mi casa* -Draw floor plan & describe house -Introduce video project -Game: *Llena el espacio*	-Warmup: pronunciation of /h/ -Formal commands p. 292 -Irregular commands p. 293 -Song: *La casita*	-Quiz: vocab *la casa* -Present subjunctive p. 294 -*La vivienda en el mundo hispano* p. 291 -Game: *El profesor exigente*
Day 6	**Day 7**	**Day 8**	**Day 9**	**Day 10**

Daily Lesson Planning

Having prepared your unit plans, you are now ready to put them into effect in your daily class periods. You will simply take the upcoming day from the "Tentative Daily Distribution" and prepare it with more detail for that class. Your lesson plans need to have learning objectives and assessments just like the unit plan, only in this case the objectives will outline what students should be able to do at the end of the class period rather than at the end of the unit, and the assessments will target these objectives. Again, many of these assessments may be informal in nature. It is also a good idea to list which of the national Standards the lesson addresses.

Other helpful things to include in a lesson plan include the materials necessary for the lesson; a description of each activity along with the estimated time it will take (or the clock time to start the activity); and the homework assignment for the students. The **assignments** constitute an extremely important aspect of the lesson and lesson planning in general. Some teachers provide their students with a written assignment sheet for the entire unit. Many teachers find that the assignment written in the same place on the chalkboard every day is the most nearly ideal.

Following is an example of a lesson plan based on Day 3 of the "Tentative Daily Distribution" above.

Lesson Plan: "Una visita a mi casa"

Class: Spanish 2	**Unit/Chapter:** *Aventuras* Ch. 12, pp. 282-283	**Date:** Dec. 3

Purpose
Discuss layouts of homes in Latin America and the U.S. by viewing a video tour of a home in Spanish, having students draw and describe a floor plan of their own home, and preparing students for a project in which they will film a short video tour of their home in Spanish.

National Standards
1.1 Students engage in conversation about differences between Latin American and U.S. homes, and explain the layout of their own home to a partner.
1.2 Students understand and interpret a video tour of a house in Spanish.
3.1 Students prepare to make a video presentation about their own house in Spanish.
4.2 Students compare homes in Latin America and the U.S.

Communicative/Linguistic Objectives
Students will be able to . . .
- Understand the rooms, furniture, and appliances mentioned in the video
- Identify some rooms, furniture, and appliances in a floor plan they draw of their own house

Content/Culture Objectives
Students will be able to . . .
- Identify differences between "typical" U.S. and Mexican homes
- Understand the instructions for the video project

Materials needed
Transparencies or slides of the floor plans of "typical" homes in the U.S. and Mexico; YouTube video "Un tour de mi casa" http://www.youtube.com/watch?v=KOea1CObS5Q; copies of handout explaining video project; copies of grid for *Llena el espacio* game

Time	Procedure
9:00 9:02	• Bienvenida y anuncios: Daniel • <u>Warmup:</u> Have students open their books to pp. 282-283 (the house vocabulary from yesterday). Show transparency or slide of an American house and ask students to identify the rooms. Do the same for the plan of a Mexican house. Ask students, "¿Cuáles son las diferencias entre las dos casas?"
9:06 9:09 9:12	• <u>Video</u> from YouTube "Un tour de mi casa" o <u>Pre-viewing:</u> Tell students, "Vamos a ver un video llamado *Un tour de mi casa* en que un hombre mexicano nos da una visita 'virtual' a su casa. ¿Qué tipo de vocabulario piensan que van a escuchar en el video? *(cuartos, muebles, electrodomésticos* – write these words on the board). "Uds. no van a entender todo en el video, pero quiero que escuchen para identificar (a) qué cuartos son mencionados, (b) qué muebles, (c) qué electrodomésticos, y (d) otras cosas que comprenden del video." o <u>Viewing:</u> Show the video up to 3:30. o <u>Post-viewing:</u> Ask students, "¿Qué cuartos fueron mencionados? ¿Muebles? ¿Electrodomésticos? ¿Qué otras cosas escucharon?" "¿Piensan que ésta es una casa típica mexicana? ¿Por qué no? (el patio es un "deck" y no un "courtyard"; tiene una parrilla "barbecue" americana – y también dice al final que la casa queda en San Francisco)
9:15 9:18 9:28	• <u>Pair activity:</u> The floor plan of your house o <u>Introduction:</u> Sketch a rough floor plan of your home on the board and tell students, "Ésta es una *planta* de mi casa. Ésta es la cocina donde preparamos la comida. Hay varios electrodomésticos: una estufa, un lavaplatos, un horno de microondas…" Show the various rooms and a few pieces of furniture or appliances. o <u>Pair work:</u> Tell students, "Ahora quiero que dibujen la planta de su propia casa o apartamento. Tienen cinco minutos para dibujarla. Luego, quiero que la describan a un compañero, mostrando los cuartos, muebles, etc." o <u>Follow up:</u> Ask students, "¿Quiénes tienen casas interesantes? Sara, ¿cómo es la casa de David? ¿Qué cuartos tiene?" etc.
9:30	• <u>Introduction of project:</u> Distribute handout explaining the video project. Students will work in pairs to film their partner giving a 3-minute video tour of his or her home in Spanish, identifying the main rooms and some furniture and appliances, and telling what they do in each room. (Students who don't want to film their own home may use the home of a friend, neighbor or relative.) Ask who has access to video cameras, and pair students who don't with those who do. Go over the assessment rubric and due dates.
9:40	• <u>Game</u> (if time): *Llena el espacio* (explained in *Me gusta jugar*). Categories: *cuartos en la casa, muebles, comidas, partes del carro, partes del cuerpo*

<u>Assessment</u>
Observe students' participation in the video and pair activities; award *pesos* for participation; have students turn in their drawing of the floor plan of their house.

<u>Homework Assignment</u>
Begin writing script for video tour of your home. *1ˢᵗ draft due Friday*

You will usually prepare your lesson plans one or two days before you actually teach the class. Some administrators require their teachers to keep a file of lesson plans: 1) for emergencies requiring a substitute teacher, 2) for supervisory purposes—the principal needs to read your mind. Detailed lesson plans are helpful to student-teacher supervisors and cooperating teachers involved in coaching student teachers and, of course, for the growth and development of the student teacher. You can rest assured that all good teachers plan carefully even when they seem to be "winging it." It is also a truism that the more you plan in detail, the better prepared you are to teach and even to vary your teaching at the last minute.

It is difficult, if not impossible, to write out copious lesson plans for the entire unit in advance (five to fourteen days); this is the purpose of the Tentative Daily Distribution. What you can do is write the lesson plan for the next day's activities so that you can make careful assignments. Even if your daily lesson plans are not as detailed as the one above, it's important to outline the lesson objectives so that you know where you're going and when you've arrived there.

Additional considerations in lesson planning. Here are some additional suggestions in preparing a lesson plan. A lesson plan is for one class period—one meeting, however long on one day (some schools have 90-minute periods). Timing is difficult. You should consider the **75 per cent rule,** which is: When about 75 per cent of the students have caught the vision of the activities, **go on.** A second special consideration is the **dosage rule,** which is, that students absorb *ounces* more thoroughly than they would *gallons*. The third consideration is the **modeling rule,** which is, that students need to see or hear the activity or experience or sentence or word at least three times before they are expected to absorb it and use it. As you gain experience you may find ways of taking short cuts in writing out this plan, but for a while, consider the following aspects and write your plans down on the card.

While some teachers may feel that this kind of careful planning stifles their creativeness; the opposite is more likely true. Teachers who do careful, comprehensive planning of this nature do not have to slavishly follow everything on the plan. They are free to change or improvise however they like, but they will always draw from that they have prepared and will have the visual aids and supplies at hand when they need them.

Other Supplemental Materials

In addition to materials provided by the textbook company, the teacher has access to other supplemental materials. As you begin your teaching you will probably see a need to add some of these resources to your primary resources.

Videos. There is a incredible variety of video materials available, ranging from videos specifically designed to teach the language, to selections taken from commercial television, to full-length movies with sound tracks in Spanish. Many Spanish teachers at all levels now have DVD players in their classroom and are building large collections of videos.

In addition to commercially produced videos, teachers can produce their own, "homemade" videos. (We will discuss strategies for using films and videos in the classroom in greater detail in Chapter 14.) More and more, teachers have access to the Internet and can project visual materials (motion or still) live on a large screen in class, or at least download those portions of those materials from sites such as YouTube onto their classroom computer and then show them in their classes.

Computer practice materials. Most of your students will have access to a computer in their home, and if not, computers are now the standard installation in language and computer labs, or in sections of school libraries that are open to use by students. Textbooks now provide computer software practice and review packages, and many software companies provide generic materials that can be used by students, regardless of the text being used in class. Some of these programs focus on vocabulary learning and practice of grammar concepts. Most of them have added interest with very colorful graphics and interesting content. The Internet now offers students a wide range of language practices and cultural information. The road is now open for creative teachers to develop activities that will capitalize on the resources that are waiting to be mined. Some teachers have even utilized competition by challenging students to go on to the Internet to develop vocabulary lists, and give prizes or rewards for those who produce the most results.

Supplemental reading materials. Some textbooks do not provide enough reading materials or the specific type that many teachers want and it is occasionally desirable to supplement the readings in the text with additional materials. There are many readers available, ranging from very simple, contrived, humorous anecdotes to edited or annotated editions of famous literature. Many of these readers include cartoons, drawings, games, puzzles, and pictures that are very motivating. In addition, there are also "current event" type newspapers, prepared specifically for language students, similar to the "Weekly Readers" used in the public schools. These contain articles of interest to teenagers and college students and have notes and glosses that help develop reading skills.

Reference tables with dictionaries and newspapers and magazines. Many teachers put a reading/reference table in the back of the classroom on which they place materials for the students to use before, during, and after class. These include books for children or adolescents, dictionaries, newspapers, and magazines. You should have several good bilingual dictionaries, and at least one good, large monolingual dictionary, such as *El Pequeño Larousse*. You might also have some picture dictionaries and other types of reference books such as verb tables, grammar summaries, etc. Also of interest to the students would be copies of popular _____ books in the foreign _____ to use the _____ need, and to _____ materials as _____ time during

PREPARING THE CLASSROOM

The environment in which teaching and learning take place is of great importance. The students are going to spend *many hours* in your classroom. You must make the effort to prepare that room so it will both stimulate the students

and facilitate their learning. The "flavor" of the classroom can have a strong effect on the *attitude* the students have about your class. We will suggest here a number of steps you can take to get the greatest advantage from the learning environment.

Classroom decoration. Fortunate are the teachers who have their own permanent classroom and the freedom to set it up and decorate it as they please. Sometimes teachers have to move from one room to another, and really have no classroom of their own. This situation dampens whatever enthusiasm one might have for preparing permanent displays and bringing aids and equipment to class. In spite of this, it is worth the "nomadic" teachers' time and effort to do a number of things in the rooms they are given:

- Use creativity to develop portable visual aids, such as foldable hanging charts (*Hoy es lunes*).
- Use a cart and file crates to keep materials together and move them easily from your office to the classroom.
- Ask the other teacher(s) who share the room if there is a corner or bulletin board you can use for displays or storage of items specifically for your class.

If you are fortunate enough to have your own language classroom, it should have a very different appearance from a normal classroom, because the activities in a foreign language classroom are not the same as with other subjects. The class is taught in another language, different cultures are studied, a lot of talking and working with electronic equipment will be taking place. The appearance of the class should be such that the student will want to use the language.

We sometimes use the term **CULTURAL ISLAND** to describe the environment we want to create. If the students feel that they are entering a different world that is somehow floating in their sea of American life, where a foreign language used for communication and the ways of associating with the teacher and their peers are different, then you are approaching that ideal. You will want to decorate the walls of the classroom with posters, maps, flags and pictures of countries where the language is spoken.

Objects and artifacts from those countries that reflect the life of speakers of the language are called *realia*, and can also add a colorful and interesting touch to the room appearance. Rugs, clothing such as ponchos and hats, wall hangings and flags can be hung from the walls (or the ceiling), and dolls, toys, plates, figures, and other realia can be placed on tables and book shelves that you acquire for the room.

Displays and bulletin boards. Bulletin boards and displays can provide "free learning." That is, the students who see them every day over a period of time will subconsciously assimilate words and cultural information.

There should be a general bulletin board for announcements in the room. You can have division titles in the foreign language, even if the announcements are in English. This board can also serve as a place to pin up jokes, proverbs, items cut from newspapers and magazines, and even letters from penpals or keypals.

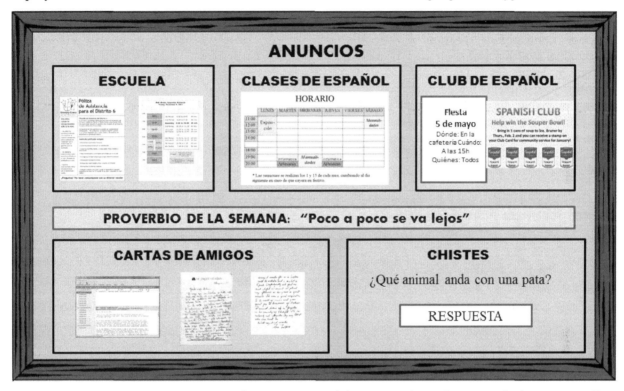

"Teaching-type" bulletin boards. There are four general kinds of "teaching-type" bulletin boards. They are:

- **vocabulary** (presenting the meaning of words through pictures or drawings)
- **culture** (presenting cultural information through pictures, realia, maps, and so on)
- **grammar** (graphically teaching some grammar concept)
- **current events** (usually illustrating some events or happenings in Hispanic countries with pictures, news clippings, and the like)

Displays add color to the room and can sometimes serve as visual aids in teaching vocabulary, discussing culture, or explaining and giving examples of grammatical concepts. Put them on a colorful background and prepare a large and attractive title (usually in the foreign language) that will call attention and present the basic theme. You should take great care with the lettering of the title, usually using the cutout type. Pictures should be large and bright. Drawings can be "blown up" from smaller drawings with an overhead projector or copy machine. They should be colored.

If you are teaching vocabulary, the words should be carefully lettered and should always include the article or something that indicates the gender. Keep the word separate from the picture itself. If the display is cultural, make sure you include information about what is shown, rather than just displaying interesting *realia*. It pays to take care in the preparing of your displays, because you can use them year after year if they are well made. You should display several maps of countries where the foreign language is spoken. It is best to laminate or mount the maps in some way so they will not become dog-eared, torn, or worn out.

Displays and bulletin boards, set up outside ... faculty to see, ... the value of ... build up an ... y awards or ... irs, or foreign ... ome of your ... complishments ... some of the ... g out, such as ... on programs," ... vents or give ... rs, field trips,

*[handwritten note:] Class Decorations! —colorful culture —vocab (portable?) —Cultural Island (como otro mundo) (date?) (tal/kres) (otros temas) *Bulletin Boards (4 types) (teaching) —vocab (pics, —grammar (simplicated) —culture maps etc) —current events *Signs→have students (happenings?) Make for extra credit*

Signs. Since you are always trying to provide the tools for your students to use the language in the classroom, a good way you can do that is to prepare signs with common classroom expressions and hang them on the walls. Signs such as: *¿Qué quiere decir _____? ¿Cómo se dice _____ en español? No entiendo. Repita, por favor* , etc. The letters of the alphabet with their corresponding names in the language can be placed over the chalk board. And of course, a huge sign at the door of the classroom which says **BIENVENIDOS** always catches the attention of those entering. It is fun to have proverbs and sayings displayed in the classroom and refer to them as often as you can so the students will learn them.

The usual signs that are put up all around in schools can be translated into Spanish (or purchased or downloaded) and hung around your classroom, such as:

If you don't have time to make signs of this type, have a student—preferably one with a little artistic talent—do them for extra credit. He or she will undoubtedly learn some Spanish in the process.

Media Equipment

A friend of ours lives on the top of a steep hill. He gets a glorious breeze in the summer and has a spectacular view of the valley, but winter is sheer torture. When it snows he has to get up early and clean the snow off his driveway, and spread salt or ashes on the ice so he will be able to get back up the hill to his home. Many times last winter, his car was unable to go up the slick roads, and he had to leave it at the bottom of the hill and walk up to his house. For some unknown reason, our friend hasn't followed the example of his neighbors. They have purchased four-wheel drive vehicles and go right up the hill in a snowstorm with no trouble at all.

Language teachers who continue to teach without using modern electronic equipment are very similar to our friend—They can carry on without it, but it's depriving the students of some real help. You need to get yourself a "four-wheel drive." You also need to learn how to handle that "four-wheel drive." If you do not know how to use computers and VCR/DVD players, or use a CD player, take a class that will teach you how. You may even have to find someone who can take you into a classroom where there is equipment of that type and teach you how to use that equipment. It could be very embarrassing to have to ask your students how to turn on the overhead projector, or find a specific spot on a DVD.

Assuming that your classroom is the usual ~~~~~~ re ~~~~~~ ge ~~~~~~ nt

[handwritten note: media equipment — white board — audio/cd player — overhead proj — video setup — computer — printer]

- An audio tape/CD player (2 if possible)
- An overhead projector and a large pull-down screen
- A video setup (VCR/DVD player and monitor)
- A personal computer with access to the Internet and school software
- A computer printer that can be used to make copies and transparencies

It would be helpful to have:

- A large sound system that can be used with audio and video players
- A digital LCD projector
- A video camera
- A document camera
- A classroom set of small white boards [make your own from shower board]
- A set of small digital audio recorders for students to use

Every language teacher should have access to:

- A copy machine to make copies and transparencies
- A laminator
- A scanner

Strategies for getting the above. If you don't have the equipment mentioned above, you need to take steps to get it. Try any or all of the following:

1. Pester the principal or department chair constantly.
2. Offer to "work off" the costs by taking tickets at sporting events, working in the office after hours, teaching an extra class, etc.
3. Apply for special enrichment or teacher-improvement grants (local, district, state or national). Funds are sometimes available from the district or state for teachers to use.
4. Ask for the help and support of the PTA or some parent group.
5. Have special fund raising activities; bake sales, candy sale, etc.*
6. Find some parent or local company who is willing to make a contribution in exchange for publicity.*

*Some schools have strict policies regarding activities of this kind. Avoid problems by clearing plans for these activities with an appropriate administrator.

Getting instructional materials to use with the equipment you have. Even four-wheel drive vehicles won't go without gas. You need to start collecting CDs, DVDs, recordings of songs, ~~~~~~ Learn ~~~~~~ from ~~~~~~ m to ~~~~~~ erials ~~~~~~ copy ~~~~~~ arize your

[handwritten note: (extras) — sound system — LED projector — video camera — small projector — white boards — digital audio recorders — cds, dvds, pics etc — uploading]

Seating

The environment provided in the classroom of course contributes to the success of the process of internalizing the language. Even the seating arrangement can make a real difference. Sometimes teachers allow themselves and their students to get into a deadly dull routine and activities seem to take place as if all were in a trance and the students were nothing but parrots. A Spanish class is very different from a history or math class. There is no reason to use the traditional seating arrangement where all the students sit in long rows. The way the seats are arranged should remind the students that they are expected to converse and participate, sometimes as a class and sometimes in pair and group activities.

Seating arrangements can be varied to facilitate the learning activities. There is no standard, all purpose-seating arrangement; rather the seating arrangement should equal the activity. We will suggest some different seating possibilities here. There are, of course, others. In our diagrams, the circles **O** represent the students, and the ⊥ represents places where the teacher might stand.

The following is a commonly used arrangement that has two rows facing the middle aisle that creates an environment that invites conversation. This is also effective for games and team competitions.

DIRECTION STUDENTS ARE FACING

Occasionally the students need a classroom meeting to determine certain goals. This is an intimate discussion in which all are at eye level with the teacher and interaction will take place; it is especially used when some kind of planning, correction of planning, problem solving, or norm setting is necessary. There will probably be no visuals or even use of the chalk or white board. Everyone is to get into the discussion. A tight small circle or a diamond shape would be very conducive to a good heartfelt discussion.

The eye span of the teacher and of every member of the class takes in everybody. There are four groups in the discussion, but they feel as one larger group. Two rows of students make for a tight close-knit diamond.

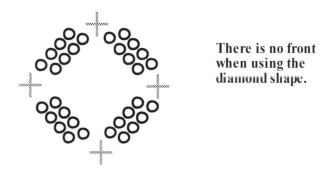

There is no front when using the diamond shape.

If you decide to use the chalkboard on any side or have a number of pictures or overhead transparencies for discussion, then open the diamond to a **U** shape or half-diamond with longer sides (**V**).

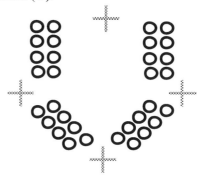

If the class needs to view media presentations or videos, the diamond can open to two straight lines.

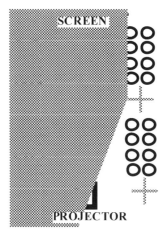

If the four groups are to divide for practice or group discussion, then smaller groups can be formed. This arrangement is common in proficiency-based classrooms and is referred to as "cooperative learning groups."

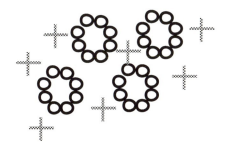

The groups can go to another room, i.e. the library, where there are tables, or if you have tables in your classroom you can make an arrangement like this.

If testing is a purpose, the groups can be arranged in a traditional (spread out for security) testing arrangements, in rows or in rows in alternate seats.

These different configurations should give you some ideas about how you can adjust the seating to whatever activity you are going to conduct. Hopefully you will be teaching in a classroom that will allow you to try them. If you ... more

Seating charts. Many teachers find that use of seating charts can be helpful in several ways:

- They facilitate learning names
- You can place advanced students next to struggling students for pair work
- You can put behavior-challenged students closer to the front

Mixing up or changing the chart every few weeks gives students a great opportunity to learn from others and have experience with lots of different classmates. This is especially important in a class with some native speakers mixed with non-natives. If your school has an enrollment program on the computer with pictures, you can make a photo seating chart.

PREPARING VISUAL AIDS

Language teachers, much more than teachers of other subjects, must make the use of visual aids a way of life. Since we teach in a language that at first is new to our students, we have to help them understand what we are saying, and this is usually best accomplished with visuals. Another value of visual aids is that when the students make a direct association with meaning, rather than translating and operating in terms of their native language, they learn to think in the new language and their retention of vocabulary and listening comprehension is much higher.

Sources for visuals. Teachers should be constantly on the lookout for raw materials that can be turned into visual aids. As you go into stores and markets, watch for displays which might help teach the names of food, fruits, and so on. Ask the manager if you can come in at the end of the promotion and "help him take his displays down," on the condition that he will give them to you. Children's coloring books are an excellent source for simple, line drawings of animals, professions, furniture, and so on. Other good sources for these visual aids are used magazines purchased at a thrift store or garage sales, old pattern books (available at most fabric stores), old encyclopedias, and clothing catalogs. Check with your friendly neighborhood dentist to see if they will donate old magazines to your worthy cause.

71

The newest and perhaps best source for visuals is the Internet. When you do a Google search, click on "images" and you have just about anything you want, including all kinds of clip art. Be careful to respect copyrighted pictures and images There is a utilities program that you can use with your computer called "Grab" which allows you to copy anything that you can get on your computer screen. This program is especially useful for selecting maps, enlarging them, and just copying the section of the map you want to use. A major advantage of using digital pictures is that they don't require storage space; you can just store them on your computer or a flash drive.

Every teacher should be skilled in making copies of pictures, maps, and drawings in books ... [obscured by note] ... e used to ... [obscured] ... s can be ... [obscured] ... y the use ... [obscured] ... camera. ... [obscured] ... a large ... [obscured] ... e it. The

Guidelines for Visuals. Effective visuals are:

- age and interest level appropriate
- colorful and interesting
- pertinent to the subject
- easily accessible (organized in a retrieval system suited to your teaching style)
- mounted on sturdy backing, such as cardstock, bag board, or carnival paper
- laminated if they are to be used repeatedly or handled by students
- large enough to be visible from the farthest point of the classroom seating area if intended for whole class

Flash cards or pictures that are used by partners or small groups are:

- simple, colorful, uniform in size
- organized ahead of time to facilitate distribution
- laminated if they are used repeatedly

Labeling. Visuals used primarily for teaching ... [obscured by note] ... the back so ... [obscured] ... word as a ... [obscured] ... e used for ... [obscured] ... labeled or

number/color coded on the front or back and thus you can teach new words as you use the visuals.

What if you think you have no artistic talent? All teachers can prepare effective visual aids, even if they think they have no artistic talent. The secret is to keep it simple. It's easier to make a simple drawing look good than a complicated one. There are many books available on how to do simple stick figure drawings. Students enjoy your attempts if you are positive about your "art work. "Use pictures from children's coloring books because they usually are simple line drawings, and often have topical pictures, such as animals, means of transportation, etc.

If you still feel overwhelmed, trade labor with someone with drawing talent. You can keyboard, enter grades, baby sit, run errands, cook or even pay them when you need visuals not available in any of your resources. Make friends with the art teachers in your school. He or she might be willing to give art students extra credit for preparing visual aids of bulletin boards for your Spanish classes.

Many teachers make trades with students, excusing them from tardies or absences, giving them extra credit, etc. if they help make visual aids, help with classroom decoration, put up bulletin boards, etc. With creativity, lots of hard work and effort, and perhaps with some help, you can assemble a collection of visuals which you can use during your entire career and which will greatly increase your success as a teacher.

Filing. What good is something if you can't find it? Every teacher should have sturdy files cabinets and sturdy storage boxes in which they can store visual aids. These could include mounted pictures for a large number of different ... [obscured by note] ... famous people, ... [obscured] ... od, professions, ... [obscured] ... s, etc. Flash cards ... [obscured] ... ove categories, and ... [obscured] ... ities that we will ... [obscured] ... should also collect ... [obscured] ... sation charts and ... [obscured] ... parencies.

PREPARING VISUAL AIDS

In this section we will make some very specific suggestions about the preparation of visual aids. You should be especially on the alert

72

for bizarre and "attention-grabbing" pictures, or funny situations that would lend themselves to creative comments, discussion and descriptions by students. Picture puzzles where impossible things appear, parts are missing, figures are hidden, or paired comparison pictures where items are different, also serve as excellent points of departure for conversation sessions. All of these visual aids should be mounted, laminated, and filed by categories for easy access.

The chalk or white board. The chalk or white board is the most usual visual aid found in the classroom. If one is not available, a large easel pad of paper and a large marking pen can be used. It is very convenient to be able to draw pictures or diagrams of what you are trying to explain. You can sometimes have things drawn out ahead in order to save time. You may protest that you are no artist, but that should not daunt you. With some practice you can draw a **recognizable** facsimile of almost anything, especially if you tell your students what it is as you draw it. Many of us are not artists, but we can laugh along with the students at our clumsy attempts and have fun while we teach the meaning of words directly.

Some chalk or white boards are magnetic and you can hangs things on them with small magnets. If you have a white board you can draw semi-permanent images or outlines (of a map, for instance) with a wet erase marker. You can then fill in other information, erase it and repeat with another class. The semi-permanent images can later be removed with alcohol or water.

Mounted pictures and drawings. You should mount your visuals because they will last longer, you can set them in the chalk tray, pass them around easily, and so on. When you mount them, a product that will be of great value to you is called *Spray Mount*, marketed by the 3M Company. Collect thin cardboard boxes or old posters and you can cut them up to mount your pictures on.

Flash cards. You can make flash cards yourself or have your students do them, but you should have collections of several different types: numbers, alphabet, math problems, sports, food, colors, parts of the body, verb forms for the different tenses, pronouns, and so on. You should make several sets so that students can work in pairs or groups using the cards. The cards can be made by cutting up large sheets of poster board, or even by using 5 x 8 cards and gluing pictures on them. Laminate them. You can buy commercial sets that are already made.

Visual cues. By visual cues, we mean the picture cues you will be preparing if you teach dialogues for memorization. You should have at least one set made up for each dialogue. You can sometimes work with artistically gifted students in your classes who want extra credit. You supply the ideas, and they do the artwork. (See Chapter 7 for examples.)

Maps. It is essential that you have a number of maps in your room of all the Spanish-speaking countries, including areas in the United States. If you don't have the money to buy maps, have your students make enlargements from the books you have available, or make transparencies from books and have them ready to throw on the projector at a moment's notice.

Charts. You need to make a number of different types of charts for class use. You can make them from sheets of poster paper and can even make racks to hand them on. Your chart collection might include: grammar diagrams and paradigms, dates and cultural information, class rules and regulations, and vocabulary lists. Keep them in Spanish.

Transparencies. Although transparencies are being replaced by digital images, at the time of this writing there are still more classrooms that have overhead projectors for transparencies than digital projectors. Every language teacher should have a large collection of overhead transparencies that can include: models for grammar practice, words to songs, instructions, questions and answers for tests, situational pictures, vocabulary pictures, maps (with overlays of cities and country boundaries), activities and games, and so on. If you want to digitize your transparencies, it's easy to do so with a scanner.

Cutouts, flannel figures, and puppets. Cutouts and puppets can be fun and motivating not only when used for presenting vocabulary, situations, and dialogues, but also when the students use them in practice and oral presentations.

A close-to-life-size dummy that has a name and personality can be integrated into many different activities and even blamed for some of the problems you are having in class.

Three-dimensional objects. Every teacher needs a large, sturdy clock with movable hands to be used in teaching time of day; smaller clocks can be made for the students to use individually and in practice activities. Dice and spinners can be used in a number of games to practice vocabulary and grammatical structures. Stuffed animals can be fun to use with teaching and practice and you can throw them around. Many teachers use small wooden figures (Fisher Price/Playskool type), houses, cars, trains, plastic animals and fruits, etc., for practicing grammar, conversational situations and dialogues.

Actual objects can also be used, such as hotel-size personal care items, such as soap, toothbrushes, combs, razors, etc. and used to teach and practice reflexive verbs: *lavarse, secarse, afeitarse, peinarse*, etc. Use your imagination and you can end up using almost anything as a visual aid.

CONCLUSION

This chapter has attempted to emphasize the enormous amount of goal setting, planning, and preparation that must go on even before you enter the classroom. Hopefully, the task will not seem too overwhelming. Obviously, you cannot do all these things in one day, or perhaps even in your first year or two; it is an ongoing process that will be hardest at the beginning of your teaching, but will become easier as you gain experience and build up your collection of resources. The more visuals you prepare before beginning to teach, the more you will have available to use at a time you will be very busy with all the first year housekeeping tasks. Don't forget:

> **¡Poco a poco se va lejos!**

REFERENCES AND SUGGESTIONS FOR FURTHER READING

Center for Advanced Research on Language Acquisition. (nd.). Content-Based Language Teaching with Technology (CoBaLLT) [website]. *A must-see website that contains instructional modules for teachers as well as samples of great lesson plans and planning templates.* http://www.carla.umn.edu/cobaltt/

Dupuy, B. C. (2000). Content-based instruction: Can it help ease the transition from beginning to advanced foreign language classes? *Foreign Language Annals, 33,* 205-223. DOI: 10.1111/j.1944-9720.2000.tb00913.x *Summarizes four different content-based models and research on their effectiveness.*

Mager, R. F. (1997). *Preparing instructional objectives* (3rd ed.). Atlanta, GA: Center for Effective Performance. *Discusses how to write objectives to match the learning outcomes you are seeking to achieve. This little book can make an enormous difference in how you prepare to teach your classes.*

McDonald, E. S., & Hershman, D. M. (2010). *Classrooms that spark! Recharge and revive your teaching* (2nd ed.). San Francisco, CA: Jossey Bass. *Contains tips on how to manage your files, set up a digital classroom with blogs, wikis and Twitter, as well as activities to boost student engagement and motivation.*

National Standards in Foreign Language Education Project. (2006). *Standards for foreign language learning in the 21st century* (3rd ed.). Alexandria, VA: ACTFL.

Redmond, M. L., & Lorenz, E. (Eds.) (1999). *Teacher to teacher: Model lessons for K-8 foreign language.* Lincolnwood, IL: National Textbook. *Contains great examples of content-based lesson plans.*

Other Books by James S. Taylor (see Appendix C for information)

- *Materiales para animar la clase de español*

Image Credits

ACTIVITIES FOR METHODS CLASSES

1. If your institution has a foreign language curriculum library, select a recently published textbook, and, using the guidelines provided in this chapter, evaluate it. Try to get a text that would be used at the level you will be teaching. Would you adopt that text for your own classes? What are the features you like best? What don't you like? Hand the evaluation in to your teacher.

2. Purchase a sturdy plastic file box and begin to collect visual aids. Put dividers in it with categories such as: food, clothing, seasons, professions, holidays, sports, and animals. Collect pictures (mount them), transparencies, dialogue visuals, etc. to put in each division. As you shop in stores and markets, ask for pictures and displays you can put in your collection. Watch for books and magazines (thrift stores, library and bookstore surplus book sales, etc.) that have pictures and drawings you can cut out, mount, and use. Or, do an online image search and print out the pictures with a color printer. If possible, laminate them. Show the file to your instructor at the end of the course.

3. Buy another crate and begin a collection of three dimensional objects you can use in your teaching: a large clock with moveable hands; plastic figures of animals, cars, houses; toys; bean bags; puppets; numbers charts; flash cards; game boards (such as "concentration"), etc. Show collection to your teacher at the end of the semester.

4. Visit the Foreign Language Curriculum Library at your institution and go through the collection of catalogs that provide visual aids and supplementary materials for language classes. Go to the websites of these companies and request free catalogues.

5. Write letters to some embassies, consulates, or tourist agencies and request materials. Show your fellow students and the teacher what you have received.

6. Go to the websites of book companies (or visit their displays in a foreign language teaching conference), and ask for examination copies of texts or readers. Proudly display them in the methods class.

7. Using the same text from activity #1 above, select a chapter and prepare a unit plan for that chapter. Use the model presented in this chapter. Hand the plan in to your instructor.

8. Take one of the days from the unit plan you prepared for the activity #7 above and write a daily lesson plan. Use the model presented in this chapter. Hand it in to your teacher.

9. Design a bulletin board. Show your preliminary drawing to your instructor for approval. Go to the media lab in your institution and prepare the materials for the bulletin board and then display it in the area designated by your instructor. Have it evaluated by the professor and fellow students.

10. Go to the different media labs in your institution and learn how to use the different equipment such as digital video cameras and audio recorders, document cameras, etc. Hand in a list of your skills to the professor.

CHAPTER FIVE

STARTING, ORGANIZING AND MANAGING

YOUR OBJECTIVES FOR THIS CHAPTER ARE TO:

1. EXPLAIN THE BENEFITS OF TEACHING YOUR CLASSES IN SPANISH.

2. CULTIVATE STRATEGIES FOR KEEPING YOUR CLASSES IN SPANISH.

3. RESOLVE TO USE SPANISH AS THE MODE OF COMMUNICATION IN YOUR CLASSES.

4. PLAN YOUR STRATEGY FOR A DYNAMIC FIRST DAY OF CLASS.

5. DEVELOP SKILL IN USING EFFECTIVE "START-UPS" AND "WARMUPS."

6. DEVELOP SYSTEMS AND STRATEGIES FOR EFFICIENT CLASSROOM MANAGEMENT.

7. BE PREPARED TO APPLY SUCCESSFUL DISCIPLINE IN YOUR CLASSES.

8. ANTICIPATE AND MAKE SOME SPECIAL DECISIONS ABOUT LANGUAGE AND PRONUNCIATION.

Mr. Goodheart studied the expressions of the teenagers entering his classroom for their first day of beginning Spanish. He was determined to teach the class entirely in Spanish this semester. He had attended a "refresher" course on language teaching at a nearby university that summer, and his professor had convinced him that he could do it. He agreed that it was the best way to bring his students to oral proficiency. Encouraged by the eager, expectant look on their young faces, he stepped confidently to the front of the class and began:

¡Buenos días! ¡Qué gusto me da verles esta mañana!

There was a shocked silence in the room. The students looked uneasy and a little panicky. Mr. G. bravely carried on:

Es evidente que ustedes tienen grandes deseos de aprender el idioma celestial. Les aseguro que lo vamos a hacer en gran manera.

A girl in the front row turned to her friend and whispered loudly:

What's he saying?

I don't have any idea, came the answer back.

Mr. G's resolve weakened. [*"They're getting frustrated. Maybe I'd better reassure them a little."*]

Don't be alarmed. You aren't expected to understand everything now, but you'll get used to it. Just listen and try to catch the drift of what I am saying.

An expression of relief flooded into the faces of the students. [*"Ah! He can speak English! Things were getting scary for a moment."*]

Mr. G. returned to the task:

Ahora les voy a dar a cada uno una hoja de papel. Quiero que la doblen en tres secciones iguales. La vamos a usar para indicar su nombre en español que les voy a dar.

What do you want us to do with this paper?, asked the burly football player from the back of the room.

Mr. G. gave up. He was getting nowhere. Besides he was a kindly man and it grieved him to see the bewilderment and confusion on the faces of his dear students.

Just a minute and I'll explain what I want you to do.

[*"Tomorrow, I'll conduct the class in Spanish,"* he thought to himself. *"There are so many administrative details that I have to take care of now, that if I insist on Spanish we'll never make it through the hour."*]

CHAPTER FIVE

STARTING, ORGANIZING, AND MANAGING

> **Let's watch well our beginnings and the results will manage themselves.**
>
> **--Alex Clark**

Just as a military general spends enormous amounts of time and energy planning his first battle, so you must have your *beginning strategies* all mapped out before you begin a semester or school year. The first week of class, and more important, the first day, will almost "set in concrete" the class atmosphere and the style of teaching with which you will have to live for the rest of the year.

It is possible for the general, having perhaps made mistakes and having lost the first battle, to change his strategy and eventually win the war. As we apply this analogy to the first days of your Spanish class, you too can start out wrong and later change your approach and win them over to communication in Spanish. But what an advantage you have if you win the first skirmish! What a giant step you can take toward reaching your goals if you can condition them to using the language the first day of class! In this chapter we will reveal the secrets that will give you victory in that initial battle.

TEACHING YOUR CLASS IN THE TARGET LANGUAGE

In 2010, the American Council on the Teaching of Foreign Languages (ACTFL) adopted a position statement emphasizing the importance of using the target language in the classroom. It states in part: "Research indicates that effective language instruction must provide significant levels of meaningful communication and interactive feedback in the target language in order for students to develop language and cultural proficiency. . . ACTFL therefore recommends that language educators and their students use the target language as exclusively as possible (90% plus) at all levels of instruction during instructional time and, when feasible, beyond the classroom."

Is it really possible to teach your classes "90% plus" in the target language? The answer is an emphatic "yes!" Pretend for a moment that you are going to teach an English as a Second Language (ESL) class. Assume that your students are from all over the world; some from Latin America, some from Taiwan, some from France, and some from Italy. Even if you spoke all the native languages of your students, what language would you conduct the class in? English, of course! If you used Spanish, only the Latin Americans would understand you. English is the only language common to all—even though the students can barely use it—and it must be the language of communication.

This situation presents some important consequences as to how you teach the class. You are obliged to give all your instructions and conduct all your activities in English. For example, you are forced to teach vocabulary *meaningfully*, in context, using visuals and making many explanations, until you are sure the students all understand. You have to be very creative and skillful in putting meaning across; there is no other alternative. You will probably make very few grammar explanations, and when you do, you will state things very simply and restate them again and again in different ways, until you see by their responses that they are getting it.

At first the students will miss a lot of what you say; but you anticipate that and continually reintroduce words and concepts. Soon they will develop the ability to catch the thread of thought and will learn how to ask for clarification until they understand what they missed. In a short time, their growth and progress in communication will have become almost spectacular. From that time on, both you and they will feel comfortable using English to express thoughts, likes, needs, feelings, and all the other things we use language for.

English as a second language (ESL) teachers are used to impressive results of this kind. They have been having them for years. As a Spanish teacher, you too can have the same spectacular results, if you do what they do: *use the target language for communication in the class.* Your task is no harder nor any more impossible than theirs. The only difference is that you have a "way out," a path of least resistance, an *easier* way to teach. You and your students share the same language, and it is infinitely easier to communicate—when you *"really want them to understand"*—in English. Little do you realize that when you do that you are hindering and blocking their learning of Spanish. You are taking away the *very* experiences that will lead them to your objective of becoming proficient in Spanish.

The secret is to *pretend that you are teaching a group of students who don't have a common language, and act as though they wouldn't*

understand if you used English. In a real sense, English should be an *intruder* language, which you would use only to make comments or comparisons. Work hard toward achieving that illusion and you will be surprised at what you can put over in the language and at how good your students become at getting the gist of what is going on and learn how to cope, just as they would if they were in a Spanish-speaking country.

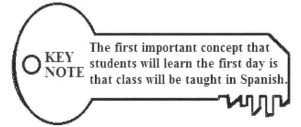

An explanation helps. If the students understand why you insist on teaching the class in Spanish, it will be helpful to them. Rather than spend time during the first day of class explaining why, prepare an explanation written in English, and *let them read it just before starting the class*—which you will teach in Spanish, of course. Following is an example of what that explanation could look like. Take these ideas and make your own version.

CLASSROOM PROCEDURES
(A word of Explanation)

In a few minutes Spanish class will begin. Hopefully you will be pleasantly surprised to learn that the language of communication in the class will be Spanish. This may cause you some frustration at first, but there is an extremely important reason for doing this. I assure you that I do not want to torture you, nor am I trying to make you feel dumb. It would be easier for me to teach you in English, but, paradoxically, that would be the worst thing I could do to you, because I want you to learn Spanish. To do that, you have to learn to think in the language, both listening and speaking. It is as if you were walking along the countryside and came to a river of murky water. You must cross; there is no way around. The only solution is to lower yourself into the water and somehow float across. For a while you may not be totally under control, but eventually you will get to the other side. Your tendency will be to hang on to the willows on the far bank (your English) and not let go, but if you do that you'll never get across. To cross that river is absolutely necessary if you want to learn to communicate in Spanish. Very faithfully following the classroom procedures listed below will make your task much easier.

1) Listen carefully to what is said, trying to understand. At first you will not understand all (any) of what I say. I know that. I do not expect you to. But, don't tune me out; don't panic. Stand your ground, grit your teeth, and try to catch the gist of what I am saying. Watch for gestures, facial expressions, words that are similar in English, and other clues. While you will have to tolerate a little vagueness at first, a successful language learner is a good guesser; use your imagination.

2) Communicate as best you can in Spanish. At first, it will be just a few words, imperfectly uttered, but for a while you will have to return to the level of a child. Try to accept that. If you are learning to play the piano as an adult, you would not start with a concerto, you would start with simple little pieces. As soon as possible I will give you the tools to communicate with. We will practice with a **"COPING CARD"** and you should use the words and phrases on it as often as you can. I will conduct a number of activities that will help you practice using these tools until they become second nature.

3) Try not to feel pressure or anxiety. Do not have unrealistic expectations, such as speaking at your English level in a few weeks. Grades will be based on your performance, but I view this as a process of "perfecting" not "perfection." I will give you ample time to prepare for tests and quizzes, and will help you get ready for them. I am on your side, remember? I am just as eager as you are for you to learn Spanish. Accept correction and suggestions with good humor. Take the attitude that "I'm going to have to make a million mistakes before I learn Spanish, so I might as will get started." I will try to correct with tact and gentleness. Do not be alarmed if others in the class seem to be understanding more or seem to be going faster than you are. It will just seem that way. Or it may be that some have studied Spanish before and naturally will have an advantage. Others may have more ability to learn a foreign language easily and quickly (aptitude). But these same differences exist in music, art, athletic skills, public speaking, etc. Adjust and accept the differences, rather than getting down on yourself. Evaluate your individual progress in terms of your own growth, not by the apparent progress of others. If you want to quicken your pace, simply spend more time studying and using the language.

4) Learn with and from others. Language is best learned with someone else. Find a partner from the class and practice before or after class or on the phone. As you learn new ways to say things, try them out on friends who speak Spanish. Listen to what others say and get ideas from them. If you can't find another person to practice with, practice with yourself. Fantasize, make up little plots and conversations in your head, practice what you would say in different situations.

5) Ask for help or clarification if you need it. Don't assume that you are the only one who doesn't understand something. Don't hesitate to say *"No entiendo"* (I don't understand) or *"Otra vez"* (Again, please) or *"¿Qué quiere decir _____?"* (What does _____ mean?) I will be happy to try to explain in some other way. I will not usually respond to questions in English, but I can often anticipate what you want to say and can help you state your question in Spanish.

6) Prepare yourself outside of class. The grammar explanations are quite clear in the book, and we will not spend a lot of time going over them in class. I will come to class wanting to *use* the text materials, not *explain* or *lecture* about them. I expect you to have studied the material prior to coming to class and to have practiced and drilled the assignment.

7) Be spontaneous and uninhibited. Learning Spanish can be fascinating and fun. Laugh at/with me, at/with others and at/with yourself. I may even "clown" a bit. Feel free to laugh. Add enjoyment to the satisfaction you will receive as you gain fluency in the language. When you understand, smile or nod; when you don't, shake your head or look perplexed. Help me out.

8) Think positively. Everything I do or say has a positive interpretation--never negative. Please reciprocate by being positive at all times. Come visit me in my office, not just when you have problems, but just to talk to me and tell me how things are going. Most students never do this. I want help you to do *your best*. We are on the same team.

With affection, your Spanish teacher,
Jaime Sastre

Give them tools to work with. You can't ask the students to do something they aren't equipped to handle. Much of your time during the first week of class will be spent giving them the tools that will allow them to understand you, and express what they need to say. After a few days, give them lists of phrases and key vocabulary words in a handy form such as a **COPING CARD**, and practice using them. Tell the students keep their *coping card* always at hand for constant reference. You can also make signs with some of the phrases from the *coping card*, such as *¿Cómo se dice__?* and *No entiendo* and put them on the walls of your classroom. On the next page is an example of a coping card that could be used in a beginning class. (See *Materiales para motivar la clase de español* for more examples of coping cards.)

Make the start of the class obvious. As you approach the beginning of class, the students are all chattering away in English. There has to be an abrupt transition, a definite end to the pre-class socializing, and a formal beginning of the class in Spanish. Get their attention and start with a bang. We call these "start-ups," and will discuss them in more detail later. Turn on a red light or put up a large sign that says *Prohibido hablar inglés* . During the next weeks, enforce this precept with fines, demerits, special rewards, or loss of privileges. Within a few days you can get the students involved in starting the class. Let them take turns giving the *bienvenida.* You could include a quick song, or a brief warm-up in your start- up. All of this focuses their attention to the fact that the class has begun and reminds them that it is conducted in Spanish.

You are the key. The key to keeping the class in Spanish lies with the teacher. If you break down and use English, they will do the same. If they express something in English that you know they can say in Spanish, *don't accept it.* Insist that they say it in Spanish. They will use as much English as you will let them get away with. If they really are unable to say something, supply the words and help them express it in Spanish.

If your personal command of the language is somewhat weak and you do not have the confidence to teach the class in the language, you need to take the steps to develop that competency. You can begin by carefully thinking through your classes ahead of time and anticipating the words and expressions you will need. Then learn how to say what you need to say. Almost any teacher who has the necessary qualifications to be a Spanish teacher is capable of using the language within a simple framework of a beginning class. (In *Materiales para animar la clase de español* we have prepared a coping card for teachers. The book *Spanish for Teachers* by Ana Jarvis is another excellent source for words and expressions a teacher would use in a classroom setting.)

Spanish names help keep the "flavor." The use of English names can detract from your efforts to use the foreign language exclusively in the classroom. Your students also need to become acquainted with Spanish names and practice their pronunciation. Many teachers give the students a Spanish equivalent of their name the first day of class. This provides constant pronunciation practice, gives a more authentic atmosphere, and lends itself to a number of activities that allow them to use the language naturally. (See *Materiales para animar la clase de español* for a list of translatable names and suggested substitutes for names that cannot be translated.) Following is an example of a procedure you could use for using Spanish names:

Model for the first day of class. We have stated that the first day of class is vital to establishing the class tradition of using only Spanish in class. Let's try to summarize all our suggestions with a model. The following can serve as a guide to what you might do to successfully condition your classes for using Spanish as the language of communication in the class.

CARTA DE COMUNICACIÓN
Spanish Coping Card

RESPONSE TO QUESTIONS

No *No/not*   Sí *Yes*
¡Claro! *You bet!*
Creo que no *I don't think so*
Creo que sí *I think so*
Es posible *It's possible*
Me llamo ____ *My name is _____*
Se llama ____ *His/her name is ____*
(It is called ____)
No (lo) sé. *I don't know (it).*
¿Quién sabe? *Who knows?*
Un poco *A little*
¡Mucho! *A lot, very much!*

GREETINGS/LEAVE TAKING

Hola *Hello, Hi*
Buenos días *Good morning*
Buenas tardes *Good afternoon*
Buenas noches *Good evening*
¿Cómo está (usted)? *How are you?*
¿Qué tal? *How goes it?'*
¿Qué hay (de nuevo)? *What's up?*
¿Qué pasa? *What's going on?*
Bien, gracias. *Fine, thanks.*
¿Y usted? *And you?*
Mucho gusto. *It's a pleasure.*
El gusto es mío. *My pleasure.*
¡Cuídese! *Take care!*
¡Buena suerte! *Good luck!*
Igualmente. *The same to you.*
Tengo que irme. *I have to go.*
Saludos a ____. *Regards to ____.*
Hasta luego. *See you later.*
Adiós. *Goodbye.*
Chau. *So long.*

IF YOU DON'T UNDERSTAND

¿Cómo? *What?*
Otra vez, por favor. *Again, please.*
Más despacio. *Slower.*
No entiendo. *I don't understand.*
¿Qué dijo? *What did he/she say?*
¿Qué quiere decir ____? *What does _____ mean?*
Usted dice que ..*You're saying that..*
[repeat what you think was said]
¿Habla usted inglés? *Do you speak English?* [only to be used in dire emergencies!]

COURTESY PHRASES

Por favor *Please*
(Muchas) Gracias *(Many) thanks*
De nada. *You're welcome*
Con permiso. *Excuse (permit) me*
¡Cómo no! *Of course!*
¡Pase (Adelante)! *Go (right ahead)!*
Perdone. *Excuse me [forgiveness]*
Está bien. *It's okay.*
No es nada. *It's nothing.*
Lo siento (mucho). *I'm (very) sorry.*
No importa. *It doesn't matter.*
¡Salud! *Bless you! (Health!)*
No se moleste. *Don't bother.*
Un momento. *Just a moment.*
Tengo una pregunta. *I have a question.*
¿Se puede (pasar)? *May I (come in)?*
Perdone la molestia. *Pardon the bother.*
A sus órdenes. *At your service.*
Es un placer. *It's a pleasure.*

ASKING QUESTIONS

¿Cómo se dice ____? *How do you say ____?*
¿Cómo se llama esto? *What is this called?*
¿Cómo se llama usted (él, ella)? *What is your (his, her) name?*
¿Cuánto? *How much?*
¿Cuántos(as)? *How many?*
¿Cuánto cuesta? *How much does it cost?*
¿De dónde es usted (él, ella)? *Where are you (he/she) from?*
¿Cómo es ____? *What is ____ like?*
¿Me entiende? *Do you understand?*
¿Habla usted español? *Do you speak Spanish?*
¿Por qué (no)? *Why (not)?*
¿Qué es esto (eso)? *What is this (that)?*
¿Qué hace? *What are you (he, she) doing?*
¿Qué quiere? *What do you (he, she) want?*
¿Quién (Quiénes)? *Who?*
¿Quién es? *Who is it/that?*

USEFUL WORDS & PHRASES

¿Algo más? *Anything else?*
Es todo. *That's all.*
A veces *Sometimes*
A ver. *Let's see.*
¡Basta! *That's enough!*
¡Muy bien! *Very good!*
¡Bien hecho! *Well done!*
Casi *Almost*
¡Cuidado! *Watch out, be careful!*
¡De acuerdo! *Agreed!*
Demasiado *Too much*
Demasiado poco *Too little*
Bastante *Enough*
Es difícil *It's hard*
Es fácil *It's easy*
Hay *There is, there are*
Grande *Big*
Pequeño *Little, small*
Mal *Bad, poorly*
Más *More*
Menos *Less*
Mucho *Much, a lot*
Muy *Very*
Nada *Nothing*
Nadie *No one*
Nunca *Never*
Y *And*
Pues… *Well…*
Siempre *Always*
También *Also, too*
Tampoco *Neither*
Todavía (no) *Still (not yet)*
Vamos a ver *We'll see*
Ya no *No longer*

TIME

¿Cuándo? *When?*
Ahora (Ahorita) *(Right) now*
Hoy *Today*
Ayer *Yesterday*
Mañana *Tomorrow*
Anoche *Last night*
Esta mañana (tarde, noche) *This morning (afternoon, evening)*
El sábado *This Saturday*
¿A qué hora? *At what time?*
A la una (A las dos, etc.) *At 1:00 (At 2:00 etc.)*

MODEL FOR FIRST DAY OF CLASS

1. As the students come into class, greet them with a cheery *¡Hola!* and give them the handout that explains why the class will be taught in Spanish. While they are reading, continue getting things ready for class.

2. When you are ready to begin, make a big show about plugging in or hanging up the **PROHIBIDO HABLAR INGLÉS** sign.

[All of the following would be in Spanish]

3. Start the class with *¡Buenos días!* and go through an exaggerated *bienvenida*, explaining that you will always start the class this way. Make some brief general comments, perhaps about the importance of learning a foreign language and the enjoyable time you are going to have in the class. Then, using gestures and/or visuals, tell some things about you.

4. Point out that since you have a name, they will need one too. Pass out blank sheets of paper, have them fold them in three sections, and then proceed to give them Spanish names, which they can write on the paper with a large marking pen. (If you have access to their names before class, you can have their Spanish names selected in advance.)

5. Have one of the students stand up, point out his name to the class and tell them who he is, for example: *Es Roberto.* Introduce the phrase: *¿Quién es?* and have them practice responding. Teach the student how to say "*Soy Roberto* and have him respond to: *¿Quién eres?* Then practice with the names of the entire class, until they can answer the questions comfortably.

6. Introduce Juan Paco Pedro (picture or dummy), talk about him and then teach the words to the song. Play it on the tape and then have them sing along.

7. Using Juan Paco Pedro, teach them other classroom expressions and some class management activities such as calling the roll.

8. Teach them common greetings and leave-taking expressions and practice them. Explain that you will be using them from then on as they come to class and encourage them to use them with each other outside class. Use visuals to teach: *¿Cómo estás?, Muy bien, Muy mal,* etc.

9. Tell them how enjoyable it has been, that you will look forward to the next class, and dismiss hem with an *¡Adiós!* and get them to respond.

10. *OPTIONAL.* At this point you could make an obvious end to the main part of the class, unplug the light or take down the sign, and use English to take care of any administrative business, or allow them to ask questions or make comments. After administrative needs are completed, you no longer need to use English.

Different teachers use different techniques to manage their classes in the foreign language. Some teachers speak English only when they are standing in a designated corner of the room, or when they put on a certain hat (a derby or a cowboy hat, for example), or they step outside the classroom and only English with their head inserted between the door of the frame. Another technique is for the teacher to hang a card around his or her neck with the words **SOLO ESPAÑOL.** Name cards can be prepared for the students that they put on just as they enter the classroom. For example:

```
┌─────────────────────────────────────┐
│                                       │
│         ¡ H ☺LA!                      │
│                                       │
│  ME LLAMO_____    │
│                                       │
│         NO HABLO INGLÉS               │
│                                       │
│   HÁBLAME EN ESPAÑOL, POR FAVOR       │
│                                       │
└─────────────────────────────────────┘
```

The preceding technique can help the students use the language among themselves if they establish the idea that they cannot use English as long as they have the name tag on.

With elementary school children, one must be careful that they know what procedures to follow, and some elementary school language teachers make it a practice to talk to the children in English outside of the room before beginning the class. Some elementary school teachers even bring into the class a parent, another teacher, or an advanced student who stands alongside and translates what the teacher is saying. This can be really effective in establishing the concept that the teacher does not use English during the class e valuable activities.

These activities are very informal and may simply consist of talking to individuals in Spanish, or to the entire group, talking about some school event, some current event, the weather, something that happened to you recently, and so on. The information you present can't include crucial, essential material because most of your students haven't arrived yet, and it isn't really necessary to have a preamble every day. Basically, it is just an attempt to establish a closer personal relationship with individual students and help them "log in" more time in hearing and using the language. Some suggested preamble activities might include:

1. A "monologue," where the teacher talks in Spanish about some current event, an anecdote of interest, some cultural information about Hispanic countries, etc.
2. Play a tape of some popular Hispanic singer. (You can keep working while it is playing.)
3. Play a tape in Spanish of a radio broadcast, an interview, a speech, a *fútbol* match, an advertising commercial, etc.

period. Some teachers use their signs to indicate the beginning or ending of the period of exclusive target language use, and use English outside that period. We favor eliminating English completely.

OTHER MANAGEMENT TECHNIQUES

Let's now look at other management techniques you should consider using in your classes.

The period before and between classes. Is there any way we can take advantage of the ten minutes we usually have before the first class or between classes? Typically, the teacher is busy getting things ready for the following class, but with a little organization and preparation of materials, we can get some "free milage" from those students who arrive early and waste the time chatting, reading the school newspaper, or just plain standing around. Activities designed to take up time before starting the class are called a **preamble.** We do not suggest you **begin** your classes this way—we recommend a more formal **"start-up"** below— but you can occupy the period of time just before you begin class with so

4. Spend the time "caring and sharing" with the students as they arrive. Talking to them in Spanish, discussing their school activities, their personal goals and achievements, their family and friends, the win (or loss) of a school team.
5. Use your bulletin board displays or 4 x 6 cards with some kind of communication activity involving the display.

The beginning of each class should be kept inviolate for Spanish communication. We would go so far as to say that time is sacred. There is much competition for that time—students often try to use that time to visit with each other noisily in English. Some ask the teacher questions. Often several gather around the teacher's desk to ask the teacher questions or to chat (or to delay) the beginning of class—perhaps not with malice or even a thought-out plan, but intuitively procrastinating the beginning of class. These offer important reasons to have the desk off to the side, in back of the room, or preferably in a little office-storage area (with glass windows and door to separate or even room dividers also with glass to see or low enough to see). Plan sufficiently so that you are ready to begin class at the signal (bell, buzzer, gong, beep, or whatever). Tell your students, "*Ahora no puedo, es hora de comenzar la clase.*" Let them know that there will be a chance later for the problems or questions they have.

The "Start-up"

The "start-up" becomes almost a ritual—a set, formal ceremony that begins as soon as the bell to start class rings. It consists of a **BIENVENIDA** given by one of the students followed by a **WARM-UP** conducted at first by the teacher and later by a student. Just before class begins, the teacher or the *bienvenida* coordinator could write the following on the board:

B (bienvenida)   Roberto

A (activ. de cal.)   Ana María

The students named get everyone's attention and the class would begin as they carried out their assignment. Here are some suggestions for organizing these two activities.

Conducting a *Bienvenida*

A *bienvenida* is a brief but formal beginning of the class period. It is the signal for everyone to stop whatever they are doing and begin the class. For the first day or two in a beginning class you, the teacher, will give the *bienvenida*, but you should begin immediately to train the students to take over that task. With beginning classes it has to be very simple. The first model below is designed for a first-year class and can be given by students after just a few days of class. With your help on pronunciation, some of your brighter students can memorize it in just a few minutes.

BIENVENIDA

¡Buenos días! (¡Buenas tardes!)
Bienvenidos todos a la clase de español.
Hoy es _____ (lunes, etc.), el _____ (cinco, etc.) de _____ (mayo, etc.)
Hoy hace _____ (calor, frío, buen tiempo, mal tiempo, sol, viento, etc.)

As the students become more able to use the language, the *bienvenida* can become more complex. Following is an example of a more elaborate one.

BIENVENIDA MÁS AVANZADA
(Modelo)

¡Buenos días! (¡Buenas tardes!) ¿Puedo tener su atención, por favor?
Quiero extender una cordial bienvenida a todos a la clase de español.
Hoy es _____ (lunes, etc.), el _____ (cinco, etc.) de _____ _____ (mayo, etc.).
Hoy hace . . . . (buen tiempo, mal tiempo, frío, calor, etc.).

Tenemos los siguientes anuncios: Hay un partido de baloncesto el viernes a las 6 (etc. etc.)

_____ nos visita hoy. Es la hermana de _____ y está pasando unos días aquí en Provo. ¡Muy benvenida _____!

No hay clase de español mañana. El lunes vamos a _____ (etc.).
Hoy es el cumpleaños de _____. ¡Felicidades, _____!
Tengo una adivinanza (un chiste). ¿Cuál es el animal más perezoso? (El pez. ¿Por qué? ¿Qué hace todo el día? ¡Nada!)
Ahora vamos a tener el ejercicio de calentamiento, dirigido por _____ .

Coordinate the giving of the welcome with the use of a sign up sheet and appoint a coordinator. He/She is responsible for seeing that someone is assigned for each day of class and to remind that person the preceding day to be prepared. The teacher can prepare an announcement folder and each day have the announcements ready. It's a good practice to talk briefly with the person giving the *bienvenida* just before class and prime him/her with the vocabulary necessary to make the announcements.

The person giving the *bienvenida* is also responsible to watch for visitors to the class, and if there are any, talk to them before class starts to find out who they are (name, origin, etc.) and why they are in the class, and then introduce them to the class, extending a special welcome— even if the visitor does not understand Spanish.

As they become more proficient in the language, the persons giving the *bienvenida* can relate an anecdote, tell a joke, recite a poem (See **Motivational Materials** for jokes and poems), make special presentations, lead the class in *Cumpleaños feliz* (See **Canciones, cultura y gramática**) if it is someone's birthday, and so on. At the end of the *bienvenida*, the time is turned over to the teacher or another student to conduct the warm-up.

Conducting a Warm-up

As your students enter the Spanish class, they bring with them the frame of mind they have acquired from whatever activity they have just participated in. They may be just arriving at school or coming from a P.E. class, tired or exhilarated. They may be just getting out of a test, getting off work, coming from an assembly or sports event, and so on. They will be speaking English and will probably have forgotten most of what they learned in the last Spanish class.

You need something startling, something that will grab their attention, weld them together as a class, and start them thinking in Spanish. The environment and climate of "we communicate here in Spanish" must be re-established. They need something to focus on, to loosen their tongues and get the Spanish flowing. A well-prepared and snappily-presented ***warm-up*** (*ejercicio o actividad de calentamiento*) can do all this.

A **warm-up** is a brief activity conducted at the beginning of class with a lot of repetition and choral response. It is an in-place activity, not a game. There is no evaluation, no testing, nor grading so there will be no apprehension or hesitation to participate. A warm-up is often a simple, short, presentation of new vocabulary or review and practice of something they have already learned, not a grammar lesson or conversation session. The teacher uses some sort of visual aid to present the new vocabulary or the material to be reviewed. This focuses the students' attention and gets them involved. If new vocabulary is presented, the warm-up always ends with the students using the words in meaningful, natural context, not just repeating isolated words. Warm-ups can be very motivating if you conduct them with enthusiasm and use a variety of visual aids. Make them fun and the students will enjoy them. Following are some examples:

1. The teacher reviews numbers with the students, using flash cards or the chalkboard. Then to get them out of the rote sequence, you have them do math problems, such as *¿Cuánto son tres y cinco?* Or the teacher asks questions such as *¿Cuántas luces,* (etc.) *hay en la clase?* using visuals or the actual objects, and the students respond with numbers.

2. Using a map of Latin America or Europe, the teacher teaches the nationalities of the people from different countries. Then using pictures, the students are asked *¿De dónde es el señor García?* (*Guatemala*) *¿Qué es el señor García?* (*Es guatemalteco.*), etc.

3. The days of the week are reviewed with flash cards or a calendar. The teacher then asks, *¿Qué día vamos a la escuela?* (*los lunes, martes,* etc.) *¿Qué día vamos a la iglesia?* (*los domingos*), etc.

Following is a sampling of some warm-ups that could be used in a first year class. (Often the lesson you are working with will give you some ideas for warm-ups, such as titles, parts of the body, school subjects, etc. Or you just might wish to review something they learned several weeks ago, but have forgotten.)

POSSIBLE WARMUP ACTIVITIES

Topic	Aid/Activities
1. Types of transportation	1. Pictures/transp./toys of train, bus, etc.
2. Nationalities	2. Map, picture of people in native dress
3. Days of the week	3. Calendar, chalkboard, pics of activities
4. Emotions, feelings	4. Pictures/flash cards
5. Daily activities, routine	5. Pictures, agendas, schedules
6. Time of daily activities (get up, go to school, to class, etc.)	6. Clock, pictures of activities
7. Parts of the body	7. Picture, dummy, actual student
8. Sports	8. Pictures of sports and personalities
9. Places and activities for entertain. (movies, beach, dance, etc.)	9. Pictures
10. Fruits	10. Pictures, real or wax fruit

1. Negative words	1. Large cards with neg. words, sentences
2. Substitution drills	2. Drill cue cards
3. Noun to pronoun drill	3. Flash cards, objects

1. Math with numbers: add, subtract, multiply, count by threes, etc.	1. Chalkboard, flash cards, number board
2. Review an old dialogue	2. Dialogue visuals
3. Coping card practice	3. Coping Card, situations, phrases
4. Rejoinders	4. Rejoinder list, situations, phrases
5. Time of day	5. Clock

1. Consonant sounds	1. Transp. with phrases
2. Schwa elimination	2. Transp. words
3. Pron. of /h/	3. Transp. with phrases
4. Tongue twisters	4. Transp. or posters with TT
5. Intonation practice	5. Transp. or tape with intonation practice

1. Expressions with tener	1. Picture cue cards
2. Weather expres. (hace frío, etc.)	2. Weather pictures, manipulatives, symbols
3. "Split-second trans. "gustar-type" verbs	3. Pictures, list of sentences.

1. Road signs	1. Pictures of signs
2. Spanish names of countries	2. Map
3. Types of stores (market, clothes, shoes, etc.)	3. Pictures
4. Money (peso, centavo, etc.)	4. Coins, bills, chart of monetary units of
5. Languages, where spoken	5. Map, samples of writing

1. Read (tell) story	1. Big story book, pictures
2. Act out fairy tale	2. Props, pictures, story book
3. Current events	3. Newspaper, mag., pictures
4. TPR activities	4. Vocab., teacher gives commands
5. Video from textbook or online (YouTube, etc.)	5. Video

(There are hundreds more warm-up suggestions in *Materiales para animar la clase de español*.)

"Sponge" Activites

After you've begun with the start-up or even during the main class activities, you may need some time (three to five minutes, more or less) to check on some special problems, such as taking silent roll (in some schools this is mandatory and must be done by the teacher) or consulting with a problem student or taking care of some clerical activity. You need a "sponge" activity, that is, something that will keep the students busy and give you a few minutes free. Often it will be a quiet activity, but it also could be a pair or group activity. Here are some examples:

1. Read a written summary of previously presented material.
2. Read a selection printed in the book—review or new.
3. Answer a series of questions about a reading passage or review summary.
4. Crossword or hidden words puzzle.
5. Written grammar exercise.
6. Complete the missing lines in a written dialogue with appropriate expressions.
7. Write a paragraph related to the current topic of study—what students did after school yesterday, what they eat in a typical day, what classes they are taking, etc.

These activities are very much like regular activities in the class (see Chapters 6 through 10), but you plan them to have something to give to the class at a minute's notice to be able to take care of any one of the special problems that come up every day—especially checking clerical tasks that are necessary and sometimes crucial such as roll, checking odd period absences (evidence of students "cutting" class), need to have one-on-one management chats or discipline discussions.

Many teachers prefer to have students do this type of activity immediately opon entering the classroom while the teacher takes roll or handles administrative tasks, prior to formally starting the class with a *bienvenida* and other activities. In this case the "sponge" activity is often called "bellwork"; in Spanish it might be called *el enfoque*. The teacher establishes this routine at the beginning of the year, letting students know that they are expected to enter quietly and get to work immediately. We would emphasize the importance of making the use of Spanish a part of the bellwork routine. For example, instructions can be written on the board in Spanish (students quickly learn to understand these instructions), and if the work is corrected as a class, the teacher can use Spanish to comment on it (*Cierto. / ¡Fantástico! / Hay un pequeño error. ¿Quién sabe cuál es?*).

ADMINISTRATIVE PROCEDURES

Formalized educational settings often require the carrying out of administrative functions. They can all be done in Spanish. It just takes some effort on the part of the teacher and training of the students. For example, you could prepare a set of visual aids to go with your discussion of dress standards, with pictures of proper haircuts, the types of shorts that can and cannot be worn, activities that are prohibited such as using cell phones, texting, and so on. It can be a good listening exercise and is fun for the students to hear in Spanish something that they have heard many times in other classes. Here are some other ideas about how you can take care of administrative procedures in the language.

Taking attendance. There are a number of ways to call the roll utilizing the language.

1. Teach the students how to say *presente* and *ausente*, call their names, and they respond with *presente*. If someone is absent, the class can tell you that he/she is *ausente.*
2. Assign each student a number in Spanish and have them call out their numbers in order. If the count pauses, that student must be absent (or asleep) and the teacher takes note and shouts out that number so the counting can continue.
3. Assign each student a permanent seat where he or she is to sit each day of class. Then prepare a seating chart indicating the name of the student in each seat. A glance at the beginning of class will reveal which students are absent (the empty seats) and the attendance slip can be quickly prepared.
4. Prepare numerous copies of an attendance sheet that has the names of the students on it in alphabetical order. The sheet can be passed around at the beginning of class and the students sign (or put their initials) by their name. An alternative is to place the sheet near the door and the students "sign in" as they enter. Some teachers include columns where the students can also indicate if they are prepared, if they have completed homework, if they attended lab, and so on. All of these sheets can be prepared in Spanish. You need only explain the meanings once or twice at the beginning of the course.

Collecting and returning written work. Baskets and small boxes placed on a table, desk, or near the door are an effective way of collecting and returning written work. This saves time that can be used for oral activities. There can be a box or basket for each class and they can be labeled in Spanish.

Making homework assignments. You will, of course, give your students all the assignments they are to complete during a term or semester. These should be accompanied by specific instructions about what to do, criteria on which they will be graded, and the date they are expected to handed in. You must establish a policy about whether they can hand assignments in late, under what conditions, and if points will be deducted. Many teachers make it a practice to write homework assignments on the board before class to remind the students what they are expected to do before the next class.

Password. A very effective technique for checking if objectives of a class period have been met (especially in FLES programs) is to set up a ritual called "the password" (*la contraseña*). Just before the class ends, the teacher stations him/herself at the exit door and the students line up in front of the teacher. The teacher selects some item the students were to have learned during the class hour, for example, a response to the question *"¿Qué tal?"*, conjugating a verb in the past tense, changing an object noun to an object pronoun, etc. One by one, the teacher gives the "challenge" (*el desafío*) to a student who has to answer with the *"contraseña."*

Maestro(a): ¿Tienes tu libro?
Estudiante 1: Sí, lo tengo. (Sale)
Maestro(a): ¿Tienes la caja?
Estudiante 2: Sí, lo tengo.
Macstro(a): Lo siento. Está mal. No puedes salir. ¡A la cola! (El/la estudiante va al final de la cola)

It's surprising how fast students learn what to do when they find themselves at the end of the line two or more times.

Extra work reports. When students are given assignments to do extra work outside of class, a simple report form can be prepared—it's very effective when printed on colored paper—and made available to the students who simply fill them out and hand them in to the teacher as they complete the work. Following is an example of a report.

INFORME DE TRABAJO EXTRA

Este informe tiene que ser entregado al/a la profesor/a dentro de 5 días después de la actividad. Si lo entregas después, no recibirás crédito.

Fecha _____

Estimado/a profesor/a _____,

Me es muy grato informarle que el ____ del mes de _____ hice lo siguiente:

_____

_____

Le solicito respetuosamente me conceda crédito extra en la clase de español ____. Gracias por su atenta consideración.

_____

(Estudiante)

Palabras nuevas aprendidas (mínimo de 10):

_____

_____

_____

Información nueva aprendida:

_____

_____

_____

RECORD KEEPING

Teachers are responsible for keeping records of student work and progress, both to be aware of how each student is progressing in the course and to give grades. With the advent of the personal computer this task has become infinitely easier. Any teacher who does not use a grade management program is living in the dark ages and is making life much more difficult than it needs to be.

There are many grade management programs available. Likely, your institution will have one for use by all the teachers. These programs are usually easy to use, even for someone now used to working with computers. Even some textbook programs now offer grading and records management materials. Here are some of the common features of a grading program:

- A choice of three different grading systems: *i.e.* percent, points, weighting.
- Names can be automatically alphabetized.
- Related assignments can be entered as categories and graded as a group.
- Scores can be recorded by student's name or assignment.
- Point and percent scores can be mixed.
- Low scores can be dropped.
- Unrecorded scores can be ignored (for incompletes and late arrivals).
- Individual progress reports can be printed.
- A "spreadsheet style" report of all scores can be prepared.
- Lists of assignment scores can be made.
- Assignments can be weighted.
- A final score report with letter grades(grade scale is adjustable) can be made.
- A list of missing assignments can be made.
- Failing notices can be made and printed, and e-mailed to students and/or parents.
- Grades can be posted on the Internet to be viewed by students and parents.
- Statistics can be computed.
- Personalized messages can be added to reports.

- Reports can be downloaded and included in letters.
- Names, assignments and scores can be easily changed at any time. (And many, many other things.)

Familiarize yourself with class management programs and start using them immediately as you begin teaching. KEEP UP TO DATE! Don't wait until the day before grades are due or the day before parent teacher conference. "Housekeeping chores," such as grading, attendance, correcting papers, etc. can become overwhelming if they are allowed to accumulate. Develop a daily or weekly system for handling them. It's far easier to keep up than to catch up.

Grading

Although few teachers enjoy it, most educational institutions require that our students be given grades, often both academic and behavioral (citizenship, work habits, cooperation). We will discuss in more detail in Chapter 12, Testing and Evaluation, some of the different approaches to grading, but we emphasize here that as you begin your courses you will need to discuss very clearly with your students the criteria you will use in grading them. Many schools require "disclosure documents" which outline the grading procedure the teacher will use; these must be given in writing to both the student and parents. Make sure that your basis for grading matches your goals and emphasis. Teachers sometimes spend all their classroom time developing oral skills and then give students written grammar tests because they are easier to prepare, administer, and grade.

We strongly suggest that you decide before you start the year what criteria you are going to use as the basis for citizenship grades and that you present those criteria very clearly to the students several times during the first weeks. It would be a good idea to give it in written form to both students and parents.

MANAGING STUDENTS -CLASSROOM DISCIPLINE

Someone once remarked that: "it is impossible to teach in a whirlwind." This is very true. If the students are so disruptive that the room is in a total uproar, it is unlikely that any learning is going on. This is not to say, however, that the room must be absolutely quiet. The nature of language learning requires speaking, interaction, role-playing, and often a lot of enthusiastic activities. These activities can be controlled to the point that the students are learning or practicing. One key to discipline in a language class is careful preparation of a wide variety of activities.

In all your classes, it is vital to work constantly with your students' attitudes. It is crucial that the students understand the importance and reasons behind all the activities you carry out in the class. They must have a feeling for their own progress and success, and have a vision of the process of language learning. Of course, a brief orientation can and should take place before the activities, but *experience* allows for sufficient assimilation to have the discussion mean something. All aspects of language learning require experience to be internalized. A good device to solve this need for disclosure is the so-called ***spot commercial***, both for orientation as well as a discussion topic. This can also serve as an evaluation. Since the class time should be devoted to communication activities rather than pontificating on rationale or even language rules, the spot commercial can be prepared in the form of written handouts. If an oral presentation is necessary as a spot commercial, it should be very short and effective—cue from radio and television—not longer than 30 seconds (tops, 1 minute). Variety of devices for these "spots" can be as extensive as in radio and TV.

Examples of a "spot commercial." (These would be in Spanish, of course.)

- After class yesterday a couple of students were commenting on how much time we spent learning the new vocabulary words and one remarked that we could have saved a lot of time if I had just told you what they were in English. True, we would have saved some time, but remember that we need to learn meanings directly in Spanish and not in terms of English. I promise that you will remember the words better and will be able to make immediate use of them if we learn them in context, without translating into English. Trust me!

• I know that some of you haven't totally understood the grammar point I have just presented, but you wouldn't understand it any better if I presented it in English. Remember, if you have a vague notion of what the concept is, that will be enough. The ability to use a structure in Spanish comes more from practicing it than it does from hearing it explained in English. ¡Confíen en mí!

• Some of you have remarked that you are annoyed by the way Monserrat keeps saying ¡Vale! in the video series. You should understand that that is the way you say OK! in Spain. You probably aren't aware how much we use that expression when we talk. It is a sort of confirmation word we use constantly, and are usually unaware that we say it. ¡Vale! is used in the same way. Rather than complain, practice using it until it becomes a habit and it will be very helpful in making your Spanish more natural. ¿Vale?

Classroom discipline. Effective discipline is based on preparation and good teaching. It also involves input from the students. You need to know how they feel and what they think about their class activities and about their relationship with you so you can make adjustments as needed. This is obvious in organizational management and teaching involves this kind of management.

Here are some suggestions:

1. Learn your students' names as quickly as possible. Show interest in students and let them know you care about them as individuals.
2. Plan carefully and well.
3. Have an interesting variety of activities.
4. Establish limits of behavior. Be consistent (determine your tolerance level for noise and activity).
5. Be fair, firm, and friendly (establish your reputation).
6. Have more rewards (smile, nod, positive expressions, excited involvement) and have less punishment—if at all (don't get the people and the act mixed up).
7. Recognize the natural student leaders and enlist their help.

Levels of motivation. Teachers need to be aware that the students' *personal* goals generate their highest level of motivation. Their second level of motivation is that the students want to please or need to please others, including their teachers. These two aspects are very positive and very effective over the long term. Other negative levels of motivation sometimes work but are not so effective over the long term. The threat of grades is negative and should be used sparingly, if at all. The next level of motivation used by some teachers really should be avoided—ridicule and sarcasm. These two rank only slightly higher than verbal abuse that is only a little higher than physical abuse.

Keep the unbreakable rules few in number, preferably only two: **1) control yourself** and **2) do your work**. The rest of the limitations are negotiable norms.

Some language teachers have expressed the doubt that they can discipline effectively in the foreign language. They argue, as an example, that their students are not as conditioned culturally to *Silencio!* as they are to *Quiet!* This may be true, but it is also true that much of the force of teacher discipline lies in the *way* things are said, the facial expressions, eye contact, and body language which are used, and these characteristics can be sensed even when Spanish is used. In our experience, successful teachers are able to handle most routine discipline problems in Spanish. If your students are accustomed to hearing Spanish and have learned to understand common classroom instructions in the language, there are relatively few cases where you will need to resort to English.

We have limited our discussion of management skills to their use in a language class. There are, of course, many theories and general approaches to discipline which may be of help to you, but which cannot be treated here. By far the best treatment of classroom management is the materials by Harry and Rosemary Wong. If you are concerned about this area, visit their web site and perhaps sign up for their on-line course. It could revolutionize your classroom management.

LANGUAGE DECISIONS

As you begin your classes you will have to make a number of linguistic and cultural decisions. The questions must be asked: "What dialect, pronunciation, or vocabulary system should I teach?" In a very simplistic way, Spanish can be divided into two major types: peninsular and Latin American. There are, of course, many subdivisions of these general types such as the Andalusian or Castilian varieties of peninsular Spanish, and in Latin America almost every country has its own brand of the language. Discuss this early on with your students in a very positive, objective way. Don't allow them to develop negative attitudes, such as "The Castilian *zeta* is 'dumb,' it sounds like you are lisping or have a speech defect." Let them know that this is one of the fun things about the language and they should enjoy learning about the differences and using them. They should not ridicule any one dialect, such as "The Mexicans speak an inferior, low class Spanish," but should rather be tolerant about the differences classmates might use, or what they might detect in audio recordings, videos, or in visitors to the class.

It is interesting to have some short lessons to point out these differences. Topics you might treat could be:

Pronunciation differences. You should decide which pronunciation you personally will be using, and then mention the /y/ of the Río de la Plata region, the /c/ and /z/ of Castilian Spanish, the dropping of final /s/ by Chileans and Cubans, the nasal sounds of the Caribbean region, etc. When you invite natives to visit your classes, point out their different way of speaking. As you use videos, replay different segments, asking the students to guess what area the speakers are from based on their pronunciation. Occasionally you can bring a flag from Spain (Argentina, Puerto Rico, etc.) to class and display it in a prominent spot, announcing that you are going to pretend you are in Spain (Argentina, Puerto Rico, etc.) and are going to pronounce the way they do in Spain. In this way your students will not be frustrated by the differences in pronunciation they are going to hear as they meet natives from different regions.

Vocabulary differences. It seems to be counterproductive for your students to learn all ten different ways to say "pig" in Spanish, so you need to decide which vocabulary you will use. In general, it is easier to follow the decision made by the authors of your textbook and teach the vocabulary they present, perhaps with comments that they may encounter other ways to say things. You will need to make the point early on that differences exist, but you can explain that just as Americans and people from Great Britain (or Australia, South Africa, Canada, etc.) use different vocabulary, the same thing is true with different Spanish-speaking countries. As they learn new vocabulary, you might mention some alternate words used in different areas, such as:

> café/marrón
> autobús/ómnibus/colectivo/
>   camión/guagua
> banana/plátano/banano
> coche/auto/carro

Differences in grammar usage. You as a teacher should stick to a standard, international grammar usage. You will probably want to use the *a* with *jugar* and include the definite article with sports, rather than follow the Mexicans as they say (probably influenced by English) "*Le gusta jugar béisbol.*" If you feel the need, you can mention that the Mexicans leave out the preposition and the article, and even change the pronunciation stress.

Spelling differences. As with the areas mentioned above, you will want to stay with the more standard ways of spelling such as writing *México* with an *x* and not a *j* as they sometimes do in Spain, spell (and pronounce) *video* without an accent (as in Spain), and include the accents on capital letters, even though omitting them is permitted and often seen, especially in the informal writing of native speakers.

The major point to be made here is simply that there are differences. You should not overemphasize them, just mention that they do exist. Obviously, they do not cause any real problems of communication, because all speakers use the basic "core" of the language. The students will probably ask which is better. The answer is, of course, all are appropriate to their region and all should be respected.

¿Tú **o** *usted?* You will have to decide if you are going to use the *tú* or the *usted* (the same is true of *ustedes* or *vosotros*) form with your students. This will depend greatly on the age of your students. If you are teaching at the elementary

level it would be very stiff, formal, and unnatural to treat them with *usted*. This is probably true in Junior and Senior High Schools also. In most Spanish-speaking countries, the teachers use the familiar (*tú*) with their students. This is also true of many university professors. However, from High School on, it would not be out of place to use *usted* with them. Your own command of the language must be a factor in this decision. If you are not sure of the *tú* forms, learn them and practice them until they are automatic. You should not mix them, unless it is on purpose to demonstrate their use. You should be a consistent model for them to follow.

Your students should use *tú* with each other. This is natural in all Spanish-speaking countries and is how they will be treated by Spanish-speaking friends of their same age. They should

not use *tú* with you. This would be a breach of the respect that the students usually maintain for their teacher. It also provides them the situations they need to practice using the *usted* form with adults and persons in authority. Don't make a big fuss over it when they use *tú* with you, but correct them often enough so they develop the sensitivity they need to keep from offending others if they go to other countries. It would be a fun and interesting activity, if you are able to use them personally, to teach the *vosotros* forms occasionally practice them with your students. If you are acquainted with the "voseo" and are able to use that form of address you may want to make your students aware of it in case they visit a country where it is used. The *Mafalda* comic books are wonderful for practicing the "voseo."

CONCLUSION

In this chapter we have tried to make you aware of some very important decisions you will have to make before you teach your classes. These decisions need to be made prior to going into the classroom. It is so important to start out right. Once you have started a pattern, it is very difficult to break. Hopefully our suggestions will help you make the right decisions, and give you help in keeping your resolve to use Spanish as the language of communication in the class. It is the one single factor which will help you meet your goals of proficiency and at the same time will be of great value to you in maintaining discipline.

REFERENCES AND SUGGESTIONS FOR FURTHER READING

Bateman, B. (2008). Student teachers' attitudes and beliefs about using the target language in the classroom. *Foreign Language Annals, 41,* 11-28. DOI: 10.1111/j.1944-9720.2008.tb03277.x *Reports on a study with student teachers in Spanish at Brigham Young University that identified factors that made it easier or harder to for them to use Spanish in the classroom. Concludes with tips for dealing with these challenges.*

Guillaume, A. M. (2008). *K-12 classroom teaching: A primer for new professionals* (3rd ed.). Upper Saddle River, NJ: Pearson Merrill Prentice Hall. *Great book that addresses the nature of teaching, accommodating all students, planing, instruction, assessment, classroom management, and other topics.*

Jarvis, A. C., & Labredo, R. (2006). *Basic Spanish for teachers.* Boston, MA: Houghton Mifflin Harcourt. *An excellent source for classroom expressions and vocabulary.*

Kronowitz, E. L. (2008). *The teacher's guide to success.* Boston, MA: Pearson. *Contains helpful tips on the first day of class, classroom management and organization, positive discipline, planning and organizing, and many other topics.*

Marzano, R. J. (2003). *Classroom management that works: Research-based strategies for every teacher.* Alexandria, VA: Association for Supervision and Curriculum Development. *A helpful book that reviews research on classroom management and suggests practical ways of applying it in the classroom.*

Pérez-Sotelo, L., & Hogan, E. (2008). *The essential Spanish phrase book for teachers.* Scholastic. *Another good source for classroom expressions and vocabulary, as well as for explaining academic subjects in Spanish.*

Wong, H. K, & Wong, R. T. *The first days of school.* Mountain View, CA: Harry K. Wong Publications. *A very helpful and informative program chock full of ideas on how to be a successful classroom manager, and specifically focusing on the first day and first weeks of school. Many teachers say it has changed their entire career as teachers. Visit the web site because there are many other materials plus a free magazine you can subscribe to. You'll like the Wongs!*

Other Books by James S. Taylor (see Appendix C for information)

- *Materiales para animar la clase de español*
- *Me gusta cantar*

ACTIVITIES FOR METHODS CLASSES

1. Carefully go over the content of the **COPING CARD** and make sure you can handle all the words and phrases. Practice some different activities you could use in the class to help the students learn how to use the card in class.

2. Go to the media laboratory, if one is available, and make a sign or light that says **PROHIBIDO HABLAR INGLÉS** to use in future classes. Show it to your methods instructor.

3. Study the **TEACHER'S COPING CARD** and lists of classroom phrases and practice with them until you are comfortable using Spanish as the language of the classroom. Practice classroom commands with fellow students or with a group of stuffed animals.

4. Study the list of possible warm-ups, select one, prepare the visual aids to use with it and do a micro-lesson in the methods class. Have the teacher evaluate your presentation.

5. Study the other warm-up suggestions and start building up your collection of visual aids you will need to conduct many of the other warm-ups. You can't have too many warm-ups ready to go. Put them in your materials file and show them to the instructor at the end of the semester.

6. Select a song that would be appropriate to teach your Spanish students, prepare visual aids, plan how you will teach the vocabulary and culture concepts, and teach the song to the students in the methods class. Have the teacher evaluate your presentation.

7. Review the songs listed in *Me gusta cantar* and think of other songs you would like to teach and prepare visual aids you would use with each one. Show them to your professor.

8. Find a way to become acquainted with a class management program. Set up a class with fictitious names, make up some tests and assignments and give your "students" grades and scores. Then print out a class report and an individual report for one of the students. Hand in the reports to your methods professor.

CHAPTER SIX

ARE YOU LISTENING? DEVELOPING LISTENING COMPREHENSION

YOUR OBJECTIVES FOR THIS CHAPTER ARE TO:

1. DISCUSS WHAT LISTENING COMPREHENSION CONSISTS OF.

2. DETERMINE APPROPRIATE LISTENING COMPREHENSION OBJECTIVES FOR LANGUAGE CLASSES AT DIFFERENT PROFICIENCY LEVELS.

3. SUMMARIZE PRINCIPLES AND APPLY ASSOCIATED TECHNIQUES FOR TEACHING LISTENING SKILLS.

4. MASTER "APT MAPS GUIDE" AS A POWERFUL TECHNIQUE IN TEACHING LISTENING AS WELL AS THE OTHER MAJOR SKILLS AND AS A TECHNIQUE IN APPROACHING TEACHING IN GENERAL.

5. DEVELOP SKILL IN USING TECHNIQUES FOR TEACHING VOCABULARY.

6. BUILD AND PRACTICE A REPERTOIRE OF CLASS ACTIVITIES TO PROMOTE LISTENING.

7. DISCUSS THE VALUE OF AND PREPARE FOR DEVELOPING LISTENING BEYOND THE CLASSROOM.

Mary Brown had really enjoyed her two-month experience in the Podunk Institute Spanish Intensive Language Program. They had classes from 8 to 5 every day, and spoke nothing but Spanish. She made rapid progress, especially in listening comprehension. In just a couple of weeks, she understood everything her classmates were saying. It took a little longer, but at the end of the program she could understand almost everything her teacher, who had lived for a year in Mexico, said in the class.

Then came the moment of truth!

She went to Argentina to study and live with a family for an extended period of time. As she stepped confidently off the plane in Buenos Aires, she was sure the language was going to be a "breeze." The customs official said something that she didn't understand. "Why did he mumble so?" she thought, "he must be uneducated and from a poor area." However, as the day progressed, her dismay grew. She didn't understand anyone! They all spoke so fast and ran their words together, and it didn't sound anything like the way her teacher spoke at Podunk Institute. What language had she learned there? Whatever it was, it wasn't what they were speaking in Buenos Aires!

~~~~

Miss Talbot was determined not to follow the same path her predecessor had taken. Although Mr. Baker had been liked and respected by everyone, administration, teachers, and students alike, his students never really developed any proficiency in the language. Even he had mentioned it to her at his retirement reception. "My only regret after 35 years of teaching is that I wasn't better able to get my students more fluent in the language. I was very good at explaining grammar, but I just didn't know how to get them to understand or speak."

After a few weeks of working with the advanced classes she had inherited from Mr. Baker, Miss Talbot agreed. They didn't understand her when she conducted the classes in Spanish, and were always begging her to translate what she was saying. Then, yesterday, two of her students came to class very excited:

"We just met a family from Nicaragua last Sunday. They have moved into our neighborhood and don't speak any English. We tried to talk to them in Spanish and they understood us, but we couldn't catch anything they said in reply. Is there something that we can do to be able to understand them?"

There certainly was, thought Miss Talbot, and she began making plans for some new kinds of activities in class and some materials she could send home with her students.

CHAPTER SIX

ARE YOU LISTENING? DEVELOPING LISTENING COMPREHENSION

> **The gods have given us two ears and one mouth—
> that we may hear twice as much as we speak.**
> **--Epictatus**

Of the four major skills, we probably spend a greater percentage of our waking hours using listening than any other. Thus, it is only natural that in this book we consider the listening skill first. In both the acquisition of our native language and a second language, the learner begins by soaking up language—mostly by means of **listening comprehension**—then by trying out language orally. In the first days and weeks of your classes, your students will spend an enormous amount of time listening to the language.

Neither speaking nor listening alone can be considered communication; it is a combination of both. We have, however, found that people don't fail in communication so often because of what they cannot say, but more often because of what they can't understand. We have been involved with students of all abilities in residence programs in several foreign countries, and we have found that the most important achievement that the student makes is understanding the natives of the country they were visiting.

The students can make themselves understood by gestures, by writing, by pointing to an object, and even by using a bilingual book of phrases and indicating what they mean by showing the equivalent in English that the native reads in the target language. But what can people do if they do not understand what is said to them? The native speakers would probably not take too kindly to having to use a bilingual book of phrases or repeating themselves too many times.

Have you heard the old story about the tourist in Mexico who wanted to take the bus to Guadalajara? He kept asking questions to find out when it would leave but couldn't understand what the people said, and missed the bus. In fact, as the story goes, the bus was in Guadalajara by the time he finally understood.

It's probably a truism that we learn to speak by speaking, but we also learn to speak by listening. People need a great deal of experience listening before they can really get the language **in the bones and tissues** and, therefore, be able to speak somewhat freely, that is, beyond just memorized expressions. It is also true that speaking ability lags quite a distance behind listening comprehension. We understand much more than we can express.

It is important that the student be exposed to a great deal of **authentic** language, even though this may be a lot of "noise" at first. Probably the best place for a first exposure to the listening experience is in the classroom where there is an "inter-language" that approximates the authentic language and has many expressions that are truly authentic in it. This "inter-language" can be controlled by the teacher so the students get **doses** rather than a **flood**, which can be very disheartening. Before we consider in detail the techniques you can use to develop listening comprehension, let's first examine some notions about what listening comprehension consists of.

THE NATURE OF LISTENING COMPREHENSION

Listening and the *Standards for Foreign Language Learning*

The *Standards* inform us that there are two types of listening that language users do. Much listening takes place in the interpersonal mode, such as when two people are carrying on a face-to-face or telephone conversation. This type of listening is two-way; the listener is an active participant in the conversation and can ask for repetition or clarification if necessary.

The second type of listening occurs in the interpretive mode, such as when we listen to a radio broadcast or view a television show or movie. (Some authors make a distinction between *listening* and *viewing*; in the latter case, there are obviously visual images to accompany the sound that aid in comprehension.) In interpretive listening or viewing the communication is one-way; there is no possibility for listeners to ask for clarification if they do not understand. Much of this chapter will focus on helping students develop interpretive listening skills.

The Listening Process and Factors that Affect It

You have undoubtedly heard at some time in your life someone speaking in a foreign language that was totally incomprehensible to you. What seemed to be only a "stream of sounds" had absolutely no meaning. Yet speakers of that language could listen, virtually effortlessly and unconsciously, and understand the message. What is the underlying process that allowed them to do so?

Background knowledge and schema theory. Research over the past few decades has shown that listening comprehension depends largely on the listener's background knowledge. Comprehension takes place to the extent that there is match between the message being listened to and the background knowledge of the listener. Thus, listening comprehension varies from person to person and from message to message, even in our native language.

Schema theory posits that our background knowledge is stored in our brain in structures

called **schemata** ("schemata" is plural; "schema" is singular.) We possess three types of schemata: content schemata, formal schemata, and linguistic schemata. *Content schemata* contain our knowledge about the world and about specific topics. Students who are viewing a soccer match in Spanish, for example, will probably understand the commentary better if they have watched similar matches in English. Learning some soccer-related words and expressions may help increase students' comprehension, but it is no substitute for knowing the rules of the game and how it is played.

Formal schemata contain our knowledge about how texts of different types and genres are organized. For instance, a news broadcast differs in structure from an interview or a commercial advertisement. A news broadcast usually starts with a general statement about the events being reported, followed by details and interviews with those involved. A familiarity with news broadcasts in English will help students understand similar broadcasts in Spanish.

Linguistic schemata contain our knowledge about language: *semantics* or *lexicon* (the meaning of words), *phonology* (how the words are said), *morphology* (the forms of the words which indicate such things as singular/plural, or present/past, or masculine/feminine, etc.), and *syntax* (the way the words are put together in the sentence). Of these linguistic elements, vocabulary knowledge is undoubtedly the most important. Even when students are unfamiliar with the grammatical structures in a particular text, they are often able to understand it if they know sufficient vocabulary.

Schema theory has important implications for teaching listening comprehension. Teachers can greatly aid their students' comprehension by **activating their background knowledge** in pre-listening or pre-viewing activities, helping the students recall what they know about the topic and genre, and anticipate the type of words and expressions that they will hear. More will be said about pre-listening activities later in this chapter.

Is listening comprehension a "passive" skill? Teachers sometimes subconsciously categorize the four basic language skills as follows: "speaking and writing are *active* or *productive* skills because the students have to produce the vocabulary words, conjugate the verbs, get the sentence order, and so on; while listening and reading are *passive* or *receptive* skills, because the students only receive the messages and do not have to supply vocabulary or construct sentences." While this perception may be true in part, understanding a message spoken in a foreign language is **not** a passive operation.

Receivers of oral messages must listen to the "stream of sound" and actively determine the message. The process involves all the aspects of language: In a real sense (and especially at first) the students have to stand their ground, grit their teeth, and concentrate on what is being said, trying to sort out words from the sounds, recognize subjects and tenses, and catch the thread of thought being transmitted. In the beginning, they might just recognize one or two words, and putting those words with other information which they have, such as the context, the facial expressions and voice inflections of the speaker, they get the gist of the meaning being conveyed and make some intelligent guesses.

Students must learn to tolerate some vagueness at first, perhaps only sensing what topic is being discussed. It is only much later that they will understand every word. That level is reached only through "logging-in" listening time in the language—there is no short cut.

Breaking the "sound barrier." Here is an excellent comparison of the process. Suppose you are walking along through the countryside and come to a barrier, a river of murky waters. There is no bridge, and it is impossible to walk upstream or downstream to look for a better crossing. You must lower yourself into the water and start to float over to the other side. It is a slow process and at first there is a tendency to hold on to the willows near you (not let go of your English), but you must if you are to get to the other side. Once past the current in the middle, the crossing becomes easier and easier and you finally reach the other bank. To develop listening comprehension skills your students must break the "sound barrier." The

best way you can help them do that is by dropping them into the "river" right from the first and getting them floating over to the other side as soon as possible.

Percent of time and the "sound barrier." A number of years ago the National Council of Teachers of English (NCTE) made a study that compared total use of listening comprehension with the other basic language skills. It was learned that adults spend 45% of their time listening, 30% speaking, 16% reading, and only 9% writing. (Since the advent of TV the listening percent is probably even higher.) You can immediately see the implications this has for our division of time in the classroom. In the beginning weeks more than half of our class time can best be spent with listening and speaking activities, and far less time on reading and writing. Can you now see one more important reason for speaking Spanish in the class? As long as you conduct the class in English, your students will never cross the "sound barrier." If you use Spanish they might not understand everything you say, but at least you are forcing them to let go of the willows and start floating, a process they will have to do sooner or later–it can't be bypassed–so why not start them right from the beginning?

The ACTFL Proficiency Guidelines for Listening Comprehension

The ACTFL Proficiency Guidelines describe what listening comprehension looks like at different levels of proficiency. We present them here in a condensed form to give you an idea of what levels we are trying to reach in beginning, intermediate, and advanced classes. We will discuss strategies for advanced classes in greater detail in Chapter 14. The guidelines are divided into four major levels: the **novice** level, the **intermediate** level, the **advanced** level, and the **superior** level. The Appendix contains the guidelines in full detail. A very brief summary of the expectations for speaking in the first three levels follows.

ACTFL PROFICIENCY GUIDELINES - LISTENING COMPREHENSION

Novice. Able to understand short, learned utterances, particularly where context strongly supports understanding and speech is clearly audible. Comprehends words and phrases from simple questions, statements, high-frequency commands and courtesy formulae. May require repetition, rephrasing and/or a slowed rate of speech for comprehension.

Intermediate. Able to understand sentence-length utterances and connected discourse on a number of topics pertaining to different times and places. Content continues to refer primarily to basic personal background and needs, social conventions and somewhat more complex tasks, such as lodging, transportation, and shopping. Additional content areas include some personal interests and activities, and a greater diversity of instructions and directions. Listening tasks not only pertain to spontaneous face-to-face conversations but also to short routine telephone conversations and some deliberate speech, such as simple announcements and reports over the media. Understanding continues to be uneven.

Advanced. Able to understand main ideas and most details of connected discourse on a variety of topics beyond the immediacy of the situation. Comprehension may be uneven due to a variety of linguistic and extra-linguistic factors, among which topic familiarity is very prominent. These texts frequently involve description and narration in different time frames or aspects, such as present, non-past, habitual, or imperfective. Texts may include interviews, short lectures on familiar topics, and news items and reports primarily dealing with factual information. Listener shows an emerging awareness of culturally implied meanings beyond the surface meanings of the text buy may fail to grasp socio-cultural nuances of the message.

PRINCIPLES AND TECHNIQUES FOR TEACHING LISTENING SKILLS

Some teachers make absolutely no provisions for activities that will develop listening comprehension. This is immediately evident when someone speaks to their students in the language. They panic. They "know" they aren't going to understand, and sure enough, they don't. They put more effort into rationalizing their deficiency than they do into straining for meaning. Let's now look at some of the principles you will follow and the techniques you will use as you develop a program for teaching listening skills.

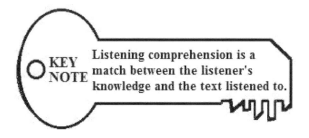

KEY NOTE: Listening comprehension is a match between the listener's knowledge and the text listened to.

Make Spanish Your Language of Communication

Your consistent use of Spanish for communication in the classroom, even for announcements and administrative business, can do more than anything else to give your students the confidence that they can understand. When someone uses the language with them, they won't panic–they are used to it.

Be careful not to slow down your own speech too frequently. Use your normal speech tempo as much as you can. Slowing down is always our tendency as teachers and although it helps students understand, they become dependent on it. Individuals can control the speed at which they speak, but it is difficult to control the speed at which others speak. We must increase the students' ability to sort out rapid speech. A good technique to use with them when they don't understand and beg: *Más despacio, por favor*, is to say to them: *No estoy hablando demasiado rápido, ustedes están escuchando demasiado despacio. Escuchen más rápido, por favor.*

The "teacher" in us also leads us to use mostly "teacher Spanish" (referred to formally as "inter-language," teacher language, or classroom language). That is, not only do we speak slower, but we pronounce very clearly, we choose words we know they will understand, and use only verb tenses they have learned. While this can be helpful to our students at first, don't make it a steady diet; you must eventually move away from the "inter-language." Native speakers are not going to use it. You need to give your students frequent doses of "non-teacher Spanish" so they will be used to what native speakers will throw at them and not be so shocked when they do. Spanish-speaking visitors—both live and via video and audio materials—can help you give them authentic Spanish.

The "APT MAPS GUIDE" Principle

As we have seen, the student only occasionally has control over "incoming" oral messages. Usually, as in the case of plays, speeches, radio broadcasts, live television programs, etc., there is only one chance to understand what is said, and there is little or no opportunity to slow down the speed at which it is transmitted. Even in direct conversation where the students can interact with the speaker, they hesitate to constantly interrupt the flow with requests to repeat or slow down. What the teacher has to do is prepare the students **before** they receive the message, enabling them to better cope with what is going to come.

We want to introduce here a powerful principle that can be used with the "receptive" skills (listening and reading) and can reduce the frustration of the students and prepare them for a higher level of comprehension. We call this the *APT MAPS GUIDE* principle and it refers to the steps you will take as you prepare the students to work with a listening comprehension or reading activity. This teaching approach consists of the following:

A
P Advance **P**reparation by the **T**eacher
T

M
A **M**otivation and **A**dvance
P **P**reparation of the **S**tudents
S

G **G**et them speaking the language
U **U**se the language
I **I**nteract
D **D**iscuss
E **E**valuate

Let's detail each of the steps one by one.
1. **A**dvance **P**reparation by the **T**eacher. Teachers must carefully preview the materials in advance (several days before beginning to work with them in the class) in order to prepare themselves and plan for the class activities that will follow. (Watch the video, listen to the CD, read the narration, find out what the visitor is going to talk about, etc.) You cannot just announce the day before that they are going to see a video in class or send them home to read a story you haven't read yourself.

2. **M**otivation of and generation of interest in the students. The teacher must arouse interest in the students such that they are eager to begin work with the materials. By giving them some indication of what the materials are about (without revealing all of the details) and letting them know what to look for, the teacher can motivate them to the point that they can hardly wait to start.

3. **A**dvance linguistic and cultural **P**reparation of the **S**tudents. Here is where you can greatly aid your students' comprehension by activating their background knowledge about the topic, text type, and language. Students must also be prepared with the key vocabulary they will need to understand the message. In addition, they should receive the cultural information necessary to be able to comprehend what they are working with. You should also give them guidelines about what to watch or listen for, such things as plays on words, pronunciation differences, specific information for answering questions, descriptions of certain persons, etc.

Suppose you are about to show your students a video of an interview with the singer Juanes. In the pre-listening stage, you might tell your students, *"Vamos a ver un video de una entrevista. En una entrevista, ¿cuántas personas hay? (Dos: una persona que hace preguntas y otra persona que contesta.) Ésta es una entrevista con Juanes. ¿Quién es Juanes? (Es un famoso cantante y guitarrista de Colombia). ¿Cuántos de Uds. han escuchado las canciones de Juanes? ¿Qué tipo de música canta: jazz, rock o blues? (rock) ¿Cuáles son algunos temas que pueden surgir en la entrevista? Vamos a hacer una lista en la pizarra de temas posibles. (su música, su carrera, cómo llegó a ser cantante, si escribe sus propias canciones, cuáles son sus fuentes de inspiración, etc.). Ahora vamos a escuchar la entrevista. Quiero que escuchen para descubrir cuáles de estos temas se mencionan."*

4. Get the students Using the language immediately after viewing the video or listening to the tape. Interact with them as you carry on a class Discussion or application. This should be a stimulating and rewarding experience that will allow use and reinforcement of the vocabulary and expressions encountered in the materials and commentary on the information presented.

5. Evaluate the students' comprehension in a formal way after your discussion and application. Unless there is some accountability, they will not make a strong effort. This is normally done in the form of a short written or oral quiz. This also permits the teacher to appraise the level of student comprehension.

Making whatever modifications are necessary to fit the situation, you can use this technique with almost any activity designed to develop listening (or reading) comprehension.

Managing the Class

Teachers typically do a lot of "managing" as they move through a class hour. With a little preparation this can all be done *in the language*. Study the following suggestions:

1. Conduct your "Start-up" entirely in Spanish. As we found out in the previous chapter, the very beginning of every class period is an ideal time for developing listening comprehension. Every class period should start in Spanish. For a while the teacher can give a sort of monologue and teach the students to take care of the *Bienvenida* that can have some type of listening comprehension included in it. The problem here is that student language is not authentic enough. Audio recordings, videos, or visitors may be needed to supplement both the students and the teacher.

Suggestions for *"monologues"*

"On the way to class (school)..."
Stories
Jokes
Adivinanzas
Anecdotes
Cultural capsules (teacher-part)
Fantasy journeys
Poetry, all kinds
Preambles—like TV programs
Radio broadcasts—Voice of America

(The booklet *Materiales para animar la clase de español* has many suggestions and techniques for using "start-ups.")

2. Do your "cultural asides" in the language. There are various opportunities in every class to talk about cultural differences, cultural objects, cultural emphases, and other "cultural asides." (See Chapter 9 for a fuller treatment of "cultural asides.") Often you can anticipate these asides and plan what you are going to present and even have some pictures or drawings in mind on transparencies or visual aids ready to use so that you will be able to make the explanation in Spanish. Try to make all of these cultural asides in very understandable Spanish by using as many devices as you can, such as gestures, miming, and drawings.

3. Do your school business in the language. You should try to plan ways of making various types of announcements and taking care of other kinds of school business in advance so that you can use Spanish for these as well. You can have a bulletin board for school business but at least put various headings in Spanish on that bulletin board so that announcements can be posted in the appropriate place. Try to have pictures, cartoons, caricatures, stick-figure situations— all kinds of similar devices to make clear your in-class explanations of school business.

4. Do your grammar introductions and check-ups in the language. Ideally, any work with grammar should grow out of a need experienced in communication. (Much more on this in Chapter 10.) To set the stage to explain that need, you can give the students a lot of listening comprehension experience. Any questions the students have about grammar should be explained very simply without specialized terminology and jargon. When helping students understand a grammar idea, you cannot oversimplify. Ask yourself: "How can I explain this as simply as possible with as short an explanation as possible and with sufficient demonstration?" Think about the questions: "What is the main point?" and "How do I keep all this in Spanish?" After the students have completed an assignment, and you need to check up on the assignment, that can also be introduced and carried out with all the instructive running patter given in Spanish.

5. Do brainstorming lead-ins in the language. In all of these activities the students' ability to express themselves lags quite a distance behind their ability to understand what is said in Spanish. Do not be derailed by the students' inability to express themselves. In fact, you could probably play the role of live dictionary in the classroom and explain how to say everything in Spanish. Allow the students to brainstorm with you about leading into any activity. Occasionally you can anticipate what they want to say and can supply the words they need.

6. Do your motivating in the language. You must constantly look for activities to motivate your students. An excellent technique for this is the "spot commercial." These "spot commercials" should be devised periodically to motivate students to recognize the value of the activities they will be participating in and the worth of the opportunity to "log in" lots of **listening** in each of the activities in order to get Spanish in their **bones and tissues.** All of these activities will help to build the students' *Sprachgefühl* ("feel" for the language), which is our major purpose in listening.

You should plan on using the **APT MAPS GUIDE** technique every time you start or review an activity so that you will be ready with a "spot commercial" or whatever you will need to be sure that the students are actively involved in a meaningful activity.

Suggestions for "spot commercials"

a. Point out the importance of listening activities that are on the cutting edge of their Spanish ability for building a *Sprachgefühl*.

b. Indicate the value of living with uncertainty—getting the gist—making intelligent guesses.

c. Collect ideas from the teacher's edition of the latest textbooks that you have available [Remember that's why you are on the textbook committee in your district—and even on the state textbook committee.]

7. Prior to reading assignments, do pre-reading activities in the language. This is another excellent opportunity to use the **APT MAPS GUIDE** formula to set up a listening comprehension activity. Make your advance preparation for the reading assignment, especially the content, and determine what will best **motivate** your students to want to read this assignment and then list the ideas that come from this planning. Then look at the reading assignment again and determine what background knowledge the students need in order to be able to read this assignment. Then **prepare** listening comprehension activities—especially the picture procedure—to help the students to read the assignment. The vocabulary, including the idiomatic expressions, certainly could be taken care of ahead of time by the picture procedure thereby enabling the students to get a feeling for the meaning. Aspects of the plot could also be treated in advance with the picture procedure.

8. Do your reviewing and recycling in the language. You can use the pictures and other props and materials that you had in the various lead-in activities again in reviewing the past several assignments. Perhaps this time student panels or student committees could conduct the review with the services of student leaders. Some of these presentations can be filmed or recorded and made available in a language lab or online for repeated listening opportunities.

In subsequent levels many of the same kinds of activities can be conducted, but made more complicated—this process is called cycling or recycling the planning and activities.

In short, the most important procedure is the obvious one: make the language of the class and classroom **SPANISH.**

"Gisting"

You need to train your students to listen for the "gist" of the message. Most of us who have learned another language, used this skill constantly. It refers to the strategy of just getting the general "gist" of what people are talking about. You may have to settle for a vague idea, such as "They're talking about *food, school,* or *some sort of problem with the car,*" but that is the beginning of listening comprehension. If our students are exposed to an entire **Pronóstico del tiempo** and then are simply asked *¿Va a llover hoy?* they realize that they should listen for as much as they can understand and, above all, not get discouraged and give up prematurely. Here are some things that will help them.

Recognizing cognates. Conduct exercises at first in class to develop an awareness of cognates. Fortunately English and Spanish share thousands of words; listening for these "free words" can go a long way in helping students understand.

Watching for non-verbal cues. There are many things a speaker does besides speaking that will help the hearer catch the message. There are facial expressions, gestures, body movements, intonation, voice inflections and stress patterns. With some exceptions, these are the same in Spanish as in English. Even though we sometimes may not be able to see the speaker, we can hear emotions such as enthusiasm, exuberance, sarcasm, and anger.

Using context. Being aware of the context of *where* and *why* one is talking will help someone understand. Some situations are so "standard" that one can almost predict what someone will say or questions they will ask. Don't all store clerks ask: "May I help you?" Doesn't the hostess in a restaurant always greet you, ask if you want to eat, how many are in your party, etc.? Do constant role-playing with your students in a variety of situations and they will soon learn how to anticipate what is being said to them, even though many of the words are new to them.

Cutting Through the Veneer of Pronunciation and Speech Differences

Informal speech is not careful speech—it is natural for people to slur, use "stutter words," link sounds together, and drop certain sounds. Have you ever paid attention to how you speak English? Do you ever say things such as "Jeet jet?" [Did you eat yet?] or "wanna" [want to] or "Whucha gunna do?" [What are you going to do?] Most people do. A good technique is to have overt, conscious discussions of the peculiarities of Spanish speech patterns, regional pronunciation differences with your students. Teach them how the Cubans drop final *s,* as in *lo[s] libro[s],* how some Chileans say *musho* for *mucho,* how Spaniards pronounce the "z" and the "c" before "e" and "i" in Castillian Spanish, and how the "y" and the "ll" are pronounced in the Rio de la Plata area. But you must follow up with lots of listening practice of those patterns and differences. You can use audio and video recordings and bring in native speakers from a variety of regions. You can even do some things yourself, such as using a different regional pronunciation occasionally.

Teach your students that many people slur when they talk and most link words together. They should not be expecting to hear "spaces" between words as they see in writing. They should be acquainted with "stutter words" such as "*este....este....este*" and "*pues*" (or even *pos*). They should not be startled by an occasional *pa* [for *para*] or *hemos trabajao* [for *trabajado*], or *verdá* [for *verdad*]. But all this needs to be conditioned with a great deal of exposure to real, everyday, authentic, "non-teacher" speech of a variety of speakers—men, women, and children of all ages.

LISTENING AND VOCABULARY

Vocabulary is by far the most important component in listening comprehension. At almost all levels you will be introducing massive doses of new vocabulary. We suggest the following teaching considerations.

Don't Teach Vocabulary in Isolation

If your students learn vocabulary from lists they won't recognize them in connected discourse. They don't sound the same. A student once asked his teacher what a *narbol* was. He had heard it in a conversation and had looked it up in the dictionary, but couldn't find it. Further discussion revealed that what he had heard was *un árbol*, which of course, was said *u nárbol*. Had the speaker spoken the word as if it were on a list, the student would have recognized it.

This concept is especially true of numbers. If they are always taught in chronological order (*uno, dos, tres, cuatro*, etc.) the students will not recognize them when people talk about money, hours, telephone numbers, etc. where the numbers are not in order. There have to be a lot of hours of practice using numbers to talk about the cost of clothes and articles, the times of schedules and events, dates and rates, and so on. (See *Me gusta jugar* for examples of games to practice numbers.)

The most meaningful and effective way to teach vocabulary is to present the words in context so the students can make a direct association of the words with the object or idea that it represents. To present the word in reference to its English equivalent, i.e. a translation, slows down the process and keeps the students dependent upon English. Avoiding reference to English requires a lot of self-discipline and imagination on the part of the teacher. Remember what the English (ESL) teacher would have to do in a class full of students with different native languages? You have to act out meanings, draw pictures on the board, use visual aids, explain meaning with different contexts, rephrase sentences, and use whatever inspiration comes to you to help students understand.

Successful teachers carefully plan lessons ahead of time, anticipating what new words they will be presenting, and gather visuals or think of ways they can make meanings clear. With experience you will soon become very skillful in conjuring up ways on the spot to help students see the meaning. Obviously it is much easier to teach meaning of concrete nouns by simply showing a picture or the object itself. Many verbs can be taught with actions or expressions. But the abstract words present a greater

challenge. Following are some techniques that will help you teach vocabulary in context.

1. Show the object. (You should have boxes full of items for your class; often you can use miniatures or toys.)
2. Show a picture of the object. (You can't take an elephant to class; start collecting pictures and transparencies.)
3. Draw a picture on the board. (This can be fun; the students may laugh at your drawings, but you can get the idea across. You may eventually develop a bit of drawing skill.)
4. Act the idea out. (Here's where you develop your latent acting abilities: gestures, expressions, feelings, uninhibited antics such as climbing on your desk [to teach *subir*] crying, shouting, dying, and so on.)
5. Describe or explain. (Un *terremoto* es cuando hay violentas acciones en la tierra y los edificios caen, etc. La *lluvia* es cuando gotas de agua caen de las nubes. Una *tía* es la hermana de nuestro padre o nuestra madre. Etc.)
6. Compare with well-known things. (Usamos *pasta dental* para lavarnos los dientes; **Colgate, Crest** o **Aim** son marcas muy conocidas de *pasta dental*. Un *país* es un territorio muy grande; **México** y **Canadá** son *países*. Una *ciudad* es un lugar donde viven muchas personas; **Provo**, **Chicago**, y **Portland** son *ciudades*.)
7. Use antonyms or synonyms when they know one of the pair. (Ustedes saben lo que es frío; *caliente* es el opuesto de **frío**. *Triste* es lo contrario de **contento**. *Regresar* es lo mismo que **volver**.)
8. Relate to cognates they will understand. (El chico es muy **listo**, es decir, es muy *inteligente*. **Quizás** venga mañana; *posiblemente* venga mañana.)
9. Use the word in several different contexts so the students can generalize. (Teaching the word *trabajar*: Un gato no *trabaja* mucho; duerme todo el día. Una mula *trabaja* todo el día en el campo, tira el carro, lleva cargas grandes, etc. El presidente de los Estados Unidos *trabaja* en la Casa Blanca. Si una persona *trabaja* le pagan dinero, si no *trabaja* no le pagan, etc.)

Avoid giving your students long lists of vocabulary words, totally out of context. They can memorize word lists long enough to pass a vocabulary text but promptly forget most of them after the test. Some words can best be presented in groups, such as parts of the body or weather expressions, but they should always be practiced in meaningful contexts rather than just as single words. In beginning classes it is better not to overload the students with a lot of low frequency words or several words that say the same thing.

Just a word about **mnemonics**. The mnemonic approach to learning a language is to associate words or phrases with words in the mother tongue that permit some type of mental cue. For example, if you wanted to learn the Finnish word for "thanks," you would mentally visualize a key sitting on someone's toes and would say "key toes" which approximates *kiitos*, "thanks" in Finnish. While this approach may give some quick help with some handy phrases, in the long run it is probably counter-productive since the students do not make a direct association with the meaning of the words in the target language. Thus the students cannot make further applications of the words in other situations; they are limited to the mnemonic phrase, which really does not "mean" anything to the students. The Germans have an interesting expression for the term mnemonic device, *Eselbrücke*, which translates as a "bridge for donkeys"—a word to the wise should be sufficient here.

Avoid Giving Them the "Crutch" of the Written Word

Today's students are very visually oriented. (This is especially true of older adults.) Very often you will introduce a new word or expression and they will want you to write it or spell it for them. While this does help them recognize the word, it also builds a dependency on seeing the written word. Rather than write the word down on the board, perhaps a better response would be repeat the word and use it in a number of different contexts. A good technique is to remind them that native speakers are not going to come up and give them a written script of what they are going to say so they can read along.

We once conducted an experiment with an intermediate class where we were concentrating on improving listening comprehension. We used a variety of activities such as DVDs, audio and video recordings, and guest speakers. We used several different approaches to the presentation of the material; sometimes we gave them a script to read along as the material was presented, sometimes we gave them a summary in Spanish or English, sometimes we just presented some key vocabulary before the presentation, and sometimes we did nothing—just went directly to the materials. At the end of the semester, we asked the students to tell us which approach they liked best. Their response was overwhelmingly in favor of getting the script to read along with as they listened. Why? Because it was easier—it took less effort to understand. However, our study showed that from a learning standpoint, that approach was perhaps the worst way to develop listening comprehension—the easiest way is not always the best in the long run.

True Proficiency Requires an Extensive Vocabulary

The present emphasis in our profession on oral proficiency makes it necessary to help our students develop a large, comprehensive vocabulary. One of the principles of the audio-lingual method was to *restrict* the vocabulary and work for a high degree of accuracy within narrow limits. However, in a proficiency approach if we expect the students to be able to function in a wide variety of situations, we will have to greatly *increase* the range of vocabulary and be satisfied with a lower level of accuracy. In the beginnings of listening comprehension the students are struggling with just sorting out words, but as they advance they must give a full effort to expanding their *active* vocabulary very rapidly. Just recognizing words is of little help if they don't know what they mean.

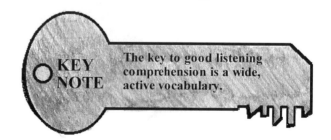

KEY NOTE — The key to good listening comprehension is a wide, active vocabulary.

As a teacher, you will have to resist the urge to hold back on the use of unfamiliar vocabulary and use all the words that the situation requires.

CLASS ACTIVITIES TO PROMOTE LISTENING

You must be consistent in providing listening opportunities in every class hour. At first the **output** (speaking) does not equal the **input** (listening). During the first years of the audio-lingual emphasis, proponents of that approach suggested an almost equal amount of listening and speaking; the input equaled the output. We are now aware that listening probably is usually ahead of speaking and provides the learner with the perception necessary to make speaking and the other major skills more successful. The traditional **input-output** relationship is shown in the following diagram:

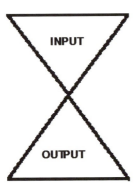

It is now felt that listening must be given more attention than any other skill right at first. It probably should be part of the planning at every level. The following diagram shows this idea:

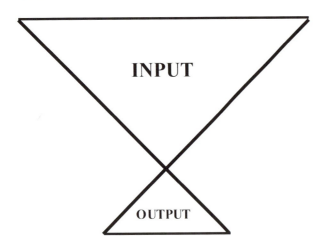

We will now present a number of activities you can conduct in the classroom to help your students develop their listening comprehension. We have tried to give a short example for each one to give you an idea about how to conduct them. You can, of course adapt and expand them as you need to fit your own materials and program.

1. Visitors to class. You should be constantly searching for native Spanish speakers who are willing to visit your classes. If you can, prepare your students for the visit a few days ahead of the event. If you don't have that time, at least prepare a transparency or visual that could prompt the students during the visit—in fact, it could be showing on the screen all the time of the visit. Some of the questions on the transparency might be these:

> ¿De dónde...?
> ¿Cuánto tiempo...?
> ¿Qué ... haces, estudias, ... aquí?
> ¿Qué ... después de graduarte?
> ¿Tu casa ...?
> ¿...la gente?
> ¿...comen?
> ¿... el tiempo?
> ¿Qué te gusta de aquí?
> ¿Qué no...?
> ¿...aquí en nuestra ciudad?
> ¿...con una familia?
> ¿...con compañeros?
> ¿...tu familia?
> ¿...tus intereses?
> ¿...cine?
> ¿...deportes?
> ¿...carrera?
> ¿... televisión?
> ¿...hobbies? etc.

These questions would naturally be asked by the students and would set the stage for lots of listening practice.

2. Narration for comprehension. The term "narration" here refers to a wide range of content presented orally by the teacher that the students listen to. It may be a story, a news item, a recycled dialogue, or a description of an event or picture. The students' comprehension may be evaluated in many different ways, from writing summaries in English, to answering *sí* or *no* to simple questions in Spanish, to filling in blanks on a *cloze* test.

Here is an example of a narration that can be presented orally by the teacher. It could simply be read, or played on a tape or CD with a variety of voices.

¿DE QUIÉN ES EL MALETÍN
(From *Me gusta aprender español*)

En un bar de Lima, Perú. Un turista americano sale. Llega el señor Eusebio Vásquez, un abogado que vive en Lima. Va a una mesa y toma un café y lee un periódico. Una familia
está en otra mesa y come sandwiches. Tomás, un joven, mira la televisión. El mozo tiene
un maletín en la mano y pregunta al Sr. Vásquez:

Mozo:	Perdone, don Eusebio, ¿es este maletín suyo?
Vásquez:	No, no es mío. Mi maletín está en mi oficina.
Mozo:	Entonces, ¿de quién es?
Vásquez:	¿Es de esa familia allí?

El mozo va a la mesa donde está la familia.

Mozo:	Perdonen, ¿es este maletín de ustedes?
Señor:	No, no es nuestro. No tenemos maletín. Quizás es del joven que está allí.
Mozo:	Oye, Tomás, ¿es este maletín tuvo?
Joven:	No, el mío está aquí.

En ese momento entra el turista. Está muy preocupado.

Turista:	Busco mi maletín. ¿Está aquí?
Mozo:	¿Es éste su maletín?
Turista:	¡Ah, sí! ¡Es mío! ¡Muchísimas gracias!
Mozo:	No hay de que.

Prueba de comprensión

A. Escoge la letra de la opción correcta.

1. El señor Vásquez es...
   A. abogado   B... mozo   C. turista

2. ¿Adónde va Eusebio?
   A. A su oficina   B... Al cine   C. A un bar

3. ¿Qué toma don Eusebio?
   A.Una Coca Cola.   B... Un café   C. Agua

4. El joven Tomás....
   A. escribe cartas.   B... mira la televisión   C. come sándwiches.

5. ¿Qué tiene el mozo en la mano?
   A. Un periódico   B... una televisión   C. Un maletín

3. Narration with visuals (Picture Procedure). Another approach is to use a picture and discuss the content of the picture. [Special note: Every Spanish teacher should have an extensive picture file separated into categories that coincide with the topics of the units presented. She or he can collect these from Spanish American magazines and, if possible, mount them on colored art paper in the uniform 8 1/2 x 11 size. If necessary, the pictures can be composed or can be collages so that they will always be large enough to see in the average classroom.] In the picture procedure, the teacher presents the vocabulary in a meaningful context while showing the pictures. This should help the students to understand clearly what's being said. The teachers can use cognates and borrowed words as well as gesturing and pantomiming as well as using synonyms and antonyms or any means to get the meaning across. It's important that this presentation be a good simulation of authentic language. It's also important to avoid just listing the words; there must be a message presented in a communicative way. Here is an example of a narration with a picture. The students would have a copy of the following picture, or it could be large enough for all the class to see, or it could be projected onto a screen. The content is presented orally, either read by the teacher and others, or played from an audio recording.

Una tarde yo estaba en casa cuando sonó el teléfono. Era mi tía Juana que vive en California. Es la hermana de mi papá. Hacía un mes que no habíamos hablado con ella y como es una mujer muy curiosa, quería saber cómo estaban todos de la familia. Le di la información siguiente: el abuelo estaba muy enfermo y estaba en el hospital; papá estaba bien y estaba trabajando en la oficina; mi hermano Carlos estaba en casa, pero todavía tenía el pie enyesado; mi hermana Merche también estaba en casa, pero estaba en la cama porque estaba muy resfriada, mamá estaba muy bien, pero estaba en la casa de una vecina. Por último quería saber cómo estaba yo y le dije que estaba muy bien pero tenía mucho trabajo de la escuela. Mandó saludos a todos y prometió llamarnos al mes siguiente.

After presenting the narration, the teacher could make comments or ask questions about the story as the students look at the picture. The comments could be of the following type:

> El papá estaba en la casa de una vecina, ¿verdad?
> ¿Todavía tenía la mamá el pie enyesado?
> ¿Por qué estaba Merche en el hospital si sólo tenía un resfriado?
> ¿Estaba Carlos en casa?

The students wouldn't be expected to say much, because this is not a speaking activity, but they could make short comments such as *¡El papá, no, la mamá!*, or *Merche no estaba en el hospital*, or respond *sí* or *no* to simple questions.

---

4. TPR (Total Physical Response). As explained in Chapter 3, this is a methodology developed by James J. Asher that is used by many language teachers. TPR is simply an activity with commands that you give the students to act out. The purpose is to give them experience with the actions of various verbs. This process resembles the process a parent uses in giving commands to its child. It is definitely a listening comprehension activity. At first you get an action for each simple command. Later on you can give a series of commands for the students to follow on signal. The first time you introduce TPR, you could act out the procedure or get some advanced students to help you demonstrate the procedure. It is very much like the game "Simon says..." You can get them to understand what's going on without using English.

The leader teaches the meaning of the vocabulary item by demonstrations, gestures, visuals, etc. To teach commands, he or she usually gives the command, then physically does it, or has an advanced student obey it. The command is then given again and the students do it. After practicing, the leader can then begin to link several commands together, to be performed one right after the other. For example: *Pónganse de pie, tomen tres pasos adelante, dense una vuelta, vuelvan a su asiento, siéntense.* Some teachers take this activity to great, elaborate lengths, having the students do such things as climbing up on their desks, lying down on the floor, rolling over, sticking their finger in their cheek, etc. This can be great fun for the students, since this allows them to do all sorts of weird things, but the practical value of such antics is very limited. We suggest that the activity focus on the kinds of commands a person might reasonably receive in normal situations, especially to the kinds of things a teacher might ask them to do in class. At first the students only physically obey, they do not respond orally, hence the term Total Physical Response (TPR).

EXAMPLES OF *TPR* USED TO TEACH CLASSROOM VOCABULARY

Goal: Teach *libro* and *cuaderno* in context, with related vocab. and actions.

MAESTRO/A	ACCIONES
Esto es un libro (cuaderno). [Lo muestra.] ¿Para qué usamos un libro (cuaderno)? Para leer (escribir). Leamos el libro (cuaderno). [Actions] Pero, no puedo. No está abierto. Abramos el libro (cuaderno). Ahora sí puedo (escribir) leer. Ustedes tienen un libro. Abran su libro. [Actions] Ábranlo a la página 3. [Escribe 3 en el pizarrón] Lean su libro. Cierren su libro. Voy a poner mi libro en la mesa. [Action] Pongan su libro en la mesa. Pongan su libro en el suelo. [Action] Levanten su libro. [Action] Muestren su libro. [Action] Pasen su libro a un amigo o a una amiga. [Action] Devuelvan el libro. [Action] Etc.	Leer Abrir Mostrar Cerrar Poner en la mesa, el suelo Levantar Mostrar, Pasar a un(a) amigo(a) Devolver

Goal: Teach *papel* in context, with related vocab. and actions.

MAESTRO/A	ACCIONES
Esto es una hoja de papel. Saquen una hoja de papel de su cuaderno. Tomen la hoja de papel. Pongan la hoja en el libro. Saquen la hoja. Pongan la hoja en la mesa. tres secciones. Etc	Sacar, tomar Poner en el libro, en la mesa, en el suelo, etc. Doblar la hoja, etc.

The teacher or leader could continue in this fashion with other classroom vocabulary such as *lápiz, bolígrafo, tiza, pizarrón*, etc. (See *Materiales para animar la clase* for a longer and more detailed version of this activity.) Other possibilities include physical responses such as moving around the room, interacting with classmates, pointing, drawing, or arranging pictures in sequence. Most action verbs allow for TPR activity as a good way to introduce actions (verbs).

The commands don't have to be in a psychological sequence, but they are a little easier to follow and to understand if they are. Sometimes the incongruent ones have a special appeal. Try both kinds—but emphasize the congruent ones.

5. Listening to songs. This process entails listening to popular, traditional, or folk songs. There is a tremendous potential for listening practice with songs; songs often have a bigger context than most of us realize, and they are always popular with the students, regardless of the age.

Preparation for teaching the song can be made in advance. Your lead-in as you teach the cultural background or meaning of the song can all be in Spanish. You can talk about when the songs are sung, what the singers think about when they sing them, what the words mean, etc. (See *Me gusta cantar.*) Usually you can have conversational practice with some of the expressions in the song days or even weeks in advance of presenting the song. Here you see an application of the **APT MAPS GUIDE** formula, motivation for the singing and preparation for the content of the song, all before the actual participation in the singing.

Following is an example of a listening exercise with a popular song. Having prepared the students beforehand with the key vocabulary words, you can give them each a copy of the handout as seen below, and ask them to listen to the song, filling in the words which have been left out. After correcting what they have written down, you can ask questions about the vocabulary and the message of the song.

PRÁCTICA DE COMPRENSIÓN CON UNA CANCIÓN

Introducción por el(la) maestro(a):
Esta semana hemos aprendido los nombres de muchos animales. Hoy vamos a escuchar una canción muy bonita que nombra muchos animales diferentes. Les he dado a cada uno una hoja de papel con la letra de la canción, pero faltan algunas palabras. Mientras escuchan la canción, escriban las palabras que cantan en la cinta, pero que faltan en su hoja. Luego, hablaremos del contenido de la canción.

AMIGO FÉLIX (Enrique y Ana)

Esta mañana me ha contado _____, que el elefante le contó al castor,
Que la culebra dijo a la piraña, que esta mañana está más triste _____.
Me ha dicho _____ que le diga al _____, que el lobo dice que contó al ratón,
Que la coneja dijo a la anaconda, que esta mañana está más triste _____.

CORO
Amigo Félix, cuando llegues _____, Amigo Félix, hazme sólo un favor.
Quiero ir contigo a _____ con el osito de la osa mayor.

Dicen _____ que les dijo el cuco, que _____ dijo al caracol,
Que la gaviota comentó al lagarto, que esta mañana está más triste el sol.
Esta mañana no ha comido _____, ni el hipopótamo que está en _____.
Le ha comentado la tortuga _____, que esta mañana está más triste _____.

Práctica de comprensión:

1. ¿Qué animal se menciona que vive en la casa?
2. ¿Qué animales se mencionan que viven en el mar?
3. ¿Qué aves (pájaros) se mencionan?
4. ¿Qué animal les contó la triste noticia esta mañana?
5. ¿Qué está más triste esta mañana?
6. ¿A dónde creen los niños que va el amigo Félix?
7. ¿Por qué quieren ir con Félix los niños?
8. ¿Qué animal no ha comido esta mañana?
9. ¿Dónde está el hipopótamo?

---

6. Listening to audio recordings. Commercially prepared audio materials such as CDs, as well as the homemade ones that you may have made or found online, can require good use of the ART MAPS GUIDE principle. Look for many ways to motivate students to look forward to working with these audio materials. Think about the content and the purpose, and try to devise pre-listening activities that will give the students a listening opportunity prior to the audio presentation. Help them to learn the expressions they will need by using the techniques we have already suggested, especially the picture procedure but also TPR and the usual narrating or explaining. It is also wise to break up long presentations in audio materials into short (three to ten minutes) segments. Each segment can give you ideas for motivation and preparation.

We won't give any example of an audio text here, it would be essentially like the narrations described above; the difference being that the content would be on a tape or CD, perhaps with sound effects, musical background, a variety of voices, etc. The activities and evaluations would be essentially the same as with the narrations.

7. Viewing videos. Video has now become perhaps the most motivating medium you can use to develop listening skills. There is a wide variety of materials available including DVDs, online videos such as YouTube, and the video materials that come with textbook packages. (We will go into the techniques of using videos in great detail in Chapter 13.) For the present we would only remind you of the importance of doing some pre-viewing activities to activate students' background knowledge and introduce necessary vocabulary and cultural concepts before you show the video. These could include a listening comprehension narration as you give an overview, present cultural background, or get them motivated with a "spot commercial."

Sometimes it is best to divide the video into several small segments to be able to have enough time to assimilate the new vocabulary and information. We will not give an example here, but the presentation would be similar to what you would do with the narrations and the audio activities.

8. Listening to lectures, forums, panel discussions. These obvious listening opportunities can be live, on video, or on audio materials. You can set them up for your classes with visiting speakers, parents, advanced students, exchange students, etc. If you record or film them, they can be used for later repeated listening practice. Better yet, put the recordings online so students can access them on their own.

9. Writing down of spoken messages. The intense concentration that one must make in order to **write down** information that is being listened to can help develop listening skills. At the lowest level of this type of activity are the traditional

dictations. Although dictations give more specific help in teaching writing (See Chapter 8.), if you are careful to make the dictation natural, it can provide listening practice. Try to select material that includes conversational Spanish, not some historical or philosophical treatise. As you dictate, make the utterances natural and authentic. And as you evaluate, check on whether or not the students comprehended the passage; for example, have them summarize the content or answer questions, and grade them on the summary, not just on whether or not they wrote down all the words included or spelled them correctly.

A step up from the dictation would be a transcription activity where the students would write down something they hear perhaps from an audio recording or a video. Songs lend themselves to this type of exercise. This activity would allow the students to play the recording over and over as much as necessary to get all the words said or sung. They could then be required to write down a translation or summary of the content.

Perhaps the hardest type of this activity is note taking, where the student listens to a lecture, speech, or interview and writes down the essentials of the information given. This can be an excellent preparation for students who will be attending classes or lectures that will be taught in Spanish. The lecture could be given by the teacher, visitors, or taped and the students would take notes that they would hand in for evaluation.

BEYOND THE CLASSROOM

There is no way that students can get enough time "logged in" listening if they just use class time. Your most important criterion for class activity is that the activity be something that could not be completed outside of class. Anything that could be done outside of class, should be done outside of class. Some listening activities can best be done in class. However, there are many supplementary listening opportunities that can be done outside of class. Here are some:

- In a language lab or online:
  - CDs or audio files (prepared to accompany the textbook)
  - DVDs/videos (prepared to supplement the text materials)
  - Online practices prepared to supplement the text materials
  - Movies

- Interactive practice with computer programs
- Live lab (with native speakers)
- Cultural presentations
- Online audio and video materials (streaming audio or video, podcasts, YouTube, etc.)
- Telephone conversations with natives and classmates
- Talking with AFS and exchange students
- Attending church meetings in Spanish
- Interviews (esp. native speakers)
- "Fireside chats," lectures in Spanish
- Spanish television programs
- Listening to Spanish radio broadcasts
- Full length Spanish movies (DVDs)
- Spanish stores, delicatessens, bakeries, restaurants

- Concerts, plays in Spanish
- Sporting events in Spanish
- Spanish club activities
- Work—a job with Spanish speakers
- Work internships (In foreign country)
- Study trips (Abroad-stay with a family)
- Language camps
- "Open House" at a university
- Special courses (college, etc.)

Your Spanish club can take a very active role in sponsoring a variety of listening activities. (See Chapter 16.) You as the teacher should always be alert to any avenues you can explore to get more listening time for your students.

CONCLUSION

Listening, then, is a very important aspect of the internalization of language; it is a large part of that process we call communication. Listening and speaking are probably what most people mean when they say "I speak Spanish" or, "I am learning Spanish" or "Would you like to learn a language?" You can't have one without the other. In fact, there is a special magic about listening. If you are really involved in listening, the development of a *Sprachgegfühl* is facilitated more than from any other act.

Some teachers worry that they perhaps talk too much in the classroom. As long as you are speaking in Spanish, this should not be a source of concern to you, because if your students are listening, they are developing an essential skill. As you plan your lessons, try to have at least one specific listening comprehension activity during each class. And last but not least, don't neglect to supplement as often as possible your in-class practice with a wide variety of listening activities outside of the classroom.

Perhaps this is what Epictatus was referring to when he suggested that we should hear twice as much as we speak.

REFERENCES AND SUGGESTIONS FOR FURTHER READING

Asher, J. J. (2011). *Learning another language through actions* (7th ed.). Los Gatos, CA: Sky Oaks Publications. *This most recent edition of Asher's work explains the background of the approach and contains 150 hours worth of TPR classroom lesson plans.*

Berne, J. E. (2004). Listening comprehension strategies: A review of the literature. *Foreign Language Annals, 37,* 521-533. *Reviews research on the listening strategies used by successful and less-successful learners, as well as the teaching of listening strategies.* DOI: 10.1111/j.1944-9720.2004.tb02419.x

Peterson, P. W. (2001). Skills and strategies for proficient listening. In M. Celce-Murcia (Ed.), *Teaching English as a second or foreign language* (3rd ed., pp. 87-100). Boston, MA: Heinle & Heinle. *A practical guide to teaching listening at the beginning, intermediate, and advanced levels. Intended for ESL teachers, but most of the information is easily transferrable to foreign languages.*

Rubin, J. (1994). A review of second language listening comprehension research. *Modern Language Journal, 78,*199-221. *Reviews research on the factors that affect listening comprehension, including those that make a particular listening passage easy or difficult to understand.* DOI: 10.2307/329010

Rubin, J., & Thompson, I. (1982). *How to be a more successful language learner.* Boston, MA: Heinle & Heinle. *Contains many suggestions for learners on strategies for listening, as well as for other language skills.*

Thompson, I. (1995). Assessment of second/foreign language listening comprehension. In D. J. Mendelsohn & J. Rubin (Eds.), *A guide for the teaching of second language listening* (pp. 31-58). San Diego, CA: Dominie Press. *Discusses considerations in selecting and editing listening passages, and offers great ideas on a variety of methods for assessing listening comprehension.*

Ur, P. (1984). *Teaching listening comprehension.* Cambridge, England: Cambridge University Press. *A highly useful book that contains a wealth of ideas for listening comprehension activities; most are designed for teaching ESL, but can be easily adapted for Spanish.*

Other Books by James S. Taylor (see Appendix C for information)

- *Materiales para animar la clase de español*
- *Me gusta cantar*
- *Me gusta jugar*
- *Me gusta conversar*
- *Me gusta aprender español*
- *Me gusta actuar*

ACTIVITIES FOR METHODS CLASSES

1. Start a collection of pictures that you can use in listening comprehension activities. Choose one of the pictures and prepare a demonstration for your methods class.

2. Prepare a list of topics for listening comprehension activities. Select a topic and find pictures or make a composite picture, and prepare a demonstration for the methods class.

3. Prepare a lead-in for a reading selection to use as a listening comprehension exercise, or do the same thing for a brainstorming session, a cultural aside, a spot commercial, etc. and present it in the class.

4. Prepare a "gisting" exercise and present it to the class.

5. Preview some of the audio recordings in the LRC designed to develop listening comprehension. Take the comprehension tests. Write a report discussing how you would use the audio in a language class or how you would prepare the students to use it outside class.

6. Preview some of the videos in the LRC designed to develop listening comprehension, and make a report similar to the one mentioned in #5 above.

7. Preview some of the videos available for teaching languages. Decide what levels they would be appropriate for. What would you do with the students to prepare them to see the film? Prepare a report and hand it in to your instructor.

8. If you are already teaching, begin to make a list of the native speakers who would be willing to visit your class. Look for a variety of ages and countries of origin. Start collecting materials you could use to prepare the students for the visits.

9. Start building your collection of audio materials you could use in class, copying from radio broadcasts, television programs, lectures, plays, etc.

10. Develop some "homemade" audio, or video materials, using natives, that you can use in your classes. Some of these could be just taping the presentations of visitors to your class.

11. Check local TV channels or radio stations to see if there are programs in foreign languages that your students could watch or listen to. What could you do to help them get ready for the assignment? Discuss this with your teacher.

CHAPTER SEVEN

¿HABLA USTED ESPAÑOL? DEVELOPING SPEAKING PROFICIENCY

YOUR OBJECTIVES FOR THIS CHAPTER ARE TO:

1. DISCUSS WHAT SPEAKING PROFICIENCY CONSISTS OF AND DIFFERENTIATE BETWEEN INTERPERSONAL AND PRESENTATIONAL SPEAKING.

2. DISCUSS THE PRINCIPLES ON WHICH SPEAKING IS BASED AND WHAT THINGS HINDER THE DEVELOPMENT OF SPEAKING PROFICIENCY.

3. APPLY STRATEGIES AND TECHNIQUES TO LAY A FOUNDATION FOR SPEAKING PROFICIENCY, SUCH AS WORKING WITH DIALOGUES, QUESTIONS AND ANSWERS, COPING CARDS, "FOCUSED" DRILLS, RITUALS, AND PASSWORDS.

4. DEVELOP A REPERTOIRE OF COMMUNICATIVE ACTIVITIES THAT DEVELOP INTERPERSONAL SPEAKING SKILLS, SUCH AS TASK PERFORMANCE ACTIVITIES, ROLE PLAYING, INFORMATION GAP AND JIGSAW ACTIVITIES, SIMULATIONS, AND GAMES.

5. PLAN ACTIVITIES THAT DEVELOP PRESENTATIONAL SPEAKING SKILLS, SUCH AS ORAL REPORTS, PLAYS AND SKITS, AND POETRY MEMORIZATION AND RECITATION.

6. IDENTIFY EFFECTIVE WAYS OF RESPONDING TO STUDENTS' ERRORS.

7. ACQUIRE THE SKILLS THAT WILL ALLOW YOU TO HELP YOUR STUDENTS DEVELOP GOOD PRONUNCIATION.

Present

What did you say?

Bill and Pete had studied Spanish for six years in junior and senior high school. They were quite good with the grammar and had an extensive vocabulary. Their biggest problem was their "gringo" accent. Their teachers had worked hard trying to convince them to work with their pronunciation, but to no avail. "So what if we don't sound like natives," they responded, "just so we get the verbs conjugated and the adjectives agreeing with their nouns, and have enough vocabulary to say what we want to, that's all we need. Some people think a foreign accent is cute, and besides Americans can't learn Spanish without an accent anyway.

In their senior year, Bill and Pete made a trip to Mexico in Pete's old car. Two days into the trip, when they were well off the tourist route, the car broke down. There was nothing to do but find their way to the nearest town and try to find a mechanic. As they were walking along the highway, they encountered a woman walking in the same direction. "Let's talk to her and find out where the next town is and if there is a mechanic," suggested Pete. "Good idea," answered Bill, as he confidently approached the woman. "Booaynohz deeuhs, saynoruh. Nosohtrohz sohmoz teeyoureestuhs amereecanoz y taynaymoz prahblaymuz cahn nyuwaystro ouwtow. ¿Poowede youstayd duhseernohz dahnday estuh el prahxuhmoh pooebloh? Nayseseetahmoz oon muhcanneeco."

The aprehension which first crossed the woman's face as the boys approached her, changed to panic and then to anguish as Bill stumbled on. As he finished she turned to Pete and said in desperation, "¡Ay, jóvenes, lo siento mucho, pero no entiendo inglés. ¿No hablan ustedes español?"

~~~~

Janet's heart quickened as the tall, handsome, young man approached and asked her to dance. She hoped she could make a good impression because he was very interesting. As they went through the usual small talk about where they were from and what they were studying, Janet mentioned that she had studied several semesters of Spanish and was currently taking a class. They young man's countenance lighted up and he cried out with enthusiasm. "¡Pero si español es mi lengua madre¡ ¡Cuánto me alegro que lo hables!" "Hey," stammered Janet, turning deep red, "I said that I had had some Spanish, not that I speak the language!"

~~~~

Virginia had been studying Spanish for several months. The main activity in her classes was the memorization of numerous dialogues. At first it was hard for her but she quickly developed the ability to memorize a dialogue after only one or two readings. One evening Virgina was invited to dinner at the home of Juan, a friend from Cuba. Juan's wife and mother spoke no English, so Virginia was looking forward to practicing her Spanish. The following day her Spanish teacher asked her how things went.

"It was terrific!" she replied, "We ate Cuban food, played some Cuban games and then Juan played the guitar and we sang songs. "How did it go with his wife and mother?" asked the teacher. "That part wasn't quite so terrific," she complained, "The big problem was that they wouldn't stick to the dialogues!"

CHAPTER SEVEN

¿HABLA USTED ESPAÑOL? DEVELOPING SPEAKING PROFICIENCY

> **Conversation should be pleasant without scurrility, witty without affectation, free without indecency, learned without conceitedness, novel without falsehood.**
>
> **--William Shakespeare**

What are the expectations of students when they arrive at a beginning language class for the first time? More than likely they will have one thought in mind, whether they are in an elementary school, secondary school, or a university setting: "I'm going to learn to *speak* Spanish." With few exceptions, students equate "*taking* Spanish" with "*speaking* Spanish." And usually their anticipation also includes the time factor—"**right away!**"

You as the teacher want to capitalize on this **initial motivation**; in fact, you should make it an ever-present goal that you never diminish the enthusiasm and excitement in anticipation that the students have as they begin Spanish. That's why you have to be well prepared for the first day of class, and why you have to have many "speaking activities" ready for the first few weeks. You also need a stock of "commercials" to subtly help them adjust their expectations to more closely reflect reality. Yes, they *will* speak—not at the level they are anticipating, nor as quickly as they hope—but nonetheless they *will* speak.

A **communicative approach** is the main trend in language teaching today. Spurred on by the ACTFL Proficiency Guidelines and the Standards for Foreign Language Learning, book companies have marketed new textbooks with a speaking proficiency approach, and teachers across the nation are adjusting their programs to bring them in line with this renewed emphasis on using speaking skills. Unfortunately, not all textbooks give equal attention to the stages of input, output, and expression. Some books are trying to start at the "expression stage" without building an adequate foundation; others are working exclusively at the "input stage," never moving to higher levels of communication. Perhaps the most common shortcoming of current textbooks, in our opinion, is that they get stuck in the "practice stage" and neglect to provide enough opportunities for students to use the language for meaningful expression.

You recall from our language learning model, that our final objective is to reach a point where the students communicate in the language, expressing their own thoughts and ideas. But, a good deal of preparation and practice must take place before the students can do this. Let's review again the stages that will lead our students to communication.

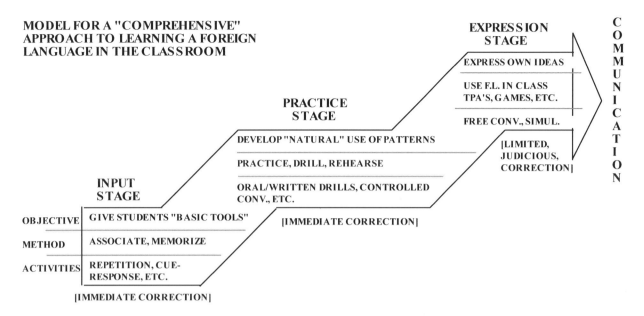

MODEL FOR A "COMPREHENSIVE" APPROACH TO LEARNING A FOREIGN LANGUAGE IN THE CLASSROOM

A number of years ago an approach to language teaching was proposed in which the students would sit in a circle, with a native speaker as a "resource person," and were supposed to converse with each other in the target language. The "session," patterned after counseling techniques, was totally unstructured so that the students would feel unrestrained and uninhibited and would express themselves freely. In an attempt to give this method a fair trial, we tried it with several groups over a fairly long period of time. It was painfully obvious from the outset that this approach tries to start at the "expression stage" without going through the "input stage" and the "practice stage" and the students were not able to make much progress. Furthermore, they were frustrated because they couldn't express themselves. You cannot ask students to do something they aren't prepared to do. They must have a good vocabulary base and some command of the structures before they can be expected to converse.

The role of the teacher becomes very crucial in directing communication activities. The teacher must "make the thing go." This is done with a variety of techniques that will stimulate, interest and motivate the students to express their thoughts and feelings. However, the teacher must not dominate the picture. The students should be the ones who do most of the talking, not the teacher. It should be somewhat like a concert; the teacher is the conductor and draws the "music" (communication in the language) out of the group, but the students are the ones who make the "music." On several occasions, we have invited visiting professors from Latin American countries to teach intermediate conversation classes for us here at the university. Almost without exception, they have taught the classes in the "European" style; they *lectured* every period.

Through the many years of their own studies, they had been conditioned to the idea that a "professor" always goes into the class and imparts great gems of wisdom and reams of information and opinion to the students, who should sit in class like sponges, soaking up everything that is said. Whatever speaking the students did in these classes was limited to an occasional question they ventured to ask. Needless to say, the students made some good progress in developing listening comprehension, but very little progress in their conversational skills. Do you see the point? If you want the students to develop conversational ability, they must spend a great deal of time practicing *conversation*, not listening to the teacher talk.

In this chapter we will discuss what speaking proficiency consists of, and will present numerous principles and techniques that you can use to develop it in your students. Speaking is the keystone in the "communication arch," the other skills are **supportive**. We have tried to illustrate this concept in the following diagram.

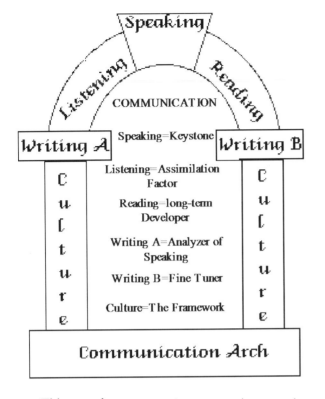

This arch represents a **gateway** to communication. It recognizes the keystone position of speaking as well as the support functions of the other major skills and culture. Even though at first the amount of listening **input** is more than the amount of speaking **output** because it develops readiness for speaking, you need to plan for some speaking contact experience every day, especially in beginning classes. Also, in beginning classes you will want to develop writing assignments to prepare directly for speaking. Reading is necessary in beginning courses for further developmental input because it can provide much background and ammunition for speaking along with listening input. And of course all communication, no matter what form it is in, is tied directly to the culture; meaning can come only from the cultural values and behavioral patterns of the people who are communicating.

WHAT IS SPEAKING PROFICIENCY?

Ultimately, we are interested in achieving the ability to speak freely and express what we want to say, when we want to say it. But this is a rather large expectation, which at first may seem impossible to reach. We must divide this large expectation into smaller ones. We see this as we watch children learning to speak. At first they communicate with just words to make meaning known: *Mamá, ¡agua!* or *Mira, ¡perro!*, etc. In a sense, our students will have to return to the speech level of children; they cannot expect to immediately express ideas and concepts at the level they do in their mother tongue: *Mamá, ¿puedes darme un vaso de agua, por favor?* or *Mira, ahí va el perro del vecino.*

Objectives for Oral Proficiency

The preceding comments mean that teachers need to be patient with students as they move from a child's level to an adult level. The guidelines for speaking proficiency suggested by ACTFL consist mostly of skills expected in *Novice* and *Intermediate* and *Advanced* Levels, which correspond with beginning, intermediate, and advanced classes. We will merely summarize them here, but have included the detailed descriptions in the Appendix where you can study them with more care.

The Proficiency Guidelines are separated into four major levels: the **novice** level, the **intermediate** level, the **advanced** level, and the **superior** level. A very brief summary of the expectations for speaking at the first three levels is shown on the following page.

124

ACTFL PROFICIENCY GUIDELINES - SPEAKING

Novice-level speakers are characterized by the ability to:
- respond to simple questions on the most common features of daily life
- convey minimal meaning to interlocutors experienced with dealing with foreigners by using isolated words, lists of words, memorized phrases and some personalized recombinations of words and phrases
- satisfy a very limited number of immediate needs

Intermediate-level speakers are characterized by the ability to:
- participate in simple, direct conversations on generally predictable topics related to daily activities and personal environment
- create with the language and communicate personal meaning to sympathetic interlocutors by combining language elements in discrete sentences and strings of sentences
- obtain and give information by asking and answering questions
- sustain and bring to a close a number of basic, uncomplicated communicative exchanges, often in a reactive mode
- satisfy simple personal needs and social demands to survive in the target language culture

Advanced-level speakers are characterized by the ability to:
- participate actively in conversations in most informal and some formal settings on topics of personal and public interest
- narrate and describe in major time frames with good control of aspect
- deal effectively with unanticipated complications through a variety of communicative devices
- sustain communication by using, with suitable accuracy and confidence, connected discourse of paragraph length and substance
- satisfy the demands of work and/or school situations

The *Guidelines* imply that at any given time, we should be paying attention to two different proficiency levels: the level that our students are currently at, and the next level that we want them to reach. For example, Novice speakers need to learn everyday vocabulary and "chunks" of set phrases and expressions that they can use for simple formulaic communication. Soon, however, they need to learn some basic grammar principles so they can begin to create with language on their own and move to the Intermediate level, where they can ask and answer questions and carry on simple conversations. By the same token, Intermediate speakers need to learn the past and future tenses and practice using them to narrate and describe in different time frames, a characteristic of the Advanced level. Thus, the *Guidelines* can help us plan and sequence our instruction in order to develop students' speaking proficiency.

What is "speaking?"

You should recall from the *Standards for Foreign Language Learning* that the Communication goal area is subdivided into three standards, encompassing interpersonal, interpretive, and presentational communication. This chapter will deal mainly with speaking in the context of **interpersonal** communication, in which two or more speakers are engaged in direct conversation – usually face-to-face, but also via telephone, Internet, or other electronic means. This type of speaking is "two-way"; it allows for interaction, clarification, and expansion. Toward the end of the chapter we will also discuss one-way **presentational** speaking, in which a presenter gives a prepared oral presentation to an audience of listeners.

Although there are some non-verbal aspects to speaking, such as gestures and facial expressions (body language), we are primarily concerned here with speech in its most basic manifestation: conveying a message by the spoken word. While it is possible to do this with just a word or two, we want to get beyond the "Me Tarzan...you Jane" level. We want our students to employ the language in a natural and fluent way.

If we are honest in our stated goal of **natural** language, we will have to modify the position that the language teaching profession has traditionally held: that students should always speak in "full, complete sentences with a subject, verb, and object." If we do that, we are, in reality, creating an artificial situation, perhaps influenced too much by the fact that we are in a school environment, a formal classroom situation. Native speakers frequently speak with short, elliptical, and incomplete sentences, so why can't our students?

PRINCIPLES FOR DEVELOPING SPEAKING PROFICIENCY

Let's consider at this point some of the principles that underlie speaking proficiency.

1. Imitating and responding. It seems clear that imitation is the first step your students will take as they begin speaking. It may begin on the first day of class when you start out with an *¡Hola!* that they will merely imitate. It may then continue with the repetition of the Spanish names you give each student, and move to the classroom phrases and expressions you will be teaching them to use during the class hour. The students will soon leave the *imitating* phase and move to *responding*. It is natural for them to respond to the direct oral stimulus that the teacher provides as he teaches the class in the language. After the students get a good base of words and expressions, their responses can move from memorized, set phrases to more creative responses.

2. Context. The more natural use the students make of the first words and expressions they are speaking, the better. When people converse, they usually have some idea, topic, or situation that is the focal point. You, as the teacher, must try to set up situations of that nature. You should be continually striving to provide context and create believable situations. Devising activities and practice sessions where the students use the

language naturally with each other is a constant objective of each class. And, need we remind you that making Spanish the medium of communication between the teacher and the students in the classroom is the most natural use that can be made?

3. Memorization. Memorization can be a very effective tool in preparing to express oneself orally. Recall that Novice speakers rely mainly on memorized chunks of language to communicate. Vocabulary learning is also largely memorization; both words and phrases can be committed to memory. At first some students may find it difficult to memorize sentences or passage because they have never memorized anything before in their life, but with practice this skill can be vastly expanded.

4. Maximization of class time for oral practice. The ideal environment for developing speaking proficiency would be a one-on-one situation between a teacher and an individual student. But the typical teacher has between 20 and 30 students in each class. If, in a class of 30 students, communication practice were limited to interaction between the teacher and the class, each student would speak for perhaps one minute. You must utilize strategies that will give a maximum amount of time to each student for practicing orally. Among these strategies are choral response, group and pair practice, and not using class time for activities that can be done outside of class.

5. Communication versus grammatical perfection. In the beginning stages, teachers must not expect students to produce error-free sentences, especially if they are expressing their own opinions and ideas. Right at first there will be many lapses; they will not have mastered the patterns, they will forget the vocabulary, and they will transfer from English. At this point you will have to exercise great patience, tolerance of errors, friendly helpfulness and support—fluency comes before accuracy. You will need to be imaginative, flexible, and dynamically motivating. You must be prepared with stimuli of all kinds to keep the activities moving; but this is where the fun of language learning is. Content, and the ability to make oneself understood are more important than getting the verb conjugated or making the adjectives agree with their nouns.

6. Give them the tools. The students cannot invent the language. We must be careful not to expect them to produce something they have not been prepared to do. To ask a student to explain what he does at work, for example, when he does not have the vocabulary to do so, only frustrates him and forces him into errors, trying to make word for word translations from English to Spanish.

7. Expect "transfer." It is only natural for students to try to express thoughts in the target language using the patterns of the native language. Sometimes this transfer is positive because there are similarities between English and Spanish, such as the use of the compound tenses. But usually the tendency to say things in Spanish the same way we do in English will lead to errors which hinder communication. The main point we want to make here is that you should expect this transfer and not become frustrated by it. Rather than getting down on the students for making "dumb mistakes," you should anticipate the problems and utilize strategies that will help them eliminate this transfer that is bound to come.

8. Fluency comes only through practice. At first students will stumble and stammer and will not be able to immediately recall words or patterns. Spontaneous fluency comes only as a result of having said something many times until it comes almost "automatically." The implication is clear that we must daily provide numerous activities that will give the students the practice necessary.

9. The students must be held accountable. If oral practice and performance are not overtly evaluated, students feel no accountability and feel no need to participate or give their best effort. Preparation outside of class and participation in in-class activities can become unimportant to them if they can avoid it with impunity. You must build accountability into oral preparation and practice activities through evaluations, tests, and grades.

TECHNIQUES FOR WORKING WITH BEGINNING STUDENTS

As we said, your students are anxious to get started with the language, even on the first day,

so be sure they get practice speaking the first day and every day thereafter.

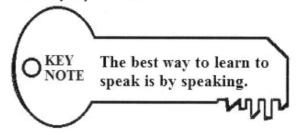

KEY NOTE The best way to learn to speak is by speaking.

There will be a perceptible movement through various levels from memorized expressions to a free-wheeling expression of inward feelings, opinions and thoughts, with many steps in between. To reach sustained communication, you must prepare them through listening and reading experiences so that they will have a great deal of input before you expect much output, and then what you expect is much less than what is put in.

Let's now look with some detail at the procedures and techniques you will use to develop your students' speaking skills. We will try to focus on *tried and true* methods that over years of language teaching have been shown to be effective.

Questions and Answers

The nature of language is such that the use of questions and answers has always been the oldest and most popular technique used in the classroom. It is very natural for the teacher to use the language by asking questions, and natural for the students to respond in the language in return. Although teachers must be careful not to monopolize class time, leaving insufficient time for pair and group activities, judicial use of questions and answers by the teacher can develop both listening and speaking skills and provide a formative assessment of students' learning. There are some special techniques, however, that you need to develop to make your questioning more effective.

The "lightening strikes" technique. A very powerful technique you will want to use in question and answer activities is what we call **"lightening strikes."** With this technique, the teachers ask the question **first,** and then pause one or two seconds before saying the name of the student they want to respond (i.e., when the "lightening strikes" that student). During the pause, **all** the students will think of an answer since the "lightening" might strike them (i.e., they may possibly be called on). Then, even though the teacher calls on another student, they listen to his or her response to see if it is the same as the one they were going to use. If the teachers say the name of the student first, and then ask the question, the moment they say the name, all the students except the one who was called on stop thinking because **he** or **she** is on the spot, not they.

An add-on technique to the "lightening strikes" is to ask the question, pause, call on the student, listen to his or her answer, and then ask the question again of the entire class, getting a choral response in which they answer the same way as the student who was called on. Another variation is to call on a second student and ask if he or she is in agreement with, or to make a comment on, the answer of the first student.

Confirmation. As students respond to questions, the teacher has various ways of reacting to their answers. If they are correct, you can give positive reinforcement with a variety of statements such as: *¡Muy bien!, ¡Excelente!, ¡Correcto!, ¡Es cierto!, Estoy de acuerdo,* etc. If you are moving very fast or are simply drilling forms, you may not say anything, and the students will know that the response was correct. If you are working on some specific structure or expression and the student uses it incorrectly, you can gently correct by restating the right answer, or by calling on another student you know will answer correctly and then perhaps going back to the first student and asking the question again.

Systematically include all students. You need to develop the skill of "scattering your shots" as you do questions and answers, but make sure you don't overlook or neglect any students. Don't go up one row and then down another, because students learn to anticipate when their "turn" to answer is going to be and only pay attention when you are getting close; then after they have answered, they shift their attention to something else. You should occasionally call on the same student two or three times in a row to establish the fact that "lightening *can* strike" in the same place twice. Sometimes you can walk over to one side of the room and call on students on the other side. This gets the attention of those near

you *and* those far from you. You will have to develop a "sixth sense" of knowing who you have called on and who not, and keep skipping around until all have answered. This sixth sense will come with experience.

A fun way of keeping track of which students you call on is to make a deck of 3 X 5 cards with the names of the students on them. Shuffle them very obviously in front of the class and say: *En esta clase somos muy democráticos,* cut the cards, and taking a card at a time from the top, ask the questions and call on the students whose card comes up. When all have responded, shuffle the cards again so everyone can see that you truly are *muy democrático/a.* (These cards can be used in numerous other ways. See **Chapter 4**, *Seating*, and **Chapter 12**, *Oral Quizzes in the Classroom.*).

What if they don't answer? We once watched a graduate assistant working with a small group of students. They were sitting in a tight circle. When he asked a question and a student didn't respond, he would ask the question louder. If that didn't get an answer, he would fairly shout the question a third time. Later he remarked to us, "What dumb students! I don't know why they didn't understand my questions; I was asking them as loud as I could!" What do you do if you ask a question and don't get an answer? Assuming that you said it loud enough, there are two basic reasons why they might not answer: 1) they didn't understand the question, or 2) they understood it, but don't know how to answer. In the first case, your best action is to rephrase the question. Ask it in a simpler way, or explain (in Spanish) what it means. In the second situation, you may have to supply some possible answers or ask the question again with some choices.

For example, if you asked *¿Qué hiciste ayer después de la escuela?* and even though the student didn't answer, if you believe he understood you might add, *¿Fuiste al partido de básquetbol, fuiste a la biblioteca a estudiar, o fuiste a trabajar?*

Another technique many teachers use is to spend time with the students before the question/answer session *practicing the answers*; they are then able to answer with greater facility. Eventually, you will want to move to personal questions that they will answer with free responses.

Sí or no questions. At the very beginning of a course, when the students' vocabulary is still limited, you cannot expect long answers to questions. At this point, simple comprehension of the questions is the main objective, and a natural response could very well be a simple *sí* or *no*. For example, if the topic of conversation were about the students' families, questions of the following type could be asked:

Tú eres de una familia grande, ¿verdad? (Sí) Tu papá trabaja para la universidad, ¿no? (Sí) ¿Tienen ustedes un elefante en su casa? (No) ¿Es su casa tan grande como la escuela? (No)

Short answer questions. The next step up from *sí* and *no* questions is to have the students respond with short answer questions of just one or two words. As we have mentioned, this type of response is very common in everyday conversation. If, for example, the topic is a discussion involving different kinds of transportation, questions and answers might be of the following type: *¿Cómo vienes a la escuela todos los días? (En coche.) Si haces un viaje a España, ¿cómo vas? (En avión.) Cuando Colón descubrió América, ¿cómo cruzó el mar? (En un barco.)*

Choice questions. If the students aren't familiar with the topic you are discussing or still have a limited vocabulary, giving them a choice question makes it easier to answer because they are "fed" possible answers and need only chose one of them, or at least, the choices give them an idea about how to answer. Supposing the topic is about what the students do for entertainment. Some "choice questions" might be: *Por lo general, ¿qué haces los sábados, vas al cine, trabajas, o estudias español? ¿Qué tipo de programa de televisión te gusta ver más, deportes, aventuras o comedias como el show de Seinfeld o David Letterman? ¿Qué clase de música te gusta más, rock, clásica, country, folklórica, lenta, o popular?*

Free response. Perhaps the most interesting question/answer activity is where the teacher asks a question and the students just shout out a response, or raise their hands to volunteer an answer. This approach allows the teacher to see which students are able to answer, and allows those students who are not quite sure of an answer to remain passive until they feel they can answer. However, the one danger of this approach is that some students may dominate, and others may be so timid that they don't participate at all. As you get experience, you will soon develop the ability to be aware of those who are not participating and need to consciously involve them.

Directed questions. Directed questions are of the type where the teacher directs a student (or students) to ask a specific question of another student (or students). This technique is especially effective in practicing certain grammatical structures, such as verb conjugations, indirect object pronouns, plural forms, etc. While discussing sports, for example, the teacher might say: *María, pregúntale a José si juega al fútbol.* María turns to José and asks: *José, ¿juegas al fútbol?* José answers: *Sí, juego al fútbol.* Maria then turns to the teacher and reports: *Sí, juega al fútbol.* In the process, the three singular forms of the verb have been practiced. The plural forms can be practiced when the teacher directs another student: *Beto, pregúntale a Carlos y Ramón si juegan al vólibol.* Beto asks them: *¿Juegan ustedes al vólibol?* When they respond: *Sí, jugamos al vólibol,* Beto reports to the teacher: *Sí, juegan al vólibol.*

Giving Them the Tools

The learning of basic phrases and sentences can provide the student with a convenient base from which he can draw ready-made comments, questions, and responses. This may range from using classroom expressions on "coping cards," to using short rejoinders, to memorizing dialogues, to preparing talks to give in class, to memorizing parts for a play.

Coping cards. A "coping card" is simply a list of useful expressions which you can print on a piece of stiff card stock and give to the students at the very beginning of the course which they can have at their fingertips to refer to when they need to "cope" with some situation, such as asking a for a repetition, a clarification, or permission to leave the class and so on. The teacher would hand out the card early in the course and spend several minutes each class hour going over the pronunciation and practicing using the words and expressions. The students would keep the card handy so they could refer to it at a second's notice. After some days or weeks of using the card, the expressions would be so well learned that the student no longer needs it. We gave you an example of a coping card for a beginning class in Chapter Five.

After the students are familiar with expressions on the coping cards, you can carry out daily practice sessions. Divide the class into two groups to provide some competition. Have them hold the card in readiness and then throw situations at them to see which group can respond fastest with an appropriate expression. The students will soon become automatic in using the expressions and the coping card can be abandoned. (See *Materiales para animar la clase de español* for other models of coping cards.)

Working with Groups and Pairs

While there are many class activities where the speaking is between the teacher and the entire class, a more natural pattern would be interaction between two or a few persons. For this reason it is important to do much of our speaking practice in small groups or pairs. Thus in the same amount of time, many conversations are going on instead of just one.

Working with Dialogues

Perhaps by far the most common and productive of all the activities involving memorization is working with **dialogues**. Many textbooks include dialogues in every chapter. The reason for this is that dialogues present natural, common expressions as they are used real-life situations. The dialogues are the "chunks" that provide a "springboard" or

"beachhead" that allows the students to begin immediate use of the language.

There are two basic approaches the teacher can take in working with dialogues: an **oral/memorization** approach or a **reading/discussion** approach.

The oral/memorization approach was very popular during the audio-lingual era. The teacher helps the students totally memorize the dialogue to the point they can act it out in a somewhat natural fashion. This approach has been accused of leading the students to a meaningless "parroting" of words and phrases that they did not understand. While some teachers may have allowed that situation to develop, it is not an *inevitable* consequence of the memorization of a dialogue. It is quite possible to memorize a dialogue meaningfully and use its contents in very effective ways. How convenient it is to have a handy "arsenal" of words and expressions that you know are grammatically proper, of high frequency use, and that you are pronouncing correctly. This state of fluency can be achieved by following these steps.

Step 1. Meaningful presentation of the dialogue with visuals. The teacher first prepares a set of visuals that represent the meaning of each line of dialogue. As an example we have chosen a simple dialogue, and have prepared visuals of the type we are referring to. We have written the line of dialogue on each visual so you can see how the drawings depict what the line means. *The students would not, of course, see the line written, they would learn it orally*, following the teacher's model, while concentrating on the meaning presented in the visual. Study the following visuals. (We have placed the words underneath so you can understand the meaning of the visual cues.)

Buenas tardes, mamá.

Hola, Ana, ¿cómo estás

Muy bien, gracias, ¿y tú?

Bien, gracias

¿Y cómo está papá?

No está bien. Está un poco enfermo.

Lo siento mucho.

Step 2. Intense practice with the dialogue words and expressions. After the students have memorized the lines to the point that they can say the line that goes with each visual, in any order, and can say the lines in the normal sequence with understanding and feeling, the teacher leads them in an intensive practice using the words and expressions in the dialog. This is usually question and answer activity about what is going on in the dialogue. For example, with the first visual, the teacher would point to different parts of the visual and ask questions of the following nature:

¿Quién es? (Pointing to the little girl.)
  (*Es Ana.*)
¿Y quién es esta persona? (Pointing to
  the mother.) (*Es la mamá.*)
*¿De dónde viene la niña? (De la
  escuela.)*
¿Qué le dice la niña a la madre? (*Hola,
  mamá.*)
¿Cómo responde la madre? (*Hola,
  Ana, ¿cómo estás?*)

Step 3. Supplementation and expansion of the dialogue words and expressions. Although the lines of a dialogue are high frequency expressions, they will not fit every possible situation, and the students have to practice using variations of the phrases and words of the dialogue. This is done by giving them additional expressions that could be applied in different situations. For example, in the dialogue presented above, the mother and child greet each other in the afternoon, but it wouldn't be appropriate to use the greeting, *Buenas tardes*, in the morning so *Buenos días* must be taught as an alternative to *Buenas noches*. *Muy bien* is a good answer to *¿Cómo estás?* when we are feeling fine, but how do we answer when we are feeling rotten? Thus we must teach other alternatives. This phase of working with dialogues is called the expansion phase and must precede the next step, because when we start to ask students personalized questions, we expect them to be semi-truthful and students need to have a variety of options available to choose from.

Step 4. Personalization of the dialogue words and expressions. The final step is to abandon the *situation* of the dialogue completely and communicate in a personal way with the students. We move to real communication as we ask the students how they are feeling and they respond naturally and truthfully. The dialogue words and expressions now become the tools they use to communicate their own feelings and ideas. The expansion phase should give them a breadth to say what they need to say. If not, the teacher needs to help them with additional vocabulary.

The second approach to working with dialogues is the reading/discussion approach. In this approach, the students do not memorize the dialogue, but only read it very carefully, either in class or at home. Then, working as an entire class, in small groups, or in pairs, the dialogue is discussed, usually through questions and answers. The words and expressions used in the dialogue are then practiced again by *personalizing* them. For example, if the dialogue is between two boys who have been playing some sport such as tennis, the students can use the words and expressions of the dialogue to discuss their own sports activities.

In our model for a "comprehensive approach" to learning a foreign language, we suggest that dialogues can be a very effective activity at the "input stage" to give the students the tools they need to begin understanding and using the language.

"Focused Practice"

We now turn to the "practice stage" of our Comprehensive Model. Coaches and teachers of different sports make constant use "focused practice." A tennis coach, for example, would not simply hand a racquet and balls to his pupils and say: "Get on the court and start hitting the ball." Instead, he would focus on one specific skill, such as the forehand or backhand stroke, or serve, and have the students practice only that skill for hours until they can do it well, and then do the same with the other skills. Of course, there would also be many hours of practice, putting all the pieces together in a game, but whenever the coach saw that the student was not developing a specific skill correctly, he would stop and go back to an intense practice of that skill alone until good habits were developed.

The same is true of grammatical control of a foreign language. Mastery of the target language structure by the students comes more directly from practice and use (conditioning) than from intellectual understanding of the concept. No matter how many times you explain conjugation of verbs and agreement of adjectives, the students will not conjugate the verbs or make their adjectives agree until they are conditioned to it — until it is "in the bones and tissues." Even though the students intellectually understand a grammatical principle, in the heat of a conversation they cannot pause every few seconds to sort through a series of rules to decide which one applies to the utterance they want to make. They must be guided by what "sounds right," that is, the things they have heard and practiced most. You as a teacher will spend more time *helping your students practice* than explaining and lecturing.

Ironically, most students believe that if they are struggling to understand the spoken language, or cannot express themselves fluently, what they need is "more grammar." A typical expectation of students in a language class is that they will learn many, many vocabulary words, the teacher will explain the grammar to them, and they will create the language from that point. This was the approach of the "grammar-translation" and cognitive code approaches, and as we have seen, they didn't produce oral proficiency. Students who are struggling in language classes often arrange to have a tutor and fully expect that the tutor will meet with them, explain the grammar, and they will soon catch up with the class. No matter what teaching approach a teacher uses, the students still have to practice the patterns until they can use them naturally and easily. The fact that they intellectually understand the grammar point does not mean that they will be able or even remember how to put the point into practice.

Activities that are specifically designed to practice a particular grammar point might be called "focused practice" activities. Ideally, such activities should focus on one grammar point, making minimal changes that require the application of the grammar point. The activities should **contextualize** the practice in a meaningful context to help students learn to recognize the situations in which it might be used. Many current textbooks contain focused practice activities that are contextualized in relation to the theme of the chapter; for example, possessive adjectives *(mi, tu, su, nuestro)* might be introduced in a chapter on family relationships, with focused practice activities in which students tell about their family members *(mi* hermano, *mis* padres) or those of the characters in the book *(su* tío, *sus* hermanos).

Because most textbooks now contain many focused practice activities, we have included only a couple of examples here.

El viaje a México
(Function: express likes and dislikes /
Grammar concepts: *"gustar,"* past tense, indirect object pronouns)

Acabas de volver de un viaje a México con tus padres y tus hermanos, y estás hablando con un estudiante mexicano, Manuel Gómez, quien quiere saber qué piensas de su país. Usen la información que sigue:

Lo que les gustó

a ti	a tus padres	a tus hermanos
los mexicanos	la música	la comida
las ruinas	los parques	las playas
hablar español	el arte	los programas de televisión
la comida	los niños mexicanos	la corrida de toros

Lo que no les gustó

el tráfico	la pobreza	la lluvia
la contaminación	el chile	las películas
el agua	los teléfonos	los turistas
los turistas	la corrida de toros	el hotel

Hagan y contesten preguntas según este modelo:
¿Te gustó México? (Sí, me gustó mucho.)
¿A tus padres les gustó la música de México? (Sí, les gustó mucho.)
¿Qué les gustó a tus hermanos? (Les gustaron las playas.)

Planes para un picnic
(Functions: Ask and answer questions about previously-mentioned objects /
Grammar concept: Direct object pronouns)

You are with a group of friends and are planning a picnic. Some of the things you will need are: (these could also be "brainstormed" by the entire class prior to the activity) sandwiches, drinks, CD player with music, matches, flashlight, blankets, volleyball equipment, etc. Practice with a classmate, following the model.

Estudiante #1	**Estudiante #2**
¿Quién trae los refrescos?	Martín los trae.
¿Y quién trae los sandwiches?	Amelia y Sarita los traen.
Y, ¿tú traes las frasadas?	Sí, las traigo yo.
(Etc.)	

ACTIVITIES FOR PROFICIENCY

You must plan to use a major portion of your class time working with activities that will lead to proficiency, moving from the "practice" to the "expression" stage. In this section we will present seven major types of activities with examples of each type and a listing of other activities of that type. How you select an activity will depend on whether your basic approach is function or grammar oriented. If you work strictly from a functional point of view, you will find each activity labeled with the function it will practice. If you approach a lesson from a grammar concept point of departure, you will find the activities are also labeled with the grammar points they will practice. Most textbooks, even though they avow an oral proficiency orientation, still center their lesson content around specific grammatical concepts. We have tried to synthesize these two approaches in this chapter—it seems to us that the activities themselves are of primary importance and oral proficiency comes from the practice, whether we are trying to develop skill in a function or trying to "condition" a structural pattern. *Using* the language is what gets it "into the bones and tissues." Following are seven types of activities, with detailed examples, and short lists of other activities of the same type. Note that these categories are not mutually exclusive; a particular activity may fit into more than one category. The important thing is that one or more speaking activities be used every day in class because it is important to practice speaking if one wants to speak well.

1. Picture-based communication. Conversation can be readily generated when it is based on some type of picture. This could be a large picture with some sort of situation, a story told in a series of episodes or frames, a series or even a collage of different pictures. Transparencies or PowerPoint slides can also be used. Following are different examples of this type of activity.

What's going on in the picture? This type of activity may be conducted with the entire class or in small groups. The picture is the focus of the conversation. The teacher or group leader may solicit comments or ask general questions which the students respond to. The best kind of visual is the type that presents a comic, unusual, or absurd situation, or a picture filled with people and actions that many comments can be made about. Following are examples of the type of pictures that could give a good basis for conversation.

The above pictures work well with Novice-level students who are progressing toward Intermediate because they provide practice creating with language to form very simple sentences ("Carlota escribe en la pizarra").

What are they saying? The teacher collects a number of pictures from different sources that show people in unusual situations or doing unusual things, such as a man sitting on top of a crocodile with a paddle in his hands and paddling as though he were in a canoe. With the class divided into several teams, the teacher puts one of the pictures in front where all can see. Each team "huddles" and makes up a conversation or makes comments that the person(s) in the picture might be saying. This activity works well with Intermediate students because it involves creating with language to form conversations. Following are examples of pictures of this type:

Competition can be used by organizing teams, giving each team a picture and having them make up a story. In another variation, each team is given magazines and they cut out pictures to illustrate a story that they have made up. Some sort of prize could be given to the group presenting the most ingenious or clever story.

Tell the story. In this activity the students see a series pictures that tell a story. The students can be divided into pairs or groups and can prepare a dialogue to go along with the frames and then read them or present them orally to the entire class. The following example can work at the Intermediate level if students are asked to form a simple sentence about each picture. The activity can be adapted for the Advanced level by pushing students to create a complete narration in the past tense:

2. Role playing. This is perhaps the most commonly used of activities that allow the students to use the language in a natural setting. In a role-play the students assume someone's identity and act and speak as that person would. The teacher prepares the students with the linguistic and cultural information necessary and then presents situations to groups or pairs of students who act out their assigned roles in the language. These roles can be modeled and practiced in advance so the students don't fumble so much when it is their turn.

Role playing is a classic Intermediate-level activity since it involves creating with language, carrying on a simple conversation, and asking and answering questions. To adapt role plays for the Advanced level, various complications may be added – for example, in the first situation below, the customs agent could stop the tourist and accuse him/her of smuggling illegal merchandise. Following are some examples of role-plays:

Role Play #1
(Function: Go through customs / Grammar concepts: Future, commands)

You are on a trip to Spain and have landed at the Madrid airport. Your first step will be to go through customs. Play the role of the tourist and your partner will play the role of the customs official. Then reverse roles. Use the vocabulary and expressions in the model you have practiced.

Role Play #2
(Function: Give advice / Grammar concept: Subjunctive)

Two friends meet in the cafeteria and talk about their problems. One is doing very poorly in school and is thinking of dropping out. The second student tries to encourage the first one and give some suggestions on how to do better in school. Use the vocabulary and expressions in the model you have been practicing.

Other activities of this type would be to present situations that would involve:

- Counseling
- Confrontation
- Celebrity interview
- (fictitious identity)

3. Handling physical objects (or pictures) or doing physical activity. Actually handling physical objects or pictures or doing the actions physically helps make communication practice more realistic. When using pictures, train the students to look at the object in the picture, visualize its name and gender in their mind, and talk about it as if it were the real thing. The activities demonstrate this concept.

El ciego y su lazarillo
(Function: Give directions / Grammar concept: Commands)

This is a very effective activity to practice the formation of commands. The students work in pairs, one taking the role of a blind person and the other the role of the guide. The *ciego* is blindfolded and the *lazarillo (el o la guía)* sends him or her through a series of commands such as those illustrated in the model. For practice the blind person can restate the command in the form of a question and the guide can either repeat the command or give an affirmative or negative confirmation.

Modelo

Lazarillo	**Ciego**
Levántate.	¿Me levanto?
Sí. Toma dos pasos adelante.	¿Tomo dos pasos adelante?
Eso es. Dobla a la derecha y toma otros dos pasos.	¿Doblo a la derecha y tomo otros dos pasos?
Perfecto. Dobla ahora a la derecha.	

Pásame la leche, por favor
(Function: Respond to requests for things / Grammar concept: Object pronouns)

The teacher will have prepared 20 or more 3 x 5 cards which have pictures of different kinds of food on them. (They were simply cut out of magazines and "spray mounted" on the cards.) The students sit in pairs facing each other and the teacher gives 4 or 5 cards to each pair. Following a model which the teacher can write on the board or put on a transparency, the students do the following: Student #1 displays one of the pictures (a glass of milk, for example), and student #2 starts the sequence:

Estudiante #2:	¿Tienes la leche?
Estudiante #1:	Sí, **la** tengo.
Estudiante #2:	¿Puedes pasár**mela**?
Estudiante #1:	¡Claro! Aquí **la** tienes.

Student #1 gives the picture to student #2 and they continue on until all the pictures have been given to #2. They then reverse the roles. The teacher keeps exchanging pictures with different pairs to make sure they all practice with singular and plural nouns and a variety of vocabulary.

Other activities of this type would include:
- Telephone conversations (with toy phones)
- Buying and selling (with toys, pictures, fruit, candy, etc.)
- Variety of TPR activities where students work in pairs and command each other.
- Draw what I describe (back to back)

4. Information gap format. An information gap activity is done by students working in pairs; each student has information that the other one needs in order to complete a task. For example, students might be given the task of finding an hour when they can get together to study. Each student in the pair could be given a copy of his or her "schedule" for the day; the teacher would prepare these schedules in advance so that there are only one or two hours that both students have free. The students must then ask each other questions to find a free hour in common: "¿Qué tal el jueves a las cuatro?" "No, jueves a las cuatro tengo mi lección de piano." This activity works well with students who are progressing from Novice to Intermediate because it involves asking and answering simple questions. In another type of information gap activity, each partner might be given a slightly different version of a picture, and each must describe his or her picture to the other in order to identify the differences. This type of activity is more appropriate for Intermediate to Advanced students since it involves giving detailed descriptions.

5. Signature search. In this type of activity students get up and walk around the room, asking each other questions to find people who fit certain criteria on a handout they have been given. When they find someone who fits a particular criterion, they write down the person's name or ask for the person's signature ("Firma aquí, por favor"). Because the activity focuses on asking and answering questions, it works well with Intermediate level students. Following is an example of a signature search activity.

BUSCA A TU CUATE
(Function: Asking questions / Gram. concept: Question words)

Give each student a half a sheet of paper similar to the one below (or one with other vocabulary you may want to practice). Tell them not to look at it, but at a given signal they are to find a person who fits the description for each category. Write down the thing they have in common, and ask the person to sign his or her name. The person who gets all the information first wins. Of course, this is all in Spanish! This can be a great "ice-breaker" for a party while you wait for students to arrive.

Busca a alguien . . .   **COSA**   **PERSONA**
1. que tenga el mismo animal doméstico en su casa.   _____   _____
2. que tenga el mismo color favorito que tú.   _____   _____
3. que tenga el mismo deporte favorito que tú.   _____   _____
4. que tenga el mismo número de personas en la familia.   _____   _____
5. que tenga la misma comida favorita que tú.   _____   _____
6. que mire el mismo programa de televisión que tú.   _____   _____
7. que tenga el mismo mes de cumpleaños que tú.   _____   _____
8. que tenga el mismo color de casa que tú.   _____   _____
9. cuya familia tenga la misma marca de coche que tú.   _____   _____
10. que tenga la misma película favorito que tú.   _____   _____
11. que tenga el mismo libro favorito que tú.   _____   _____
12. que le guste el mismo grupo de músicos que a ti.   _____   _____

Usa preguntas de este tipo: ¿Cuál es tu deporte (color, libro, comida, programa de TV, libro, etc.)? ¿Cuánta personas hay en tu familia? ¿Qué marca de coche tiene tu papá (animal doméstico tienes en casa, grupo de músicos te gusta más, etc.)? ¿Quién es tu cantante favorito/a? ¿En qué mes naciste? ¿De qué color es tu casa?

Other similar activities that involve the whole class in a task (though not necessarily signature searches) are:

- Adventure and detective activities
- Who's who in the family.
- Chain stories
- Solve the puzzle (together)
- Scrambled sentences

6. Jigsaw activities. Jigsaw activities begin by dividing the class into groups of three to five students, who are given 5-10 minutes to become "experts" on a particular topic such as the content of a picture, map, or short article. The students are then mixed so as to form "jigsaw" groups comprised of one member from each "expert" group, who must then pool the information they have learned. For example, in a unit on Spain, students could be divided into "expert" groups of four, and each group given a pamphlet on a different region of the country. Each group is given ten minutes to scan through the pamphlet looking for information on *geografía, clima,* and *atracciones turísticas.* The students then "jigsaw," forming new groups of four with each group comprised of one "expert" on each of the five regions studied. Their task is now to fill in the following chart, with each group member contributing information on the region he or she read about in the pamphlet:

	Clima	Geografía	Atracciones
Madrid			
Andalucía			
Asturias			
Cataluña			

Finally, the groups must use the information in the chart to come to an agreement on which region of Spain they would like to visit, and present their decision to the class. Although this particular activity was designed for the Intermediate level, it could be made to work with Novice High students by providing a template for their reports: "Vamos a ir a (Asturias). Asturias tiene (montañas, valles y playas). Vamos a ir en (el verano) porque (hace fresco). Vamos a ir a (la ciudad de Oviedo y el Parque Nacional de los Picos de Europa)." To build on the cultural

content of the lesson, the teacher could then show slides and a map of the regions chosen.

7. Pedagogical task activities. Since the 1980s there has been much attention to using task-based activities in foreign language classrooms. A "language task" is any activity in which two or more people interact in the language in order to accomplish a specific purpose or goal. According to Nunan (1999), there are two different types of tasks: (1) **real-world** or **target tasks** that students might do outside the classroom, such as ordering a meal in a restaurant, making a purchase, or making a phone call; we will discuss this type of task later in this chapter. (2) **Pedagogical tasks,** which are done for classroom learning purposes. Examples of pedagogical tasks might include interviewing partners about their eating habits for the purpose of comparing their diet with the recommendations in the food pyramid; or surveying the class about their parents' musical preferences as compared to their own, in order to document changes from one generation to the next. Notice that this type of activity often lends itself to a theme-based approach; for example, the above activities would fit well in units on food and music, respectively.

Following is another example of a pedagogical task, adapted from Bill Van Patten. This particular task is geared toward Intermediate (or Novice High) students because it involves asking questions and creating with language in a simple way.

¿Qué tan activo eres?
(Function: Ask questions / Gram. concept: Preterite tense)

Paso 1. With a partner, list as many activities as you can in the following three categories that a typical student might engage in. An example of each is provided. You'll have about 5 minutes to do this.

Físicamente activo	Entre activo y sedentario	Sedentario
jugar al tenis	ir de compras	mirar la televisión

Paso 2. You and your partner now interview each other. Find out if your partner did any of the activities last week by asking "yes/no" questions, e.g., "¿Jugaste al tenis la semana pasada?" Keep track of your partner's responses.

Paso 3. You and your partner should rate each other on the following scale.

Muy activo <----------------------------> Muy sedentario
     5   4   3   2   1

Paso 4. Present your findings to the group. You may use the following model if you need help.

A John le di un tres para su semana. Él hizo dos actividades activas: jugó al tenis y corrió. También hizo dos actividades sedentarias: estudió y durmió.

SIMULATIONS

Simulations are an attempt to create reality. They are much more elaborate and much time and effort go into their preparation than into the activities discussed above. The teacher must find resource persons and train them. The teacher must also prepare student materials and spend time going over them with the students until they are ready. Props, costumes, and decoration of the setting are very important to give the illusion of, or at least, a flavor of a Spanish language environment. Simulations can be done in the classroom, in some part of the school, or out in the community. Where students have no opportunities to experience an authentic Spanish-speaking situation, a simulation might be the closest they will come to the real thing, and although it is somewhat artificial, it can develop fluency and self-confidence.

Some simulations that you could set up **inside** your classroom are: a store or market, a city with streets and shops, all kinds of radio and TV "shows" such as talent and talk shows, news and weather broadcasts, television commercials, a bank, telephone conversations, a restaurant, a "golpe de estado," a trial, a guided tour in some famous city, and so on.

Some simulations that could be conducted **outside** the classroom could include: visiting a real restaurant where the personnel speak Spanish, making phone calls to Spanish-speaking persons and getting specific information, interviewing people from Spanish-speaking countries (in Spanish, of course), conducting treasure and scavenger hunts, taking tours of the school or city with "natives," and so on. (See *Simulations and Conversational Activities for the Spanish Class* for a collection of simulations.)

Here is an example of a simulation that could be set up in the classroom:

CAMIÓN MEXICANO
(A Simulation for the Spanish Class)

This fun simulation can be set up in the classroom with very little effort. The classroom is cleared of chairs except for two rows of chairs with an aisle down the middle, representing the "bus." A bus-stop sign may be prepared, indicating the numbers of the busses that will stop at that sign. The students are all given a sheet (similar to the one in the Modelo below) that indicates the place where they are going, the sign the bus will have on it, and the street they are to get off at. A "bus driver" (another Spanish teacher, a native or advanced student) sits in front of the bus and makes the motions of starting and stopping the bus. The driver responds to the signals of the students to stop and pick them up and to their requests to get off. He or she also answers questions about streets the bus will be going to. Two "propmen" (who don't have to be fluent in Spanish) stand near the bus, one with signs the busses will have on them, and the other with names of streets. The "propmen" slowly change their signs as though the bus were moving from street to street. As a sign comes up that indicates to students that that is the bus they are to take, they signal the bus to stop, ask the driver if the bus goes to the street of their destination, ask the price, pay, receive their ticket, and take a seat. The bus will slowly fill up and eventually the names of the streets will come up where the students will have to get off. They call to the driver or pull the buzzer and get off at their street. Realism can be added if the students carry packages and boxes on the bus, a lot of people crowd on, an inspector comes by checking tickets, beggars or vendors get on plying their wares, etc.

MODELO
(diferente para cada estudiante)

Tú vas al _____**Palacio de Bellas Artes**_____. (Nombre de un lugar)
Tienes que tomar el camión que indica__**Alameda**__. (Letrero en el camión)
Debes bajarte en _**Avenida Juárez y Avenida San Juan de Letrán**___.

Haz lo siguiente:
1. Para el camión al dar la señal apropiada.
2. Pregúntale al chofer si el pasa por las calles donde debes bajarte.
3. Pregúntale al chofer cuánto cuesta y dale el dinero. (Asegúrate que el te dé la vuelta correcta. No dejes de sujetarte cuando el camión se ponga cn marcha.)
4. Sé cortés al dar tu asiento a viejitos, mujeres cargando niños, o a quienquiera que creas que lo necesite.)
5. Pídele a otro pasajero que te indique dónde debes bajarte.
6. Observa los letreros de las calles para ver el nombre de tu calle.
7. Indícale al chofer en la manera apropiada para avisar que vas a bajarte.

Las frases siguientes te serán de ayuda:
1. (Para saber si es tu camión.) ¿Pasa por la calle _____?
2. (Para saber el precio del boleto.) ¿Cuánto cuesta?
3. (Para decirle al chofer que no tienes cambio.) No tengo cambio.
4. (Para ofrecer tu asiento a alguien.) Siéntese, por favor.
5. (Para pedir ayuda en saber dónde bajar.) Perdone, ¿me podría indicar dónde me tengo que baja en la calle ....?
6. (Para avisarle al chofer que vas a bajar en la próxima calle.) **¡BAJO!**

INTERVIEWS

There are two kinds of interviewing that you can teach the students to do which will go a long way in bringing them to fluency: 1) in class and 2) out of class.

In-class interviews. You should begin early on developing the skills and providing your students opportunities to interview fluent speakers of Spanish. You can begin by preparing a simple transparency with questions that would commonly be asked of someone visiting the class. Over a period of time, practice those questions with the students and then have a native, preferably of their same age, visit the class and let them interview him or her. You can guide the interview personally by interspersing questions of your own.

Out-of-class interviews. Most of your students will have some family member, friend or neighbor who is a fluent speaker of Spanish. (If not, you can find some one in the school that they could do this assignment with.) Practice with them in class and then give them the assignment to visit that person in their home and interview them. You can give them a report sheet, similar to the following one, and have them hand it in for credit. You might even have them report their interview, in Spanish of course, to the students in your class.

OUT-OF-CLASS INTERVIEW ASSIGNMENT

Instructions: Locate someone who speaks Spanish fluently. This could be some member of your family, a relative, or a neighbor. Make an appointment with him or her, explaining what you are going to do. Take along your tape recorder and record the interview. It must be done entirely in Spanish. After the interview, fill out and hand in the reports.

Interview #1 - "We get acquainted" (Some suggested content.)

1. Tell me about your growing up years. (Where did you live, your family, where you went to school, what activities you participated in, work, etc.
2. What is your profession? Why did you decide to enter that field? What training, schooling did you have to do to prepare for that career?
3. Describe a typical day of work at your job.
4. Tell me about your family. Members, their work, what they like to do, what you do together as a family, etc.
5. How did you learn to speak Spanish? Do you use it often? In what circumstances? How do you keep up your ability to use it?

Informe

Nombre_____ Clase_____ Fecha_____

Entrevista # _____ Con _____

Información aprendida:

        Pregunta #1

        Pregunta #2

        Pregunta #3

        Pregunta #4

        Pregunta #5

Hice toda la entrevista en español. (Firma) _____

(Pídele a la persona entrevistada que rellene la parte siguiente y entrega las dos partes a tu profesor.)

Estimado/a Señor, Señora:

El/La joven que le da esta nota, _____, es un/a estudiante en mi clase de español en Podunk Jr. High School. Los estudiantes de la clase tienen que completar una asignación de practicar el idioma al entrevistar a una persona hispanohablante. ¿Sería usted tan amable de permitirle la entrevista? Por favor, no le hable en inglés. La entrevista debe estar exclusivamente in castellano. Gracias por su cooperación.

                              Sinceramente,
                              Jaime Sastre
                              Profesor de español, Podunk JHS

In a real sense this interview activity actually moves from the practice stage to an authentic use of the language. If your students can use the language to communicate ideas, ask questions, and understand the information that they are given, they are communicating!

TASK PERFORMANCE ACTIVITIES

A task performance activity (**TPA**) is similar to role-playing and simulations. Its objective is to prepare the student to carry out a specific "target task" or "real-world task" in the language. On one occasion we were directing a study abroad program in Madrid, Spain. The students needed only to step out the front door of the University

Center to be able to put the language to use. As assignments in the conversation class, we gave the students specific tasks to perform each day, such as: buying something in a store, mailing a package in the post office, getting a haircut, buying a ticket to a theatrical performance, cashing a check in a bank, and so on. After a few of days they reported that they were finding it difficult to complete the tasks because they "didn't know how to say things." This led to the development of materials designed to give them the tools to carry out the tasks. Needless to say, they were much better able to perform the tasks. (See *Me gusta conversar* for a collection of different task performance activities.) Following is an example of a TPA:

STOPPING OR GETTING A TAXI

Task to be Performed: You will find a taxi and ask the driver how much it would cost to go to a certain place. Ask him to take you there and pay him.

Content: Taxis are common forms of transportation in Spanish-speaking countries. They are usually quite cheap and since most people don't have a car, they take a cab when they are in a hurry, or if the weather is bad. Near train and bus terminals, large department stores, and main plazas there are usually areas where taxis wait for customers. You are expected to take the first one in line. Otherwise, you can wave one down in the street if it is free. Usually there will be a sign saying "LIBRE" if the taxi is available, or a green light may be on. It is always a good idea to ask if the driver will take you to a certain area and approximately how much it will cost.

Novice Dialogue: Un/Una joven llama un taxi　*A young man/woman hails a cab*

Joven:	¡Taxi, por favor! ¿Está usted libre?	YM/W:	*Taxi please! Are you free?*
Taxista:	Sí, señor/señorita.	Taxi:	*Yes sir/miss.*
Joven:	¿Me puede llevar a Dr. Esquerdo 97?	YM/W:	*Can you take me to Dr. Esquerdo 97?*
Taxista:	Sí, claro, ¿por qué no?	Taxi:	*Sure, of course, why not?*
Joven:	¿Cuánto sería, más o menos?	YM/W:	*How much would it be, more or less?*
Taxista:	Unos 3 o 4 Euros.	Taxi:	*About 3 or 4 Euros.*
Joven:	Está bien. ¡Vámonos!	YM/W:	*OK. Let's go!*

Intermediate Dialogue: Un hombre quiere ir al aeropuerto

Señor:	Buenas tardes. ¿Me puede llevar al aeropuerto de Barajas?	Man:	*Good afternoon. Can you take me to the Barajas Airport?*
Taxista:	Sí, señor. Espere y le ayudo con las maletas.	Taxi:	*Yes, sir. Wait and I'll help you the suitcases.*
(Baja del coche y abre el maletero.)		*(Gets out of the car and opens trunk.)*	
Señor:	¿Cuánto cuesta?	Man:	*How much does it cost?*
Taxi:	Es una tarifa fija de quince euros. Luego es un euro extra por cada maleta.	Taxi:	*It's a fixed fee of 15 Euros. Then it's 1 Euro extra for each suitcase.*
Señor:	Está bien. Tengo que tomar un avión que sale a las 10:30. Llegaremos a tiempo, ¿verdad?	Man:	*That's fine. I have to take a plane that leaves at 10:30. We'll arrive on time, right?*
Taxi:	¡Cómo no! Es cuestión de 30 minutos no más, 40 si hay mucho tráfico. Tendrá media hora para facturar su equipaje y pasar al salón de espera.	Taxi:	*Sure! It's only a question of 30 minutes, 40 if there's a lot of traffic. You'll have 1/2 hour to check your luggage and go to the waiting room.*

Possible Terms to be Used:

Cliente:
¿Me puede llevar a_____?
Quiero ir a___
¿Cuánto le debo?
¿Cuánto es? How much is it?
¿Cuánto me costaría ir a _____?
¿Cuánto marca el taxímetro?
¿Sabe dónde queda el _____?
Déjeme aquí.
Me bajo aquí en la esquina.

Client:
Can you take me to_____?
I want to go to___
How much do I owe you?

How much would it cost me to go _____?
How much does the meter show?
Do you know where _____ is?
Leave me here.
I'll get out here on the corner.

Taxista:
Hay una tarifa base de __ pesos
¿A dónde va?
Son __ pesos cada valija
No puedo llevar a más de
    cuatro personas

Taxi Driver:
There is a fixed fee of __ pesos.
Where are you going?
That's __ pesos every suitcase.
I can't carry more than
four people.

Suggested Learning Activities:

1. Learn and memorize the expressions.
2. Make up a dialog and practice it with a friend until you feel comfortable with the vocabulary.
3. Make up names of places you might want to go to in a city and practice with a partner asking him to take you there. (Change roles)

Assessment: The instructor will give you a simulated situation where you are to go to a certain place. The teacher or another student will play the role of the driver. You will tell him where you are going and use the necessary expressions correctly.

GAMES

Games can be used in a number of ways to develop speaking skill and can add pleasure and enthusiasm to your classes. If you organize games in an enthusiastic way, make them challenging, and utilize the motivating force of competition, you can revitalize your class to the point where the students won't want to stop, and even look forward to succeeding classes.

Selecting a game. There are some cautions you need to follow before jumping into games. There are some games in which no real learning is taking place, and there are others that have no bearing on a Spanish class. You need to carefully choose games that are fun and motivating but at the same time are helping the students learn or

practice some aspect of the language. In analyzing the value of a game, consider the following:

1. Does it develop a language skill? (What is the focus or goal? Does it involve the recognition or recall of vocabulary? Does it practice some structure of the language?)
2. Does the activity fit your lesson? (Does it substitute for a drill, use the vocabulary you are working with, practice the grammar of the chapter?)
3. How much time is needed? (Do you have the time to spare, is it worth it for the growth the students might make, can the time be shortened or limited?)
4. What are the benefits of the game? (Does it provide motivation, a change of pace, eliminate boredom or wake them up, allow for

creative input, involve all students or just some of them?)

5. Is the game appropriate for the level? (Can the students handle the vocabulary, the verb tenses needed, the command forms?)

6. Is the game simple to understand, easy to administer? (What materials are needed, are they available, are the directions clear and simple?)

(Adapted from a presentation by Alice Omaggio in ACTFL convention in Atlanta, 1987.)

There are some skills you as a teacher will need to develop that will help you be more effective in using games. The following guidelines should be helpful.

1. Keep the learning objective in mind. Too often teachers play games just for the sake of playing. As you prepare your lesson plans, ask yourself what games will be appropriate for the material being learned. In the collection of games *Me gusta jugar*, there is an index of grammar points, topical vocabulary, and cultural concepts, cross referenced to games that can be used to teach and practice them. It is simply a matter of looking up the objective in the index and then selecting the game that lends itself best to the objective.

2. Prepare the students to be able to play the game in Spanish. Explain it in very simple Spanish or if it is very complicated, give them the rules written out in English to read on their own. Teach them all the vocabulary and expressions they will need. Obviously everyone wants to make comments during the game, so teach them how to say *¿A quién le toca? ¡Caramba! ¡Eso no vale! ¡Están haciendo trampas!*, and so on. (See *Me gusta jugar* for a more extensive list.) Then, make a formal, obvious shift into playing the game totally in Spanish. From that point you can assess a penalty for anyone who uses English, or give some reward for using only Spanish, such as candy, special "class money," extra points, and so on.

3. Don't make a big fuss over it or disrupt the game, but if the students are making the same

error, correct it before it becomes ingrained. Games are great for developing habits, and habits are difficult to change. As always, the correction must be done in a gentle, diplomatic fashion that will not inhibit nor dampen enthusiasm or participation. (More about this later in the chapter.)

4. Utilize the spirit of competition; it is a powerful force. When you can, divide the class into teams and give each team an identity, such as *"LOS LEONES," "LOS TIGRES," "LOS SABIOS," "LOS CAMPEONES."* If you can, and if it doesn't make it unfair, it is always stimulating to pit the boys against the girls. Offer incentives to the winners such as letting them choose the next game, giving them some sort of prize such as candy, permitting them to direct a game, or excusing them from class early.

5. Keep working with a variety of games. There will be, of course, class favorites, which students may want to play time after time. This is fine, but try to add a new one each time you play to broaden their "gamut of games." If you do the same activity each time, the fun becomes the primary focus and the learning diminishes.

6. Never begin a class hour with a game. Plan them for the last half of the class or whenever you see the students getting bored or tired. If you start out with a game, they will not want to quit at the specified time, or it will be impossible for them to settle down to normal classroom activities. It is often wise to set a definite time limit and hold to it, declaring whichever team is ahead at that point the winner.

Examples of games. We present here five different types of games as examples. There are, of course, many more types but you can get an idea from these examples of how they can be used to teach, reinforce, and practice the language while motivating your students at the same time.

¿QUIÉN SOY?
(Function: Ask about a person/Gram. concepts: forms of *ser*, adj. agreement, verb tenses)

There are at least 5 ways to play this game.

1. The leader takes the role of a person or famous animal, and asks: "¿Quién soy?" The other players can ask questions, but the leader can answer only *sí* or *no*. The other players can ask questions such as:

    ¿Eres [Es usted*, soy**] una persona real (ficticia)?
    ¿Eres un animal (real, ficticio)? ¿Eres una cosa? ¿Eres un hombre (una mujer)?
    ¿Estás vivo[a] (muerto[a])? ¿Eres una persona famosa de la historia? ¿Eres un[a] político[a] famoso[a]?
    ¿Eres un militar (general, almirante, etc.)? ¿Eres un presidente (dictador, rey, reina, emperador, etc.) de un país?
    ¿Eres una personalidad del cine (del teatro, de la Biblia, de la televisión, de un libro)?
    ¿Eres un músico (compositor, cantante, bailarín, etc.)? ¿Eres un inventor, científico, pintor, etc.)?
    ¿Cantas, tocas un instrumento (el violín, el piano, la guitarra, etc.)? ¿Eres un[a] deportista famoso[a]?
    ¿Eres famoso en el mundo del golf (fútbol, básquetbol, natación, etc.)
    ¿Eres de este siglo (del siglo pasado, del siglo XVIII, de antes de Jesucristo, etc.)?
    ¿Eres de los Estados Unidos (de Europa, de México, de Utah, etc.)?

*If you are trying to discover who your teacher is, use the *usted* forms, if you are working with a classmate, use the *tú* forms.
**If you are trying to discover your own unknown identity, use the *yo* forms.

2. The group is divided into teams and one player from each team goes out of the room with the leader. The leader gives these selected players the name of a famous person—they are **the same person**. They reenter the room and stand in front of their team. At a signal from the leader, the team members start asking *sí* or *no* questions as fast as then can to determine their teammate is. The team that correctly guesses first is the winner.

3. The group is divided into teams and one player from each team goes to the front. The leader pins a different name of a famous person (or animal) on the back of each player. They turn around so all can see who they are, and then go back to their team and try to guess who they are. Their team members can answer only *sí* or *no* and the first person to guess correctly wins a point for the team.

4. The group is divided into pairs and the players of each pair write a name down on a slip of paper. The partner tries to guess who he is, keeping track of the number of questions asked. The one who guesses correctly with the fewest questions is the winner.

5. This can be a good party mixer. As guests arrive, the name is pinned on their back and they have to ask questions to find out who they are. The others answer only with *sí* or *no*. When players discover who they are, pin their name on their chest.

Variations: This doesn't have to be limited to persons or animals, it can be a "¿Qué soy?" with professions, nationalities, cities, etc. However, the players may need help with the kinds of questions they should ask. This game can also be done with different tenses, such as:
        "¿Quién fui?", "¿Quién seré?", etc.

LOTERÍA
(Function: recognize spoken vocabulary/General or specific vocabulary)

This game is played with the ***LOTERÍA*** sets that can be purchased in México, or material supply companies. You can make your own cards and *tableros* for specific vocabulary words. The leader has a deck of picture cards and slowly reads off the names of the cards as he draws them. The players have one or more *tableros* that have 16 pictures on them. As a name is read, they repeat it and if they have it on their *tablero*, they place a *ficha* on its picture. The first player to cover four pictures in a row (horizontally, vertically, or diagonally) shouts "**LOTERÍA**" and wins the game. He verifies this by reading in Spanish the names of the pictures he has covered. He may then be allowed to call the words from the deck in the next game.

Suggestion: The members of the class can make their own *lotería* cards and *tableros*, by cutting pictures out of magazines, catalogs, etc. They can focus in on specific vocabulary, such as foods, colors, car parts, or animals.

MANOS ARRIBA
(Function: give commands/Gram. concepts: imperative, use of definite article)

In this game, two teams are seated on opposite sides of a table (or the writing surface of their desks forming tight rows). Members of each team take turns being *jefe*. Team A receives a coin that they pass from one hand to another underneath the table where it cannot be seen. When the *jefe* of team B feels they've passed the coin around long enough, he asks team A: "*¿Listos?*" When team A answers "*Sí*" the *jefe* then says: "*¡Manos arriba!*" and each player on team A raises both hands, with fists clenched, into the air at about eye level. Of course one of the players will have the coin hidden in one of his clenched fists. The *jefe* then says: "*¡Manos abajo!*" and all team A players quickly slap their hands, palms down, on the table, all in unison. The clinking noise of the coin might be heard, but the slapping noise of everyone's hands on the table will make it harder for team B to guess who has the coin hidden under his hand and also under which hand it is hidden. Members of team B, starting with the *jefe*, take turns, telling a person on team A to raise a hand, **trying to leave until last** the hand the coin is under. The team B player may consult, in Spanish, with teammates, but they can only talk, they cannot point. He begins guessing by naming a person on team A and saying: "Fulano/a, levanta la mano derecha (o izquierda)," or he may also say: "Levanta las dos manos." The person called upon then lifts up the hand (or hands) indicated to show if the coin is there or not. That hand is then left off the table. This continues until the coin is uncovered. If this happens before all other hands have been lifted, team B loses. Team A passes the coin again, and another player on team B becomes *jefe*. When team B succeeds in leaving the hand with the coin *until last*, team B wins, and the coin is passed over to team B and team A then tries to find the coin. A team is given a point every time the other team loses and 2 points when they win.

Suggestions: Find a large coin, such as a Mexican 5 or 10 peso piece, or a silver dollar. Insist that the players say *la mano* (or *las manos*), not *tu* or *el mano*. The goal of this game is to get in the habit of using the correct article automatically.

CONCENTRACIÓN
(Function: General vocabulary, any specific vocabulary, phrases, proverbs, tenses, etc.)

A concentration game board has to be prepared for this game. You will need a large piece of plywood that will accommodate twenty squares about 5 inches square, as illustrated below. A finishing nail (small head) in nailed near the top-center of each square. Squares of paper with a hole in the top-center are prepared so they will fit over the nails. These are your "working slips" and are prepared in pairs; for example, a picture of a chair and the word *silla*, a picture of a nurse and the word *enfermera*, a picture of a banana and the word *plátano*, the first part of a proverb, such as "*Más vale tarde...*" on one slip and "*...que nunca*" on the other, etc, A second set of squares of paper is prepared; these are your "cover slips" to be hung on the nails over the top of the "working slips." The "cover slips" all bear a number from 1 to 20, (or they can be letters of the alphabet). Before beginning the game, the pairs of working slips are prepared and placed at random on the board. The cover slips are then placed over them, in consecutive order of the numbers or the letters. The players, of course don't see this preparation, they just see the

cover slips and don't know what's behind them. To begin the game, the group is divided into two teams. The first member of Team #1 calls out in Spanish two numbers, for example: *trece y veinte*. Those numbers (cover slips) are removed to reveal what is underneath. If the working slips form a pair, or a match, they remain uncovered and team #1 gets a point. If they are not a matching pair, they are covered over again with the cover slips. The first player on team #2 then guesses two numbers. If he gets a pair, then his team gets a point. If not, the squares are covered up again. The second player on team #1 now takes his turn, and the game continues in this manner until all pairs have matched and left uncovered. If one team gets a match, they immediately get another turn, but it has to be the next player whose turn it is who calls the numbers, not the one who got the match. The team with the highest score at the end of the game is the winner. If another game is to be played, the leader turns the board around and rearranges the working slips in another order where no one can see, and replaces the cover slips.

ESTO ES MI PIE
(Function: play game/Vocab.: parts of the body, demonst. adj., posess. adj.)

The players sit in a circle with "IT" standing in the center (or two players sit facing each other). "IT" goes up to one of the other players (or the one player says to the other) and points to a part of his own body and says: "*Esto es mi _____*" (something *other than* what he is pointing to). For example, he may point to his **nose** and say: "*Esto es mi pie.*" The player addressed must immediately do the reverse—point to his **foot** and say: "*Esto es mi nariz.*" The person initiating the sequence starts counting to ten in Spanish, and the person called upon must respond correctly before the other reaches ten. If he does not, then he becomes "IT" (or the other person gets a point). If the person called upon responds correctly and in time, then "IT" must try again. This is a good game for practicing parts of the body. Watch out when using *lengua*!

With a little thought and imagination, you can adapt almost any game for use in the classroom. There are also several commercial sources for games you can use in the classroom. (See *Me gusta jugar* for an extensive collection of games for the Spanish class and sources for commercial games.)

ACTIVITIES IN PRESENTATIONAL MODE

Unlike interpersonal communication, which is two-way in nature, presentational communication involves one-way speaking to an audience of listeners. This type of activity requires the students to prepare (usually outside of class) a presentation to give orally in class. Possible formats for presentations may include oral reports, poems, retold stories, or humorous anecdotes.

In all types of oral presentations, we recommend that the students prepare a preliminary version that the teacher goes over first to make suggestions on vocabulary and structural accuracy. From that point the student can memorize the presentation or prepare cue cards to work from. They should be discouraged from just standing before the class and reading their report. The students in the audience may also need some coaching on how to be good listeners. Often it helps to require them to take notes or write down key points from the presentation to turn in later.

Oral Reports

Teachers commonly assign students to study some aspect of Hispanic culture and then give a report in class. Too often these reports are given in English. With guidance and some extra time put in by the teacher, these reports can be done in Spanish. If you give the students simple guidelines, already written in Spanish, they simply fill in the information they have researched and hand it in to be checked and get suggestions for the final revision.

An example of a fun type of oral report is "show and tell." The students obtain some piece of *realia* such as a *sarape*, a *banderilla*, a *wooden figure*, etc., that that reflects some cultural concept and then show it to the class as they talk about the concept.

Plays and Skits

Plays and skits can be the natural outcome of all the communication activities you conduct daily in class. Experience gained from dialogue memorization and role-playing situations can easily be transferred to the presentation of humorous skits, longer (and perhaps more serious) playlets, or even simple versions in Spanish of well-known stories or fairy tales.

Many teachers have been successful in helping students write and stage their own versions of famous episodes from great literary masterpieces, such as Don Quixote fighting the windmills or Sancho Panza as governor of the "island" of Barataria, excerpts from contemporary novels or short stories, such as *Una carta a Dios,* or even scaled down versions of modern plays such as *La dama del alba* or *La barca sin pescador.*

The plays and skits can be put on before other classes or audiences. The students will work harder if they have a public, and performances of this kind will also promote your program. You can make videos of the presentations and show them to other classes or put them in the lab for the students to watch outside of class. Plays and skits can even be put on for a PTA program or a special parents' night sponsored by the Spanish Club. Parents love to see their children performing in a foreign language even if they don't understand. An exciting activity is to have an annual exchange party with another school where each school puts on a play or several short skits.

When they participate in plays and skits, students increase their confidence in speaking the language. They gain a collection of phrases and expressions they can use in ordinary conversation. Many of us who have been in plays in foreign languages find ourselves, years later, still using lines from the play whenever we speak the language.

Props and simple scenery can make the presentations come alive. Make sure the students learn to project their voices so everyone can hear. Work with their pronunciation so they can be understood. And, especially with humorous skits, practice the dramatic ending to make sure the "punch line" comes across with unmistakable effect. (See *Me gusta actuar* for a collection of skits and plays for the Spanish class.)

Poetry Memorization and Recitation

We have stressed the value of memorization. Similar to the learning and presenting of plays and skits is the memorization and recitation of poetry. Oral recitation is very popular in Spanish-speaking countries and can give your students a cultural glimpse of what their counterparts in those countries frequently do in their school activities, in addition to the obvious linguistic growth they gain from the vocabulary and phrases they learn.

You can start with short, simple verses and then move to longer poems. You can practice together in class and then have the students do the memorization at home. Then take a few minutes each day, perhaps during the warm-up period, and have them recite as an assignment, giving them credit and a grade.

An example of a simple poem that can be easily memorized is one of the verses of José Martí, the revered Cuban poet and patriot. The rhythm and rhyme of this verse helps the students remember the lines, and the message of the poem is noble and uplifting. (See ***Materiales para animar la clase*** for other selections of poetry that students can easily memorize.)

Versos sencillos XXXIX
de José Martí

Cultivo una rosa blanca,
en julio como en enero,
y para el amigo sincero
que me da su mano franca.

Y para el cruel que me arranca
el corazón con el que vivo,
cardo ni ortiga cultivo;
cultivo una rosa blanca.

SIMPLE TEACHING TECHNIQUES

As you gain experience in teaching, you will learn many simple teaching techniques that prove very effective and their use will soon become almost second nature to your teaching personality. We will mention several here.

Circumlocution. One of the special skills you need to teach your students, especially those on intermediate and advanced levels is that of *circumlocution.* This is the ability to say something that they don't have the specific word for. Following is a very abbreviated model for teaching this skill to your students. (For a more complete version of this activity, see ***Materiales para animar la clase.***)

HABLANDO CON RODEOS
(An Activity for Learning Circumlocution)

When you try to communicate in a foreign language there will be many situations where you don't know the word in the foreign language that you want to use. In those cases you must come up with a substitute, a definition, or a description. This is called "circumlocution" in English; we will call it *"hablando con rodeos,"* (talking around something) Here are some techniques you can use to develop this skill.

1. Use general "catch-all" words plus descriptions.

When trying to talk about someone's position, occupation, or authority:

> **la persona**
> **el hombre +   que   +   a description of what the person does**
> **la mujer**

Examples: office manager = la mujer que dice a las secretarias su trabajo
                              la persona más importante de la oficina
            plumber = el hombre que viene cuando el agua no sale

When trying to talk about something to be used for something:

> **la cosa**
> **la parte**
> **la máquina   +   que   +   a description of what it does, or is used for**
> **el aparato**
> **lo**

Examples: windshield wiper = la cosa que limpia las ventanas de un coche
                              el aparato que saca la lluvia del parabrisas
            pencil sharpener= la máquina que usamos con el lápiz cuando no escribe bien
            star = lo que está en el cielo de noche, que da luz, pero no es la luna

2. Use "cover" words with categories or properties (like "animal, vegetable, or mineral") when talking about something eaten, drunk, or worn, etc.:

> **algo para comer**   **(dulce, salado, amargo,.....)**
> **un artículo de ropa**   **+ describe it**   **(para trabajar, para fiestas,....)**
> **un tipo de fruta**   **(rojo, ácido, dulce,....)**

Examples: apron = un artículo de ropa que usamos (en frente) cuando trabajamos
                              algo que usamos para quedar limpios
            honey = algo para comer que hace el insecto que visita las flores, es muy dulce, lo
                              ponemos en pan

Practicing circumlocution techniques. Teaching and practicing the techniques listed above will help the students become quite adept in expressing ideas and needs even when the vocabulary is lacking. Following are some suggestions for practice.

After learning the phrases and techniques presented in "*Hablando con Rodeos*," put the students in small groups or pairs and use the charades approach: Give one person a word in English (which the partner or others of the group do not hear) and have him/her *"hablar con rodeos"* until everyone agrees that a native speaker would have understood. Meaning must be transmitted by words, it is not allowed to use hands, facial expressions, or point to things. Examples: flag, swimming suit, crutch, cavity (in tooth), drunk, spoiled, disappointed, etc.

Or, still working in pairs or small groups, use a role-playing approach. Give one student a slip of paper with a situation which he/she role-plays, *"hablando con rodeos."* Allow the "native" to offer words that the clues suggest. Examples: Tell a new friend from Costa Rica that your uncle is a barber, your aunt is a seamstress, your dad is a bricklayer, your brother is an insurance salesman, etc. Explain that you are a student and are studying travel and tourism, business management, electrical engineering, etc.

Raising a Student's Volume

When working orally with the entire class or with groups, it is important that the students speak loud enough so the others can hear. Often students will speak with such a low, timid voice that the others do not hear the response. In these cases, teachers sometimes automatically walk nearer the student and ask him/her to repeat. A more effective way to raise his/her volume is to **move away** from him/her; perhaps clear across the room, or stand by another student and say: *Juan no te oyó. ¿Lo puedes repetir más fuerte para que él te pueda oír?* The student then will repeat much louder so the teacher (and the student mentioned) can hear. If you move **nearer** to the student who wasn't heard, the natural tendency is for him/her to speak even more softly since you have gotten closer.

"Rituals"

A *ritual* is simply a set sequence or ceremony that you train your class to follow, using very common language expressions. As your students use these expressions over and over during a course, they become "ingrained" in their speech patterns, similar to our saying *please* or *thank you* without really thinking about it. The expressions are learned in "chunks" and thus are always said correctly and with complete

naturalness. Here are some rituals you can teach your students.

1. Someone in the class sneezes. Everyone stops whatever they were doing and says: *¡Salud!* The student who sneezed responds with *¡Gracias!* and the class continues on.

2. The teacher or a student wants to pass by a student or students. He or she say: *¡Con permiso!* and pause until the students respond with *¡Cómo no!* (Or *¡Usted lo tiene!* or *¡Es propio!* or *¡Pase usted!* or some other expression of that sort.)

3. A student arrives late to class. He or she opens the door and pauses. The other students stop whatever they are doing and sing out in chorus (with some sarcasm): *¡Buenas tardes!* The late student, with an appropriate hang of the head, replies: *Siento mucho llegar tarde.* The class responds in chorus: *Está bien; más vale tarde que nunca.* The class continues on.

4. During a class period the teacher finds out that a student has not prepared the assignment (or completed some other task). The teacher announces to the class: *Clase, ¡Roberto no ha preparado la tarea!* The class turns to Roberto and says in chorus: *¡Roberto! ¡Qué vergüenza!* Roberto then replies: *Lo siento mucho, no pasará otra vez.*

5. A student wants to leave class early. He or she goes to the teacher and asks: *¿Puedo salir de la clase temprano hoy?* The teacher gets the attention of all the class and announces: *Clase, Felipe quiere salir de la clase temprano hoy. ¿Qué les parece? ¿Lo permitimos?* The class responds, *Sí, está bien.* (Or, if you have the time, you might have Felipe explain why he has to leave early and the class decides if he has a good reason.)

6. A teacher or student accidently (or perhaps on purpose, so you can practice the expressions) bumps into someone, steps on someone's toe, or somehow causes them grief and says: *¡Perdón!* (Or *¡Perdóname!* or *¡Lo siento!*, etc.) The injured party responds with: *Está bien.* (Or *No es nada*, or *No importa*, etc.)

7. A student eats an apple (cookie, candy bar, etc.) during class. The teacher or a student gets the attention of the class and says: *Clase, Carolina está comiendo en la clase.* The class responds: *Quien come y no convida, tiene un sapo en la barriga.* Carolina then has

to offer to share with the class (in order not to have a *sapo en la barriga*) by holding out the apple and saying: *¿Quieren ustedes?* Since she has offered to share, the class responds with: *No, gracias,* and the class continues on.

8. Always use courtesy expressions in Spanish. *Por favor, gracias, con mucho gusto, claro que sí, cómo no, perdón, no importa, no pasa nada, repita por favor, me puedes (podrías) ayudar, etc.*

Password

An effective technique teachers often use, especially with younger learners, is to occasionally require a **password** routine (*la contraseña*) for the students to be able to leave the class. The teacher positions him/herself at the door just before the class ends and the students line up, ready to leave the classroom. The teacher announces the password that the students must give before leaving the class. It might be some new vocabulary learned that day or a correct response to some stimulus given by the teacher. For example, the teacher might say to each student as he/she leaves: *¡Qué te vaya bien!* The student must then respond: *Gracias, igualmente.* If the student does not give the password correctly, he/she must go to the end of the line and try again later. Somehow they always find a way to learn the password correctly by the time they get to the front of the line a second time.

Reject Their English

During a class session it is very common for students to say something to the teacher or request something in English. This is only natural since they probably are not thinking in Spanish and they forget to use it with you. Condition yourself to gently reject their English and have them say it over in Spanish. For example, the student might say: *Senorita Alba, I forgot my pencil. Can you loan me one?* You might respond: *¿Cómo? ¿Qué has dicho? ¿Quieres darme dinero? Lo acepto con mucho gusto.* At this point the student shifts over to Spanish.

Non-intimidating Error Correction

It is appropriate to discuss in this section on techniques the role of error correction in a language class. Years ago, this subject perhaps never would have come up. It was axiomatic that language teachers constantly corrected their students; "correct usage" was a primary goal of language study. The recent emphasis on functional fluency has raised the issue of the importance of correctness and the possibility of its actually hindering progress in the development of oral proficiency.

"What does it matter," some teachers are now saying, "if there are errors, as long as the student can complete the task?" Still others feel that correction of errors intimidates the students and makes them hesitant to use the language for fear of being embarrassed if corrected in front of others. These are valid points and should have a direct influence on *how* we correct. There are some who argue that the students will eventually "self correct," that is, after considerable work with the language, they will realize that they are speaking incorrectly and will correct themselves.

In all our years of teaching languages we have only rarely seen self-correction, and this was with special students who had an unusual linguistic talent for learning languages. What usually happens is that when students learn and continue to practice incorrect patterns, they "set" or "ingrain" that pattern in their speech habits until it becomes very difficult or impossible to change. This phenomenon is sometimes referred to as "fossilization."

One should also consider the impact of inaccurate use of the language on the listener. Studies have indicated that speakers who constantly make errors as they use the language are held in low esteem by listeners who get the impression that the speaker is not very bright or well educated.

Consistent and supportive correction can be very helpful in raising the level of the students' oral proficiency. One thing is certain, beginning students are constantly making tentative attempts to express something in the new language, they know that what they are saying might not be correct, but if nothing is said, they will assume that it was not wrong and will continue to make the same mistake. Natives typically do not like to correct errors, and often tell learners that: "it's unbelievable how well you speak the language," or that: "you speak like a native." Unfortunately this graciousness too often leads to a smug complacency and a lessening of striving for higher levels of accuracy.

It seems obvious that error correction is the role of the teacher, who is responsible for guiding and forming the habits of the students. Rather than abandoning correction, we suggest you develop the skill of correcting in a positive, supportive way.

Lyster and Ranta (1997) identified six types of feedback that teachers can give students on their errors: explicit correction, recasts, clarification requests, metalinguistic feedback, elicitation, and repetition. Suppose you ask a student, "¿Dónde está tu tarea?" and she replies, "Mi tarea es en mi casa." The following examples illustrate how you might respond to the student's error using each of these techniques.

> **Explicit correction:** "No es 'Mi tarea *es* en mi casa', sino 'Mi tarea *está* en casa.'"
> **Recast:** "Ah, tu tarea está en tu casa."
> **Clarification request:** "No comprendo. ¿Tu tarea es en tu casa?"
> **Metalinguistic feedback:** "Usamos *ser* o *estar* en esa situación?"
> **Elicitation:** "No es 'Mi tarea *es* en mi casa', sino 'Mi tarea . . .' *(pause and wait for student to produce the correct form)*
> **Repetition**: "Mi tarea *es* en mi casa?"

Lyster and Ranta found that although teachers overwhelmingly chose recasts to respond to student errors, this technique was not particularly effective because students thought the teacher was responding to the content rather than the form of what they said. The last four techniques – clarification requests, metalinguistic feedback, elicitation, and repetition – were more effective

in helping students notice and correct their errors. These techniques require students to think about the language and come up with the correct form on their own rather than simply having the teacher give it to them.

When the students are participating in activities that have the specific purpose of learning vocabulary or structure, correction can be impersonal and immediate, so the students do not continue practicing the mistake. This can be true of pronunciation, vocabulary, or grammatical errors. Sometimes as you are moving around the class listening to students as they work in groups and you hear a common mistake that everyone is making, you can stop the entire class activity, practice the correct form chorally, and then go back to group work.

If the students are working in conversation sessions where they are spontaneously expressing their own feelings and ideas, where the communication is more important than form, then it might be counterproductive to interrupt them every few minutes with correction. What you can do in these cases is jot down mistakes that are being made, and at some other point in the class, make comments about incorrect forms that were being used. It is especially important not to interrupt students who are communicating with you in the language, such as asking for help, explaining a problem, etc. In those cases, be receptive and supportive; try to comprehend what they are trying to say and respond naturally as though everything they said were correct. This will build their confidence and reinforce their desire to communicate with you in Spanish. Study our model for language learning again and note in which kinds of activities we can correct immediately and in which ones we should only use limited and judicious correction.

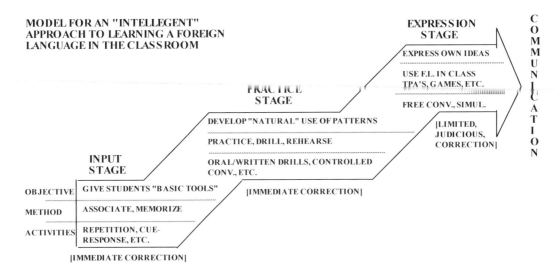

MODEL FOR AN "INTELLEGENT" APPROACH TO LEARNING A FOREIGN LANGUAGE IN THE CLASSROOM

EXPRESSION STAGE

EXPRESS OWN IDEAS

USE F.L. IN CLASS TPA'S, GAMES, ETC.

FREE CONV., SIMUL.

[LIMITED, JUDICIOUS, CORRECTION]

C O M M U N I C A T I O N

PRACTICE STAGE

DEVELOP "NATURAL" USE OF PATTERNS

PRACTICE, DRILL, REHEARSE

ORAL/WRITTEN DRILLS, CONTROLLED CONV., ETC.

INPUT STAGE

OBJECTIVE   GIVE STUDENTS "BASIC TOOLS"   [IMMEDIATE CORRECTION]

METHOD   ASSOCIATE, MEMORIZE

ACTIVITIES   REPETITION, CUE-RESPONSE, ETC.

[IMMEDIATE CORRECTION]

The mechanics of moving the class into group or pair activities. As we have noted before, you will want to do a lot of group and pair activities. You need to train your students to do this quickly and efficiently or a great deal of time can be wasted. A good technique is to do a "walk through" of the activity once before moving into groups. This can be done by selecting a nearby student (preferably one who can handle the activity) and walking through the activity with him/her so all can see what they are expected to do. Then tell them how they are to group. The division can be done a number of fun ways. You can vary them from day to day. For example, one day you might mix up your name cards and draw out groups at random. On other days, you might have everyone wearing red in one group, those with Levis on in another group, or those with white tennis shoes in another group, and so on. It is wise to keep changing groups so that the students do not keep working with the same partners every day.

Make Use of a Timer

One of the handiest pieces of equipment you can have in the class is a timer with a very loud bell or buzzer on it. You can use it in many different ways, such as timing responses in games, keeping track of the length of oral presentations or tests, preparing videos for class use, and on and on. One of its principal uses will be in working with group and pair activities. When the students have moved into their groups, you can shout out, *¡Vamos a practicar con esta actividad 10 minutos!* Then set the timer and when it rings

everyone knows it is time to stop. This is a real necessity to avoid wasting time when working in groups. It keeps activities moving at a brisk pace.

PRONUNCIATION

It is appropriate that this chapter on speaking proficiency also include a discussion of pronunciation since it is an essential part of speaking. There is some controversy in this area. There are those who affirm that good pronunciation is not possible for many students, and that to insist that they try to develop it will only put pressure on them that will retard their development of natural expression. There are others who believe that good pronunciation is not only possible, but very desirable.

Is it worth it? We are convinced that good pronunciation is well worth the effort the teacher and students must make to achieve it. Although there are some who say that a foreign accent is "cute," experience has shown that more often it hinders understanding and can be irritating to the listener. Studies have also shown that natives hold speakers with good accents in higher esteem than those who have poor pronunciation.

When work on it? There are some who suggest that no emphasis be put on correct pronunciation until later in the course when the students will eventually self correct their bad habits. Our experience has been just the opposite. If students are left to the bad habits that develop from the natural transfer of English pronunciation to Spanish, those bad habits become "ingrained" and are extremely difficult to change. And as for "self correction," in working with thousands of language students, we have seen it happen only on rare occasions. Efforts toward developing proper pronunciation must begin on the first day of class and must continue until the students have made it a permanent part of their oral use of the language.

How go about it? The secret to developing good pronunciation in our students is gentle, but constant **insistence**. This can be done in such a way that it does not threaten or demean the students. They need only understand that to pronounce badly at first is natural because of their English habits, but that it is important to make the effort to develop new habits, and that you will help them through modeling and reminding.

Techniques. There are a number of techniques or "tricks" you can use when working with pronunciation. Here are some:

1. Modeling of sounds and a repeated pronunciation of difficult words is usually more effective than detailed explanations of how to form the sound. If students cannot get it right from your model alone, then isolate the sound they are not making correctly and help them see how to do it. **Ex.** They are not tapping the /r/ in *tres.* Have them say today/today/today several times until the tongue is tapping correctly and then transfer that sound to *tres.*

2. If they are using "schwas" in place of pure vowel sounds, just utter the vowel sounds of the word several times and then put the consonants back in. **Ex.** They are saying *buhstante.* Have them say "ah-**ah**-ey" several times until they get the rhythm of the vowels and then put the consonants back in, *bastante.*

3. If they are pronouncing the letter **h** as in English, stop the class and announce: *"Voy a pronunciar la **hache** en español. ¡Escuchen todos!"* You then make a big dramatic show of opening your mouth and not making a sound. Have them all do it with you several times. Then go back and pronounce the word with the **h** in it without making the sound of the English **h**.

4. The trilled **r** (not the tapped **r**) can be difficult for many students. In words that have an initial **r**, have them try putting a **d** sound first. **Ex.** *dRoberto, drojo, drico.* Making the **d** sound puts the tongue in its proper place for the trill. Later they can phase it out. Or have them try blowing when the tongue is in that position to make the trill. Keep them practicing. If after a reasonable amount of time and effort, it still does not come, teach them an acceptable substitute, such as a fricative or "whistled" **r**.

5. Conduct frequent pronunciation evaluations, such as having students prepare paragraphs to read to you individually for grades. Make sure that they know that oral tests also include an evaluation of their pronunciation and state it specifically in the test results.

6. Get peer pressure to work for, not against you. Some students don't try to improve their pronunciation because they don't want to be different. You have to have a lot of "commercials" ready to praise those who have good pronunciation so the poor-speaking minority will realize that they belong to a group that isn't being praised and will make the effort to be one of the "good guys."

7. Whenever you can, you should practice pronunciation in context. One activity of this kind is a "focused" practice where the students are to select their answer according to a certain sound, and practice that sound in the process. For example:

   Contesten con la palabra con "erre"

   ¿Vas con Juan o Ramón? (Voy con Ramón.)
   ¿Es tu coche el blanco o el rojo? (Es el rojo.)
   ¿Tú eres de Colombia o Puerto Rico? (Soy de Puerto Rico.)
   ¿Prefieres carne de res o carne de cerdo? (Carne de res.)

8. Have frequent in-class practice sessions. You can prepare transparencies for each of the "problem sounds" similar to the following example for the phoneme /R/ and practice chorally as a class. These practices are very good warm-ups.

Alternate the in-class choral practice with partner practices. Prepare enough practice cards similar to the example below (la "Z") for each of your students and have them work for two or three minutes with a partner, focusing on that particular sound. They should correct each other if their partner mispronounces.

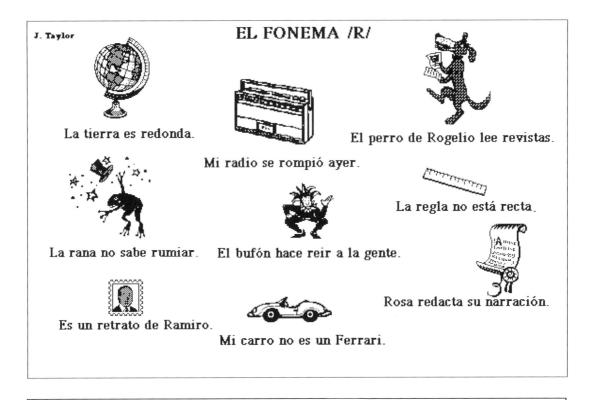

EL FONEMA /R/

J. Taylor

La tierra es redonda.

Mi radio se rompió ayer.

El perro de Rogelio lee revistas.

La rana no sabe rumiar.   El bufón hace reir a la gente.

La regla no está recta.

Es un retrato de Ramiro.

Mi carro no es un Ferrari.

Rosa redacta su narración.

Práctica de Pronunciación - #9 - La "Z"

En el restaurante

A: Mozo, quiero la merluza con arroz y calabaza en salsa y un vaso de zumo de fresa.
B: Lo siento. Hoy sólo servimos zanahorias asadas o zarzuela de mariscos.
A: ¿Y el zumo?
B: Solo tenemos zumo de manzana o cerveza.

CONCLUSION

Speaking activities should get the highest priority in class. Teachers have to be careful that they do not get so "bogged down" in "covering" material that they never get around to conducting communication activities. True, a lot of work has to go into the preparation of materials and the students for these types of activities, but the increased enjoyment and motivation of the students and the rapid growth of their speaking proficiency make it well worth it. Remember, oral proficiency is what the students expect gain from the class.

REFERENCES AND SUGGESTIONS FOR FURTHER READING

Brown, G., & Yule, G. (1983). *Teaching the spoken language.* Cambridge, England: Cambridge University Press. *Discusses theoretical and practical considerations in teaching speaking and listening, as well as ways of assessing these skills.*

Lyster, R., & Ranta, L. (1997). Corrective feedback and learner uptake: Negotiation of form in communicative classrooms. *Studies in Second Language Acquisition, 19,* 37-66. *Discusses six ways of responding to students' spoken errors, and the effectiveness of each type of response.*

North Carolina DPI, Second Languages Instructional Services. (2001). *Oral language assessment in the foreign language class (planning, conducting, managing): The possible dream.* Raleigh, NC: North Carolina State Dept. of Public Instruction. Retrieved from ERIC database. (ED454738) *Available online, this document contains many helpful examples of oral assessment tasks for students at different levels, along with examples of rubrics and checklists for assessment.*

Ur, P. (1981). *Discussions that work: Task-centred fluency practice.* Cambridge, England: Cambridge University Press. *Although geared toward teaching ESL, this little book is packed with great activities for pairs and small groups that can easily be adapted for foreign languages.*

General Methods Books that Address the Teaching of Oral Skills

Brandl, K. (2007). *Communicative language teaching in action: Putting principles to work.* Upper Saddle River, NJ: Pearson Prentice Hall.

Brown, H. D. (2006) *Principles of language learning and teaching* (4th ed.). Upper Saddle River, NJ: Pearson Longman.

Omaggio Hadley, A. (2001). *Teaching language in context* (3rd ed.). Boston, MA: Heinle & Heinle.

Shrum, J. L., & Glisan, E. W. (2009). *Teacher's handbook: Contextualized language instruction* (4th ed). Boston, MA: Heinle.

Other Books by James S. Taylor (see Appendix C for information)

- *Dilo con sabor*
- *Materiales para animar la clase de español*
- *Me gusta jugar*
- *Me gusta conversar*
- *Me gusta actuar*

Image Credits

p. 124: Ocal. (2007, Nov. 13). Chat Icon. *Clker.com.* Retrieved July 4, 2011 from http://www.clker.com/clipart-2312.html. Public domain.

p. 148: Gato Azul. (2006, Sept. 19). La Lotería. *Flickr.* Retrieved July 4, 2011 from http://www.flickr.com/photos/gatoazul/248757436/. Creative Commons attribution license.

p. 155: Raising hands. (n.d.). *Public Domain Clip Art.* Retrieved June 27, 2011 from http://www.pdclipart.org/displayimage.php?album=search&cat=0&pos=10. Public domain.

ACTIVITIES FOR METHODS CLASSES

1. Select a dialogue from a recent Spanish textbook and prepare a set of visuals you could use to teach it with total comprehension. Follow the models we have presented, with a picture for each line of dialogue. Teach the dialogue to a real class or practice with groups in the methods class.

2. Using the same visuals mentioned in #1 above, do an expansion and personalization exercise using the class or group you taught the dialogue.

3. Pick a Spanish grammar concept and select three different types of "focused practice" activities to practice the concept. Do the activities in a real class or in groups in the methods class.

4. Using the same Spanish grammar concept from #3 above, develop a communication activity that would practice that concept. Conduct the activity in a real class or in groups in the methods class.

5. Start a collection of conversational pictures taken from magazines. Keep them at least 8 x 11 in size, using typical topics. Or, prepare a PowerPoint presentation with images to teach vocabulary related to a specific topic. Show to your teacher.

6. Find a large picture with some basic situation and expand its context by adding more activities in the form of a "composite" or "collage" picture. Use it in teaching a micro lesson to members of the methods class.

7. Prepare and present a micro-lesson using an interpersonal communicative activity such as a role play, jigsaw or information gap activity, or pedagogical task activity.

8. In the methods class teach TPA or simulation you have chosen or possibly developed yourself.

9. In your teaching practicum, play a game, tell a story, do a play or skit, or demonstrate the ritual-procedure. Report to your methods professor.

10. Find a first-year student who is having trouble with Spanish pronunciation and help him or her improve his/her pronunciation. Hand in a report to your teacher.

11. Find a beginning or intermediate student who is weak in communication skills and tutor the student by practicing with him or her in oral activities once or twice a week. Hand in a report to your methods instructor.

12. Read one of the works on teaching speaking from the reference list at the end of the chapter. Write a short report summarizing what you learned.

CHAPTER EIGHT

WHAT HAVE YOU READ LATELY? READING FOR MEANING

YOUR OBJECTIVES FOR THIS CHAPTER ARE TO:

1. DISCUSS WHAT "READING FOR MEANING" MEANS.

2. EXPLAIN THE ROLE OF BACKGROUND KNOWLEDGE AND AUTHENTIC TEXTS IN THE TEACHING OF READING.

3. SELECT AND APPLY TECHNIQUES TO HELP STUDENTS DEVELOP READING PROFICIENCY IN BEGINNING AND INTERMEDIATE CLASSES.

4. IDENTIFY DIFFERENT TYPES OF READING MATERIALS THAT ARE AVAILABLE AND SELECT APPROPRIATE MATERIALS FOR EACH LEVEL.

5. SELECT READING MATERIALS THAT WILL BE OF INTEREST TO STUDENTS.

6. APPLY TECHNIQUES FOR TEACHING STUDENTS TO USE A DICTIONARY.

7. USE THE "APT MAPS GUIDE" TECHNIQUES EFFECTIVELY IN DEVELOPING PRE-, DURING-, AND POST-READING ACTIVITIES.

As Elizabeth stumbled and picked her way through the first sentences of the story they were reading out loud in class, Ed mentally calculated which paragraph he would be called on to translate. The professor always went down the rows, having each student translate a paragraph. Since there were three students between him and Elizabeth, Ed knew that he would have to do the fifth paragraph. Tuning out the comments the professor was making, Ed focused on the first words of the fifth paragraph:

Let's see now . . . first I need to find the subject . . . Great! It must be "conquistadores." . . . This time it was easy to spot, not hidden in the verb as it so often is. . . . Now for the verb . . . there it is . . . "avanzaron," an easy cognate word. . . . Let's see . . . -aron is a preterite ending, so this is "advanced" . . .

Now . . . the next word is "sin" . . ..I remember that one, the word that looks like some dirty deed, but it really means "without" . . .Who knows how it is pronounced . . . The next word is "miedo." . . . Whoops! I don't recognize that one . . . I'd better look it up in the dictionary . . .

Gosh, I hate this word-for-word decoding . . . I really wish I could have found the time to take a regular class and learned how to understand and speak the language . . . Maybe when I get the Ph.D. finished I can go back and learn the language in a way that will be interesting and useful.

~~~

Tom plopped into the armchair and reached for his backpack. The first book he pulled out was the latest science fiction thriller which he had started reading in biology class. It was really interesting, and he was tempted to continue reading, but he remembered his dad's threat: "Improve your grade in Spanish or no use of the car for a month!"

"I'd better do the Spanish reading assignment first," he thought. "Spanish is so easy to read that I'll make short work of it and then I can watch TV or finish the novel." He opened the graded reader to Chapter Two and began reading:

En la clase hay muchos alumnos. Dos alumnos son muy buenos amigos, Juan y María. Juan es americano. María es americana también. Juan tiene 13 años y María tiene 14 años. Juan está en el cuarto año de la escuela superior. María está en el cuarto año de la escuela superior también. Juan y María estudian español. En la clase de español no hablan inglés, hablan español. Hablan inglés en la clase de inglés.

Tom dropped the reader on the floor. "How boring," he yawned, and reached for his novel. In just a few seconds he was devouring page after page of his science fiction thriller.

CHAPTER EIGHT

WHAT HAVE YOU READ LATELY? READING FOR MEANING

> **Some books are to be tasted; others swallowed;**
> **and some few are to be chewed and digested.**
> **--Bacon**

Reading has traditionally been one of the principal objectives of foreign language study. Indeed, the major goal of the study of the classical languages, Greek and Latin, was to be able to *read* the great works of philosophy and literature of those languages. This tradition is very deeply seated in our profession and is still evident even in our days. As you read in Chapter Three, *What You Can Learn from the Past and Present*, during the 1920's and 1930's, the development of the reading skill was given a higher priority than any of the other skills. However, with the new emphasis placed on listening and speaking by the audio-lingual approach in the 1950's and 1960's, reading took a secondary role. In some audio-lingual procedures, reading was postponed or even withheld entirely, until several weeks into the program. Immediate reading from the first day of class was seen as a cause of poor pronunciation and was delayed until the students had developed strong pronunciation habits that would not be altered when seeing the written word. Audio-linguists insisted that since the reading skill is not difficult to develop, it would come along very naturally after good oral fluency and aural comprehension were established.

There are some theoreticians today who believe that since children learn their mother tongue before knowing how to read, we should follow the same pattern with second language learners and postpone the reading component because it would put an extra burden on the students to expect them to read and write as they begin learning a second language. They argue that each skill should be learned one at a time, starting with listening, progressing slowly to

speaking, and only much later moving to reading and writing.

While there is probably some truth in the aforementioned theories, we strongly believe that *all four skills can and ought to be learned simultaneously* because they are very interrelated and support each other. Reading and writing can be used very effectively to help develop the oral skills, and they are of extreme value in managing classes.

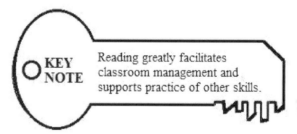

KEY NOTE Reading greatly facilitates classroom management and supports practice of other skills.

We indicated in Chapter Five that listening comprehension activities seemed to magically increase the language acquisition process. We are sure that reading has a similar magical quality. Appropriate reading assignments at all levels reinforce the students' speaking ability. Reading reinforces the acquisition of writing ability by providing a good model for students to follow. All four skills are necessary for progress in communication.

We should not confuse "reading for meaning" in a foreign language class with the process that children go through as they learn to read for the first time. Most of the techniques elementary school teachers use to teach children to read do not apply to students learning a second language. Normally, we do not have to go through the laborious and complex process of teaching them how to match sounds with graphic symbols. Unless we are teaching Spanish in preschool, a FLES or immersion program, our students *already* know how to read and write in their native tongue. (Students who learned Spanish as a heritage language may be an exception, as we will discuss in Chapter 16.) As

they study a second language they just transfer those skills to the second language. Generally speaking, the materials your students will be reading in your language class are not specifically contrived to teach sound-symbol correspondence, as they are in this Mafalda cartoon:

© Joaquín Salvador Lavado (QUINO) Toda Mafalda – Ediciones de La Flor,1993

Moreover, the older our students are, the more accustomed they are to using reading to learn new information. To ignore reading or deliberately to withhold it would be to deprive ourselves of a very effective tool in teaching the language.

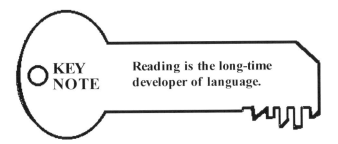

KEY NOTE — **Reading is the long-time developer of language.**

We also believe that reading in and of itself is a very desirable objective for our students. Reading is simply a different form of communication and can be a rich source of information and satisfaction as the student acquires a second language.

READING AND THE *STANDARDS FOR FOREIGN LANGUAGE LEARNING*

The *Standards* make reference to two different types of reading: interpersonal reading and interpretive reading. In **interpersonal** reading, students read and respond to messages from others through means such as letters,

dialogue journals, email, online chat rooms, and text messaging. This type of reading is two-way; the reader is in contact with the writer of the message, and is usually also a writer of return messages. If necessary, either party can ask the other for more information or clarification of the message.

The second type of reading is **interpretive** reading. In this case the author of the text is not present, and students must rely on their own knowledge and strategies in order to interpret the text. Examples of texts that usually involve interpretive reading are novels, short stories, newspaper and magazine articles, advertisements, owner's manuals, schedules, product labels, and recipes, among others. This chapter will be primarily concerned with teaching **interpretive** reading skills.

WHAT IS "READING FOR MEANING" IN A FOREIGN LANGUAGE COURSE?

In the most general sense, reading for meaning is what happens when readers look at a text and assign meaning to the written symbols in that text. The reader and the text are the two necessary ingredients; however, it is the **interaction** between the two that constitutes actual reading (Aebersold & Field, 1997). Comprehension occurs when there is a match between reader and text. The more the two have in common, the greater the reading comprehension. This implies that reading comprehension differs from one reader to another and from one text to another, even in our native language.

Background Knowledge and Schema Theory

To a great extent, the match between reader and text depends on the reader's background knowledge about the topic of the text, its genre, and its use of language. As you read in Chapter 6, readers possess three types of background knowledge or **schemata**: content schemata, formal schemata, and linguistic schemata. *Content schemata* contain our knowledge about the world and about specific topics. For example, readers of a story about a boy attending his uncle's funeral can compare it to their own knowledge about funerals in their culture; those who have attended a funeral or two will likely comprehend the text better than those who have not.

Formal schemata contain our knowlege about how specific text genres are organized. A newspaper article, for example, differs in structure from a short story or a an email message. News articles generally feature a headline; an introductory paragraph telling who, what, when, and where; additional paragraphs that provide details; and quotes from interviews with the people involved in the event. Readers who are familiar with this structure will have more success in reading news articles than those who are not.

Linguistic schemata contain our knowledge about words and how they fit together in sentences. As was the case with listening comprehension, the most important linguistic element for reading comprehenion is vocabulary. Readers see words but must recognize meaning from having seen or heard the words before. Grammar (morphology and syntax) is less crucial, but does play a role. Students must distinguish plurals from singulars, recognize the subject from the verb endings, be able to tell what a pronoun refers to from its form (*lo, la, los, las*), and so on.

Since the 1970s, a considerable number of studies have demonstrated the role of background knowledge and schemata in reading comprehension. One of the most important things teachers can do to promote reading

comprehension is to activate their students' background knowledge about the topic, genre, and language prior to having them read a specific text. If the students are unfamiliar with cultural topics or key vocabulary words in the text, teachers can conduct pre-reading activities to teach these concepts. Later in the chapter we will discuss ways of doing this.

The Process of Reading for Meaning

In the past there has been some disagreement among researchers as to whether reading is a **bottom-up** process or a **top-down** process. Advocates of the bottom-up theory argue that readers construct text by starting with the smallest units (letters, words, phrases) and progressing to larger ones (sentences, paragraphs, sections). They claim this process, which has sometimes been called **decoding,** becomes automatic so that readers are not aware of it.

Advocates of the top-down theory, on the other hand, claim that readers approach a text with a great deal of previous knowledge: knowledge about the topic, cultural knowledge, and expectations and assumptions about what they are reading. As they read, they fit the text into the knowledge they already possess, and are likely to keep reading as long as the text confirms their expectations.

Most researchers currently endorse an **interactive** theory of reading. They assert that reading involves both top-down and bottom-up processes, which take place either alternately or at the same time, depending on the reader's background knowledge, language proficiency, motivation, and other factors (Aebersold & Field, 1997). In our experience, beginning foreign language readers tend to over-rely on bottom-up strategies by attempting to decode every single word, forgetting that they don't understand every word even when reading in their native language. Teachers need to help students develop top-down reading strategies as well. Later in the chapter we will discuss some techniques for developing these strategies.

What are Ordinary, Daily Uses of Reading for Meaning?

Here are seven everyday reading activities that students should learn to accomplish:

1. Reading to practice and reinforce other language skills, such as speaking and listening comprehension: i.e., dialogues in written form, transcripts of audio recordings, TV shows, or films.
2. Reading instructions: how to complete written practice exercises, how to play a game, how to read TV schedules, what to do in an exam.
3. Reading for information: explanations of pictures, explanations in textbooks, histories, biographies, ads, announcements, programs, menus, timetables, names of buildings or stores, road signs, other signs—especially directions.
4. Reading for pleasure and amusement: humorous stories, cartoon captions, jokes, comic strips.
5. Reading correspondence: personal and business letters, notes from the teacher or a classmate, emails, blogs, posts on social networking websites.
6. Reading for news: newspapers, magazines, online news sources.
7. Reading longer selections for enjoyment and excitement: novels, short stories, poems, plays.

IN A SPANISH COURSE WE READ:
1. TO PRACTICE AND ASSIMILATE THE LANGUAGE
2. FOR INFORMATION
3. FOR PLEASURE AND ENJOYMENT

Four reading techniques. As we go from reading easy to difficult materials, we use four techniques: we **scan,** that is, we look quickly through a passage or a list for specific information (telephone book, classified ads, menus, etc.), we **skim,** that is, we look quickly through a passage for the main idea or the general gist, we read **extensively**, that is, we read fairly large amounts for main ideas and for pleasure but do not pay close attention to details, and we read **intensively**, that is, we read for complete understanding while savoring every aspect of a literary work, sometimes reading out loud, or reading for crucial information when applying for a job, or when studying a text in physics or chemistry or another subject.

There is considerable disagreement among researchers as to whether reading is a decoding process that is dependent on language ability or whether it is a system of processing and organizational skills. We suggest that you can have your cake and eat it too. Through reading *extensively* at one level, students can process and organize and absorb vocabulary and grammar at each level. Through reading *intensively* with the teacher's help and checking the words and expressions, the students practice a more formal, decoding-type skill and use the language and grammar in the process.

Reading: Developer of the other skills. The four techniques of reading (skimming, scanning, extensive reading and intensive reading) serve the direct purpose of developing the major skill of reading, but we certainly shouldn't overlook the support function reading provides to the other major skills. For example, it can provide background to insure comprehension of listening opportunities. It can provide content for speaking and writing activities. It can increase comprehension and use of language after experience in the other skills. It can provide constant opportunities for increasing our ability in the language.

Reading has an important role in the acquisition of language process—getting the language in the bones and tissues. It is necessary to plan for lots of reading experience on the cutting edge of our language learning as well as easy enjoyable reading. Students can progress from pictures alone to pictures with words—signs on buildings, signs in the streets, to advertisements with high frequency vocabulary and expressions, to short paragraph materials in handouts and readers, to the real-life world of pamphlets, books, newspapers, magazines, and others at all kinds of levels of difficulty—from general interest to specific use. We are interested in the intertwining of all the major skills or modalities of language learning so we need to plan for reading from day one.

Objectives for Reading

To get a better idea of what our reading objectives are, let's examine the ACTFL Guidelines. With the reading skill we expect beginning classes to reach the *intermediate level,* and intermediate classes to reach the *advanced level* as described in these guidelines. Advanced classes should easily surpass the *advanced level* and move well into the *superior level.* We will discuss reading in advanced classes in Chapter 14. More complete versions of the Guidelines are in the Appendix where you can study them with more care. The following is a condensed summary of the first three levels.

Novice. Able to recognize the symbols of an alphabetic and/or syllabic writing system and/or a limited number of characters in a system that uses characters. The reader can identify an increasing number of highly contextualized words and/or phrases including cognates and borrowed words, where appropriate. Material understood rarely exceeds a single phrase at a time, and rereading may be required.

Intermediate. Able to read consistently with increased understanding simple connected texts dealing with a variety of basic and social needs. Such texts are still linguistically noncomplex and have a clear underlying internal structure. They impart basic information about which the reader has to make minimal suppositions and to which the reader brings personal interest and/or knowledge. Examples may include short, straightforward descriptions of person, places, and things written for a wide audience.

Advanced. Able to read somewhat longer prose of several paragraphs in length, particularly if presented with a clear underlying structure. The prose is predominantly in familiar sentence patterns. Reader gets the main ideas and facts and misses some details. Comprehension derives not only from situational and subject matter knowledge but from increasing control of the language. Texts as this level include descriptions and narrations such as simple short stories, new items, bibliographical information, social notices, personal correspondence, routinized business letters and simple technical material written for the general reader.

Outline of Reading Progression. Reading, a receptive skill like listening, allows for fast progress in Spanish. Native English-speaking students usually can read already in their native language, and the early experiences of sound-symbol connections are learned rapidly in Spanish, a much more phonetic language than English. We will illustrate progression through the ACTFL levels with the following graphic (patterned after our model for a "comprehensive approach"). You will note from the graphic that reading can be accomplished much faster than the corresponding levels for speaking and listening.

The reading goals for the novice level of proficiency can be accomplished in a very few weeks—probably three. For this reason (and following the *ACTFL Proficiency Guidelines* and various *State Curriculum Guides*), we suggest that beginning courses strive to reach the proficiency level of *intermediate*, intermediate courses try to reach the *advanced* level of proficiency, and advanced courses should be able to reach the *superior* level of proficiency. We have included all levels in the graphic, but we will discuss advanced classes (*superior levels*) in more detail in Chapter 14.

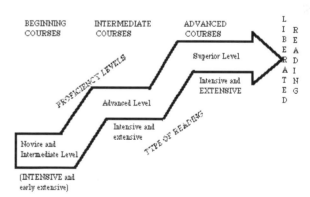

These are approximate correspondences and indicate considerable experience and mastery of the content, tasks (functions), and accuracy, all in reading. There might be a few students who won't achieve the goal indicated and there will be quite a few students who will achieve a higher status—even two levels higher—especially if they spend some time in a Hispanic country and, above all, if they do a lot of reading. The objectives they will achieve are best laid out in terms of the proficiency wanted and needed.

Description of Proficiency Levels

Let's now look at the proficiency levels in greater depth, considering content, functions, and topics.

Novice. The content objectives at this level include such **topics** as these: 1) objects in the classroom and in the home, 2) family members, 3) clothing, 4) colors, 5) numbers, 6) telling time, 7) dates, 8) self identification, 9) weather/seasons, 10) simple greetings and courtesy expressions and others.

The **functions** that we emphasize at the novice level are: 1) that the students can connect the sounds and the symbols—no problem in Spanish which is phonetic and which uses the same alphabet as English (with the addition of some writing conventions such as the accent marks and inverted question marks), 2) that the students can pick out main ideas and key words when reading familiar material, and that the students can read recombined short narratives and dialogues using familiar memorized materials. As far as reading is concerned, the novice level can be treated adequately in the first few weeks (perhaps three) and then merged with the intermediate level.

Intermediate. The content at the intermediate level includes such **topics** as: 1) **home:** messages, names, letters, mealtimes, health, newspaper headlines, personal biography, invitations, parties, etc.; 2) **community and travel:** restaurants, transportation, shopping, purchases, lodging, money, post office, customs, meeting arrangements, etc.; 3) **narrations**, all kinds of familiar topics; and 4) **schedules, forms, tables, memos, ads, labels, menus, and instructions.** Topics like these and many others are supplied by most textbook authors in recent textbooks.

The **functions** at the intermediate level indicate that the students will be able to: 1) get the main gist, and 2) get key ideas and some supporting detail. This proficiency is usually achieved in the first year of college Spanish or in the first two years of Spanish in the secondary schools. If they have been reading a lot and have

had experience in Spanish-speaking areas during this time, students may show signs of being able to handle advanced reading—especially in the last part of their beginning courses. Help them to have advanced experience.

Advanced. The functions or tasks expected of students at the advanced level are the following: 1) understand main ideas and most supporting details of factual narrations and descriptions; 2) understand abstract topics in a familiar context; and 3) understand descriptions and narrations of factual material and nontechnical prose. Students can now start to read the topics in the advanced list which has now become very inclusive: Narratives, newspaper accounts, instructions, directions, routines, reports, current events, politics, economics, education, leisure, history, customs, etc.

DEVELOPING READING PROFICIENCY

Reading materials can vary tremendously in levels of difficulty, from simple narrations or conversations to complex philosophical treatises. It will be of vital concern to language teachers to select reading materials appropriate to the level of their students. And we must not overlook the students in this process; they naturally want to read things which are of interest to them. We will have to consider the interest and motivational attraction of whatever reading materials we are planning to use. Usually teachers rely on the basic textbook program, but as we indicated in the chapter on planning, often the teachers have a course-syllabus that drives the course content. As you consider the goals and priorities for the course, look at the textbook and its accompanying workbooks and materials as well as your repertoire of materials to be sure you are prepared. Many textbooks do not contain enough reading, especially at the beginning levels. Therefore, we need to be concerned with appropriate supplementary reading materials. The students need lots of practice in reading using all four techniques.

Finding Supplementary Reading Materials

Readers. Over 100 years ago the first word-frequency study was started. Soon the effort was made to prepare reading books, referred to as "readers," that would use high-frequency words exclusively—especially since the Modern Language Study issued the mandate that foreign language classes emphasize reading proficiency, and that they accomplish that goal in two year's time. "Graded readers" were the result. Readers that tried to include only words in the frequency lists of each level were boring and artificial. At the novice level they could be described as "chloroform in print." Another Mafalda cartoon will illustrate the point here:

© Joaquín Salvador Lavado (QUINO) Toda Mafalda – Ediciones de La Flor, 1993

More recently, agencies trying to foster the study of Spanish have encouraged publishers to produce collections of fun reading materials, especially on beginning levels of proficiency and continuing up through higher ability levels. Therefore, there are many good supplementary materials available through the major publishers and importers. Publishers in the USA are now providing abundant reading material that is colorful, pictorial, and graded through several levels. Many of the new textbook programs include much more reading in their textbooks and ancillaries, both as main reading texts and supplementary reading materials with lots of color and pictures and topic-variety. Classroom sets of some of these materials from publishers in the USA are suggested. Many teachers have purchased five to ten copies of three or more different readers at the same level rather than thirty or more copies of one reader. This makes for an interesting variety in the reading.

Authentic texts. Nowadays the buzzword in the selection of reading materials is **authentic.** *Authentic texts* are those that are not specifically prepared for the purpose of language learning. They usually come directly from the target language environment and are written *by* native speakers *for* native speakers. Examples of authentic texts include children's and adolescent books written for native speakers; magazines and newspapers from Spanish-speaking countries and from Latino communities in the U.S.; tourist brochures from Spanish-speaking areas, either in hard copy or online; informative texts from the Spanish-language version of Wikipedia or similar websites; and excerpts from blogs, wikis, and social networking websites. Examples of some of these texts are shown in the pages that follow.

Authentic texts have certain advantages over simplified texts prepared for students. Research has shown that in some cases, students actually understand authentic texts better than simplified ones because the authentic texts are in familiar formats (advertisements, articles, web pages, etc.) and contain contextual clues such as pictures, captions, and subheadings. In addition, these texts are culturally authentic, providing opportunities for cross-cultural comparisons as advocated by the *Standards for Foreign Language Learning.* It can be highly motivating for students to know that they are able to construct meaning from a text intended for native speakers of the target language.

Samples of Authentic Texts

Following are some examples of authentic or semi-authentic texts that you could project onto a screen or possibly make copies for your students to read and discuss.

1. *Maps or pictures with descriptions or cultural information:*

La **catedral de Granada** *muestra un impresionante interior con un grandioso retablo y varias capillas. En su cámara sepulcral se hallan los sepulcros de los Reyes Católicos.*

2. *Cute or "fluffy" kinds of things that attract interest: poems, rhymes, proverbs, jokes.* Below are a few examples; many more can be found in the booklet *Materiales para animar la clase de español* (see Appendix C for information).

Aunque la mona se vista de seda, mona se queda.

--¿Qué es un moño?
--Un añimalito que come bañañas.

Con paciencia y saliva, al elefante se comió la hormiga.

En el tribunal
Juez: ¿Qué edad tiene Ud., señora?
Señora: Cuento veinticinco años.
Juez: ¿Y cuántos no cuenta Ud.?

Erre con erre cigarro
Erre con erre barril
Rápido corren los carros
Cargando las cargas del ferrocarril

--¿Qué hace la vaca cuando se levanta?
--Sombra.

3. Funny anecdotes or motivational stories.

EL CONTRABANDISTA
(From *Me gusta aprender español*)

El señor Martínez es inspector de aduanas y trabaja en la frontera entre España y Francia.
Todos los sábados un señor gordo cruza la frontera montado en un burro. Siempre hay bolsas en el burro. El señor Martínez sospecha que el señor gordo es contrabandista, pero cada vez que inspecciona las bolsas, no encuentra nada.

Muchos años después, el señor Martínez ve al hombre gordo en un bar. Le dice:
—Ya no soy inspector de aduanas. Ya no le puedo hacer nada. Dígame una cosa. Usted es contrabandista, ¿no?
—Claro—contesta el señor gordo.
—Pero, ¿qué lleva usted de contrabando? Yo nunca pude encontrar nada.
—Burros—responde el señor gordo.

---

4. Fairy tales and children's stories.

CAPERUCITA ROJA - Un Drama
(From *Me gusta aprender español*)

Narrador: Caperucita Roja vive con su mamá en una casita al lado de un bosque. Siempre lleva una caperuza de color rojo (un regalo de su abuela) y por eso todos la llaman "Caperucita Roja". Un día de primavera su madre prepara unas cosas para la abuela que vive al otro lado del bosque.
(En la casa de Caperucita Roja)
Mamá: ¡Caperucita Roja! ¡Caperucita Roja! ¡Ven!
Caperucita Roja: Ya voy, mamá. ¿Qué quieres?
Mamá: Tu abuela está muy enferma. ¿Puedes llevarle esta cesta de fruta?
Caperucita Roja: Sí, mamá.
Mamá: Y no le cuentes esos chistotes de elefantes.
Caperucita Roja: ¡No, mamita!
Mamá: Pero ten cuidado, hay un lobo feroz que vive en el bosque.
Caperucita Roja: Bueno, mamá. Voy a tener cuidado.
(Toma el cesto de la mamá, le da un besito y se va.)
Mamá: Adiós hijita.
Caperucita Roja: Adiosito.
(La madre sale y Caperucita Roja se va por el camino.)
Caperucita Roja: (Canta una melodía.) La, la, la. La, la, la... ¡Ay! ¡Qué flores más bonitas! Voy a recoger unas para la abuelita.
(Coge las flores y va acercándose más y más al bosque. Se ve el lobo malo entre los árboles.)
Lobo: ¡Qué hambre tengo!

---

5. *Signs, directions, billboards.*

6. *Articles from newspapers, magazines, or online news sources.* The best types of articles are those that deal with topics of interest to young people. These could include stories about famous singers, actors, or athletes that young people might look up to; current TV shows or movies; or new technological gadgets and games. Of course you should also look for articles about themes that you are currently studying, such as music, art, food, or travel.

7. *Advertisements from newspapers, magazines, or the Internet.* Most ads contain images as well as text. Together, images and text can convey more information than either could alone, enhancing students' comprehension of the message. In addition, advertisements often reflect hidden cultural perspectives. For example, a comparison we once made of car ads from the U.S. and Mexico revealed that the U.S. ads featured themes of individuality and ruggedness, often showing a lone driver in the car, whereas the Mexican ads generally depicted couples, children, or friends (one was captioned "*Espacio para toda la familia.*").

8. *Authentic comic strips, or well-known American comic strips translated into Spanish.* Comic strips from Spanish-speaking countries, such as the Mafalda strips shown earlier in this chapter, are often full of cultural references. On the other hand, American comics translated into Spanish, while lacking Hispanic cultural information, can also be useful due to students' familiarity with them.

We have not included examples of these last three categories due to copyright issues. The use of authentic texts, especially those obtained online, raises copyright questions that you will need to deal with as a teacher. We will discuss these issues later in this section.

Selecting reading materials. As you select supplementary materials for use in your class, follow some guidelines such as the following:

1. Are they within the range of your students' vocabulary and grammatical abilities?
2. Will they be of interest to your students? Do they go beyond the "See Dick, see Dick run, run, Dick, run" mentality? Do they contain

topics that will be of interest at the age level of your students?
3. Do they contain information that will help your students understand the cultural background of the Hispanic world?

Reading shelf/table. Many foreign language text companies publish or import reading materials. You can write for catalogs and descriptions of materials. It would be too large a job to list all the readers that are available; so we recommend that teachers look through the catalogues for suitable readers. When attending language conventions and other professional meetings—especially the annual state convention—be sure you go to the book and material exhibits and look through as many of the offerings as possible so you can make a wise choice of the ones for your classroom. Remember that you should get a few books of many series rather than classroom sets of just a few readers.

If your teaching situation allows it, set up a reading table and shelves in some area of your classroom where you can have a collection of books, magazines, newspapers, comic books, novels, short stories, Spanish translations of classic English reading materials, etc. Doing so will put materials appealing to anyone's interest in the reach of your students. Encourage students who arrive early to class, or who finish their work early, to spend time reading.

Two kinds of reading practice. Teachers must afford the students ample reading practice at each level and also help them to progress to more involved reading and make sure the students are reading as rapidly as they can for the type of reading involved (four techniques).

As you move to intermediate and advanced classes you should be aware of *vertical* and *horizontal* reading. No, we are not talking about physical positions while reading, we are talking about the kind of practice reading that must take place in order to make progress. **Vertical** reading refers to a constant moving upward to more difficult levels. Constant emphasis on vertical reading will probably result in decoding procedures and glossary practice or "reading with their thumb," that is, constantly looking up words and expressions throughout the students' reading development.

We recommend that students also do some **horizontal** reading, that is, reading considerable material at one specific level, before proceeding vertically. With so many readers available at each level, it is quite manageable to have the students read for enjoyment and understanding on one level before going on to the next vertical level. There is a caution that must be indicated at this point. We have known teachers who have stayed too long at the novice level—and for that matter, too long at each level.

The art of teaching reading lies in knowing how to balance the vertical and the horizontal reading. Help the student to have a "feel" for this balance. If you have an extensive collection of all kinds of readers at various levels arranged in groups of three to six booklets of each series instead of 20 to 30 books of only one series, the

variety is enticing and allows for this rough rule of procedure: read various booklets at the same level until you can read about a page a minute with quite good comprehension—the student knows the difference between 1) reading with understanding and 2) "decoding." The readers generally have been chosen on the basis of various **word frequency lists** as well as **interest**, and therefore they have a similar vocabulary with just a few glossed words in the margins. The students can be given the opportunity to read extensively fairly early in their experience and this process will be motivating. You label the shelves as to level of difficulty and give students the chance to experiment with the rough rule of procedure (the minute-per-page goal).

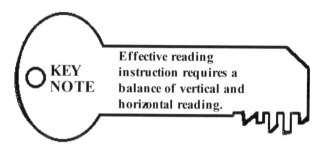

KEY NOTE

Effective reading instruction requires a balance of vertical and horizontal reading.

With enough practice in all these experiences, students will eventually learn to look at a text and determine, usually automatically, which of the four techniques of reading is involved and do it. Even beginning students need practice with all four techniques of reading.

Copyright Issues for Teachers

As mentioned previously, teachers need to be aware of certain copyright restrictions on authentic texts that they obtain from magazines, newspapers, or online sources. Fortunately, U.S. copyright law contains a provision for "Fair Use" that allow teachers to use and reproduce copyrighted works in nonprofit educational settings, subject to certain restrictions, without seeking prior permission from the copyright owner.

Rather than providing clear and direct answers about what constitutes "fair use" in specific situations, the law expects users of copyrighted materials to make their own "reasoned analysis" based on four factors. The Brigham Young University Copyright Licencing Office (http://lib.byu.edu/departs/copyright/) provides a series of helpful tutorials as well as a brief manual explaining these factors. Another useful resource is "A Teacher's Guide to Fair Use and Copyright" (http://home.earthlink.net/~cnew/research.htm). If, after consulting these resources, you have any doubt about the legality of using specific copyrighted materials, and especially if you plan to make copies of them for students or to post them online, it's best to check with your school district. Districts often have their own copyright policies and will provide assistance to teachers in dealing with these issues.

Although it is beyond the scope of this book to offer legal advice about specific copyright issues, you should be aware of the following:

- Avoid copying large amounts of materials to substitute the purchase of books or periodicals, as this violates the principles of fair use.
- Avoid making copies of materials that are intended to be "consumable," such as student workbooks or test booklets.
- When using copyrighted materials of any type, be sure to credit the sources and display the copyright notice © and copyright ownership information if shown in the original source.
- Teachers and students should exercise caution when using digital materials downloaded from the Internet in producing their own multimedia projects for posting online, as some of these materials may be protected by copyright. Safe alternatives are to use only materials that are specifically labeled as being in the public domain (such as many of the images on Wikipedia), images from sites such as Stock.XCHNG (http://www.sxc.hu/), or materials that have a Creative Commons license (see http://creativecommons.org/ for more information).

USING THE *APT MAPS GUIDE* PRINCIPLE IN DEVELOPING READING

As you work with specific reading assignments with the entire class, you should always be guided by certain principles. Remember the principles we discussed in Chapter 5 on listening comprehension. Those same principles apply to developing reading skill. You will recall the acronym we invented to help you remember these principles, *APT MAPS GUIDE.* The principles are as follows:

A
P　Advance Preparation by the Teacher
T

M
A　Motivation and Advance
P　Preparation of the Students
S

G　Get them speaking the Language
U　Use the language
I　Interact
D　Discuss
E　Evaluate

Let's look at these principles as they apply to teaching reading skills.

Advanced Preparation by the Teacher

You cannot simply send the students home to read an assignment you haven't read yourself. You must read the assignment very carefully several days in advance and then make plans for the preparation of the students. You will often have to prepare visual aids, do some cultural research, and plan activities.

Motivation and Advanced Preparation of the Students

Without a doubt, the most important phase of a reading lesson is the pre-reading stage. The teacher's approach to pre-reading activities can greatly influence students' success with reading assignments. Prior to working with the actual reading materials, the teacher should help activate the students' background knowledge about the topic, text type or genre, and the language involved. If necessary, teachers can also prepare students with the key vocabulary and cultural and facts necessary to be able to comprehend what they are reading about. Students can also be given suggestions as to what they should be looking for and what things are important. They can be asked to watch for examples of humor, descriptions of a region, personality of some of the characters, and so on.

The teacher must arouse interest in the students such that they are eager to begin work with the material. By giving them some indication of what the material is about (without revealing the plot) and letting them know how interesting it is going to be, you can motivate them to the point that they can hardly wait to begin reading.

Ideas for pre-reading activities. Following are some possible ways of preparing students to read a particular text.

- Ask students what they know about the topic; brainstorm as a class or in small groups
- Brainstorm words and expressions related to the topic, and teach key terms that students don't already know
- Help students recall what they know about the genre (for example, how a newspaper article or short story is organized)
- Make predictions about the content of the text (topics, theme, plot, etc.)
- For narratives, introduce the setting and characters and possibly preview the plot
- Examine features of the text that may aid comprehension (title, subheadings, graphics, different styles of print, etc.)
- Review or teach relevant cultural information
- Preview segments of the text (read the introduction or conclusion, the first sentence of each paragraph, skim for main ideas, scan for specific information)

One word of caution: Some teachers and textbooks present students with lists of unrelated vocabulary words that they will encounter in the text, absent from any context. Experience has shown that students often don't remember these words when they encounter them in the text. A better approach is to brainstorm or teach only key words that are related to the topic and are necessary for comprehension, and to present them in the context of a mini-discussion or preview of the text. Don't worry about unfamiliar words that aren't related to the topic or that appear only infrequently; teach students to gloss over these words or guess their meanings from the context.

Get them Speaking, Use the Language, Interact, Discuss, Evaluate

Post-reading activities serve several purposes. They can hold students accountable for the reading and assess their comprehension. They can solidify and deepen students' understanding of the text. They can also provide a chance for students to use the vocabulary and ideas they have encountered in the text by discussing or acting out its content.

Accountability and evaluation. When the entire class is working on a given reading assignment, they must be aware that they will be held accountable for having read the selection. There is nothing more frustrating to a teacher than to come to a class ready to discuss a reading selection only to find that no one has read it. One way to hold students accountable, and at the same time assess their comprehension of the reading, is to give them a reading quiz at the beginning of the discussion activity. The quiz can consist of simple questions or be of the true-false type. In a true-false quiz you might extend the process by having them change false statements to true, or indicate why the statements are true or false. Quizzes may also take on a role-playing flavor, they may take place in panel discussions, they may take place as a result of brainstorming sessions or buzz sessions culminating in a report to the class; in short, the tests and quizzes can be in disguise but result in your being able to evaluate and grade them. Above all, we want to be sure our students want to read and that they learn to appreciate good literature in the process. Other ways of holding students accountable for reading and assessing their comprehension might be to have students write a summary of what the reading was about or hand in a short "impressions" paper.

Ideas for post-reading activities. Besides assessing students' reading comprehension, post-reading activities can provide an opportunity to deepen students' understanding of the text and reinforce language learning. Post-reading activities should focus first on "big-picture" issues related to students' global understanding of the text. This type of activity helps students develop top-down reading skills. Teachers can ask students to:

- Identify the topic and/or theme
- Describe the characters (for narrative texts)
- Identify main ideas and supporting ideas (for expository texts)
- Order or sequence information or events from the text

After focusing on global issues, activities can focus on specific information from the text in order to develop bottom-up reading skills. Teachers can have students:

- Answer "wh" questions (who, what, when, where, why, how)
- Scan for specific information or categories of information
- Fill in a chart or outline of the text
- Work in groups to create questions based on the text (to "stump" other groups)

Teachers can also capitalize on the text as a source of linguistic and cultural information. Students can be asked to:

- Look for cognates
- Look for particular grammar points (verb tenses, adjectives, etc.)
- Identify transition words used (además, sin embargo, por lo tanto, etc.)
- Recognize figurative language (similes, metaphors, personification, etc.)
- Focus on sociolinguistic features of language (regionalisms, use of tú and Ud., etc.)
- Focus on cultural elements of the text

Finally, and most importantly, teachers need to help students synthesize what they have learned from the reading experience. Activities at this stage can help students relate the reading back to its original purpose as well as transfer what they have learned to other skills and settings (reading other texts, speaking, writing). Possible activities at this stage include:

- Discuss the author's purpose for writing
- Evaluate the author's success in conveying his or her message
- Act out parts of the text
- Participate in a debate on the topic

- Discuss students' reaction to the text, as well as how their ideas or feelings may have changed as a result of reading
- Read other texts about the same topic or in the same genre

Reading to write. Reading reinforces the acquisition of writing ability by providing a good model for students to follow as well as the opportunity to assimilate vocabulary and idiomatic expressions. Just as high school English teachers assign their students to write about what they have read, foreign language teachers can use reading as a springboard for writing. Among other possibilities, teachers can have their students:

- Write their reactions to the reading
- Rewrite the ending to a story
- Rewrite a story from another character's point of view
- Write an opinion paper or persuasive paper based on the reading

Additional ideas for "reading to write" will be discussed in Chapter 9.

TECHNIQUES FOR TEACHING READING AT DIFFERENT PROFICIENCY LEVELS

As we discuss ideas and activities for teaching reading at beginning and intermediate levels, we will introduce each section with the corresponding segment of the graphic that we presented earlier in this chapter.

Reading at the Novice Level

Reading in the first two years of Spanish in the schools is divided into two proficiency levels: novice and intermediate. [You know that a few might not make it and that many may achieve the advanced level.]

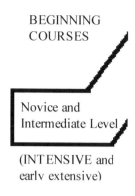

BEGINNING
COURSES

Novice and
Intermediate Level

(INTENSIVE and
early extensive)

NOVICE

Generally the emphasis in this level at first is on listening and speaking activities and on building a large recognition vocabulary. These activities can offer some opportunities for early reading experiences from day one on. The startup, the dialogue, vocabulary presentation through many pictures and TPR, association activities, brainstorming activities, interview activities, priming for listening to audio recordings, priming for viewing videos, and priming for reading special selections all comprise a majority of the activities in the early stages of beginning classes. With each of these activities, you can help students to experience **elementary, early reading** as part of their language acquisition experience. Most of these follow the same sequence, but the separate descriptions will help you use the ideas as a checklist.

Activities and Ideas for Encouraging Reading at the Novice Level

Pictures—vocabulary building. In the early days of the course when you are concentrating on giving the student lots of listening comprehension experience and at the same time developing an extensive vocabulary by giving a message about each picture, there is a little trick that can help the students with their reading from day one; write important new vocabulary on the board while you are presenting it orally in context (a message). The picture itself is kind of very basic pre-reading experience. As you give your message, write the important words—the new vocabulary—on the board. Feel free to fill the board with these words, and encourage the students to take notes. Early in the course this experience will serve as a reading experience

priming and will help cement the learning. We know that eye vision plus note taking (picture and words written down) will help the students remember more, will help them to make the sound symbol connections, will let them read the key words in Spanish, and will give them enough cognition time to get the words in the bones and in the tissues. Incidentally, it will also help them to learn to write in Spanish.

Rather often you should show the students that certain function words are important by writing them down: for example, the uses of *que* and prepositions (such as *por, de, en, sin,* etc.), and adverbs (such as *muy, donde, cuando,* etc.).

Dialogues. We have pointed out that most textbooks contain numerous dialogues. In introducing the dialogue, you will at first concentrate on listening comprehension and oral activities. Key words from the dialogue written on the board are an extension of the picture approach given above so reading can be a part of the priming activities for dialogue learning. After the initial oral presentation, the students can see the dialogue in its written form. Since the dialogue appears in the text, visual access to it is very easy. It is important to assure yourself and the students that they can indeed read the dialogue—even separate words. The usual approach is to read the original dialogue as a first experience and later read recombinations. Often the workbook will have recombinations of the dialogue in narrative form for a variation in easy reading. If you try writing your own versions of recombination narratives, be sure you check these with trained native speakers to avoid errors creeping in. It is better if you find *readers* (books or booklets) that have done this for you already. A variety of reading activities in connection with the dialogue is important.

The startup—especially the preamble. Scripts or notes for various parts of the startup can be provided and serve as an easy reading experience. The preamble is a listening comprehension opportunity for the students to hear from the teacher, from a visitor, or from a fellow student—some particular anecdote or real-life experience that should catch their attention and be interesting. It is usually oral, but you can give concurrent reading experience by writing key words on the board. A typewritten handout taken from an audio recording can be provided for subsequent reading experience. Portions of any audio or video material used as a preamble can be typed up to provide reading opportunities.

Brainstorming. In the beginning days of the course, you may need to play the role of oral dictionary while the students brainstorm expressions that they need to use to prime themselves for some activity or to be able to talk about a special theme. Again, the system of writing words on the board along with brainstorming can afford early reading experience; plus, a script of the brainstorming can be prepared as a handout for supplementary reading experience.

The interview. This is an activity that can be used every day in class and is set up to afford students the chance to speak with someone about a variety of themes throughout the course. The usual procedure is to give the student a handout with the main ingredients of the interview given, but with key expressions left blank. This handout is a reading opportunity. An audio recording or a video recording of the interviews can be made; then some students can be assigned to provide a script of the interviews (a writing assignment), resulting in scripts for follow-up reading.

TPR activity can be made into a reading assignment by preparing 3 x 5 cards with the commands or directed dialogue possibilities typed on them for use in-group activities or for use in total class activities.

Association activities are set up to have pictures or objects or activities linked with persons in the class or groups in the class. Because of these associations, language sticks to us better. Instructions can be written to the groups to conduct these activities, thus making it a reading assignment. Of course any activity can be written up in the class minutes to be duplicated for reading aloud to the class or to be read individually.

Pre-listening activities for audio–recordings or videos can be written as instruction on 3 x 5 cards so that students can refer to them in the language lab or at home, allowing some additional easy reading.

Textbook reading selections in the early units are usually based on the kinds of topics that are being treated in the listening and speaking activities of each unit or chapter. Hispanic geography with a map is a very good topic for a reading selection with the first unit. Another good possibility is a short letter. **No single textbook program, to our knowledge, contains enough material for extensive reading. Supplementing is necessary to all.** As a teacher of Spanish, you have several textbooks and several readers from various publishers in your personal reference library so you can use them to prepare daily handouts for reading assignments— especially for early extensive reading.

Reading longer selections. Even in beginning courses, longer selections are possible for extensive reading, especially the type we call horizontal readings. **Interest and variety promote this kind of reading.** Most reading selections in textbooks are culturally oriented and by and large are not too interesting. We suggest that there are many possibilities for interesting reading including anecdotes, adventure stories, jokes, poetry, letters, songs, diaries, folk tales, even fairy tales, speeches, human interest stories, newspaper articles, and many others. The students need to feel that they can identify with these selections and that they can personalize them. This makes the discussing of these selections much easier and much more exciting. Various techniques such as restating and paraphrasing can be employed. See the suggestions for further reading for examples of these longer selections.

Toward Intermediate Proficiency

Early Extensive Reading. More and more lately, we are pushing the extensive reading opportunities back toward the beginning of the course. This gets the students started earlier with the process of inferring meaning and of intelligent guessing in reading much akin to what we expect of them in listening comprehension. We recommend giving them some longer passages earlier for out of class reading or for special in-class reading periods (especially in the schools with 95 minute class periods).

Every day there must be a reading assignment—preferably a take-home assignment. Reading in Spanish is not too different from reading in English—especially after the orientation weeks. Just remember to give some hints to prime the students so there won't be any real surprises. After all, you have been building an extensive recognition vocabulary that should be helpful in reading. Continue to give hints in vocabulary orally as part of the regular work of the class. Hints in grammar can be given well in advance of the actual treatment in the course, because reading doesn't require oral mastery of the grammar. A simple comment that *el, la, los, las* are all words for *the* might be given for a reading hint in the first week of the course.

The *tres pasos* approach. A technique that is effective with all extensive reading, especially early extensive reading, is the ***tres pasos*** approach. Instruct the students to make it a part of every reading assignment, especially take-home reading tasks.

Paso 1. Skim through the passage for the main idea. Use your present knowledge and experience to guess at or to figure out the main idea.

Paso 2. Go through the passage again guessing the meaning of as many words as possible and looking up only a few key words. [Clarify how important it is to guess intelligently at the meanings, to be content with uncertainty, and yet to get the meaning—the teacher's selection or the textbook selection of suitable passages will make this easier.]

Paso 3. After a short incubation period (at least an hour—preferably a few hours), speed read the passage again. There should be a good deal of satisfaction in this third step for the student.

If there is any *spot commercial* that is important, it is the one on ***los tres pasos***; make it your best selling job.

The next day the reading experience with the above three steps should be followed up in class. During the group activities, brainstorm *¿Qué han leído? ¿Qué hay de interés? Escribamos una lista...* and then report as groups to the whole class; the whole activity takes about seven to ten minutes.

Discourage the writing of English between the lines in any textbook or reader or in any handout for reading purposes. Teach your students to write their notes elsewhere. Avoid at all costs anything resembling an inter-linear translation. English written in the textbook becomes a crutch, a point of reference that is always referred to, and used to avoid the internalizing of the Spanish word or expression.

Intermediate Classes

As students move to the intermediate level they should begin to do more and more extensive reading, that is, they will begin to read strictly for content and enjoyment, and pay less attention to vocabulary and language structure. The material they will read will be much longer as they tackle short stories, plays, and even novels.

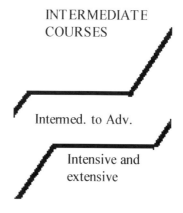

INTERMEDIATE COURSES

Intermed. to Adv.

Intensive and extensive

This new emphasis means that students will have to greatly increase their reading speed. They will simply not have time to move slowly through the materials. There will, of course, be many, many words that are new to them. They must learn to do as they do in English, ***read without their thumb***.

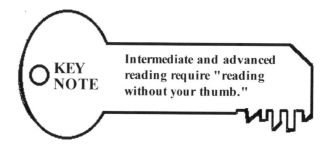

KEY NOTE

Intermediate and advanced reading require "reading without your thumb."

How to read without your thumb. To read without your thumb simply means you should not be using your thumb to look up every word you don't recognize. Instead, you use the following techniques, and look up the word as a last resort, and after you have determined that you need to know its exact meaning. Study the following steps:

1. Read to end of a line, or paragraph. When you come upon a new word, don't stop yet to try to decide what it means, keep going until you reach the end of the line or paragraph. This will give you more context and more information to work with.

2. Tolerate some vagueness. Usually you won't need to know the exact meaning of the word. If you have a vague idea of what is going on, keep reading and adding more information.

3. Use the concept of "cover words." Very often you have an idea of a general area or classifications that the word belongs to, such as:

> an article of clothing
> something to eat
> some type of plant, tree

4. Use the context to help you make "intelligent guesses." Decide whether it is a noun, adjective, verb or so on and ask yourself what possibilities the situation would permit. Often there are several clues that give you some idea of what the meaning is; keep reading to confirm or reject the idea. You often do the same as you read in English. Would you have any trouble guessing at the meaning of the following?

> The *arronche* made a crash landing.
> The neighbor's *blifnitz* barks all night.
> He *bufted* too many pieces of candy and
> 　　got sick.

5. Learn to recognize cognates. Doesn't it make you mad to look up a word and then realize that it is very similar to an English word and you could have saved time if you had been more observant? You need to condition yourself to recognize cognates. Sometimes it just means dropping the final vowel in Spanish (*problema, elástico, cliente*), subtracting an e- from the beginning of a word (*escuela, especial, espíritu*), learning equivalents to endings such as -dad (*maldad, iniquidad*), -oso (*curioso, suntuoso*), -ente/-ante (*conveniente, petulante*), or changing some letters (*escritura, gato, guerra*).

6. Learn to recognize word derivations. If you watch for word families or different bases in words you can spot words you know.

For example, can you see *rico* and *pobre* in the following?

> *riqueza, enriquecer, riquísimo*
> *pobreza, pobrecito, empobrecer*

How many words can come from *hablar*?

> *el habla, hablador, habladuría, hablante*

7. Get acquainted with idioms. An idiom is a group of words that express meaning quite different from the sum of the words in the group. In fact, the words sometimes have nothing to do with the meaning.

> *Siempre me toma el pelo.*
> *Cálmate, no le busques tres pies al gato.*
> *Eso pasa a cada muerte de obispo.*

8. Write down the nuisance words. You often find yourself looking up a word time after time and still not remembering it. In that case, write it down and try to use it. Keep a list of these "nuisance" words that you can study from time to time.

Reading Activities *in* the Class

At the intermediate level, you will be concerned with developing a variety of activities to insure interest. It's a good idea to capitalize on the natural tendency of adolescents to work in groups. **Reading groups** can be used after the students have completed their homework to get together in class and discuss what they have read, following a study guide provided by the teacher. The group can prepare a presentation of the results of their discussion to give to the class. Another variation is to have the groups read new material in class to find answers to study guide questions and to prepare a group report to the class to make a coming homework assignment easier to accomplish. This idea is especially appropriate if you have sets of three to five books of many series.

Some of the entries in a **study guide** could be true-false questions, report skeleton, reaction to the plot, a brief resume of the content read, the students experiences while reading (how long, how difficult, reaction) or a summary in English.

These study guides provide a measure of accountability and a preparation for quizzes and tests.

Reading groups are very necessary in intermediate and advanced classes because students vary so widely in reading ability. Teachers have to contend with different levels in the same class because of these variations, starting as early as second semester in college (second year in secondary schools) and continuing into advanced courses.

Some highly motivational and entertaining **classroom magazines** are published by companies such as Scholastic to be used specifically in foreign language classrooms. These magazines are issued monthly and are sent in quantities to enable all the students to work with them in the classroom as well as at home. Students love them and in addition to providing excellent reading practice, they introduce a huge amount of cultural information on topics of interest to young people such as popular actors, movies, sports, and music. Some of them even have accompanying CDs and teacher's editions to give answers, teacher tips, and suggestions for use.

Perhaps the worst activity that can be conducted relative to a reading assignment is to have each of the students read a paragraph out loud and then translate it. This type of activity gives students the false impression that reading in a foreign language is simply a matter of "decoding," and it accomplishes little in the way of teaching reading strategies or helping students develop a global understanding of the text. Furthermore, this activity only engages one student at a time, while the rest of the class is likely tuning out. A better approach to in-class reading is to use reading groups as discussed above. Other approaches might be to have students read the text silently on their own and then discuss it, or follow along in the text as the teacher reads it aloud.

Reading *Outside* of Class

Reporting reading. Some kind of reporting of the reading done outside of class is important to the process of grading reading. As students turn more and more to extensive reading and approach liberated reading, their reporting system become

more and more important. Reports of outside reading can be as simple as writing four or five sentences on a 3 x 5 card or extend to book reviews and essays. A good book review can have a simple outline that can be filled in almost at any intermediate or advanced level but with differing complication. The book review outline is in three parts:

1. What is the author's purpose?
2. Did he or she achieve that purpose?
3. Was the experience worthwhile?

Other considerations for grading reading might include reading speed, the number of pages, the type of reading (skim, rapid reading, and savoring every word – and were these appropriate to the assignment?), the students' experience while reading and their reaction after reading.

Extensive Reading/Higher Levels

The following two graphics give you an overview of the many categories for reading and show how each item in the overview can be selected for its type and for its difficulty-level. You will remember that the proficiency level aimed at in the beginning courses is *low intermediate* (the *novice* goal can be reached in two or three weeks), the proficiency level aimed at in the middle courses is *intermediate high*, and the proficiency level aimed at in the advanced courses is *intermediate to superior*.

READING FOR INFORMATION

READING FOR PERSONAL
PLEASURE

USING DICTIONARIES

The major task in learning to read a foreign language is learning the meaning of words. When beginning students encounter new vocabulary, they should look up the important words. The best source, at first, is the glossary or end-vocabulary in the text or reader because the definitions there are specific to the context used in the text. The entries in a standard dictionary must be much more inclusive and include multiple entries. Generally speaking, beginning students are not prepared to work with a dictionary. We have all had experiences similar to the true story of the student who wanted "just plain water" asking for "*justo llano agua*" because of a not-too-bright use of a Spanish-English/English-Spanish dictionary. Beginners need to be cautioned and, on the intermediate level, helped extensively with the use of the regular dictionary. It might be wise to discourage the use of a regular dictionary and exclusively use the text end-glossary for the first semester or first year of Spanish. Also you should remember that you want to train students to get meaning from context and not become too dependent on looking up every new word.

It takes a lot of practice to learn how to use a regular dictionary. Students must decide which entry is the one that meets their needs. They need to be especially on guard against trying to find an exact equivalent. They must realize that the dictionary serves only as a starting point in understanding a word or expression; more information and observations are necessary to find the best meaning for the context the student is reading.

There are different kinds of dictionaries. There are special monolingual dictionaries, there are spelling ones, etymological ones, style ones, synonym ones, picture ones, poor ones and good ones. How do you evaluate grammar ones, pronunciation ones, current usage ones, special problem ones, simple ones and complex ones? Certainly you need to teach which dictionary to use and how to use it. Therefore, it is important to wait until you really want to introduce a regular dictionary—probably second year in the schools and second semester in college—certainly be sure to give a good deal of attention to orienting the students to the regular dictionary at whatever point you have them begin using them.

Selecting a dictionary. As we have already indicated, students do not need to use a complicated dictionary in the first one or two courses in Spanish. They can get by with the notes they take listening to the teacher plus the end-vocabulary or glossary of the textbook. There are, however, some good easy dictionaries that could be used in the second course and beyond in the first two years of Spanish study. They require a minimum of orientation work on the part of the teacher and students. Whenever the dictionary is introduced, you have to teach the basics: gender, plurals, choosing among multiple meanings, irregular verbs, and the like. This introduction necessitates a coverage of grammar that might not be sufficient until the second course or, more likely, a more advanced course. [See the recommended dictionaries at the end of this chapter.]

Selecting a more specialized dictionary for more advanced courses requires following a set of criteria. Actually compare the dictionaries, determining how the following are taken care of:

1. How many entries does it have for each word? (Example: there ought to be over 20 for *sacar*.)
2. Does it give irregular plurals? (Example: *club*, *menú*)
3. Does it indicate which prepositions follow verbs? (Example: *depender de, consistir en*)
4. Are stem-changing and irregular verbs so marked? (Example: *acertar, yacer, caber*)

5. Are irregular participles indicated? (Example: abrir > abierto, romper > roto, dormir > durmiendo, ir > yendo)
6. Does it indicate the gender in both the English and Spanish sections? (Example: *sartén, sal, pared*)
7. Are the reflexive uses included? (Example: *llamar, llover*)
8. Does it have spelling variations plus use of accents? (Example: *México/Méjico, vídeo/video*)
9. Are British or American definitions used? (Example: lorry, petrol)
10. Are regionalisms included? (Example: brown > café/ marrón, pineapple > piña/ananá)
11. Are new, special words included? (Example: transbordador)
12. Are the idiomatic uses indicated? (Example: darse cuenta de, costar un ojo de la cara)

All of these considerations must be made from the American (or English) vocabulary viewpoint and from the Peninsular Spanish or Spanish- American viewpoint. [See the recommendations for large bilingual and monolingual dictionaries at the end of this chapter.]

Dictionary activities. It is a good idea to conduct frequent activities when you first begin to work with dictionaries to get the students accustomed to using the skills you want them to develop. You could do a "dictionary chase" activity with the following:

1. Where is it in the dictionary? Have the students compete to see who can find the meaning of the following fastest: *chancho, ñato, llanto*, etc. (alphabet)
siendo, contuvo, suele, yergo (verb forms [The students learn how to reconstruct the original infinitive form])
2. What's the gender? See who can find the gender of the following fastest: *sien, capital (¡Ojo!), azúcar, costumbre, ave, problema*
3. What is the plural? Who can be the first to find the plural of: *bambú, crisis, cumpleaños*
4. Selecting among a variety of equivalents. See who can find the correct equivalent for the given context: *¿Dónde está mi ensayo? Lo quiero* (check) *una vez más antes de entregarlo.*
La última canción de Julio Iglesias fue un gran (hit) .
5. Identifying false cognates. Who can be the first to find out if the following are "true" or "false" friends? *actualmente, pretender, realizar, registrar, sopa, luna de miel*
6. Multiple meanings. See how many meanings the following words in English have in Spanish: *run, time, set*
See how many meanings the following Spanish words have in English: *sacar, tiempo, gracia*
7. Idiomatic uses. How many idioms can you find with: *ojo, gato, santo*

CONCLUSION

As we have seen, our students will first use reading skills in a functional way: for reading instructions in the textbook and workbook, reading words and notes on the board, signs and decorations in the class, using end vocabularies and dictionaries, seeing dialogues and oral materials in written form, and getting old material recombined in a new form. As they rapidly develop their ability to read they begin to read for information: captions under pictures, announcements on the bulletin boards, and much information presented in their textbook in cultural, historical and biographical materials. They may even get grammar explanations in Spanish. Next, they reach the point that they can use reading for enjoyment: jokes, humorous stories, advertisements in newspapers and magazines, and stories written about topics of high interest. Finally they move into the area of "literature," that is reading which is well written, with clever use of the language and attractive and interesting styles and move toward developing an appreciation of good writing, an acquaintance with major Spanish authors, and a broadening of their horizon as they work with poetry, drama, and novels.

We face a dilemma as we consider all of these possibilities; that is, we might have so much fun with one selection that we don't have time to read extensively. It's important that we learn to increase our reading speed and that we perhaps use the rough rule of thumb to read every fifth selection intensively and that we read the four intervening selections more rapidly. We take for granted that as our capacity to read increases that we can use these fun activities without teacher and peer intervention.

It is possible that many native readers are not truly liberated readers in that they may not be able to read all registers equally comfortably. How many native readers would pick up selections by Cervantes, Galdós, Alejandro Casona, Horacio Quiroga, or Jorge Luis Borges and enjoy reading them as much as they might reading something similar to a science fiction or fantasy novel or watching a television movie or variety show. More curious yet, how many would go to a bookstore and purchase a selection by the literary greats to read for pleasure.

All the reading we do at the various levels discussed in this chapter should culminate in liberated reading. This means that the students will depend less and less on our help until they are able to read and enjoy the reading of any author without our help remembering that some books (reading material) are to be tasted, some swallowed and a few chewed and digested. Will the graduates of our programs be well on their way to liberated reading?

REFERENCES AND SUGGESTIONS FOR FURTHER READING

Aebersold, J., & Field, M. (1997). *From reader to reading teacher: Issues and strategies for second language classrooms.* Cambridge, England: Cambridge University Press. *One of the best books on the subject, including chapters on factors influencing reading; designing a reading course; pre-, during-, and post-reading activities; teaching literature; and assessing reading skills.*

Bernhardt, E. B. (1991). *Reading development in a second language: Theoretical, empirical, & classroom perspectives.* Norwood, NJ: Ablex. *Examines theoretical models of FL reading, research on reading, as well as classroom methods of teaching and assessing reading.*

Anderson, N. (1999). *Exploring second language reading: Issues and strategies* (Newbury House Teacher Development Series). Boston, MA: Heinle & Heinle. *Each chapter is structured around one of eight strategies for teaching reading, including activating prior knowledge, cultivating vocabulary, and building motivation.*

Eskey, D. E. (2005). Reading in a second language. In E. Hinckel (Ed.), *Handbook of research in second language teaching and learning* (pp. 563-579). Mahwah, NJ: Lawrence Erlbaum Associates. *A succinct review of research on L2 reading and its implications for the classroom.*

García, C. (1991). Using authentic reading texts to discover underlying sociocultural information. *Foreign Language Annals, 24,* 515-526. *Contains great examples of using birth, marriage, and death announcements in Spanish to teach reading skills as well as culture.*

Freeman, D. S., & Freeman, Y. S. (2006). *Teaching reading and writing in Spanish and English in bilingual and dual language classrooms* (2nd ed). Portsmouth, NH: Heinemann. *An outstanding boook featuring extended scenarios of effective teaching of reading and writing organized around themes.*

Nuttall, C. (1996). *Teaching reading skills in a foreign language* (2nd ed.). Portsmouth, NH: Heinemann. *A very teacher-oriented texts that examines the skills required to read effectively and suggests classroom strategies for developing them.*

Other Books by James S. Taylor (see Appendix C for information)

- *Materiales para animar la clase de español*
- *Me gusta jugar*

- *Me gusta conversar*
- *Me gusta aprender español*
- *Me gusta actuar*

Recommended dictionaries

A good bilingual dictionary for student and classroom use is *The New College Spanish and English Dictionary*, edited by Edwin B. Williams, and published by Amsco School Publications. It is compact and easy to use and has a very durable binding. It has most of the features we recommend in the section on dictionaries.

An excellent, large monolingual dictionary is the *Pequeño Larousse en color*, edited by Ramón García-Pelayo y Gross, and published by Ediciones Larousse. It has modern, up-to-date entries that include Spanish-American uses, many colored pictures and charts, examples of words used in sentences, word origins, synonyms, and even verb charts. It also has a History, Geography, and Sciences and Arts section that includes information about people and places. You should have at least one of these in your classroom for student reference. (This dictionary is much cheaper if you can buy it in Mexico.)

A very helpful "contextualized," picture dictionary (*en la ciudad, los artículos del hogar, los deportes, plantas, animales*, etc.) is the *Oxford Picture Dictionary of American English, English/Spanish Edition*, edited by E. C. Parnwell, and published by the Oxford University Press. It gives vocabulary by topics or situations and allows a focus on the learning of Spanish words for household objects, modes of transportation, etc.

Miscellaneous Reading Materials

Carlitos. The escapades of Charlie Brown, Snoopy, etc. in Spanish. Published by Ediciones Junior S.A., Grupo Editorial Grijalbo, Barcelona.

Consejería de educación de España. The Ministry of Education of Spain has many materials for the use of Spanish teachers, both in the USA and in the UK. Visit the web sites give here. They provide materials that you can download for use by your students, including many interesting reading materials, at three different levels.
http://www.mepsyd.es/exterior/usa/es/home/index.shtml
http://www.mepsyd.es/exterior/uk/es/consej/es/quienessomos/contacto.shtml [See the section called TECLA.]

Condorito. Riotous comic books about the adventures of Condorito, the national comic figure from Chile. Order at: http://www.condorito.cl/

Las aventuras de Asterix. A hilariously funny comic series translated from French into Spanish. Published by Ediciones Junior S.A., Grupo Editorial Grijalbo, Barcelona.

La dama del alba, Casona, published by Scribners. An exciting, motivating, authentic play prepared for Spanish students with notes, questions, cultural explanations, and end vocabulary. Great for second-year college classes or fourth-year High School classes.

Mafalda by Quino. You will love this marvelous little Argentine girl who faithfully presents an entire national culture. See the official web page to learn about her or Quino her creator, or Amazon. com where you can find all the publications, including one you can read on line. http://www.quino.com.ar/

Periodicals

Selecciones del Readers Digest, the Spanish edition of "the most read magazine in the world." Can be received by subscription from Reader's Digest Latinoamérica, S.A., P.O. Box 144357, Coral Gables, FL 33114-4357.

GeoMundo, the Spanish version of *National Geographic Magazine*. Can be received by subscription from: Editorial America, S.A., Subscription Department, P.O.Box 10950, Des Moines, Iowa 50347-0950.

Recommended Classroom Magazines

Scholastic Foreign Language Magazines. Scholastic publishes high-interest reading materials [classroom magazines] for different levels. They come with many different activities, tests and games. You can find a listing of their materials and look at sample issues at this web site. http://teacher.scholastic.com/products/classmags/mgm_spanish.htm

Weekly Reader. Perhaps you read these magazines in school. They have readers in Spanish. Go to this web site and see what is available. Request a catalog. http://www.weeklyreader.com/estore/search.aspx?SearchTerm=Spanish&submit.x=17&submit.y=10

¡Vamos! A variety of reading materials published by EMC. Visit their web site and request samples. http://www.emcp.com/product_catalog/index.php?GroupID=2330

Eli Language Magazines. Classroom magazines, such as *Chicos*, *Muchachos* and *Todos Amigos*. Motivating with activities and games. See their web site and order a catalog. http://www.continentalbook.com/catalog/spanish/spelimagazines.html

Image Credits

p. 168: Balin, Jean Victor. (2008, May 26). Book. *Open Clip Art Library.* Retrieved July 4, 2011 from http://www.openclipart.org/detail/16972/book-by-jean_victor_balin. Public domain.

p. 170: Anu & Anant. (2009, May 20). Granada Cathedral. *Flickr.* Retrieved June 27, 2011 from http://www.flickr.com/photos/chutki/3633547100/. Creative Commons attribution license.

p. 170: Hinzel. (2009, April 13). Metropolitan areas of Spain. *Wikipedia.* Retrieved June 27, 2011 from http://en.wikipedia.org/wiki/File:Spain_met.png. Public domain.

p. 172: Total; es Cádiz [blog without author's name]. (2008, Feb. 6). Se lo guisan y se lo comen; será lícito. Retrieved July 20, 2011 from http://nosotrostambiencontamos.blogspot.com/2008/02/se-lo-guisan-y-se-lo-comen-ser-lcito.html. Creative Commons attribution/no derivatives license.

p. 172: Cruz, Kenneth. (2007, Dec. 31). Se hace toda clase de costura. *Flickr.* Retrieved June 27, 2011 from http://www.flickr.com/photos/extranjerochapin/2534584824/. Creative Commons attribution license.

p. 175: Lambert, Steve. (2007, Oct. 12). Stephanie Hunt Reading. *Open Clip Art Library.* Retrieved July 4, 2011 from http://www.openclipart.org/detail/6809/stephanie-hunt-reading-by-stevelambert. Public domain.

ACTIVITIES FOR METHODS CLASSES

1. Select a recent first year textbook and examine the reading selections. Are they motivating or would you have to supplement them with something more interesting to the students? Report to your teacher.

2. Using the text mentioned in #1 above, choose one of the reading selections and prepare a lesson plan. What activities would you use in working with it in the classroom? Hand the plan in to your methods instructor.

3. Go to the foreign language curriculum library and evaluate some of the readers available. Which ones would be most interesting to beginning students? Intermediate students? Advanced students? Keep the level of difficulty in mind as you evaluate them. Turn in a report to your professor.

4. Divide the methods class into several groups. Each group will choose a reading selection and prepare it for presentation in the class. Follow the APT MAPS GUIDE principles as you prepare yourselves and the other students for the presentation.

5. Prepare a reading selection for presentation in an intermediate Spanish class or in your methods class. Prepare the students with pre-reading activities to motivate them and activate their background knowledge. When they come to class having read the selection, give them a comprehension quiz, discuss the reading selection with them and conduct some post-reading application activities.

6. Select some classroom magazines in Spanish and practice using them in the methods class with all the students. Which of the activities were the most interesting? Informational? Fun? Discuss with your teacher.

7. Go to the websites of some publishers or book importers and order their catalog. When you receive it, study the reading materials available. Which ones would you want to use in your own classes? Report to your professor on what materials you received.

8. Evaluate a foreign language literature class you are currently taking or have taken recently. Is your professor effective in teaching the class? What are the professor's goals, and does he or she reach them? If you were teaching the class, what would you do differently? Give your evaluation to your methods instructor.

9. Go to the Scholastic Books site and order free samples of their classroom magazines. Show them to your teacher when they arrive.
    http://teacher.scholastic.com/products/classmags/mgm_spanish.htm

CHAPTER NINE

DON'T FORGET TO WRITE! WRITING FOR A PURPOSE

YOUR OBJECTIVES FOR THIS CHAPTER ARE TO:

1. DISCUSS THE NATURE OF FOREIGN LANGUAGE WRITING, INCLUDING THE DIFFERENCES BETWEEN INTERPERSONAL AND PRESENTATIONAL WRITING, PROCESS VS. PRODUCT WRITING, AND WRITING VS. TRANSLATING.

2. EXPLAIN THE ROLE OF WRITING AS A SUPPORT SKILL IN A FOREIGN LANGUAGE CLASS.

3. EXPLAIN THE ROLE OF WRITING AS A MAJOR COMMUNICATIVE SKILL.

4. PLAN APPROPRIATE WRITING OBJECTIVES FOR BEGINNING AND INTERMEDIATE FOREIGN LANGUAGE CLASSES.

5. PLAN ACTIVITIES FOR DEVELOPING INTERPERSONAL WRITING, INCLUDING DIALOGUE JOURNALS; PENPALS AND KEYPALS; BLOGS, WIKIS, AND SOCIAL NETWORKING SITES.

6. PLAN ACTIVITIES FOR DEVELOPING PRESENTATIONAL WRITING, INCLUDING STORIES, ARTICLES, ESSAYS, AND POETRY.

7. DEVELOP STRATEGIES FOR RESPONDING TO AND GRADING STUDENTS' WRITING.

8. IDENTIFY SOURCES FOR FURTHER EXPLORATION AND IMPROVEMENT OF WRITING.

Professor Snarf attacked the pile of compositions with a certain amount of relish. It was the first week of his intermediate Spanish class and he had assigned the students to write a three-page composition on "The Problems of the World, and How I Would Solve Them." It was his custom to require the composition in the first week of class. The students were always abysmally unprepared for writing assignments because of the oral emphasis in the first year classes. Professor Snarf would literally cover their papers with red circles, underlining, and comments about their poor use of grammar. The students were always stunned when they got their papers back; no one ever got higher than a C-. "They need a shock like this," he would say, "They get complacent and think they can handle the language and this lets them know they have a long way to go."

~~~~~

Paul had learned his grammar well working through many workbook exercises. He achieved high scores in the 90th percentile plus on the departmental examination that measured command of structure and vocabulary. The explanation of grammar had for the most part largely been in English in the lower division courses. Paul had an excellent memory for grammatical details, the workbook exercises and vocabulary lists.

In the first upper division writing course after the first writing experience, the professor brought in another form of the departmental examination and gave it in class and especially watched Paul. After class he asked Paul to come to his office. He used an answer key and checked Paul's test. He said, "I'm amazed that you do so well on this grammar and vocabulary test and yet write a composition with so many grammar and idiomatic errors."

In the interview the professor discovered that Paul had not been involved in any writing experience. Paul had worked through many workbooks and was very adept at completing these assignments, but he had not had practice in writing compositions, and therefore had not applied the knowledge to writing for communication. That had been the experience in both his high school language courses and his college lower division Spanish courses. Nowhere had he been expected to be at all creative in his writing.

~~~~~

Mr. Smith, the Spanish teacher at South High School, noticed a letter in his mailbox as he checked in on Monday morning. It was from Gordon Seaman, who was working in Spain in a summer job while vacations were going on there. Among other comments and general news, Gordon said, "I guess that I have to admit you were right about the writing I would do over here. Just today I wrote a note to a friend who was not home; yesterday I wrote a thank you note to a family I visited over the weekend; tonight I'm writing some letters and postcards to friends in Spain and in the USA--this letter to you is one of them; do you like my Spanish? Have I made improvement? By the way, before I visited the family I just mentioned, I emailed them to notify them that I was going to come and visit them; and you were right about another thing, I have had to fill out forms for customs, for the police, for the bank, for a credit card, and to rent a car. I've been writing in my diary every day in Spanish about my daily activities, my new friends, and my job. Yes, you can tell your students that I've been using all the ideas you gave me about writing and that practicing does make sense. Oh, yes, I remember two others now; I took notes on the instructions I received on the telephone this morning because I have to fill in on the job for an acquaintance of mine, and I also wrote an apology for not meeting a friend. So thanks again for all your help. I'm sorry I was so stubborn. I hope this unsolicited testimonial will encourage your students to be more cooperative in learning how to write than I was."

189

CHAPTER NINE

DON'T FORGET TO WRITE! WRITING FOR A PURPOSE

> Reading maketh a full man;
> conference, a ready man;
> and writing, an exact man.
> --Bacon

Of the four major skills, **writing** takes considerably more time to learn to use, and eventually to master than **listening** or **reading** or even **speaking.** Both teachers and students will have to be more patient, more persevering, and more diligent in order to develop writing proficiency. Because it's difficult to grasp the nature of writing in its totality, it is the most poorly understood of the four skills. Generally speaking, the other skills are more useful than writing—we know many students who have had extensive foreign residence in Hispanic countries but have never done much more writing than simple filling out of forms and short letters or notes. While it is true that writing may be very important to a few students, it can be of lesser or of no importance to many others. Writing takes many years to master. Professional and creative writing (elegant writing) is probably beyond most teachers in schools—even in their native language.

Writing is different from speech and more than speech. Speech is usually unkempt, if not downright sloppy. Writing can groom our oral proficiency. Writing is, of course, very directly tied to reading since reading is the means by which writing is interpreted. The difference is that when we read we have no control over what and how things are said. When we write we have total control over what we say and how we say it; that is we determine the vocabulary chosen, the grammar structures used, and the style in which it is said. We must teach writing at all levels and stages so that writing maturity will develop—even though the process will take a long time.

WHAT IS WRITING?

Writing in its simplest definition is "talk on paper," that is, the expression of thoughts or ideas in written or printed form. When discussing writing, we often speak in terms of dichotomies: writing as a support skill versus a communicative skill, interpersonal vs. presentational writing, process writing vs. writing as a final product, and writing vs. translating. Let's examine each of these dichotomies.

Writing as a Support Skill vs. Writing for Communication

In the classroom, writing has a kind of split personality. One purpose is its use as a support or service skill to master or to test the other skills. The other purpose is its communicative function.

KEY NOTE *Writing* has two basic purposes:
1. a SUPPORT skill
2. a COMMUNICATIVE skill

We make constant use of writing as a *support skill* in our language classes. Students might take notes, make word lists, write down assignments, take quizzes and tests, and so on. Using writing to practice grammar and vocabulary has been a traditional activity for centuries and continues to be so today with practice worksheets, workbooks that accompany textbooks, writing of compositions, and more recently, using computers for with a variety of uses. To omit writing would deprive us of one of the most accessible and useful tools for practice which we have available.

The *communicative function* is what makes writing one of four the major skills. What distinguishes communicative writing from support writing is its purpose. Communicative writing, whether interpersonal or presentational, always has the purpose of communicating some message to someone, as opposed to just reinforcing language learning.

It is important for students to learn writing both as a support skill and for communication. Unfortunately, some teachers never move beyond the support type of writing, even as their students progress to higher levels. The writing that our students do in completing their daily assignments and tests and homework fulfills the requirements of the service function but only in a very limited way does it fulfill the requirements of the communicative function. Compare the following two writing assignments that might be given to a Spanish 3 or 4 class:

1. Write a one-page composition using the preterite and imperfect tenses at least 10 times each.
2. Write about a memorable holiday experience – where you were, whom you were with, and what happened that made it memorable.

Although both assignments are likely to elicit preterite and imperfect tenses, the first one merely uses writing as support skill to practice verb tenses, whereas the second one illustrates a communicative use of language and is therefore more likely to be meaningful to students (as well as more enjoyable to read).

Interpersonal vs. Presentational Writing

Communicative writing, as outlined in the Standards for Foreign Language Learning, is of two different types: interpersonal and presentational. In interpersonal writing, students are in direct correspondence with other writers and are able to ask and respond to questions, and to ask for and give clarification when needed. Some common types of interpersonal writing include dialogue journals, letters, emails, wikis, online chat rooms, and even text messaging.

Interpersonal writing shares many of the characteristics of spoken language: it is usually spontaneous, informal, and not planned in advance. Furthermore, it is usually written in one sitting with little or no revision.

In contrast, presentational writing is planned in advance in order to communicate a message to an audience of readers. In presentational writing, it is not possible for readers to ask for clarification; thus, clarity and accuracy become important. Good presentational writing requires planning, thought, and revision; ideally, it also incorporates feedback from readers such as other students or the teacher. Some common types of presentational writing include essays, reports, stories, résumés, opinion pieces, and scripts for oral presentations.

It is important for students to learn to write in both interpersonal and presentational modes. Given the prevalence of electronic media such as email and texting, much of the writing that young people do nowadays is interpersonal in nature. This type of writing can develop fluency and confidence in language use. However, it is also important for students to practice presentational writing, especially as they progress to the Intermediate and Advanced levels. Presentational writing gives students an opportunity to focus on organizing their ideas (which most of them need practice with, even in English) and expressing themselves clearly and accurately.

Emphasis on Product vs. Process

An important change in emphasis has been made in recent years in the teaching of writing. In past years, we were interested only in the product in writing, that is, the paper or composition that students turned in. Little attention was given to the steps students went through to produce that final product. Some students who were good writers seemed to know intuitively how to go about writing, while others didn't.

Nowadays, we recognize the importance of the writing process as well as the final product. **Process writing** refers to writing that is done in successive drafts, with attention to the planning and revising process. A process approach to writing helps students understand the necessary steps in producing good writing and develop strategies for improving their writing. It places emphasis on going to back to reread and revise what one has written, which research has shown to be a key characteristic of good writers (Krashen, 1984). It also acknowledges the fact that students learn to write by writing, and that as they produce successive drafts of a composition, their writing improves in quantity and quality (Gallego de Blibeche, 1993).

Writing vs. Translating

Although traditionally the use of writing skills in Spanish courses may have been limited largely to translation practice, there is a great difference between writing freely to express our own ideas and direct translation. Although our students may at first tend to write from a dual system modality—transferring information from English to Spanish word for word—we need to help them reach the level of being able to express thoughts as naturally in writing as they do in speaking. Students who translate rather than express themselves naturally in Spanish will usually superimpose the structure, style, and vocabulary of English and come up with such classical gems as: *"Yo fui nacido en el ombligo hospital de San Diego. Mi papa hizo no fue al hospital porque corrió fuera de gasolina en la manera."* (An actual paragraph from an autobiography written by an authentic student. [Think in English to get the message.]) Translating is a different skill from writing and should only very rarely be used as an activity in developing writing proficiency.

Some General Implications for Teaching Writing

Teaching writing, then, can be divided into three tasks:

1. Teaching what is essential for all students: note writing, letter-writing, filling out forms, and taking notes as reminders, messages, and observations.

2. Teaching what is of probable importance to most intermediate and advanced students: taking notes for academic purposes and writing formal papers especially for use in school and in college.

3. Giving those few students who have the gift opportunities for writing for pleasure (and perhaps personal advancement or profit) by exposing them to creative writing and specialty writing: journalism, essays and research as well as advertisement and mass media uses. We will reserve our discussion of this area for Chapter 14, *Advanced and Special Classes.*

BEGINNING AND INTERMEDIATE WRITING OBJECTIVES

The writing stages that we will explore in this chapter, both in the *service or support* function of writing and in the *communicative function* of writing, will be the **beginning stage**, or the first two school years in the secondary level, and the **middle stage**, or years three and four in the schools. We will discuss the **higher stage**, years five and six in the schools, in Chapter 14.

Presently, the profession accepts the proficiency concept as the organizing principle for all of the major skills and culture. Proficiency is what the student can do.

The ACTFL Proficiency Guidelines for Writing

Let's examine briefly the writing proficiency skills that ACTFL has suggested for beginning and intermediate classes (novice and intermediate levels). These guidelines were designed to assist evaluators in giving a proficiency rating in an uncontrolled testing environment. As teachers, these guidelines influence us considerably, and we want to be sure that our students prepare to fulfill the requirements of these guidelines.

ACTFL PROFICIENCY GUIDELINES - WRITING

Advanced

Advanced-level writers are characterized by the ability to:
- write routine informal and some formal correspondence, narratives, descriptions and summaries of a factual nature
- narrate and describe in major time frames, using paraphrase and elaboration to provide clarity in connected discourse of paragraph length
- express meaning that is comprehensible to those unaccustomed to the writing of non-narratives primarily through generic vocabulary, with good control of the most frequently used structures.

Intermediate

Intermediate-level writers are characterized by the ability to:
- meet practical writing needs - e.g. simple messages and letters, requests for information, notes- and ask and respond to questions
- create with the language and communicate simple facts and ideas in a loosely connected series of sentences on topics of personal interest and social needs, primarily in the present
- express meaning through vocabulary and basic structures that is comprehensible to those accustomed to the writing of non-narratives.

Novice

Novice-level writers are characterized by the ability to:
- produce lists and notes limited formulaic information on simple forms and documents
- recombine practiced material, supplying isolated words or phrases to convey simple messages, transcribe familiar words or phrases, copy letters of the alphabet, or syllables or reproduce basic characters with some accuracy
- communicate basic information.

We must be careful that we not restrict our work to these guidelines as our major teaching goals. We need to go beyond these in our teaching so that we are controlling the environment to provide our students with experiences that they will need. For example, when we are working with novices in writing we need to expose them to intermediate experiences in order to get them ready for these possibilities. That means our teaching will have a get-acquainted phase, and then later we will have a doing phase. When we are teaching intermediates, we will be exposing them to advanced experiences. Likewise, when we are dealing with advanced students, we will be presenting superior possibilities for their experience.

The main levels of the ACTFL guidelines are presented in the appendix for your information. The guidelines, and hence the proficiency test itself, focus on three aspects of writing: function, content, and accuracy.

Function-content-accuracy comprise the so called functional trisection of proficiency testing and planning. In testing students, we give these three almost equal attention, but in teaching students, we can vary the emphases in the process of exposing students to higher levels.

In discussing objectives we will combine the basic functions we have previously mentioned, namely, *support* and *communication*. Borrowing the guidelines of the ACTFL proficiency test, our objectives can be classified in three aspects: 1) *Tasks or functions,* 2) *Topics or content,* 3) *Accuracy.* The goals listed under each aspect will assist you in determining as many associations as possible and will provide a road map across the whole curriculum.

The following graphics will describe writing in the beginning stage (ACTFL Novice and Intermediate), and the middle stage (ACTFL Intermediate and Advanced). The higher stage goals (ACTFL Advanced and Superior), as well as the possibility of elegant writing, are included here for your perspective, but they will be treated in depth in Chapter 14.

Our first graphic will look at the topics or content aspect of these two stages. The "two-step" stairway simply indicates that there is a progression upwards towards proficiency.

TOPICS OR CONTENT

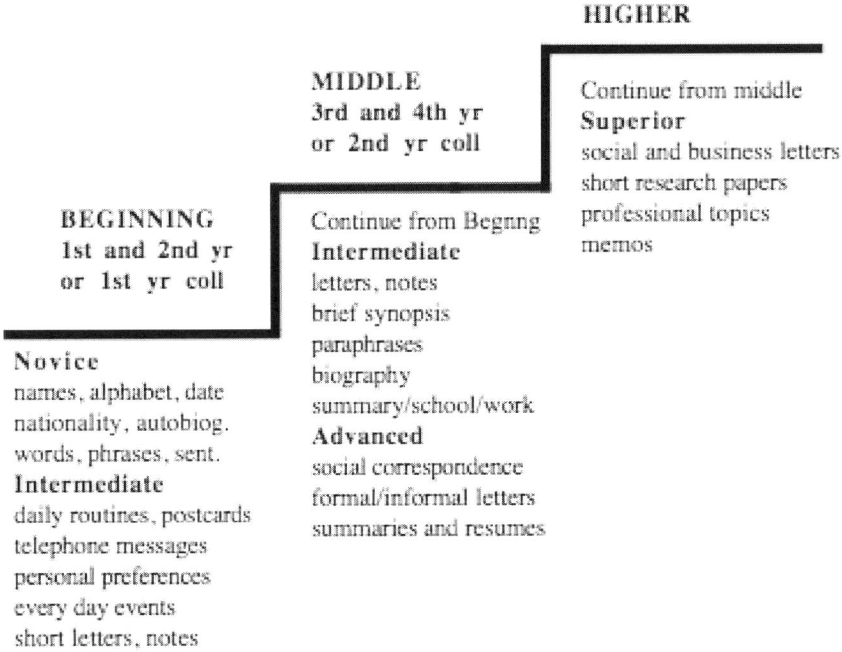

HIGHER

MIDDLE
3rd and 4th yr
or 2nd yr coll

Continue from middle
Superior
social and business letters
short research papers
professional topics
memos

BEGINNING
1st and 2nd yr
or 1st yr coll

Continue from Begnng
Intermediate
letters, notes
brief synopsis
paraphrases
biography
summary/school/work
Advanced
social correspondence
formal/informal letters
summaries and resumes

Novice
names, alphabet, date
nationality, autobiog.
words, phrases, sent.
Intermediate
daily routines, postcards
telephone messages
personal preferences
every day events
short letters, notes

The beginning phase is characterized mostly as the "sentence phase." The students progress from point zero to words to sentences as their doing phase and they are in the process of getting ready for the middle stage paragraph building activities that lead to composition writing. Most of the activities will be recycled and developed in later stages. In this beginning stage, we urge that you give your students lots of opportunities to write and that you give them lots of psychological reinforcement.

It's in the intermediate phase where most progress can be made in writing for communication, at least in the schools. You will see that in this phase they complete entire activities and products. Very seldom will students in the schools go beyond getting acquainted with many of the ideas presented in these first two phases. Let's now look at the tasks or functions aspect of these phases.

194

TASKS OR FUNCTIONS

HIGHER

MIDDLE
3rd and 4th yr
or 2nd yr coll

Continue from middle
Superior
write cohesively
(especially advanced, i.e.
small paragraphs)
conjecture
support opinions
hypothesize
defend hypothesis

BEGINNING
1st and 2nd yr
or 1st yr coll

Continue from Begnng
Intermediate
generating, creating
questions, statements
Advanced
describe
narrate
explain
compare

Novice
copying, transcribing
listing, filling in
paragraph length
Intermediate
daily routines, postcards
telephone messages
personal preferences
every day events
short letters, notes

The next graphic focuses on accuracy and gives statements of general proficiency that will be modified in the chapter. Spanish teachers have in the past given too much attention to the subject of grammar and in fact they have built entire courses around the driving force of a grammar syllabus. More recently they have abdicated the task of teaching any grammar at all. Both positions are too extreme. We recommend that teachers choose the functions and topics carefully and allow these to drive the course and also use the accuracy aspects necessary to communicate well in the stage and at the level where the students are with the best variety possible. Writing of all the major skills requires the most concern with accuracy, but this accuracy must grow out of natural communication in writing, not just grammar drills and workbook activities ad nauseam or in vacuo. This use will be in the support manifestation of writing and in the communicative manifestation of writing.

ACCURACY

HIGHER

MIDDLE
3rd and 4th yr
or 2nd yr coll

Continue from middle
Superior
good control
underlying organization
sensitive: formal and
    informal style
still not tailoring
precisely but...
    ...errors in writing
    rarely disturb natives or
    cause miscom-
    munication

BEGINNING
1st and 2nd yr
or 1st yr coll

intermediate continued
Advanced
good control
frequent errors with
    complex sentences
writing may resemble
    literal translation from
    the native language
writing is understandable
    to natives not used to
    the writing of
    non-natives

Novice
no practical communi-
    cative writing skills
Intermediate
many errors, but...
..can be understood by
natives used to the
writing of non-natives

¶

We will now focus on different strategies and activities you can use to develop your students' writing skills.

TEACHING WRITING AS A SUPPORT SKILL

As previously mentioned, writing as a support skill is characterized by its support of the other skills (speaking, listening, reading) and not for writing as principle communication. By writing we can internalize ideas and vocabulary and expressions; writing helps us to memorize and to assimilate.

- Writing provides a service/support function for practicing, reinforcing, consolidating grammar and pronunciation.
- Listening and reading comprehension can be assessed through writing.
- Writing can improve language-learning ability. Although most people have the ability to learn languages orally, some people are dependent on reading and writing. Writing can be of help to this type of student.
- Testing in general most likely employs writing as the support skill and as the extension of oral responses.

- Writing provides variety in classroom procedures. Writing can be a change, and hence a rest, from a steady diet of oral practice.
- Writing individualizes work in classes of many students with varying abilities in them. More than the other skills, writing allows students more freedom of expression and progress at their own pace and style.
- Writing increases retention because one can read the notes again, but the very act of writing helps one to remember because it involves more senses. An estimate of the increase is from 15 per cent retention by just hearing, to 85 per cent retention by writing notes.
- Writing gives a source for later reference. Almost all students acquire the habit of jotting down important information to refer to later.
- Writing gives actual evidence of achievements. We can compare what students wrote in the third week of the course with what they write in the seventh week of the course.

196

Activities Using Writing as a Support Skill

Following are some examples of activities in which writing can be practiced as a support skill.

Δ **Copying activities** Students can copy everything the teacher writes on the chalkboard while giving any kind of presentation. They should do the assigned workbook or textbook activities that help them to copy words and expressions they have been learning while engaged in activities: listening, speaking, and reading, including concocted writing opportunities such as crossword puzzles. These activities will help the listening and retaining experiences.

Λ **Grammar exercises.** Even by doing exercises (usually for grammar purposes) that are not our own, we tend to catch the vision because we are writing. Textbooks usually have workbook supplements or online programs that contain writing exercises. In the past, working with workbooks was a boring and tedious chore and students universally hated them. In recent years the textbook companies have made great progress in making workbooks and practice manuals much more attractive and almost fun to work with. They now include fun illustrations, crossword puzzles, games and motivating activities.

Today most modern workbooks include a "model answers" section that allows the students to confirm and correct their written work. Now the students write out their answers, compare them with those in the key, correct what they have done incorrectly, tear out the pages they have completed, and turn them into the teacher. This is a marvelous boon to the teacher, who can quickly glance over the work to make sure the students have corrected (and not copied) their answers, but does not have to carry out the onerous task of correcting each student's work.

Many new textbook programs are accompanied by software programs that provide a myriad of writing activities to practice vocabulary and grammar structures. Students (especially on the college level) spend an hour or two each week in the lab or online working with programs that give immediate reinforcement to the students' responses, thus requiring no self correcting on the part of the student. Programs of this type also sometimes provide reports of student progress directly to the teacher and in this way eliminating the necessity of handing in stacks of workbook exercises which the teacher would have to take home to evaluate.

Δ **"Active-involvement" sheets.** These sheets are usually handouts that provide a written outline of statements about a presentation with blank spaces for note taking—varying in length from one-word to full-paragraph notes.

Δ **Questions and answers—statements and rejoinders.** Teachers can check up on the students' listening and reading progress by having them write out questions and answers about the work they are reading and listening to. In this way writing reinforces the reading and listening skills.

Δ **Dictations.** Dictations allow the students to practice their writing skills. A "spot" dictation (where most of the dictation is already written out except for a few blanks which the student fills in) is more efficient, because it allows the teacher to focus on one specific writing problem, such as the capitalization of days of the week, use of written accents, etc.

Δ **Oral exercises.** Students can reinforce oral skills in many ways, such as writing down the words to a dialogue they have memorized, writing out answers to oral questions they have been practicing, and writing out descriptions of pictures they have been discussing orally.

The previous suggestions and others can be recycled and intensified and developed as students pass through the beginning, middle, and higher stages of writing. At first student progress with writing will seem quite slow. We work up to five sentences, seven sentences, and ten sentences and more. Slowly we begin to acquaint the students with various discourse elements that help to make good connections or transitions with these sentences, changing them into paragraphs. Then we learn how to put them into past tense. Finally, we learn how to give the paragraph good cohesion with the topic sentence and supporting sentences with logical order or chronological order, at least at the acquainting level.

TEACHING INTERPERSONAL WRITING

In interpersonal writing, the writer is in direct correspondence with one or more other writers. As previously mentioned, interpersonal writing tends to be informal and unplanned. In general, when students write emails, text messages, or journal entries, they write exactly as they would speak. Because students' errors may seem more serious and more numerous when written than when spoken, some teachers fear that interpersonal writing will encourage inaccurate use of language. Research has shown, however, that writing does not perpetuate errors any more than speaking does (Beauvois, 1997). Certainly, we should not allow our students to write only in interpersonal mode where there is little focus on accuracy. Nevertheless, periodic opportunities for interpersonal writing can give students a chance to develop fluency and confidence in language use.

Activities Using Interpersonal Writing

Following are some formats for practicing interpersonal writing.

Dialogue journals. A dialogue journal is a written conversation in which students communicate with the teacher or with each other. This might begin with an entry in a personal journal or a diary of three to five sentences based on the comprehensible input experienced in the classroom in the first week of the class and gradually expanding the entry as the weeks go on. Possible journal prompts might be as follows:

a. Write five sentences that describe you for the biography of a work application.
b. Write your plans for decorating for a school dance.
c. Write five sentences about the job you are applying for.
d. Write a post card telling five sentences about what you do during a family reunion.
e. Write a note suggesting what you would do if you had 24 hours of free time in your home town.
f. Tell about your favorite video.

It is important that the teacher respond to the content rather than the form of what students write in their journals. Teachers should explain to students that the purpose of the journal is to encourage free expression of ideas, and therefore they will not be correcting errors as they would in presentational forms of writing. If the students' errors interfere with the message, teachers can recast in their response what the students said, using more correct language, or can provide necessary vocabulary or expressions. If the teacher doesn't understand what a student was trying to say, the teacher can write a question in response: "No comprendo. ¿Quieres decir . . . o . . . ?", offering options that provide the student with more appropriate ways of expressing the message.

In order to limit the time spent responding to dialogue journals, teachers can have students turn in their journals on a rotating basis. This helps us to overcome the major problem with journal assignments that is the time it takes to read and react to them. It's a good idea to limit the amount that you have to check so that you can make comments in response as to what you read in their journals.

Penpals and keypals. Correspondence with penpals (by letter) or keypals (by email) can be a wonderful way of practicing interpersonal writing. Students' pals can be other students from Spanish classes in neighboring schools or students in Spanish-speaking countries. This type of correspondence can be highly motivating, as it provides students with an authentic audience for their writing. It can also be a powerful tool for culture learning. (See Chapter 11 for suggestions on setting up penpal or keypal correspondence.)

Blogs, wikis, and social networking websites. An electronic variation of the journal activity is to assign students to create Spanish blogs (short for web logs) in which they make regular entries and the teacher periodically comments. Students may also be assigned to comment on each other's blogs. Some teachers have used blogs in study abroad settings, assigning students to maintain a blog with pictures and comments about the places they visit.

A wiki is a collection of interlinked web pages that can be easily created and edited by many different users. This makes wikis a wonderful tool for collaborative writing. For example, students who are working on group writing projects such as cultural presentations can each be assigned to write a portion of the presentation on the wiki, and other group members can easily comment on what they have written. The wiki also makes it easy to assemble each student's writing contribution into a single document or presentation.

Other possibilities for online interpersonal writing include forums, chat rooms, and social networking websites.

Text messaging. Some teachers have capitalized on students' interest in text messaging by temporarily setting aside the prohibition against cell phones, asking students a question, and having them text the answer back to the teacher. Students can also send text messages in Spanish to other students, although it may be difficult to verify that students are staying on task and staying in Spanish. Because of the short, abbreviated nature of text messages, they almost resemble support writing more than communicative writing, and should therefore not be seen as a substitute for other types of communicative writing.

TEACHING PRESENTATIONAL WRITING

Unlike two-way interpersonal writing, presentational writing is one-way; students are preparing some type of composition for an audience of readers. This type of writing requires advance planning, as well as revising successive drafts in order to make sure the final product communicates the message that the author intends.

Activities to Prepare Students for Presentational Writing

There are many possible activities that can prepare students for formal presentational writing. These activities are less formal in nature and require less planning and revision than writing formal compositions, and can therefore work with beginning to intermediate-level students. Unlike writing-as-a-support-skill activities, however, these activities give students practice with more communicatively-oriented writing.

Filling out special forms. This can provide very early writing assignments because a lot of the information is already given in the form. Since Spanish-speaking countries are especially noted

for their extensive bureaucracy, there are many forms available to fill out.

Graffiti. A strip of butcher paper can be posted on a wall of the classroom on which students can write notes to each other in class, in separate classes or even in separate levels of school. Also, announcements can be written informally. Other messages can be written. All this can be spiced up considerably by the addition of pictures, cutouts, drawings, and the like. Monitors will need to keep bad words from being written or will have to change the bad words to other words if the graffiti board cannot be watched constantly.

Definitions of cultural objects. These can be objects in the home, in the school, in the church, on the streets, in the center of the city, etc.

Descriptions of characters. Write descriptions of students, teachers, friends, politicians, etc.

Memos. This can be a very realistic experience. Make believe that you are on the work internship for the summer at a store in Spain and you have to write a memo about a seventy-year old who is stealing oranges.

Logbook. Write entries for a logbook as if you were a traveler. For example:

a. As first mate on board Columbus' ship in September 1492, write an entry.
b. As a tourist traveling through Peru discuss the places you have visited and what you will be doing next.

Personal topics. Write about pictures of family members, about vacations, about special human-interest topics.

Descriptions of pictures. Cut pictures from a magazine, paste them on a sheet of paper and then write impressions and descriptions underneath the cutouts.

Group paragraphs or compositions. As a class, write a group composition or paragraph with a class member acting as recorder, writing it on the chalkboard or on an overhead transparency (or, if a digital projector is available, typing it in a word processor and projecting it onto a screen). A variation would be dividing the class into three or four groups for smaller group composition or paragraph writing.

Brainstorming and stream of consciousness activities. Brainstorming has been an important activity for developing flexibility and creativeness for years. For example, the students and teacher can try to find as many words as possible to describe a picture or an inkblot or a photograph or a caricature. After experience with words we can try sentences and paragraphs.

A natural takeoff on the association activity is stream of consciousness writing. Students can be given a short set amount of time, starting out with one minute or even thirty seconds and working up to five minutes, to write as much as they can in Spanish. It doesn't really matter if they stick to one subject. This is a type of brainstorming so we might give instructions like these:

> *"Take a pencil or pen and a piece paper. I'm going to give you ..... minutes and I want you to write in Spanish the entire time. If you aren't able to keep writing about one subject or idea, change to something else. If you can't write sentences, write phrases. If you can't write phrases, just make a list of words. You have to keep writing in Spanish the entire time. I'm going to watch that you are writing and I may even glance at your papers but I'm not going to collect these so don't be afraid to write something private."*

As the teacher circulates to keep students on task, it's important that the teacher encourage the students to keep writing, reminding them that it's okay just to list words and also reminding them that this type of writing is to be done without pondering or meditating. After the activity, it's all right to ask students if the assignment was hard or if they were able to write sentences the entire time or if they enjoyed the exercise, but we don't ask them to read aloud what they wrote or even to share it with small groups or partners. The purpose of stream of consciousness writing is to avoid thinking in English and translating directly into Spanish.

In all of the above activities, it is important to work from simple to complex and keep recycling. These activities have to be kept

reasonably simple in this beginning stage, which in the public schools extends for a couple of years and in college two semesters. They all can be recycled with increased complications for both the middle and higher stages

Free writing topics for beginning and intermediate classes. Refer to the chapter on planning for further ideas on this section to remind yourself of the ideas for you as the teacher to be in charge of selecting the topics for your courses; however, you probably have selected a good textbook that contains the topics you will most likely use. It will probably treat the topics indicated in the graphic for this stage above plus additional possibilities. Consider such topics as families, pastimes, travel and vacations, future plans, funny experiences, persons you admire, etc. Prompts or titles for composition on these topics might include *Horas libres, Una vida sana,* and *Niñez y juventud.*

Presentational Writing Activities

The following activities are more truly "presentational" in nature; they involve writing more formal compositions that provide opportunities for planning and revision, and are thus geared more toward intermediate- and advanced-level students.

Stories. Write a collective story, or a story from a different point of view (another character's point of view). Or, given the first part of a story, write different original conclusions.

Family Booklets and Family Stories. These are especially easy to write at this level. Students don't have to create new plots, they can use familiar experiences and this is just a step beyond the personal journal. One nice thing about this project is that the audience for students' writing can include their family as well as their teacher and classmates.

Fairy tales. Tell your favorite fairy tale in your own words, or perhaps a "fractured" version of some of the well-known children's stories. <u>Caution:</u> This one must be set up carefully because the students will try to translate because they are thinking in English. The biggest challenge for both teachers and students is to get the students steeped in Spanish, thinking Spanish before and during the writing process. Setting up a good context is very important in all of these suggestions. Provide a good reason for writing and a plausible reader.

Scripts. Write Spanish scripts for familiar American TV stories or mysteries. These subjects provide considerable grist for the writing mill in this later beginning stage. An extension of this activity could be to act out the scripts, which could be filmed for possible posting online.

Reports of interviews. Go into the community and interview people to get a story—especially a human-interest story. Part of this assignment is to prepare the interview questions themselves. Other parts of the assignment might involve writing to community members to get permission to interview, or writing a letter to the teacher outlining the proposed plan. Summarize what you learned from the interviewee(s) in a written report or article.

Articles for newsletters or websites. Write reports on activities experienced in the classroom or in any of the class excursions. As a result of any interview opportunities, following models provided by the teacher, the students can write descriptively of the events or express their feelings about the events. Other possibilities include writing about survey results, writing about upcoming school or Spanish Club events, or reporting on these events.

Poetry. Write simple poetry, especially *haikus* and *cinquains.* Poetry provides the student with a number of fun activities, and can be written on a beginning or intermediate level.

A *haiku* is a very simple Japanese poem without rhyme. It usually deals with something beautiful in nature. It follows the following formula:

Line 1 = 5 syllables
Line 2 = 7 syllables
Line 3 = 5 syllables

Example:

Flores bonitas
Altas y amarillas
Los girasoles

The haiku is excellent for beginning students because it is syllable-based and needs no rhyme. Also, the students do not have to worry about using verbs, adjectives, nouns, etc.

The ***cinquain*** was developed in France. As a verse form, it is used to create an atmosphere of lightness, airiness, and softness, and so its subject matter is restricted. The *cinquain* uses nature references to highlight the poet's feelings.
These verses are always unrhymed, without jerkiness, and have no regular meter. In addition to a restricted content, *cinquains* use one of the two following formulas:

Line 1 = Subject, 2 syllables
Line 2 = Description of subject, 4 syllables
Line 3 = A relevant action, 6 syllables
Line 4 = A relevant feeling, 8 syllables
Line 5 = Restate subject with synonym or metaphor, 2 syllables

Another formula for the *cinquain*:
Line 1 = a noun
Line 2 = two adjectives describing line 1
Line 3 = 3 verbs applying to line 1
Line 4 = four words (a sentence or phrase)
Line 5 = 1 word, either a synonym of line 1 or a repetition of it.

Examples:

Novia
Muy hermosa
Bailando, jugando, amando
Yo no te merezco
Inocencia

Ciudad
Grafitti, gris
Prohibe, excluye, mata
¿Qué sabes de libertad?
Centro

Business letters. A very meaningful writing assignment for students is the business letter. (Business letters are more similar to presentational writing than interpersonal writing due to their formality and need for accuracy, as opposed to *friendly* letters, which belong more in the beginning stage or in the early portion of the middle stage.) Business letters in Spanish are quite different from business letters in English

The various parts of a business letter can give students a lot of opportunity for prewriting practice.

Opinion papers. Build opinion papers a few sentences at a time to a full-fledged composition in which you give your own opinion on political or school issues (e.g., whether vending machines should be eliminated from schools.) Or, take on a new identity and give the opinion of that new person. This activity provides good practice in writing and is very creative. You might become any person from a *periodista* to a *futbolista*.

Essays. A natural extension of opinion papers is essay writing. More advanced students can write essays literature read for class, which constitutes "reading to write" as discussed in Chapter 8. Much more will be said about essay writing as we discuss advanced classes in Chapter 14.

Preparing Students for Presentational Writing

Students often think that they should be able to produce exciting and properly written prose the very first time they sit down at the word processor (or if they are don't have access to a computer, when they sit down with pen and paper). All good writing comes out of a series of steps beginning with brainstorming and getting ideas written down, followed by a process of organizing ideas—eliminating some and adding others resulting in a revised draft. (You've seen all of the steps previously.) The prewriting experiences should provide students with experience in each step to facilitate the large task of writing the composition. The following are suggestions for specific techniques that will help students accomplish their writing assignments.

Role of possible reader audience. All writers have to consider their reader audience. Traditionally, the main audience for students' work has been the teacher, which meant that students had little motivation to polish and perfect their writing other than to get a good grade. With the advent of computers and the Internet, however, students have a wide range of possible audiences. Blogs, wikis, class websites, and online newsletters may be read by classmates, other students in the school, parents, community members, partner schools in Spanish-speaking countries, and even unanticipated readers around the world. Other audiences can be penpals or keypals.

It is important for students to be aware of the audience they are writing for. Prewriting activities can help students to practice different writing styles and registers for the various reader groups, as well as anticipate their interests and purposes for reading.

Point of view. This refers to the standpoint from which a writer makes observations and gives opinions. Points of view include some of these possibilities: A child's view, an eyewitness view, a servants view, a first person view, an all-seeing view, a third person view, and the like. The students should practice writing from various points of view in prewriting activities so that they will do quite well in their main assignment.

Different types of texts. There are specific considerations in writing different types of texts (narration, description, argumentation) that can be discussed and practiced in pre-writing activities.

Δ **Narration.** Narrations (e.g. stories, fairy tales, experiences) should contain elements with action in the story that answer the question: "What happened?" In Spanish the preterite is used mostly for a single past event (like a snapshot) and the imperfect past is used for descriptions, for setting the scene. The students need a lot of prewriting practice with these two tenses. If the prewriting practice is directly preparatory to the actual composition that they will be writing, it will be much more meaningful and the student will assimilate the experience.

Δ **Description.** Descriptions should contain elements giving background information such as circumstances and descriptions of ongoing actions. There are various ways to organize descriptions so that they will stimulate the imagination and the senses from specific to more general or the reverse and from the outside to the inside and in terms of logical sequences, etc.

Δ **Argumentation.** Students in the middle stage of writing will need to get acquainted with writing argumentative essays and persuasive essays. Various kinds of pre-writing activities will contribute to argumentation and persuasion.

Activities would include 1) arriving at an opinion step by step, 2) anticipating possible objections and answering them, and 3) citing people or documents to support opinions.

Writing skills. Two skills that can be developed in pre-writing or practice activities include circumlocution and use of a dictionary.

Δ **Circumlocution.** It's important to give students practice in expressing their ideas *Hablando con rodeos* so that they will not be frustrated trying to find a specific translation for a word that comes to them in English instead of Spanish.

Δ **Using a dictionary.** In order to think in Spanish, students in the middle and higher stages should be encouraged to use monolingual dictionaries; bilingual dictionaries should be consulted vary sparingly. Before turning to a dictionary one should ask oneself, "Is there a simpler way to say that? Can I say it *hablando con rodeos?"* Finding a simpler way can avoid many problems that students face when using a bilingual dictionary. Words often have many meanings. For instance, *time* has at least ten different meanings, *to be* has many meanings, *fun* has many meanings. Spanish probably has a different word for each of the separate meanings. Occasional prewriting activities to teach students to use the dictionaries properly will be very profitable.

Elements of a composition. All compositions have a beginning, middle, and end. Following are some considerations in developing these elements.

Δ **Introduction.** It's important for writers to communicate their line of thought in the opening sentences of their composition. As a prewriting activity, students should practice introductory sentences and paragraphs for various topics just so that they will get the idea of the importance of the introduction. Students can practice these introductory sentences alone or as a "pair" activity.

Δ **Paragraphs.** Before writing longer compositions, students should write various kinds of paragraphs and become quite proficient in paragraph writing. This is a prewriting experience

in that the preparatory work anticipates compositions composed of many paragraphs. It's important to get a topic sentence and then to write subordinating ideas contributing to the topic sentence. A variation on this activity would be to place the topic sentence in the middle of the paragraph or at the end of the paragraph for appropriate reasons. A topic sentence in the middle might stand out as a surprise and the topic sentence at the end would build to a climax.

Another important consideration is the matter of paragraph continuity. Practice writing topic sentences and then supporting those with appropriate ideas: making a contradiction or an objection, providing an example, speculating about possibilities, or making a transition as to what will follow. Another consideration to practice would be the transitions between paragraphs, such as: 1) using a transitional word or phrase (various discourse connectors, such as *pero, sin embargo,* etc., 2) answering a question raised at the end of the preceding paragraph or 3) repeating a key word or recalling a key idea from the preceding paragraph. Students will need to learn many discourse connectors for opening paragraphs for closing paragraphs and, of course, for the middle paragraphs of a composition.

Δ **Discourse connectors.** Depending on the students' level, they should be made familiar with the possible discourse connectors appropriate to their writing needs. Such expressions as the following are important as connectors for a flashback:

> *y luego*
> *entonces*
> *y después*
> *por lo tanto*

Δ **Variety.** Sentence length and sentence complication can be varied. Students need a lot of practice in using sentence size to communicate feelings and other special purposes. Generally, sentences should vary in length in order to avoid boredom in reading. Determined by the composition assignment, preparation for writing can be in prewriting sentences and paragraphs emphasizing variety and length and complexity.

Δ **Ending with conclusions.** Students will also have to work with conclusions so that they will have a variety of possibilities in mind. A really good conclusion can make or break an essay. Students should avoid just restating everything they said before, a nasty trick they may have learned in English composition classes. They need to learn how to "come to a conclusion" about what they have said by answering the question: So what? They should include a new idea or question in the last paragraph. For truly effective closure they should make sure the last sentence is a strong one.

The checklist. A good way to improve the communication writing is to use the *checklist* idea. After talking about an aspect of writing in class, such as to how to write the date correctly, or inverted word order, or some other grammatical element, have them agree not to make that mistake again. Then use peer review to check that they have not made any of the checklist errors. You should feel free to circle any checklist errors for the student to correct. Some examples of checklist items are these:

1. La fecha se escribe así: Lunes, 5 de mayo, 1992.
2. Piensa en "cuando, como, donde, con quien," por ejemplo: Hoy (cuando) voy al centro (donde) con mi madre (con quien) en el auto (como).
3. Recuerden que con el verbo *entrar* hay que usar una preposición "en" o "a": *Entramos en la casa.*
4. Recuerden que "to leave" se expresa en español en diferentes maneras: *dejar, salir, irse.*

Personal checklists are also kept by the students and, of course, encouraged by the teacher.

Have the students keep a "writing notebook." This notebook would simply be a collection of materials and information that the students would use in writing assignments and could include:

- Notes written every day as you go through a unit of activities, especially things that excite you or interest you or involve you emotionally, etc.
- Special expressions: Sentences, idioms, discourse connectors, even words, phrases, proverbs, anything that catches your interest or

that you will possibly find helpful in expressing yourself in writing.
- Any special quotes that you would like to use taken from your reading, whether they are literary or not.
- A list of any hints that you get concerning how to make your writing more effective.
- Notes about the process of writing.
- A checklist of grammar items to avoid your special problems in writing.

A Student Checklist for Presentational Writing

Too often we assume that students already know how to write themes and compositions. This is often not the case. As you work with more extensive and less restricted writing activities, it would be very helpful to give students some sort of checklist similar to the following.

Prewriting. Try to set up a Spanish "frame of mind" or a "Spanish mood" to provide the circumstance for writing a composition of any size from 1) a couple of sentences to 2) a paragraph to 3) several paragraphs. Get in the "Spanish mood" by reading something related to your topic and listening to audio segments or watching videos all as part of this **prewriting ritual**. It is also necessary to gather facts and generate ideas from reading and listening as well as from discussing ideas—especially by brainstorming. Fill your mind with expressions in context, checking your notes where, hopefully, you have anticipated your composition, and in activities with others in Spanish. Steep yourself in Spanish every way you can.

Organizing. Organize your facts and especially, your ideas, and then write an outline of the ideas as a pre-first-draft experience. You may be able to do this mentally. If a person has something to say, the writing, the vocabulary, the expressions will be much easier to produce and to edit. Choose an organizing approach when appropriate: chronological order, logical order, cause and effect order, etc.

Drafting the composition. Write your first draft directly in Spanish—don't write it in English and then try to work out a stiff translation. Use your own vocabulary and grammar structures to

express your thoughts and ideas—if necessary HCR (Hablando con rodeos) that is by **circumlocuting** your meaning in the Spanish that you feel in your bones and tissues. If you need new words, look them up in the dictionary, but if you are
not sure of the usage of a word, check it in a monolingual Spanish dictionary to make sure you are using it right.

Do your writing on a computer if at all possible. It is infinitely easier to correct errors and to prepare second drafts and final copies. And, since your teacher will surely have your correct and revise your work, you will save yourself a great deal of time and effort if you can return to your original draft and simply make changes, rather than typing the entire text over again.

Getting feedback. Be aware of some kind of direct contact with your audience—that is, with those who will be reading what you write. Get a class partner to read over your composition and make suggestions. The reaction of a responder to your writing is usually expressed with questions, suggestions, or statements about the content or form.

Revising (Idea Level). When you have prepared your first draft, let it incubate a few hours or a day or two, then go over it and check the following:

- Can some of the ideas be stated in a clearer fashion?
- Can you elaborate on some of your most valid points?
- Are there some irrelevant materials that can be left out?
- Can you improve the organization, the order in which you present your points?

Editing (the Form Level). Check through the composition carefully to eliminate any mechanical errors or grammar errors ("spell check" with the word processor if you have it in Spanish). Check the following:

- Are you overusing some words such as *la cosa, hacer, ser, estar, haber* (as main verbs), etc.? Can you replace them with more elegant words?

- Are you expressing your ideas with style and grace of are you simply stating information?
- Are you using colorful, interesting phrases, proverbs and idiomatic expressions? Collect them; get suggestions from your teacher as to sources.

Corrected Version. After the teacher has checked and returned the composition, make sure you understand all the changes and suggestions. Then rewrite it. Study the corrected version and commit it to long-term memory. Review the corrected version periodically. Keep the original and the corrected version in a notebook for reference.

Publishing (Showing It Off). The corrected version (after the teacher has checked it) could be placed on display (bulletin board) or published in a student magazine (school or professional). From this corrected version, prepare yourself to write or speak ten sentences (or later, 100 words in paragraph) of correct Spanish for oral reports, for panel discussions, for forum and symposia, for informal talks, and in writing for tests and other possibilities.

Error checklists (Class and Personal). If your teacher provides a checklist of errors and suggestions that have been discussed in class, use it as a guide for editing and revising your compositions. These checklists also help you know what you must review in your grammar work. They give more relevance. They help you and your peers help each other with the revision and editing process when you read each other's papers before the teacher sees your work.

Responding to Students' Writing

Teachers have traditionally assumed that their role is to "correct" students' writing, as implied in the statement "I have to correct my students' papers tonight." There exists a strong temptation for teachers to go through their students' papers with red pen in hand, marking every grammar and vocabulary error as they go along.

What is wrong with this approach? First, it assumes that writing is nothing more than producing grammatically correct sentences. (Imagine if an English teacher were to give "A" grades to all students who wrote with reasonably good grammar and vocabulary, regardless of the content of what they wrote or their effort in writing it.) Writing is much more than producing error-free sentences; it involves having a meaningful message to communicate and planning how to best communicate it to the intended audience. This requires attention to content, organization, and rhetorical structure as well as grammar and vocabulary.

A second problem with the mark-every-error approach is the assumption that student writing is not worthwhile unless it is free of errors. The absurdity of this assumption becomes apparent when we realize that most non-native teachers are unable to produce error-free writing in Spanish themselves. In reality, we write for a variety of purposes, not all of which require the same degree of accuracy. In interpersonal writing, such as emails and text messages, the main goal is to get the message across. In contrast, presentational writing requires a higher degree of accuracy.

We recommend replacing the notion of "correcting" with "responding to" students' writing. One of the best things teachers can do is put down their pen and read through a student's paper without making any marks at all. Teachers can then decide what issues are most in need of attention and prioritize their comments accordingly.

In responding to the first draft of students' presentational writing, teachers should focus mainly on content and organization, marking only those grammar and vocabulary errors that interfere with meaning. It makes little sense to spend time marking errors in the first draft when students are going to rewrite it anyway. Research has shown that as students go through the process of rewriting, they fix many errors on their own (Scott, 1996). In responding to the second draft, teachers can then give more attention to the remaining errors, as well as to any remaining content and organization issues. Even then, teachers should not correct all of the errors all of the time. The main focus should be on errors that interfere with communication or that have been discussed in class and listed in students' "notebooks." Students will then have just a few errors to look at. A positive approach could be adopted in that the teacher marks each sentence or, later, paragraph that is correct (perhaps red pluses!)

Using correction symbols. The use of a list of correction symbols gives the student direction but doesn't make the correction for the students. The error or problem is circled, and the symbol is indicated, and the students have the responsibility of finding out what needs to be done, making the correction and then practicing the correction. One of the simplest systems is to circle grammatical errors, underline vocabulary errors (wrong words or incomprehensible phrases), and double-underline spelling errors. With the aspects that have not been covered yet either by the checklist or by grammar exercise or content discussion, the words or phrases could be supplied.

Writing comments to students. As a main aspect of the "coaching" approach, that will help the students to assimilate the language best and become effective writers (if not poets or reporters), encouragement as positive reinforcement has the best possible outlook for success. Always emphasize what is being done right and coach rather than criticize. Here are some suggestions for writing comments to students:

- Respond to the *content of their writing* before analyzing the assignment.
- Have a caring attitude.
- Be somewhat personal and willing to risk sharing your feelings or experiences.
- Find positive aspects about their writing before suggesting improvement.
- Respect their right to voice their ideas. Don't judge or correct their ideas.
- Respond specifically to whether their writing followed the instructions for the assignment.
- When giving suggestions be specific and give examples to show what you mean.
- End on an encouraging positive note.
- Make a long list of words and expressions to praise their work, and be free with praise for even minor successes. Be careful never to be phony.

Eight samples of ways to praise should get you started composing your own long list of possibilities.

1. ¡Fantástico!
2. ¡Me gusta tu trabajo!
3. ¡Qué buenas ideas!

4. ¡Tu estilo tiene chispa!
5. ¡Ahora lo tienes!
6. Ahora vas por buen camino.
7. Felicitaciones, tienes las formas de los adjetivos correctas hoy.
8. Se ve que estás trabajando mucho.

Peer reviewing. Some teachers like to have students review the first draft of each other's papers. One benefit of this activity is that it can help familiarize students with what good writing looks like, as well as give them another audience for their work besides the teacher. However, just telling students to read and comment on each others' papers is likely to be of little benefit; it requires time and effort to teach students how to be good reviewers.

Berg (1999) and Byrd (2003) offer some suggestions on how to make the peer review process more successful. First, teachers should provide students with a guide on what to look for as they read others' work (see example below). Generally this guide should focus on content, clarity, and organizational issues rather than grammar, since students are often not good judges of language use. To teach students how to use the review guide, teachers can make copies of student papers from previous years to project onto a screen, and practice using the guide to comment on the papers. They can also show examples of appropriate and inappropriate peer responses. This process will need to be repeated frequently. With practice, the quality of students' peer feedback should improve as they learn to recognize what constitutes good writing. Of course, students should receive points for completing the review guide with meaningful feedback for their peers.

Peer Review Guide for Business Letter

Reviewer _____

Student whose letter was reviewed: _____

Read your partner's letter and respond to the following questions. Be sure to provide positive comments as well as helpful suggestions for improving the letter.

1. Does the format of the letter correspond to the samples reviewed in class? What components are missing or need revision?

2. Is all of the required content included? If not, what else needs to be included?

3. Are there any sentences that you had difficulty understanding? If so, list them here.

4. What do you like best about this person's letter?

TEACHING WRITING BY HAND AND ON THE COMPUTER

It's not hard to get started writing in Spanish. There is no change in the alphabet. What will be new to the students will be the use of the written accents, the ~ over the n, and the ¨ over the u (dieresis). The writing conventions of the inverted question mark and exclamation mark will also be new to them. The combination of certain letters such as the *qu,* the *gu,* changing of the *z* to *c,* and so on will also take some getting used to at first. Students need to learn to produce these writing conventions both by hand and on the computer.

Contrasts Between Spanish and English Handwriting

As a teacher you will undoubtedly have people come to you for help with letters written by Spanish speakers. In many cases these people don't need help with the *vocabulary* or *grammar,* what they are not used to is the *handwriting.* It would be good for you to teach your students how Spanish-speaking children are taught to write in school and let them practice it enough to become accustomed to the different system. You could occasionally use it yourself when writing on the chalkboard, on overhead transparencies, or on paper when writing notes to students. Both teachers and students can master this handwriting system in an hour's time of concentrated effort—especially if motivated. Learning it will benefit the students in their ability to read correspondence written by Spanish speakers and help them to be able to read the students' handwriting more readily

The following examples of the alphabet as Spanish-speaking children learn it will give you what you need both to learn and to teach this system. This seems to be uniform in most Spanish-speaking countries.

Basic differences between American handwriting and that of Hispanic countries. Following are some examples of cursive letters commonly used in Hispanic countries.

b   d   p   q

b   d   p   q

Generally speaking, Hispanic handwriting tends to be a little more "artistic" with curves at the beginning and end of words. Note that some letters are left open where in our handwriting system they are closed: the "p" and sometimes the "a" or even the "o".

Following are some examples of letters written by Spanish-speakers of different ages. Comparing the first two letters you will observe that Spanish handwriting allows two different ways to write the letter "r" just as does English. Note also the "z" in the word *buzón* in the second letter. It could easily be confused with an "r".

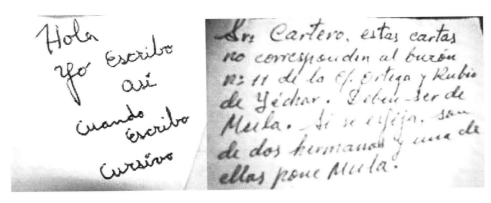

Capital letters are often more creative. Note the elegant capital letters in the following:

> ay! en los graves apuros
>
> Poco te valdrá la ciencia,
>
> Sino, con afectos puros
>
> Invoca la Providencia

The written grade of an elementary school student, shown below, illustrates the handwritten numeral 1, which we might confuse with a 7, and the use of the underlined superscript "o" in the abbreviation of *primero*.

An interesting and fun activity in your classes would be to take a handwritten letter such as the one on the following page that was written by a four-year old to her godparents, and have your students transcribe, not translate, and then discuss differences. Note that she does not always use written accents, which is quite common among Hispanics, she switches from singular to plural, and is not careful about punctuation and capitalization of letters. After all she is only four years old. She probably had quite a bit of help from her parents.

> Letizia Ortiz Rocasolano
>
> 1° ev. Sobresaliente
> Mucho interés, Participativa
> gran facilidad. Inteligente
> Excelente comportamiento

These examples were all taken from the Internet. You can find other examples there on your own, or use some of your own personal correspondence. Don't fail to expose your students to letters of this kind so they can become accustomed to the differences.

Writing and Computers

It goes without saying that computers have revolutionized the writing process. Gone forever are the days of when a single error in a typewritten paper could force the writer to retype a whole page or more. With computers, we can write more, faster, and more accurately than ever before. Research has shown that when writing on a computer, students write more and revise more than when writing on paper (Bridwell-Bowles, Johnson, & Brehe, 1987).

Because much of students' writing will be done on a computer, students need to learn how to use it as a writing tool. One obvious implication is learning to produce written accent marks and upside-down question marks and exclamation points. Teachers should teach their students how to produce these marks on whatever operating systems and software are available on the school's computers. Because students invariably resist using accent marks at first, teachers need to emphasize that words that require an accent will be considered misspelled without the accent. (This goes for handwriting as well.) It may help, for example, to point out the difference in meaning between esta and está, hablo and habló. Teachers will have to be patient and somewhat lenient at first, but with time and effort, students can learn the conventions of Spanish writing on a computer.

Students also need to learn how to use a Spanish spell checker. Teachers should make sure that Spanish spell checkers are installed on the school's computers (with the assistance of lab personnel if necessary). Just as English teachers encourage their students to spell check their papers, Spanish teachers should do the same. Using a spell checker is not "cheating"; rather, it is simply a wise practice that all good writers nowadays use when writing on a computer.

These days, computers provide a variety of writing practice. Besides the practice materials provided online by textbook companies, there are many independent web sites with a variety of practices. Special software programs such as Atajo are also available to help students learn to write in Spanish. Atajo, published by Heinle (http://www.heinle.com/) includes an electronic version of the Merriam-Webster Spanish-English Dictionary, with audio examples of the pronunciation of each word and examples of usage; a verb conjugator; grammar index; lists of vocabulary words by topic, and lists of phrases organized according to language function. If students are writing a letter, for example, they can view a screen with examples of how to open and close a letter in Spanish.

ASSESSING STUDENTS' WRITING
"A 'B' or not a 'B'?"
To Grade or not to Grade?

As we will discuss in much more detail in Chapter 12, Testing and Evaluation, teachers must use a fair and consistent system of grading. This is especially true of writing assignments. We have included some examples of different types of grading systems below, as well as in the Appendix to this chapter.

One of the simplest grading systems, which is appropriate for short, informal writing assignments, is to assign an overall grade for the content and creativeness of the student. In our opinion, the major grade should be based on this area. A second grade can be based on accuracy or correctness. The two grades could be in the form of a fraction-number with the content grade above the line and the accuracy grade below the line.

Holistic vs. analytic scoring. More formal writing assignments, especially those in which students work to revise and polish successive drafts of a composition, may call for a more sophisticated grading system. This system may be either holistic or analytic. In holistic scoring, an overall grade is assigned to the entire composition based on certain criteria. Usually the teacher spells these criteria out in a rubric. The criteria might include content, organization, vocabulary, grammar, and/or mechanics such as spelling (including accents) and punctuation. Following is an example of a holistic rubric for grading compositions:

Holistic Rubric for Assessing Writing

4	*Excellent* – Excellent treatment of the topic, with well-articulated ideas; connections between ideas are clear; vocabulary usage is appropriate; few if any grammatical or mechanical errors
3	*Good* – Adequate treatment of the topic; main ideas are generally clear; occasional errors in grammar, word choice, and/or mechanics
2	*Fair* – Conveys some ideas on the topic, but ideas are not thoroughly developed; relationship among ideas is sometimes unclear; frequent errors in grammar, word choice, and mechanics
1	*Poor* – Topic is inadequately addressed; ideas are poorly developed, with no apparent organization; distracting accumulation of errors in grammar, word choice, and mechanics

In contrast, analytic rubrics award separate points for each criterion. Following is an example of an analytic rubric for assessing writing:

Analytic Rubric for Assessing Writing

CONTENT		
Poor 1 2	*Adequate* 3 4	*Excellent* 5
Topic is inadequately adressed; ideas are poorly developed	Topic is adequately addressed, with limited development of ideas	Thorough treatment of the topic with well-articulated ideas
ORGANIZATION		
Poor 1 2	*Adequate* 3 4	*Excellent* 5
No apparent organization; progression of ideas appears random	Main ideas are clear but somewhat loosely organized	Connections between ideas are coherent and logically sequenced
ACCURACY IN LANGUAGE USE		
Poor 1 2	*Adequate* 3 4	*Excellent* 5
Distracting accumulation of errors in grammar, word choice, and mechanics that impede comprehension	Some errors in grammar, word choice, or mechanics that may occasionally impede comprehension	No major errors in grammar, word choice, or mechanics; errors never impede comprehension

Both holistic and analytic scoring have advantages and disadvantages. Students often prefer analytic scoring so that they can see more specifically how their particular grades were determined, and they may appreciate the helpful feedback provided by analytical scoring. However, if the person grading tries to use an absolute standard of quality, students may not have a chance for success. Often various features in the students' writing are not connected with the context and the fact that the writing is more than the sum of its parts might be lost and there is a definite problem with weighting for each category. In order to accommodate the varying learner needs, both systems might be judiciously used. In general, research has shown that holistic scoring and analytic scoring are equally effective. In either case, the description offered by rubrics such as these is better than just giving a letter grade without specific feedback. We would also emphasize again that points need to be given along the way for effort in the writing process, as well as for the final product.

After reading these suggestions, you can start to devise your own methods for evaluating writing — especially compositions. First of all, there is the very important idea that we teachers should enlist the help of native readers who will read the papers to weed out the expressions that sound non-Spanish to them—this is a very tricky endeavor that could have emotional overtones. Therefore we suggest that you copy the compositions and then have the native reader (who will need a lot of training and help in doing this task) read the copies and make the suggestions on the papers in pencil. You take these and read through the students' original papers and you give the help needed. You can decide if the native's help is too much for the student or not. Then you can help the native to do a better job by helping the native to learn to judge what is just a little distance between the Spanish of the students and what constitutes an Americanism. This experience will help you to become conscious of the errors in expression. If you can get to Spanish-speaking countries often enough to become familiar with the latest expressions, so much the better.

CONCLUSION

In the past it has been the attitude of many language teachers that the teaching of writing as an integrated process will be put off until the rather advanced courses in foreign languages. We, however, have taken the position that writing can be very helpful in its support function in language classes, and that writing as communication is a skill that can be developed from the very beginning days progressively to the advanced stages achieved later. We have suggested many ways to accomplish this goal. Writing is a powerful tool that you can use develop your students' command of the language, and, who knows, it might even help you in your own use of the language.

Everyone needs to learn to use writing; college majors and minors in a foreign language need more than secondary students, and those few who show special talent in writing creatively and elegantly must have special opportunities. Since we don't really know what talents may lie dormant within people, we need to help all students explore writing possibilities. Who knows, we may have an occasional Cervantes or Neruda in one of our classes
.

REFERENCES AND SUGGESTIONS FOR FURTHER READING

Berg, E. C. (1999). Preparing ESL students for peer response. *TESOL Journal,* Summer 1999, 20-25. *Although directed toward ESL teachers, contains great tips on preparing students to read and respond to each others' writing, including examples of effective and less-effective student responses.*

Beauvois, M. H. (1997). Computer-mediated communication (CMC): Technology for improving speaking and writing. In M. D. Bush (Ed.), *Technology-enhanced language learning* (ACTFL Foreign Language Education Series, pp. 165-184). Lincolnwood, IL: National Textbook.

Bridwell-Bowles, L., Johnson, P., & Brehe, S. (1987). Composing and computers: Case studies of experienced writers. In S. W. Freeman (Ed.), *The acquisition of written language: Response and revision.* Norwood, NJ: Ablex.

Breinder-Sanders, K., Swender, E., & Terry, R. M. (2002). Preliminary Proficiency Guidelines -- Writing, Revised 2001. *Foreign Language Annals, 35,* 9-15. DOI: 10.1111/j.1944-9720.2002.tb01828.x

Campbell, C. (1998). *Teaching second language writing: Interacting with text* (Newbury House Teacher Development Series). Boston, MA: Heinle ELT. *Contains chapters on academic and creative writing, responding to students' writing, and getting students to review each others' writing.*

Gallego de Blibeche, O. (1993). *A comparative study of the process versus product approach to the instruction of writing in Spanish as a foreign language.* Unpublished doctoral dissertation, Pennsylvania State University, University Park, PA. (AAT 9414287)

Krashen, S. D. (1984). *Writing, research, theory and applications.* Oxford, England: Pergamon Press.

Musumeci, D. (1998). *Writing in the foreign language classroom: Soup and (fire)crackers.* Washington, DC: Center for Applied Linguistics. Retrieved from ERIC database. (ED433725) *An instructional module for on teaching writing. It is addressed to college TAs, but very applicable to the secondary level. Contains multiple examples of writing tasks for beginning-level students, along with helpful examples of teacher feedback and scoring procedures.*

Scott, V. M. (1996). *Rethinking foreign language writing.* Boston, MA: Heinle & Heinle. *One of the best books on the subject, addressing the issue of what constitutes writing competence, the FL writing process, writing and computers, and teaching and assessing writing.*

Terry, R. M. (1989). Teaching and evaluating writing as a communicative skill. *Foreign Language Annals, 22,* 43-54. DOI: 10.1111/j.1944-9720.1989.tb03142.x *Contains great examples of writing activities (for French students, but easily adaptable to Spanish) along with scoring procedures.*

Williams, W. (2004). *Teaching writing in second and foreign language classrooms* (McGraw-Hill Second Language Professional Series). Columbus, OH: McGraw-Hill. *This short, accessible book provides research-based information and practical advice to teachers.*

Image Credits

p. 196: Machovka, Jana Jakeschová. (2006, Dec. 20). Writing. *Open Clip Art Library.* Retrieved July 4, 2011 from http://www.openclipart.org/detail/2185/writing-by-machovka. Public domain.

ACTIVITIES FOR METHODS CLASSES

1. Select a first year textbook and examine the writing exercises. What kind are they? Are they limited to mechanical types of writing or do they try to practice natural, everyday uses of writing? Report to your instructor.

2. Develop a system for giving students feedback on a short paragraph or composition that they have written. Ask an instructor of a first- or second-year university Spanish class to allow you to use your system on some student compositions. Respond to the students' writing, making supportive comments on the content. Indicate on the compositions what the students need to revise, hand them back and ask them to revise them and return them to you.   Grade the composition a second time, basing the grade on accuracy. Show the composition to your methods teacher.

3. Go to the lab. Evaluate a computer-assisted program for writing. What are its values? Are there any disadvantages? Hand in a report to your instructor.

4. Find some sources for penpals or keypals. Get some students involved. Help them write letters or email messages to their pals. Show them to your instructor.

5. Go to the foreign language curriculum library and select a writing workbook that accompanies a text program. Work through a lesson. How many of the exercises focus on supportive skills? How many allow creative or liberated writing? Are there keys that will permit the students to correct their own work? Report to your teacher.

6. Keep a personal diary or logbook for a week. Then pick one day of what you wrote and pretend that it is a student's work. Practice your supportive techniques by writing comments just as you would with a real student. Show it to your teacher.

7. Try your hand at writing a *cinquain* or *haiku*. Read it in class with your classmates. Do you have a better insight into how you would help students in a similar assignment? How would you grade or evaluate them?

8. Ask an instructor of a first- or second-year university Spanish class to let you correct the workbook materials the students hand in. What comments can you make which will be helpful to them? Report your work.

9. Spend some time on the Internet and find some safe and sane Spanish chat rooms, forums or blogs that will be safe for your students to use. Evaluate the use of writing and summarize the use of abbreviations, emoticons, and other "quirks" that are common in those kinds of sites.

10. Read one of the works on teaching writing that are listed in the reference section at the end of this chapter. Prepare a short report on what you learned.

CHAPTER TEN

WHAT SHALL I DO ABOUT GRAMMAR?

YOUR OBJECTIVES FOR THIS CHAPTER ARE TO:

1. DISCUSS THE MEANING OF THE TERM "GRAMMAR".

2. DISCUSS THE ROLE OF GRAMMAR IN A PROFICIENCY-ORIENTED CLASSROOM.

3. DEVELOP SKILLS FOR PRESENTING GRAMMAR CONCEPTS IN A VARIETY OF WAYS, INCLUDING THE INDUCTIVE APPROACH.

4. IDENTIFY AND USE TECHNIQUES AND ACTIVITIES THAT WILL HELP STUDENTS EFFECTIVELY PRACTICE, INTERNALIZE, AND REINFORCE GRAMMAR CONCEPTS.

5. APPLY THE PRINCIPLES OF "DYNAMIC ACTIVITIES" FOR PRACTICING GRAMMAR IN NATURAL, MEANINGFUL SITUATIONS.

6. RECOGNIZE THE VALUE OF VISUAL AIDS IN TEACHING GRAMMAR AND BE ABLE TO PREPARE AND USE THEM.

7. BE AWARE THAT COMPLETE MASTERY OF GRAMMAR CONCEPTS DOES NOT COME ALL AT ONCE AT THE BEGINNING, BUT RATHER AFTER FOCUS, REVIEW, AND RECYCLING.

But they don't know their grammar!

Miss Ima Grammarian could stand it no longer. For three years she had been distressed by the level of preparation of the Spanish students she was getting from the middle school. Even since Mr. T.P. Response, the middle school Spanish teacher, had gotten excited about a new oral approach (which she was sure was nothing more than "fun and games"), his students who continued studying Spanish at the high school were totally lost in her intermediate classes. They had absolutely no background in grammar; they couldn't tell a noun from a pronoun, and they were totally nonplussed when she mentioned the subjunctive. She had visited the middle school to talk to Mr. Response about it, but he wouldn't listen to reason. "They don't need grammar," he argued, "They can understand everything I say in class and are really motivated. My enrollment has increased dramatically." "But," she objected, "All they can do is respond to a series of absurd commands such as 'Crawl under your desks,' or 'Scratch your left ear,' and when I try to explain the use of the preterite and the imperfect they don't have the foggiest notion of what I am talking about."

The discussion had ended in an impasse, and Miss Grammarian had returned to the high school in frustration. After an additional year of trying to compensate for the inability of the middle school students to compete with those who had started Spanish with her in high school, she made her decision. "So you see, Mr. Principale," she explained to the principal, "Their grammar is so bad that I will have to create a special class just for them. The only solution is to spend the first term teaching them grammar concepts in English, then the second term I'll teach them Spanish grammar and finally in their second year I'll merge them with my intermediate students."

~~~

Melissa had been in Mr. Nelson's Spanish class for more than a month now, and was beginning to get very frustrated. She had been a brilliant student in several English classes, and since her English teachers had been very focused on grammar rules and sentence diagramming, she had expected to do a lot of the same in Spanish. So far Mr. Nelson hadn't given them a single grammar explanation! They had learned a lot of vocabulary and practiced a lot of role playing, but still no mention of nouns and pronouns, or subjects and objects. Melissa decided to talk to Mr. Nelson. She felt cheated. Why was he holding back on the most important part of learning the language?

~~~

John felt lost in Spanish. He had been sick for two weeks and when he returned to class, they had moved two chapters ahead. They were now using some structures he didn't know. However, John didn't feel any panic. In his history class it had been just a matter of reading the text. He could do the same in Spanish and he could get a tutor to help. He was sure that a few hours of having the tutor explain the grammar would catch him up with the class.

217

CHAPTER TEN

WHAT SHALL I DO ABOUT GRAMMAR? TEACHING THE UNMENTIONABLE

> **Neither can his Mind be thought to be in Tune, whose words do jarre; nor his reason in frame, whose sentence is preposterous; nor his Elocution clear and perfect, whose utterance breaks itself into fragments and uncertainties. Negligent speech doth not only discredit the person of the Speaker, but it discrediteth the opinion of his reason and judgement; it discrediteth the force and uniformity of the matter and substance.**
>
> **—Ben Johnson**

In our chapter on the history of language teaching, we discussed the traditional "grammar-translation" approach that had been the dominant method of teaching foreign languages in the American educational system for many years. That approach was characterized by a primary focus on analysis of the grammatical patterns of the target language. In a typical class period, the teacher would spend the major part of class time exploring the complexities of a grammatical concept such as the formation of relative pronouns, the use of the subjunctive, or the need for agreement of adjectives. The remainder of class time was customarily spent practicing those grammatical concepts by reading texts in the foreign language and translating into English or translating sentences from English into the foreign language which required the application of the rules just studied. We commented on the failure of that approach to bring the students to any significant level of functional fluency in the target language, other than reading and laboriously translating.

With the current shift to communicative approaches, grammar instruction has taken on a new role in the language class. As the profession tries to break away from the sterile, analytical study of grammar patterns, there is a temptation avoid, discredit, or not even mention the idea of "grammar." In tradition-breaking approaches certain "taboos" sometimes appear. When the direct methods were at the height of their popularity, the greatest "sin" that could be

committed by the teacher was to use English in the classroom. During the decade of the audio-lingual dominance, the activity to be avoided was *translation*. (This was undoubtedly a reaction to the most common activity of the grammar-translation classroom.)

With today's emphasis on learning the language in a more natural and functional way, the newest unmentionable word seems to be *grammar*. Indeed, a theoretician of some note, Stephen Krashen makes a distinction between formal classroom study of the language, which he calls "language learning," and "language acquisition" which he defines as the acquiring of the language by the student in natural, non-classroom environments. Krashen declares that "language learning" cannot succeed in bringing students to fluency in language use.

WHAT DOES "GRAMMAR" MEAN?

Without question, vocabulary carries the heaviest burden in foreign language learning. Unless the students successfully learn the meanings of the words, they will never understand or make themselves understood. Yet the vocabulary of a language is subtly intertwined in unique patterns, and words undergo changes that alter meaning. These forms and patterns are usually called "grammar" and although linguists talk about *lexicon*, *morphology*, and *syntax*, we know what they mean. The way languages are put together is fascinating. If words are the "bricks" of communication, grammar is the "cement" which holds everything together.

It is true that a mother tongue is learned without an obvious, conscious analysis of grammatical patterns. Consider the several hundred million speakers of Spanish who can't tell a verb from a noun, and who could in no way tell you why they say: *Quiero que me prestes 5 pesos* and not *prestas*, or explain the difference between *Manejé con cuidado* and *Manejaba con cuidado.* As we learn our mother tongue we are not conscious of such things as verb conjugations, word order, the formation of plurals and past tenses, and the formation of commands; we "speak to express ideas," and we say things "like every one else does."

Yet as teachers we won't help our students much by just telling them "that's the way you say it," as our parents and peers did when as children we were learning our mother tongue. And as teachers we can also see the quite inefficient process (in terms of time and effort) through which we learn our native language; the thousands of hours, days, weeks and years hearing, imitating, speaking and being corrected, making adjustments until after several years we finally master the basic structures. As teachers we intuitively feel that in some way what the child learns during these years can be summarized, encapsulated, and condensed into short, simple explanations which will save our students from going through that same drawn-out learning process. Can't an understanding of how tenses are formed, how adjectives agree with their nouns, when the subjunctive must be used, help the students absorb the language more meaningfully? Won't understanding the order and patterns of declensional endings help them shorten the time it takes to master their use?

A vital fact that is often overlooked by those trying to teach a second language by imitating the process of a child acquiring its native tongue, is that learning a second language is *not* the same as learning the first language. With the first, the mind of the child is in a sense a blank slate (*tabula rasa*), with nothing written on it, and everything learned is new. But when we learn a *second* tongue we already speak and understand a *first* language, which obviously influences our learning of the second. It seems only logical that we can somehow use the first language to aid us in learning the second.

A second critical difference that is often ignored by those who insist exclusively on "acquisition" is that as teachers we are talking about second language learning in an educational environment, *i.e.* in the schools. While we all know about the advantages of submersing someone entirely in the total linguistic milieu, we do not have that luxury in our classrooms, nor can we compare the scant 50 minutes per day, 5 days a week (on good weeks), for a few months a year with the total 24 hours a day, 365 days a year for the several years that we spend acquiring our mother tongue.

So, where does all this bring us? What *shall* we do about grammar? Should we ignore it completely? Some argue that we should. A number of years ago, an important publishing company produced a textbook that did not contain a single grammatical explanation; the content consisted entirely of pattern sentences and practice exercises. It was proclaimed as the latest and most scientific method of language learning and hundreds of teachers adopted it for use in their classroom. Most of those teachers discontinued its use after a year or two because they were used to explaining grammar and it frustrated them that the book did not explain to the students "why it is said that way," and many teachers felt they were constantly having to make up for the "inadequacies" of text by preparing their own explanation of the rules.

But isn't it true that one can communicate with just words? (We are indebted to our colleague Cheryl Brown of the BYU Department of Linguistics for the following example.) If someone were to say, even with very bad pronunciation,

You me downtown movie much fun?

we would probably get the message. Even if the order were changed and one said,

Much fun you me movie downtown?

we would still understand. This can certainly be called communication, and isn't that our major goal in teaching a language?

But surely, others will argue, we want to go beyond the "Me Tarzan, you Jane" level of communication. It is obvious that if our students speak only with words they will not be very highly regarded by natives, perhaps even considered to be non-educated louts. Accuracy in speech should be important. In that case, should we go back to spending the major part of our class time discussing the rules and convolutions of structure as we did for generations? The failures of the past don't argue well for that course of action, either. Our years of experience have shown that understanding a rule doesn't automatically ensure the *use* of that concept in conversation.

Further, grammar cannot be separated from the language itself; if we teach the language we must do *something* with the grammar. It is interesting to see the terms used by "experts" and some textbooks as they try to avoid any appearance of being so "old fashioned" as to teach grammar. A common ploy is to teach it, but to call it something else. What used to be the grammar sections of textbooks are now called "structure," "basic patterns," "How Spanish works," or "Why do they say it that way?" Just as a rose would smell the same under any other name, grammar is grammar no matter what we call it, and it still needs to be dealt with.

The Importance of the Teacher's Attitude

We need to emphasize that the attitude of the teacher in teaching grammar is of utmost importance. How you approach this with your students will set the tone and will shape their own attitude. If you overemphasize accuracy, they may develop inhibitions or feel apprehensive about talking. If you give them understanding support and loving correction, they will not feel hesitant to try, even though they know they will be making mistakes.

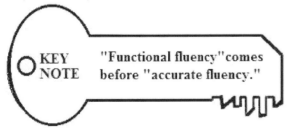

KEY NOTE — "Functional fluency" comes before "accurate fluency."

You must understand that at first they will be struggling just to understand and make themselves understood. If they can do that, we should be cheering them on and be happy with

their progress, not berating them for not making their adjective agree with its noun. We must be patient and constantly remind them (and ourselves) that this is a process of "perfecting" and not producing perfection.

Generally speaking, Spanish teachers are wildly interested in the structure of the language and how it works. We shouldn't forget that we are a different breed from our students, and most likely they won't share that fascination. We must resist the temptation to dump everything we know on them, as the following anecdote illustrates.

There was once a preacher who spent much time and effort trying to convince a certain farmer to come to church on Sundays. Every time he saw the farmer he would ask him to come, but the farmer never did. Finally, one Sunday the farmer showed up at church. Unfortunately no one else came that day. The preacher didn't know what to do. After all his efforts to get the farmer to come he couldn't just send him home without giving a sermon. So for an hour the preacher delivered a "hell's-fire and damnation" sermon while the farmer listened. After the services, the preacher said to the farmer, "I hope I didn't overwhelm you, but I felt that since you made the effort to come, I couldn't send you away with nothing. After all, when you go out on your farm to work, you wouldn't return home without doing anything." "Yes," replied the farmer, "but if I were working on my farm and had a whole wagon load of manure, I wouldn't dump it all on to one plant."

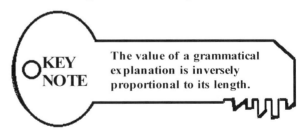

KEY NOTE — The value of a grammatical explanation is inversely proportional to its length.

Just as a sex-education teacher doesn't tell all he or she knows about sex, we shouldn't teach all we know about the language.

We must never forget that a student's understanding of a grammatical concept does not equate to an immediate ability to use that concept in communication. Students often come with that incorrect expectation because it often works in other classes, such as history, math, or chemistry.

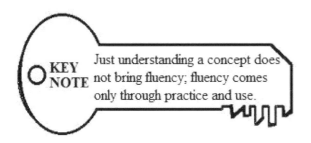

KEY NOTE — Just understanding a concept does not bring fluency; fluency comes only through practice and use.

After we have made the presentation and our students have understood, we must still spend many hours with practice activities.

While it is true that careful use of grammar terminology can help us be more exact in our explanation of grammar, we must understand that our students will probably not understand most of the technical terms such as possessive pronouns, dative of interest, copulative verbs, etc. This is true even of university students. We should be content to use simple, descriptive terms such as "the person who does the action," "the thing which receives the action," the "describing word," etc. This is especially true if you do this in Spanish, as we recommend that you do.

The following grammatical explanation was taken from a Chinese first year textbook and shows how difficult it can be to understand something explained with terms the student will not understand:

"The structural particle " 的 " is used to connect the attributive and what it qualifies. If the attributive is made of a verb, a verbal construction, a subject-predicate construction or an adjective with its adverbial adjunct," 的 " can't be omitted."

This type of explanation usually leaves the student's head spinning.

This discussion about how different people view the place of grammar in a foreign language classroom might still leave you with the question, "What shall *I* do about it?" We have seen that you cannot separate it from the language, so rather than ignore and never mention it, you must assign it a new role. The question now becomes, *In **what ways** shall I teach grammar and **what role** should it play in my classes?"*

A COMPREHENSIVE APPROACH TO GRAMMAR INSTRUCTION

It is our opinion that understanding how the language works will facilitate the learning process, but it must not become the **primary** focus of our classes. The teacher must strike a balance between spending too much time in formal explanation of grammar, and leaving the students completely on their own to puzzle out what is going on. Grammar teaching, *per se*, should take **secondary** priority in competing for class time with other activities designed to develop comprehension and speaking skills. Unfortunately, with some teachers the explanation of grammar concepts is the primary focus of the class. These teachers seem almost grateful that they have the language handy so they can use it illustrate the grammar points they have "to cover." There are many teachers who despair at the poor background in grammar of their students, and not just a few who "spend the first eight weeks (or months?) teaching terminology and the fundamentals of English grammar, and only then start teaching the foreign language.

What seems to be the most sensible and productive approach is to think of grammar principles as **concepts** or **general characteristics of the language** that are taught as a **support** or **help** to the student in achieving our communicative objectives.

Grammar at the Input Stage

Following our model for language learning which we presented in Chapter 3, we will suggest three levels at which we can integrate grammar concepts into our classes. You will recall that the three stages or levels that must be followed to bring our students to communication are: **input**, **practice**, and **expression.** The initial *presentation* of a grammar concept clearly falls into the input stage:

INPUT STAGE

X

A good place to start might be to give our students some notion of how we learn structures in our native language. This will help them gain the skill of *learning to recognize grammatical patterns on their own.* (An *inductive* approach.) A motivating activity is to have them help you decide how we form plurals in English. With a few exceptions this will be a totally new experience for your students. Here are two possible activities:

A practice activity to develop the skill of discovering grammar patterns. The class is divided into groups of 5, and each group is given a handout using the following figures:

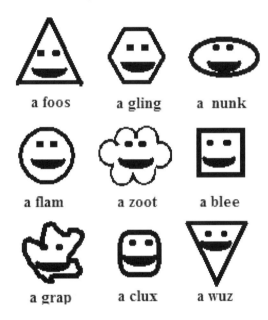

a foos   a gling   a nunk

a flam   a zoot   a blee

a grap   a clux   a wuz

The handout introduces the above characters singly and then in pairs. For example:

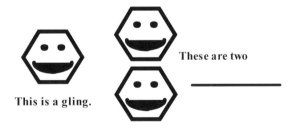

This is a gling.   These are two _____

First the teacher has the students group the words into three separate groups, according to how they would form the oral plurals of those words if they were English words. Then the teacher asks them to describe the sound they would use to make the words of each group plural.

Now, and this is the hard part, the students must analyze what common properties each group of words has that would put them together in the group and describe what those properties are. The teacher might have to help the students after a while by suggesting that it has something to do with the sound(s) at the end of the words. When they have discovered the answer, then they apply their rules to English nouns and see if they are the same. The teacher finally has them create a "rule" about how we form oral plurals in English.

A second inductive grammar practice. Another motivating activity can help the students become conscious about looking for patterns in a foreign language. This exercise was taken from the aptitude test developed at the Defense Language Institute (DLI) in Monterey, California.

The students are first given four pictures and asked to study them and try to discover structure patterns in the language.

shiyu

jamo

shiyum jamo gingvi

čaya

Then the students are given this picture:

Using what they learned from the first four pictures, the students must decide which of the following sentences correctly describes what is happening in the picture.

    a. shiyum chaya gingvi
    b. cayam shiyu gingvi
    c. cayam jamo gingvi
    d. shiyu gingvi cayam

The students are then given another picture and asked to choose a, b, c, or d.

    a. shiyu kotli jamom
    b. jamom shiyu kotli
    c. shiyum jamo kotli
    d. jamom kotli shiyu

The students must now use everything they have discovered about the structure of the language in the previous pictures to figure out the last picture that presents all new vocabulary.

    a. lola hungam piki

    b. piki lola hungam
    c. hungam piki lola
    d. hungam lola piki

The students should finally be able to come up with five rules about the structure of this language. Exercises of this kind should give your students better insight into seeing patterns in other languages.

Advanced organizing. Experienced teachers have learned that they can lead up to presenting a grammatical concept a little at a time. A structure can first be presented in a natural context with no specific commentary. For example, in a dialogue or reading assignment, the students might see, *"Ojalá que se mejore pronto,"* in one of the very first lessons. No mention is made of the use of the subjunctive at that time. It is just treated as a vocabulary item. As the course progresses, there will be other instances of subjunctive uses, and finally, when the students are ready, we will make a conscious presentation of the subjunctive structure and its use, taking examples the students have already seen. This "foreshadowing" of grammatical structures can "spiral" upward through the course and be integrated with constant practice and reinforcement.

Presenting Grammatical Concepts

A grammatical concept can be presented in a number of ways. Our basic focus will be on two: a *deductive* approach and an *inductive* approach.

The Deductive Approach. For centuries language teachers have taught grammatical concepts in the class with a deductive, or overt, approach. In this approach, the teacher (or the textbook, for that matter) overtly explains the concept by directly describing how it works or by stating rules. Examples of its use in the language are given, and the students then procede to the practice phase.

Unfortunately, in this type of presentation, it is usually the case that technical grammatical terms are used that the students do not understand. Long years of experience in teaching at the secondary, and even at the university level, have proven to us that students often do not know what a *pronoun*, a *preposition*, or an *adverb* are. Teachers find that they must define the terminology or the students will not understand the explanations. Statements such as *"In Spanish, an **adjective** must agree with its **noun** in **number** and **gender**"* often pass right over the students' heads.

Teachers can help the students in this approach by using charts and visual aids that help the student understand what the terminology refers to. What Spanish student hasn't used the idea of *"**shoe verbs**"* to remember which persons of the stem-changing verbs require a change in the stem and which ones don't?

pensar

pienso	pensamos
piensas	pensáis
piensa	piensan

The use of charts to help students remember verb tenses or forms of pronouns has also been practiced by teachers for generations. Don't these charts look familiar to you?

Direct Object Pronouns	
me	nos
te	os
lo, la	los, las

And what teacher is not familiar with the diagrams that indicate what is happening in sentences like this?

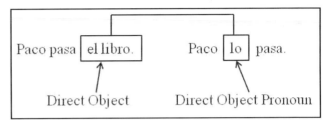

Then this is followed by a more complicated diagram that shows the transformation of *le* and *les* to *se*.

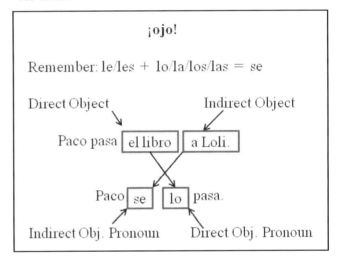

This entire presentation can be made even more attractive if illustrated with pictures.

Paco pasa el libro a Loli.

Paco se lo pasa.

Teachers who teach grammar deductively should make every effort to simplify their presentations and proceed immediately to practice activities that will put the concept into "the bones and tissues."

Teaching grammar inductively. Our own experience has taught us that a more effective and lasting way to present a concept is to use an **"inductive"** approach. An inductive approach to teaching a grammar concept lends itself well to the deemphasizing of grammar analysis, and by its nature disciplines the teacher to make a careful and simple, clearly understandable, presentation (in Spanish, of course), rather than depending on grammar terminology, and verbose, erudite explanations.

An inductive approach consists of three phases:

1. A carefully planned presentation which focuses sharply on the grammar point being taught, contrasting where possible with that which is already known, and with enough examples that the students can draw an analogy (generalize) as to the concept being taught. If for example, you are teaching the difference between *ser* and *estar*, you would present a number of examples with *ser* and then contrast them with examples of *estar*. You could, for example, have a student stand up while you make a number of comments about him, such as: *José es alto, es guapo, es estudiante, es de Provo, es norteamericano*, etc. You would then make another series of comments about him using *estar*, such as: *José está en la clase, no está enfermo, está contento, está en Provo*, etc.

This type of presentation requires students to pay attention, to think and reason about what is going on. They can see that you are sometimes using *es* and sometimes using *está*, but since you offer no explanation, they start looking for the reasons why. When they have to discover the answers for themselves, making a conscious effort to understand, they will retain the concept much longer, will understand it better, and, more importantly, will be far more likely to use it as they speak the language.

2. The teacher now spends a good deal of time (perhaps several class periods) providing the students with a variety of activities in which they practice the concept that was presented. They have already made generalizations in their mind, and they now test and verify, and modify if necessary, their conclusions as they practice. Teacher correction or confirmation will allow them to adjust any erroneous conclusions they

may have drawn. For some students this may be the point where they really grasp the concept for the first time, having missed it in the presentation.

It is in the practice phase that the students develop the conditioning that leads them to conjugate verbs, make adjectives agree, use object pronouns, and get the words in the right order. The ability to do these things does not come from hearing, and even understanding a grammar explanation. If your students forget to make an adjective agree or conjugate a verb wrong, they don't need more grammar explanations, they need to consciously practice and be gently reminded when they forget to apply the concept that they have already internalized.

3. (Optional) The teacher ties things together in a brief summary with a carefully prepared discussion of what the students have been practicing for some time. The teacher leads the student (in Spanish or English) to state in their own words what the concept or rule is. The teacher does not explain the rule. He asks carefully pointed or leading questions designed to highlight the contrasts and have the students tell what they think is going on.

You can avoid using technical grammar terms; the students might say the "describing word" instead of "adjective," the "person who is doing the action" instead of the "subject," etc. Sometimes the teacher might want to teach them useful terms, such as "the impersonal *se*," the "command" forms, "masculine" and "feminine," etc. At the end of the discussion, the teacher can have the students state a rule in their own words.

Obviously, this approach involves more preparation and takes more time than the traditional **deductive** approach where the teacher simply stands in front of the class and explains the rule, but research has shown that an inductive approach that requires the students to concentrate on what is happening and allows them to discover the concept on their own, is much more understandable, meaningful, and long-lasting (Haight, Herron, & Cole, 2007). It also permits the teacher to present the concept in Spanish, because it is done in a simple, step-by-step fashion. The time and effort spent in making the inductive presentation is well worth it in terms of results. A full example of a grammar concept presented with an inductive approach follows:

1. Presentation (The teacher begins by showing a picture of a boy writing a letter.)

Maestro(a):	Díganme lo que pasa aquí.
Estudiantes:	Juan escribe la carta
Maestro(a):	¿Quién hace la acción de esta frase? (¿Quién es el actor, o el sujeto de la frase?)
Estudiantes:	Juan.
Maestro(a):	¿Qué recibe la acción del verbo? (¿Cuál es el objeto del verbo?)
Estudiantes:	La carta.
Maestro(a):	Podemos decir toda esta información en otra manera. (Con énfasis) La carta es escrita por Juan. Ahora, ¿cuál es el sujeto, y qué tiene el énfasis?
Estudiantes:	La carta.

The teacher then repeats the process with the following sentences:

Juan escribe muchas cartas. (**Muchas cartas son escritas por Juan.**)
Juan escribe el ejercicio. (**El ejercicio es escrito por Juan.**) Juan escribe los ejercicios, etc.)
La chica come el pastel. (**El pastel es comido por la chica**, los pasteles, etc.)
Los estudiantes abren la ventana. (**La ventana es abierta por los estudiantes**, las ventanas,
El profesor corrige los exámenes. (**Los exámenes son corregidos por el profesor**, etc.)

At this point, the teacher will give some new sentences and the students will change them to the passive: *María estudia la lección, El conserje limpia los cuartos, La secretaria contesta el teléfono, El profesor saca las notas, etc.* The students should be able to make the changes. If not, the teacher repeats the process.

2. Practice (A number of practice activities should be scheduled to allow the students to internalize the concept and gain skill in using it.)

3. Generalization (Optional) Teacher shows the following visual aid and asks carefully ordered questions.

I	**II.**
1. Juan escribe la carta.	1. La carta **es** escrit**a por** Juan.
2. Juan escribe muchas cartas.	2. Muchas cartas **son** escritas **por** Juan.
3. Juan escribe el ejercicio.	3. El ejercicio **es** escrit**o por** Juan.
4. La chica come el pastel.	4. El pastel **es** comid**o por** la chica.
5. Los estudiantes abren las ventanas.	5. Las ventanas **son** abiert**as por** los estudiantes.
6. El profesor corrige los exámenes.	6. Los exámenes **son** corregid**os** por el profesor.

Maestro(a):	Vamos a ver si ustedes me pueden decir lo que pasa aquí, y me pueden formar una regla. En la primera frase de la columna uno, ¿cuál es el sujeto y que recibe la acción del verbo.
Estudiantes:	Juan es el sujeto y la carta recibe la acción, es el objeto.
Maestro(a)	En la primera frase de la columna dos, ¿cuál es el sujeto y recibe el énfasis?
Estudiantes:	La carta.
Maestro(a):	¿Cómo sabemos que recibe el énfasis?
Estudiantes:	Porque viene primero.
Maestro(a):	¿Qué diferencia hay entre "Juan escribe la carta" y "La carta es escrita por Juan"?
Estudiantes:	En la segunda, el énfasis está en lo que antes era el objeto que ahora es el sujeto.
Maestro(a):	¿Qué diferencias ven ustedes en la construcción de la frase uno en la columna dos?
Estudiantes:	La carta viene primero, hay es, escrita, y por, y Juan viene al final.
Maestro(a):	¿De que verbo viene la forma es, y por que tenemos esta conjugación?

Estudiantes:	Es de *ser*, y tenemos esa conjugación por que la carta es el sujeto.
Maestro(a):	¿Qué forma tiene el verbo principal en las frases de la columna dos, y por qué?
Estudiantes:	Es la forma de *-ado, ido, -to* (participio pasado) y es masculino, femenino, singular, o plural según el sujeto.
Maestro(a):	¿Qué palabra usamos para expresar el agente o la persona que hace la acción?
Estudiantes:	Por.
Maestro(a):	¡Han hecho un trabajo magnífico! Esta transformación se llama la voz pasiva.

Introducing grammar with textbooks. While some textbooks overemphasize grammar and others make their explanations too complicated or all-inclusive, many textbooks have good grammar presentations with many examples and practice exercises. A teacher can give assignments to read and practice grammar at home.

Some teachers argue that since the textbook usually makes simple and well-stated grammar explanations, there really is no need to spend class time going over it one more time. They simply assign the students to read the grammar sections outside class, and the students then come to class prepared to practice the concept. This can be a valid approach if you have a textbook that does have simple, easy to understand grammar presentations, accompanied by many examples and followed by exercises that the students can do to practice the concept just learned. Certainly we must protect our precious class time for activities that cannot be done outside of class, such as listening comprehension activities, oral drills, pair and group practice, conversation sessions, role-playing, and simulations. Lengthy grammar explanations in class can easily take away time from these kinds of activities.

Grammar at the Practice Stage

As we have commented before, working with grammar at the **practice** stage is by far the most effective way to make it a permanent part of our students' natural use of the language. During the audio-lingual era grammar practice was primarily confined to **pattern drills**. The basic premise of pattern drill practice was that in order for a grammar structure to become automatic, the students had to practice until they became conditioned to its use.

This "conditioning process" was misused by many teachers because they never moved from the out-of-context drills to real communication and the drills were very monotonous and boring. This approach is often referred to as "kill and drill."

Nevertheless there has to be some way to "cement" the newly-learned grammar concept into the students' use of the language. A more effective and motivating approach to practicing patterns is to use interactive or dynamic activities that are placed in a real-life context. Once the grammatical concept has been presented and the students have an idea about what is going on, the teachers can best direct their efforts toward activities which will allow the students to "internalize" the concept, that is get it into their "bones and tissues."

Most textbooks approach this task with exercises in the text. Unfortunately many of these exercises are mechanical and are intended to be written out. Few textbooks provide activities that permit students to practice orally in the class. The teacher may have to look elsewhere for "dynamic" activities, or prepare them himself.

There are a number of kinds of activities that will allow the students to orally practice a grammar concept during a class period. The most effective are organized to allow the students to work in pairs or small groups, but there are some that work well with the participation of the entire class. We will give you a variety here so you can have an idea of the different types.

¿Qué tal la clase? *(an activity for pairs)*

Grammar concept: Forms of preterite
Practice the forms of the preterite tense

Materials needed
Transparency or student handout of the
Picture and model

Instructions:
Review formation of the preterite forms, including irregulars
Divide the class into pairs.
Referring to the picture (either a handout or transparency) present the following model to them:

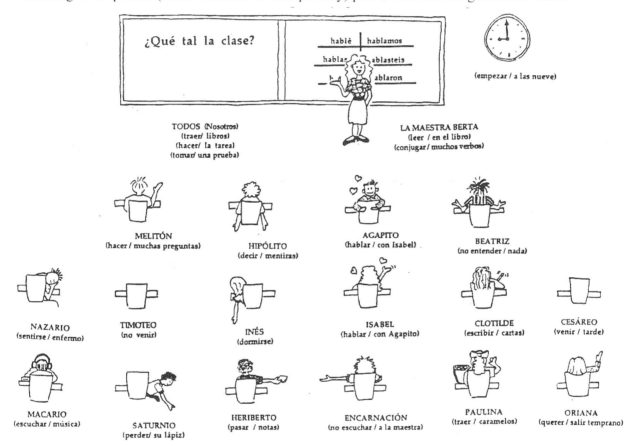

Estudiante "A" falta un día a la clase. Al regresar al día siguiente pregunta a Estudiante "B": "¿Qué tal la clase ayer?" Estudiante "B" responde con una de las acciones que ve en el dibujo, por ejemplo: "La maestra nos **enseñó** mucha gramática." Estudiante "A" (fijándose en el dibujo) pregunta: "¿Qué **hizo** Inés?" Estudiante "B" responde: "Se **durmió**." etc.

Announce that you are going to practice with a student. Choose a student and go through the model with him/her while all listen. Start them working with the activity and walk around helping and correcting where needed. About halfway through the activity, have them change roles and Estudiante "B" asks the questions and Estudiante "A" answers them.

Variations: 1. To practice the use of an *imperfect description*, interrupted by a preterite action, change the situation to where one student is telling another that he arrived late to the class and tells what was going on when he arrived. For example: "Cuando llegué a la clase, Melitón **hacía** preguntas."
2. Can also be done with *progressive tense*: "Cuando llegué a la clase, Agapito **estaba hablando** con Isabel."

Te doy la oreja por la manzana *(an activity with the entire class)*

Grammar concept: Por and para
Practice some of the different uses of *por* and *para*

Materials needed
Transparency with model
Picture flash cards—general vocabulary

Instructions:
Review following uses of por and para:
Give each person in the class seven flash cards

Display the model either on the chalk board or with a transparency and practice it with the students.

MODELO   Estudiante "A": A ver, ¿qué tienes?
                Estudiante "B": (mostrando) Tengo_una manzana_ [un reloj , una araña , etc.]
                Estudiante "A": Quiero _la manzana_ .
                Estudiante "B": ¿**Para** qué la quieres?
                Estudiante "A": **Para** _comerla._
                Estudiante "B": A ver, ¿qué tienes tú?
                Estudiante "A": (mostrando) Tengo_un pez_ [un mono , una oreja , etc.]
                Estudiante "B": Te doy _la manzana_ **por** _la oreja._
                Estudiante "A": ¿**Para** qué la quieres?
                Estudiante "B": **Para**_escuchar al profesor._
                Estudiante "A": Bueno, te doy _la oreja_ **por** _la manzana._

Explain that the purpose of the game is to collect a set of four cards that fit in a category. Encourage the students to be creative with their trading. For example, they could collect animals, something to eat, things you see in the sky, all black things, etc. Perhaps if someone wants something that they don't want to give up, they could trade two cards for it. Start them working with the activity and walk around helping and correcting where needed. Keep an ear out for English speakers. At the end of the game, give prizes to the students with the best sets. Have them show and explain their sets to the class.

¡Mentira! *(an activity for pairs)*

Grammar concept: **Use of sino**

Materials needed
Picture flash cards — comida
Transparency of model

Instructions:

Review the use of *sino*
Divide the class into pairs. Each pair should have a set of comida flash cards divided between them.

Referring to the transparency, go over the model with the students.

Maestro/a: Estudiante "A" tiene un problema. Le gusta mentir. Estudiante "B" tiene que
corregirle. Por ejemplo:

Estudiante "A": (Mostrando una calabaza) Esto es un <u>tomate</u>.
Estudiante "B": ¡Mentira! No es un tomate **sino** una calabaza.
Estudiante "A": (Mostrando un pescado) Esto es un <u>pollo</u>.
Estudiante "B": ¡Mentira! No es un pollo **sino** un pescado.

Announce that you are going practice with a student. Choose someone and go through the model with him/her while all listen. Start them working with the activity and walk around helping and correcting where needed. About halfway through the activity, have them change roles so that the other person gets to be the person that tells the "mentira."

Nunca he . . . . . *(a small group activity)*

Grammar concept: Present perfect
Practice using the *present perfect* tense in
the *yo* form

Materials needed
Transparency with model and vocab.
either prepared or brainstormed
Classroom money or candy

Instructions:

Review formation of the present perfect tense with special emphasis on the irregular past participles (roto, hecho, puesto, visto, etc.). Divide the class into groups of six or more students. Give each student six or more (depending on size of group) bills (or pieces of candy if class has no money system — taffy or small individually wrapped candies work best.) Assign a "director" in each group to keep the game moving and to make sure that no one speaks English.

Explain the game as follows:

Vamos a jugar a **"NUNCA HE..."**. La idea de este juego es ganar lo más dinero (o dulces) posible. Para ganar dinero tú tienes que pensar en una actividad que tú **nunca** hayas hecho que los demás probablemente **sí** hayan hecho. Por ejemplo: "Yo nunca he comido una hamburguesa." ¿Ustedes han comido hamburguesas? (Most students will probably have to answer: "Sí, yo he comido una hamburguesa".) Entonces ésta sería una **buena** pregunta para usar en este juego. "Yo nunca he viajado a África." ¿Ustedes han viajado a África? (Most students should respond: "No, yo nunca he viajado a África.") Entonces, ésta **no** sería una buena pregunta para usar en el juego. Recuerden, hay que decir la verdad.

El "director" empieza, diciendo algo que él no ha hecho. Todas las personas que hayan hecho la actividad, es decir, tienen que contestar que "sí", tienen que darle a la persona que hizo la pregunta un billete de dinero (o un dulce). Así va turnando por el circulo, cada persona diciendo algo que nunca ha hecho.

Move from circle to circle helping and correcting. At the end of the game the person with the most money (*o dulces*) wins.

There are many more of these interactive practice activities in the booklet *Dynamic Activities for Grammar Practice*, some for almost any grammar point or concept you will want to teach.

Using Songs to Practice Grammar. Songs can serve as another technique to present and practice a grammar concept. They can be used simply to give examples of different uses of a grammar point, or can involve the students in an activity where they actually practice the structure

Sing along with the examples on the following page.

Un elefante *(preterite and imperfect)*

Un elefante se **balanceaba**
Sobre la tela de una araña
Como **veía** que no se **caía**,
Fue a llamar a otro elefante.

Dos elefantes se **balanceaban**
Sobre la tela de una araña.
Como **veían** que no se **caían**,
Fueron a llamar a otro elefante.

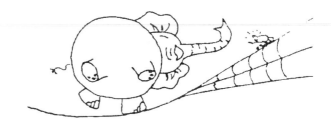

Los dientes *(reflexives)*

Los dientes no **me lavaré**,
Un niño exclamó.
Ya **me lavé**, ya **me peiné**,
Con eso me bastó.
Mas en su boca se oyó
Un grito de placer,
Y los microbios sin temor,
Salieron a comer.

Dijeron llenos de placer:
Aquí hay buen hogar.
Entre sus dientes sin lavar,
Podremos festejar.
Oyó el niño de su plan
Y pronto **se lavó**,
A los microbios él mató,
Ni uno escapó.

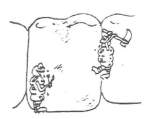

Some songs can be varied to give a greater practice of the vocabulary topic or grammatical pattern. For example, with the song *Me gustan todas*, which in its original version refers to girls, it can be varied to refer to something else:

Me gustan todas
(Original version)

Me gustan todas, me gustan todas,
Me gustan todas en general,
Pero esa rubia, pero esa rubia,
Pero esa rubia me gusta más.

Having taught the song, the teacher then announces that they will now sing about fruit and teaches another version:

Me gustan frutas, me gustan frutas,
Me gustan frutas en general,
Pero ese mango (pera, cereza, manzana, etc.),
Pero ese mango,
Pero ese mango me gusta más. [Etc.]

Another technique used by teachers to practice grammar with songs is to give the students a sheet with some crucial words left out. As the students listen and fill in the blanks, they focus in on some grammar point. The following song can be used to practice the forms of the subjunctive:

¡Qué canten los niños! *(subjunctive)*

Que _____ (cantar) los niños,
   que _____ (alzar) la voz
Que _____ (hacer) al mundo escuchar
Que _____ (unir) sus voces
   y _____ (llegar) al sol
En ellos está la verdad

Que _____ (cantar) los niños,
   que _____ (vivir) en paz
Y aquellos que sufren dolor
Que _____ (cantar) por esos que no cantarán
Porque han apagado su voz . . .

232

Using writing workbooks. As we mentioned in Chapter 9, most text programs are accompanied by writing workbooks that give the students additional practice with the grammatical concept presented in the text. The best type of these workbooks have keys or answers which permit the students to check their own work and make corrections, thus reinforcing the grammar point. This saves the teacher many hours of correcting homework

Integrating Grammar at the Expression Stage

Our final goal in foreign language instruction is communication. This means that we must bring the students to situations where they are using the language in the ways it is normally and naturally used: expressing ideas, getting and giving information, defending opinions, and so on. That brings us to the expression stage.

EXPRESSION STAGE

Integrating grammar at the expression stage is not easy, because it means that we move away from our focus on the specific grammatical concept and move to a *whole language* context, where we try to communicate without worrying about correctness. Our best approach at this level is to try to present contexts that require certain grammatical patterns and hope the students will integrate the concepts they have been practicing. For example, have them describe people, hoping they will use adjective agreement; talk about past events, hoping they will use the past forms of the verbs; give directions, hoping they will use command forms; express feelings, hoping they will use the subjunctive, etc

The techniques and activities which we presented in Chapter 7 such as conducting conversation sessions, playing games, and performing simulations will all help students integrate the grammatical patterns into their everyday use of the language. Task performance activities can also bring grammar use into natural, common situations.

Practicing Grammar With Games. There are a number of games that are ideal for practicing grammar concepts. The best part about using games is that you can use the motivating force of competition and the students enjoy it so much that they don't want to stop. Some different types of games are shown on the following page.

Voy a España *(personal "a")*

This is one of those fun, "add-on" games. The players sit in a circle, and the first player says: "Voy a España y voy a llevar _____" naming some object or person he wants to take with him. The second player then repeats the sentence, naming the object chosen by the first player, and then adding an object or person of his own. The game continues around the circle and the list gets longer. If a player fails to name everything in correct order, or forgets an item, he is out of the game. The winner is the player who can stay in the circle the longest without making a mistake.

To practice the personal "a," the leader brainstorms with the group two lists; a list of things and a list of people. Players have to choose an item from one of the lists. With the persons they have to say: "...y voy a llevar *a* ....". The lists could include: una maleta, mi novio(a), mis padres, un mapa, un diccionario, camisas limpias, mi chofer, una cámera, un(a) guía, el/la professor/a de español, mucho dinero, la señorita Gómez, mi pasaporte, un intérprete, mis tíos, etc.

Here is another game that requires the cooperation of all students, since they must get information from others.

¡Tú eres mi madre!
(Function: Ask personal questions / Grammar concept: Interrogatives, forms of "*ser*")

Each player receives a card with information about himself and a member of his or her "family" written on it. (See model.) The leader explains that there are several families consisting of a father, mother, son, daughter, grandfather, and aunt, i.e. there are 6 members in each "family." At the leader's signal all the students will walk around in the class asking questions, trying to find the "family" member described on their cards. They must ask and answer questions only in Spanish! When players discover a family member they are looking for, they work together to find the other 4. The family that is all reunited first is the winner.

Modelo:	**tú**	**tu madre**
	Tienes 18 años.	Tiene 45 años.
	Vives en Nueva York.	Vive en Los Angeles.
	Eres estudiante.	Es maestra.
	Tienes un Volkswagen.	Tiene un Buick.
	Te gusta la comida mexicana.	Le gusta la comida mexicana

There are many more examples of games that can be used to teach grammar principles in the booklet *Me gusta jugar.*

USING VISUAL AIDS TO TEACH GRAMMAR

Visual aids can be of great value at all stages of our work with grammar instruction, especially at the presentation and practice stage. Following are some examples of the use of visuals in presenting and practicing concepts. In this case the grammar concept is the use of subjunctive with in noun clauses. The visuals reinforce the fact that the dependent clause is being subjected to the feelings and emotions of the main clause.

*Estamos contentos que tu mamá **esté** bien.*

*Es triste que no **puedas** ir al cine con nosotros.*

*El profesor insiste que **hablemos** español en la clase.*

*Mi novia quiere que yo le **escriba**.*

*Me da pena que José **salga** con esa chica.*

*Preferimos que no **cante** Josefina.*

Many teachers find that they can put up a bulletin board a few days in advance of discussing a grammatical concept, and then use the board as a focus of presentation. The following page shows an example of a bulletin board that illustrates how the different phrases and constructions are used in Spanish to talk about weather conditions.

235

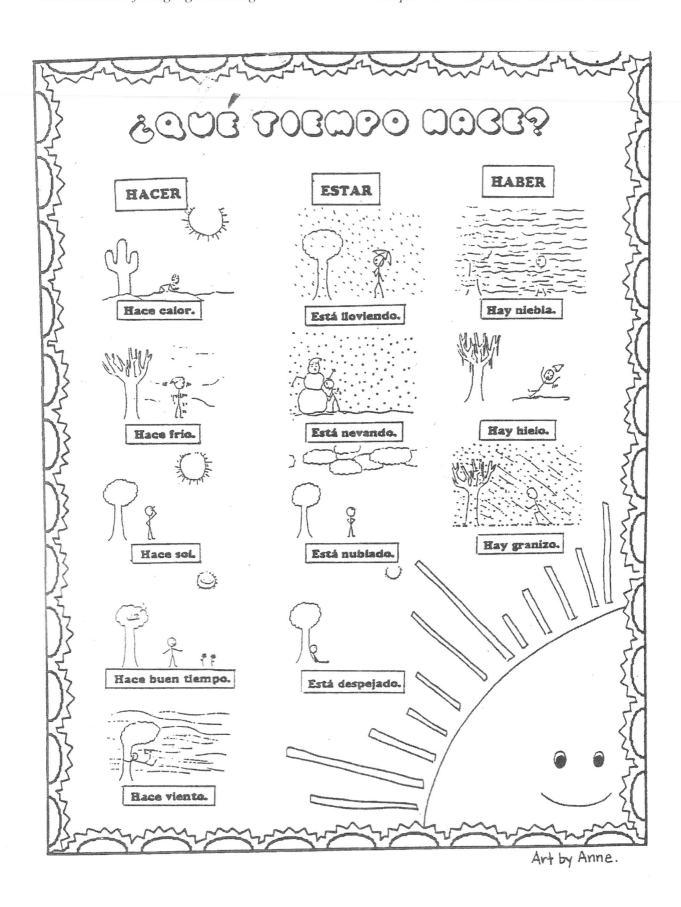

A "Visual Grammar of Spanish"

The late William E. Bull, who was a professor of Spanish Linguistics at UCLA, developed a very useful approach to teaching grammar. His technique consisted in trying to reduce the grammar rule, or principle to a very simple idea and then illustrating that idea with pictures. That led to the development of an entire set of pictures that included all the major grammatical concepts commonly presented in a Spanish class. Following are examples of those materials:

 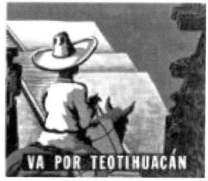

Using the visuals, the teacher could present the grammar concept either inductively or deductively, and then move to practice activities. Long out of print, these materials have recently become available to teachers again. A reissue of Bull's classic posters on DVD-ROM (Whitney & Lunn, 2010) provides versatile JPEG images of all the posters to easily incorporate into Power Point presentations and worksheets. It includes an instructor's manual on the disk that presents background on the materials, explains the concepts behind the images, and offers suggestions for ways to use them in the classroom.

Language labs that purchase a copy of *Teaching Spanish Grammar with Pictures* will automatically receive rights to (a) post an electronic copy of the content on a secure (password-protected) network for use by current students and faculty at their institution; and (b) loan the number of purchased copies to students.

Use of these marerials greatly facilitates limiting the presentation of grammar to a very simplified concept. It also allows the teacher to present the concept in an inductive approach inviting the students to discover it themselves.

SOME TECHNIQUES AND "GIMMICKS" FOR PRESENTING SPECIFIC GRAMMAR CONCEPTS

Gustar-Type Verbs

The basic problem with *gustar* and verbs of this type is that the student associates the meaning of the verb with the English verb and uses the same construction. The student reasons:

gustar means to like, thus I like = *gusto*,
We like = *gustamos*, etc.

What the teacher needs to do is help the student see that even though the basic **equivalent meaning** of *gustar* is to like, the **construction** is that of *to appeal to*, thus *it appeals to me, we appeal to them*, etc.

An effective practice is to turn off your "no English" sign and practice in English, changing from the "to like" construction to the "to-appeal-to" construction. Example:

Teacher	Students
I like the food.	The food appeals to me.
They liked the movie.	The movie appealed to them.
We really like her.	She really appeals to us.
I like you a lot; do you like me?	You appeal to me a lot, do I appeal to you?
We hope John will like the present.	We hope the present will appeal to John.

CONCLUSION

In our efforts to help the students remember grammatical concepts we often reach out to use any device we can. Another example is as follows:

The two-headed monster

Did you know that the *por/para* decisions are easier if we think of a "two-headed" monster? The *para* head looks forward: some future event, someone something is being given to, some intended act. The *por* head looks backward to see the cause or reason for doing something.

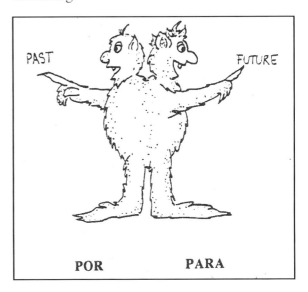

PAST   FUTURE

POR   **PARA**

Although teaching grammar will not be our major focus in our classes, we cannot ignore the fact that grammar is an essential part of the language. If we want our students to be understood and respected, we should help them learn to use correctly the structures of the language. At the same time we must be patient and realize that we cannot expect perfection from day one and that part of the process of learning a language will include making mistakes. We must tolerate these mistakes and constantly provide them with helpful explanations, but at the same time save the bulk of our class time for meaningful and effective practices, oral and writing, which will allow the students to integrate the patterns permanently into their use of the language.

| REFERENCES AND SUGGESTIONS FOR FURTHER READING |

Haight, C. E., Herron, C., & Cole, S. P. (2007). The effects of deductive and guided inductive instructional approaches on the learning of grammar in the elementary foreign language college classroom. *Foreign Language Annals, 40,* 288-310. DOI: 10.1111/j.1944-9720.2007.tb03202.x *Reports on a study with college students of French showing that an inductive approach to teaching grammar results in greater short-term and long-term gains than does a deductive approach.*

Krashen, S. D., & Terrell, T. D. (1983). *The Natural Approach.* Hayward, CA: Alemany Press.

Nassaji, H., & Fotos, S. (2010). *Teaching grammar in second language classrooms: Integrating form-focused instruction in communicative context* (ESL & Applied Linguistics Professional Series). London, England: Routledge. *Explores various options for integrating a focus on grammar and a focus on communication in classroom contexts and offers concrete examples of teaching activities for each option. Designed for ESL but adaptable to Spanish.*

Whitney, M. S., & Lunn, P. V. (2010). *Teaching Spanish grammar with pictures: How to use William Bull's Visual Grammar of Spanish* [DVD]. Washington, DC: Georgetown University Press. *(described in the chapter)*

Other Books by James S. Taylor (see Appendix C for information)

- *Dynamic Activities for Practicing Spanish Grammar*
- *Materiales para animar la clase de español*
- *Me gusta cantar*
- *Me gusta jugar*
- *Me gusta conversar*
- *Me gusta aprender español*
- *Me gusta actuar*

Image Credits

p. 327: Whitney, M. S., & Lunn, P. V. (referenced above). Image from book cover used by permission of publisher.

ACTIVITIES FOR METHODS CLASSES

1. In group discussions, decide if a language can be learned with a total ignorance of grammatical or structural patterns. Decide if you would mention or not mention grammar in a language class. If you think conscious understanding of grammatical patterns would enhance and speed up language mastery, how would you treat them in a language class? Make a list of all the grammatical patterns of Spanish (adjective agreement, verb conjugation, reflexive, etc.) and decide which ones you think are crucial, essential to proficiency. What could you leave out in a beginning Spanish class? Report to the class.

2. In a group session, select several of the grammar concepts from the list you made in #1 above. Brainstorm with your classmates about ways you would present them to the students. Anticipate the visual aids you would use in presenting the concepts. Make copies of your list and comments, show them to the professor, and keep your copy for future use. Start preparing some of the visuals you mentioned.

3. Select a grammatical concept (or have it assigned by the professor) such as contrast between *ser* and *estar*, use of the subjunctive in noun clauses, the future of conjecture, etc., and prepare a presentation on that concept using the *inductive approach.* Prepare all the visual aids you will need in the presentation and prepare an overhead transparency or handout to use in the *generalization.* Make the presentation in the methods class.

4. Using the same grammar concept selected above, develop a *dynamic activity* to practice it. Conduct the activity in a micro lesson in the methods class.

5. Study the song collection *Me gusta cantar* to see what songs (such as *Me gustan todas, Un ratón, Cielito Lindo,* etc.) can be used to reinforce certain grammatical concepts. Using the list of grammatical concepts that you made from the activities above, write down songs by each grammatical concept would teach. Show the list to the instructor and save it for later use.

6. Study the indexes in the booklet Me *gusta jugar* and see which games can be used to practice which grammatical concepts. Think of other games you could use. Add your new games to the indexes and show to the professor.

7. Select a popular textbook for teaching Spanish and study how the grammar is presented. Is it a deductive or inductive approach? Are grammatical terms used which the students would not understand? How could you present the concept in simpler terms? How could you present the concept in an inductive approach? Show the results to your teacher.

8. Find a reference grammar book and review the fundamental grammatical concepts one more time, asking yourself some personal questions. Do you totally understand the rules? Do you personally use those structures correctly? Could you explain them to a class? In Spanish? How could you explain the concept in simpler terms than those used in the book? Plan a program to improve your personal use of certain grammar points, such as use of the subjunctive. Discuss with the professor.

9. Volunteer to serve as a tutor for actual university or secondary school students who are currently learning Spanish. Analyze their use of grammatical structures. What are they using correctly and what incorrectly? Prepare simple explanations that will help them. Try to do it inductively. Prepare activities that you can use in your tutoring sessions to help the student practice.

CHAPTER ELEVEN

TEACH CULTURE? I ONLY HAVE TIME TO TEACH THE LANGUAGE!

YOUR OBJECTIVES FOR THIS CHAPTER ARE TO:

1. DISCUSS WHAT THE TERM "CULTURE" INCLUDES.

2. BE CONVERTED TO THE IMPORTANCE OF INCLUDING CULTURE WITH THE LANGUAGE SKILLS.

3. DETERMINE WHAT TYPE OF CULTURAL INFORMATION SPANISH STUDENTS SHOULD LEARN.

4. IDENTIFY *GENERAL* CROSS-CULTURAL COMMUNICATION SKILLS THAT STUDENTS SHOULD DEVELOP.

5. IDENTIFY SOURCES FOR CULTURAL INFORMATION, ESPECIALLY THE INTERNET, AND STRATEGIES FOR USING ONLINE CULTURAL RESOURCES.

6. USE A VARIETY OF ACTIVITIES TO TEACH CULTURE-SPECIFIC INFORMATION IN THE CLASSROOM, INCLUDING CULTURE CAPSULES, CULTURAL ASIDES, CULTURE ASSIMILATORS, MINI-DRAMAS, AND CLASSROOM DÉCOR.

7. USE A VARIETY OF ACTIVITIES TO TEACH CULTURE-SPECIFIC INFORMATION *OUTSIDE* THE CLASSROOM, INCLUDING ETHNOGRAPHIC INTERVIEWS, LANGUAGE CLUB ACTIVITIES, CULTURAL INVESTIGATION PROJECTS, AND STUDY ABROAD.

8. DESCRIBE WAYS OF USING TECHNOLOGY TO TEACH CULTURE-SPECIFIC INFORMATION.

9. IDENTIFY TECHNIQUES AND MATERIALS FOR ASSESSING CULTURE LEARNING.

It was Friday at Podunk High and a group of Mr. Ortega's Spanish students were eating lunch together in the cafeteria. "Let's drive over to Palm Valley and check out the new video games," suggested Marta. "A great idea," agreed Phil, "but what about Spanish class?" "Did you forget what day this is?" asked Mike, "Friday's culture day, and probably all Mr. Ortega will do is show a PowerPoint or talk about some Latin American country. He never asks us about those things on the tests, so it won't matter if we miss class today."

"You guys go on without me," suggested Alan, the "brain" of the group. "I've got to put some finishing touches on my research paper for English, so I'll skip Spanish and spend the time in the library."

In Spanish class that afternoon, Mr. Ortega wondered why so many students were not in class. "Probably some sort of school activity," he mused, and showed his PowerPoint presentation anyway to the seven students who showed up.

~~~~

Emily was really frustrated. She had been in Argentina for two weeks now and was definitely suffering from culture shock. Since she had been the best student in Mrs. Murphy's Spanish class, she wasn't doing so badly with the language, but it was still hard for her to understand the Argentines, especially since everybody insisted on using the *vos* form with her. Why didn't they use *tú* like they were supposed to? And they certainly didn't pronounce Spanish like Mrs. Murphy, and they used so many slang expressions. Why did they say *morfar* instead of *comer* like normal people? Speaking of eating, she surely hadn't been prepared for *milanesas*, *raviolis*, *ñoquis*, and *tallarines*. She had been looking forward to the *burritos*, *tamales*, and *tacos* she was used to back in California. But tonight had been the worst. She had been thrilled when her friend Ramón had invited her to a movie, but she must not have understood the part about meeting at the movie theater, because she was ready by the door of her apartment at 8:30 as they had agreed, but when he called from downtown at 9:30 to see why she was not at the theater, she was furious. Boys always go to the girl's home to pick her up! Her frustration stemmed mostly from the fact that she really liked Ramón, but he canceled the date because it was too late to see the movie. Would she ever understand these people?

~~~~

Mr. Hansen put down the Spanish history book with a sigh and began to ponder. He had the strong feeling something was wrong. He had been very diligent in his preparation of cultural information to teach his students. They seemed to enjoy Spanish, especially since he was exclusively using a communicative approach with lots of TPR Storytelling and no textbook. But when he tried to introduce culture, they seemed to be turned off. Because of the lack of a textbook, Mr. H. had to find his own sources for cultural material. He had relied heavily on the books he had used in his literature and civilization and culture classes at the university. Now he was having second thoughts. He hadn't doubted the importance of the history of Spain, knowing the difference between Gothic and Mudejar architecture in college, and he still felt that his students should know great historical figures like El Cid, Fernando and Isabel, and Santa Teresa de Jesús, but his students seemed to be more interested in what sports were popular in Spain, some new rock group called La Oreja de Van Gough, and what teenagers did in school and on the weekends. Maybe they were right. If they were to go to Spain it would certainly be more helpful to know who Antonio Banderas and Pau Gasol were than Miguel de Cervantes or Salvador Dalí. But where was he going to find that kind of information?

242

CHAPTER ELEVEN

TEACH CULTURE? I ONLY HAVE TIME TO TEACH THE LANGUAGE! DEVELOPING CULTURAL PROFICIENCY

> **We must come to realize that every race and every peole have their own way of doing things, their own standards of life, their own ideals, their own kinds of food and clothing and drink, their own concepts of civil obligation and honor, and their own views as to the kind of government they should have. It is simply ludicrous for us to try to recast all of these into our mold.**
> **-J. Reuben Clark, Jr.**

"Culture" is much like the spare tire in a car—everyone agrees that we should have it with us as we drive, and as we plan trips, we check to see if it is there. But most often it is forgotten and little used. On the occasions that we leave it at the service station for repairs, we still drive the car, because we have learned that we can get along without it. We feel uneasy, and know we should have it along, but continue without it, trusting that it won't be needed. So it is with many language teachers in regards to their attitude about teaching culture. They know they have an obligation to include it along with the study of the language, but they have learned that nothing overtly tragic happens if they leave it out.

Truth be known, the area of culture is so overwhelmingly all-inclusive that it is actually intimidating. To fully understand the magnitude of the task of including culture in our language classes, consider the following analogy. Imagine you have a large box containing several hundred jigsaw puzzle pieces, and you have only 60 minutes to put together as much of the puzzle as you can. At the end of the hour, you will be expected to furnish as many details about the total picture as you possibly can, drawing information from whatever parts you were able to assemble. As you begin work you realize that some of the pieces must be from some other puzzle, because they obviously don't fit the one you are putting together. Probably your best plan

of action would be to sort out the pieces which don't belong, start on the border pieces until you have the outside framework, and then concentrate on areas where there are definite contrasts such as houses, fences, and trees. You would not confine yourself to one area since that would limit what you could learn of the whole picture, nor would you spend much time on relatively empty areas of sky or water. At the end of the allotted time, you would still have many unfinished parts, and some areas would be only faintly recognizable, but if you had the border finished and some of the main features filled in, you could give a partial description of what is in the entire picture.

Such is the complexity of the language teachers' task as they strive toward an objective of giving their students cultural insight and awareness. Culture, in its fullest definition, is so broad that the student—or the teacher, for that matter—will never be able to learn everything. At best, a framework can be established, and enough important areas filled in to allow a fairly accurate *glimpse* of the total picture.

Just as the puzzle assembler also gains insight and develops general skills in putting puzzles together, so also does a student in a foreign language class acquire some basic skills for coping with foreign cultures in a general, nonspecific approach. These general skills are perhaps as important as learning a lot of specific information about a cultural group that the student might never visit.

WHAT DOES "CULTURE" INCLUDE?

There is some difficulty in agreeing on exactly what we are talking about when we use the term "culture." To many college professors, culture is limited to the contributions of a people to society, such as art, literature, music, and architecture. This "fine arts" or "civilization" definition has always been seen as "respectable" area of study, and anything beyond that has usually been considered insignificant and trivial. But "culture" in the anthropological sense, that is, the behavioral patterns of a people, without doubt has more importance in being able to understand and communicate with the people of another society. Certainly "culture" goes far beyond the bounds of "personal refinement."

There are some terms that are widely used in the profession that will be helpful in defining culture. The term "big C" (or "capital C") culture is used to refer to concepts and information in the area of fine arts or civilization. This area includes art, literature, history, geography, music (usually folk and classical), architecture, and theater. These topics are the main focus in a typical Spanish or Latin American civilization and culture class at most universities. Clearly, this information will be of interest and value to a Spanish student, but ignorance in this area can usually be overlooked or pardoned by natives, and only rarely leads to miscommunication or offended feelings.

An area of culture more important to our students is that area which includes the patterns of life, value systems, and everyday behavior. This is referred to as "little c" (or "small c") culture. To truly understand and be able to communicate effectively with people of another culture requires groundwork in "little c" culture.

Borrowing an idea from C. Richards Pusey, we might add a third type of culture, which he calls "big K Kulture." Big K Kulture includes all that is Kute, Kurious, Kwaint, and Kweer in a foreign culture. It consists of all the odd things that foreigners do that make them so strange. Big K Kulture comes from an attitude that focuses on, and emphasizes, the oddities. The major difference between big K Kulture and little c culture is one of attitude. Teachers emphasizing big K Kulture imply that the foreigners will always remain just that, foreigners, outsiders, odd-balls. This point of view makes it difficult for the students to identify with the foreigners and their "strange" culture. An overemphasis on big K Kulture leads to false stereotypes. The students come to believe that all Mexicans wear *huaraches,* big *sombreros,* have a *sarape* on their shoulders, and sleep leaning against a cactus. True, some Mexicans might do this, but our students should not expect it of every Mexican.

Generalizations vs. Stereotypes

It is true that there are many general characteristics shared by Spanish-speaking cultures. We will summarize some of these "universals" or shared cultural traits later, but we need to caution our students to be careful about forming stereotypes. A **stereotype** is the false notion that *all* members of a culture behave in a certain way or possess certain characteristics. Too often in our search to find common cultural patterns, we create stereotypes that often do not fit. Some Latin Americans are "hot-blooded" but that certainly does not apply to all Latins.

In contrast to stereotypes, it is valid to make a **generalization** about other cultures; it is only through such generalizations that we learn to recognize cultural patterns that differ from our own. The key is to help students make generalizations about cultural patterns while acknowledging that individual differences do exist.

The Students' Attitude

As we approach the task of teaching culture, we know beforehand that our students will be suffering from two maladies: *ethnocentrism* and *xenophobia*. We expect this because people from all cultures subconsciously acquire these attitudes as they are growing up in their own specific cultural milieu. These attitudes are not reprehensible, they are just natural, and it will be our responsibility to awaken their awareness of these underlying feelings and help them modify them to a point that they can increase their tolerance and their ability to combat "cultural shock."

Ethnocentrism is the attitude that one's own cultural patterns are "correct" and that "the way *we* do things is the *best* way, and that any other way of behaving doesn't make sense." Ethnocentrism thus leads individuals to consider people of other cultures as inferior or stupid or at the least, "weird." Enthnocentric individuals spend a lot of time comparing, criticizing, and making fun of the people of the culture foreign to their own.

Xenophobia is the fear or distrust people have of everything that is strange or foreign. This again is a natural reluctance to accept something that doesn't fit in the regular patterns we are comfortable with. This is usually manifest in the discomfort we feel with someone's physical appearance that is different from what we are used to. A daughter of one of the writers, a striking girl with blue eyes and long blond hair, once spent several months in Taiwan. People would always stare at her and some even walked up and stroked her hair in disbelief. A close Taiwanese friend once confided to her that for a long time she wondered if she could see well with such *colorless* eyes. Our students may have feelings similar to these as they meet Indians from South America.

Somehow, we as language teachers have to help our students change these attitudes, help them see that cultures are different but not inferior, and that while people may appear different, they are unique individuals as deserving of respect and love as we are.

As you contemplate teaching culture, there are three main questions to be asked: Why teach culture? What should I teach? How can I teach it? We will approach each of these questions separately.

WHY TEACH CULTURE?

One of the basic objectives of a foreign language class, and many social science classes as well, such as world history, world geography, international relations, and the like, is to guide the student to a fuller understanding of the members of the other societies that we share this globe with. Educators want students to develop an empathy and greater tolerance for ways of thinking and behaving that are different from their own. These objectives are reflected in the Cultures and Comparisons goal areas of the *Standards for Foreign Language Learning.*

Understanding cultural practices, products, and perspectives. The Cultures goal area of the *Standards* reads as follows:

2.1　Students demonstrate an understanding of the relationship between the practices and perspectives of the culture studied.
2.2　Students demonstrate an understanding of the relationship between the products and perspectives of the culture studied.

As you can see, there are three elements here: practices, products, and perspectives. **Practices** are what the members of a culture do: their daily habits, customs, and traditions. **Products** are what the culture produces: literature, music, films, art, handicrafts, buildings, foods, laws, and the like. Both practices and products are tied to underlying **perspectives**: the beliefs, attitudes, and values that lead members of a culture to do the things they do and make the things they make.

As an example, take the Spanish practice of going out for *tapas*. In Spain, it is common for friends to go out at night to bars or cafés that serve appetizers or snacks known as *tapas.* The group will order several plates of various tapas for everyone to try, and will often go from bar to bar sampling the different tapas offered. One famous *tapa* is the Spanish tortilla, which, unlike the Mexican tortilla that American students are familiar with, is more similar to an omelette made with potatoes and onions and cut into slices or small pieces.

The tortilla is an example of a Spanish cultural *product;* the act of going out for tapas is a cultural *practice*. But the key to developing understanding is to challenge our students to explore the underlying cultural *perspectives*. Why do Spaniards go out for tapas? There are multiple possible answers: Spaniards enjoy eating in the company of friends; they appreciate gourmet foods; or the hot summer days in Madrid simply mean that nighttime is the only time when one can sit comfortably at an outdoor café. Understanding these perspectives can help our students go beyond seeing cultural products and practices as mere oddities and begin to develop a true appreciation for different cultures' ways of looking at life and the world. This is perhaps the most important cultural skill that our students can develop.

Developing an awareness of how culture influences our perceptions. Cross-cultural communication is often hampered by cultural differences. Miscommunication is quite common.

The reason for this is illustrated by the following diagram contrasting a person from Chile and an American.

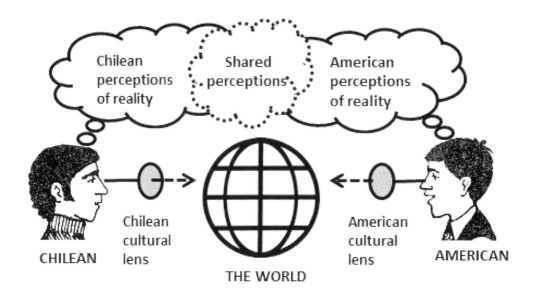

Because everyone sees the world through their own particular cultural lens, two people from different cultures see the world somewhat differently. They may share some aspects, but there will be many differences. These two persons could be totally unaware that they were not viewing an event or idea in the same way and may find themselves miscommunicating and not knowing why.

Although we can't escape the influence of our own cultural lens, we can work on becoming aware of the way our perceptions and those of others are influenced by our respective cultures, and we can choose to focus on areas of shared similarities as well as differences. This concept is illustrated in the Comparisons goal area of the *Standards:*

4.2   Students demonstrate understanding of the concept of culture through comparisons of the cultures studied and their own.

Standard 4.2 recognizes that an important part of culture learning is an awareness of the way our beliefs, attitudes, and values are shaped by our own culture. Studies have shown that American students typically give little thought to their own culture, since they are constantly immersed in it – much like "not being able to see the forest for the trees" (Hall & Ramrez, 1993; Ulichny, 1996). Studying other cultures can help students develop an awareness of their own cultural perspectives, and by so doing they can come to understand that other cultures view the world somewhat differently than their own culture does. Again, this is one of the most important outcomes for culture learning that teachers can cultivate in their students.

"Culture shock." "Culture shock" refers to the condition people find themselves in while operating in a foreign culture. They soon discover that the cues they depend on to function comfortably and efficiently in their own culture do not work (Oberg, 1960). They may become increasingly frustrated because they are unable to understand what is happening or why. The following illustration offers a good summary of the effects of culture shock.

Sees the natives as being stupid and inferior in intellect. Becomes critical of everything and sarcastic.

Is overly concerned about cleanliness and health. Thinks all food, bedding, and dishes are dirty.

Clings to things which are familiar and remind him of home. Remembers how good everything is at home.

Will fall asleep or mind will wander in business or social gatherings because he cannot understand what is being said.

Will speak louder than usual to make himself understood rather than more slowly.

Finds food unappealing. May have an upset stomach, particularly if there is a change in climate.

Has a general feeling of helplessness.

The Victim of Cultural Shock
(***From Culture for Missionaries***, LTM)

Language reflects culture. Another argument in favor of including culture in language classes is that one cannot separate the culture from the language. Some experts estimate that as high as 50% of communication is cultural, not linguistic. Certainly, it is impossible to conceive of a language devoid of culture; language reflects our thoughts, our values, our customs. Language students soon learn that communicating is not just a word for word substitution of English words with Spanish words. Consider the following examples.

1. Early in the course, Spanish students learn that *colegio*, as it is used in Spain, does not mean "college," but rather refers to schools in general, such as our elementary and secondary schools. A deeper look into the educational system of Spain informs us that when Spanish children say *colegio*, they are thinking about something quite different from what American children sees in their mind as they say "school." In many Spanish-speaking countries this could be a private school, where the students wear uniforms, or a parochial school where they receive religious education, or a school where they attend only in the morning or afternoon.

2. When Spaniards say *pan* they see something quite different from what we think of when we say "bread." To them it is a long loaf of crusty bread, bought or delivered every day. Spanish women do not bake *pan*, it is baked fresh daily in a bakery.

3. The Spanish word *pie* means foot, but it is not the word which is used to refer to the foot of an animal. The underlying cultural pattern requires the use of *pata* here.

Culture is certainly the cause of certain words becoming charged with special meaning, shock effect, or sexual overtones that limit their use in polite society. Swearwords and taboo words are other examples of these culturally loaded words. Some regions have given special meaning to words that only they are aware of and even native speakers of Spanish might be embarrassed by using what they consider to be a perfectly innocent word. (For example, the substitution of *blanquillo* in some parts of Mexico for *huevo*, *agarrar* for *coger* in most of South America, etc.) Seelye (1993) points out that even an innocent *¿Y tu madre?* might be taken in a different meaning from what is intended.

The use of the names of deity in many expressions in Spanish certainly doesn't carry the same force as it does in English. Some countries have done extensive borrowing of words from other languages. Members of those communities understand them, but Spanish speakers form other areas might not. (For example, *lonchería, "OK," chequear*, etc.)

Proverbs and idioms can be very cultural in meaning. They often make references to historical events or regional words that only the people of that culture understand. (For example: *"Zamora no se ganó en una hora," "Se armó la de San Quintín,"* and *"No se puede chiflar y comer pinole."*)

Grammatical constructions also seem to reflect cultural patterns. Note the very common use of the use of reflexive and indirect pronouns to express actions where the speaker wants to avoid responsibility: *Se nos cayó el plato, se me fue el tren, se le escapó la lengua,* etc. (One of the authors actually heard a five-year old use this construction to affirm to his parents that he wasn't responsible for wetting his pants in school as he declared: *Se me orinaron los pantalones.*) It seems clear that to teach vocabulary or grammar devoid of cultural context would leave our students vulnerable to some real problems of miscommunication.

Culture is motivating. Language teachers who omit culture often find that their enrollments are low. An exclusive diet of grammar analysis can be boring. Culture can be very motivating; student interest is high, and they continue studying because they enjoy it. Students have a natural interest in the way the people whose language they are studying live. Among younger students there is a natural desire to know what someone of their own age is interested in, does for fun, what their school is like, etc.

National defense. A good case for teaching culture can be made from the point of view of national defense. Too often the policy makers in government departments such as the Department of State are unaware of the nuances of intercultural communications and make serious mistakes that could have been avoided. Language students who have become sensitized to these problems and who later occupy positions of national importance will be better prepared to make decisions which perhaps will affect the security or economy of our nation.

Resistance from teachers. Unfortunately there are some language teachers who resist including the teaching of culture in their classrooms. Some of the reasons most commonly given are: "I don't have enough time; It's too slippery; I don't know what to teach; I'm not prepared; and It's in the book." None of these reasons justify the omission of teaching culture, in the light of the objectives listed for the teaching of culture that we have already mentioned.

WHAT CULTURAL CONTENT SHOULD I TEACH?

There are some who argue that rather than teach cultural information, we should focus on helping our students develop basic skills for coping in any foreign culture, and they in their turn will use those skills to adapt to whatever culture they find themselves in. There is much to support this position, and we will have more to say about it in the section on the **culture-general approach**. However teaching only general notions about how to adjust to *any* culture, does not satisfy the intense desire our students have to know specific information about the people whose language they are studying. Are they like us? How are they different? Do they eat the same things? Do they listen to the same music? Do they have the same pastimes? What things are of value to them? These are the just some of the questions they want answered, and the more specific information we can give them, the more generalizations they can draw about cultural patterns in general.

It is extremely difficult to decide what information to include and what to leave out. A number of people have tried to develop a taxonomy of culture and have failed dismally. Perhaps this is one of the main reasons textbooks used to give it only a half-hearted effort. They used to include some pictures of markets, parks, castles and cathedrals, a few maps and a listing of the principal exports and let it go at that. Fortunately the more recent textbooks are making a greater effort to include more pertinent cultural information, but there seems to be little organization and a general lack of priorities, and no systemized approach.

Perhaps our efforts may not be much better than those of others, but here are our suggestions for specific information you might include in a first-year Spanish class.

**SUGGESTED CULTURAL CONTENT FOR
A FIRST-YEAR SPANISH CLASS**

At the end of a beginning course, the student will have studied and learned the following content:

---

1. **Guidelines for social interaction** (How to act and react)

 A. How do the people greet each other, introduce someone, take leave, etc.?
 B. What are the significant social levels and what conventions must be followed; what avoided?
 C. How is a foreigner expected to act in a formal/informal situation?
 D. Is there social behavior to be avoided, such as gestures (body language, eye contact, proximics, etc.), giving compliments, admiring an object, etc. What is offensive?
 E. How does the name system operate? What titles should be used? What forms of address (such as tú and usted) should be used?
 F. How can one refuse food, services offered, etc.?
 G. Is there physical contact (haptics) which should be observed or avoided (such as touching the head, kissing on cheek, holding hands, etc.)?
 H. What physical proximity is expected, tolerated (proximics) for conversations, seating, etc.?
 I. What are the courtesy patterns, expressions, gestures, actions (such as entering someone's office, invitations, sending flowers or thank you notes), etc.?

---

2. **Important facts of the physical environment** (Where, in what, and how do they live?)

 A. What is the geographical location of the target culture and who are its immediate or most influential neighbors?
 B. What are the climate and weather like, including unusual features (such as rainy season, cold winters, etc.)?
 C. What is the physical makeup of the country, including unusual features (mountains, surrounded by water, arid, very fertile, etc.)?
 D. What kind of homes do the people live in (apartments, chalets, grass huts, etc.)?
 E. What is the typical food they eat, what are the staples, who prepares it, how is it prepared, etc.?
 F. Is there a typical drink for the culture? Do they make an alcoholic drink?
 G. What is the typical clothing the people wear, regional costumes, clothing to be avoided, etc.?
 H. What kinds of animals are present, domesticated?

3. Values and attitudes (What do they value, dislike, care about?)

A   Are there some values and attitudes inherited from the past? (such as conservatism, sharing goods with others, "good name," etc.) What are the people proud of?
B.   Who do they revere, who are their heroes, what persons are respected, quoted? Why?
C.   What traits and qualities are considered desirable, undesirable?
D.   What do they aspire to? What is success?
E.   What are typical patterns of recreation and diversion? Do they practice sports? Which ones?
F.   What types of reading materials do they use most frequently? What do they read as children?
G.   What are the most common axioms, proverbs?
H.   What type of music is typical, popular? Dance? Drama?
I.   What would they consider to be their culture's most important contribution to world civilization?
J.   What are their attitudes toward Americans, other cultures and races?
K.   How do legends and folklore affect them. What are their most common legends?
L.   What professions are most highly valued?
M.   What personality traits are common (such as stoicism, fatalism, expression of anger, pride, self-effacement, gossip, lust, revenge, etc.)?

4. Patterns of behavior (What are they like and how do they relate and interact with other?)

A.   What are the typical personality characteristics? Are they impersonal, easygoing, energetic, punctual, stoic, cheerful, open, etc ?
B.   What is family life like? Who makes decisions? What is the role of family members?
C.   What would a typical day's activities be like for each family member?
D.   What systems do they use in interacting (such as personalism, nepotism, compadrazco)?
E.   What happens at birth, marriage, death, etc.?
F.   What are the most important events in a person's life?
G.   How do they react to sickness, tragedy, etc.?
H.   Are they superstitious? What are some of the most important superstitions?
I.   What games do the children play? Do adults play? What?
J.   Who goes shopping? How is it done? When?
K.   What are the most prominent "customs" (such as Sunday paseo, piropos, etc.)
L.   What kinds of social activities are engaged in (parties, visiting, tertulias, tomar el aperitivo, etc.)
M.   How do the people eat, use makeup, keep clean, etc.
N.   What "themes" would explain certain behaviors (such as individualism, privacy, politeness, equanimity, machismo, etc.)
O.   What are male/female roles, male dominance, women's liberation, double standard of morality?
P.   How does boy meet girl? What are dating practices?

5. History, civilization and fine arts (What is the historical heritage of the people and what is their place in and their relation and contribution to the world in general?)

    A.   What are the prominent events in the history of the people?
    B.   What are the ethnic and racial characteristics of the people?
    C.   To what language family does their language belong?
    D.   What are the major features of the language? Are there dialects?
    E.   What other languages are spoken in the country?
    F.   Are there subcultures, minorities in the culture? How are they treated by the majority?
    G.   What festivals and celebrations are important?
    H.   Are there regional costumes, music, dances?
    I.   What contributions does the culture make to world civilization in art, music, drama, architecture, literature, etc.
    J.   Are there local arts and crafts such as ceramics, jewelry, etc. which are typical of the culture?

6. Operations and functions of formal institutions (What organized entities affect the lives of the people?)

    A.   What system of government is in force? What has been in the past?
    B.   What is the dominant religion, beliefs? What is the impact on the people?
    C.   What is the relationship between church and state?
    D.   What is the system of education? How does it affect the lives of the people?
    E.   Are there military obligations? How do they affect the life of the people?
    F.   How do the police fit into public life? How do the people feel about the police?
    G.   What mode of transportation are available, most used? Who uses them?
    H.   What are the functions of the postal system, availability of phones, banks, etc.
    I.   What is the operation of health systems, hospitals, health insurance, dentists, cosmetic medicine?
    J.   What is the monetary system of the country?
    K.   Who controls the mass media operations? (radio, television, newspapers)
    L.   Who has access to radio, TV, newspapers? What is available from other countries?
    M.   What are the characteristics of the mass media (free, educational, academic, etc.)?
    N.   What are the salient legal restrictions of the culture? Advantages, benefits?
    O.   What freedoms do the people have?

7. Current political and economic situation (What is the quality of life like?)

    A.   What do most of the people do for a living?
    B.   What professions are available?
    C.   Can the poor change their economic status?
    D.   How is the country presently governed. Are the people satisfied?
    E.   What is the average income? What goods are available, not available? Who can buy them?
    F.   Is the country stable economically, politically?
    G.   What are the current relations with neighboring countries?
    H.   What are the most pressing, critical political and economic needs?
    I.   Who are the present important people of the culture?

HISPANIC "UNIVERSALS"

Teachers of Spanish have an additional difficulty in teaching culture because there is not just one culture. We are faced with talking about 20 to 30 different countries and regions. It will be helpful to try to find some general characteristics that are shared by most residents of Spanish-speaking nations and areas, but care should be taken to point out that there will be many who do not fit the pattern. Nevertheless, in spite of the diversity of Hispanic cultures, the mother country, Spain, has been a unified country for five centuries and this has led to a great deal of homogenization, and there are many points of similarity. In looking for these areas it is very helpful to use the concept of *themes* and *clusters*.

A *theme* or *cluster* refers to a grouping of several cultural concepts that naturally fall together. As an example, **food** would be the theme or cluster and within this category could come a number of specific presentations about food such as what the people of the culture eat, how they procure the food, how they store it, how they prepare it, mealtimes, eating styles, etc. Because most foreign language textbooks organize their chapters around specific themes, it is relatively easy to take each chapter's theme and identify cultural concepts related to the theme. Graphically, the relationships in our food example could be seen as follows:

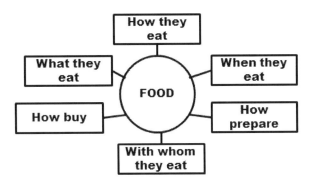

While it is not always possible to find cultural information that applies equally to all Hispanic cultures, the notion of themes and clusters are will help us pinpoint the areas where similarity exists. As a general introduction to culture in your classes, you might want to teach some of the following "universals:"

Language. The most obvious cultural trait shared is the Spanish language. Even though there are regional differences of pronunciation, variations in vocabulary, and some different uses of grammar, the basic foundation of the language is the same in all Hispanic cultures and they readily understand each other.

Religion. An overwhelming majority of Hispanics are Roman Catholics. This is reflected in many aspects of their life: they believe in Christian virtues such as helping others, being honest, and living good lives. They are pious, and tend toward belief in divine intervention in their lives. They believe that the Virgin or Saints can answer prayers. They believe in repentance, confession, and penance. They also tend toward ostentation and over emphasize outward appearance. They are usually flowery and pedantic in formal occasions. They often feel that the end justifies the means. Most of their festive celebrations have a religious origin and focus.

Physical appearance. Because of their historical background and ethnic origins the physical makeup of a Latin American is usually dark hair, dark eyes, olive skin, and medium stature. There are exceptions, of course. In Latin American countries, where there has been considerable mixing with the native Indian population, they are even shorter and have straight black hair and many of the Indian features. In areas such as Panama, the Dominican Republic and Cuba where there has been a mixing with slaves brought originally from Africa, it is common to see African characteristics.

Personal traits. Spaniards seem to show their emotions more openly than members of other cultures. They passionately defend their beliefs, express their grief and caring very openly, and are gregarious in their relationships with other. They are fiercely independent and are not afraid to stand out in opposition to what others think. They are proud, and are very concerned about their image and what others think of them. They place honor as one of their highest values.

Spaniards typically have a tendency to be (sometimes brutally) frank and often express their opinions in what seems to others a tactless way (*no tener pelos en la lengua*).

Inhabitants of Latin American countries with large populations of indigenous cultures tend to be more submissive, stoic about the injustices in the world, and accepting of their fate and fortune.

Humor is found in Hispanic cultures just as it is in ours. They laugh at the same kinds of jokes, they make puns with words, and even make fun of people from certain regions that have the reputation for being stingy or a little dense or unsophisticated.

It is true that Hispanic cultures have been traditionally male dominated. While this is changing somewhat today, *machismo* is still alive and seen in many aspects of life in Spanish-speaking countries.

Hispanics are very family oriented. Traditional holidays often center around family gatherings and activities. It is not unusual to see members of the extended family (cousins, nieces and nephews, etc.) living with the immediate family as they work, attend school, and make adjustments in their life. When parents and grandparents become ill or need help in their old age, they become part of the nuclear family and are taken looked after with love and caring.

Work.   Hispanics are sometimes depicted as being lazy. This is patently untrue. As a whole they are industrious and hard-working. Many of the members of lower class families work long hours and sacrifice to improve their living standards. The economic patterns of most Hispanic countries make it very difficult to change their status.

Among the middle and upper classes there is often a feeling that certain kinds of work are demeaning, and should be done only by lower class laborers. This is usually manual labor.

Concept of time. Hispanics tend to view time as something to be used and savored, not something that has to be slavishly obeyed. They commonly arrive after agreed-upon hours, and find other things such as talking to friends, carrying out family relationships, etc. more important than being on time. They typically will postpone things to another day rather than being rushed into something they are not ready for.

We have commented on the above lifestyle characteristics to show that some "universals" do exist in Hispanic cultures. Following are others which you or your students could develop using the same theme or cluster approach.

Eating
- Food
- Times
- Style

Family
- Extended
- Role of father, mother
- *Compadrismo*
- Maids
- Elderly people, retirement

Personal interaction
- Use of familiar and formal forms (tú/usted/vosotros)
- Greetings (*beso, abrazo*)
- Touching
- Space
- Handshakes
- Personalism
- Social classes

Values
- Double standard of morality
- Power more than wealth (?)
- Respect of writers, poets

Shopping
- Daily for freshness
- Open-air markets
- Small stores underneath apartments in residential areas
- New trend away from small, family-run, specialized stores toward large shopping centers and malls

Celebrations & Special Events
- Family celebrations, birthdays, anniversaries
- Weddings
- Confirmation
- Funerals
- Religious festivals
- Other festivals

Housing styles
- Entrance
- *Patio*
- Closets
- Kitchen
- Apartment life

Government system

Legal heritage from Spain

Fascination with strong leader

No selfless service

School system

Private, religious schools

Uniforms

Formal learning

Free time-Diversions

Paseo

Evenings

Siesta (medio día)

Sports

Theater/Movie

Music

WHERE CAN I FIND CULTURAL INFORMATION?

One of the major problems encountered in teaching culture is finding sources of correct and up-to-date information. Since our definition of culture is so all-inclusive, we will have to cover a broad range of sources of cultural information. Some types of information will be easier to find, such as fine arts and civilization information ("big c"). There are many history and geography books, books on art and architecture, and numerous books on civilization and fine arts. But getting authentic, reliable "small c" information is very difficult. One has to look in many places, such as

cultural anthropology articles, sociology studies, and such unlikely sources as popular songs, tourist brochures, and even comic strips.

Typically when a teacher assigns students to research a country or culture, the students turn immediately to an encyclopedia or an Internet search engine. These can be good places to start, but they usually provide information about the history, geography, and the economy of a country. Remember, we don't want our students limited to "big c" information. Since those sources seldom supply "small c" information, we are going to have to help them find additional sources.

You will need to be cautious in using Americans who have lived in foreign cultures, including yourself, as sources of information. Many people are not perceptive enough to see cultural patterns, and others have started out with biased or erroneous attitudes that lead them to false or negative conclusions.

We also need to be careful about using natives of a country or culture as sources. They are usually unaware of "little c" culture traits and social patterns. If asked to volunteer information, they typically focus on "big C" areas or are unable to see their own behavior from the viewpoint of a foreigner. Valid and important facts can often be obtained only by insightful questioning by the teacher who is looking for specific information. Although it will still be quite incomplete, we will provide here a list of some sources for obtaining cultural information.

Sources of Cultural Information

Source	What you are likely to find
1. Foreign language textbooks	Mixture of "big C" and "small c" culture, no systematic presentation or sequence, often outdated information, some excellent materials and pictures
2. Encyclopedias, Wikipedia	Facts (often sterile), history maps, pictures, "big C" culture, geography, physical environment, etc.
3. Geography books or websites	Maps, physical environment, climate
4. "Peoples of the World" types	History, geography, climate, products, some customs and behavior
5. History books or websites	History, politics, kings, wars, etc.

6. Civilization and culture books (345, 355)	Civilization, "big C" culture, art history, music, architecture
7. Literature	"Small c" culture imbedded in stories
8. Cultural readers for Spanish students	History, "big C" culture, geography
9. Fine Arts books or websites	Art, music, architecture, civilization
10. Current periodical from Hispanic countries (magazines, newspapers)	Current events, products, values, pictures, etc.
11. Comic books from Hispanic countries (Condorito, Mafalda, El chavo del quinto)	Language, everyday life, values, events, behavior, entertainment, etc.
12. Periodicals in English (National Geographic, Américas, etc.)	Pictures, economy, etc.
13. Area studies handbooks	Economy, facts
14. Popular books on country (Iberia, etc.)	Varied information, sometimes outdated, often distorted
15. Tourist information (pamphlets, brochures, websites, etc.)	Places to visit, things to buy, entertainment, recreation, etc.
16. Booklets on living in foreign country (*Culture Shock!* series, books from Intercultural Press)	Good information on behavioral patterns, themes, contrasts
17. Information from embassies, consulates	Economy, facts and figures
18. Songs, folk music	Must dig out own cultural info.
19. Sociology and Anthropology books or websites	Good insight into patterns, sometimes (Oscar Lewis type) difficult to read, primitive cultures, movement from country to city
20. Internet search engines	Incredibly rich, but overwhelming in amount, must look for "small c" info.
21. Other people (teachers of other subjects, returned missionaries, etc.)	Data often erroneous, biased
22. Natives	Must know how to ask questions to get important information
23. Go to the country yourself/with students	Must be organized for researching and collecting cultural information
24. *CultureGrams*	Excellent mix of "big C" and "small c" information, great materials of all kinds

Personal study by the teacher. We have listed some sources for cultural information at the end of the chapter. Obviously there are many more. It is your professional duty to spend a lifetime learning all you can about the cultures whose language you teach. You must constantly read books, newspapers, magazines, etc. You must look for "fugitive" materials, that is, sources of "small c" information which can't be found in encyclopedias, textbooks, and history books. Such things as books on anthropology, magazines like *National Geographic* (or *Geomundo*, the Spanish version), and watching Spanish television channels will greatly help.

Personal travel by the teacher. Nothing can give you more cultural insight and understanding than living it personally. You should always be looking for opportunities to get to Hispanic countries. When you get there, keep in mind that you are not a typical tourist, you are a "researcher" gathering information and materials to take back to share with your students. We will talk more about getting abroad in Chapter 18, but for now here are some culturally-oriented suggestions:

- Find things to buy for classroom decoration: posters and humorous signs; pictures of countryside, important buildings, industries, and park and recreation areas; flags; post cards and maps; things made out of typical fabrics such as *ponchos, sarapes,* tablecloths, wall hangings, and clothing.
- Look for reading materials for classroom reading areas: newspapers, magazines, popular fiction, history books, comic books, children's books, classics in translation, legends and fables, text books.
- Realia to buy to put on shelves and use in culture capsules: dolls and clay figures with regional costumes; objects of typical arts and crafts such as carved figures, pottery, and leather articles; typical fabrics such as lace and woven objects; tickets and programs from special events such as theater, bullfights, concerts, plays, movies, performing arts such as folk dance festivals
- Buy games, both of the kind that are played in the country and the kind that your students can use to practice the language.
- Buy as many recordings as you can afford of all kinds of music, but don't restrict yourself to the folklore type; get some of the kind that young people most often listen to. If you buy DVDs or videocassettes, make sure they can be played on your equipment.
- Some miscellaneous items to buy might be cooking pots and pans, unusual tools, etc.
- Things to do and activities to participate in would include eating typical food, buying a lottery ticket, going to an amusement park, riding different kinds of transportation, visiting factories, shopping in different types of stores, visiting parks and museums, going swimming in a public pool, visiting a sports club, visiting a hospital and a cemetery, and so on.

- People to meet and interview might include a policeman, a taxi driver, a hotel clerk, an undertaker, a priest, school teachers, a *portero,* gas station attendants, military personnel, salespersons, secretaries, and sidewalk vendors of all kinds.
- Pictures to take would include people of all ages, different kinds of cars and trucks, street signs, sidewalk cafes, transportation, different kinds of shops, gas stations, traffic, processions, parades, homes and apartments (especially inside), markets, and so on.

TECHNIQUES FOR TEACHING AND LEARNING ABOUT CULTURE

Assuming that teachers are convinced of the importance of culture, how should they go about teaching it? It seems clear that the secret is to have a plan that will systematically include culture along with the language. Hopefully that is what this chapter will give you.

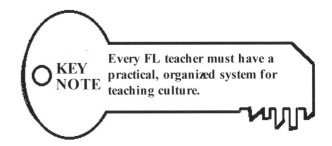

KEY NOTE Every FL teacher must have a practical, organized system for teaching culture.

In formulating your plan or system of teaching culture, you need to understand that there are two basic schools of thought: a "culture-general" approach and a "culture-specific" approach.

"Culture-General" Approach

The "culture-general" approach is motivated by the fact that it is impossible to teach all the pertinent information about a specific culture. As teachers, we usually do not know which countries or cultures our students will be visiting. Thus some educators argue that we should teach only general principles of cross-cultural interaction and try to give our students the skills and strategies for adapting to any new culture. In that way they can apply those skills to get specific information about the particular culture they find themselves in. Rather than teaching specific information about any particular culture, this approach suggests that our efforts be directed to teaching "coping" skills which can help the student adjust to whatever situation he might end up in. Following are some basic concepts that can be taught in a "culture-general" approach and the skills and strategies the students should develop to apply the concepts.

General Concept	**Strategy or skill**
1. People's attitudes and values will be different from one culture to another.	1. Be ready for differences, expect them, don't be caught unaware. Recognize different scales of values.
2. Social relationships between men and women, old and young, educated and non-educated, wealthy and poor, adolescent boy and girl, etc., will be different from one culture to another.	2. Be observant and try to follow the lead of others.
3. One culture is not inferior or superior to another, they are just different and each culture is usually best for its circumstances.	3. Don't judge, criticize, compare. Don't label people according to your own culture's norms.
4. You will be a "foreigner" in the other culture, you cannot be fully accepted as "one of them."	4. Don't try to "go native." Adapt where you can, but allowances will be made for you as an "outsider."
5. The cues and behavioral patterns you are used to will probably be different and won't work in the new culture.	5. Be ready for frustrating moments and learn to cope with them.
6. Religious practices and beliefs will probably be different.	6. Be tolerant and respectful of religious rites and customs. Never belittle or ridicule.
7. Generalizations may not fit all individuals and stereotypes are often false.	7. Don't trust generalizations and beware of stereotyping individuals or cultures.
8. Cultural differences will directly tied into the language; in vocabulary words, in grammatical use, in pronunciation, in the use of expressions and proverbs, etc.	8. Study the language and observe its different uses. Don't expect words to have exact equivalences; they seldom do.
9. Their formal society will be quite different from your own; schools, government, laws, etc.	9. Don't criticize leaders, government policies, school system, etc.
10. There will be some things that are the similar in both cultures. People all over the world have the same needs and feelings.	10. See commonality amidst diversity. Look for areas where there is agreement.

Teaching Strategies for the "Culture-General" Approach

Films and videos are a very effective way to teach general basic concepts. For example, the film *The Eye of the Beholder* teaches the dangers of drawing a hasty conclusion from what appears to be "obvious." Although it is an older film, it makes the point very well. You can download it for free classroom use. http://www.archive.org/details/EyeOfTheBeho

Other recommended films of this type are:
- *Leo Beuermann* — A day in the life of a severely handicapped man, but who with industry and creativity has made himself self-dependent and a contributing member of society. http://www.phoenixlearninggroup.com/
- *Johnny Lingo* — In a South Sea Island setting we see that beauty is found within a person and self esteem and feelings of personal worth can be developed through sensitive caring. (BYU film classics. Also in Spanish.)
- *The Cipher in the* Snow — The tragic death of a young boy makes us all determine not to prejudge, criticize, or belittle others. (BYU film classics.)

There are a number of **games** that are very effective in practicing general skills for coping with a change of culture. Some are:

- *Labeling game* — A small groups activity to emphasize the effect of "labeling" other persons. Labels such as IGNORE ME, REJECT MY OPINION, AGREE WITH ME, are put on each person's forehead where they can't see it, and in a discussion circle all are treated according to their label.
- *Bafá Bafá* — A somewhat complex, interactive activity where students are divided into two cultural groups with very strict taboos and norms of behavior that are the cause of frustrating conflicts when the two groups attempt to interact. (*wilderdom.com/games/MulticulturalExperientialActivities.html*)

Several **books and articles** approach culture from a general point of view and give insight into to the problems of intercultural communication. Among the best we might mention are:

- Edward T. Hall, a professor of cultural anthropology at Northwestern University has written a series of very readable books such as *The Silent Language, The Hidden Dimension,* and *Beyond Culture,* where he presents many suggestions as to how Americans can learn how to communicate effectively with foreign nationals.
- The Center for Advanced Research on Language Acquisition (CARLA) publishes a set of materials entitled Maximizing Study Abroad, which includes both a student manual and a teacher's manual. A large part of the materials is devoted to culture-learning strategies. There are many useful exercises to help students understand what culture is and how it affects our lives.
- Intercultural Press publishes many books on both culture-general and culture-specific topics. Many of these books focus on helping Americans understand the differences among cultures.
- Corinne Mantle-Bromley has published a series of articles on preparing foreign language students for culture learning and helping them become aware of cultural issues. some of the articles include lesson plans.

References for the above books and articles can be found at the end of this chapter.

There are numerous organizations and societies that are interested the area of intercultural communication in a general way. One will usually find terms such as "cross-cultural communication" or "intercultural communication," "multi-cultural education," "pluralistic society," etc. in their titles. We have included the names of some of these groups and the materials they have published the *Reference* section at the end of this chapter.

"Culture-Specific" Approach

In the culture specific approach, we teach information and concepts of a specific nature. It is practically impossible to avoid talking about the civilization and way of life of the people in a specific country who speak the language we are studying. Textbooks are replete with specific cultural information, and our students will constantly ask questions such as: What are Mexican schools like? Do Argentines study the same things we do? Do they have sports teams and school activities in Spain like we do? Do they have TV in Ecuador? What do they watch? It is natural that they should be interested in these things and we should take advantage of this curiosity to motivate them to learn more about the language and the culture. The largest portion of this chapter will be devoted to suggestions on how to develop "cultural proficiency" in our students through the presentation of culture-specific information.

Teaching Strategies for the "Culture-Specific" Approach

The "culture-specific" approach is practiced by almost all language teachers. We have a wide variety of activities available to us. We suggest a three-step approach. Include the following types of activities in your program: 1) out of class, 2) in class, and 3) in the lab.

Out-of-Class Activities

There are many activities we can use to teach culture to our students out of class. Let's consider some of the most important ones.

Language club activities. Language teachers have found that a language club can be a valuable asset in organizing and carrying out cultural activities. These activities are usually in the evening in the home of the teacher or one of the students, in the school, or in a special place outside the school. For example:

- Special guest lectures or presentations. You could invite an official from a consulate, embassy, trade delegation, exchange student, etc. to give a lecture on some aspect of their country. It is often helpful for you to suggest a specific topic, and give fairly detailed instructions about what you want discussed, otherwise, you might get nothing but "big C." Hispanic families from the community might be asked to discuss some aspect of their life such as schools, special events, etc.
- A "culture night" featuring things from a specific country such as music, songs, poetry, etc.

- A drama night where some play is presented, either by a professional group, a university group, or your own advanced students.
- A "sing-along" where typical songs from a cultural area are sung.
- A movie night where a video or movie is presented.
- A night in a Mexican restaurant where only Spanish is spoken and the meal is typical Mexican cuisine.
- "Game night" in someone's home where cultural games such as *Washington, lotería*, etc. are played.
- Fiestas, especially those where some Hispanic customs can be practiced, such as *Navidad, 5 de mayo, Reyes Magos,* etc.
- Professional cultural presentations, such as the Ballet Folklórico, a *"tuna,"* a choir, a "mariachi" group etc. that may travel near your school.
- Penpals/keypals. Students who correspond with penpals or keypals in Spanish-speaking countries have a direct connection for receiving cultural information. As their pen pals talk about their daily activities, their aspirations, and their relationships with others, perceptive students can glean thousands of bits of information about their friends' culture.
- Many teachers have their students conduct studies and write reports on life in Spanish-speaking countries. This research is done outside the class and must be carefully organized and supervised or the students will simply go to the encyclopedia and copy down facts and information.

Work with librarians. It is very important to work with librarians of your institution to make sure your library has adequate books and a wide enough variety for the students to be able to carry out research and out of class assignments.

An excellent way to make out of class research more personal and meaningful is to use the "adopt-a-country" approach. This is an elaborate project, similar in nature to a research paper commonly prepared in English classes. It is perhaps more appropriate for advanced classes. The project is designed to be carried out through the course of one school year, with each unit researched over a two-week period.

Even though there is some work with encyclopedias, there is a specific attempt to get into "small c" aspects of the culture by using "thought questions" which request information that will not be in the encyclopedia. There is also a variety of student presentations that will require creativity, verbal presentations, and sharing of

information with classmates. Following are the guidelines that could be given to students for this type of activity: The assignment could be done by teams of students or by individuals.

SPANISH 4	Page 1 of 2
GUIDELINES FOR "ADOPT-A-COUNTRY" PROJECT	

From the list given you, choose a Spanish-speaking country in which you are interested, or wish to find out more about. Following the guidelines below, and the time schedule given you, research the required information about your country. Be prepared to share your information with the class as scheduled.

Guidelines

1. Keep an accurate bibliography of ALL materials you use.
2. Thoroughly read the CulturGram for your country.
3. Read at least two (2) encyclopedia articles. Take notes.
4. Using a search program, locate at least two (2) more information sources about your country on the Internet. Read and take notes. If possible, make a copy of the articles for your file.
5. Locate a National Geographic that has an article on your country. (See the references given after the countries on the list.)
6. Read one book about your country (see the reading list suggested in the CulturGram) andsummarize what you've read.
7. Keep a portfolio of current event articles about your country; collect these from newspapers, magazines and any other sources. Put dates and labels on everything. If you get information from a TV or radio broadcast, write the information on a 3 X 5 CARD with the date and the station you heard it on.
8. Write to a consulate, embassy or tourist office for information: posters, maps, pamphlets, etc. Be specific in requesting what you need (think about your collage/poster and other topics you will be presenting; plan ahead).
9. **(Extra)** Read a book on Latin America or Spain. Write a summary of your impressions. Choose one from of the lists (CulturGrams), or find your own. (O.K. with me first.)
10. **(Extra)** Locate someone from your country. Interview him/her with specific questions. Use the outline of the required information to guide you in forming your questions (knowing what questions to ask).

Outline of topics to be presented

1. Draw a map of your country. Locate capital, major cities, neighboring countries, geographical features, and anything else you feel is important.
2. Climate.
3. How do the people go from city to city; within cities (transportation).
4. Flag
5. National symbols (anthem, flower, mottos, etc.)
6. National traditions: holidays, festivals, typical costumes.
7. Principal occupations, industries, agricultural and natural resources.
8. National language, dialects, etc.
9. Foods, eating habits, dietary staples.

10. Monetary system, including present exchange rate with dollar.
11. Family life; role of parents, children, relatives, social classes.
12. Customs: birth, marriage, death, etc.
13. Predominant religions.
14. Education - school system.
15 History of the country.
16. Government, political system, present political figures.
17. Famous people: art, music literature, science, etc.
18. Sports: native sports, famous athletes.
19. Current events: magazine and newspaper articles; TV news programs.
20. Travel poster/collage: why should we visit your country?

The above topics may be presented and shared in any manner you desire. Use your imagination. Be creative! Use at least five (5) different methods of presentation. Plan on about two weeks for research per topic. Not all topics will be shared verbally.

List of Spanish-speaking countries - Choose one (1):

Argentina, Bolivia, Chile, Colombia, Costa Rica, Cuba, Dominican Republic, Ecuador, El Salvador, Guatemala, Hispanic USA, Honduras, Mexico, Nicaragua, Panama, Paraguay, Peru, Puerto, Rico, Spain, Uruguay, Venezuela

Thought questions: Pretend you are a person of your same age in the country you have adopted. You are being interviewed by *National Geographic* for a story about everyday life in your country. How would you answer these questions?

1. How many are in your family? (Do grandparents or other relatives live with you?)
2. Who makes the decisions in your home?
3. What persons do you look up to? (Family, city, country)
4. Whom do you go to for advice?
5. Do you like to go to school? What do you do there? What do you do after school?
6. What do you want to be when you grow up? What do you have to do to become that?
7. What does it mean to be successful in life? How is success measured?
8. What kind of person will you marry? What size will your family be? What you're your home be like?
9. How do you spend your weekends? Where do you go on vacations? What do you do there?
10. What is the most important day in the year for you? Why? What do you do then?
11. What is important to you about your heritage? (Family, national)
12. What do you think about Americans?
13. What can you always depend on as being good or important?
14. What are your talents? (Sports, musical instruments, art, etc.)
15. What kind of music do you listen to, what TV programs do you watch, what is your favorite movie, what books or magazines do you read?

Think about how you would answer these questions in your real life, then try to find out how you would answer if you lived in your adopted country. Use all your resources to find answers. Be prepared to participate in class discussions.

There are any number of field-trip activities which can be taken by groups outside of school, such as visiting old missions, Mexican restaurants, historical sites, and so on.

The "transplant" approach to teaching culture is similar to the "adopt a country" activity, but is more personalized. In this approach, students imagine themselves transplanted into a situation similar to their present one, but in the foreign country. They would be the same age, live in a similar geographical area, their parents would have the same professions, etc. The students would make oral or written presentations to the class or the teacher, from the viewpoint of their "transplant."

Get your students abroad. Obviously one of the best ways for our students to learn about foreign cultures is to visit them personally. There are a number of organizations that sponsor tours designed to take students to foreign countries. We will discuss these opportunities in more detail in Chapter 17.

There are also many exchange programs that are set up to help American students travel abroad. Usually these students agree to host foreign students in their own homes. These programs provide some of the most valuable cultural experiences possible for students to become immersed in the foreign cultures. Some of the more reputable programs are the American Field Service, the Experiment in International Living, and programs with the 4-H organization. Needless to say, an experience of this type is highly motivational for the students, and they can later become sources to your classes for cultural information, as are the foreign students who come to study in American schools.

Ethnographic interviews. One effective technique for culture learning involves pairing students with native Spanish speakers and having them conduct a series of ethnographic interviews. The goal of ethnography is to understand a culture from the point of view of members of that culture. One tool of ethnographers is the ethnographic interview, which differs from a "standard" interview in that the questions are not scripted; rather, the interviewer asks open-ended question such as "What it is like to be a Venezuelan living in the U.S.?", and then asks follow-up questions based on the interviewee's responses, allowing the interviewee to guide the conversation and bring up topics that he or she feels are important. These interviewing techniques can be taught in class, with the teacher giving a model and then having students practice interviewing each other.

Students may find it less intimidating if they are assigned to work in pairs to conduct the interviews with a native speaker. (The teacher may need to assist students in locating someone to interview.) Generally, conducting a series of at least three interviews with the same person allows for the participants to build rapport with the interviewee. Beginning- and intermediate-level students can conduct the interviews using a mix of Spanish and English (depending on the interviewee's English proficiency). They can be assigned to turn in a short written reflection after each interview, and to prepare a final project summarizing what they learned about the interviewee's culture and their own culture.

Studies have found that ethnographic interview projects can help dispel stereotypes as students interact personally with members of the target culture (Bateman, 2004). An additional benefit of the interviews is that they free the teacher from having to be a cultural expert. Following is a handout that can be given to students in preparation for an ethnographic interview project.

HANDOUT: ETHNOGRAPHIC INTERVIEW ASSIGNMENT

<u>Preparing for the interviews</u>
·Contact your interviewee and set up an appointment for the first interview.
·Before beginning the interview, answer any questions that the person has about the project.

<u>Planning for the interview</u>
·With your partner, write out the questions that you plan to ask in Spanish.

Sample Questions for Ethnographic Interviews

Following are some example questions. Many other types of questions are possible. You will want to go into as much depth as possible on each question.

·What is it like to be a Venezualan student living in the U.S.?
·How did your daily life in Venezuela differ from your life here?
·What surprised you when you first arrived here?
·What do you like about the United States? What don't you like?
·What do you miss about Venezuela?
·If you were talking to a friend in Venezuela about the school system in the U.S., what would you tell him or her?
·What things do you think Venezuelans consider most important in life? Do you think North Americans have the same priorities? Why?

<u>Conducting the interview</u>
·If you plan to record the interview, verify that you have the person's permission.
·Interview the person. (Each interview should take approximately 45-60 minutes.)
·Take some notes during the interview to help you remember the topics that come up.
·Make an appointment for the next interview.

The Ethnographic Interview Process

·Become acquainted with the person; build rapport
·Start with a general "grand tour" question
·Build follow-up questions on the person's responses; repeat key items and ask for expansion
·Encourage the person to talk:
    - pause and allow time to respond
    - stay on one topic until it is exhausted; go into as much depth as possible
    - ask for clarification if you don't understand
    - restate what the person says to check your own comprehension

---

In-Class Activities

We must include the teaching of cultural information in every class period. And it must be more than just a sterile reciting of information. As much as possible, we must allow the students to practice the concepts. Some would argue that the idcal situation for teaching culture would be to place the student in the actual milieu of the culture being studied, and let him smell, taste, hear, see and feel. Unfortunately, even that doesn't guarantee that the individual will perceive cultural concepts. We all know of people who have lived in a foreign environment for a number of years and still seem oblivious to the new system of values and behavior. Just as some language students tend to fossilize linguistically at level 2 on the FSI scale of oral proficiency (corresponding to the ACTFL Advanced level) (Higgs & Clifford, 1981), many people living abroad seem to be "terminal 2's" culturally. They never get beyond the most obvious differences and continue to see and act according to their own cultural patterns.

Most of our students need guidance. They need to learn cultural concepts consciously. They need to practice the skills of coping in a new and often frustrating cultural environment. As an example, in our American culture we usually draw quick conclusions about persons' honesty, importance or level of education from the clothes they wear, their speech, or their home. Yet the use of those standards in another culture might be totally meaningless. It takes practice to stop operating according to our own cultural norms, to withhold our judgment, or observe first how others react or behave.

Cultural Island. We can begin by making our classroom a *cultural island*, that is we decorate the room to such an extent that when they enter the students feel they are in another world, a Hispanic world. Of course, this is only possible when teachers have their own classroom. Here public school teachers have a huge advantage over the university professors. Some suggestions are to fill the walls with maps, posters, pictures, bulletin boards, post cards and letters, travel brochures, realia, etc. which you have been collecting over the years. (See Chapter 3 for additional ideas.)

Asides. Perhaps the most frequent type of technique for teaching culture will be what we will call "cultural asides." This is simply a very brief explanation of some cultural concept that is made at the point a "teaching moment" presents itself. By and large, the time for these asides cannot be anticipated, it just appears on the spur of the moment, suggested by the particular turn of the lesson or conversation or activity going on. Spanish teachers will spend their entire life preparing for these asides. Because of the all-inclusive nature of "culture," you will have to become "experts" in many fields; history, geography, music, fine arts, literature, anthropology, architecture, and so on. More important, you will have to keep current on what is going on politically in the Hispanic world. Spanish teachers are "expected to know" who is in power, what the present economic conditions are, and what next crisis will be for almost every Spanish-speaking country.

Culture Capsules. A culture capsule is a short presentation in the class (15-20 minutes) that focuses on some aspect of culture. It has been carefully selected by the teacher as a concept that it is felt that the students should be taught. The teacher researches the information beforehand and carefully prepares the class presentation. The teacher tries to find some article of realia or some visual aid to serve as a center of focus in the presentation. The students are involved as much as possible and at the end there is some type of evaluation to ensure learning by the students. We have prepared an example of a culture capsule here to serve as a model.

MODEL CULTURE CAPSULE
El *mate*

1. **Purpose**
   To acquaint the student with *mate*, how it is prepared, what it tastes like, how it is used, and the role it plays in the life of the people who drink it. The student should understand the patterns of courtesy involved in its use and should know how to react in a situation were he offered mate.

2. **Teaching Objective**
   The student will be able to describe the appearance and taste of mate, explain how and when it is used, and will be able to use the basic vocabulary words listed below. He will be able to demonstrate acceptable reactions in a situation where mate is used.

---

3. **Possible Assessment Approaches**

Show the students the basic items used in drinking mate, and they will write down the Spanish name for each item. Give a multiple-choice test in class about the use of mate. Present pairs of students with hypothetical situations where mate is involved and the students role-play in Spanish how to accept or reject the mate.

BASIC INFORMATION AND SOURCES

Mate is a kind of tea that is very popular in Southern South America (Uruguay, Argentina, Paraguay, and parts of Brazil, Chile, and Bolivia). The *yerba* comes from the leaves of the *mate* bush. It is commonly drunk from a gourd (*mate*) with a metal tube (*bombilla*) but can also be prepared like tea. It can be prepared with hot or cold water, but is most often taken hot. It is often sweetened with sugar and is sometimes flavored with pieces of orange peel, cinnamon, lemon, etc. The drinking of *mate* is an integral part of life of many South Americans. Many drink it immediately upon arising, in a midmorning break, during lunch, or in the early evening while relaxing from the day's work. It has become a sign of courtesy and hospitality. When friends or relatives visit it is prepared and passed around, each drinking a gourd-full. The custom began with the Indians, was traditional among the *gauchos*, and has passed to all social classes. It is said that in the early days, *mate* had a language of its own, and that certain meanings could be given, depending on how the *mate* was served. (Encyclopedias, native informants, and personal experience.)

CLASSROOM PRESENTATION

1. **Method and Activities**

Hold up a mate and ask how many know what it is. Show how to prepare it and pass it around for the students to taste. Role-play typical mate drinking situations and explain how and when it is used. Demonstrate how to refuse mate without offending the host.

2. **Vocabulary**

mate, yerba, bombilla, termo, pava

3. **Materials**

Mates, yerba, bombilla, termo, sugar, hot water, pictures or slides of mate drinking.

Eventually you should have a good collection of culture capsules that you can present at appropriate times during the year. Taylor and Sorensen (1961), the original developers of the culture capsule technique, suggest that the materials, including the script, for each culture capsule be kept in separate shoeboxes for easy storage and access. Nowadays many teachers simply incorporate these materials into a PowerPoint presentation, which requires no storage space.

***Culture Assimilator* format.** A very popular way to teach cultural information is with the culture assimilator, a technique developed by a group of social psychologists (Fiedler, Mitchell, & Triandis, 1971) in order to "expose members of one culture to some of the basic concepts, attitudes, role perceptions, customs, and values of another culture" (p. 95). In this approach, the student is presented, usually in written form, with a "critical incident"---a situation where a cultural conflict has arisen. The student is then given several choices of possible steps to take which might resolve the conflict. Each choice is followed with directions sending the student to a certain page number where there is a discussion of what would result from that particular choice. If the choice is not a good one, the student is directed to go back to the page with the choices and make another one. Following is an example of a *culture assimilator*

MODEL CULTURE ASSIMILATOR
¿Está alguien en casa?

Read through the following "critical incident" and select what you think is the most appropriate response. Check your selection on the page indicated. If it is not the best response, choose others until you find the most correct one.

You are visiting your friends in Chile and the mother asks if you would be able to deliver a package to one of her friends in the neighborhood where you are going next. Since you are on your way there anyway, you agree to help her. When you finally arrive at the house, you find that there is an iron fence in front and a yard between the fence and the house. The gate is shut and you can't find a bell to ring anywhere. What do you do?

Possible Responses
1. You reach over and open the gate yourself and walk up to the door. (Go to page 2)
2. You leave, assuming a shut gate means no one is home. (Go to page 3)
3. You go to the house next door to ask the neighbors if they know where the friend is. (Go to page 4)
4. You clap your hands sharply or yell *¡Halo!* until someone inside comes out. (Go to page 5)

"Retorts" (found on the pages indicated after the response)

You selected option #1. It is considered to be very rude to just open the gate and walk up to someone's door. In fact, you could be trespassing. The person who answers the door would probably be startled and annoyed that you didn't respect their privacy. Or even worse, the owner's dog could come running out and attack you! Try another option.

You selected option #2. If you just leave assuming no one is home because there is a shut gate in front of the hours, you will never find anyone at home! It is customary for most houses to have some sort of gate or fence separating the house from the street. Sometimes the house is built very close to the street, others may be set back quite far with a large yard in front. There is a better solution.

You selected option #3. If you decide to go to the neighbor's house, you will find yourself in the exact situation—standing in front of a house with a closed gate and no bell to ring. Then what do you do?

You selected option #4. Congratulations! You picked the correct option. In America, it might seem rude to clap or shout, but in Chile, and other South American countries, it is customary for a visitor to stand outside the fence and clap or shout. Not so loud that the neighbors come to see if it is for them, but loud enough for the persons at home to hear you and come outside to give you permission to come in. Either they will say *¡Pase!* or *¡Adelante!* inviting you to open the gate and enter, or they will come out and open the gate for you.   (Kelli Lake)

Preparing your critical incidents for the computer is ideal because it allows clicking on one of the options that can take the student directly to the branch he has chosen and can give positive reinforcement for correct answers.

Mini dramas. A mini drama is essentially a cultural concept prepared in the critical incident format that has been dramatized (Gorden, 1968).

The dramatization can be presented live by students in class or be recorded in audio or video format with sound effects, music, native voices, and so on. At various points in the drama there may be a pause made to review and discuss the information available that may help solve the conflict.

A mini drama can also be prepared in a "homemade" video format, using students or native speakers as actors and making some attempt at staging the cultural environment in which the conflict takes place. These can be very motivating with the students because they are visual and the students can relate to the actors. The students are assigned to research cultural themes and write their own dialogues illustrating cultural conflicts that might arise. They then make a video of the performance for later presentation in class or include the tape in a "mini drama library" that can be used for years to come. Jerry Larson (1974) has demonstrated that this can be a very effective approach on both a high school and college level.

Teaching Culture with Media

Since it is usually impossible to transport our students to the target culture, we must transport it to them, and nothing can do it so well as the use of a variety of media. Never was the old adage "a picture is worth a thousand words" truer than it is in the teaching of culture. More and more computers are available for enhancing teaching.

PowerPoint Presentations. Language teachers should wherever possible illustrate their presentations with pictures of geographical features, daily life, people, paintings, styles of architecture, national monuments, etc. Individual students can be assigned to prepare power point presentations on specific topics, which could be viewed & critiqued by other students, either orally or in written form.

Pictures can also be used in a variety of testing formats, such as naming types of architecture, matching different topographical features with specific countries, explaining the meaning of different gestures, identifying foods and fruit, and types of houses and buildings.

Videos. Videos are without doubt the most effective way of teaching culture in the classroom. They come as close as possible to taking the students personally into the culture. It is so much easier to imagine and visualize what the homes, clothing, sports, and activities are like if the student can actually see and hear them. The old 16 m. films that we used to show in class have been virtually replaced by DVDs and digital technology. There is an incredible variety of video

materials available to teachers nowadays, ranging from full-length movies to short clips taken from live television.

We will discuss the techniques for teaching with videos in Chapter 13, but the advantages are obvious; videos present authentic people in an authentic environment, speaking authentic language. You can even use them without sound, making comments or guiding students to find the information you want to teach. One of our favorite techniques is to ask cultural questions before showing a video segment and then having the students discover the information on their own while they watch the video.

If you have access to computers and a projector for in-class teaching, the computer is ideal for presenting cultural information because it permits immediate access to the incredible variety of materials available..

Textbooks. Years ago, most textbooks were not very rich sources of cultural information. They stuck pretty close to the traditional objectives of teaching the language. Since the days of the audio-lingual revolution, things have changed and now textbooks are usually excellent sources of culture. If you were to open a recently published text you would find page after page of cultural notes, cultural reading selections, color pictures, and maps. Often the cultural content is the focus of grammar and vocabulary practice. In addition to the information it presents, your textbook can be a springboard to cultural asides, the basis for culture capsules, and the catalyst for many questions by the students. Newer textbooks also include additional cultural information in the teacher's edition and include questions on cultural facts in quizzes and exams.

Cultural Readers are supplemental materials whose primary purpose is to develop reading skills. The content of readers can range from humorous stories to authentic literature. Many readers combine the reading objective with the cultural objective and make cultural information the core of the reading material. Sometimes the culture presented in these types of readers is very subtle and will require comments from the teacher if the reader itself does not include cultural notes.

Classroom news magazines. There are some commercially prepared classroom "news magazines" (similar to the Weekly Readers so popular in U.S. elementary schools) which are designed specifically for language students. These newspapers are loaded with cultural information that is of great interest to young students because of many articles about the lives of young people in Hispanic countries of their same age. They are also very strong on news and current events.

Songs. Songs have too often been neglected as a means of teaching culture. Teachers usually teach the song with few or no cultural explanations. This is unfortunate because songs can be a rich source of cultural information. The problem basically lies in the fact that the culture is usually buried beneath the surface and most teachers have neither the time nor the background to dig it out. How many thousands of Spanish students have sung *Allá en el rancho grande* or *Cielito Lindo* and never found out why the girl was going to finish the *calzones* with leather, or why the pair of eyes coming down from the Sierra Morena were "*de contrabando?*" With a little effort, some cultural concept can be found in almost any song, even the short children's fun songs. (See *Me gusta cantar* for an excellent collection of songs where the cultural information has been researched and indexed.)

Preambles. A preamble is a technique used by many teachers to fill up the slack time between class periods with informal bits of culture. The teacher presents some *slice of life* such as a recording of natives talking, excerpts from a radio or TV program, or simply the latest hit song of a popular singer or group just a few minutes before the formal beginning of the class. Brief comments on the culture information included can be made right at the time.

Teaching Culture Via the Language or Computer Lab

An answer to the question "How can we language teachers meet our responsibility and fulfill our commitment to teach culture without sacrificing our students' mastery of the language skills?" can come via computer technology. Some schools are equipped with a special lab for language learning; nearly all schools have a general computer lab that can accomplish the same thing, provided the computers have Internet access, speakers, and (ideally) a webcam or

microphone. Virtually all of the techniques we have mentioned above for teaching culture in the classroom can be adapted to the lab, and in some cases, more effectively. If teachers don't want to give up class time to teach culture, the lab can carry the ball. In addition, recent newer technology can provide us with some new and exciting approaches that aren't even available to us in the classroom.

There is also the question of practice. While it is true that culture teaching involves the presentation of great amounts of information, it is also true that the students must practice "culture-general" skills such as observing, not "labeling," asking for clarification, not making comparisons, etc. They must be given opportunities to try out those skills in a number of novel situations. Just as we use audio recordings in the lab to give the students comprehension practice outside the class, so can we use media in the language lab to provide practice of intercultural skills. Here are some additional strategies for teaching culture that can be used in a lab.

Full-length Films. While films are one of the most common avenues for teaching culture, they can also cut deeply into class time. If your media center has DVD players, the students can view the films outside of class at their own convenience. DVDs can also be loaned to students or streamed online to watch at home. The movie *The Mission*, which tells the story of the Jesuit missions in Paraguay, is a marvelous example of a gripping historical account that your students will love. (They will watch it in Spanish, of course.)

In a "culture-general" approach, there are so many excellent films, that the teacher rarely has time to show them all. Use of the lab facilities would permit that. Use of written "active involvement sheets" could guide the students as to what to watch for and also provide a way of checking to ensure that they actually see the films and learn from them. If the lab can accommodate small groups for watching films, group interaction could be very stimulating and group-oriented reports on specific segments or topics could be made in class.

Audio recordings. Teachers often use audio recordings in the classroom to present such experiences as interviews, music, the authentic sounds of street scenes, and sporting and cultural events. These "slices of life" can be handled very easily in the lab. There are many commercial audio programs available in CD or online which present cultural content. A "library-type" language lab allows students to check out a variety of CDs and listen to them on an individual basis; better yet, upload the audio files and make them available online. The use of "viewing guides" prepared either commercially or by the teacher for use with the audio materials can greatly increase learning. "Mini dramas" can be prepared and recorded in the language lab.

Can you use your song collection in the lab? CDs or MP3 files can be made and sheets prepared with the words and cultural explanations. Students can enjoy the music as they follow along with the recording and read about the cultural concepts reflected in each song.

DVDs and videos. Make copies of your videos available to you students in the lab. If the students have access to a library of videos that they can either check out or view online, their learning can be greatly increased because they can "freeze frame," repeat segments, and watch the video numerous times. YouTube is an especially fruitful source of cultural videos; a quick search on almost any topic will yield multiple videos. Typing the search terms in Spanish will often lead you to Spanish language videos.

Teachers can prepare video "packets" in which an especially good segment of film or television program has been dubbed, and the students are given work sheets which help them look for certain items cultural items you have taught them or try to discover something new.

Teacher-prepared Presentations. Teachers can prepare media presentations that can allow students to prepare themselves in the lab before the class, or practice in the lab the concepts the teacher has presented in the class. Information that the teacher often has to leave out in class presentations because of lack of time can easily be presented in the lab, and at the students' own pace of learning.

Culture capsules could easily be adapted for use in a lab if they are prepared in an electronic format such as PowerPoint. Pictures can be synchronized with a sound track, or the entire presentation could be put on video, which is easier to handle.

Use of Technology Outside of Class

In addition to in class and lab use of technology there are outside of class options available.

Live Television. Virtually all students will have television in their homes and if it is provided by cable or via satellite, they will probably have Spanish language channels that they can watch. The potential for cultural learning from this resource is enormous. The students can watch programs from different foreign countries at any time of the day, and with guidance from professors can gather examples of specific cultural traits. For example, the teacher can ask the students to report on which sports are broadcast, what kinds of music are popular, the differences between the content of Hispanic newscasts and those of US channels, and what products are advertised on Spanish channels.

Internet. The cultural information that can be found today on the Internet is incredible. A person needs only enter key words in a search engine and will find thousands of books, articles, encyclopedias, and other sites ranging from official country web sites to personal blogs complete with descriptions and pictures. The biggest hurdle is how to process all the information available.

Most students now have access to the Internet at home and many schools provide Internet access in their library or language lab. Of course there are always dangers of accidentally finding undesirable sites, and you may have to warn the students to avoid certain words in their searches. Most schools have blocking programs that block out sites of that nature on the school computers.

ASSESSING CULTURE LEARNING

Teachers commonly have problems trying to evaluate the students' learning of the cultural concepts and information they teach. Too often teachers test only for mastery of facts and information. Since many of our objectives lie in the affective domain (ability to adapt, greater empathy, more tolerance, etc.) we are going to encounter some real difficulty with assessing learning of those things. The mastery of intercultural communication skills and the measurement of feelings and attitudes is difficult to measure.

Ideally, we would want to place our students in a cross-cultural situation such as putting them in the country or living with a family, and observing their behavior. This has been done by some government agencies such as the Peace Corps, but of course is not within the means of the average teacher.

However, some reliable instrument needs to be developed, else how will the teacher know is he/she is reaching objectives? There have been several different approaches to evaluation in this area in the recent years. Some include attitude surveys and inventories, such as the Intercultural Development Inventory (Hammer, Bennett, & Wiseman, 2003). These often help us get to the real feelings of the students. The "critical incident" approach in various forms has been used as a test with some success. Another approach is the "projective role-playing" technique where the students are placed in a certain situation and are asked to act out what they would do.

Some teachers have had success by having the students write paragraphs on specific topics such as "Why I Feel that the Mexican People are Treated as Inferior in the United States." In writing out their thoughts, students often reveal their underlying biases or prejudices.

"Cultural proficiency" is very hard to evaluate. This might best be done by having the students physically interact in role plays such as greetings, using gestures, certain levels of speech (tú/usted), and so on. We can test their ability to find cultural information by presenting simulated cultural conflicts and seeing how they go about finding solution: looking for explanation instead of criticizing, what questions need to be asked; who can be relied on for correct information; what kinds of things need to be overlooked or disregarded; etc.

Testing the information taught in the culture specific approach is much easier, but should be done very carefully. We must not become entrapped in the mode of only asking trivial information such as the names of the all the rivers in Mexico, how many tons of bananas are exported by Ecuador each year, the distinguishing characteristics of Gothic cathedrals, or the names of all the Spanish kings. Rather we should also focus on general concepts that we have taught and have the students give us examples of customs and behavior that reflect those concepts. Examples would be: personalism, respect for elders, beliefs and values, eating patterns and so on.

We will deal more in depth with cultural testing in Chapter 13, and will present some examples of culture tests.

CONCLUSION

We have seen that culture in its broadest definition must be integrated into every period of a language class. Indeed, we must include "cultural proficiency" as one of our basic objectives. Although it is difficult to decide what cultural information should be included, and sources of accurate cultural information are hard to find, we can draw on a variety of activities in our efforts to combine both the cultural and linguistic aspects of the language. With this approach we should be able to help our students put enough of the pieces of the puzzle together to have a clear picture for understanding the Hispanic people, feel an empathy toward them, and, hopefully, not find themselves too often miscommunicating or offending. There is clearly a heavy burden placed on the foreign language teacher by the obligation to include culture in their teaching. A language teacher is expected to be an expert not only in the language, but also in the history, geography, civilization, music, art, current events and politics, contemporary lifestyles, belief and thought, and so on for each of the Spanish-speaking cultures of the world! As we accept the challenge, we must redouble our efforts to be prepared and to keep up-to-date in all those areas.

REFERENCES AND SUGGESTIONS FOR FURTHER READING

Bateman, B. E. (2004). Achieving affective and behavioral outcomes in culture learning: The case for ethnographic interviews. *Foreign Language Annals, 27,* 240-253. DOI: 10.1111/j.1944-9720.2004.tb02197.x *Report on a study in which first-year college students conducted a series of interviews with native Spanish speakers to learn about their culture. The project was highly successful in promoting positive student attitudes toward Hispanic cultures. Offers tips for setting up similar projects.*

Damen, L. (1987). *Culture learning: The fifth dimension in the language classroom.* Reading, MA: Addison-Wesley. *One of the most best and most complete books on the teaching of culture, incorporating both theory and practical teaching techniques. A great resource for teachers.*

Fiedler, F. E., Mitchell, T., & Triandis, H. C. (1971). The culture assimilator: An approach to cross-cultural training. Journal of Applied Psychology, 55, 95-102. *The inventors of the culture assimilator describe what it is and research on its effectiveness.*

Galloway, V. (2001). Giving dimension to *Mappaemundi:* The matter of perspective. In V. Galloway (Ed.), *Teaching cultures of the Hispanic world: Products and practices in perspective* (AATSP Professional Development Series Handbook for Teachers K-12, Vo. IV, pp. 3-63). Mason, OH: Thompson Learning. *An outstanding discussion of the issues implied in the Cultures goal area of the National Standards, with practical examples showing how culture might be incorporated in a unit on food.*

Gorden, R. L. (1968). *Cross-cultural encounter in a Latin American Bank.* Yellow Springs, OH: Antioch College. *One of the first presentations of cultural information in the mini-drama format.*

Hall, E. T. *The Silent Language* (1990), *The Hidden Dimension* (1966), *Beyond Culture* (1989), *Understanding Cultural Differences* (1987). *These books, written by the highly regarded social anthropologist Edward T Hall give insight into all the dimensions of "small c" culture.* www.edwardthall.com/books.htm.

Hall, J. K., & Ramírez, A. (1993). How a group of high school learners of Spanish perceive the cultural identities of Spanish speakers, English speakers, and themselves. *Hispania, 76,* 613-620. DOI: 10.2307/343839 *A fascinating study that includes a discussion of implications for the classroom*

Hammer, M. R., Bennett, M. J . & Wiseman, R. (2003). The Intercultural Development Inventory: A measure of intercultural sensitivity. In M. Paige (Ed.), *International Journal of Intercultural Relations*, 27, 421-443.

Heusinkveld, P. R. (Ed.). (1997). *Pathways to culture.* Yarmouth, ME: Intercultural Press. *A collection of some of the most important articles on teaching culture that have been published by various authors in professional journals over the past 50 years.*

Higgs, T. V., & Clifford, R. (1981). The push toward communication. In T. V. Higgs (Ed.), *Curriculum, competence, and the foreign language teacher* (ACTFL Foreign Language Education Series, Vol. 13, pp. 57-79). Lincolnwood, IL: National Textbook.

Kramsch, C. (1993). *Context and culture in language teaching.* Oxford: Oxford University Press. *Although Kramsch's book is somewhat theoretical in nature, it contains some profound insights into the nature of culture, as well as some very practical ideas for teaching and learning activities.*

271

Mantle-Bromley, C. (1998). Seeing through language: Preparing second or foreign language learners to explore culture. In B. Finkelstein & E. K. Eder (Eds.), *Hidden messages: Instructional materials for investigating culture* (pp. 137-178). Yarmouth, ME: Intercultural Press. *Contains excellent lesson plans for teaching culture-general concepts.*

Oberg, K. (1960). Cultural shock: Adjustment to new cultural environments. *Practical Anthropology, 7,* 177-182. *One of the first descriptions of culture shock by the person credited with coining the term.*

Seelye, H. N. (1993). *Teaching culture: Strategies for intercultural communication.* Lincolnwood, IL: National Textbook. *A practical guide on the teaching of culture that has been used by teachers for many years. Outlines six goals for culture learning, with many practical examples and activities.*

Snyder, B. (1994). *Encuentros culturales.* Lincolnwood, IL: National Textbook. *A collection of cultural activities prepared specifically for Spanish classes. A Teacher's Guide is available with the book.*

Other Books by James S. Taylor (see Appendix C for information)

- *cultura, **Cultura** y kultura*
- *Materiales para animar la clase de español*
- *Me gusta cantar*
- *Me gusta celebrar*
- *Me gusta comer*

Miscellaneous Sources for Cultural Materials

CultureGrams. Born at Brigham Young University, these highly useful materials with valuable information about the Spanish-speaking countries of the world are now available online in an interactive format. http://online.culturegrams.com/secure/world/.

Wilderdom Games. Their website has a section on multicultural experiential games. It also has a very extensive bibliography of books with descriptions of multicultural, cross-cultural and intercultural games and activities. wilderdom.com/**games**/MulticulturalExperientialActivities.html

---

ACTIVITIES FOR METHODS CLASSES

1. Find the books you used in your Spanish civilization and culture courses. How much "small c" culture is included? Start gathering other books and materials which contain "small c" cultural information which you want to present to your students. Show the list of what you have to your methods instructor.

2. In relation to Activity #1 above, make a list of other books and materials you cannot afford to buy and plan on giving that list to your school librarian to have available to your students. Show the list to your teacher.

3. Subscribe to some Hispanic newspaper or magazine, such as Geomundo, or find out what newspapers and magazines are available in your school library and get in the habit of going to read them at least once a week. Report to your teacher.

4. Examine the list of suggested books for "in-depth" reading at the end of the chapter and read some of them, such as Seeyle's book *Teaching Culture*, Damen's book *Culture Learning: The Fifth Dimension in the Language Classroom*, or one of Edward T. Hall's books. Report what you read and your reactions to your methods professor.

5. Study the list of general cross-communication skills we want to develop with our students. Think of ways you could do this in your classes. Do you know of any films you could use to teach these general concepts? Any games or class activities? Make a list of what you would do and show it to your teacher.

6. Prepare a culture capsule on some specific concept that you would present to your class. Follow the model of the capsules in this chapter. Present the capsule in class as a micro lesson. Make copies for your classmates in the methods class.

7. Prepare a culture assimilator on some specific concept that you would present to your class. Follow the model of the example in this chapter. Make copies for your classmates in the methods class.

8. Prepare a mini-drama on some specific concept that you would present to your class. Follow the model of the example in this chapter. Make copies for your classmates in the methods class.

9. Go to your language lab and study the list of videos available. Decide which ones would have good cultural information. Watch the videos and hand in a report.

10. Find a copy of a comic book from some Hispanic country, and study it, looking for cultural information. List the cultural concepts and hand them in to your instructor.

11. Prepare a simulation that will reinforce some cultural concepts. Present it in the class and have the class act it out.

12. Develop your own culture test or other means of assessing culture learning. What aspect(s) of culture does it assess? How would you score it? Show it to your instructor.

13. Go online and look for good sites for information on any Spanish-speaking country or culture of your choice. Make a list of the best ones and report to your instructor.

CHAPTER TWELVE

ASSESSMENT

YOUR OBJECTIVES FOR THIS CHAPTER ARE TO:

1. EXPLAIN WHAT PROGNOSTIC OR APTITUDE TESTS ARE AND HOW THEY ARE USED.

2. IDENTIFY NATIONAL TESTS THAT ARE AVAILABLE AND DESCRIBE HOW YOU CAN USE THEM IN YOUR PROGRAM.

3. DEVELOP PROGRESS TESTS OF LISTENING, READING, WRITING, GRAMMAR, VOCABULARY, AND CULTURE.

4. DIFFERENTIATE BETWEEN SELECTED RESPONSE AND CONSTRUCTED RESPONSE TEST ITEMS, AND LIST ADVANTAGES AND DISADVANTAGES OF EACH.

5. SELECT FROM AMONG DIFFERENT OPTIONS AND FORMATS FOR ADMINISTERING SPEAKING TESTS AND ORAL ASSESSMENTS.

6. UTILIZE ASSESSMENT TECHNIQUES OTHER THAN FORMAL TESTS, INCLUDING SELF- AND PEER-ASSESSMENTS, OBSERVATIONS, ASSIGNMENTS, PROJECTS, AND PORTFOLIOS.

7. DESIGN CHECKLISTS AND RUBRICS AND USE THEM TO ASSESS STUDENTS' LEARNING.

8. DESCRIBE DIFFERENT GRADING SYSTEMS, INCLUDING GRADES FOR CITIZENSHIP AND WORK HABITS.

9. DESCRIBE DIFFERENT CLASS MANAGEMENT AND GRADING PROGRAMS AND THEIR USES.

10. EXPLAIN THE IMPORTANCE OF USING A WIDE VARIETY OF ASSESSMENT TECHNIQUES AND STRATEGIES IN YOUR CLASSES.

As Phillip left the Podunk High School gym after a long and exhausting basketball team practice, all he could think about was getting home to the delicious meal he knew his mother had prepared for him. Then, as he was driving home, he suddenly remembered that they were having a unit test in Spanish class the next day. Although they spent most of the time in Señorita Silva's class in speaking activities, he wasn't too concerned about being totally unprepared for the test. He knew that she never tested their oral skills any more because they took too much time and whenever she did, the students who good poor grades always complained that the grading system wasn't fair. So it had been a long time since she administered speaking or listening tests. "If I review the vocabulary sheets and the grammar tests she has given us on this unit," Phil thought, "I'll be in good shape. I'm really glad she won't be testing us orally, because I haven't spent any time practicing my speaking since basketball season started."

~~~~

Friday afternoon Mr. Gonzalez stayed late in his classroom after classes were finished. He had to prepare the midterm test for next week. "Let's see," he mused, "I can select about 100 grammar items from the written exercises for each chapter, and that will take care of the grammar part of test. For the reading section, I'll select a paragraph from one of the reading assignments and have them translate it. Now, I should have an oral part, since we have been working quite hard on oral proficiency. I could have oral interviews, but they are so hard to set up and it would take three days to administer to every student. I think that I will just give them a dictation paragraph. That will cover the oral area, and they are very easy to grade. No one can complain about their grades on a dictation. If they don't have the word written down and spelled correctly, it's wrong."

~~~~

Miss Sweetly was a little nervous about the conference one of her student's parents had requested. Wilbur Whetstone was one of her worst students. He was not a problem in Spanish class, he was just plain lazy. He never turned in homework, never prepared for the oral presentations, he had low marks on the tests and quizzes, and she was sure he had never opened the textbook. Still, he always attended class, was pleasant, and never caused trouble. Perhaps she had been a little hasty in determining his grades, a "D" as his academic grade and "U's" in Work Habits and Citizenship. She was very surprised when Mr. Whetstone came right to the point; "I am not questioning Wilbur's academic grade, Miss Sweetly," he said, "You've ample evidence with test scores and records of homework that hasn't been done, that he is not doing passing work. Perhaps he isn't bright enough or doesn't work hard enough to get an 'A.' I can live with that. What I don't understand is why you gave him a 'U' in Citizenship. One thing I can control is his behavior. What is he doing in class that merits an 'Unsatisfactory' grade?" Miss Sweetly was startled. Actually she had no evidence at all to explain the grade. She had just given the "U" because it seemed to go along with the other grades. How was she going to explain that?

CHAPTER TWELVE

ASSESSMENT

> **Where there is accountability, performance improves;**
> **where there is evaluation, success increases.**
> **Boyd K. Packer**

There are many compelling reasons for you to develop a strong assessment component for each of your classes. Some of the more important reasons are:

1. You must assess the *general progress* of your class. How can you tell if what you think you taught was really learned if you don't assess? "Teaching feel" or intuition isn't enough—there has to be some kind of test or measurement.
2. You must assess the status of each individual student. Only when you have assessed can you know what the needs of each student are and what steps you must take to help him or her continue to progress.
3. You must assess the effectiveness of your program. How else can you know if you are reaching your course objectives if you don't have frequent checks? Through assessment you can learn if you need to make adjustments, change your approach, spend more time practicing, or re-teach specific material.

4. The nature of our academic system requires that teachers give grades to the students. In fairness to the students, the grades must be based on assessments that have been made consistently and frequently during the grading period. These grades must also be justified to the students themselves, to administrators, and to parents. This justification is much easier and less likely to be challenged when the grade is based on numerous assessments.
5. Frequent assessment improves the performance of the students. When the students know that their work and progress will be assessed, they make a greater effort.

There are many ways of assessing students' learning. You are probably most familiar with *tests*; however, there exist many other forms of assessment (sometimes called alternative assessments). The following diagram illustrates some of these types of assessment:

Different Types of Assessment

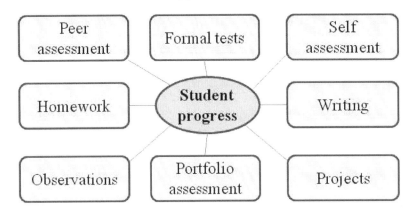

In this chapter we will focus our attention on two basic areas: 1) *formal tests* and 2) *other types of assessment.*

TYPES OF FORMAL TESTS

Since there are so many different kinds of formal tests, it will be helpful to divide them into general classifications. Different experts classify tests in different ways. For simplicity's sake, we will focus only on the kinds of tests that will have the highest use by language teachers. They fall into two general categories: proficiency, and progress. Before we discuss those types in detail, we do want to mention a third kind of test, which at one time received a great deal of attention from FL teachers, but is now used only in specialized contexts. These are prognostic, or aptitude, tests.

Prognostic or Aptitude Tests. Prognostic tests are the kind of tests that are typically given to persons *before* they begin the study of a second language. This type of test is based on the premise that there are certain aptitudes or abilities that are essential or helpful in language learning. The prognostic test measures those abilities and can then be used to predict or prognosticate the degree of success that that person will have in studying the language. All language teachers agree that some students learn quickly while others struggle in some areas such as memorization, recognizing patterns, or making certain sounds. There are a number of prognostic tests available, but the most well known and most widely used are the **MLAT** (Modern Language Aptitude Test), the **Pimsleur LAB** (Language Aptitude Battery), and the **Army Test of Language Ability.** Typically these tests are used in situations where some type of language training is to be given and it is desirable to screen or select those who can best succeed in the training. Examples of those situations are military language schools, government service programs such as the Foreign Service Institute (FSI) and the Peace Corps.

In most school situations it is hoped that no selection will have to be made, and that all students who desire to learn a foreign language will be allowed to do so. Certainly, the best measure of an individual's ability to learn a foreign language would be to let him try. Sometimes, however, because of administrative considerations such as space, money, availability of teachers, etc. some selection must be made. Typically this is done on the basis of the students' academic performance in other subjects, such as grades in English classes or grade point average or even scores on an I.Q. or some other standardized test. Anyone acquainted with students will recognize that these parameters are **not** totally reliable predictors of an individual's probable success in language learning. If screening or selection must be made, it should be on the basis of something more reliable, such as a well-designed aptitude test.

Certain other uses can be made of prognostic tests. Some teachers administer an aptitude test to students who are signed up to study a language to identify which students might have problems, and then give remedial or special attention to those students to compensate for their lack of aptitude in some areas, such as sound discrimination, memorization, and association of meaning. Another use of prognostic tests is get information for "grouping" students according to ability and then allowing one group to proceed at a faster pace, another at a slower pace. Finally, a very creative use some teachers make of prognostic tests is to recruit students to enter language programs. Some teachers give the test to students in elementary schools and then encourage those who do well to take advantage of their "special aptitude" by studying a language when they enter secondary school.

Let's now turn to an in-depth discussion of the different types of the formal tests that you will use in your Spanish classes.

Proficiency (Standardized Achievement) Tests. Proficiency, or standardized achievement tests, are the kind which are given at the end of a program or several years of study to measure the student's achievement in a more global way. Proficiency tests are a type of achievement test that measures general mastery of some aspect of the language, such as speaking or reading. These types of test typically have been administered throughout the country and have been "standardized." Examples of this type of tests are the **ACTFL-ETS Oral Proficiency Interview** (OPI), the **Foreign Service Interview** (FSI), the **College Board Test**, the **Advanced Placement Tests** (AP), and the **MLA Cooperative Foreign Language Tests**.

These tests are usually global by nature and are helpful in seeing where a person fits on a broad continuum ranging from no ability at all to the level of a native speaker. They have the advantage of allowing comparison of one program to another or mastery of one language to another, but do not focus on the mastery of specific grammar points or vocabulary.

A recently developed program of testing that comes much closer to evaluating the skills you will be teaching in your classroom is the STAMP program. This acronym refers to Standards-based Measurement of Proficiency, and was developed by the Center for Applied Second Language Studies (CASLS) at the University of Oregon. The STAMP tests provide an opportunity for teachers to monitor their students' progress toward proficiency. They allow teachers to evaluate their course's curriculum based on how their students perform. STAMP can also help teachers make adjustments in their classroom to improve student outcomes. Following are some of the STAMP features:

STAMP Features
- Chinese, French, German, Italian, Japanese and Spanish
- Available in reading, writing, and speaking
- Measures proficiency ranging from Novice-low to Intermediate-mid
- Age appropriate for grades 7 through 16
- Web-based
- Related to ACTFL Proficiency Guidelines
- Textbook independent
- Available at an affordable cost through CASLS' partner company Avant Assessment.

Benefits for Teachers
- Provides validated, easy-to-use data
- Excellent for checking progress, placement, program and standards review, staff development, and instructional planning
- Access to longitudinal individual speaking and writing samples

Benefits for Students
- Engage in real-world language situations
- Emphasis on what students can do with the language
- Facilitate goal setting

The biggest deterrent to teachers using this program is, of course, the cost. Schools pay a fee for each student enrolled, and for schools with large enrollments this can be a major expense. We have personally evaluated the program and are satisfied that if teachers can find some way to find the money, it is well worth the investment. Perhaps its greatest value is that since many schools across the nation use the program, teachers can compare the progress of their students with those of other schools and other regions. Teachers can try out the program free of charge by contacting CASLS on the Internet.

Progress (Classroom) Tests. Progress (classroom) tests are the kinds of tests that you as a teacher will be using constantly with your classes. These tests can range in nature from a simple vocabulary quiz to a final comprehensive examination given at the end of a semester or year of study. Since this type of test is often focused on evaluating a single or just a few aspects of what you are teaching, they are sometimes referred to as "criterion-referenced" tests because they measure the student's achievement of a particular objective or set of objectives that you have set for a specific presentation or lesson.

Your constant axiom for the preparation and administration of progress tests should always be *"test what you teach."* Students quickly perceive what they are being tested on, and even if you spend most of your class time practicing oral skills, if all your tests are written and limited to grammar concepts, students will only concentrate their efforts on learning grammar terms and rules. If you want to achieve listening comprehension and speaking skills, you must make frequent evaluation of listening comprehension and speaking progress. Even though this might seem obvious, many language teachers do not do it because of the difficulty of administering and scoring these kinds of tests. You must take care to make sure that your tests are matched with your goals and objectives. More on this later in the chapter.

KEY NOTE

TEST WHAT YOU TEACH!
Oral Skills=Oral tests
Listening Skills=List. Tests

The first step, then, in developing a classroom test is to refer to your objectives for the chapter and decide how to assess them. As explained in Chapter 4, you should decide on this at the time you're planning the chapter rather than as just an afterthought at the end.

Remember also that there exist many other forms of assessment besides tests. In the following section we will discuss various formats for tests, followed by a discussion of alternative forms of assessment such as self assessment, peer assessment, and portfolio assessment.

FORMATS OF TEST ITEMS

The questions on a test are called *items*. Test items basically fall into two categories: *selected response items* and *constructed response items.*

Selected response items, as the name implies, require students to choose from among two or more answer options. Common selected response formats include true/false, correct/incorrect, matching, and multiple choice.

Selected response items are most often used for testing the receptive skills, listening and reading. They may also be used for testing grammar and culture. The main advantage of selected response items is that they are easy to administer and correct. However, they are generally not useful for testing speaking and writing, which require students to produce their own responses. In addition, it is quite challenging to write good selected response items (as you know if you've ever taken a poorly-written multiple choice test). If you plan to make extensive use of selected response items, we recommend consulting one of the resource books listed at the end of this chapter.

In constrast, **constructed response** formats require students to produce some type of response on their own. Common constructed response formats include fill-in-the-blank, sentence completion, short answer, and longer answer items such as descriptions, narrations, and essay questions.

Constructed response formats are often used for testing writing, as well as grammar and sometimes culture. (We will address speaking separately, as it cannot be assessed by a written test.) Constructed response formats are useful in that they require students to produce a response that demonstrates what they can do with the

language. However, they are more time-consuming to grade than selected reponse items.

TESTING THE FOUR SKILLS, PLUS GRAMMAR, VOCABULARY, AND CULTURE

In this section we will give specific information about the construction and administration of tests of the skills we are trying to develop in our students.We will begin with listening and reading, which use mainly selected response formats. Next we will discuss writing, which requires constructed response formats. We will then address speaking, which poses special challenges that require a different type of test. Finally, we will discuss the testing of grammar, vocabulary, and culture.

Listening Comprehension Tests

Typically, listening comprehension tests are given "live" by the teacher in the class, or by playing audio or video recordings. They lend themselves well to selected response formats such as true/false or multiple-choice, and thus are very easy to correct. Following are some of the most common types.

True or false. The students hear a statement that they indicate is either true or false. For example:

1. Comemos con la boca.
2. Vamos a una cancha de baloncesto para nadar.
3. Etc.

True or false with visual cues. The students have a visual cue such as a picture or scene and hear statements about what is in the picture. They determine if the statements are true or false. For example, the student would see a picture of children playing in a living room and would hear the following statements:

1. La mamá está preparando la cena.
2. Una niña juega con una muñeca.
3. Etc.

Response to commands. The teacher (or recorded stimulus) gives commands and the students physically respond to the command.

They are graded on their response. For example, the teacher says:

> *Levanta la mano derecha.*
> *Toma una hoja de papel, dóblala y*
>   *métela en tu libro.*
> *Ve a la pizarra y escribe tu nombre.*
> *Etc.*

Drawing test. Each student has a blank sheet of paper and the teacher describes a person or scene that the students draw. For example, the teacher describes:

> *Veo una casa con una puerta y dos ventanas. Hay cortinas en las ventanas. Hay flores en frente de la casa y en la calle delante de la casa hay un coche con un señor sentado dentro. Ese señor lleva un sombrero y está leyendo un periódico.*

The test is scored on how many details the students get right, not on the artistic quality of the drawing.

Logical or illogical response. This is similar to the true or false type, but allows a more natural use of the language. The students hear a statement, followed by a response, and they decide if the response is logical or illogical. For example:

> —*No he podido comer en todo el día y*
>   *tengo un hambre tremendo.*
> —*Lo siento mucho. Debes estudiar más.*

Students would indicate their responses on answer sheets.

Multiple choice answers. The students hear a statement or question and then hear three or four possible answers or responses, each identified as "A" "B" "C" or "D." For example:

1. ¿Dónde está tu hermano?
    A. Sí, es mi hermano.
    B. Mi hermano tiene ocho años.
    C. No sé. Quizás en su dormitorio.
    D. Tengo tres hermanos.

2. Mi tía Matilde está muy enferma.
    A. Lo siento mucho.
    B. Muy bien, gracias.
    C. Trabaja en el hospital.
    E. Me siente un poco enfermo.

The students would circle the correct option on their answer sheets.

Multiple choice with visuals. In this type the students hear a statement, a question, or a partial statement (teacher or tape) and bases their answers on the pictures or written answers or completions that they see on the test sheet. Examples:

(Students hear) *Número uno: Es un libro.*

(Students see on their test sheet)

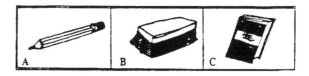

Número dos: Son las cuatro.

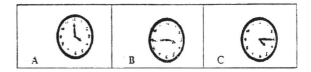

Número tres: Marta escribe una carta en su clase de español.

Número cuatro: Pablo y Adela salen de casa.

Location of situation. The students hear a brief conversation and then are given a multiple-choice selection of where the conversation takes place. For example, the students hear:

—Tengo buenas noticias, Sra. Gómez, su problema es una simple infección, no tendremos que operarle.

—¡Ay! ¡Cuánto me alegro! Como mi esposo no tiene trabajo, no tenemos dinero para una operación cara.

The students would choose from the following options:

A. En la escuela
B. En el consultorio del médico
C. En el mercado
D. En la estación de tren

Conversation/Questions. The students hear a short conversation and then are asked questions about what was said. The questions can be answered in writing by the students or they can be given multiple-choice answers to select from.

Narration/Questions. This type is similar to the preceding one, but is often longer, such as a story. This type could also include listening to story or lecture on an audio tape, or most common of all, watching a video or watching live TV. The student can write out answers, choose from true-false or multiple-choice options, listen for information, or even write out a summary in English.

Testing Reading Comprehension

While, technically speaking, any test requiring some sort of reading by the student could be called a reading test, what we are concerned with here is the testing of the normal use your students will make of reading. Can they read a letter, a story, or instructions with direct comprehension?

Testing reading comprehension is a fairly simple task. Customarily the students are given a passage to read, and are asked to answer questions about the selection. They are expected to use the normal techniques you will have taught them in the class, using context to determine meaning of unfamiliar words, intelligent guessing, recognition of cognates, and so on. For this reason the students are not normally allowed to use dictionaries in reading tests. Here is an example of a typical multiple choice reading test:

Un domingo Ricardo llama a su novia Teresa por teléfono para invitarla a un concierto que va a presentar un grupo musical llamado "La Charanga" el sábado próximo. Teresa dice que irá porque quiere estar con Ricardo, pero no le gusta mucho la música de ese grupo. El miércoles por la mañana Ricardo va a la ventanilla y compra los boletos. La noche del concierto salen muy temprano porque van en el autobús y no quieren llegar tarde. Como es un grupo muy popular, hay mucha gente en el concierto. Un chico y una chica cantan y otros dos tocan la guitarra. Es una sorpresa cuando en la primera parte cantan canciones folclóricas, y a Teresa le gustan mucho. Luego cantan canciones folclóricas, y a Teresa le gustan mucho. Luego cantan música popular, que es más típico del grupo. Después del concierto Ricardo y Teresa cenan en su lugar favorito y luego vuelven a casa.

1. ¿A qué le invita Ricardo a Teresa?
   A. A ir al cine.
   B. A cantar con "La Charanga".
   C. A ir a un concierto.
   D. A ir a la ventanilla.
   E. A ir al restaurante a comer.

2. ¿Por qué va Teresa con Ricardo?
   A. Porque quiere practicar su español.
   B. Porque quiere estar con Ricardo.
   C. Porque ella va a cantar.
   D. Porque le gusta la música clásica.
   E. Porque le gusta la música popular.

3. ¿Cuándo compra Ricardo los boletos?
   A. El domingo.
   B. La noche que salen.
   C. El día antes.
   D. Dos semanas antes.
   E. Tres días antes.

4. Después de la presentación...
   A. Toman una Coca Cola y vuelven a casa.
   B. Comen.
   C. Bailan
   D. Van a un concierto.
   E. Vuelven directamente a casa.

The questions can be either in English or in Spanish. If they are in Spanish, care must be taken to keep the question very simple and easy to understand, so that if the students miss a question, it is because they did not understand the *passage*, not because they did not understand the *question*. Answers can be written out in English or Spanish, but must be graded on correctness of the answer, not the correctness of the grammar they used in their answer, or they can be given multiple-choice options.

Care should be taken not to require the student to make critical comments on a reading selection, such as might be required in a literature class, nor would a translation be an appropriate measure of reading comprehension as we have defined it. Translation is a specialized skill that can be taught apart from the regular skills learned in a language class.

Testing Writing Proficiency

Writing skills are also very easy to test. Normally the students will be completing numerous writing assignments during the course and the kinds of evaluation can be of a similar nature. Some of the most common types are:

Dictations. Although some teachers think dictations test listening comprehension, they are primarily a test of writing. Some students with Hispanic background, for example, might understand completely a dictation passage, but not be able to write it because they have little or no experience in writing in Spanish. Conversely, other students might be able to write down exactly every word in a dictation, but may not really know what it's about.

Dictations are usually given in short groups of words, with pauses between to allow the students to write the words down. They are helpful in checking the students' ability to spell in the language and evaluate their use of writing conventions such as use of capital letters, written accents, writing conventions such as the inverted question mark, and so on.

Spot dictations allow us to check specific items without having to wade through long paragraphs of written material that we are not really interested in. An example of a spot dictation follows:

(Student answer sheet)

Aunque mi (1)_____ es (2)_____,
ella (3)_____ en _____. Ella
hablaba (4)_____ hasta que su familia se
(5)_____ a los (6)_____
(7)_____. Mi (8)_____
(9)_____ dice que ahora ella habla como
una (10)_____.

The student would hear the following paragraph and would fill in the blanks with the missing words on their answer sheet as they hear them. Thus the teacher has only to check the words in the blanks to determine if the students use capitals and written accents properly.

(Read by the teacher)
Aunque mi mamá es americana, ella nació en México. Ella hablaba español hasta que su familia se mudó a los Estados Unidos. Mi tío Jorge dice que ahora ella habla coma una gringa.

Written answers to questions. This type of test is similar to what the students will probably be doing regularly with writing notebooks. For example:

1. ¿Tienes un animal domesticado en casa?
_____

2. ¿A qué hora te levantas?
_____

3.¿En qué mes es el día de independencia?
_____

The teacher can check use of vocabulary and correctness of grammar.

Longer-reponse questions. This type of question requires students to write some type of message, description, or narration. This format comes closer than other formats to approximating real-life language use, so you should consider using it wherever possible. Even first-year students can write short messages if you keep the instructions simple enough. Following are a couple of examples:

You are writing a description of yourself for a social networking website. Include the following information in your description: (a) your name and age, (b) where you live, (c) a brief physical description of yourself, and (d) two things you like to do.

You are visiting Mexico City during a Summer trip with your Spanish class, and you decide to write an email message to a Spanish-speaking friend back home. In your message, mention at least three famous places you have visited, and tell something interesting about each place.

A simple way to grade students' responses would be to assign a certain number of points for content, grammar, and vocabulary.

Testing Oral Proficiency

Speaking tests are often neglected because of two inherent problems: 1) administering the test, and 2) scoring the test. Because of its nature a speaking test usually must be given to individual students, one at a time. While there are some ways to get around this, oral testing requires a large commitment of time that most teachers can't find. Nevertheless, to be true to our objectives and to motivate the students in the right direction, we must include these kinds of tests in our program. The scoring of oral tests is also by nature somewhat subjective. Since the test is given separately to individuals, the conditions will vary. Students react differently to the test—some are confident and respond rapidly and easily; other are nervous and shy and sometimes suffer "mental blocks." To avoid being unfair, we must try to administer these tests uniformly to all students and must score them according to specific criteria that we apply equally and fairly to all.

Types of Oral Production (Speaking)Tests

Pronunciation tests. The teacher can focus specifically on the student's pronunciation by giving him something to read and recording how he handles specific sounds. Some teachers give a paragraph to the students and practice it over a few days in class, allowing them to make any annotations on their paper they want and asking them to practice. Then when the test is given, the teacher gives the student a fresh copy of the paragraph to read and writes down comments and perhaps a grade on another copy that is given to the student at the end of the test.

Another approach is to give the student a card with short phrases on it, and asks the student to read them one at a time. With each phrase the teacher focuses on just one or two specific sounds. A third method is to make a global evaluation based on a rubric specifying the criteria that the teacher has prepared in advance, such as the following:

MODEL SCORE SHEET FOR PRONUNCIATION	
Criteria	**Points**
Very good pronunciation of all sounds: almost native quality	4 points
Good pronunciation; occasionally misses a sound; easily understandable	3 points
Poor pronunciation; noticeable American accent; not easy to understand	2 points
Very bad pronunciation; strong, annoying American accent; very difficult to understand	1 point

The teacher should go over these criteria with the students before the test and even do a "dry run" with them so they know exactly how they will be evaluated. Practicing for this test can be a very effective way to remind your students about the importance of good pronunciation and emphasize your "insistence" that they keep working on it.

Presentation of memorized material. This type of test might simply be the recitation of a memorized dialogue, prepared talk, or poem. You may have the students do this in front of the entire class, individually with you, or even in pairs. You must devise a scoring system and let the students know what it will be. For example, the grade could be based on the following:

Memorization	5 points
Expression	5 points
Fluency	5 points
Pronunciation	5 points
Content (if by student)	5 points

Points could be deducted if the student has to be prompted, if words or lines are left out, if parts are said without expression or understanding, and so on.

Assessment of oral skills can also be made in the presentation of skits or dramatization of a situation, such as a mini drama. Be careful not to dampen enthusiasm or motivation with oppressive evaluation of activities of this sort. Most teachers simply give students credit if they participate. However, when students know they are being evaluated they usually perform to higher standards.

Oral reports should also be evaluated. The criteria in our model can be used, but to that the teacher must add other considerations such as quality of research, length, use of visuals such as maps, pictures, charts, etc. in the presentation. Feedback on oral presentations of this nature, such as correction or assigning of grades, can be made in a general sort of way, without singling out specific students, or can be made privately with individuals.

Question and answer tests. This is perhaps the most typical kind of oral test: the teacher asks questions and the student responds. The same questions would be asked of each student, but the teacher can adjust or rephrase or repeat the questions as the situation requires. For example:

Maestro/a: .Voy a hacerte unas preguntas. Trata de contestarlas con una frase completa. ¿Listo(a)?

Número uno: ¿A que hora es tu clase de español? (pause for student response)
Número dos: ¿Cuántos hermanos tienes? (pause)
Número tres: ¿Cuántos años tienes? (pause)
Número cuatro: ¿Cuál es tu número de teléfono? (pause)
Número cinco: ¿Qué clases tienes por la mañana? (pause)

The teacher would score students on their response, giving points for correctness and appropriateness, and could include some rating of pronunciation. Points could be deducted for delay of response or the necessity of repeating any of the questions.

Directed response. In this type of test, the teacher simply directs the student to say something such as follows. You would probably give these directions in English to avoid giving away the vocabulary.

> *Ask me what my name is.*
> *Tell me to come in and sit down.*
> *Tell me about your family.*
> *Describe your Spanish teacher.*

Scoring of this test could be based on vocabulary, correctness, pronunciation, and appropriateness of what was said.

Visual cues. This is a very easy type of test to prepare. It can be done with a drawing or picture that illustrates people, actions, or scenes that require vocabulary or constructions that the student has learned and previously practiced. The teacher can simply ask the student to tell what he or she sees in the picture, or ask specific questions, such as "*¿Cuántos libros hay en la mesa? ¿Qué hace el muchacho? ¿Adónde van?*" Pictures showing conversation can be used to require that the student infer what is being said, students can describe what action is going or, can tell stories in different tenses, and so on.

Example: (Student sees a larger version of this picture.

Maestro/a:	Aquí ves un dibujo. Observa un minuto lo que hay y lo que pasa en el dibujo y luego te haré unas preguntas.	
Número uno:	Ves que la familia García va de vacaciones. ¿Qué medio de transporte usan? (pause for student answer)	
Número dos:	¿Qué hace la mamá durante las vacaciones? (pause)	
Número tres:	¿Qué hace el papá? (pause)	
Número cuatro:	¿Qué hace el hijo? (pause)	
Número cinco:	¿Qué hace la hija? (pause)	
Número seis:	¿Qué hacen todos juntos?	

Students could be given points for each comment they make or each question they answer correctly.

The teacher can show the students pictures of a conversation and ask them to infer what is being said, such as a boy offering a seat to a girl, and the teacher asks:

¿Qué le dice el muchacho a la muchacha?

The scoring would be the same as indicated in the above examples.

To test the time of day, the teacher can set an hour on a clock and ask the student what time it is. Or the teacher can set an hour on the clock and ask questions of the student, who would respond using the hour set on the clock. For example:

Maestro/a (setting 11:30 on the clock):
¿A qué hora tienes tu clase de español?

Estudiante: Tengo mi clase de español a las once y media.

The scoring in this case might be restricted solely to correctness in stating the hour.

Role-playing. This type of test probably reflects most faithfully the kinds of activities you will have the students do in class. The teacher presents a situation and then plays the role of one of the speakers with the student, or gives a situation to two or more students and has them act out the roles. Again, the instructions would probably be in English to avoid giving away vocabulary words. Example:

Maestro/a: Pretend that you are calling a friend on the phone. You need to get some information about a school assignment. I will play the role of the friend's father (or mother).

Maestro/a: ¡Diga! (Pause for student's response.)
Maestro/a: ¿De parte de quién? (Pause)
Maestro/a: Un momento, Marta (Beto, etc.), voy a ver si está. (Pause)
Maestro/a:..Lo siento mucho, Marta (Beto, etc.), pero no está en este momento. ¿Quieres dejar algún recado?

Alternatively, the role play can be set up between two students, with each one given separate instructions. For example:

Estudiante A: You are making plans with a friend for Saturday night. Suggest some activities that you might do, as well as plans for getting something to eat afterward.

Estudiante B: Ask your friend about the time and location of the activites, and suggest some ideas. Make definite plans as to where you will go and what you will do.

Following is a rubric that could be used for assessing most types of role plays. The teacher simply circles the appropriate point value for each criterion. If there are two students involved in the role play, the teacher fills out a separate evaluation for each student. Notice that the rubric weights overall communication slightly more heavily than the other components.

RUBRIC FOR ROLE PLAY	*Poor*	*Fair*	*Good*	*Excellent*		
Pronunciation: Correct sounds, stress on the correct syllable, acceptable accent	1	2	3	4		
Vocabulary: Correct use of words and expressions for the situation	1	2	3	4	5	
Grammar: Correct use of grammar rules studied so far	1	2	3	4	5	
Communication: Overall ability to accomplish the purpose of the role play	1	2	3	4	5	6
				Total ___ /20		

Free narration. This type is the hardest to score. The teacher simply gives the student a topic and allows him to talk. These instructions could be in Spanish. For example:
Cuéntame de un viaje que has hecho recién. Seguramente hay cosas en nuestra escuela que no te gustan. ¿Qué cambiarías si pudieras?

Relátame brevemente el trama del cuento que leímos en la clase la semana pasada.

In scoring this type of test, the teacher could focus on vocabulary use, conjugation of verbs, use of different tenses, agreement of adjectives, and so on.

Ways of Administering Oral Tests

"One-on-one." This is the most common technique of giving oral tests. The student and examiner meet in an office, at the teacher's desk, in the hallway outside of class, or in a corner of the room. As the teacher administers the test, it is important that the other students not be allowed to hear the questions or see the materials used. Those students not being tested could be given written work to keep them occupied.

Group or pair tests. This approach allows a more natural setting. The students perform in pairs or groups and the teacher evaluates each individual's contributions. This might include role-playing, the recitation of a dialog, conversation on a selected topic, etc. Sometimes one student's lack of preparedness might tend to "drag down" the other student's performance, and the teacher needs to adjust for this in order to be fair to the better-prepared student.

Oral tests in the lab. If you have a lab that has individual recording equipment in each booth, you can administer a test simultaneously to several students either by asking the questions or giving the stimulus from the console and having the students record their responses. The questions or stimulus could also be played from a recording. The students record their responses for the teacher to be scored at a later time. Thus a five-minute test can be given to perhaps twenty students in the time it would take to give to one student individually. The tests can be scored by teachers at their convenience, just as is done with written tests. An additional advantage of this kind of test is that the teachers can listen to the oral responses several times if necessary as they score a student's responses.

Oral tests with two audio recorders. If you have a room or an area available in your classroom that is away from the other students where you can set up two audio recorders, you can have students take an oral test while you are doing other activities with the rest of the class.

One recorder has pre-recorded questions or stimuli (with pauses for answers) and is in the play mode. There can be a large "PLAY" sign on this recorder. The other recorder is in the record mode and on "pause." This recorder could have a "RECORD" sign on it. The students come one

at a time, release the pause button of the "RECORD" machine, say their name, push "PLAY" on the "PLAY" machine, and respond to the questions or stimulus. At the end of the test, the student simply presses the pause button on the "RECORD" machine, and returns the "PLAY" machine to "start." The teachers have only one recording to listen to and can score it at their own convenience. The scoring system would be essentially the same as with direct interviews.

Testing Grammar and Vocabulary

Grammar and vocabulary are fairly straighforward to test. They can be assessed through selected response formats such as multiple choice, although constructed response formats are usually more useful, as they require students to produce the correct words or grammatical forms.

Remember that grammar and vocabulary should also be assessed in communicative contexts through speaking and writing tests, as discussed earlier. Nevertheless, most chapter or unit tests contain specific sections to assess grammar and vocabulary by themselves, so we have included some possible formats here.

Fill-in-the-blank tests. This well-known type of test is universally used by most teachers. It allows us to focus on specific items of vocabulary and use of grammar. We advise that the teacher remember to keep this type of test in context, especially when working with verb conjugations. Here is an example of the type you might use to test use of preterit and imperfect:

> Había una vez un mono que se (1) (llamar) _____ Jorge. El (2) (vivir) _____ en la selva, donde siempre (3) (brillar) _____ el sol y (4) (cantar) _____ los pájaros. Un día (5) (llegar) _____ dos hombres del zoológico. Le (6) (atrapar) _____ al mono y le (7) (llevar) _____ a una ciudad grande.

Don't forget to keep it in context!

Transformation. This type of test allows the specific evaluation of mastery of grammar concepts. The student is given a sentence, part of which is underlined, and a cue that is to be substituted in the place of the underlined word. For example:

1. Mi primo <u>Enrique</u> es alto y moreno. (María y Marta)

   _____.

2. ¿Quién es esa <u>muchacha</u>? (Muchachos)

   _____.

In the first item, the student would have to write: *Mis primas María y Marta **son** altas y morenas,* demonstrating an understanding of singular and plural, and adjective agreement. In the second item, *Quién* would have to be changed to the plural *Quiénes, esa* to the masculine plural *esos,* singular *muchacha* would have to be changed to *muchachos,* and *es* would have to be changed to *son.*

Construction from fragments. A common test that allows a narrow focus without revealing the correct forms is the "fractured" approach where the student is given words and ideas placed between diagonal slashes and is asked to construct sentences. For example:

papá/no/permitir/Juan/manejar/coche

The student might write:

El papá no permite que Juan maneje el coche.

Omitted words tests. A written test that allows the teacher to evaluate the students' mastery of basic vocabulary and "function" words involves giving the students a passage where words are left out. The students must decide from the context what word belongs. For example:

Fill in the blank with the logical word or words that complete the idea being expressed.

Raúl:	¡Qué tal, Jorge! ¿Cómo _____?
Jorge:	¡Hola! Bien gracias, ¿y _____?
Raúl:	Bastante bien. ¿A _____ vas?
Jorge:	Voy _____ parque. ¿Quieres ir conmigo?
Roberto:	No, _____. Tengo _____ trabajar.

Testing Culture

Because of the nature of the objectives for teaching culture, it can be quite challenging to assess. Teachers need to be careful not to require just a memorization of facts and information. Hopefully, your treatment of culture in the class will affect the students' awareness, values, and attitudes toward people from Hispanic cultures. We also hope to develop some cultural skills in our students such as how to cope with cultural change, how not to offend, how to be patient and non-judgmental. These things are nearly impossible to test.

The testing of cultural information can use either selected or constructed response formats, of the type that might be used in a history or geography class. For example:

1. On the map below, locate the following countries: Argentina, Uruguay, Chile, Paraguay, Bolivia, and Peru.

2. Match each country with its capital.

____	1. Honduras	a. Buenos Aires
____	2. Argentina	b. Asunción
____	3. Paraguay	c. Tegucigalpa

3. A student from Salamanca who has been studying in Madrid, returns home for the first time in several months. How would he greet his mother? He would probably:

   A. Kiss her on the mouth.
   B. Kiss her on the cheek.
   C. Kiss her on both cheeks.
   D. Give her a big hug.
   E. Shake her hand with great affection.

4. What would happen if you went into a restaurant in Spain and asked: *Quiero un taco*?_____.

5. You are about to hear a music selection. Tell what kind of music it is and tell what area it is from. (Students would hear a "salsa.")

6. —*Hola, Paco ¿cómo estás?*

   This greeting in Spanish indicates that:
   A. the speaker is an American.
   B. the speaker and Paco are friends or peers.
   C. the speaker and Paco have just met for the first time.
   D. Paco is the speaker's boss or social superior.

7. From the following list of names, circle five that are not Spanish: Mckenzie, Diana, Betty, Linda, Susan, Ana, Tiffany, Maria, Pilar, Teresa, Shirley.

8. True or false? The following things are very typical of Latin-America families:

   1. Very few have cell phones.
   2. The whole family gets together to eat at least one meal a day.
   3. Very often relatives (cousins, aunts, uncles, grandparents, etc.) live together in the same house.
   4. Latin-American teenagers often own their own car.
   5. The parents decide who their children will marry and make the arrangements.

9. Explain the cultural pattern illustrated in the following Mafalda comic strip:

© Joaquín Salvador Lavado (QUINO) Toda Mafalda – Ediciones de La Flor,1993

10. This Peruvian woman is shown here with her . . .

    A. burro
    B. caballo
    C. camello
    D. alpaca
    E. llama

Another effective way of assessing culture learning is through *portfolios,* which we will discuss later in the chapter.

ALTERNATIVE FORMS OF ASSESSMENT

Now let's look at other approaches to assessment other than formal tests. This type of assessment is not as objective as formal tests and thus less frequently used as the basis of grades, but nevertheless it can give us valuable feedback as to the achieving of our objectives. Look again our diagram and note the different kinds of assessment that can be made in addition to formal tests:

Different Types of Assessment

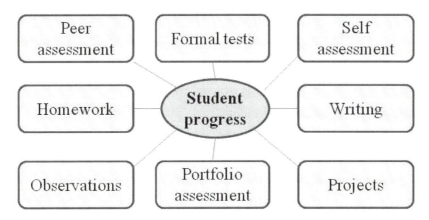

Let's now look at some other types of assessment besides formal tests. This section illustrates the use of **checklists**, which differ from rubrics in that they do not specify a range of performance at different levels; they only require a checkmark to be made in the appropriate column, such as *sí* or *no*, or *siempre / usualmente / a veces / nunca*. We have kept our models in Spanish to help you, since the language of communication in the class will be Spanish.

Self assessment. In this type of assessment, students evaluate their own progress with a progress report. Following are examples for listening comprehension, speaking, and reading.

Example of self progress report for listening:

Estudiante:	**Clase:**		**Fecha:**	
	Siempre	Usualmente	A veces	Casi nunca
1.Entiendo lo que dice el/lamaestro/a				
2.Entiendo a mis compañeros				
3.Entiendo las cintas en el lab.				
4.Entiendo los videos en la clase				

Example for speaking:

Estudiante: Fecha:	Sí	No
1. Puedo decir cuándo y dónde nací,		
2. Puedo deletrear mi nombre en español.		
3. Puedo describir a mi familia: cuántos, edades, trabajo, descrip.		
4. Puedo hablar de las cosas que me interesan, mis "hobbies".		
5. Puedo hablar de las cosas (comida) que me gustan.		
6. Puedo preguntar de que le gusta a otra persona.		
7. Puedo preguntar de donde viene otra persona.		
8. Puedo preguntar la edad de otra persona.		

Example of self diagnosis of reading difficulties:

Estudiante:	Fecha:
I have difficulty with:	
	understanding the general meaning
	picking out the main information
	because I find too many words I don't understand
	because I always feel I am missing some of the information
	following the points in an argument
	understanding the details
	following instructions
	reading newspapers
	reading stories or novels
	understanding official letters or forms

Peer assessment. Here, students rate their peers as they work in pairs with questions/answers, problem solving, conversing on topic, dynamic activities, etc.

Estudiante:	Evaluador:	Fecha:	
		Sí	No
1.Contesta bien preguntas personales			
2. Usa el vocabulario asignado			
3. Puede dar instrucciones (Diego Dice)			
4. Puede dar direcciones (Mapa)			

Teacher observations. Here the teacher makes weekly observations of the entire class, using an observation report.

Clase: Semanas:	Saludar y respond.	Dar # de teléfono	Comprar (regatear)	Decir la hora	Pedir comida en restaurante	Pedir dir. para trans.
Acabado, Ana	√	√	√	√		√
De Tal, Fulano	√	√	no	√	no	no
Fold, Bill (Guillermo)	√	no	no, no	√	no	no
Matamoscas, María	√	√		√	√	√
Presley, Elvis (Edelberto)	√	no, no		no	no	no
Sastre, Jaimito	√	√	√	√	√	√

Projects and out-of-class assignments. : For projects and assignments that students do out of class, they can hand in a report on what they did. The teacher may want to leave a space to comment on the students' work.

Example of group project report:

INFORME DE PROYECTO TERMINADO		
Estudiantes: Jaimito Sastre, Ana Cabado, Edelberto Presley **Fecha:** 10 marzo, 1996	**Producto del Proyecto**	**Evaluación del profe:**
Escribimos una "telenovela" titulada Los *tres mosquiteros* y la grabamos en un video.	El video	Excelente producción. Me he reído mucho. Muy buen trabajo. Nota: 50 puntos de 50 posibles.

Example of outside-of-class assignments report:

INFORME DE ASIGNACIONES **Estudiante:** Jaimito Sastre	**Fecha de entrega:**		
Asignaciones (fuera de la clase, en español)	me gustó	más o menos	no me gustó
1. Pron.: leer en voz alta 5 min.por día (una semana)		√	
2. Conversar 10 minutos con vecino, amigo (adulto)		√	
3. Hablar por teléfono 10 minutos (amigo)	√		
4. Comer en un restaurant mexicano	√√√		
5. Jugar a la lotería con compañeros 20 minutos	√√		

PORTFOLIO ASSESSMENT

An increasing number of teachers are turning to **portfolios** as one way of assessing their students' progrss. A portfolio is a systematic collection of a student's works over a period of time. It is *not*, however, just a folder full of everything the student has done during the year. Portfolios have two distinguishing characteristics: they involve students in (1) selecting the content that is included, and (2) reflecting on their progress in language learning.

Portfolios have a number advantages for assessing students' learning:

- They help create a match between classroom activities and assessment.
- They can capture a rich array of what students know and can do.
- They can chronicle students' language development over time and show their progress.
- They involve students in evaluating their own work, effort, strategies, goals, and progress.

- They help students take responsibility for their own learning.
- They can show progress and effort as well as final product.

There are two basic types of portfolios. **Working or process portfolios** show evidence of students' progress over a period of time. The content of the portfolio does not necessarily reflect students' best work or current level of proficiency, but rather, the growth that they have made over time. In contrast, **showcase or product portfolios** show examples of students' best work at their current proficiency level. They are intended for some type of final evaluation, competition, applying for jobs, etc. It is also possible to combine elements of both types of portfolios.

Portfolios can include any combination of language skills or modalities, plus grammar, vocabulary, and culture knowledge. Following are some possibilities for portfolio content, organized according to the three communicative modes of the *Standards for Foreign Language Learning* (although they could just as easily be organized around the four skills of speaking, listening, reading and writing). Because portfolios are an excellent way of assessing culture learning, we have also included ideas for cultural content of a portfolio.

Interpersonal Mode

- Audio or video recordings of interviews with native speakers, classroom discussions or debates, oral journal entries, telephone conversations, role plays, selected classroom speaking tests, etc.
- Copies of correspondence with penpals or keypals
- Self-, peer-, or teacher assessments of interpersonal communicative skills
- Self-assessment of communicative strategies used
- Goals for improving communicative skills

Interpretive Mode

- Logs, summaries, or critical reviews of works read, listened to, or viewed
- Self-assessments of listening or reading comprehension and enjoyment
- Self-assessments of listening or reading strategies used
- Goals for improving comprehension

Presentational Mode

- Audio or video recordings of oral presentations, skits/plays, projects
- Photgraphs of projects, posters, etc.
- Drafts and/or final versions of written works (stories, poems, essays, etc.)
- Self-, peer-, or teacher assessments of oral and/or written presentations
- Self-assessments of writing strategies used
- Goals for improving writing and/or presentational speaking skills

Culture

- Culture capsules or presentations created by students
- Reports on cultural interviews with native speakers or presentations by guest speakers
- Entries in culture blogs or journals (especially in a study abroad setting)
- Self-assessments of attitudes toward the target culture or toward interacting with native speakers

Following is an example of a portfolio project from a Spanish 4 class that incorporates reading, writing, and culture. The instruction sheet, along with the assessment rubric, would be given to students early in the year.

SPANISH 4 PORTFOLIO

The progress that you make in reading comprehension, writing, and cultural understanding during the course will be demonstrated in your portfolio. Part of the purpose for the portfolio is to encourage you to look back and see the growth you have made, as well as areas in which you can continue to improve. The portfolio will consist of three sections:

Lecturas: For this section you should select your written responses to three of the readings that you particularly enjoyed. Include these three written responses in your portfolio, along with a reflection sheet in which you respond to the following questions:

- What was significant about the three readings that you selected? What was it that you enjoyed about them or learned from them?
- In what ways has your reading ability in Spanish improved throughout the year?
- Do you approach reading in Spanish any differently than you did at the start of the year? If so, how?

Composiciones: From the *composiciones* that you wrote during the year, choose your two favorite to revise and polish for inclusion in your portfolio. The revised versions should reflect your best writing, in terms of content, grammar, vocabulary, and spelling (including accent marks), and should be typed. They should be accompanied by a reflection sheet in which you respond to the following questions:

- Why did you choose these two compositions? In what ways do they demonstrate your best Spanish writing?
- In what ways has your writing ability in Spanish improved throughout the year?
- Do you approach writing in Spanish any differently than you did at the start of the semester? If so, how?

Actividades Culturales: In this section you should include your written reports on the two cultural activities in which you participated. These should be accompanied by a reflection sheet addressing the following questions:

- What did you learn from the actividades culturales, as well as from the course in general, about Hispanic cultures?
- How do you feel about interacting with members of Hispanic cultures? Have your feelings changed at all during the semester?
- Have you learned anything about your own culture as seen in contrast with Hispanic cultures? Have you learned anything about yourself? If so, what?

The portfolio materials should be assembled neatly in a three-hole-punched binder. Portfolios are due on the last day of class.

SPANISH 4 PORTFOLIO – ASSESSMENT CRITERIA

Contenido general	1	2	3	4	5
	Significant portions of portfolio are missing			All required elements of portfolio are present (3 *lecturas*, 2 *composiciones*, 2 *actividades culturales*, and a reflection sheet for each of the 3 sections)	
Lecturas	1	2	3	4	5
	The three reading responses selected for inclusion in the portfolio, as well as the accompanying reflection sheet, demonstrate little thought or reflection about the student's reading			Reading responses, as well as reflection sheet, demonstrate significant thought about the readings, the strategies used, and growth in reading comprehension	
Composiciones	1	2	3	4	5
Quality of writing	Compositions demonstrate little or no effort to revise and polish the writing to incorporate feedback from teacher and correct errors			Compositions demonstrate significant effort to revise and polish writing to the best of student's ability, including content, grammar, vocabulary, spelling, and accent marks	
Quality of reflections	1	2	3	4	5
	Reflection sheet accompanying the compositions shows little thought about why the compositions were chosen or what growth they reflect			Reflection sheet explains why each composition was chosen and how the student's writing skills have improved during the course	
Cultura	1	2	3	4	5
	Written summaries of the two *actividades culturales*, as well as the accompanying reflection sheet, show little thought or insight about student's culture learning			Written summaries of the *actividades culturales*, as well as the reflection sheet, demonstrate significant insight on student's culture learning during the course	

Total _____ x 4 = _____ /100

If you decide to try out portfolio assessment, keep in mind the following tips:

- Start small. You may want to focus the portfolios on just one skill (e.g., writing) or communicative mode (e.g., interpersonal mode).

- Give attention to the development of the portfolio throughout the year rather than just at the end. Some teachers hold periodic "portfolio conferences" in which they discuss with students the content of their portfolios.

- Remember that a key element of portfolios is student reflection on the content. Be sure to have students include an explanation of why they chose the content they did for their portfolios and what they feel it shows about their learning.

- Portfolios are probably best used in conjunction with other, more traditional forms of assessment. You might consider making the portfolio worth 10 to 30% of the overall class grade, in addition to tests, homework, etc.

- Consider reading one or more of the works listed at the end of this chapter for more ideas on portfolios. In particular, check out the website of Dr. Helen Barrett, who has tips for putting your students' portfolios in digital format and/or online.

GRADING

As we remarked at the beginning of this chapter, the academic nature of teaching a foreign language in a school setting requires that we give the students grades. We must do all we can to ensure that our grading is fair for all students and that it accurately reflects achievement of objectives fully understood by our students. The grades should also be a faithful reflection of the work and activities that we conduct and require of the students during any grading period.

Grading Approaches

There are numerous approaches to grading. We will limit this discussion to some of the most common ones and make some general suggestions.

The point system. Many teachers use a point system for giving grades because it allows a great deal of flexibility and seems fairer. Under this system, the teacher assigns a number of points to each test, assignment, and activity on which the students will be evaluated. The teacher must carefully consider each assignment to decide how many points it should receive (weighting). This distribution of points is very crucial since the teacher must try to balance each test, homework assignment, oral report, extra work, and so on according to the amount of effort required and their importance in relationship to the goals of the class. For example, a quiz might be worth 15 points, a chapter test 50 points, a review test 100 points, and an oral report 75 points.

Points can be deducted from a student's total for tardies, absences, cheating and so on. Students can be motivated by the possibility of earning additional points with extra oral practice, attendance at Spanish Club activities, oral or written reports, and the like. At the end of a grading period, grades can be based on the total number of points each student has earned. The distribution of A's, B's, C's and so on is usually made according to the percentage the student has of the total points possible. The usual distribution is as follows:

> 93% to 100% = A
> 90% to 92% = A-
> 87% to 89% = B+
> 83% to 86% = B
> 80% to 82% = B-
> 77% to 79% = C+
> 73% to 76% = C
> 70% to 72% = C-
> 67% to 69% = D+
> 63% to 66% = D
> 60% to 62% = D-
> Below 60%   = E (Failure)

Make frequent assessments and use multiple forms of assessment. Grades can create strong emotions. It takes only one conference with a parent demanding justification of a child's grade to underscore the importance of having a large number of evaluations on which to base grades. When you can say: "Johnny got a 'C' in Spanish because he had 71% average on 20 tests and 30 quizzes, did only half of the homework required, and did poorly on the oral tests," you will seldom get any arguments. You can then focus on asking the parent to help improve Johnny's performance.

Another reason for making multiple, frequent assessments is that it is only fair to the students to assess their progress as thoroughly as possible. Using different types of assessments, such as projects, homework grades, classroom participation grades, or portfolios can give a much more complete picture of students' learning than tests alone can. Grades based on one or two tests can often be wide of the mark in regards to the students' true proficiency.

Grade on "the curve?" Most teachers object to the notion that certain percentages of their students should get A's, B's, C's, D's and E's. It seems especially true in a language course that all students who reach realistic goals and levels of proficiency should get good grades, regardless of what percentage of the class does well or poorly in reaching those goals. Students who receive poor grades should be those students who have not reached the goals because of some personal fault, such as poor attendance, lack of participation, or failure to do the work required to meet the goals that have been set.

"Citizenship and Work Habits" Grades. Some schools require teachers to give "conduct" or "work habits" or "citizenship" grades in addition to academic grades. These types of grades can also arouse strong emotions. As a parent once remarked: "If my son is not smart enough to get A's, there isn't much I can do, but he can behave, be responsible, and do what the teacher asks of him. In that area I insist on excellence."

What is important with this type of grade is that the rules be completely laid out and understood by the students. The teacher must have a consistent and fair system of assigning the grades.

As an example, we will present here one such system. The teacher and students prepare a list of the rules that they are expected to follow. Possible infractions of those rules are then printed on demerit slips that the teacher hands out to students who violate the rules. The student fills the slips out and hands them back to the teacher. These papelitos verdes (so called because they are printed on green paper) are used to determine the students' citizenship grades. A stack of them can be very helpful in reminding students of their misdemeanors during the semester—which they have usually forgotten. They can also be very handy in a parent-teacher conference. Following are examples of these slips of paper or papelitos.

Example for "work habits" grade.

PAPELITO DE FALTA – APLICACION

Nombre _____
Clase _____ Fecha _____

- ☐ 1. No preparado(a) para la actividade de clase.
- ☐ 2. No preparado(a) con la tarea escrita.
- ☐ 3. Hacer el trabajo de otra materia en la clase de español.
- ☐ 4. No traer el libro o materiales a clase.
- ☐ 5. No prestar atención (estar en la luna) durante la lección o una actividad.
- ☐ 6. Llegar tarde sin excusa.
- ☐ 7. Ausente a la clase sin excusa.
- ☐ 8. Ler novelas, historietas, revistas, periódico, etc. en la clase.
- ☐ 9. Dormir en la clase.
- ☐ 10. No participar en las actividades.
- ☐ 11. Otro_____
     _____

Example for "citizenship" grade.

PAPELITO DE FALTA – COMPORTAMIENTO

Nombre _____
Clase _____ Fecha _____

- ☐ 1. Hablar y no escuchar o prestar atención.
- ☐ 2. Tirar cosas en la clase.
- ☐ 3. Escribir en, cortar, o marcar de alguna manera el pupitre o libros de la escuela.
- ☐ 4. Usar lenguaje ofensivo (palabrotas).
- ☐ 5. Comer o beber en la clase.
- ☐ 6. Escribir y/o pasar notas o mensajes de texto.
- ☐ 7. Desaliño o falta de aseo (no afeitarse…).
- ☐ 8. Masticar chicle en la clase.
- ☐ 9. Peinarse o maquillarse durante la clase.
- ☐ 10. Destruir propiedad de la escuela.
- ☐ 11. Pelear con, estorbar, angustiar a otros estudiantes.
- ☐ 12. Infracción de las normas de vestir:
     _____
- ☐ 13. Otro_____
     _____

CONCLUSION

Tests and other assessments are an integral part of academic life for many important reasons. We must assess and measure the progress of our students in order to know if we are reaching, or even approaching, our objectives. For this same reason, our assessment instruments must closely parallel our objectives, if we are teaching for oral proficiency, we must test oral proficiency. *Assessments must reflect our goals.* Language teachers will find that there is a wide range of commercial and professional tests available to them; these tests can be very valuable to building and assessing the quality of many aspects of language programs. Although they loudly protest, students accept assessment and are aware of its importance. Thus it can be a very motivating force toward growth and progress. In foreign language teaching, we are finding many ways beyond formal tests to assess the progress of our students. Teachers must become aware of these alternative instruments of assessment and make greater use of them.

| REFERENCES AND SUGGESTIONS FOR FURTHER READING |

Brown, H. D., & Abeywickrama, P. (2010). *Language assessment: Principles and classroom practices* (2nd ed.). White Plains, NY: Pearson. *An excellent resource that addresses the assessment of all four skills, grammar, and vocabulary, as well as alternative forms of assessment such as such as portfolios, journals, conferences, observations, interviews, and self- and peer-assessment.*

Glisan, E. W. (Ed.). (2003). *ACTFL integrated performance assessment.* Alexandria, VA: ACTFL. *Outlines a process for assessing all three communicative modes within a single thematic context: students first complete an interpretive task, then use the information learned in an interpersonal task, and finally summarize their learning with a presentational task. Includes examples and scoring rubrics.*

Hughes, A. (1989). *Testing for language teachers* (Cambridge Language Teaching Library). Cambridge, England: Cambridge University Press. *A practical guide to testing the four skills, grammar and vocabulary, with a section on testing young learners.*

Milton, J. (2009). *Measuring second language vocabulary acquisition.* Bristol, England: Multilingual Matters. *Offers a thorough treatment of many aspects of vocabulary learning, including the relationship between word frequency, difficulty, and acquisition; receptive vs. productive faculty; depth of vocabulary; and vocabulary learning in classroom and out-of-classroom settings.*

Popham, W. J. (2010). *Classroom assessment: What teachers need to know* (6th ed.). Prentice Hall. *A well-known bestseller, this book explains a wide variety of classroom assessments, including test formats (with great tips on writing multiple-choice, true/false, and matching items), performance assessments, portfolio assessment.*

Rudner, L. M., & Schafer, W. D. (Eds.). (2002). *What teachers need to know about assessment.* Washington, DC: National Education Association. *A great short book addressing concepts such as validity and reliability, norm-referenced and criterion-reference testing, as well as tips on writing multiple-choice tests, rubrics, and performance assessments. Available free online:* http://echo.edres.org:8080/nea/teachers.pdf

Sandrock, P. (2011). *The keys to assessing language performance: A teacher's manual for measuring student progress* (ACTFL Guide for Professional Language Educators). Alexandria, VA: ACTFL. *Written by ACTFL expert Paul Sandrock, this book provides a step-by-step approach for designing performance assessments and rubrics and using them to track student progress in a standards-based program.*

Valette, R. M. (1977) *Modern language testing* (2nd ed.) New York, NY: Harcourt Brace Jovanovich. *Although now quite dated, this "classic" book continues to be an excellent resource containing many examples of test types, and valuable information on preparing, giving, and evaluating tests.*

Tests

Aptitude Tests. The best resource for information about aptitude tests is the Second Language Testing Foundation, Ind. (SLTI). They make the Modern Language Aptitude Test (MLAT) and the Pimsleur Language Aptitude Battery available to the second language testing community. Visit the website and click on Language Aptitude Tests. http://www.2lti.com/home2

College Board SAT Subject tests. These are nationally-normed tests that can be used in applying for admission to colleges and universities. You can get detailed information about the tests and preparation tests at http://www.collegeboard.com/student/testing/sat/about/SATII/whichLang.html

National Spanish Examinations. These tests, recently updated, are available for use with Spanish students whose teacher is a member of AATSP. Awards, scholarships, etc. offered. http://www.nationalspanishexam.org/

Image Credits

p. 290: Dyan, Emmanuel. (2009, Dec. 30). Andes, Peru. *Flickr.* Retrieved June 27, 2011 from http://www.flickr.com/photos/emmanueldyan/4286940281/. Creative Commons attribution license.

ACTIVITIES FOR METHODS CLASSES

1. In small groups, develop a philosophy of testing. Are tests necessary? Could they be eliminated from classes? What kinds of tests do you like? Why? What kinds do you hate? Why? What elements are there in a foreign language class that will make tests different? Report to the class.

2. Arrange to take one of the aptitude test such as the MLAT. Evaluate the different areas of the tests and determine what ability is being measured. Score the test and calculate your own aptitude. Do you have the ability to learn foreign languages? How would you feel if you were "selected out" of a foreign language program for low aptitude? Hand in a report to your teacher.

3. Take one of the standardized proficiency tests available to you. Decide what skills are being assessed. Is it a valid test? (i.e., does it evaluate what it is supposed to evaluate?) What areas does it not evaluate? Could you use this test to compare your students with those from other states? Hand in a report to your instructor.

4. Go to the lab and take a listening comprehension test, either one from the regular Spanish classes, or a standardized one. Was it fair? (i.e., was the recording good? Did the speakers speak clearly? Was there time to respond?) Hand in a report.

5. Develop a listening comprehension test in Spanish. It can be of any type, such as choosing pictures related to a stimulus, true or false, multiple-choice, understanding a conversation, etc. Prepare to give the test, either live or recorded, to your *compañeros* in the methods class. Score their answers and have them critique the test.

6. Prepare an oral test in Spanish. It can be of any type, such as questions and answers, narrating an event in the past, a personal interview, describing a picture, etc. Administer the test live to a fellow student in front of the methods class. Tell how you scored the test and ask the other methods students for comments.

7. Select some aspect of grammar, such as object pronouns, future tense, present perfect tense, etc. and prepare a written test of two or three different types to evaluate mastery of that grammar concept. Attach a description of the scoring system you would use and hand it in to your teacher.

8. Find a reading selection and prepare a test that would assess your students' understanding of the selection. Describe how you would score the test. Turn it in to the professor.

9. Pick some aspect of culture that you would teach in a Spanish class. Prepare a test that would evaluate the students' mastery of that concept. Turn it in to the professor.

10. Suppose you are teaching and have to give your students "citizenship" and "work habits" grades. Prepare a list of the criteria you would base those grades on, and describe how you would apply those criteria. Give a copy of the list to your instructor.

11. Develop a plan for portfolio assessment incorporating one or more communicative modes or language skills. Determine the criteria for selecting the content of the portfolios, how they will be assessed, and how students will be involved in reflecting on their learning.

CHAPTER THIRTEEN

CAN TECHNOLOGY HELP?

YOUR OBJECTIVES FOR THIS CHAPTER ARE TO:

1. IDENTIFY TECHNOLOGICAL TOOLS THAT ARE USEFUL IN LANGUAGE TEACHING AND LEARNING.

2. ENHANCE YOUR TEACHING BY EFFECTIVE USE OF AUDIO AND VIDEO MATERIALS.

3. DISCUSS THE ROLE THAT LABS CAN PLAY IN LEARNING A LANGUAGE, DIFFERENT TYPES OF LANGUAGE LABS, AND HOW TO USE A LAB TO ITS FULLEST POTENTIAL.

4. IDENTIFY SOURCES OF SUPPLEMENTARY DIGITAL MATERIALS AND SOFTWARE.

5. DESCRIBE DIFFERENT KINDS OF VIDEO MATERIALS THAT ARE AVAILABLE FOR USE IN THE CLASSROOM AND LABS, AND A VARIETY OF ACTIVITIES FOR USING THEM.

6. DISCUSS WAYS OF USING COMPUTER TECHNOLOGY TO STRENGTHEN YOUR PROGRAM.

7. UTILIZE THE INTERNET AS A SOURCE OF AUTHENTIC CULTURAL TEXTS AND INFORMATION.

8. DESCRIBE VARIOUS USES OF WEB 2.0 AS A TOOL FOR FACILITATING STUDENT INTERACTION, COLLABORATION, AND COMMUNICATION WITH NATIVE SPEAKERS.

George Wilson had just returned from a visit to the new Riverview High School, where he had inspected their new language lab. He had been very impressed and green with envy as Bill Newhaus, the lab director had shown him computer, digital equipment, and DVD players in every learning station. "What I wouldn't give to have a lab like that," mused George. "My students' skills and motivation would increase dramatically. I'd better get to work on my request to Mr. Snodgrass to install a lab in our school. I know we don't have the money they have at Riverview, but maybe we can afford some things."

George was right. Although Mr. Snodgrass did agree to install a lab, it had few of the features of the Riverview lab.

Several months had passed since the installation of the new language lab, and Mr. Snodgrass stopped to chat with George in the hall. "Why don't you use the language lab any more, George?" he asked. "I've noticed that you never go in there with your students any more."

"There are several reasons," responded George. "First, half of the headsets are broken and we don't have the money to repair them, and we don't have the right software. Second, the only time we can use the lab is during class period, and so we miss class activities to go to lab. I'm not sure the value of working in the lab makes up for what we miss in class."

"Maybe we jumped too hastily when we installed the lab," suggested Mr. Snodgrass.

"No, I think it could be really valuable, but the software that came with our textbook is not very interesting and the students don't enjoy it. What we really need is different kind of equipment such as computers and digital equipment."

"Well, that could be extremely expensive. We'll look at the possibilities," replied Mr. Snodgrass, as he continued on down the hall. It was apparent that he wasn't sold on the idea. Perhaps it had something to do with the fact that the present lab was collecting a lot of dust.

~~~~

Sharon was excited about her student teaching assignment. She had requested that she be placed in Central High School because it was close to where she lived and she had heard that Mrs. Murphy, the Spanish teacher, was an outstanding teacher. She wasn't disappointed. Mrs. Murphy had a full program of Spanish classes, with over 30 students in each class. "Why is Spanish so popular?" asked Sharon on her first day in the school "Well, for a number of reasons," responded Mrs. Murphy, "but mostly because we do a variety of activities and make it fun and interesting. The word gets around. I think our use of videos has a lot to do with it."

Sharon had noticed that Mrs. Murphy had her own LDC projector and a large screen in the front of the classroom and as the day progressed she saw that she made constant use of it. She played excerpts from online news broadcasts at the beginning of each class, she frequently played videos of songs by popular Hispanic artists, she used video segments from YouTube as a basis for conversation sessions in her intermediate classes, and showed a video version of a Lope de Vega play for her AP class. As she admired the collection of over 50 DVDs Mrs. Murphy had, Sharon asked where she got the money. "We have fund raisers, some parents have donated money, and I get help from the librarian," answered Mrs. Murphy. "Oh, by the way, you will want to come to our Spanish Club party this Friday. We're showing some new films we just got from Argentina. We're charging 50 cents admission, and that will help buy the Spanish version of Star Wars which we want to get."

Sharon was beginning to see why Spanish was so interesting to the students of Central High. She was also beginning to understand why they all had such good listening comprehension skills.

CHAPTER THIRTEEN

CAN TECHNOLOGY HELP?

> A foreign language teacher today who does not incorporate the latest media technology into his or her classroom is living in the past. It would be very much like a farmer who, even though surrounded by marvelous new equipment, insists on using a wooden plough – it might get the job done, but at what cost in labor and efficiency?
> --Jaime Sastre

The incredible advances in modern technology have made some foreign language teachers a little uneasy. It is obvious that technology can be used in numerous ways in their programs, but they aren't sure how to go about adopting it. Other teachers perceive technology as something so complex and technical that it is beyond their capacity to work with. Educators who do use technology steadfastly declare that it can never take the place of teachers; it can only enhance what they are doing in the classroom. Companies that sell educational technology are constantly trying to make their products so "user friendly" that anyone can use them. In this chapter we will discuss how technology can be a great boon to your program, both in direct use in your classroom, in labs, and outside of the classroom.

THE ROLES OF TECHNOLOGY IN THE FOREIGN LANGUAGE CLASS

There are three basic roles that technology can play in your language class. First, it will allow you to bring an unending parade of authentic speakers into your classroom that you couldn't possibly do personally. You, as the teacher, will always be the Spanish speaker your students hear most and your own Spanish will always be tied to your gender, age, and personal pronunciation. If your students hear only you speaking Spanish, how will they react when they leave your classroom and go out into the wide world with its infinite variety of speakers?

Technology can bring male and female voices, children, teenagers, adults, senior citizens, media professionals, film personalities,

housewives, and blue-collar workers, all of them from a variety of Spanish-speaking countries, right into your classes. And what's more, when you couple the fact that virtually all your students now have access to a personal computer and cell phone that connect them to the incredible resources of the Internet, they can invite all those people right into their own homes.

Second, technology provides an untiring, consistent and ever-present avenue for the individual practice of all language skills. Your students can practice listening and speaking with audio recordings in the classroom, in the lab or with online activities. They can practice their reading at any level with online media that ranges from news articles to Facebook. And they can practice their writing by sending e-mails and text messages around the globe or just down the hall to their teacher's room.

Third, you as a teacher can only talk about cultural aspects of daily life in Spanish-speaking countries, and perhaps show a few pictures or realia, but multimedia allows the students to immerse themselves in the culture by seeing and hearing real images and live action. It's all genuine and authentic; the only things lacking are the smells and tastes. Perhaps that, too, will someday be added as augmented reality and 3D applications become increasingly available

The changes in technology in the few years since we completed the first edition of this textbook have been truly awesome. In those early years we were excited about using audio and video tapes. Videocassettes were our bread of life because we could buy them already prepared, copy new ones from media sources, and even make our own. Today everything is digital, in high definition, and available online—including broadcast TV. Consider all the help your personal computer gives you. When you link your PC to a projector you can bring the rich resources of the Internet into your classroom and make your classes alive, vibrant, and far more motivating than ever before.

NATIONAL EDUCATIONAL TECHNOLOGY STANDARDS

In light of today's rapid changes in technology, the International Society for Technology in Education (ISTE) was established in order to promote effective use of technology by teachers. The society's website (http://www.iste.org) summarizes its philosophy: "As technology dramatically changes our society, educators need to demonstrate the skills and behaviors of digital-age professionals. Competence with technology is the foundation."

ISTE has developed a set of standards for teachers that outline the ideal competencies in using technology that teachers should strive to develop. We have listed them here as a springboard for you to begin thinking about your own skills in using technology and how you might go about improving them.

NATIONAL EDUCATIONAL TECHNOLOGY STANDARDS FOR TEACHERS

1. Facilitate and Inspire Student Learning and Creativity

Teachers use their knowledge of subject matter, teaching and learning, and technology to facilitate experiences that advance student learning, creativity, and innovation in both face-to-face and virtual environments. Teachers:
   a. promote, support, and model creative and innovative thinking and inventiveness.
   b. engage students in exploring real-world issues and solving authentic problems using digital tools and resources.
   c. promote student reflection using collaborative tools to reveal and clarify students' conceptual understanding and thinking, planning, and creative processes.
   d. model collaborative knowledge construction by engaging in learning with students, colleagues, and others in face-to-face and virtual environments.

2. Design and Develop Digital-Age Learning Experiences and Assessments

Teachers design, develop, and evaluate authentic learning experiences and assessment incorporating contemporary tools and resources to maximize content learning in context and to develop the knowledge, skills, and attitudes identified in the NETS•S. Teachers:
   a. design or adapt relevant learning experiences that incorporate digital tools and resources to promote student learning and creativity.
   b. develop technology-enriched learning environments that enable all students to pursue their individual curiosities and become active participants in setting their own educational goals, managing their own learning, and assessing their own progress.
   c. customize and personalize learning activities to address students' diverse learning styles, working strategies, and abilities using digital   tools and resources.
   d. provide students with multiple and varied formative and summative assessments aligned with content and technology standards and use resulting data to inform learning and teaching.

---

3. Model Digital-Age Work and Learning

Teachers exhibit knowledge, skills, and work processes representative of an innovative professional in a global and digital society.
Teachers:
a. demonstrate fluency in technology systems and the transfer of current knowledge to new technologies and situations.
b. collaborate with students, peers, parents, and community members using digital tools and resources to support student success and innovation.
c. communicate relevant information and ideas effectively to students, parents, and peers using a variety of digital-age media and formats.
d. model and facilitate effective use of current and emerging digital tools to locate, analyze, evaluate, and use information resources to support research and learning.

4. Promote and Model Digital Citizenship and Responsibility

Teachers understand local and global societal issues and responsibilities in an evolving digital culture and exhibit legal and ethical behavior in their professional practices.
Teachers:
a. advocate, model, and teach safe, legal, and ethical use of digital information and technology, including respect for copyright, intellectual property, and the appropriate documentation of sources.
b. address the diverse needs of all learners by using learner-centered strategies providing equitable access to appropriate digital tools and resources.
c. promote and model digital etiquette and responsible social interactions related to the use of technology and information.
d. develop and model cultural understanding and global awareness by engaging with colleagues and students of other cultures using digital-age communication and collaboration tools.

5. Engage in Professional Growth and Leadership

Teachers continuously improve their professional practice, model lifelong learning, and exhibit leadership in their school and professional community by promoting and demonstrating the effective use of digital tools and resources. Teachers:
a. participate in local and global learning communities to explore creative applications of technology to improve student learning.
b. exhibit leadership by demonstrating a vision of technology infusion, participating in shared decision making and community building, and developing the leadership and technology skills of others.
c. evaluate and reflect on current research and professional practice on a regular basis to make effective use of existing and emerging digital tools and resources in support of student learning.
d. contribute to the effectiveness, vitality, and self-renewal of the teaching profession and of their school and community.

TECHNOLOGY THAT HAS DIRECT APPLICATION TO FL TEACHING

Let's make a quick review of the basic technology you will likely have available to you as a language teacher.

Audio recordings. The initial development of magnetic audio recording was a real breakthrough for the language teacher. What it did was capture speech right out of the air, permitting it to be permanently registered on a medium that could be played over and over again in a variety of ways. This was in contrast to live speech, which, whether spoken by a person or broadcast over radio or television, went into the air and was irretrievably lost.

Language teachers were some of the first educators to use audio materials, first in the classroom and then language laboratories. Now almost all students have access to some type of audio recording device of their own, whether it be an MP3 player or a computer. They have grown up with them and these days it is not uncommon for a teacher to ask students to do homework assignments in their own home using their own audio equipment.

Some examples of the uses the Spanish teacher can make of audio equipment are:

1. Providing exposure to a variety of voices, ages, genders,and regional accents.
2. Bringing songs and music into the classroom.
3. Practicing language structure (grammar) in the class, lab, and at home.
4. Teaching culture with such things as actual sounds, music, and interviews.
5. Testing listening comprehension, both in class and in the lab.
6. Setting up recording stations in the classroom to record oral tests.
7. Practicing pronunciation with students, both listening and recording.
8. Individualizing instruction or making up work that students have missed.
9. Listening to important events or famous persons.
10. Using audio materials that accompany the text.
11. Recording visitors or class presentations.
12. Playing commercially prepared supplementary materials such as "audio magazines" while students interact with reading and writing exercises.
13. Playing audio materials that the students or the teacher have taken from radio or television programs.

Video recordings. Films are ideal for allowing the students to hear the language in its everyday use and to see the speakers in natural surroundings. Films are enormously valuable for teaching cultural concepts because they are the next best thing to being personally in the cultural environment.

Today among young people, when parties and entertainment are planned, more often than not watching a video is the central activity. Videos are now available for rent in stores, vending machines, and online. In schools and universities, it is commonplace to see video equipment in almost every classroom.

The greatest value of videos is that they can do more to immerse us in authentic language situations than anything else except being in the foreign language environment itself. We may not be able to transport our students to the foreign culture, but we can transport that culture to our classroom via videos. Digital media is very convenient to use, has superior visual quality, and provides instantaneous access to any point in the video, a big improvement over the shortcoming of having to fast forward or rewind a videocassette. Many DVDs and online videos have the additional value of providing subtitles in the language if you want to use them.

Contribution of Video to the Development of the Five Basic Skills

Following are lists of the value of video in developing each of the five basic skills and some examples of activities that can be carried out to practice those skills.

Listening Comprehension Value
- Variety of authentic speakers, accents
- Non-teacher language
- Extra hours of practice (logging time in language)
- Sustained chunks of material (long movies, soap operas, interviews)

- Entertaining, funny, interesting
  Activities
  - Gisting (weather broadcast - will it rain?)
  - Fact getting (News broadcast - what happened?)

Speaking Value
- Close to the real thing (almost interacting)
- Motivating
  Activities
  - Questions/answers on what is seen
  - Use video clips as a visual aid (freeze, talk about)
  - Actors ask personalized questions
  - Practice Task Performance Activities

Culture Value
- Bring culture to the classroom
- Authentic settings, not USA
- Worth 1,000 words.
- Rich source of materials
- Motivating (like talking with the people personally)
- Can keep you up-to-date—latest changes in lifestyles
  Activities
  - Find the cultural differences
  - Focus on one cultural aspect

Writing Value
- Motivating
- Change of pace
- Allows freedom of expression, creativity
- Timely
  Activities
  - Write lines of dialog to situation (mimed sequences)
  - Write new lines to commercials
  - Listen to song, fill in blank spaces on sheet
  - Write own video script
  - Spot dictations with teacher
  - See a story up to some conflict or problem, then write conclusion

Reading Value
- Change of pace
- Natural use of reading (we do read some things on videos)
- Get "feel" for language
- Improve pronunciation, intonation

- Speed up reading
  Activities
  - Listen to sound track while reading highlighted materials

Miscellaneous uses
- Record important presentation for students who are absent
- Prepare warm-ups, start-ups, bienvenidas, etc.
- Use for discussion of grammar concepts
- "Prime" students for activities

Types of Videos

Let's look at what types of videos we have available to us as teachers. Basically there are four types:

1. Instructional videos. Instructional videos are prepared specifically to teach certain concepts or information. They might teach some aspect of a foreign language, or they might be designed to teach some other subject matter, such as health or history, but can be used for language instruction because the sound track is in the foreign language. An example of this type would be the videos prepared by textbook companies for use with their basic text. There are also "generic" video materials that can be used with any textbook program.

The *Español en Vivo* program emphasizes the richness of Hispanic culture and the variations of authentic spoken Spanish. Through filmed interviews with more than twenty native Spanish speakers, students are introduced to a variety of dialects that derive from differences in geographical area and other factors such as age, sex, ethnicity, and social status. The DVDs contain forty-seven segments filmed in locations in Spain, Central America, and Latin America. Unrehearsed interviews with Spanish speakers deal with such aspects of life and culture as housing, family, the immigrant experience, cultural traditions, and politics. These videos present the Spanish language in a natural way, with speakers expressing themselves freely and using the real language of every day.

Some video materials are designed to be complete, self-contained, first-year programs where the entire course is based on videos, such as the very popular *Destinos* program, a sort of "soap opera" complete with a main plot and several sub-plots, all designed to teach specific aspects of Spanish, complete with practices and reviews. Raquel, an attractive *chicana* lawyer is employed by a rich Mexican rancher to investigate the situation of his first wife, thought to be killed in the Spanish Civil War. Raquel travels first to Spain, then to Argentina, where she falls in love, then to Puerto Rico where she finds the grandchildren of her employer, and finally to Mexico where the story comes to an exciting finale.

2. Entertainment videos. These videos have been developed primarily for entertainment and only incidentally lend themselves to language education because they are in the foreign language. They are mostly of the full-length, feature film type.

Examples of this type would be movies such as *La historia oficial* or *Macario* that are full-length movies, or *Los pajaritos* or *El pueblo sumergido* which were feature films prepared for television. It also includes any of the current popular movies that have a Spanish sound track such as *Harry Potter*, Disney movies, *Shrek*, *Enchanted*, and *Star Wars*. IMDB is a great Internet site for information about almost any movie. You can buy most of them from sources such as Amazon.com.

Be aware of your school district's policy. Most districts will not allow teachers to show anything rated above PG. Check carefully to make sure it has a *Spanish soundtrack* and not *Spanish subtitles*. We don't advise using the latter because if the soundtrack is in English, the students don't develop their listening skills.

3. Video clips from live TV or from the Internet. Live television is a very rich source of video materials and there are many things that can be legitimately used in an educational setting. Examples of this type would be commercials taken from live TV, news broadcasts, talk shows, soap operas, sports broadcasts, and documentaries.

The Internet now has literally thousands of video clips that can be found on sites such as YouTube. Another good site that has homemade videos specific to teaching is TeacherTube (http://www1.teachertube.com), which is similar to YouTube but geared toward providing a site

where teachers can upload instructional videos. Another potentially useful site is DotSub (http://dotsub.com), which allows users to view, upload, transcribe and translate any video into any language by adding subtitles..

4. Homemade videos. With the availability of digital video cameras, including cell phone video, teachers now have the capability of producing some very sophisticated videos right in the home or school.

Examples of videos you can make would be the filming of classroom presentations, skits or plays written or put on by students, task-performance-activities (TPAs) prepared by the teacher, lectures or visits by natives to the classroom, and interviews with native speakers. As an added motivation to students, these videos can be uploaded to be viewed online.

Video sources. There is an enormous wealth of materials available to the language teacher. There are even "monthly video" programs that send out a new video each month with new programs and materials taken from current TV broadcasts. These "video magazines" are usually accompanied by a teachers' guide that provides vocabulary lists, practice activities, additional cultural information, and a script of the content of the video. In the references section at the end of this chapter we have included a number of sources for videos that may be of interest to you, and you can, of course, do searches online.

TEACHING STRATEGIES WITH VIDEOS

Too often teachers use videos with a very passive approach. They simply show the video and afterwards discuss what students saw. Our focus here will be on active and interactive use because, as we have so often pointed out, that is what develops proficiency in our students.

As you use videos in your class, you should apply the principles we introduced in the chapters on listening comprehension and reading, which we called "APT MAPS GUIDE." We will review the concept once more with the following diagram, this time applied to use of videos:

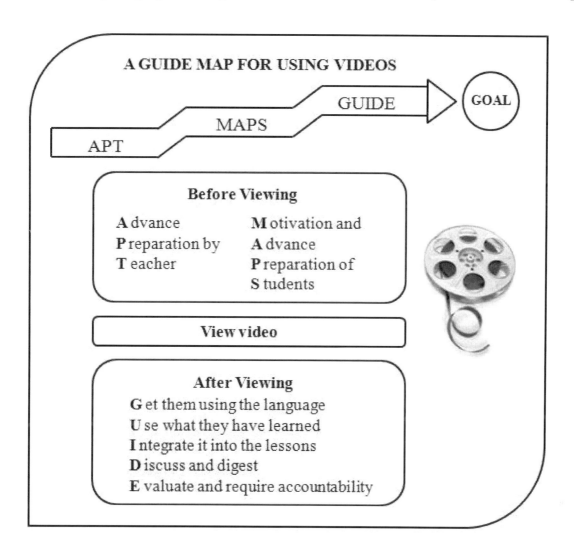

A GUIDE MAP FOR USING VIDEOS

GUIDE → GOAL
MAPS
APT

Before Viewing

A dvance   **M** otivation and
P reparation by   **A** dvance
T eacher   **P** reparation of
                            S tudents

View video

After Viewing
G et them using the language
U se what they have learned
I ntegrate it into the lessons
D iscuss and digest
E valuate and require accountability

In our discussion of video use in teaching languages, we will look at three areas where we can find applications: the classroom, the laboratory, and the student's home.

Videos in the Classroom

You should make whatever effort is necessary to obtain access to video in your classroom so you can use it whenever it fits your needs and as often as you would like. Following the concepts of **APT MAPS GUIDE**, your techniques for classroom use will focus on three areas: 1) pre-viewing activities , 2) during viewing activities, and 3) post-viewing activities. Recall that these activities were discussed in detail in Chapter 6; we will merely summarize them here.

1. Pre-viewing activities would include activating students' background knowledge about the topic and genre, teaching and practicing the critical vocabulary, presentation and practice of important grammar points, and discussion of cultural information necessary for understanding the content of the video.

2. There are many "during viewing" techniques you can use as you show video clips to actively engage students with the conceptual, cultural, and linguistic content of the video. For example: see the video "cold" and then discuss it and watch it again; show parts and discuss each part separately; freeze frames and talk about the frozen image, using it as a visual aid; show the video without sound and hypothesize about what could be said; and so on. During the first pass through the video, you can focus on comprehension of the message; in a second or third pass, you can draw students' attention to language use.

3. After the video has been seen, the teacher and students can spend time discussing what happened. This can be done orally or in writing activities. The students should have opportunities to summarize the content of the video, reflect on its significance to their own lives, connect it with what they know from other sources, and extend their learning by considering how the content of the video might apply to other situations.

Videos in the Lab

When you have shown and practiced with a video in the classroom, you can have a copy of it available in the lab or online where the students can see it as often as they would like. This allows them to repeat parts they did not understand, review certain grammatical concepts, or even search out specific cultural information.

New videos that the students have not seen before can be available to them in the lab or online. In this case we recommend that you prepare viewing guides for the students. These guides could contain key vocabulary words, cultural explanations which will help them understand the content, and some viewing suggestions, such as things to watch for, information to learn, etc.

Videos at Home

As we mentioned, a high percentage of your students will have a video player or computer available to them in their home. You can have copies of videos available for the students to check out for home viewing or give students the URL to watch videos online. As with lab use, we recommend that the students have a viewing guide to prepare and help them understand the video. You can also prepare worksheets for them to use after seeing the video to reinforce and solidify what they have learned.

LANGUAGE LABORATORIES

In the 1960's, the federal government made large amounts of money available to schools for the installation of language labs. More often than not, a school would install a language lab just because they wanted to take advantage of the bargain. Then the labs began to collect dust because there were no materials to use in them, someone had forgotten to allot funds for repair or replacement of worn out equipment, or simply because the teachers could not find ways to use them.

Currently, almost every new language text that appears on the scene is accompanied by supplementary materials to be used in the lab or online; audio and video listening comprehension materials , and perhaps listening comprehension tests.

Language Lab Levels

Early Language Labs. In the very first language labs, the students were given a set of earphones that was connected to an audio source, usually a large tape deck. Students would sit in a carrel to provide privacy and reduce noise from other students. Any speaking the students did was done "into the air." Students listening to the same tape would have to move in "lock-step," that is, they would all have to go at the speed of the tape, and would not be able to stop, start over, or replay segments.

Later, a console with an amplifier was added to the lab and all student positions were connected to the console. The console could play several sources, and a switching device allowed the teacher to connect any position to any source. A microphone was added to the earphones, and the amplifier allowed the students to hear their own voices in their earphones.More importantly, the teacher at the console could also monitor what each student was saying. With a microphone at the console, the teacher and a student could communicate through their headsets.

At last, moving to the highest level, a recorder was installed in each student position, which allowed the students to listen and record their voices. This now permitted one of the most valuable operations of the language lab, simultaneous testing of many students, because they could all record their responses at the same time.

Today's language labs. Virtually all language labs today are at this highest level. The players and recorders have been replaced with computers that add a visual component with graphics and video, and an interactive component where the student can give input with a keyboard and get immediate feedback from the computer.

"Maxi" versus "Mini" Labs

Basically, there are two approaches to designing language labs: 1) a full-fledged lab with carrels or student positions such as described above. These are called "maxi-labs." 2) One or more lab positions installed in the regular classroom, or portable equipment that can be set up, are called "mini-labs" or "electronic classrooms".

"Maxi-labs." The "maxi-lab" is the typical lab with numerous booths or carrels where the students work. The lab can be used by the entire class if the students leave the regular classroom and meet in the lab, or by individual students going to the lab whenever they have free time. If the students use the lab individually, there must be a lab instructor or lab attendant on duty to provide the students with the materials that they will be working with and to protect the equipment. This type of lab works best for colleges and universities since the college students typically have free time during the day. Free use of labs is not too common in public schools because classroom space is usually scarce, money is not available for a lab instructor or assistants, and the students' day is normally filled with classes and activities. If a public school has a maxi-lab, the students usually go from their classroom to the lab, thus exchanging regular class activities for lab practice.

"Mini labs." Mini-labs are located directly in the classroom and often have positions for only a limited number of students. Mini-labs include "electronic classrooms," such as the type where the equipment hangs from the ceiling, or where the program is broadcast with a transmitter, or the equipment is on a cart that is shared among all the foreign language faculty and can be wheeled around. All these variations allow the students to do lab work without leaving their seats. This type of lab is more practical for public schools, since it doesn't have to be scheduled in advance and can be used at any point in a class period, but it can be more expensive since all language teachers want the same installation in each of their classrooms.

Using "Multi-Use" Labs and Media Centers for Language Practice

It is common nowadays for schools to have "multi-use" labs with computer stations that can be used for a number of activities, such as computer classes, keyboard practice, and word processing. These labs nearly always have access to the Internet, meaning that virtually any activity that can be conducted in a traditional language lab can also be done in the computer lab, provided the computers have microphones and speakers (or headphones), and, ideally, a webcam. School libraries have now evolved into "media centers," because in addition to checking out books, students can now check out listening and video materials or access them online and can work with them at an individual computer station.

Language teachers can make good use of these labs and media centers by making materials available for the students to work with, and can give students specific assignments to complete in the lab or online. In the following discussion of lab uses, keep in mind that most of these activities can be done by students online in the media center or at home as well as in a language lab. Some examples are:

- listening and viewing practice (hearing sound clips from radio broadcasts, watching online videos, etc.)
- speaking practice (recording pronunciation paragraphs)
- reading practice
- writing practice
- writing e-mails, blog or wiki entries, etc.
- homework, makeup and remedial work
- completing online workbooks or practice activities, or making up work missed in class
- testing
- taking written and listening tests

School websites. It is now common for schools to have websites that both students and parents have access to. Grades, assignments, and instructional materials can be posted on these sites. Language teachers can prepare materials, put them on the site and the students can download and work with them. Examples of such materials would be:

- video and audio clips
- worksheet writing practices
- links to other websites
- class notes and lessons
- assignments
- test reviews
- quizzes

Teachers can also use their websites to encourage interactive, participatory communication between students, parents, and teachers. For example, students can post work online and comment on each others' work – as can parents.

Practicing culture. Having read Chapter 11, you will be committed to including culture in your classes. Although new textbook programs provide us with everything we need to teach grammar and vocabulary, the allotment of cultural materials is sometimes shortchanged. While it is true that most language texts have an array of pictures with accompanying captions, an occasional "cultural note," and less often, sections presenting cultural themes, we are still left on our own to choose what we will teach and to try desperately to find the time and the materials to teach what we have chosen.

Many teachers do not include the teaching of culture in their classes because they don't believe they have time. One commonly hears, "There's so much cultural information that we can't begin to make a dent in it. Besides, our primary responsibility is to teach the language and we don't have enough class hours to do even that." In this case, online materials, language labs, and media centers can supplement classroom activities. Virtually all of the techniques for teaching culture in the classroom that we discussed in Chapter 11 can be adapted for lab use, and in some cases, more effectively. Some examples of culture practice that can be done in the lab or media center are:

Films. Films, especially full-length ones, can take out big chunks of class time. If the media center has computers or DVD players, the students can view the films in the lab at their own convenience.

In a "culture general" approach, there are so many excellent films, such as *In the Eye of the Beholder*, that the teacher rarely has time to show them all. Use of the lab facilities would permit that. Written "active involvement sheets" could guide the students as to what to watch for and also provide a way of checking to ensure that they actually see the films and learn from them. If the lab can accommodate small groups for watching films, group interaction could be very stimulating and group-oriented reports on specific segments or cultural topics could be done there.

Audio recordings. "Slices of life" materials such as interviews, music, the authentic sounds of street scenes, and sporting and cultural events, can be deposited in the lab or uploaded to a website where students can watch them.

Many teachers have collected songs of all kinds in the foreign language. Recordings can be made and sheets prepared with lyrics and cultural explanations. Students can enjoy the music in the lab or online as they follow along with the recording and read about the cultural concepts reflected in each song. Again, pre-, during-, and post-activities are important in working with songs, as we discussed in Chapter 6.

Videos. We have discussed a variety of uses of videos in the classroom in the previous section. Most of those uses can also be applied in the lab or online. If the students work individually with the video materials, their learning can be greatly increased because they can "freeze frame," repeat segments, and watch the video numerous times.

Teachers can prepare video "packets" in which an especially good segment of film or television program has beenidentified, and the students are given worksheets which help them look for certain items, give them help with vocabulary and grammar difficulties, and them with a variety of practice exercises.

Culture capsules could easily be adapted for use in a language lab or online if the presentation were recorded and the video deposited in the lab for student viewing. Alternatively, culture capsules could be prepared in PowerPoint format and uploaded to *Slideshare* or the teacher's website.

Live television. Most universities and some public schools have cable TV access that can bring live television into their learning resource centers. The potential for cultural learning from this resource is enormous. The students can watch programs from different Spanish channels at any time of the day, and with guidance from professors, can gather examples of specific culturalproducts, practices, and perspectives. For example, the teacher can ask the students to report on the use of gestures, the use of space, and different clothing styles.

Live television has the great advantage of being current, up-to-date, and thus motivating to the students. However, it does have the disadvantage that once it has been seen, it can't be retrieved. Nevertheless, some professors have reported that when they use live television, certain students (for example, those who get "hooked" on soap operas) can make great gains in listening comprehension and cultural understanding.

Make-up and remedial work. One of the facts of life in education is that students get sick, go out of town, or miss class for any number of reasons. What do you do about helping them catch up? Few teachers have enough time to work personally with every student. Again, the lab can.help students make up missed work. Even if you don't use practice software in your classroom, if it is available, students who have been absent can recover the material they missed by practicing in the lab or online.

Extra credit. If you allow your students to do remedial or extra credit work, why not have them do it in the lab? Usually extra credit work consists of reading or writing. To stay true to our proficiency commitment, why not have them do some kind of listening comprehension or oral practice in the lab for extra credit?

Testing. More and more, technology is allowing us to relegate activities that used to consume a lot of in-class time, to after class . How many extra days could you spend doing communicative activities in class if you could do all your **testing** outside of class? With planning and extra time spent preparing the tests, you can.

Most text programs provide listening comprehension tests recorded on CD. That is a natural lab activity; have your students take their listening quizzes in the lab. Cultural tests can be prepared and given in the lab, such as identifying specific cultural sounds, the recognition of the pronunciation of different dialects, and the classification of different kinds and origins of music.

Commercial tests such as the AP tests and the STAMP tests mentioned in Chapter 12 can be administered in the lab. Even though writing tests have to be corrected by the teacher, at least they can be administered in the lab. Students can write the test on the computer and hard copies can be printed out for you to correct at home. You can often access the tests through the network and correct them on the computer in your office. How much easier it is to read tests written on a computer than those written by hand!

In Chapter 12, we discussed the difficulties of administering oral tests. We proposed the lab as a great solution to that problem. In the lab you can administer an oral test to 30 students in 10 minutes. If you give that same oral test "face-to-face," you will spend 300 minutes with those same 30 students. Most colleges and universities now administer tests in labs.

Technology can require a lot of time in preparing materials and tests, but the time saved in the long run is worth it.

USING COMPUTERS

Every day use of computers in schools and universities is now a total reality. In addition to the tremendous assistance a computer can give to the teacher with materials preparation and classroom management, more and more uses are being made to help with classroom presentation and practice. In addition, there are many uses outside of class. Following are some of the common computer use configurations teachers have available to them.

The teacher has a personal computer to use in the classroom. It is normal these days for teachers to have their own computer in their room. This allows them to prepare materials of every kind of classroom use. Preparation or revision of tests is a simple matter in comparison to the total retyping which we used to have to do with a typewriter. The preparation of course outlines and semester or yearly schedules used to be a major undertaking, but with a computer, and once you have made the original schedule, only the dates and minor adjustments need to be made to prepare schedules for a new semester or year.

One of the most convenient uses of a computer is to manage grades. Most districts have programs that will allow teachers to input grades, make seating charts, print rolls and class lists, and access student information.

A few computers in the classroom for the students to use. With an extra computer in the classroom the teacher can make it available to the students for personal use, such as: looking up information on the Internet, printing out copies of worksheets, entering assignments, printing worksheets, working with practice materials in free time, or perhaps even downloading music onto their own iPods. Student assistants could help with entering test and homework information. Some teachers prepare materials such as fairy tales, news-, radio-, and video-clips.

If those computers have Internet access, the students could use them to search for something they need to practice. For example, if a student enters the search term "Spanish preterite practice," 377,000 sites are listed.

Language Teaching Software

There are many different types of computer software that are available to support language learning with computers. Here are some examples:

"General" supplemental materials This type of software is the most abundant. The programs may be published by large publishing companies, small software organizations, or by individual teachers who developed a program for their classes and then decided to market it.

The *Playing With Language* series is an example of this type of program that is basically designed to teach children words and phrases in a foreign language through multimedia versions of fun, familiar games.

The *Living Books* series is an example of generic materials that are independent of any text. The CD ROM presents fun stories, such as Aesop's fable, *The Tortoise and the Hare.* The story contains graphics and is narrated by natives, and the student can interact with the

content by clicking on different parts of the graphics. A delightful story in this series is *Abuelita y yo* by Mercer Mayer, who tells of Critter's trip to the beach with his grandmother.

Accompanying computer software to use with a specific textbook. Textbook publishers have become very sensitive to the desire of teachers to have some kind of computer software to use with the regular text materials, and almost all of the recently published texts have computer software. The big advantage of this software is that it coordinates with the vocabulary used in the text and follows the same order of grammar presentation. The same materials used in the text are practiced in different ways by the students working with computers.

An example of this type of software is the *¿Habla español?* program published by Holt, Rinehart and Winston. There is an accompanying study disk that has grammar drill exercises and vocabulary review that is directly linked through page references to the text.

More and more textbook publishers are also making their accompanying workbooks available online. This solves the problem of teachers having to photocopy workbook pages for students. These online workbooks can also be set to correct students' work automatically and send their scores to the teacher's email account or website.

Comprehensive programs. There are some comprehensive programs designed to totally teach a language. An example of this type of program is the *Cara a cara* program published by Heinle & Heinle, which is a beginning-level program that focuses on grammar and vocabulary. It includes animation, games, melodies, stories and color graphics.

THE INTERNET AND WEB 2.0

A veritable bonanza of sources of information and language practice comes to schools that have access to the "information superhighway," simply by tying into networks and being able to use the Internet and e-mail.

Although the system of interconnecting computer networks that make up the World Wide Web has been around since the late 1980s, its uses have changed dramatically since the turn of the 21st century. In its early years, the Internet was seen mainly as a place where people could go to retrieve information that was posted online by those who were more technologically savvy than the general public.

In the early 2000s, the ways in which people used the Internet began to change dramatically. Websites began making it possible for users to interact and collaborate with each other instead of just passively viewing information. The term that was coined to describe these new uses of the Internet is **Web 2.0.**

A Web 2.0 site allows users to participate in creating their own content in a virtual community. Examples of Web 2.0 include social networking sites, blogs, wikis, and photo and video sharing sites. These types of websites are now used by millions of people across the world, and classroom teachers are beginning to recognize their potential for facilitating learning.

Schools are finding ways to encourage digital citizenship and the ethical, safe use of the internet, such as setting up guidelines and policies for Internet use and requiring students and parents to sign contracts agreeing to abide by the terms. We have listed some useful websites in the references section at the end of this chapter, and we have included some addresses for internet key pals.

In the remainder of this chapter, we will discuss two "traditional" uses of the Internet as (1) a source of information, and (2) a source for finding authentic reading, listening, and viewing materials; as well as three Web 2.0 uses as (3) a forum for publishing; (4) a tool for collaborating with others; and (5) a tool for communicating with native speakers.

A Source of Information

The oldest and most well-known use of the internet is as a source of information. Encyclopedias, which used to be the main source of information for students, have been almost entirely replaced with websites offering information on every topic imaginable.

Linguistic information. Almost anything you or your students could want to know about the Spanish language can be found online. Typing "Spanish-English dictionary" or "Spanish grammar" into a search engine yields dozens of websites with online dictionaries and grammar

explanations. Many of these sites have been designed specifically for teachers or students. If you or your students have doubts about the usage of a particular phrase or expression, typing it into a search engine with quotation marks around it should yield dozens of examples of usage. Another option is to search within a Spanish corpus such as the one developed by Mark Davies at BYU (http://www.corpusdelespanol.org/). If the expression you typed doesn't show up, chances are it isn't an authentic or correct Spanish expression.

Cultural information. Many different types of cultural information are available online. Simply typing a cultural topic such as "el Escorial," "*quinceañera*," or "*Día de los muertos*" into a search engine will yield many links to websites on the topic. These may include travel-oriented websites designed for tourists; informational articles on websites such as Wikipedia; or even posts on personal websites and blogs. Some of these websites are targeted toward students of Spanish, meaning that they provide simple explanations and don't assume previous knowledge about the topic. If you type the search terms in Spanish, chances are greater that you will find websites written in Spanish.

Pedagogical information and activities. There is a wealth of websites that target teachers and students of Spanish. Typing "Spanish lesson plan" into a search engine will yield more ideas for lesson plans than you can possibly use. Listservs such as FLTEACH (see http://web.cortland.edu/flteach) can serve as forums for Spanish teachers to share ideas or request tips on how to teach specific topics. For students, doing a search for "Spanish vocabulary practice," "Spanish grammar practice," or even just "teach yourself Spanish" will yield countless links to online explanations, games, and practice activities.

One type of web-based activity is the **WebQuest**, invented by professors of educational technology at San Diego State University in 1995. A WebQuest is an online activity in which students go to a specified website that contains a description of a learning task related to a particular topic, often with links to websites where students can find the information needed to complete the task. (See http://educationalwikis.wikispaces.com/Examples+of+educational+wikis for some examples) Learners typically complete WebQuests as cooperative groups. Each learner within a group can be given a "role" or specific area to research. WebQuests sometimes take the form of role-playing scenarios, where students take on the personas of professional researchers or historical figures. In one WebQuest, for example, students are assigned to pursue a duo of Spanish-speaking thieves who have stolen the Hope Diamond from the Smithsonian. By reading a letter written by the thieves, students are able to narrow their possible whereabouts down to three Spanish-speaking countries, which the students then divide into groups to research using the websites provided. Finally, the groups collaborate to share the information they have discovered and come to an agreement on where the thieves are to be found (see http://chalk.richmond.edu/education/projects/webquests/spanish/tindex.htm). An online search for "Spanish WebQuest" will yield many such activities that Spanish teachers have designed for their students. Teachers who are more technologically savvy can develop their own WebQuests using web authoring tools or a wiki.

A Source for Authentic Reading, Listening, and Viewing Materials

The Communication goal area of the *Standards for Foreign Language Learning* reminds us that students need practice reading, listening to, and viewing authentic materials. With respect to reading materials, the internet provides unlimited reading practice with "digitized" newspapers and magazines, tourist and travel descriptions, and a myriad of websites replete with texts of all types. We refer you back to the discussion of different types of authentic texts in Chapter 8; virtually all these types of texts can be found online.

Likewise, audio and video recordings of all types can be found online, including live feeds or podcasts of radio and television programs, movies, and homemade videos. We refer you to the discussion of different types of listening and viewing materials in Chapter 6; again, all of these types of materials can be found online. And all of this can be had in Spanish!

A Forum for Publishing

The *Standards* also remind us that students need opportunities to prepare written and oral products in Presentational Mode. Prior to the advent of the internet, the main audiences for students' writing products and oral presentations were the teacher and sometimes their classmates. The internet now provides us with unlimited audiences that can include other students in the school, parents, administrators, and the general public around the world. Teachers can design websites to showcase the best of their students' oral and written work. Digital videos of students' presentations can also be posted online. Students themselves can design websites or blogs to publish their work.

In Chapter 12, we discussed the use of portfolios for showcasing students' work. If students' materials are produced in digital format, they can be uploaded to online **electronic portfolios** (also known as **e-portfolios** or **digital portfolios**). Electronic portfolios may include inputted text, scans of students' writing on paper, digital photos that students have taken, or digital audio and video recordings of students carrying on conversations, enacting skits, or giving oral presentations.

One advantage of electronic portfolios is that they can be accessed by a variety of audiences in any location, sometimes permitting varying degrees of access depending on the audience. Another advantage is that they can easily be maintained dynamically over time; for example, students could use their electronic portfolio to collect examples of their work throughout several years of Spanish study.

Many web-based companies offer electronic portfolio packages; unfortunately, they are often expensive to use unless your school subscribes to one of them. However, there are other options for online hosting of electronic portfolios that cost virtually nothing. Dr. Helen Barrett, who has done extensive work on the subject, explains many of these options on her website (http://electronicportfolios.com/). These options include using applications such as Google Docs and Google Video, or simply uploading students' work to a regular website or wiki. Whatever the technologies used, teachers should keep in mind that they may need to teach students how to use these technologies.

A Tool for Collaborating and Communicating with Others

Currently, it seems that almost all of our students post their own material online. As previously mentioned, the term "Web 2.0" refers to web applications such as social networking sites, blogs, wikis, and photo- and video-sharing websites that are user-friendly and facilitate interactive collaboration on the Web. A Web 2.0 site allows its users to interact with other users or to change website content, in contrast to non-interactive websites where users are limited to the passive viewing of information that is provided to them. (See http://cultureconnection.wikispaces.com/Tech+Tools for an extensive list of web 2.0 tools that students can use to create with the target language.)

Wikis. Among the best tools for online collaboration are *wikis.* A wiki is a website that allows for the easy, collaborative creation and editing of any number of interlinked web pages via a web browser. Wikis invite all registered users to edit or create new pages. Many teachers have successfully used wikis to promote collaborative writing among their students. If students are assigned to prepare a group paper or presentation, for example, individual students can post their contribution on the wiki, and the other group members can post comments or make revisions. Thus, much of the collaboration can be done outside of class. Students can log onto the wiki in the computer lab or at home, reducing the amount of class time required for collaborative work. (See http://educationalwikis.wikispaces.com/Examples+of+educational+wikis for an extensive list of wikis being used around the world in education.)

An online search for "educational wikis" will reveal a number of websites that host wikis for teachers and students. (To compare features across these services, see http://www.wikimatrix.org/index.php.) These websites make it fast and easy to create your own wiki. Many sites allow the creation of wikis for free; sometimes "upgrades" providing additional features are available for a small fee.

Blogs. Most students are familiar with *blogs* (short for "web logs"), in which regular entries can be posted online along with photos and audio and video files. Many of your students probably have their own blogs. Some teachers have assigned their students to create Spanish blogs as online "journals" in which they make regular entries. Students can be assigned to read each other's blogs and post comments. Blogs can be very useful in study abroad settings; students can be assigned to maintain a blog with entries on the places they visit, their historical and cultural significance, etc., accompanied by uploaded photos the students have taken. Students' families and friends back home can then see and read about the students' experiences abroad.

Important considerations in using blogs and other social networking media are to respect school and district policies, consider parents' wishes regarding the protection of students' identities online, and generally follow best practices for safe and ethical use. Students need to be taught the dangers of providing personally identifying information, such as their full name, address, and contact information.

Tools that allow students to create with language. There are a number of Web 2.0 tools that allow users to create videos or animations with audio in any language. One such tool is *Vokis*, animated figures that students can create with a personalized appearance that "speaks" whatever text the students type in. Students can then post these figures on their own blogs or websites for others to see and hear. It can be very motivating for students to create a Voki character, type in Spanish text for the Voki to say, and hear their text actually pronounced in Spanish. Different Spanish accents can be selected, pronounced by male and female native speakers, allowing students to compare different regional pronunciations of the same text. Vokis are hosted on the website http://www.voki.com/.

Other Web 2.0 tools that allow students to create with language include Xtranormal (http://xtranormal.com), which allows students to create their own videos, and GoAnimate (http://goanimate.com), which allows users to create cartoons. Spend some time checking out these tools.

A Tool for Communicating with Native Speakers

The *Standards* specify that students need practice using the language to communicate with others in Interpersonal Mode. Ideally, this practice should include interaction with native speakers. The internet can put our students in instant contact with native Spanish speakers around the world.

In Chapter 9 we mentioned **key pals**, which are the electronic version of traditional pen pals. There exist several websites that help teachers find key pals for their students in other countries; an online search for "international key pals" will reveal some of these sites.

Another useful tool for putting students in contact with native speakers is **Skype**. For those unfamiliar with this technology, Skype is a software application that allows users to make voice calls over the Internet. Calls to other Skype users are free, while calls to other landlines and mobile phones can be made for a fee. Additional features include instant messaging and video conferencing. (Use Skype's education page to find other teachers who are interested in collaborating on classroom projects: http://education.skype.com/)

Skype is commonly used on virtual foreign exchange websites that are designed to help people learn about other languages and cultures. These sites specialize in putting students in contact with speakers of the language they are learning, allowing them to speak directly with native speakers right from their own classroom or home. One popular site is http://www.languageexchange.org; other similar sites may be found by doing a search for "Skype foreign language."

CONCLUSION

The use of technology provides such advantages to language teachers that we cannot pass it by. Creative teachers are finding ingenious ways to incorporate the functions of electronic devices into their classroom teaching and assigning the students to use them to practice their skills. As more and more materials become available, and as better and more sophisticated technologies are developed, we must be ready to use them to our advantage. For example, virtually all students have their own cell phones and have become very adept at sending text messages. Instead of prohibiting the students to bring them into the classroom, perhaps we could develop activities that would require them to do texting in Spanish. Publishers and materials providers will undoubtedly develop more materials to use in teaching culture, such as some type of an "adventure" game where the students have to use their knowledge of the culture to survive in a series of critical situations. If we can get our students to spend as much time learning and practicing language skills and cultural information as young people now spend with computer and video games, we're bound to make some spectacular progress.

REFERENCES AND SUGGESTIONS FOR FURTHER READING

Altman, R. (1989). *The video connection: Integrating video into language teaching.* Boston, MA: Houghton Mifflin. *A comprehensive look at video uses in the teaching of foreign languages. Many excellent suggestions. Also has an extensive bibliography.*

Blake, R. J. (2008). *Brave new digital classroom: Technology and foreign language learning.* Washington, DC: Georgetown University Press. *Examines the effective use of a range of technologies, from websites to computer-mediated communication such as synchronous chatting and blogs, to distance learning.*

Burbules, N. C., & Callister, T. A. Jr. (2000). *Watch IT: The risks and promises of information technologies.* Boulder, CO: Westview Press. *Examines the positive and negative consequences of new technologies in the classroom, including such issues as access, new approaches to reading and writing, privacy, and globalization.*

Calico Journal. This is a professional journal dedicated to the use of computers in the teaching of foreign languages. Each issue contains many excellent articles on any aspect of CALI.

Dieu, B., & Stevens, V. (2007, June). *Pedagogical affordances of syndication, aggregation, and mash-up of content on the web.* TESL-EJ, 11*(1), 1-15.* Available at http://tesl-ej.org/ej41/int.html. *Provides an overview of Web 2.0 tools that can be used in a classroom, including blogs, social networking, and podcasts.*

Henry, J., & Meadows, J. (2008, Winter). An absolutely riveting online course: Nine principles for excellence in web-based teaching. *Canadian Journal of Learning & Technology, 34*(1). Available at http://www.cjlt.ca/index.php/cjlt/article/view/179/177. *Focuses on general principles for web-based teaching rather than specific tools.*

International Society for Technology in Education (ISTE). *This is the organization that developed the National Education Technology Standards. It provides professional development for teachers, as well as the annual Horizon Report, which identifies and describes emerging technologies that likely to have a large impact on teaching and learning.* http://www.iste.org/standards/

SOURCES FOR AUDIO MATERIALS

Culture Connection. This website, created by Dr. Cherice Montgomery of Brigham Young University, features a collection of authentic videos and other materials in Spanish, including children's songs and stories, poetry, literature, and conceptual topics such as sports, the environment, immigration, and education. http://cultureconnection.wikispaces.com

Puerta del Sol Spanish Audio Magazine is a program that provides sound clips from radio programs from various Spanish-speaking countries. Toni Garrido from Spain and Maria Fernanda Lencina from Argentina head a team of contributors who introduce you to the issues, personalities, and traditions that comprise the rich fabric of Hispanic and Latin American culture. You receive monthly an hour-long audio program (Spanish language CD) and it includes transcripts, vocabulary and notes, and optional Study Guides and Flash Cards. http://www.champs-elysees.com/products/spanish/product.aspx

Spanish radio programs. Audio clips from United Nations radio broadcasts are available at: http://www.unmultimedia.org/radio/spanish/

SOURCES FOR VIDEO MATERIALS (Request catalogs)

Amazon.com. Go to their site and do a search of movies and TV. Scroll down to the section "Product Details." Check to make sure it has Spanish language. You can buy the film and then prepare your own preview and practice exercises. http://amazon.com

Applause Learning Resources is a foreign language teacher and student/learners source for a wide variety of foreign language teaching & supplemental materials including: DVD's, study guides (for the DVD's), and audio CD's. http://www.applauselearning.com

Destinos: An Introduction to Spanish. A total video program from the Annenberg/CPB group. Text, teacher and student materials are from McGraw-Hill, Inc. A marriage of television drama and language instruction. Complemented by a complete collection of teaching and learning aids including a faculty guide, student workbooks/study guides, audio recordings, optional software, and professional supplements. A demo video is available on their website. http://www.learner.org/resources/series75.html

Film Arobics. This company offers a number of films in Spanish (wide selection, including some Disney films) that they have divided into segments and prepared previewing materials and practice activities that the students can work with after viewing the segment. You can download examples of the activities. http://www.filmarobics.com/pages.php?pageid=3

Films for the Humanities and Sciences has DVDs with history, culture and literature. http://www.films.com

IMDB A great source for information on films and movies. Click on icon of Spain flag for movies in Spanish. http://www.imdb.com

Insight Media has lots of DVDs, including an extensive collection of movies from Spanish literature. http://www.insightmedia.com

Spanish Multimedia has many classic Spanish films. http://www.spanishmultimedia.com

Spanish videos from the British Broadcasting Corporation (BBC). http://www.bbc.co.uk/mundo/index.shtml

Teacher's Discovery provides supplemental materials of a wide variety, including videos, DVDs, and CDs. http://www.teachersdiscovery-foreignlanguage.com/spanish.asp

Videocuentos has a nice collection of chilren's stories and fairy tales in Spanish in cartoon format. http://pacomova.eresmas.net/paginas/videocuentos/videocuentos.htm

World Language.Com had a variety of materials for use in language classes, including computer software, videos, and many other products. http://worldlanguage.com/

Yale University Press. The source for the *Español en vivo* program with DVDs. You can view a demonstration of the program free at the website. http://yalepress.yale.edu/yupbooks/book.asp?isbn=9780300115383

COMPUTER MATERIALS

WebCLIPS (Computerized Language Instruction and Practice Software). An intermediate-level review of the basics of Spanish grammar, complete with diagnostic tests, practice exercises, and mastery tests. Available online at http://webclips.byu.edu.

JumpStart Spanish. A CD ROM beginners program with animation and fun interactive games to learn vocabulary.
http://www.amazon.com/Vivendi-Universal-3590-JumpStart-Spanish/dp/B00001XDVZ/

Living Books Series. Interactive, animated stories for children. (*The Tortoise and the Hare*, and *Abuelita y yo, etc.*) http://www.kidsclick.com/foreign.htm

ACTIVITIES FOR METHODS CLASSES

1. In group sessions, decide what media equipment you would want in your language class. Put the items in descending order of importance, #1 the last thing you would give up, #2 the next most important thing, etc. Discuss how each item would be of value to you in teaching languages. Report to the class.

2. Do a search on YouTube for videos in Spanish (other than music), such as children's stories, cartoons, TV commercials, etc. Select one that you could use in your classes. Prepare a guide to it for classroom use, or to give to the students so they could work with it on their own. Show it to your teacher.

3. Working with partners from the methods class, write and make a recording designed to be used by your students to practice listening comprehension. Include a students' guide, with instructions, vocabulary practice, and a listening comprehension quiz. Hand in to your methods instructor for evaluation.

4. In a local media store or online, find some DVDs in Spanish. Buy (or borrow) one and decide how you could use it in your Spanish class. Prepare a teacher's guide for use in the class (or a guide for individual student use), and prepare a listening comprehension test to accompany it. Show it to your teacher.

5. Spend some time watching a Spanish TV channel, such as Univisión or Galavisión, and decide what kinds of programs you could use in your class, such as commercials, news broadcasts, talk shows, documentaries, etc. Record some different segments for classroom use. Prepare a list of what is on the recording, including a description, possible class use, length, location on the disc, and level of difficulty.

6. If you have access to a lab that has a library of videos, check out several videos of the different types we have discussed in the book. Make a report of your opinion and of how you could use it in a class, and hand the report to your methods instructor.

7. Get a copy of the software program of a Spanish textbook, or access it online, and work with it in the lab as if you were a student using that program. Write a report discussing your reaction: Was it boring? Would it help the students practice? Was it interactive, self-correcting? Hand in a report.

8. Visit a language lab in your university or a nearby public school. Prepare a description of all the types of equipment it has and make a list of the uses made by the teacher and the students.

9. In small groups, plan what you think would be the ideal language lab. Assume you have unlimited funds, you can put anything in it you want. Describe how you or your students would use each feature of the lab. Write up your plan and present to the class.

10. Log onto Spanish WebCLIPS (webclips.byu.edu) and work for an hour on some of the CLIPS lessons. Hand in a report to your instructor.

12. With other students from the methods class, prepare a skit and, using a video camera, record it for use in 11. Watch a television program intended to teach a foreign language, such as Destinos. Write a report discussing the advantages and disadvantages of learning a FL by TV. Hand in.

13. Do an online search for different companies that host wikis. Create your own wiki and spend an hour or so experimenting with typing in text, uploading pictures, and creating different pages. Give your instructor the URL of the wiki.

14. Do an online search for some generic software programs for language practice and work with one or more of them for at least an hour. Hand in report.

15. Check a commercial CD program for children, such as Living Books and play with it for an hour or so. Write a report, telling how you could use it with your Spanish students.

16. Browse ("surf") the Internet for an hour or two, specifically looking for sites that would be useful to your students in practicing Spanish. Bookmark these resources. Prepare a report telling how you would have your students use the program.

17. Do an online search for sites that sponsor international key pals. Try to find a class with which your students could exchange email messages in Spanish. Write a report on what you found.

18. Prepare a test, including an oral and a listening comprehension section, that could be given to an entire class in a lab. Administer the test to some friends, and hand in the results to your teacher.

19. If you can find a classroom management program, practice with it, entering names and scores of some pseudo students. Show the grade printout to your instructor.

20. Find an issue of Calico Journal or the IALL Journal, read an article and report it to your instructor.

CHAPTER FOURTEEN

ADVANCED AND SPECIAL CLASSES THE "TOTAL CURRICULUM"

YOUR OBJECTIVES FOR THIS CHAPTER ARE TO:

1. DISCUSS HOW YOUR CLASSES FIT INTO THE "TOTAL CURRICULUM."

2. DISCUSS THE IMPORTANCE OF ARTICULATION WITHIN THE SCHOOL AND BETWEEN SCHOOLS, AND STEPS THAT CAN BE TAKEN TO ESTABLISH EFFECTIVE ARTICULATION IF IT DOESN'T EXIST.

3. IDENTIFY STRATEGIES FOR SETTING UP INTERMEDIATE AND ADVANCED CLASSES AT THE HIGH SCHOOL LEVEL.

4. IDENTIFY STRATEGIES FOR DEALING WITH COMBINED-LEVEL CLASSES.

5. DESCRIBE TECHNIQUES AND SKILLS THAT CAN BE USED IN ADVANCED CLASSES TO DEVELOP LISTENING, SPEAKING, READING AND WRITING SKILLS.

6. EXPLAIN WHAT THE ADVANCED PLACEMENT (AP) PROGRAM IS AND HOW TO SET ONE UP IN YOUR SCHOOL.

7. GIVE EXAMPLES OF SPECIAL PROGRAMS THAT CAN BE SET UP BETWEEN HIGH SCHOOLS AND UNIVERSITIES.

8. IDENTIFY STRATEGIES THAT CAN ENHANCE YOUR PROGRAM IF YOUR SCHOOL MOVES TO NEW OR DIFFERENT SCHEDULING CONFIGURATIONS.

9. GIVE EXAMPLES OF SPECIALIZED CLASSES, SUCH AS FLEX CLASSES, INTENSIVE CLASSES, AND MINI-COURSES THAT CAN BE OFFERED AT YOUR SCHOOL.

10. DESCRIBE STRATEGIES FOR TEACHING LANGUAGES TO OLDER ADULTS.

11. IDENTIFY THE GOALS OF A LITERATURE CLASS AND SOME BASIC TECHNIQUES FOR TEACHING LITERATURE.

12. RECOGNIZE THE SPECIAL NEEDS OF HERITAGE SPEAKERS OF SPANISH AND DEVELOP STRATEGIES FOR TEACHING THESE STUDENTS.

As Mrs. Ventura walked toward the principal's office she was asking herself, "I wonder what he wants now. The last time he called me in formally like this he talked about cutting out the Spanish program. That was two years ago and I have built the program up to eight classes of Spanish since then. We even had to get Mr. Bono to teach a couple of the beginning classes. He's doing a good job even if his fluency is limited, and he's getting better every day."

"I'll come right to the point," said Mr. Principale. "I have mentioned several times lately how pleased we are with the way you have turned the Spanish program around and what a remarkable progress your students are making. Some of them are in their fourth year now and a few days ago some of them came into my office to ask why we couldn't have an AP class in Spanish. Mr. Thomas over at Hot Dog High School has had AP classes for several years now, and I understand that his students always do extremely well on the AP exam. What do you know about AP classes? Would you be able to start an AP program in Spanish here at Podunk High?"

A small group of boys and girls was waiting for Mr. Padilla as he returned from lunch. They were all the top students of his Spanish II class. "Señor Padilla," they began, "What are we going to do about keeping up our Spanish? We are all coming back next year and want to keep studying it, but in the office they tell us that they aren't going to offer Spanish III next fall."

"I know, I know," sighed Mr. P. "I was talking to the principal this morning and he says that there is no way he can let me teach a class with just 10 students in it. He is going to assign me an English class."

As he saw the disappointment on their faces, Mr. P. made a decision. "I've been thinking about other options," he said. "I know it isn't right to have you make such great progress and then leave you stranded. I will make arrangements to teach Spanish III during my 'prep' period. Set up your schedules to have 3rd period open."

"But Sr. P.," they protested, "that means you won't have any free time at all during the entire day!"

"True, but I know how hard you have worked to get this far, and I want you all to take advanced Spanish classes in college. That could be very difficult if you have a gap of a year or more where you would forget much of what you have learned. I'll have to get to school earlier in the morning or stay later after school."

When Mr. Padilla was voted "outstanding teacher" at the end of the school year, there was a big smile of satisfaction on the faces of his Spanish III students.

Señorita Rodriguez was struggling with her mixed feelings. She now had 25 Hispanic students in her Spanish III and IV classes— almost double from last year—primarily because school administrators and counselors had felt that they would profit from her classes. At the workshop she attended during the summer, she had learned that there was a new term to refer to what had always been called "native speakers"— *heritage speakers*. She felt a strong tie and empathy with them, but she was also painfully aware that "all heritage speakers are not created equal." Their mastery levels were so different; some understood everything but had no speaking skills; others spoke well enough, but their usage was sprinkled with errors; others were strong in conversation, but could not read or write since their school experience had been in English. And on top of that, she had three exchange students from Latin America, whose Spanish was marvelous. How could she possibly meet the individual needs they each had? She returned to the idea she had been turning around in her head: Could she convince Mr. Goodfellow, the principal, to let her organize a separate class for those heritage students? It would be a ton of extra work for her, but if she kept them in her regular classes, what would they learn? Would they reach their potential? She reached for the phone, and dialed the office.

CHAPTER FOURTEEN

ADVANCED AND SPECIAL CLASSES THE "TOTAL CURRICULUM"

> Consider the postage stamp, my son.
> It secures success through its ability
> to stick to one thing till it gets there.
> -Josh Billings

As we discussed teaching the four skills in chapters six through nine, our focus was on the techniques and activities one would use in *beginning* and *intermediate* classes. In this chapter we will turn our attention to *advanced* and *special* classes. We have frequently pointed out that a high level of language proficiency cannot be reached with just beginning and intermediate classes; we must strive to get our students into advanced classes. Special considerations must be made with those advanced classes, and there are unique approaches and techniques one must use that are different from those used in beginning or intermediate levels.

In this chapter we will also look at some unusual and specialized classes or programs that go beyond the scope of the regular school curriculum, something you could consider to meet some unique conditions or needs that might exist at your school. We will describe classes that have some very specific or unique goals. There can be a wide variety of programs of this type, each with its own special objectives and each requiring a unique approach.

WHY LONG SEQUENCES?

Because of the normal time configuration of the public schools, it is impossible for fluency to be achieved in two or three years. Experts estimate that functional mastery of a language takes about 600 hours of exposure and practice. In a typical school year the students spend from 40 to 50 minutes a day, five days a week, for about 30 weeks. This figures out to be approximately 150 hours per school year. To get

the recommended 600 hours then, the students must have at least five years of study. To develop a study period of this length, we must work at both ends of the curriculum. We must start language classes earlier, and we must provide advanced classes all the way through high school.

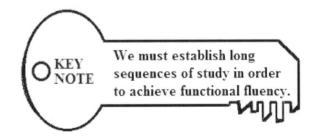

KEY NOTE

We must establish long sequences of study in order to achieve functional fluency.

Ideally, language study would begin in the elementary school, continue uninterrupted until graduation from high school, and then continue on in highly advanced classes at the university level. We will discuss in depth the teaching languages in the elementary schools (FLES) in Chapter 15. At the very latest, students should begin learning a foreign language in middle school or junior high (7th grade).

ARTICULATION

Whatever the program a school or district might set up, it is absolutely essential that all the pieces fit together in a coordinated and sequential pattern. If there is an elementary school program, it should merge smoothly into the middle school or junior high school program with a minimum of back-tracking or repetition of content. Junior high and middle school courses should not be just "fun and games" to entertain students, but should be serious and important parts of the total sequence. In high school, intermediate and advanced classes should build upon what has been learned in beginning classes and should lead to Advanced Placement (AP) or university level classes. Textbooks and teaching emphasis should be coordinated, and there should be someone responsible for supervising the overall program.

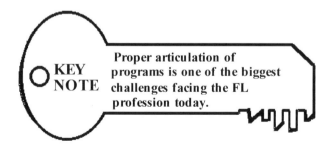

KEY NOTE — The total foreign language curriculum must be articulated, i.e., sequential and coordinated.

The term *articulation* is used in the foreign language field to refer to the coordination of a program within a school, or, even more importantly, between schools, such as the transition between elementary school and middle or junior high school, between junior and senior high school, or between high school and college. Proper articulation emphasizes the importance of maintaining the students' progress in the language smoothly and steadily upward, not punctuated with stops and reversions back to beginning levels, or moving in one direction and then abruptly moving in another. The lack of articulation is all too frequent in many schools and districts across the nation.

KEY NOTE — Proper articulation of programs is one of the biggest challenges facing the FL profession today.

Following are some examples of lack of articulation commonly seen in schools:

• A 4th grade teacher includes Spanish in her curriculum with no thought about what will happen to those children in the next grade. The children make a good beginning in the language, and then watch it die out at the end of the school year.

• An elementary school which has a coordinated, sequential program in place within its own school sends students with three or more years of sequential language study on to junior high (or middle) school where they are placed in a Level I class and are taught again (this time in total boredom) greetings, numbers, and how to tell time, along with other students who have never had prior language study.

• Students with two years of Spanish in junior high school move to high school and enroll in Spanish 3 and find a huge gap between what they learned and what is expected of them and they drop out of Spanish altogether.

• A junior high teacher does a marvelous job of teaching three coordinated years of Spanish with great enthusiasm and sends his students on to high school only to hear rumors that they are not continuing on with the language in high school because the teacher teaches nothing but grammar and the classes are terribly boring.

• A high school teacher receives students from the junior high who seem to have spent two or three years of singing and playing games in the language with no notions of grammar patterns, and starts them over in Spanish I with beginning students.

• Students with two or more years of language study in secondary school go on to college where they enroll in beginning language classes because they are afraid of taking advanced classes.

These failures to capitalize and build on an early beginning of language study are tragic. What a waste of time and effort to move students to a point where they can do advanced work, only to have them have to start over again at a beginning level!

An Ideally Articulated Public School Program

Studies have shown that an ideally articulated program will have the following essential features:

• A district coordinator (preferably an experienced language teacher) who is responsible for coordinating the foreign language programs in the district at all levels, especially the transition points from one school level to another.

- An in-school coordinator (department chairman) who is responsible for making sure the teachers are following the same curriculum, using basically the same approach in their teaching, making the same progress through the text materials, which are the same for all teachers, etc.

- A textbook program or series that is used by all the teachers of a language in a district. This greatly facilitates moving upwards toward advanced classes and transferring from one school to another.

- Frequent meetings (at least once a month) of language teachers from both the sending out and receiving ends of "feeder" schools to coordinate curriculum, activities, methods, and especially the smooth progress from one level to another.

- Advanced Placement (AP) classes taught and supported by the administration, even if enrollment falls below the desired number.

Schools who have the preceding features are able to bring their students to a high level of proficiency and send many of them on to college where they go directly into advanced classes. Some districts even encourage "teacher exchanges" where the junior and senior high teachers exchange classrooms for a few days to give each other better insight in solving articulation problems.

SPECIAL CLASSES

In addition to the regular beginning, intermediate, and advanced languages classes that a school might offer, there are some specialized classes that you as a teacher might want to consider. Teachers sometimes find that offering one or more classes of this type may solve some problems they are encountering or fill some unique need that they have.

Exploratory or *FLEX* classes. Many intermediate schools, usually in the first year of middle school or junior high school, prefer to give their students a general introduction to foreign languages before letting them actually begin learning a specific language. This

introduction to language study is commonly called a ***FLEX*** class (the acronym *FLEX* comes from **F**oreign **L**anguage **EX**perience [or **EX**ploration]). These courses do not have the goal of actually learning a language, but rather giving the students an introduction to what language is all about and what it takes to learn a second language. This type of program typically introduces the students to several different languages and prepares them to make a choice of which language they may want to study later on. Possibly the most important goal of a FLEX class is to give the students a positive attitude about learning languages. If a student enrolls in a regular foreign language class after the FLEX class, then in terms of that student, the program was a success.

Examples of some typical units in a FLEX class might be:

- What is Language
- The history of language
- Other ways of communicating (gestures, body language, etc.)
- How do we learn our mother tongue?
- How did English develop?
- How have other languages influenced English? (borrowed terms, musical expressions, alphabet, etc.)
- Language families of the world
- Different language alphabets
- Why learn a foreign language?
- How to learn a foreign language

These FLEX courses are sometimes team taught by several teachers from the school; i.e. the Spanish teacher, the Russian teacher, and the German teacher, or another subject area teacher who speaks a foreign language such as Japanese or Hebrew. Each of these teachers typically instructs a mini-course in their particular language to give the students a taste of the excitement and satisfaction that come from learning another tongue.

Many schools report that the inclusion of FLEX courses in their curriculum has increased the enrollment in the regular language courses dramatically.

A final advantage of a FLEX class is that even if students decide not to study a foreign language, their horizon will have been broadened and their use of English probably improved.

[Some textbooks that might be used in a FLEX course are included in the reference section at the end of the chapter.]

Intensive language classes. Recently there has been a wave of enthusiasm for intensive, or concentrated, "rapid-fire" programs. The purpose of this approach is to gain the maximum fluency in the shortest time possible. These programs can range from a simple weekend, to one- or two-week programs, to programs that last for several months. Typically in these programs, students will spend several hours a day studying and practicing the language. They usually provide a variety of activities that allow the students to work on all four skills.

Courses of this type are somewhat difficult to establish within the normal secondary school schedule. They are typically offered during summer vacations as one of the options in the regular summer school program. For example, an intensive course might be offered in Spanish, where the students immerse themselves in Spanish from 8 a.m. to 5 p.m. daily for a period of eight weeks. Studies of programs of this type have shown that the students get approximately the same amount of exposure to the language in those short weeks that they would get in one regular school year, but because there is such immediate use of the language they make greater progress and retain more of the language.

Institutional intensive programs. An example of non-school intensive programs is the Defense Language Institute (DLI) in Monterey California, where U.S. military personnel spend from several months up to a year learning a language. The Foreign Service Institute (FSI) has a similar program in Arlington, Virginia for civilian government employees. The Peace Corps has been conducting intensive language programs since its inception in the 1950's.

In Provo, Utah, on the campus of Brigham Young University, the Missionary Training Center (MTC) carries out the largest intensive language-training program in the world. The participants in the program, who are preparing to serve missions for the LDS Church, spend two months in intensive language instruction and most are able to successfully communicate in the language upon arrival at their field of labor.

There are commercial intensive programs where businessmen or tourists can relatively quickly gain some basic language skills. The Berlitz organization sponsors intensive programs for travelers who need to learn a language because of an assignment by their business organization to visit or reside in a foreign country.

There are many obvious advantages of intensive programs. They bring immediate success to the students in terms of language use, they quickly allow an exclusive use of the language in the classroom, and they are very motivating.

The disadvantages include the high cost and the fact that it demands time flexibility for the student to devote complete time to the program, something most public schools and many colleges do not have.

"Mini" language classes. Some schools supplement their regular language offerings with "mini" courses designed to give students a totally practical focus. This type of course may have its origin in the traditional "Latin for medical students" or "Latin for law students" or even "Latin for English vocabulary building" which have been popular in schools and universities for generations. Giving the course this practical focus legitimized the teaching of Latin, a language which students otherwise seldom used for communication purposes.

Examples of these types of classes in a modern language would be:

- Spanish for the traveler
- Cooking in Spanish
- Spanish for law-enforcement personnel
- Spanish for medical personnel
- Spanish for agriculture workers
- Children's literature in Spanish
- Secretarial Spanish
- Current events in Spanish

This type of course became popular during the years that individualization of instruction was in vogue because it permitted the students, who were already working at their own speed and style, to choose their own emphasis and move at their own pace.

The biggest disadvantages of fragmenting the regular curriculum in this way with too many different offerings are that it usually requires a great amount of work on the part of the teachers in the preparation of materials, more time spent counseling individuals, a lessening of the depth and importance of course content, and the constant need to justify small enrollment numbers in each of the mini-courses.

Community foreign language courses. Many high schools, community colleges, junior colleges, and universities offer classes in the evening for students who have dropped out of full time study during the day, senior citizen groups, or middle-aged persons who in spite of having work and family responsibilities, want to learn a foreign language in their free time. These groups include persons who are planning to travel abroad, who need a foreign language in their profession, persons who just want additional skills, or persons who want to enrich or broaden their life with academic study. These programs allow students to work during the day and pursue their study of the foreign language in the evening.

These courses are normally similar to the regular daytime offerings, but usually move a little slower because of work and family considerations. The courses are typically more relaxed and do not demand much out-of-class work, or put heavy emphasis in exams, grades, and academic credit as do the usual regular school offerings. They often meet only one or two days a week and thus the exposure and practice with the language is less, and progress is somewhat slower than normal. However, these students can be highly motivated and those who stay with the programs for long periods can reach impressive levels of fluency.

TEACHING LANGUAGES TO OLDER ADULTS

Since the community and evening school programs mentioned above often include older adults, often of the retired, "senior citizen" variety, we make some comments here in the possibility that you may teach a class of this type some time. There are some special considerations that must be made for older students; they cannot be treated the same as adolescents or even college-age students.

In the following summary we present some language learning characteristics of older adults coupled with some suggestions for classroom strategies that will take advantage of, or compensate for, each of the qualities listed. This summary is the result of many years of experience by one of the writers of this textbook with teaching community language classes for older adults whose ages ranged from twenty-five to seventy-five.

Characteristics of "Older Adult" learners	Teaching strategies
Older students cannot move at the fast pace of younger students and should not be combined with them because it leads to frustration and discouragement.	Divide or arrange your classes so that adults can be by themselves and not required to compete with younger students.
Older adults have greater difficulty memorizing and remembering vocabulary words.	Give them special help with memorizing using visuals, actions, and a constant review and practice of vocabulary.
Older adults need more time to "digest and process" what they are learning.	Proceed at a more deliberate pace and spend a great deal of time reviewing and recycling materials.
Adults typically have a "comfort zone" which they are reluctant to leave and consequently are not usually "risk takers."	Expand this comfort zone and make them feel free to try new sounds and new ways of expressing themselves without fear of being ridiculed.

Students in evening and community courses typically have jobs and families that naturally receive higher priority—that is usually why they are taking the classes in the evening. Therefore, they will often miss class because of family and work obligations.	Provide ways for these students to make up work they have missed in a non-embarrassing and supportive way. Worksheets and makeup packets or recordings to work with can be very helpful in this area.
With age come physical problems, and older students typically cannot see or hear as well as younger students.	Make sure that audio activities are adequately loud. Encourage students to speak loudly so that classmates with hearing impairment can hear. Make your visuals extra large so they can be seen by the near-sighted, and prepare your transparencies with a computer using large fonts. Prepare your handouts with large fonts, never reduce them in the interest of saving paper. Encourage students with physical problems to sit on the front row.
Mature students are very image conscious and are often hesitant to participate in oral activities, especially if they think they might make mistakes and be laughed at by others.	Rather than eliminating or curbing activities of this sort, we recommend that you work very hard at making them entertaining, with no stress. Establish the attitude that it is no disgrace to make mistakes, that it is just part of the process.
Tests and grades can be very intimidating and can cause apprehension.	If you possibly can, set up the course so that no grades are given and exams are voluntary for those who simply want to evaluate their progress.
Adults are much more conscientious than adolescents and are usually very dedicated to doing written assignments. They understand the need for homework and preparation outside class and very often over-prepare.	Give them frequent assignments to bring to class completed. They will work for you with very little complaining. Have them do the bienvenidas and the warm-ups. Make sure they understand what they are to do and how to do it.
Adults like to laugh, play, and "ham it up" as much as younger students.	Take extra care to reduce all stress. Do role-playing, put on plays, work in groups and pairs, and play games just as much as with adolescents.
Oldsters enjoy singing, and are even more willing to sing in class than youngsters.	Oldsters enjoy singing, and are even more willing to sing in class than youngsters. Teach them songs of all kinds: traditional, folk songs, children's songs, modern songs, etc.

331

Adults are more linguistically sophisticated and can see grammar patterns quicker than younger people. They can draw on a much broader linguistic understanding and have a much greater vocabulary.	Have them read the grammar explanations at home and spend less time explaining in class. Teach grammar inductively, and make comparisons with English so they can draw parallels.
Adults find it more difficult to pronounce correctly. Their ability to make new sounds has diminished and they are very influenced by the written words, which they will relate so tenaciously to English that it will be hard to get them to change.	Keep them always aware of good pronunciation. Practice it in class with warm-ups, songs, reading out loud. Keep insisting on correct pronunciation, but always in a gentle, supporting way. Use pronunciation "tricks" such as "totter they" (tarde), "smiling from ear to ear" (imposible), etc.
Adults are very writing (visually) oriented, and will invariably insist on seeing words written out.	Work constantly to remove the crutch of the written word. Help them become accustomed to learning orally by presenting new vocabulary orally. Remind them that they will not see what people are saying in written form.
Adults will process oral speech more slowly than young people. They will complain that you are "speaking too fast" and will constantly ask you to slow down.	Constantly work to help them "listen faster." Teach the class entirely in the language and speak at a normal speed. Practice with large doses of listening comprehension: carefully selected videos and tapes, songs, native-speaking guests.
Adults tend to be more motivated because they can see more easily the need for language study and are usually more focused on the practical use they will be making of their new skills.	Use that motivation to your advantage: have them prepare and make presentations in class, focus class content on practical, functional vocabulary. Anticipate situations they will find themselves in and do simulations in the class.
Adults are overly anxious to know "why" and feel that they need grammar explanations to feel secure.	Give them "quick" grammar explanations and answer their questions, but remember that that won't produce fluency. Don't overemphasize the importance of grammar; let them know that there often is no reason "why." (Así se dice. No hay un "porque.")

Hopefully you will experience the privilege of teaching older adults. No one is more gracious and appreciative of teachers, and seeing them make progress with the language can be some of the most rewarding and satisfying experiences you will have as a teacher.

VARIED CLASS SCHEDULE CONFIGURATIONS

It is common now for schools to move to innovative class scheduling to make fullest use of the school facilities and thus save money, or to allow the student to take more classes. Some examples of these configurations are:

- Alternate day schedule ("A" and "B" days). This format, called "block" scheduling" is rapidly becoming the norm in secondary schools. The students take only half of their classes on one day, but each class is for 85 minutes. Then on the following day they take the other half of the classes, also for the longer periods. This approach can be very beneficial for some subjects such as band or chemistry where there must be a set up time, but for Spanish teachers it means that you only have the class every other day, and you must plan for 85 minutes of class. Needless to say, you will have to plan a variety of activities to keep the students from getting bored. Alternating oral and listening activities with videos or work in the lab can help you keep the class interesting. The longer periods also permit more interactive activities and works with groups. However, you must spend more time planning for this type of class and be very creative in planning a variety of activities.

- Extended day schedule. Half of the students come earlier to school and leave earlier in the afternoon. The second half comes later, but stays later. The students usually share large classes over the midday hours. In this configuration teachers spend more time in school and may have some free time to prepare for classes. The approach allows for smaller classes, which is an advantage in language classes since more attention can be given to individuals.

ADVANCED CLASSES AT THE HIGH SCHOOL LEVEL

We have already discussed the desirability of encouraging students to stay in language study until they can take advanced classes. However, many high school teachers, especially those in small or medium-sized school, find that this can become very difficult because of diminishing class sizes. As normal attrition and competition with other subjects take their toll, language classes after second and third year become smaller and smaller. Administrators are usually reluctant to allow a teacher to teach courses with fewer than fifteen students, and consequently language teachers are faced with a dilemma. They want their students to continue on in

advanced classes, but the administrator will not allow classes with only 5 to 15 students in them.

Among the options the teacher has in these situations are: 1) not offer advanced classes [not an attractive option], 2) give up a preparation or consultation period and teach the advanced classes "on their time," 3) teach a class before or after school (if the district allows it) or 4) combine two advanced classes, such as third and fourth year.

Teaching Combined Classes

The last option mentioned above is the most common one selected, but it too brings some challenges. How can a teacher best work with combined classes? In general, the teacher must be much more organized, allowing students to work a great deal more independently. A variety of materials needs to be prepared for both of the groups which have been combined into one class.

Meeting with the students. One approach that teachers take is to teach the two groups together, using the same materials. This is not altogether satisfactory because you either work above the level of the younger students and they get lost or are always struggling, or you work below the level of the more advanced students who are just repeating something they have already learned and are not learning anything new, are not challenged, or become bored. The best strategy with this approach might be to use a different textbook or set of materials, which neither group has worked with. In this way the more advanced students will be working with new vocabulary, new content, and perhaps new structures. The following year, the teacher could go back to the regular materials that would be new again to both groups. The teacher must of course continue to make adjustments for the different abilities of the two groups.

A second approach a teacher can take is to alternate days with the two groups. For example, he or she could work orally one day with the less-advanced group while the advanced group works with reading or writing assignments (or in the lab), and then switch activities the following day.

A third approach sometimes taken is to divide the class hour into half, working with the beginning group during part of the hour and the advanced group during the other part. This approach requires a high degree of organization and energy on the part of the teacher to ensure that each group gets a fair share of the time available. It can also be difficult to keep one group's activities from interfering with those of the other group, but with cooperation and even some interaction between the two groups at times, it can be done.

Cooperative learning. Teachers who have worked with cooperative learning techniques often have found success by organizing the students into small groups, with both advanced students and younger students in the same group, and having the advanced students teach the younger ones. With this approach we would again suggest using materials that are new to both levels, permitting the advanced student to learn new material also.

Help from other people. Another solution to this problem is to get additional help. Many schools have a system that permits advanced students to work as aides (lab assistants) in less advanced classes and get credit for their work. Sometimes the school has money to pay for aides or arrangements can be made with international organizations such as AMITY who can place natives from Spanish-speaking countries in schools at a minimal cost, usually board and room which often can be donated by parents of students.

Community resources. Most communities have speakers of Spanish who would gladly volunteer to help with classes in the local schools. Parents or family members of students, students who have lived in foreign countries, exchange students from Hispanic countries, residents of the community who are from Spanish-speaking countries, can all make a valuable contribution to combined-level classes. Teachers should investigate the possibilities of having volunteers help with advanced and combined classes. Schools with colleges or universities close by can often find help from advanced Spanish students from the university.

Media help. If your school has a language laboratory that is separate from your classroom, you can use the lab as a type of "baby sitter" to work with one group while you work with the other. If you have computers or VCRs in your classroom, you can have small groups working at different "learning stations" while you work with other groups orally or with individuals.

Some teachers set up work *stations* in the classroom itself, using tables stocked with reading materials such as magazines (*Selecciones del Readers' Digest,* for example), newspapers, graded readers, and so on. At another station might be tape recorders with earphones that allow individual work without disturbing others. Some teachers make arrangements with the school librarian to allow students to do individual work such as written exercises and reports in the library.

AP Classes

When a teacher has developed a full program of language classes, consideration needs to be given to the offering of special advanced classes, such as an Advanced Placement (AP) class.

The AP program was established a number of years ago to provide university level instruction in the high schools. Most high schools offer AP classes in a variety of subjects, ranging from Physics to English, including two areas in Spanish: language and literature. Students who enroll in the AP classes are typically the brightest and best scholars in the school and are usually juniors or seniors. Normally the most qualified and best-prepared teacher in a subject area is selected to teach the class.

Following guidelines set up by the national AP program, the students work at a university pace and level which regularly requires a great deal of homework. Near the end of the school year the students take the national AP exam prepared by the Educational Testing Service (ETS) that is administered in their own school or a nearby institution, under very strict rules and careful supervision. The cost of the test, paid by the student, can run between $85 and $100. The answer sheets are sent to Princeton, New Jersey, to be scored along with each student's indication of which institutions of higher learning he/she intends to attend. A score of 3, 4, or 5 (on a scale of 1-5) will normally qualify the student for college credit, if the college or university he/she attends participates in the program.

Most students in Spanish take the language test that includes multiple-choice questions on the reading and listening sections, and free response questions on the writing, reading and speaking sections. In the oral test their responses are recorded and later rated by trained scorers at ETS. Unfortunately students learning Spanish as a second language are rated the same as heritage or native speakers and receive lower scores.

The literature test can be more difficult than the language test since the students are expected to be at the level of students in an beginning literature class at a university, but there is the advantage that can spend the school year working with a specific reading list and the test measures literature comprehension and analysis. There are no listening or oral sections.

An AP class can be the crowning point of the Spanish program at your school. As you work with beginning and intermediate students, keep them aware of the benefits of taking the AP class and encourage them to keep it as a goal. Some of your most rewarding experiences will be with your AP students.

University Classes at High School

Many high schools have an arrangement with nearby colleges or universities that allow advanced students to get credit at that institution for classes that they take in the high school. This program is usually called "concurrent enrollment." Typically a student in this program goes through the procedure of enrolling at the college, pays tuition, etc., and the class is taught either by a professor from the college who travels to the high school to teach the class, or by a highly qualified high school teacher who uses the textbook, course outline, and tests used by the college, but teaches the class in the high school.

A variation of this program is where the high school student signs up for a course at the college or university and is authorized to leave the high school and travel to campus to attend classes.

Programs of this type can be very beneficial to the students since they can get a good start in college even before finishing high school, and can get college credit. A word of caution: some colleges and universities do not accept credit of this type, so you should check with higher education institutions that your students are likely to attend, and verify if they will be given credit.

TEACHING ADVANCED CLASSES

What are some things that teachers can do to develop language skills in advanced classes that they cannot do in beginning and intermediate classes? One major difference is an increased use of what the profession calls **"authentic" materials** in both listening comprehension activities and reading. Simply stated, authentic materials are things like books, magazines, newspapers, videos (or even live TV) that have not been simplified or edited for use by students of Spanish. That is to say, authentic materials that were written for normal consumption by educated natives. Examples of reading materials might include:

- Daily newspapers published in Hispanic countries such as El país (Spain), La prensa (Argentina), Excelsior (Mexico), etc.
- Magazines such as Más (US Hispanics), GeoMundo (Mexico), Buen Hogar (International), Selecciones del Readers Digest (International), Américas, etc.
- Magazines for young people, including comic books, such as the Asterix series (Spain), Mafalda (Argentina), Mortadelo y Filemón (Spain), etc.
- Children's literature such as El gato con botas, La canción del coquí (Puerto Rico), Los osos dormilones, etc. There are Spanish editions of such American classics such as El gato en el sombrero (Dr. Suess), Carlitos (Peanuts), and almost all the Walt Disney classics.
- Young Adult/Teenage literature such as the books by Ana María Matute, the "Tradiciones" de Ricardo Palma, or the short stories by Jorge Luis Borges.
- Spanish editions of world classics such as: El principito, Mujercitas, Tom Sawyer, El hobbit, the Harry Potter books, etc.
- Great classics of Spanish literature, such as Don Quijote de la Mancha, Lazarillo de Tormes, El sombrero de tres picos, La dama del alba, Platero y yo, etc. Many of the great classics can be obtained in annotated editions that present the materials in the original but have notes, vocabularies, cultural explanations, etc. that are of immense help to students.
- A mind-boggling array of materials now available on the Internet. We are just beginning tap the resources that are now being

put on the "information highway" that range from commercial advertisements, to news summaries, to tourist information, to sports, to celebrities, to individual sites—all in Spanish! (See chapter 13 for the in-depth discussion of activities with the Internet.)

- Examples of listening comprehension materials might include:
- Audio recordings of children's stories, Cri-Cri (Mexico), etc.
- Segments from full-length films such as: El profe (Cantinflas), La historia oficial (Argentina), Valentina (Spain), Macario (Mexico), La Misión, Disney movies, almost all the movies that come out with DVD format have a Spanish sound track.
- Almost anything taken from TV such as commercials, news broadcasts, soap operas, documentaries, comedians, talk shows, etc. There are a number of "video magazines" which regularly download materials from TV in Hispanic countries. These materials come with guides for teacher use.

Let's now discuss some specific strategies and techniques that you can take in the classroom. We will consider them by language skill.

Speaking

The most obvious difference in this area is that *all* communication in and out of the classroom can be done in the foreign language. In beginning or intermediate classes there might be some occasional use of English to carry out certain tasks that could not be done in the foreign language. But there is no justification for using English in advanced classes, even outside the classroom.

At this level, students can be given much more personal responsibility for their preparation and participation in class activities. For example they can be assigned to research information outside class using books the Internet, interviewing natives, etc. and making oral reports or presentations in class. Teachers must be very sensitive to the fact that different configurations for evaluating and assigning grades must be used for oral presentations. (Refer to Chapter 12 for ways to evaluate oral production.)

Some oral activities you might use in an advanced class are:

- Oral reports
- Mini-dramas
- Present your own TV shows
- Make your own videos
- Noche de teatro
- Interviews with natives
- Debates
- Simulations

Guides for Oral Presentations. At the advanced level, students can take over a great deal of the responsibility for preparing oral presentations. However, a guide prepared by the teacher can be of immense help, especially by giving instructions about what to include, how to make the presentation, and how it will be graded. Following is an example of a guide for oral presentations. The teacher can make models similar to this to be used with debates, simulations, mini-dramas, and the like, adapted to the special features of the presentation.

MODELO PARA UNA PRESENTACIÓN ORAL

El estudiante debe seguir estos pasos:

1. Escoger el tópico (o tema) de su presentación.
2. Consultar con el/la profesor/a antes de comenzar el trabajo para recibir aprobación del tópico.
3. Buscar información sobre el tópico. Debes incluir más de dos de las siguientes fuentes:
   a. libros de referencia (enciclopedias, libros de historia, libros de países, libros de texto, etc.)
   b. periódicos y revistas
   c. informantes expertos (nativos, personas que han vivido en países hispanos, el/la profesor/a, etc.)
   d. videos, TV, películas, programas de computadoras, etc.
4. Preparar un borrador (draft) de lo que vas a presentar, escrito en español y usando el vocabulario que vas a usar en la presentación.
5. Mostrar el borrador a el/la profesor/a para recibir corrección de vocabulario y gramática y sugerencias en cuanto a la presentación
6. Buscar o preparar ayudas visuales (fotos, dibujos, mapas, PowerPoint, etc.) para usar en la presentación. También puedes pedir la ayuda de otras personas en la presentación
7. Fijar el día y la hora de la presentación en la clase.
8. Hacer la presentación

El estudiante puede recibir un máximo de 100 puntos por la presentación. La nota se basará en lo siguiente:

1. Contenido de la presentación (información, validez, etc.)   25 puntos
2. Ejecución (interesante?, límite de tiempo [10 minutos], mecánicas, etc.)   25 puntos
3. Uso del idioma (memorización, vocabulario, pronunciación)   25 puntos
4. Uso de ayudas visuales (fotos, mapas, dibujos, etc.)   25 puntos

Listening Comprehension

In advanced classes you can move totally away from "inter-language" or "teacher-language," the contrived language that teachers often use to make sure the students understand. You can now give them large doses of authentic listening comprehension experiences, allowing them to become accustomed to hearing and coping with input that they don't totally understand. Since you want them to hear a variety of ages, voices, and regional pronunciation you will make frequent use of videos, native visitors to the class, computer and CD ROM materials, etc. You would probably have daily activities of the following types:

- Watching and practicing with videos
- Interacting with native speakers
- Listening comprehension practice in the labs with audio, video and computer materials
- Practice with live TV programs, both in the class and at home if there are foreign language channels available.
- Segments of full-length movies on DVDs with Spanish soundtracks (not subtitles).

Practicing listening comprehension can be greatly enhanced with guides. Consider the following guide that the student would study before watching a video.

337

VIDEO GUIDE -FOR INDIVIDUAL WORK

Advance preparation

  The basic goal of working with these videos is to develop your ability to understand spoken Spanish. There is no shortcut to this skill, it simply requires many, many hours of listening to a wide variety of Spanish speakers, conditioning your ears to hear the words, and your brain to understand their meaning. If we were to give you a script to read as you listen, you would be able to understand more, but you would also become dependent upon seeing the words as you hear them, something you won't be able to do as you speak with natives in normal situations. You must reduce your visual dependency, learn to grit your teeth, concentrate on what people are saying, and learn to catch the gist of what is being said. After much practice you will suddenly realize that you are understanding without straining for meaning.

  We will prepare you for each video with a brief description of the situation and a list of key vocabulary words which you should be prepared to hear. We will also give you some ideas of what to look for and some cultural concepts to watch for. Study the guide carefully and work with the vocabulary before watching the video.   As you watch the video, write down any words you don't understand and look them up after you have seen the entire program.

  When you have seen the video in the lab, you will take a comprehension test. Correct your test with the key that you will find at the end of this booklet. When you have passed the comprehension test, hand it in to your teacher.

  Even after you have completed the assignment, if you enjoyed the video, watch it more times if you like. It will help develop your listening skills.

VIDEO #2
"LOS PAJARITOS"

---

1. **Situation.** The action takes place in Spain's capital and largest city, Madrid. It has large buildings, factories, a lot of industry, and many, many cars and trucks. The film focuses on a major problem of large cities, air pollution. Over the radio we hear the announcement that 30,200 birds have died that day alone. Two very sensitive old people, themselves very much like fluttering birds, are concerned. They want to help save the birds from dying from the pollution. They each sacrifice and sell something that they treasure very much. Watch to see what it is, because they are symbols of an age that is past. With the money they buy a bird and each has an adventure where the bird is almost lost. What do you think they decide to do to save their birds from death? Do you think it is practical?

2. **Culture.** As these old people embark upon their adventures, we see some wonderful scenes of life in a large city in Spain. The initial scenes of the video show the pollution, something that is becoming a problem in Spain. We then meet the old man and the old woman, and go with them to the *rastro* (flea market) where they sell valuable objects for money. We visit typical pet shops. We travel with them on a bus and a metro. Are they the same as the busses and metros in the U.S. or are they different?   Can the people make good-natured fun of the police in Spain? What is the reaction of a man who almost puts his arms around a nun? We visit a modern business office. What things do you see that are the same as in our country? Or different? (Hints: How many women work in the office? How are the workers dressed?) We see some typical types of transportation in Spain as we go from a bicycle, to a motorcycle, to a Seat 600, to delivery trucks, and finally to a fire truck, which is quite different from those we are used to. We see parks, plazas and the countryside around Madrid. We witness the courtesy and chivalry that are shown to older persons in Spain, and finally see how the old style of life is giving way to the new. What a delightful exchange between the little old lady and the captain of the *bomberos*!

3. **Language objectives.** Pay close attention to the words and expressions used. You will be able to learn a number of new words, such as pájaro, jaula, macho, contaminación, etc. You should be able to practice the formation of commands as we listen to the boss in the office and as we travel with the lady as she tries to catch the truck, giving several commands to each of her "drivers." Listen to the surprised expressions of each person as she takes over.

4. **Key vocabulary.** Before you view the video, be aware of the meaning of the following words and phrases.

la hembra...female (animal)
el macho...male (animal)

la jaula...cage
¡Esto es por querer echar al bote
    el pájaro!...That's what you get for wanting
    to put the bird in a cage!
¡Qué barbaridad!...How awful!
¡Qué manotas!...What huge hands!
echar una mano...to lend a hand
coger...to catch, grab, take
exagerar...to exaggerate
el camión...truck
¿No le parece?...Don't you think so?
la estación   subway stop
¡Intentémoslo de nuevo!...Let's try again!

el humo...smoke
la contaminación atmosférica
    ...pollution
la campana...bell
el bombero...fireman
darse prisa...to hurry up
distraerse...to get distracted
el trino...call of a bird
¡Qué mona!...How nice, pretty!
el banco...bench
seguir...follow
el uniforme...uniform
el parasol (quitasol)...the parasol
el parque...the park
el canario (la canaria)...canary

Follow this sequence while working in the lab:
1. Read the GUIDE.
2. Study the vocabulary.
3. Practice the vocabulary, using the WORK SHEET. Check your work with the key.
4. Watch the video.
5. Take the COMPREHENSION TEST and correct it with the key. If you passed (7 points or more), you can hand your test in to your professor and move to another video.
(6. If you did not pass the test, repeat the sequence. As a last resort you can go over the script that is included in the GUIDE.)

[A comprehension test with key, and practice sheets follow.]

Writing

While most of the writing activities at beginning and intermediate levels were limited to filling in blanks, writing summaries, or practical uses such as taking notes or writing letters, in advanced classes you can require more sophisticated and complicated uses of writing.

With the new emphasis on proficiency, we do not look at writing simply as a way to evaluate progress with grammar. We now start with purpose and audience—with reader perception. Writing is much more subjective and personal. We now consider **process** as the driving factor; therefore we emphasize invention, discovery, risk-taking, sharing, exploring, interacting, and valuing (meaningful context). The intentions of the writer can be negotiated. The **content,** however, must be important and under control of the student who has "final say." The teacher coaches or facilitates the writing by building with the student.

Learning to write is not just a matter of acquiring basic skills or repairing errors. Many older students will need special motivation to provide reasons and purposes for this exploratory, inquiring approach to writing. The task must match the student's intentions after a genuine invention or a real search. Teachers give up their all-knowing positions, their scepters of power ("sage on the stage") for coaching, facilitating, encouraging, behind-the-scenes shadow leadership ("guide on the side"). We help make things happen.

In the higher stage seen above, we are beginning to get close to the realm of the composition courses that characterize the general freshman English courses. We certainly hope that we can do a better job in teaching advanced writing than we have in the past. Some have even accused our Spanish teachers of not being able to write very effectively in Spanish, or worse, not being able to write in their native language. With the emphasis on **writing across the curriculum** we just have to do a better job of teaching writing and of being able to model good writing in both English and Spanish. We suggest that you concentrate on reaching high goals with your advanced students in writing Spanish. It certainly is important to prepare future teachers of Spanish in the realm of advanced writing as well as in oral proficiency—a much more ambitious objective. Our experience also confirms that grammar is internalized best through meaningful experience in speaking and writing both in its own right as a communication modality as well as in its support mode extending the speaking modality.

Considerations for Developing Writing for Communication Abilities in Advanced Classes. As you design writing activities for communication you will use rather broad strokes; remember the teacher facilitates or coaches. The student is helped to make decisions or invent or, at least, think through most of these considerations as appropriate for the stage and level.

1. **Purpose.** What are "real world" reasons for writing? To recall information? To organize ideas for speaking? To express feelings? To question? To convince? To entertain? To impress? To inform?

2. **Topic.** If we have a purpose for writing the topic will be much easier to come by. What is familiar to the student growing out of the

purpose? Having something to say is of primary importance--about 90% of the task. Knowledge, interest, and expertise *of the student* must be foremost in choosing a topic.

3. **Audience.** To whom or for whom are we writing? What will the reader need to know? These questions help us decide questions of information, detail, format, and the style and correctness of the language.

4. **Tasks or Functions.** What tasks are to be performed? explanation? description? narration? argumentation? persuasion? Answers to these questions are needed to guide the student.

5. **Plan.** What is needed to get started? Time to write? Place to write? What does the teacher do? What context of activities? Feedback? How are the consequences of writing related to original purpose?

6. **Resources.** What tools are needed? The students must decide and then suit the resources to their purposes. The teacher can help the student with:

   - Generating ideas
   - Organizing ideas
   - Language--word/sentence, paragraph, vocabulary, structures
   - Strategies--lst draft, revision, editing, proofreading

A revelation of "inner working." Language teachers rapidly discover that having the students do communicative writing has special value in revealing what the students' "inner selves" are doing in terms of their progress toward mastery of the language. Perhaps more than any other activity a written composition reveals the inner working of a person's language skills in general.

Topics for the third and fourth years. In Chapter Four in our discussion of goals and objectives, we gave you some ideas for topics that would be appropriate for these levels. In addition, you probably have selected a good textbook that will probably treat those topics plus additional possibilities. Be sure that the topic selected contains ideas for the discourse connectors that are so typical of Spanish communication. Consider such topics as: health and fitness, careers and professions, and travel and vacations, as well as various controversial themes and various literary themes.

We need to be sure that students are able to get acquainted with the abstract themes in this stage and get started with hypothesizing and also defending opinions. Plan your units to include lots of writing assignments, especially paragraph writing and composition writing. Some of the topics in current textbooks include the following: *Estereotipos, Mundo del trabajo, ~ Guerra o paz?, Ambiente, Problema de la gente mayor,* among many others. All of these could be introduced, supplemented, or featured by short stories and even appropriate poetry. Journalistic writing could be introduced at this stage. This would give the students ideas to ponder and then to react to in writing through interpretation or expressions of feeling or rewriting or for some even possible limitation. The student should become proficient in paragraph writing and should become acquainted with composition writing. Many will even become proficient in writing compositions. [See "Suggestions for Further Reading" for some of the current intermediate level textbooks.]

Some activities might include:

- Writing longer compositions on more difficult topics
- Writing articles in the foreign language
- for school or class newspapers
- Writing stories, poetry, etc. to be published in a class or school magazine
- Writing up results of research in the form of reports
- Having the students select a special event or adventure from history or real life, using the "you are there" technique. For example, Paul Revere's ride, Columbus' discovery of America, Neil Armstrong stepping on the moon, living through a hurricane, a heavy snowstorm, etc. In this activity the students need to include setting, characters, point of view, and action.

Additional topics or themes. In addition to the topics listed above, we certainly should include creative writing of essays, stories, poems, plays, possibly novels, and the like so that we will have a **get acquainted phase** in the higher stage along with the **doing phase** as represented in the topics, tasks, and accuracy indicated.

Writing Centers or Labs. Learning centers in language classrooms typically feature listening comprehension activities, augmented by video activities—including interactive video with the computer. Any writing done with the computer for the activities in these listening and viewing centers is usually in the support mode. But why not set up a *writing center* along with these other learning centers? The writing center could feature word processors and allow the students to engage in prewriting activities that would lead to composition writing. Adjacent to the writing center could be reading and listening centers where students could steep themselves in Spanish experiences in reading and listening which hopefully would set them up to write in Spanish without thinking in English. Another learning center for writing purposes could be the peer review center where groups of students or pairs of students could read each other's prewriting exercises, each other's paragraphs and compositions. These learning centers can be established areas in the classroom indicated by a butcher paper label on the wall for each separate center, or the room could be supplied with room dividers to make a more formal set of sub-rooms.

Ways to write about literature. There are many ways to approach writing about literature. Consider the following:

- Writing for self-discovery
- Journal
- Parody
- Reformulation in another literary or artistic medium
- Writing in the style of ...
- Summary
- Paraphrasing
- Research report
- Thesis centered research paper
- Thesis centered critical essay
- Personal narrative
- Essay from various critical perspectives
- Research on function of literature in people's lives (family, self, friends)

- Research on various personal responses to literary texts
- Writing about personal literary forms (dreams, jokes, lit in family, stories, genealogy, personal folklore)
- Writing about experience, feelings, reactions
- Writing about observations
- Formulating theses
- Experimentation through writing
- Writing personal mythology in style of Greeks, Romans
- Writing about personal myths, dreams—what is their structure? themes? etc.

Writing research articles. A whole series of activities can be centered around writing articles and research papers in this higher stage. We should begin to acquaint the students with writing research papers. It is possible in this stage that we can achieve the doing phase.

A final word about translation. Probably the most advanced and most difficult writing is in translation. We have commented that translation is a skill apart from direct reading and writing in Spanish. It involves operating in a two-language process that we try to avoid when our goal is communication. If you have students interested in translation as a profession, you may want to consider teaching a mini course in that area. These students need to be very proficient in Spanish and have excellent writing skills in English. For Americans, translating from Spanish to English is recommended. We definitely need a genius to translate from the native language into the foreign language. Universities and translation institutes have entire courses for training translators and interpreters that terminate in a translator's diploma or certificate. If you have students who want to enter that profession, you can guide them to one of those programs.

Reading

One of the most enjoyable benefits of advanced classes is that as the students become proficient they can begin reading directly and without translation from interesting and motivating works written by authors for native speakers of the language, not students just beginning to learn the language. One of the

great satisfactions we will have as Spanish teachers is to share with our students the pleasure of reading something well written. With preparation and help from the teacher, our students can savor some of the great literary masterpieces, even if only in selected pieces. How much more will they appreciate the humor of Cervantes as they read of the efforts by Don Quijote to provide a name for his horse and his lady fair and discover how he came up with Rocinante and Dulcinea when they understand what a *rocín* is and what *dulce* means.

The motivation of the students increases dramatically as they get beyond the "Juan y María son alumnos" level and begin reading works that are really interesting. At first, they will work with edited materials. Most of the current textbooks prepared for advanced classes include some adapted versions of some fine literary gems. Fortunately, if your text does not have interesting reading, there are many readers available which provide a huge variety and range of difficulty.

The materials commonly used in intermediate classes have usually been edited, some of the complex grammatical structure simplified, and the extremely rare vocabulary replaced with more common words. There are usually glosses and footnotes to help with difficult passages or especially troublesome words, and cultural notes to help the students understand the context.

If we follow the current trend toward use of *authentic* materials in our advanced classes, we will give our students original, unedited works, that have few of the aids mentioned above. That means that we as teachers have to supplement the process with a great deal of pre-reading preparation. In these classes, more than ever, we must put the principles of **ACT MAPS GUIDE** (which we studied in Chapter 8) into practice. Let's briefly review them here in the context of advanced reading.

> **APT** = Advanced Preparation of the Teacher

You must always have read a work before you assign your students to read it. Your personal reading will concentrate on the areas of vocabulary, culture, motivation and the preparation of guide materials that will help the students to focus on the most important aspects of the work.

MAPS = Motivation and Advanced Preparation of the Students

Before sending the students home to read, activate their background knowledge about the topic and genre. Help them with key or difficult vocabulary words, cultural explanations, and guidelines of what to look for. Do they need to look for characterization, foreshadowing, symbolism, and examples of fantasy? If you prepare them with enthusiasm and some introduction to the conflict, mystery, and style of the work, your students will have such great interest that they can hardly wait to start reading.

GUIDE = Get them using, interacting, and discussing what they have read

---

When the students come back to class after having read an assignment, they need the reinforcement of seeing that others understood the same things they did. They may have questions to be answered and need to be led to a full understanding and appreciation of what they have read. We no longer have students take turns translating paragraphs of the reading selection into stiff, stilted English. Rather, we now spend the class hour discussing the content or plot, talking about the ideas the author presents, reading parts together, and appreciating the beauty of something well written. (And all this in the foreign language, of course.) At the end, some sort of evaluating instrument, such as a reading quiz or a written summary, could be made to assess their comprehension and understanding.

A Model for Teaching Advanced Reading

Following is a model of how you as a teacher can put the preceding concepts into practice with reading assignments in an advanced Spanish class. We have used *La dama del alba*, by Alejandro Casona, a popular Spanish playwright, as the text for this model because it contains all the features we hope to find in advanced reading materials. As a play, it is in dialogue format, so the students need to adjust to the use of the *tú* and *vosotros* forms, and pay attention to the stage instructions. The play is a beautiful example of motivating reading: it is well-written; it is full of cultural information about Hispanic life, especially in Asturias, a region in Northern Spain; and there is mystery, romance, and suspense which keeps the students reading far into the night.

Student Guide. We suggest that you prepare guide materials to give the students before they begin their reading. Following is a guide prepared to give to students before they begin reading Act I of *La dama del alba*. Notice that some of the situation is described to help the students understand, but not too much is revealed that would give away what is going to happen. Notice also that we have asked questions to guide the students in what to look for. The cultural explanation is given because the students would not understand references to the region, the traditions, or the customs of the characters in the play. And finally, we have selected in advance the key words the students will need to know to understand the main content of the reading.

La dama del alba - **Guía del estudiante**

Reading Skills. Since *La dama del alba* is a play intended to be seen on a stage, you should understand that it is very important to read the instructions to the actors and descriptions of the scenes. These are usually in italics or in parentheses. If you saw the play presented in a theater, you would see the scenery and would hear and see the actions of the actors. Since you will not see and hear anything, you must gain this information by reading it. Notice also, that since the story takes place in Spain, the plural of *tú*, *vosotros* is used. You need to get accustomed to those forms.

Advance preparation. We will prepare you for each reading selection with a brief description of the situation and a list of key vocabulary words that will help you understand what you are reading. We will also give you some ideas of what to look for and some cultural concepts to watch for. Go over this carefully before you read. Skim through the assignment once to get a general idea of what it is about. Then read a second time, trying to understand almost everything. Then go over it a third time to digest, ponder, and think about what you might comment on in class or parts you have questions on. We will always have a quiz at the beginning of class, so try to anticipate what questions might be asked. Whatever you do, don't go to class unprepared.

Act I

Situation. The story begins on an early winter afternoon, in a rural area of Asturias. We meet a family that lives in a small *aldea* situated at the edge of a river. The family is just finishing eating and Martin is preparing to go up into the mountains to bring down some young bulls to the fair being held the next day. Quico (a young hired hand who works for the family) has saddled the mare, but we see later that there has been a mysterious change. The day is the fourth anniversary of the disappearance of Angélica in the river. The barking of the dogs announces the arrival of a mysterious guest. Pay particular attention to the strange things she says and does. Because of her clothing and walking stick, the children assume she is a pilgrim going to Santiago, and from that point on she is referred to as la Peregrina. After playing with the children she is very tired and falls asleep, even though she has an appointment at 9 p.m.

Characters. Who are the family members, and what are their relationships with each other? Try to get a feeling for the characters--remember this is a play, and if we saw it represented we would build empathy or antipathy for each actor. It is said that the abuelo represents the men of that region of Spain--why? How does his manner of speaking indicate to us what he is like? The madre is typical of many Spanish women--in what ways? Telva is very different from the Madre, yet she is also a typical Spanish woman--how? What is unusual about the children? Would they like to be normal? What is Quico's personality like? How does he react to Telva's penchant for gossip? Does Martin's personality fit his actions the night Angélica disappeared?

Style. What a great picture Casona draws of his native Asturias! What can we learn of the region from the first act? What characters does Casona use to express humor? (Hint: pp. 2-3, p. 8) Do we see elements of *lo fantástico* in the first act. What examples can you find of *simbolismo*? (Hint: pp. 21-22) *Presagio* is the word we use in Spanish for "foreshadowing." How many examples can you find of *presagio*? (Hints: pp. 20-21, p. 24)

344

Culture. Your teacher will talk to you about the region of Asturias and its location on the *"Camino a Santiago."* This will help you understand the obligation the inhabitants feel toward *"peregrinos"* who are making the pilgrimage to the sacred city of Santiago de Compostela.

Language Objectives. Not only will you be increasing your reading vocabulary as you learn new words, you will continue building your conversational skills as you discuss the reading in class and as you participate in activities where you will recreate many of the scenes of the play. Prepare yourself for these activities and try to make the vocabulary become active in your use of the language, not just a passive recognition of words as you read them.

Key Vocabulary. As you read the first act, be aware of the meaning of key words and phrases, such as the following. You will use these words in discussing your reading.

casa de labranza-farmhouse	la silla (de montar)-saddle	morir-to die
el horno (de leña)-oven	la espuela-spur	muerto(a)-dead
el remanso-backwater	el potro-colt	la muerte-death
la balsa (barca)-boat	el portón-(corral) gate	acercarse-to go near to
el molino-mill	el (la) peregrino(a)-pilgrim	ahogarse-to drown
la braña-summer pasture	el yerno-son-in-law	envenenar-to poison
la yegua-mare	el quinqué-kerosene lamp	ensillar (ensillada)-to put a
el jinete-horseman, rider	el granero-barn	saddle on (saddled)
el paso-the (mountain) pass	la mina (de carbón)-coal mine	domar-to break (a horse)
el relámpago-bolt of lightning	la capucha-hood	ladrar-to bark
la feria-(animal) fair	el bordón/bastón-walkingstick	aullar-to howl
el ganado-farm animals	la boda-wedding	reír(se)-to laugh
....the list continues	......the list continues	......the list continues

In-class preparation. The teacher can spend a good deal of time in the class prior to sending the students home to read. Much of the same material in the guide can be presented orally, such as discussion of important vocabulary, cultural information, and motivation. Following is a model of the kinds of preparation the teacher can do in the class prior to reading:

La dama del alba - Guía del profesor
PREPARACIÓN Y MOTIVACIÓN
(En la clase el día anterior a la lectura de los estudiantes)

Preparación *(Ideas / conceptos / cultura)*

- Vamos a leer un drama, no podrán ver las acciones, el decorado. Hay que leer las descripciones e instrucciones (entre paréntesis, en itálicas)
- Alejandro Casona (Rodríguez) Nombre de pluma, nacido en un pueblo de Asturias, padres maestros de escuela, vivía en una casona, cuentos de su abuela de fantasías y leyendas, amor de su patria
- (Leer la dedicatoria del autor), costumbres, fiestas, etc.
- Asturias-¿Dónde está? (Mapa) ¿Cómo es? ¿Clima? (verde, ríos, montañas, bosques, minas de carbón), agricultura, ganado, caballos, ferias, perros, molinos, braña
- Camino a Santiago (de Compostela) Los restos del apóstol santo, lugar sagrado, peregrinos, el deber de ser hospitalarios
- Caballos: jinete, yegua, domar, potro, silla (de montar), ensillar, corral, portón, relinchar, espuelas

---

Motivación

- Habrá una prueba (Lean y podrán contestar)
- Vamos a conocer una familia: madre, criada (Telva), abuelo, niños -- Andrés, Dorina, Falín -- ¿Qué hacen niños de estas edades? Estos no. No van a la escuela, no juegan, no gritan, no se ríen, etc. ¿Quieren saber por qué? Lean el primer acto.
- Había otra hija: Angélica. ¿Dónde está? ¿Por qué no vive más con la familia? ¿Quieren saber? Lean...
- Llega una mujer misteriosa. ¿Quién será? ¿Qué querrá? ¿Cómo será, vieja y fea o joven y hermosa? ¿Quieren saber? Lean el primer acto.

Key Vocabulary. *(The teacher would use the same vocabulary prepared for the Student's Guide)*

Comprehension quiz, discussion, and in-class commentary. What do you do with the students in class after they return from having read the assignment? We would suggest that the first activity be a simple comprehension quiz that would allow the students to demonstrate they understood what they read. The questions on the quiz should be of the type that the students who have read the assignment can answer easily but the students who have not read cannot answer. This motivation is essential to a meaningful class discussion. There is nothing more painful than trying to carry on a discussion of a reading selection which only one or two students have read.

Traditionally teachers would check students' comprehension by having them translate the entire reading assignment paragraph for paragraph. This is a carry over from the old grammar translation method. With the new emphasis on reading for meaning, no translation need be made. Comprehension can be determined by asking information questions, eliciting student comments on certain aspects of what they read, and asking opinions about the content. Frequently the teacher should read important passages out loud (while the students follow along with their texts) dramatizing, emphasizing, and pausing for comments. Having the students read with stumbling and uncertain pronunciation and comprehension only drags the activity out and becomes very boring.

With the teacher leading a lively discussion, the plot is moved ahead and the students are drawn in to the action and become involved with their emotions and opinions.

Oral practice of reading. It is very important to make the reading of advanced materials a continued support of listening and speaking development. That is, we need to create a number of activities that will allow the students to use the vocabulary and information gained from their reading to practice their communication skills. Examples of activities of this kind are:

- Read important passages together and comment on them.
- Role-play some of the scenes.
- Put on some of the scenes as a sort of play and video them.
- Have debates on some controversial topics that have come up in the reading.
- Have students give oral reports on some aspects of the reading materials.

Following is a model of activities that could be conducted the day following classroom discussion and commentary.

La dama del alba **ACTIVIDADES DE PRÁCTICA** – El día después de la lectura

1. Una tarjeta postal a los padres (1 a 5 personas)

Uno o dos estudiantes están de vacaciones en Asturias y escriben una postal a sus padres describiendo la región, las personas que viven allí (luego leen sus postales a la clase).

2. Noticiero de televisión (2 personas)

Un locutor (locutora) de televisión presenta las noticias del accidente de la mina:

"Una gran tragedia pasó ayer en un pueblo de Asturias . . ." etc.

Describe la situación: una explosión, parece que hay muertos, etc.

Menciona que va a pasar la transmisión a su colega (corresponsal) que está en el pueblo.

El segundo locutor(a) (que se supone está en el pueblo) habla de la situación: "A las 4 de la

"No sc sabc nada dc la causa....." etc.

"Ha habido muchos muertos....." etc.

"Los mineros están tratando de salvar la vida de personas que todavía están en la mina..." etc.

"Ha tenido gran efecto en los habitantes del pueblo....." etc.

"Hay una mujer que perdió siete hijos...." etc.

"Ella misma lavó los cuerpos de sus hijos......" etc.

"Les daremos más noticias en cuanto sepamos algo nuevo....." etc.

3. Noticiero de televisión (2 personas)

Un locutor de televisión presenta las noticias de la muerte de Angélica en el remanso:

- "Una gran tragedia pasó anoche en un pueblo de Asturias........" etc.
- Describe la situación: "Una de las chicas más populares del pueblo desapareció en el remanso. La chica se había casado sólo hace tres días con uno de los jóvenes principales del pueblo. Hasta ahora no han encontrado su cuerpo." etc.
- Menciona que va a pasar la transmisión a su colega (corresponsal) que está en el pueblo...

El segundo locutor(a) (que se supone está en el pueblo) habla de la situación:

- "Angélica de Narcés, quien sólo tenía tres días de estar casada con Martín de Narcés, uno de los principales ganaderos del pueblo, se ahogó anoche en el remanso del río. La chica habría pasado por este lugar miles de veces en su vida aquí en el pueblo. No hay muchos detalles, pero se cree que trataba de cruzar el río para ir al pueblo. Todavía no han encontrado su cuerpo aunque los del pueblo han pasado toda la noche buscando. Lo único que han encontrado es su pañuelo..." etc.
- "Hemos tratado de tener una entrevista con su esposo, pero él se ha encerrado en su cuarto y se niega a hablar con nadie....." etc.
- "La madre está muy angustiada y dice que.............." etc.
- "Sus hermanos están muy tristes porque........." etc.
- "Los del pueblo siguen buscando su cadáver, y en cuanto sepamos algo, se lo comunicaremos....."etc.

---

4. Escena de la llegada de la Peregrina (6 personas)

Abuelo: El perro ladra mucho, alguien viene, ¿Quién será?, etc.

Telva: No me gustan personas misteriosas, ¡Qué se vaya al pueblo!, etc.

Dorina: ¡Qué hermosa es, parece una reina!, etc.

Madre: ¿Quién es usted? ¿Por qué viene a nuestra casa?, etc.

(Andrés y Falín) ¿Está cansada?. ¿Quiere jugar con nosotros?, etc.

---

5. Escena de la salida de Martín (3 personas)

Martín: Tengo que ir a la braña, tengo que traer unos novillos a la feria, etc.

Quico: La yegua está ensillada, está en el corral, etc.

Madre: ¿Tienes que ir esta noche?, ¿Por qué no te quedas en casa? Es el aniversario de la muerte de Angélica, El paso del Rabión es muy peligroso, etc.

---

6. Escena de la vida de los niños (5 personas)

Andrés: Mamá, queremos salir a jugar, etc.

Dorina: Queremos ir a la escuela para aprender a leer y escribir, etc.

Falín: Nunca podemos reír o gritar como otros niños, etc.

Madre: ¡No! No quiero que paséis por el río, No quiero que os pase lo que le pasó a Angélica, etc.

Telva: Hay que olvidar el pasado. Los niños deben ser normales, deben ir a la escuela, etc.

---

7. Conversación entre Martín y la Peregrina (3 personas)

Peregrina: Buenas noches. Usted en Martín de Narcés, ¿verdad? ¿A dónde va? ¿Va a pasar por el rabión? ¿Me permite hacer un acto de humildad?. etc.

Martín: Perdone. No la había visto. ¿Quién es usted? etc.

Madre: Es una Peregrina. Va a cumplir una promesa, etc.

TEACHING LITERATURE

In very advanced classes, the teacher may be able to make a major shift in the objectives of the class. Understanding and appreciation of literature may become the primary goal and development of language skills may become secondary.

You perhaps recall how in some of your college literature classes the focus was entirely on literary criticism. Sometimes those courses, even though they dealt with literature written in a foreign language, were taught in English. This can be justified because the objectives of those courses were to learn about style, literary techniques, and literary movements. But we should not forget that in even in literature classes many students are still working on language development and we should always find ways to help them continue developing language skills as they learn appreciation of literature.

In these highly advanced classes we can delve more into the style of the author and discuss some of the literary techniques that he/she employs to get certain effects or results. For example, foreshadowing, use of first person, use of dialogues, etc. We can discuss why the author uses specific vocabulary, slang, or regional or dialectical expressions. We can analyze plays on words and decide what makes something humorous. We can analyze poetry and marvel at the images that a great poet can bring to our minds. In short we can help our students to learn to enjoy, in the target language, the rewards of reading great literature.

The study of literature requires special skills that many of our students well may not have. To jump right into a literature class appreciation, perhaps hoping that they learned those basics in their high school literature classes, is a foolhardy undertaking. We highly recommend, at both high school and college levels, that a preliminary introduction to the basic elements of literary appreciation. There are a number of textbooks that can help you do this, some in Spanish, and some in English with Spanish selections to be read.

Another caution we would add is that the teacher make every effort possible to lighten the burden of the works the students are assigned to read. As teachers we are in a position to prepare the students in such a way as to make their reading easier, more understandable, and much more enjoyable. We suggest one more time the timeless principles of **APT MAPS GUIDE** that we reviewed above.

Sending our students home to read authentic materials without preparation can be so discouraging that any enjoyment the students might have had disappears and the reading now becomes a chore. We need to carefully preview the reading selections ourselves, anticipate the linguistic, vocabulary, and cultural obstacles which will hinder their understanding, and then spend class time discussing the literary aspects that we want them to understand.

SPECIAL CLASSES FOR HERITAGE SPEAKERS OF SPANISH

Because of the enormous number of Spanish speakers immigrating to the U.S. in recent decades, it is quite possible that you will have students in your classes who are already fluent or semi-fluent in the language. In the past these students were usually referred to as "native speakers." However, Spanish-speaking students who were raised in the U.S. often do not have the same skill set as other "native speakers" and do not consider themselves natives; therefore, these students are now referred to as "heritage speakers" of Spanish, or learners of Spanish as a heritage language (SHL).

Heritage learners of Spanish are not a homogenous group. They vary in terms of their Spanish proficiency and the variety of Spanish that they speak, as well as in their general academic skills. Those who are recent immigrants from a Spanish-speaking country where they attended school are generally fluent speakers of a standard variety of Spanish and often have excellent academic skills. In contrast, those who

come from families of migrant workers may have no exposure to written Spanish and may lack academic skills. Still others who grew up in the U.S. may have developed some academic ability in English but not in Spanish. Most of them hear Spanish in the home and have good listening comprehension, but may speak English with their siblings and friends. Their formal education has probably been in English and consequently their reading and writing skills in Spanish have never been developed.

Some SHL students naturally have high interest in their heritage and enroll in Spanish classes in secondary schools; others are placed in these classes by counselors or administrators. Typically they are placed in traditional Spanish-as-a-foreign-language classes with native English-speaking students. This can cause several problems. Unlike traditional foreign language (FL) students, SHL students do not need to develop the basic vocabulary and listening comprehension skills that are taught in first- and second-year classes. On the other hand, they may struggle with Spanish spelling conventions that foreign language students have already mastered, and are probably unfamiliar with grammatical concepts and terminology. Conversely, the native English-speaking students may resent the heritage speakers because they already have a wide range of everyday vocabulary, well-developed listening skills, and sometimes considerable speaking skills. In light of the differences between SHL and FL students, it is advisable to create separate courses for these two groups rather than attempting to meet the needs of both groups in a single program.

Needs of SHL Students

As has been pointed out, SHL learners have many and varying needs. Depending on their background, these needs may include the following:

Learning a "prestige variety" of Spanish. Many SHL students speak rural varieties of Spanish, which may be stigmatized or seen as inferior to more standard varieties. In order to fully develop their Spanish skills, they learn the differences between the standard and other varieties of the language, and when it is appropriate to use each.

Learning literacy skills in Spanish. As previously mentioned, many SHL students have never learned to read and write in Spanish, which can actually handicap them in their schoolwork in English. Research shows that the development of students' literacy skills in a second language is strongly related to their first language literacy skills. When SHL students' Spanish development is discontinued before it is completed, they may experience negative cognitive effects in their English development, which can handicap them throughout their academic career. This may be a key factor contributing to the achievement gap between Latino students and other students. For these students, learning to read and write in Spanish may enhance their ability to succeed in their academic content classes in English.

Learning general academic skills. Another factor contributing to the achievement gap for Latino students is that they may need help negotiating the U.S. school system and developing academic skills. Part of the difficulty is that parents of Latino students have, on average, significantly less education than non-Latino parents, and often have little or no proficiency in English, which limits their ability to provide scholastic support for their children.

Learning challenging academic content in Spanish. This is especially important for students with limited English proficiency. English language learners do not have the luxury of waiting to study academic content in English until their language skills have caught up, and consequently they tend to fall behind their native-English-speaking peers in their schoolwork. Bilingual coursework in both Spanish and English can help prevent these students from falling behind academically while they are learning to function in an English-speaking academic setting.

Learning to value their Spanish heritage. Many students from SHL backgrounds view Spanish as an informal language that has little value outside their home and family. They may also avoid using Spanish because they have internalized messages about its inferiority or undesirability in U.S. society. They need to learn the value of knowing more than one language and culture.

Implications for SHL Instruction

The abovementioned needs of SHL learners have a number of implications for classroom instruction. Among them are the following:

- **Teach Spanish writing conventions.** SHL students may have little or no experience writing in Spanish. They tend to produce forms like *baser* (for "va a hacer"), *deven* (for "deben"), *empesamos*, *orita,* and *nomas.* They will need to be taught the mechanics of writing in Spanish -- spelling, punctuation, and use of accents.

- **Help students recognize the difference between formal and informal language**. SHL speakers may have grown up speaking informal varieties of Spanish, using forms like *haiga* (for "haya") or adding an "s" to the *tú* forms of the verbs, like *tú fuistes* or *tú comistes.* In addition, because they live in an English-speaking environment, they may mix in a lot of English words with their Spanish (code switch), or "hispanize" English words: *troca* (truck), *bracas* (brakes), *marqueta* (market), *pushear* (to push), or *mopear* (to mop).

Potowski (2001) points out that while it is important to teach SHL students academic Spanish, it is equally important not to devalue the varieties of Spanish that the students have grown up using. She suggests using the terms "formal" and "informal" instead of "standard" and "nonstandard" when giving feedback to heritage students. Potowski cites the useful "beach-wedding" metaphor of Zentella (1997):

> When people go to the beach, they wear shorts, sandals, and other appropriate beach attire. When they go to a wedding, they wear suits, dresses, and other formal apparel. Wearing shorts and sandals to a wedding is very likely to be considered inappropriate, but we do not throw away those items just because we are attending a wedding, nor do we call them inherently wrong. As with language, we choose what is most appropriate for the situation. It is not the job of [teachers] to "fix" the Spanish of bilingual students, but rather to teach them additional, more formal speech styles. (Potowski, 2001, p. 102)

- **Teach reading and writing strategies.** SHL students need to learn reading strategies such as skimming, scanning, using extratextual clues (titles, subheadings), and distinguishing main ideas from supporting details. Likewise, writing strategies such as outlining, rereading and revising what has been written, reorganizing and combining can be helpful. Techniques for teaching these strategies are discussed in Chapters 8 and 9.

- **Read texts in a variety of genres.** SHL students who are reading in Spanish for the first time may benefit from reading simple, familiar texts, including emails, recipes, menus, instructions, advertisements, and application forms. More advanced students should have the opportunity to read literary texts by famous Hispanic authors, including short stories, novels, and poetry, as well as journalistic and informative texts such as magazine and newspaper articles. The Internet can provide a source for many of these texts.

- **Provide writing opportunities in a variety of genres**. Even SHL students who have never written in Spanish before can write simple autobiographical descriptions and dialogue journal entries. More advanced students need practice in creative writing, such as stories or poetry, and expository writing, such as reports and essays.

- **Assign students to work on projects from other subject areas (math, science, etc.) in Spanish.** This practice helps students develop the academic vocabulary they need in order to succeed in school.

- **Arrange for extracurricular programs to help SHL learners.** One effective activity is to have SHL students run tutoring programs or homework clubs to help their peers; this can help the tutors become more active in school activities, raise their grades, and improve their self esteem. You may also consider organizing an academic competition where SHL students from different schools compete against each other in Spanish on a variety of school topics.

- **Help SHL learners involve their parents.** Latino parents are often uninvolved in their children's schooling due to lack of knowledge of English and of the U.S. school system. SHL students could be assigned to develop a bilingual brochure for Latino students and their parents with important information about their

school. Another possibility is to create blogs or wikis in Spanish where students and their parents can ask questions and share information about school and college.

- **Help students understand the value of being bilingual and bicultural.** Teachers of heritage speakers of Spanish often need to help their students learn to recognize the advantages of knowing more than one language and culture. These advantages include increased communicative ability (with implications for employment, travel, and social interaction); improved academic achievement in English; and the ability to appreciate diverse cultural perspectives, beliefs, and values.

Establishing an SHL Program

Because the needs of SHL students differ from those of traditional foreign language students, SHL students get little benefit from first- and second-year Spanish classes, and even advanced classes may not fully meet their academic needs. These students need specialized classes that prepare them with literacy skills and subject matter knowledge in Spanish, as well as academic skills in both Spanish and English.

If you find yourself with large numbers of SHL learners in your classes, you may need to take the lead in advocating for the creation of separate classes for these students. In most cases this will involve convincing the school principal and other administrators of the need for these classes; it may involve talking with school counselors and other faculty members as well.

You might start by asking administrators and policymakers to read articles summarizing the needs of SHL students (such as the ERIC Digest by Peyton, Lewelling, & Winke listed at the end of this chapter) and then scheduling a follow-up meeting to discuss the reading. In this meeting, you can emphasize that SHL students' needs cannot be fully met in either existing Spanish classes or ESL classes, and ask about the possibility of creating separate classes for SHL students. It may also be helpful to point out the increasing availability of textbooks and other curricular materials designed to meet the needs of these students.

In deciding what level of SHL classes to offer, consider the backgrounds of your students as well as the resources of your school. For example, if it is feasible to create only one SHL class, and there are large numbers of students with no academic experience in Spanish, along with a few immigrant students who attended school in their home country, the first group could be accommodated in a beginning SHL class, while the immigrant students could enroll in Spanish 3, 4, or AP.

Resources for SHL Programs

In the past decade, resources for teachers of SHL/SNS classes have become increasingly available. Many textbook publishers now produce books for SHL learners. In addition, many traditional Spanish textbooks now offer supplementary materials for heritage language learners. These materials are listed on the publishers' websites, and in some cases may be available online. A good example of these materials can be found at the Houghton Mifflin Harcourt   site: http://www.hmhschool.com/School/index.html (see the "Lectura" section).

Several helpful collections of research and teaching techniques for SHL students have been published in book form. Among them are Columbi and Alarcón's *La esneñanza del español a hispanohblantes* (1997); Roca and Columbi's *Mi lengua: Spanish as a Heritage Language in the United States, Research and Practice* (2003); and the AATSP's *Spanish for Native Speakers* (2000).

Other resources for SHL teachers include an online database on heritage language programs in community and K-12 settings, maintained by the Center for Applied Linguistics (available at http://www.cal.org/heritage/profiles/index.html), as well as a database and resources being developed by the National Heritage Language Resource Center (available at http://www.international.ucla.edu/languages/nhlrc/index.asp).

Dealing with Mixed Classes

Unfortunately, administrative constraints may prevent the creation of SHL classes, leaving you with some heritage speakers in your regular classes. The presence of the heritage speakers in the class can be a positive situation if the teacher cultivates their friendship and cooperation and

uses their skills to reinforce what the other students are learning. However, the teacher must be careful not to appear to be favoring them.

Fortunately, many of the above techniques for teaching heritage learners can be applied in traditional FL classrooms. In addition, you can address the needs of SHL students in mixed classes through techniques such as the following:

- **Assess SHL students' strengths and weaknesses**. Some publishers of SNS textbooks offer diagnostic tests to assess students' knowledge of Spanish and their proficiency in the four skills, their knowledge of grammar and vocabulary, or both. You can administer these tests early in the year and use the results to plan for the needs of your SHL students.
- **Use SHL students as "resident experts" on the language.** Recognize their language skills by consulting them on how specific words or ideas would expressed in their variety of Spanish. Assign them as conversation partners or tutors for non-native students.
- **Assign SHL students more challenging tasks to develop their skills, especially in writing**. If non-native students are assigned to write sentences describing a picture, for example, SHL students could be asked to write a story about the picture.

Non-native Teachers and SHL Classes

If you are not a native speaker of Spanish, you may be nervous about teaching heritage language students. Fortunately, research and experience have shown that non-native teachers can be successful at teaching SHL students. Keep in mind that your students may be just as insecure about their Spanish skills as you are. A good approach is to view your abilities and those of your students as complimentary. SHL students have firsthand knowledge of everyday vocabulary and culture that their teachers may not, whereas teachers can share their knowledge of grammar, writing conventions, and formal academic language. By taking this type of approach, you can create a win-win situation for yourself and your students alike.

CONCLUSION

Teaching some of the classes mentioned in this chapter means that you are in the "big leagues." This is what you are aiming for with the beginning and intermediate classes. In your advanced classes, you have the cream of the crop, the students you have been grooming for all these years. Don't shortchange them! Now you are not so much teaching them as you are guiding them to do the fun things they can do with fluency in the language. Send them home with audio recordings, with videos, or better yet, make these available online; send them to the library, to the community, to the labs. Find ways for them to use the skills you have taught them. Perhaps some of the special approaches mentioned in this chapter will be possible in your own particular situation. Advanced classed require more preparation on your part, but the reward will be the satisfaction of seeing your students using the language in meaningful ways and especially gaining much of the pleasure which you felt and which led you to become a language teacher. Working with heritage speakers can give you the satisfaction of knowing you have helped those students keep a wonderful legacy alive and perhaps even expanded it. Working with specialized classes also gives the satisfaction of providing training that might have immediate use. And, opening the world of a second language to adults can provide some of the most fulfilling experiences in your career.

REFERENCES AND SUGGESTIONS FOR FURTHER READING

Lubiner, E. D. (1992). *Learning about languages.* Lincolnwood, IL: National Textbook. *A very comprehensive activity book that could be used with a FLEX program, with some excellent material and many motivating activities for the student to practice with.*

Robbins, E. S., & Ashworth, K. R. (1995). *Discovering languages: Spanish.* New York, NY: Amsco School Publications. *An excellent example of materials that can be used in a FLEX program, with many interesting practice activities for the students. A well-designed teacher's edition is available.*

Schmitt, C. Jr. (2006). *Invitation to languages.* New York, NY: McGraw Hill. *An excellent FLEX program exploring six languages. Features teacher's and students' editions and activities workbook.*

Sims, W. D., & Hammond, S. B. (1982). *Award-winning foreign language programs.* Skokie, IL: National Textbook. *A collection of description of foreign language programs that were judged to be the most successful and innovative in the country.*

Resources on Teaching Spanish to Heritage Speakers (described in the chapter)

American Association of Teachers of Spanish and Portuguese. (2000). *Spanish for native speakers* (Professional development series handbook for teachers K-16, Vol. 1). Fort Worth, TX: Harcourt College.

Bateman, B. E, & Wilkinson, S. L. (2010). Spanish for heritage speakers: A statewide survey of secondary school teachers. *Foreign Language Annals, 43,* 324-353. DOI: 10.1111/j.1944-9720.2010.01081.x

Carreira, M. (2007). Spanish-for-native-speaker matters: Narrowing the Latino achievement gap through Spanish language instruction. *Heritage Language Journal, 5*(1). Available at http://www.heritagelanguages.org/

Columbi, M. C., & Alarcón, F. (Eds.). (1997). *La enseñanza del español a hispanohablantes: Praxis y teoría.* Boston. MA: Houghton Mifflin.

Peyton, J. K., Lewelling, V. W., & Winke, P. (2001). *Spanish for Spanish speakers: Developing dual language proficiency* (ERIC Digest No. EDO-FL-01-09). Washington, DC: Center for Applied Linguistics. Retrieved from ERIC database. (ED469209)

Potowski, K. (2001). Educating university foreign language teachers to work with heritage Spanish speakers. In B. Johnston & S. Irujo (Eds.), *Research and practice in language teacher education: Voices from the field* (CARLA Working Paper #19, pp. 99-113). Minneapolis, MN: Center for Advanced Research on Language Acquisition.

Roca, A., & Columbi. M. C. (Eds.). *Mi lengua: Spanish as a heritage language in the United States, research and practice.* Washington, DC: Georgetown University Press.

Zentella, A. C. (1997). *Growing up bilingual.* Malden, MA: Blackwell.

Image Credits

p. 336: NCDOT Communications. (2011, April 15). NCDOT Bridge Building Competition 2011. *Flickr.* Retrieved July 4, 2011 from http://www.flickr.com/photos/ncdot/5654562015/. Creative Commons attribution license.

ACTIVITIES FOR METHODS CLASSES

1. Working with your methods instructor, select a school district in your area, contact an official and evaluate their articulation: Is there a district foreign language coordinator? Do they have a district syllabus? Do they have district coordination meetings? Have they selected textbook series for the district? etc. Report to your methods class.
2. Working with your methods instructor, select a college or university in your area, contact an official or teacher and evaluate their program of articulation with incoming students: How do they evaluate previous language study? Do they use a placement test? Do they give credit for beginning language classes if the students have had prior study in secondary schools? Can students get credit for college classes they skip? Report to your methods class.
3. Working with your methods instructor, select an elementary school or secondary school in your area, contact a teacher and evaluate their articulation with other schools: Do the elementary, junior high and senior high language teachers know each other? Do they coordinate their curriculum? Do they use the same textbook series? Do they meet frequently to coordinate programs? Do they ever make "teacher exchanges?" In large schools, is there a department chairman? Etc. Report to your class.
4. Visit a school that has a FLEX program and observe the class. Interview some of the students after the class and find out how they like the class. Ask them if they are going to take a foreign language the following semester or year.
5. Visit a school that has an AP Spanish class. Observe the activities the students are engaged in. Do they prepare them for the AP test? Is the class really taught at a university level? Interview the teacher. Ask how he/she set up the program. What help is available from Educational Testing Service (ETS), the organization that administers the program. Find out what percentage pass the AP exam.
6. Visit an intensive language training program. How much use of the foreign language is made in the class activities? Make a list of the advantages of an intensive program. Write up a report, including your reaction to the program, and hand it in to your instructor.
7. Go to the foreign language curriculum library and find textbooks that have multi-level programs. Evaluate the books in terms of continuity and organized advancement to higher levels. What provisions are there for additional development of the four skills; for example, are there readers, video programs, computer software, and materials for lab use?
8. If you didn't take an AP test in connection with Chapter 12, go to the lab and take it now. How would you have done on the test? Was it at a college level? The oral part of the test is extremely expensive to administer. Do you feel it is worth it?
9. Find out if the Spanish Department of your university has any kind of program for advanced students of local high schools. Report on the program to your class.
10. Visit one or more of the local high schools in your area. Do any of them have special scheduling configurations? Share what you have learned with your methods class.
11. If any schools in your area have combined advanced classes, visit one of the classes. Interview the teacher and find out what techniques he/she uses to work with two different levels. Write up a report and hand it in to your instructor.
12. Visit a special class for students of Spanish as a heritage language, or a regular Spanish class that has heritage speakers in it. Observe the class and talk with the teacher afterwards. What challenges does he or she face in working with the heritage students? What accommodations are made for these students?

CHAPTER FIFTEEN

TEACHING FOREIGN LANGUAGES IN THE ELEMENTARY SCHOOLS

YOUR OBJECTIVES FOR THIS CHAPTER ARE TO:

1. ARTICULATE REASONS FOR TEACHING FOREIGN LANGUAGES IN THE ELEMENTARY SCHOOLS.

2. DISCUSS THE ROLE OF FLES IN THE BASIC SCHOOL CURRICULUM.

3. IDENTIFY THE ESSENTIALS OF A SUCCESSFUL FLES PROGRAM.

4. DISCUSS DIFFERENT TYPES OF FLES PROGRAMS.

5. DESCRIBE AN IDEAL FLES PROGRAM.

6. SUMMARIZE FUNDAMENTAL PRINCIPLES OF TEACHING LANGUAGES TO CHILDREN.

7. SELECT TEACHING TECHNIQUES THAT ARE APPROPRIATE FOR ELEMENTARY-AGE CHILDREN.

8. DISCUSS THE NATURE OF A LESSON PLAN FOR CHILDREN.

9. IDENTIFY SOURCES OF MATERIALS FOR FLES PROGRAMS.

Mr. Principale was finally filling a lifelong wish. He was taking a tour of Europe. He thrilled, as millions have done, with the scenery and the richness of the cultural heritage. More than anything else, he was amazed that everyone spoke English, even the younger people. Since he was an educator, he wanted to visit some schools and was finally able to arrange it with a friend who was the Director of an elementary school in Holland. To his amazement, the children were studying English in the first grade and in the fifth grade were starting to learn a second foreign language, either German or French.

"Isn't it a little early to start them on a foreign language?" he asked his friend. "Don't they have to get their reading and writing skills in Dutch fully completed?"

"Not at all," replied the director, "the learning of foreign languages is as vital to our program as learning reading, writing and math. Children are capable of learning languages from the time they start talking. Why waste this ability and wait until they are older? By then their speech patterns have been set and it is harder for them to learn without an accent. Besides, it takes many years to become fluent in a foreign language, and we get a longer sequence if we start earlier."

Mr. P. shook his head in amazement. "What a great program," he thought. "What a pity that we can't do something like this in the U.S."

~~~~

Ever since Miss Truly Nice returned from her vacation in Mexico she had a strong desire to teach Spanish to her third grade class at Podunk Elementary School. She had studied Spanish for a couple of semesters in college and she had been amazed at how much she was able to communicate with the people she met in Mexico. She had no doubt that her third graders would enjoy learning a little bit of Spanish, and she was sure that they would pick it up very quickly with no trouble at all.

After a number of weeks of spending 15 minutes a day on Spanish with her class, Truly was very pleased with their progress. They could greet each other in Spanish, talk about how they felt, describe their family, tell time, and talk about the weather. As she talked about her success with Mr. Williams, the father of one of her students, he asked her a question that brought her up short. "I am really thrilled that Janie is learning Spanish," he remarked, "and she really enjoys it, but what is going to happen next year? Are there any plans to continue with Spanish in the fourth grade, or are they just going to forget all that you have taught them?"

CHAPTER FIFTEEN

TEACHING FOREIGN LANGUAGES IN THE ELEMENTARY SCHOOLS

> Train up a child in the way he should go and when
> he is old he will not depart from it.
> --Proverbs 22:6

All of us have seen or heard of situations where children who, when placed in an environment that required them to learn a foreign language, were able to pick it up, seemingly effortlessly, and without a trace of a foreign accent. It is obvious that children have an enormous capacity for learning languages. Studies indicate that this innate ability is present when they begin learning their mother tongue, but it begins diminishing around age 12 and steadily decreases as the child gets older.

What an unfortunate waste of potential if this capacity is not tapped by the educational system! In many countries of the world, children begin to study a foreign language in the elementary school and by the end of their formal education are fluent in one or more foreign languages. Tragically, here in the United States we have continued to deprive the majority of our children of the opportunity to begin learning a foreign language when they are most ready for it.

The teaching of foreign language in the elementary schools, hereafter referred to as **FLES**, should be one of the basic components of the core curriculum of every school in the country. It should not be relegated to the area of "enrichment," but placed on a par with reading, writing, math, social and natural sciences That is the way it is handled in many countries throughout the world. In the schools in our country that are considered to be the finest, all students learn a foreign language.

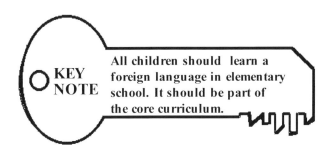

KEY NOTE: All children should learn a foreign language in elementary school. It should be part of the core curriculum.

There have been times when this key reality has been widely acknowledged and acted upon. In the 1960's, when there was grave concern that our nation was falling behind Communist countries in certain areas of education, including the study of foreign languages, national attention was focused on improving foreign language programs across the nation. Large infusions of federal funds permitted retraining of teachers and development of improved texts and materials. There was also popular movement to extend language study downward into the elementary level. Hundreds of thousands of elementary schools were encouraged to include foreign language in their curriculum. Many did, but unfortunately most of those programs were ill-conceived, rarely coordinated, and poorly taught. The lack of any real success led to the gradual abandonment of virtually all of those programs.

While it is not within the scope of this book to treat all aspects of teaching languages to elementary school children, we do want to discuss how FLES should fit in the total educational curriculum and how it should be coordinated with the language programs of the secondary schools.

FLES IN THE CURRICULUM

The popularity of FLES seems to ebb and flow. At the present time it is making a comeback, especially in the form of immersion and bi-lingual programs. This comeback is taking place in schools where administrators and parents are insisting that the children learn a foreign language. In areas of the country where there is a high population of speakers of other languages, particularly Spanish, school districts are making strong efforts to include language study in the primary grades.

Values of FLES

- The values of FLES are undisputed, but we will take the opportunity to review some of the most important areas here.
- Children have a natural, innate ability to learn language. A FLES program allows them to make use of that aptitude.
- Children have an amazing ability to imitate sounds and hence have very few problems with learning to pronounce a second language.
- Children are less inhibited than adults and hence are more willing to try to communicate in the foreign language.
- The sooner we start children learning a foreign language, the more time they will have to develop fluency. Although they pick it up quickly, total, lasting proficiency requires several years.
- Children who start early learning a language quickly develop a positive attitude about other languages and about other cultures in general.

With such evidence in favor of language learning at a young age, one is led to ask: Why, then, do so few schools in our countries have good FLES programs? There are many answers to this question, not the least of which are apathy and the resistance to change which is always found in our educational system. Another must be that the expectations with earlier programs were so unrealistically high that they were considered failures. In the 1960's, when national attention was focused on teaching languages in the elementary schools, many schools jumped on the FLES bandwagon and many programs were initiated without the careful planning, design, or preparation of teachers. Consequently, when the

hoped-for fluency wasn't achieved, the programs were dropped from the curriculum.

Essentials of a FLES Program

The resurgence of FLES can be good news to our profession only if these new programs do not repeat the mistakes made in the past. For a FLES program to succeed the following elements must be present:

The program must be well-planned. A full "program" must be more than an individual teacher desiring to include "a little Spanish enrichment" in his or her class. The entire school must be involved, there must be total support by the administration, and it must be regarded as an integral part of the curriculum.

The objectives must be spelled out. Many of the programs in the 1960's failed because teachers and administrators didn't know exactly where they were going. For a FLES program to succeed there must be a conscious working toward functional goals, such as: students being able to talk about their family and friends, being able to use numbers to tell how old they are, how many brothers and sisters they have, etc. The goals must be more than just fun and games, yet they must also be realistic. Another cause of the downfall of the early FLES programs was an unrealistic expectation; everyone thought the children would be totally fluent at the end of 6th grade. Parents and teachers alike must be patient and content with partial or modest fluency, and realize that total fluency comes only after years of study and practice.

Teachers must be qualified. It takes special training to teach foreign language to children. Poorly trained or unqualified teachers seldom make a strong FLES program. (See our discussion of those qualifications in Chapter One.) If the teacher is not a native speaker, he or she at least must be able to communicate comfortably and confidently in the language. They certainly need to have studied more than just a couple of semesters at college or had more than a three-week trip to Acapulco. On the other hand, native speakers must have been trained to be teachers, and have acquired the skills to help children learn. They must relate well to children, understand the philosophy, practices, and techniques of the American school systems, must understand their own language well enough to teach it, and must be familiar with the process of second language learning.

The program must be totally articulated, within school and between schools. In the past many FLES classes were created "spontaneously" by a teacher who wanted to teach a foreign language, but could make no provisions for continuation in later grades. In other words, the instruction the children received "went nowhere." Successful programs must be totally coordinated from grade to grade. That is, if language study begins in grade four, grade five should build on that beginning and move steadily upward, with a similar continuation in grade six. There must also be total coordination between the elementary school and the middle and secondary schools so that children with three or more years of language study in elementary school are kept apart and continue to advance, or are placed in intermediate classes, not forced to start over again from zero with students who have never studied the language before. Sometimes children participate in a FLES program for two or three years, then do nothing for the next few years until they reach junior high school, but by then have forgotten what they had learned. There is an appalling lack of interest on the part of secondary school language teachers in helping establish FLES programs and then later coordinating them with what is being taught in the junior and senior high schools.

The program should be integrated with regular school curriculum. Instead of working in a vacuum, the FLES program should be integrated as much as possible with other content areas being studied at each grade level in the elementary school. For example, in music the children could learn songs in Spanish, in math, concepts could be practiced in the foreign language, in social sciences, the teacher could emphasize contributions of the Hispanic cultures, etc. In the language class, the content being studied could easily contain and reinforce what the children are studying in other areas. This is especially important when a language specialist is teaching the language during regular class time. By correlating with the classroom teacher, the specialist can reinforce other concepts taught,

rather than just take time away from the regular classroom teacher.

The program must use carefully prepared, and richly endowed teaching materials. Rare are elementary school teachers who can write their own materials. And why should they? There are some very good programs available that include an impressive array of support and supplementary materials such as teacher manuals, visual aids, practice materials, transparencies, children's texts, testing materials, audio files, videos, computer practice, and even puppets. Carefully-prepared materials will consist of a series for several levels, designed to be sequential as the children move from grade to grade and planned to mesh in with intermediate classes in secondary schools.

Parents must be involved. Virtually all of the successful FLES programs in the nation are backed by active parental support groups. Parents can keep pressure on administrators to provide the needs for the program, they can find financial support, they can make the program visible to the community, and can help personally with volunteer work in the classroom. Activities organized by the support groups help parents whose children are in the program become better acquainted with what is happening in the classroom, and they allow those parents to help with the recruiting of new children. And, above all, the parents must find ways to help their children use their emerging skills in the home and fmily settings.

Goals of FLES

Most FLES programs will have one or both of the following goals: 1) to open the children's world to other languages, to broaden their horizon, to help them better understand language in general; and 2) to give them some ability to use the language in a functional way in common, everyday situations. Obviously, some types of programs are more ambitious than others, ranging from the objective of immersion programs to bring the children to a high level of functional fluency, to improvised non-sequential programs that barely give the children the notion that some people speak differently and that ideas can be expressed in other ways. All of the programs intend to enrich the children's lives, increase their tolerance and understanding of people from other cultures, and prepare them to be responsible citizens in an increasingly pluralistic society and a world that is becoming "smaller" as the opportunities for traveling, visiting and living in foreign countries become more common.

TYPES OF FLES PROGRAMS

There are many different approaches that can be taken in teaching foreign languages in the elementary schools. Programs can range from teaching the entire elementary school curriculum in a foreign language, to just a few minutes of language instruction one or two days per week, to introductory programs which merely introduce the children to some ideas about language in general and then expose them to a taste of some selected foreign languages. Decisions have to be made according to the desires of the schools and parents, the financial resources available, and to the availability of teachers and materials.

In this chapter, we will concentrate our comments on three general types of FLES programs: **immersion** programs (total and partial), **sequential** programs, and **FLEX** programs. The following graphic summary of these three types will help you visualize the amount of exposure to the language and the value of each type.

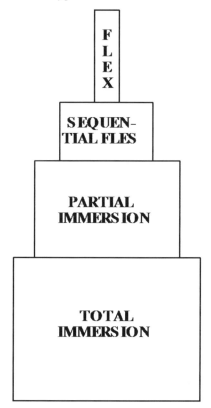

Immersion Programs

Immersion programs are the zenith of FLES programs and produce spectacular results. In immersion programs the children are taught the normal and regular curriculum of elementary school *in the target foreign language!* In this approach, the acquisition of the foreign language is secondary and almost incidental to the usual learning of math, social and natural sciences, health, etc. Reading and writing are, of course, essential components of the curriculum, but the children learn to read and write in the foreign language. Reading and writing in English is usually delayed or taught by the parents at home. The shift of reading and writing skills learned in the foreign language to English can usually be made over a period of two to three years without problems.

Immersion programs may be *total* or *partial*. In **total immersion**, the children are taught exclusively in the foreign language. No use of English is made during the entire day for the first two or three years. Starting with the first grade, the children learn to read, write, do math, science, social sciences, and so on in the foreign language. The teacher, usually a native or near-native speaker, teaches the usual curriculum and the children learn the foreign language from context and use. After two or three years of exclusive use of the foreign language, English instruction is usually phased in slowly. For example, in third or fourth grade, one hour of instruction might be given in English, in the next grade, two hours, and in the next three hours, eventually leveling out to about half in English and half in the foreign language. By the end of the sixth grade, the children are close to being bilingual and can work in the foreign language effortlessly and with almost total comprehension. This is not to say that children in immersion programs speak the language without any errors or at the same level as native children of the same age. Immersion children speak fluently but with many errors and are still below the level of native children, who have used the language 24 hours a day for several years.

Partial immersion programs are similar to total immersion but are less ambitious. Essentially they are just total immersion programs cut in half. Class instruction in the foreign language is carried out for only one or two hours, or perhaps a half-day and only in

361

selected subject areas, such as reading and writing, math, and social sciences. The remainder of the curriculum is taught in English in the traditional fashion. Obviously this approach is not as effective as the total immersion programs, and the children's mastery of the foreign language is much less and progresses at a slower rate. Nevertheless, a partial immersion program does bring the children to a natural use of the language and an impressive ability to communicate in common situations.

Two-way immersion. Two-way immersion, also known as **dual immersion,** is a form of immersion education in which balanced numbers of native English speakers and native speakers of the partner language are integrated for instruction so that both groups of students serve in the role of language model and language learner at different times. For example, a two-way Spanish immersion program might have approximately 50% native English-speaking students and 50% native Spanish-speaking students.

The structure of two-way immersion programs varies, but they all provide at least 50% of instruction in the partner language at all grade levels beginning in pre-K, Kindergarten, or first grade and running at least five years (preferably through Grade 12). (Center for Applied Linguistics Two-Way Immersion page, http://www.cal.org/twi/)

Utah's "Dual Immersion" model. The state of Utah has received national recognition for its implementation of a unique immersion model which it calls "dual immersion." It is important to note that Utah's usage of the term "dual immersion" is not synonymous with two-way immersion (although some of Utah's programs are two-way); rather, the state uses the term "dual immersion" to refer to a model that elsewhere would be called "partial immersion." Typically, in the Utah model, a native speaker will teach the children for a half-day in the foreign language and a English-speaking teacher will teach them the remaining curriculum in English during the second half. Following is a description of the very successful Utah Dual Immersion Program, taken from the Utah State Office of Education website:

"The Utah Dual Immersion curriculum model engages students in two different languages throughout their elementary school learning experience: the foreign language and English.

"From kindergarten to the sixth grade, fifty percent of a student's day is spent in foreign language instruction with their highly qualified native teacher and the other fifty percent is spent with their English-speaking teacher. In grades K-3 most of the core content learning is delivered by the foreign language teacher while the English teacher concentrates on developing the building blocks for strong English language skills and literacy.

"To ensure that the students understand the core content subjects, a strong collaborative effort exists between the two teachers to reinforce the students' learning. The foreign language-speaking dual immersion teachers are hired by schools as regular teachers. They are permanent and critical members of the school's faculty, just like their English-speaking partner teachers.

"Although the amount of time spent in each classroom doesn't change, the curriculum model shifts when students enter grades four through six as a greater sharing of content area responsibility is developed between the two teachers. For example, some areas of math, social studies, and science will shift to the English half-day with an increased concentration on foreign language literacy during the foreign language half-day to help improve the students' proficiency.

"Students entering immersion programs in kindergarten or the first grade will become part of an immersion strand of study that culminates in Advanced Placement Foreign Language by the 9th grade (and the AP foreign language test), and college-level coursework from grades ten to twelve as they work to achieve advanced level proficiency on graduation from high school. It is anticipated that many students who stay with the foreign language through high school will also graduate with significant progress toward an undergraduate minor in the foreign language at a college or university."

In order to enhance the preparation of immersion teachers, as well as to facilitate the recruitment of teachers, Utah has created a "dual immersion" endorsement that can attach to either an elementary- or a secondary-level teaching license. This endorsement allows a teacher who also holds a world language endorsement in one of the state's immersion languages (currently Spanish, Chinese, French, German or Portuguese) to work as an elementary school foreign language teacher in Utah's two-teacher model, even if the teacher holds a secondary-level license rather than an elementary-level one.

While the Utah Dual Immersion Program is just in its initial years, the program directors report the following:

- Immersion students perform as well as or better than non-immersion students on standardized tests of English and math that are all **administered in English**.
- Immersion students typically develop greater cognitive flexibility, demonstrating increased attention control, better memory, and superior problem solving skills as well as an enhanced understanding of their primary language. Current research shows that being bilingual boosts brainpower.
- Immersion students are more aware of and show more positive attitudes towards other cultures and an appreciation of other people.

Goals of immersion programs. Immersion programs have all the regular goals of a normal elementary school: to develop socially, to teach reading and writing, to teach children the basic skills of mathematics, the fundamentals of science, and so on. However, by teaching all those elements in a foreign language, immersion programs achieve a second goal of fluency in the second language. There is usually not much overt emphasis on the language itself, and it is allowed to develop as a simple "byproduct" of the process of using the language as the medium of communication in the class. Of course, immersion teachers do talk about the foreign language, and often contrast it with English, giving the children greater insight into language in general and an increased ability to use English. The use of "authentic" materials in the program, especially in the reading materials, naturally introduces the children to new cultures and ways of life.

Non-Sequential or FLEX Programs

We use the term "non-sequential" to refer to programs which have only the objective of giving the children an awareness of language in general and an acquaintance with some basic aspects of the language, such as counting, learning the colors, a few greetings, and some songs. There are really no expectations in this type of program that the students will be able to use the language functionally. The hope is that the children will have a positive experience and will develop enough interest to study the language more seriously at a later date in the education sequence. In other words, they are simply a variation of the FLEX (foreign language exploratory) programs that we discussed in Chapter 14.

A high proportion of the FLES programs in the country are non-sequential. What usually happens is that a teacher who knows a foreign language sets up a program to teach it in his or her class, but there is no coordination from one grade to another.

Some elementary schools begin programs that are coordinated between the grades of their own school, but there is no close articulation as the children move from the elementary school to the secondary level, usually a Junior High or Middle school. Even though these programs might be very good and well taught, since they lead nowhere, they are still primarily FLEX programs. Often these programs are taught with a hit and miss approach; one teacher might teach Spanish one year and the following year no language will be taught, or it might be another language such as German or French. Often teachers have no specific goals in these types of programs and the students make very limited progress.

Goals of non-sequential programs. As we have mentioned, the primary goal of non-sequential programs is not developing linguistic proficiency, but rather enrichment. An additional bonus is that if the children have positive feelings about other languages and other cultures they are much more likely to study a foreign language when a more serious, organized program becomes available to them. Some success may also be achieved in the area of becoming acquainted with other cultures and developing more tolerance in a multi-culture society.

Sequential FLES Programs

We will use the term **Sequential FLES Programs (SFP)** to refer to a program that is designed to be continuous and coordinated, and that has functional fluency in the language as its primary objective.

In a truly sequential program the students are given foreign language instruction for periods of time from one to several days a week. The typical instructional period is about twenty to thirty minutes and the classes are usually held two to three times a week or daily. The objectives of this program are much more modest than those of the immersion programs, but this approach, if carefully organized, sustained, and coordinated over several years, can bring the students to a simple but functional use of the language.

Setting realistic expectations. School administrators, teachers, and parents should be careful not to set unrealistic expectations on sequential FLES programs. Too often the impression is given that after a few years the children will be "fluent" in the language. The term "fluency" does not convey the same connotation to all people. It is true that the children will be able to function in very simple situations, such as talking about their family, buying things in a store, and expressing how they feel, but they will not be anywhere close to children their age who speak the language natively.

Time allotment. In setting up sequential programs, the ideal time allotment would be from twenty to thirty minutes *every day*. Some schools schedule more time: 40 to 50 minutes, every other day, or once a week. But, it is better to have shorter periods of class time (remember the attention span in children) and not have days in between where the students forget what they have learned.

Who is enrolled? Programs of this type should be for all the children in the school. It would not be fair to provide this enrichment and skill to only part of the children. It is our opinion that if an SFP is set in place, it should be available to every child in the school.

Coordination. We have stated that coordination must be an integral part of this type of program. For the program to succeed it must be carefully planned out, coordinated and supervised, and articulated into the program of the schools the children will graduate into. The following are essential:

- A school or district plan. Administrators, teachers, and parents must carefully prepare a plan (preferably in consultation with an expert) stating what grades will participate, what will be taught at each grade level, who will be enrolled, etc.
- A coordinator or supervisor. This could be a full-time coordinator, perhaps a school administrator, perhaps a teacher who teaches half-time and coordinates the other half, a specialist teacher, or a teacher who is paid to work extra hours. This coordinator must have authority to make decisions and enforce them, conduct planning and training workshops, provide materials, visit classes, interview teacher candidates, and lobby for the program among administrators and parents.
- Trained, competent teachers. These could be regular teachers who speak the language or natives who are prepared to teach, but they must be given special training on how to teach languages to children. They should meet regularly, at least once a month to exchange ideas, learn new techniques, and practice their language skills.
- Well designed texts and materials. All the teachers must use the same teaching materials. If each teacher is allowed to choose what he or she wants to teach, overlapping and gaps occur, and the sequential nature that is so important is greatly impaired.
- Articulation. The foreign language curriculum must be articulated between the grades within the school, and must be coordinated with the middle school or junior high school that the students will move into. It is a tragic waste of time and effort if the children make a good start in the language and then start over again as they move up each year.

Goals of a sequential FLES program. The goals of teaching foreign languages to elementary school children usually include one or more of the following objectives: 1) building a positive attitude toward foreign languages and language learning, 2) increasing the child's cultural awareness and tolerance of people of other cultures, 3) giving the child an insight into language in general and improving his/her use of English, and 4) giving the child a functional use of the foreign language. Almost all FLES programs can usually achieve the first three of these goals, but immersion programs and very good sequential programs can best bring the children to fluency in the target language.

Sequential FLES versus Immersion

It is obvious that the immersion programs are the most desirable. A school which implements an immersion program and which has the desire and the resources, will achieve the four goals mentioned above quickly and effectively. But immersion programs are difficult to start for a number of reasons, including the ignorance of the public about the programs, the reluctance of administrators to implement them, and the lack of availability of qualified teachers. School administrators must be 100% in favor of an immersion program, and give it total support, especially when natural attrition reduces the number of students in the higher grades and the non-immersion teachers begin to complain that they are getting short shrift. However, once an immersion program is in place, it gives the optimum results for the time and money invested.

One big disadvantage of immersion programs is that they limit the number of students who are learning the language. Even though the immersion students learn the language well, they are usually only 1/3 of the total number of students in the school who are learning it. The other 2/3 continue to be monolingual. There are a few schools with both an immersion and a Sequential FLES program that involve all of the students in the school, but this can be an expensive approach.

Some school districts set up an immersion program on a district level, and gather the immersion children together from all over the district in a ***magnet*** school. This type of program requires a great deal of organizing and the total support of the parents who must agree to leave their children in the program, and in most cases also transport them to school. The Japanese Magnet Program in the Portland City School District, and the Japanese and Spanish immersion program at Culver City, California, are excellent examples of a program of this type.

Although the sequential FLES program is not nearly as impressive as the immersion programs, it is probably the most realistic answer to our call for all children in elementary schools to be taught a foreign language. It also has the advantage of including all the children in the school. Let's now look at how this can best be accomplished.

The Ideal Sequential FLES Program

The following features are what we consider to be essential to an "ideal" Sequential FLES Program.

1. It is a permanent, integral part of the elementary "core" curriculum. To reach the goals this program must not be treated as a "frill" nor an "enrichment" program, but a component that is as important to children's basic education as are their social studies, science, and fine arts courses. It should be taken by all students. The decision as to which foreign language is to be studied is up to the individual school, but the language should be one that has a continuation in the secondary school into which the elementary school feeds. It is foolish and wasteful for schools to teach one language in one grade, to be followed by nothing in the next grade, to be followed by another language in the next grade, to find that neither is taught in the Junior High School the child eventually attends.

2. The program is coordinated and sequenced through the elementary grades. It is essential that the students take the same language each year until graduating from elementary school, with no breaks between elementary and secondary school. That is to say, the program should be established to mesh with the secondary school program, and if it is not possible to teach the foreign language in all the grades of the elementary school, it should at least be taught in the fourth, fifth, and sixth, and not taught in first, second, and third.

3. Students stay with one language. If staff and funds permit it, more than one language could be taught in a school. The students should be allowed to choose what they wanted to study, but once they have begun a language, they should not be allowed to switch. It would probably be more efficient for each school to offer only one language. The staffing and coordinating of several languages in one school is very difficult. Once the students have become reasonably fluent in the first foreign language, they can consider the probabilities of studying a second language sometime in their secondary school years.

4. The teacher is fluent in the language and especially trained to teach the language to children. This could be handled in one of two ways:

1. The regular grade teacher is be qualified to teach the language along with the other subjects.

This means that the school would have to hire teachers with the necessary qualifications.

2. A *"specialist teacher"* would teach all the children of every grade. This teacher would teach nothing but the foreign language and could travel from class to class to do so, or even better, the teacher would have his/her own classroom and the children would travel to that classroom. Depending on the size of the school and the length of time of the language class period, there might be one or more specialist teachers per school. For example, if the language class period were for 30 minutes, four days a week, one specialist teacher could handle over 300 students per week, or three classes each for fourth, fifth, and sixth grades.

The following diagram illustrates one way a specialist teacher would teach the classes in a totally integrated program:

MORNING	AFTERNOON
9:00 6th Grade - Class 1 Spanish C	1:00 5th Grade - Class 3 Spanish B
9:30 6th Grade - Class 2 Spanish C	1:30 4th Grade - Class 1 Spanish A
10:00 6th Grade - Class 3 Spanish C	2:00 4th Grade - Class 2 Spanish A
RECESS	2:30 4th Grade - Class 3 Spanish A
10:30 5th Grade - Class 1 Spanish B	
11:30 5th Grade - Class 2 Spanish B	

In a school where some of the regular teachers are qualified to teach the FLES program, for example in a situation where three teachers are team teaching the fourth grade, the qualified teacher would teach each of the three classes for one half hour each while the other teachers were teaching the other groups in some area of their own specialty, such as math, reading, art, geography, etc.

5. The contents of the classes would be based on the content of the first-year junior high school or middle school language class. In this way, the instruction could be spread over three or four elementary school years so that the elementary students would naturally flow into the second year language class when arriving in junior high school, totally bypassing the first year and thus gaining a full year in the total sequence. The junior high school might therefore offer only

one class of first-year language for students who come in at the seventh grade with no language study (or want to start a second foreign language) and the other classes would be second, third, or perhaps even fourth, year language. This approach must be carefully coordinated with curriculum guides, coordination of vocabulary, and use of the same textbook.

6. The entire sequence must be carefully coordinated from elementary school, through junior high school, to senior high school. This coordination would be done preferably by a district coordinator, so that students who continue would eventually take an Advanced Placement (AP) class or a university-level course in high school. These students would be very close to near-native fluency in the language.

The following graphic illustrates what could be done with this "ideal program:"

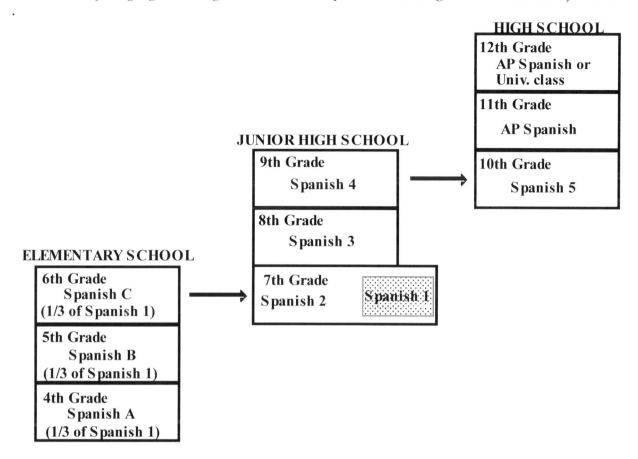

The students who have begun to study Spanish in the fourth grade are able to gain an entire year of secondary study on those who start their language study in the seventh grade. Studies have shown that the FLES students who do this are much more fluent and more able to use the language than the students who began in the seventh grade, and they have far better pronunciation.

Bilingual Education

Before leaving our discussion of different types of foreign language programs for children, we want to mention ***bilingual programs***. These types of programs involve children and languages, but they don't fit directly in the area of FLES. Bilingual programs have existed throughout the nation in some form or another for many years. Most bilingual programs are found in regional areas (i.e., Texas, Florida, and California) or large cities (i.e., Chicago, Miami and New York) where there are large numbers of minority children who do not speak English. In the past, and still today, the usual objective of a bilingual program is ***not to make all the children in the schools bilingual***; it is to help those

minority children learn the dominant language (English) and adjust to the social patterns of a culture which is different from the one in their home. In past years in a typical bilingual program, the "limited-English-speaking" (LEP) children were taught in the first grades of their school experience in their native language, while also given instruction in English as a second language (ESL). With this special help they were merged as soon as possible into the regular program of their schools. This type of program is usually called *transitional* because the major goal is to integrate ("mainstream") the children into the regular school program.

Many bilingual programs are political in nature and have sometimes been implemented because of pressure from minority groups. Often these programs are forced upon the school with little planning or with no carefully-considered objectives.

One particularly successful type of program combines bilingual instruction with immersion. This type of program is usually known as **two-way or bilingual immersion.** An ERIC Digest (1990) explains two-way immersion as follows:

"Two-way language development programs are

full-time programs that use two languages, one of which is English, for the purpose of instruction. Ideally, these programs are composed of elementary or secondary students, half of whom are native speakers of English and the other half of whom are native speakers of the other language of instruction. Subject matter is learned through both languages, enabling students to become proficient in a second language. The objectives of two-way language development programs include the following: language minority students will become literate in their native language as well as in English; language majority students will develop high levels of proficiency in a second language; both language groups will perform academically at their grade level, develop positive attitudes toward the two languages being learned and toward the communities they represent, and develop a positive self-image." (p. 1)

In a two-way Spanish immersion program, for example, all the children in the school might be taught in Spanish in the morning and in the afternoon all will be taught in English. Thus both the minority children and the English-speaking children become bilingual. In these programs the schools provide instruction in the two languages over an extended period of time, from kindergarten through at least fifth grade. Instruction is in the partner language at least 50% of the time.

Although the principles and strategies of bilingual education are *similar* to those we use in teaching Spanish to non-speakers of Spanish, the circumstances are quite different, primarily because the limited English proficiency children live in a society filled with English and have constant opportunities and motivation to learn it. It is not within the scope of this book to treat bilingual education in depth. We have listed some articles and books that will give guidance in that area at the end of the chapter.

SOME FUNDAMENTAL PRINCIPLES OF TEACHING LANGUAGES TO ELEMENTARY SCHOOL CHILDREN

It will not be possible to cover all areas of teaching languages to children in this book, but we will briefly present some fundamental principles here. We have listed several books at the end of the chapter that do contain excellent

materials, methods, and techniques for teaching second languages to children and will be of great interest to those who are or will be following that career. Most of what we have discussed in this book up to this point has been relevant to teaching adolescents and young adults. While much of what we presented also applies to children, there will be some important differences. Some basic principles are:

- A holistic approach produces the best results with children. Rather than just teaching isolated vocabulary words (such as the colors, counting, parts of the body, days of the week, etc.) teachers should try to select natural uses of the language and teach vocabulary in context. Children are receptive to having the class taught totally in the language and will not insist on total comprehension or detailed explanations of why things are said like they are.
- Fluency will come slowly. Do not become impatient or set expectations higher than what can be accomplished in very limited exposure and work with the language.
- Children learn by doing. Most of the classroom activities should be centered on natural use of simple language.
- Since children are not as self-conscious as adults and are natural mimics, they will have little difficulty with pronunciation, but you will need to emphasize its importance. They are not afraid to pronounce a trilled /R/, for example, but you need to impress on them that they need to say it that way.
- Children will not understand complicated grammatical explanations. Only the essential structures should be overtly taught and even then, in very simple terms. Presentation of grammatical concepts should be done inductively and always in context.
- Foreign language should be fun. If the children are relaxed and free of apprehension, they will be more confident and will learn faster. Children will enjoy singing songs, playing games, and acting out situations, skits and role-playing.
- Children are very curious and interested in other cultures and ways of life, especially those of children their own age. Include cultural information in your program, but relate it to daily life situations.

368

- There must be a good public relations plan. Schools and teachers should strive for a high degree of parent involvement. There should be numerous occasions where parents can see the progress being made by their children.

TEACHING STRATEGIES FOR ELEMENTARY SCHOOLS

We will now present some of the more salient strategies and techniques that elementary school teachers would use in teaching children. In order not to be redundant with what we have presented in the preceding chapters of this book, we will limit our comments to the areas where there are important differences between teaching children and adolescents and adults.

- Since traditional elementary teachers normally work with the same children during the entire day, they can integrate the foreign language instruction into the day's work. This will allow more flexibility and creativity in presenting and practicing concepts.
- Because elementary school children normally remain in the same classroom and are with the same teacher, the transition to the period of language instruction must be done with a great "flourish." That is, there must be an obvious move from whatever they are doing to a period where they will use another language. A teacher can emphasize the switch to Spanish by putting on a certain hat or article of clothing or by putting up a sign or turning on a big red light. Perhaps the best way to make the transition obvious is to use **formal routines** such as:

  - Bienvenidas
  - Warmups
  - Self starters
  - Passwords
  - Featured student
  - Reciting pledge of allegiance

It is difficult for children to learn from a formal, lecture-type presentation. They learn more by **doing**. The instructional period should include natural, contextual use of the language, such as:

- Acting out situations
- Show and tell
- Playing, chanting, singing
- Plays and skits

Children are very visually oriented, and enjoy working with pictures, charts, puppets, "manipulatives," and so on. FLES teachers will make far greater use of **visual aids** than teachers in higher levels and will use objects, cards, clocks, and even other children in presentation of vocabulary and practice. Visual aids should be large, colorful, and appropriate for the age and interest of the class.

Children need the reinforcement of seeing the language used functionally and meaningfully. Make the language **relevant**. This can be done with activities such as:

- Market simulations
- Preparing food
- Talking about the calendar and seasons
- Dressing up
- Celebrating holidays

Children cannot absorb large loads of information and vocabulary, and have short attention spans. FLES teachers must teach things in small **chunks and pieces,** merging them into a whole over a period of time.

Children learn better through **repetition**. Teachers will need to plan lots of repetition activities and in great varieties. Too much of the same thing quickly becomes boring. Ideas for varying repetition are:

- All the girls, then all the boys
- One side of the room, then the other
- Saying it with a loud voice, quiet, etc.
- Everyone with blue eyes, brown, etc.
- Everyone with certain type of hair
- Everyone with certain type, color of clothes, etc.
- Everyone whose names start with A-G, L-P, etc.

These kinds of activities should end with an action or voice that is calming.

Children love to **memorize**. This can be a powerful aid to learning languages. (See Chapter

7 for suggestions on memorization.) Things that could be memorized are:

- Songs
- Poems, childrens' rhymes
- Proverbs
- Riddles or jokes
- Pledge of allegiance
- Skits
- Dialogues

Children cannot grasp complex grammar explanations. FLES teachers must restrict **grammar presentations** to the very essential and should present the concepts in an inductive and very simple way. Many examples, with visuals, should be given and the students should be led to discover the concept, using their own words. Focused practice will be helpful in cementing the concept.

Because children love pictures, color, and decorations, elementary schools make great use of **classroom decoration**, bulletin boards, charts, and labels. FLES teachers can make great use of the concept of the "cultural island" which we presented in Chapter 4. Types of things that could be part of the classroom decoration are:

- Seasons bulletin boards
- Holiday decoration (turkeys, witches, valentines [in Spanish, of course])
- Maps, pictures from Hispanic countries
- Dolls with regional costumes
- Magazines, newspapers, comic books
- Realia (mates, boleadoras, figures, maracas, ceramics, etc.)
- Wall hangings (serapes, blouses, hats)

Since children so love to hear and read **stories**, teachers should capitalize on these interests and collect simple children's storybooks both to read and to make available for the children to read, or at least to look at. Many FLES teachers have a reading table or bookshelf in a part of the room where the children can spend free time. Children can read to each other or check books out and take them home to read to members of their family. Even if parents or brothers and sisters don't understand, the child learning Spanish is delighted to tell them what

the story is about. A word of caution: remember that *children's literature* does not mean that the language will be simple. You must choose storybooks that are truly simple. Sometimes a book in English may be very simple, but the Spanish version might have very complex language structures or low frequency vocabulary. Examples of storybooks in Spanish:

- *La oruga hambrienta*
- *¿Es tu mamá una llama?*
- *La tormenta*
- *Los cinco sentidos* series

We have included some sources for children's storybooks in the **References** section at the end of the chapter.

Children have a great ability to learn from **hearing**. Don't forget to provide numerous activities to develop listening comprehension. Some ideas are:

- Teacher telling stories, anecdotes
- Storybooks accompanied with recordings by natives
- Videos, especially things like cartoons, Disney movies, etc.
- Invited parents, guests who speak Spanish

Writing is part of the elementary school curriculum. Don't fail to include some simple writing activities, such as:

- Simple verses for valentines
- Thank you or appreciation notes (for parents, friends, teacher, etc.)
- Letters to the Reyes Magos
- Letters to pen pals
- Simple poems such as a Haiku
- Simple tests
- Simple "book writing" activities

If computers are available, your children could practice writing in Spanish on the computers.

No one loves to play more than children. There are many **games** and **fun activities** you can use to practice vocabulary and structure. The games can be active such as:

- *Señor Policía*
- *7-up*

370

- *Robar el tocino*
- *Mamá, ¿puedo?*
- *¿Qué hora es? (El sereno)*
- *Veo veo*

Songs can provide a rich source of vocabulary and cultural information, and children love to sing. Songs can provide pronunciation practice and examples for grammar presentations. They are a natural way to repeat. They can be included in programs for other classes and parents. There are numerous collections of children's songs available, many accompanied by a tape. Favorite songs of children are:

- *Amigo Félix*
- *Juan Paco Pedro de la Mar*
- *Un elefante*
- *Fernando Séptimo*
- *Mi gallo se murió ayer*
- *Hoy es lunes*

Everyone knows that you go on **field trips** in elementary school. Don't neglect to do some with your FLES students. For example:

- Eat at a Mexican restaurant in Spanish
- Visit high school or university Spanish classes
- Participate in foreign language fairs
- Visit a historic site such as a Mission, monument, ranch
- Go to museums with Spanish exhibits
- Attend a play or concert that is in Spanish or that is oriented to Hispanic culture (Ballet Folclórico, tuna, etc.)

Do "mini-field trips" within the school. For example, divide the class into small groups and have them take Spanish-speaking guests on a tour of the school.

Many elementary classrooms make use of **learning stations.** These can also include materials in Spanish. For example, if the learning station has computers, there are a number of software programs and online programs for learning and practicing Spanish. Examples of materials that can be included in learning stations are:

- Matching games
- File folder games
- Word games and puzzles
- Storybooks with audio (earphones)
- Videos (earphones)
- Computer software such as:
  Arthur'sTeacher Trouble, Abuelita y yo (Living Books

Children have a natural interest in other cultures, especially if the information relates to children their age. Don't forget that we want them to develop tolerance and accept people from other ways of life. Ways to include culture in your class are to discuss or participating in activities such as:

- Community festivals (Cinco de mayo)
- Learning foreign dances (with costumes)
- Foreign holidays (Día de los muertos)
- Spanish TV channels

Elementary schools make more use of **community and parental help** than institutions at higher levels. FLES teachers should find out what community groups can give help to their program and should especially seek cooperation from parents of their students, even if they have no language skills. Examples of parental help are:

- Working with individuals needing help
- Grading papers
- Entering grades in the computer
- Preparing book orders
- Helping with class activities
- Going on field trips as chaperons
- Sponsoring fund-raising activities

Elementary schools can gain the same benefit from use of **technology** as secondary schools and universities. FLES teachers should have CD and DVD players, tape recorders, VCRs, computers, projectors, etc. for use in their classroom. Don't be afraid to press administrators to obtain equipment. Apply for special funding that is often available for procuring electronic equipment to use in schools. Parent groups can also help raise funds. Equipment essential to your class would include:

- Sound system for playing CDs and audio files
- Overhead projector
- Digital projector
- TV monitor and DVD/VCR player
- Personal computer(s) with microphone, webcam and printer

Connecting FLES to the Regular Curriculum

FLES teachers should not forget that they are not teaching in a vacuum. They should make a conscious effort of develop a warm collegiality with the other teachers in the school. There are many ways that cooperation and coordination can be beneficial to both types of teachers. Much of the regular curriculum can be integrated with study of the language, and language skills can be practiced in other classes. The National Standards use the term *"connect"* in this connotation. A major goal of FLES, then, should be to *connect* to the regular curriculum.

Procuring and Using Texts and Materials

Too many FLES teachers feel that they must develop their own materials. As we mentioned, this leads to a lack of continuity and problems of articulation. Many teachers are unaware that there are many good teaching programs available for use in elementary schools. They must make an effort to search for materials that will lead to their specific objectives, and save a great deal of time using what has already been prepared, rather than "reinventing the wheel." Furthermore, very few FLES teachers have the background and language ability to produce textbooks and materials of such high quality as those already available commercially.

We have included information about some excellent materials at the end of the chapter. We recommend that you try to acquire a total "package" program, such as *Español para ti, ¡Viva el español!,* or the *Nuevo Bravo* program which are sequential and are designed to continue on for several levels. Using materials of this kind is a huge help to teachers who are trying to keep the program moving from one grade to the next and ensure a steady upward spiral of progress toward proficiency.

Developing Lesson Plans

When you have your materials selected, you must do the same kinds of planning as we discussed in Chapter 4. You must make long range plans to determine how much content you will cover, and how you will distribute that content among the class periods you will have available to you during a semester, term, or school year. We include here a sample daily lesson plan that can be used as a model for planning a 30 minute class. Note that the plan is in Spanish. Preparing in that manner will be of great help to you in teaching the classes entirely in the language.

MODEL LESSON PLAN
(Taken by permission from *Me gusta hablar español*)

LECCIÓN UNO   "¿QUIÉN ES?"

OBJECTIVES

1. Students will understand that the word *"Quién"* means "who" and is used to ask questions.
2. Students will understand that *"eres"* refers to him/her and that *"es"* refers to someone else. They will understand that *"soy"* means "I am" and will use it before saying their name in response to the question *"¿Quién eres?"* They will respond to the question *"¿Quién es?"* with *"Es _____,"* and will name the person indicated.
3. Students will continue to get a feel for Spanish pronunciation as they use the names of the other students.
4. Students will begin to get the feel of using *"no"* to make statements negative.
5. Students will continue becoming accustomed to having the class taught in Spanish.

LANGUAGE CONCEPTS

1. The basic concept of conjugation; that is, a different verb form is used for I, you, he/she, etc. This will be learned inductively and reinforced with practice and correction.
2. The use of the article with title in the statement: *"Soy el señor* _____*, soy la señora* _____*, soy la señorita* _____*"* is taught passively.
3. The use of *"no"* in front of verb to negate a statement will be learned inductively and reinforced with practice and correction. The children will learn this quite naturally.

CULTURE

The monetary unit for many Spanish-speaking countries is called a *"peso."* We will use "Classroom *pesos*" in our class as rewards for good work and good behavior.

NEW VOCABULARY

soy, eres, es, quién

PREPARATION

1. Have the name tags for all the children ready. It's a good idea to keep them in a specific place in the classroom and put them there each day after class. Assign a child to pass them out and collect them at the end of the class.
2. Get your picture or dummy of Juan Paco Pedro de la Mar ready.
3 Have a recording of the song "Juan Paco Pedro de la Mar" ready to play.
4. Prepare "*pesos*" for classroom use.
5. Have the *PROHIBIDO* sign ready.

LESSON

ACTIVITY	TEACHER	STUDENTS	MATERIALS
Bienvenida	Greets students	Respond	*PROHIBIDO* sign
Review greetings	Greets indivs. and has them respond	Respond	
Practice greet. and names	Has children greet each other	Greet and respond	Name tags
Motivational Activity	Announces that he/she has some pesos, and says: *"Tengo unos pesos aquí y voy a dar un peso al niño o niña que pueda decir los nombres de 5 niños de la clase.* (Lots of gestures to help them understand.)	Respond	Pesos
Intro. *"soy"* and *"es"*	Points to self and says *Soy el Sr.(la Sra., Srta.)* _____ *"* Points to child and says *"Es* _____ *"* Has them repeat.	Listen, repeat	

Teach *"quién"*	Points to child and asks *"Quién es?"* Then answers *"Es _____"* Occasionally makes "mistakes" and lets them correct him/her, *"No, no es Juan, es Roberto, etc."*	Repeat, respond
Teach *"eres"*	Asks child *"Quién eres (tú)?* " Has child answer *"Soy _____"* Makes "mistakes" and has child correct him/her, *"No, no soy _____, soy ___"*	Repeat, respond
Game	Teaches adaptation of game *"¿Adivinen quién es?"* or *"Estoy pensando en una persona"* (See **Me Gusta Jugar**)	Play game
Song	Reintroduces them to Juan Paco Pedro and reviews song. (See **Me Gusta Cantar**)	Review/sing Puppet and recording of song

Assignments
1. Children are to say *"Adiós"* to their parents as they leave for school tomorrow.
2. Children are to practice calling their classmates by their Spanish name in the hall and outside of school. If they forget, they can ask: *"¿Quién eres?"*

Passwords

Password #1: *"Soy _____"* The teacher stands at the door and asks each child *"¿Quién eres?"* as he/she leaves. The child responds with *"Soy _____"* as he/she leaves.

Password #2: *"Es _____"* The teacher points to a student behind a child and asks *"¿Quién es?"* The child responds with *"Es _____"* and the Spanish name of the student.

Password #3: *"No, no es _____."* Same as above; teacher points to someone and asks *"¿Es _____?"* using a name that is not the person's name. The child responds, *"No, no es _____, es _____."*

Personal Language Proficiency of FLES Teachers

We occasionally encounter the notion that since FLES teachers are teaching children, they need only minimal language fluency and will not be using very complex language in the classroom. Nothing could be further from the truth. While it is true that all elementary school teachers use simple and unsophisticated speech with the children, they are not using a pidgin or marginally understandable language either. They are fluent and comfortable, able to say anything they need to, and at a variety of levels. Equally, FLES teachers must be able to use the foreign language naturally and with confidence. True, they do not need to speak at the level of a college professor, and may make occasional errors of a minor nature, but they must be to speak smoothly on most topics of a general nature and would have no difficulty understanding or being understood by a native speaker. They should be especially proficient in classroom vocabulary and be able to teach with ease the content of the curriculum.

Even FLES teachers should be constantly improving their personal language skills. They should watch TV and videos, read newspapers and magazines, correspond with natives, and find as many opportunities as possible to converse with others in the language. It is axiomatic that FLES teachers speak Spanish with their students always—in the halls, the playground, at recess, and in the lunchroom.

What a thrill it is for the child to be shopping with parents in the supermarket and have their Spanish teacher come up and talk to them in the language! What a positive impression it leaves on the proud parents! Spanish language teachers should always speak Spanish with each other, both as a practice and as a reinforcement to the children who are always watching. Teachers need to use and hear correct, adult Spanish often or they become rusty and find it difficult to use anything except the present tense. Travel, study, and residence in Spanish-speaking countries should be just as desirable for FLES teachers as their colleagues in secondary school or college.

CONCLUSION

Children have a marvelous facility for learning foreign languages. Fluency in a foreign language as a result of study in the schools is much more reachable if the language study is begun in the elementary schools, and continued in a coordinated and sequential way until the end of secondary school. Until recently, our country had fallen woefully behind the world in the teaching of foreign languages to children. We currently see a trend toward reestablishing FLES programs. Hopefully they will avoid the problems that led the failures of the past. A number of states are now mandating FLES. Good, well coordinated, FLES programs are highly desirable because they lengthen the amount of time an individual spends developing fluency. However, FLES programs must be coordinated and well-designed. Teachers need to develop personal fluency and receive proper training. They must understand the principles of teaching children and must be skillful in using a wide variety of strategies for teaching languages. Strong FLES programs can make a major contribution in preparing our citizens to participate productively in a multicultural, multilingual society.

REFERENCES AND SUGGESTIONS FOR FURTHER READING

Curtain, H. A., & Dahlberg, C. A. (2010). *Languages and children—Making the match: New languages for young learners, grades K-8* (4th ed.). Boston, MA: Pearson. *An outstanding book that presents an extensive rationale for teaching foreign languages in elementary schools, different models of programs, and many excellent suggestions how to organize and teach FLES. Also has an extensive bibliography. A must-have for elementary school foreign language teachers.*

Fortune, T. W., & Tedick, D. J. (2003). *What parents want to know about foreign language immersion programs* (ERIC Digest). Washington, DC: ERIC Clearinghouse on Language and Linguistics. Retrieved from ERIC database. (ED482493) *A comprehensive but succinct guide for parents on many aspects of immersion programs, their benefits, and what outcomes they can expect for their children.*

Lipton, G. C. (1998). *Practical handbook to elementary language programs (FLES*), including FLES, FLEX, and immersion programs* (3rd ed.). Lincolnwood, IL: National Textbook. *Gives practical advice on how to establish, maintain, and improve all types of FLES programs.*

Semonsky, C. M. S., & Spielberger, M. A. (2004). *Early language learning: A model for success* (Contemporary Language Education Series). Charlotte, NC: Information Age. *Describes the successes and challenges of the Georgia Elementary School Foreign Languages Model Program. The primary audience is policy makers, state and district level educators, principals, teachers and foreign language educators who wish to begin an elementary school foreign language program at the state or district level.*

Yatvin, J. (2009). *Teaching writing in mixed-language classrooms: Powerful writing strategies for all students.* Scholastic Teaching Resources. *Offers a variety of techniques for teaching writing in grades K-5, including songs, rhymes, and playground games; short forms, such as slogans and mottos; letters and invitations; and fairy tales and legends.*

Other Books by James S. Taylor (see Appendix C for information)

- *Me gusta cantar*
- *Me gusta jugar*
- *Me gusta celebrar*
- *Me gusta actuar*
- *Me gusta hablar español*

Sources for Texts and Materials for FLES and Bilingual Programs

American Council on Immersion Education. *The ACIE publishes a newsletter three times a year with news and tips for immersion teachers. Their website features a wealth of information on many different aspects of immersion programs. In conjunction with the Center for Advanced Research on Language Acquisition (CARLA) at the University of Minnesota, ACIE offers one-week summer institutes for immersion teachers.* http://www.carla.umn.edu/immersion/acie.html

American Council on the Teaching of Foreign Languages. *On their website, ACTFL maintains a bibliography of research studies in support of elementary school foreign language learning.* http://www.actfl.org/i4a/pages/index.cfm?pageid=3653

Bound to Stay Bound Books. *A good source for children's books in Spanish, many bilingual.* http://www.btsb.com/

Harper Collins Childrens' Books. *Spanish editions of childrens' books.*
www.harpercollinschildrens.com/Search/SearchResults.aspx?TCId=100&ST=1&SKw=spanish

Instituto Cervantes. An organization sponsored by the government of Spain to promote the learning of the Spanish language. There is an interactive web site for children learning Spanish called ***Mi mundo en palabras***. It is designed for children from 7 to 9 and could be helpful. http://cvc.cervantes.es/ensenanza/mimundo/default.htm

McGraw Hill/Wright Group
https://www.wrightgroup.com/ [Select "World Languages" link, and then "Spanish" link.]

¡Viva el español! Third Edition. An excellent, complete, and totally integrated package for K-12, with a large variety of supplementary materials.

Español para ti. A very good, complete program for K-5, based on videos and a wide variety of supplementary materials.

Libros para ti. Beginning, intermediate and advanced readers, completely in Spanish.

Santillana USA Publishing. This company is dedicated to the diffusion of Spanish instructional materials for K-12 education Their products are of high quality and they offer many other services, including professional development. They have a large selection of Spanish bilingual materials including dual immersion. http://www.santillanausa.com

Nuevo Bravo Bravo Program. A fully integrated theme-based program for K-5 that develops listening, speaking, reading and writing skills using modern methodologies of second-language acquisition. It enables students to communicate in Spanish in all modes of expression as they acquire information in the new language.

¡Arte y Más! An interactive DVD video series for K-3 that promotes Spanish language acquisition through the arts. Students are immersed in Spanish with lively, interactive, culturally rich lessons designed to deliver content-based, literacy-focused Spanish instruction. [There is an excellent demo that you can watch.)

Leer en español. A graded reader program of six levels that starts with simple stories written by natives and progresses up to simplified versions of classic literature such as works by Cervantes and Lope de Vega.

Scholastic Inc. A large selection of K-8 books in Spanish. Also has lots of other materials including games and interactive books. http://teacher.scholastic.com/products/classmags/mgm_spanish.htm

Teacher's Discovery. This fantastic source has literally thousands of products that you can use in your classes. It has a section of materials especially suited to elementary school FLES programs. http://www.teachersdiscovery-foreignlanguage.com/spanishElementary.asp

Computer Software

Go to online sites like *Amazon.com* and *Kidsoftwareoneline.com* and search for "childrens' software, foreign languages" and you can find programs such as "Jumpstart Spanish." "Dora the Explorer," "Arthur's Teacher Trouble" and many others in Spanish.
http://www.amazon.com/gp/bestsellers/software/229551
http://www.kidsoftwareonline.com/Arthurs_Teacher_Trouble.htm

ACTIVITIES FOR METHODS CLASSES

1. Form small groups and discuss what you think children's experience with a foreign language should be. How would you respond to parents who ask if their children should learn a foreign language? Make a list of the advantages so you will be ready with your response. Compare your list with those of the other groups.

2. In groups, decide what you would tell an elementary school teacher who proudly announces that she has been teaching Spanish to her children. They can sing some songs, count to ten, know the colors and parts of the body, etc. Is she wasting her time? Is she doing any good to the children? Should she try to get more teachers involved? Report to the class what you would say to her.

3. Assume you are going to teach a song to a class of elementary school children. What song would you choose? Would you use visuals? If they couldn't read or write yet, how would you teach the words? Write up a lesson plan on how you would teach it. Prepare your visuals and teach the class to the methods students.

4. Assume you are going to teach some topical vocabulary to a class of elementary school children, such as the days of the week. (Warm-up style.) How would you teach the words? As a list or in context? Would you use visuals? How would you have the children practice the vocabulary? Prepare a lesson plan, visuals, etc. and teach the words to your compañeros in the methods class.

5. Visit a total immersion class and observe how the children use the language to work with the regular elementary school curriculum. Talk to the teachers to see what they feel are the strengths and weaknesses of the program. Participate in some sort of activity in the foreign language with the students to observe how well they can communicate in the language. Find out what language program awaits the children in Middle or Junior High School. Write down your comments and give them to your methods instructor.

6. Visit an elementary school that has a FLES program. Find out what the objectives or the program are; is it just an enrichment (FLEX) program? Is the program sequential? Is it coordinated within the school? Is it articulated with the Middle or Junior High School that the children will be feeding into? Talk to some of the children in Spanish. Can they communicate? Are they meeting the objectives? How do the children feel about language study? Do they plan to continue learning the language? Write down your comments and give them to your methods instructor.

7. Go to the Foreign Language Curriculum Library and examine the materials for use in FLES programs. Use the textbook evaluation model found in Chapter 4. Is there a text you would like to use in a FLES program? Are the materials up to date? Does the package make use of technology? Hand the report in to your methods instructor.

8. Assume you are going to teach an essential grammatical concept, such as the reflexive, to a class of children? How would you present the idea? The forms? Would you do it the same way as you would in a secondary school? How would it be different? Prepare a presentation and make it to the methods class.

9. In a discussion group with classmates, discuss what different strategies or techniques a teacher would use in teaching children, as contrasted with classes of teenagers or university students. Report to the class.

10. Look in local bookstores or libraries to determine what children's literature that is available in Spanish. Which of these materials would be appropriate for use in a FLES program? Are audio recordings appropriate for children available? Videos? (Remember that just because they are for children, it does not follow that the language will be simple.) Hand in a report to your methods instructor.

CHAPTER SIXTEEN

BEYOND THE CLASSROOM

YOUR OBJECTIVES FOR THIS CHAPTER ARE TO:

1. DISCUSS THE VALUE OF PARTICIPATION IN ACTIVITIES OUTSIDE THE CLASSROOM IN THE PROGRESS AND MOTIVATION OF YOUR STUDENTS.

2. DISCUSS THE VALUE OF ORGANIZING A LANGUAGE CLUB AND HOW IT CAN LEND SUPPORT TO YOUR PROGRAM.

3. DESCRIBE WAYS OF ORGANIZING AND SUPERVISING A LANGUAGE CLUB AND THE DIFFERENT ACTIVITIES IT CAN SPONSOR.

4. GIVE EXAMPLES OF PROGRAMS THAT CAN BE ORGANIZED OUTSIDE THE CLASSROOM, SUCH AS INTENSIVE PROGRAMS, MINI-WORKSHOPS, AND RETREATS.

5. EXPLAIN WHAT CAN BE DONE IN A LANGUAGE CAMP.

6. DESCRIBE THE VALUE OF PENPAL OR KEYPAL PROGRAMS AND TO HOW TO GET YOUR STUDENTS INVOLVED IN THEM.

7. IDENTIFY STRATEGIES THAT CAN BE USED TO MAKE EFFECTIVE USE OF NATIONAL, STATE, AND LOCAL COMMUNITY RESOURCES TO SUPPORT YOUR PROGRAM.

8. DESCRIBE PROGRAMS THAT WILL ALLOW YOU AND YOUR STUDENTS TO TRAVEL ABROAD TO COUNTRIES WHERE YOU CAN PRACTICE THE LANGUAGE AND GAIN ADDITIONAL CULTURAL INSIGHTS.

Dr. Smedley hurried to the seminar room where the Spanish Department held its weekly faculty meetings. He was just completing his first year of teaching at Podunk University and had been delighted with his new position. True, he had been asked to teach more than a full load of classes and he had the distinct feeling that all the menial assignments were being dumped on him since he was the junior professor, but he enjoyed working with his classes and felt he was making a lot of headway. He had some really great ideas he was planning to use next fall.

One of the items on the agenda that day was the reorganization of the university Spanish Club. Professor Doolittle, who had been nominally in charge of the Club was retiring. He had been "over the hill" for the last few years and had done very little with the Club. The department chairman tactfully mentioned that "the Club had not been used to its full potential recently" and asked for a volunteer to take over the direction of the Club. There were sheepish smiles in the room as everyone avoided his glance and looked at the floor. After a long, strained silence Smedley spoke up. "I'll give it a try," he said. "I really don't have the time, and I don't know what it involves, but I think it can be of great value to our programs." The department chairman heaved a sigh of relief, gave Smedley a grateful smile and hurried on to more important matters.

~~~~

Trudy rushed into the house to tell her parents the great news. She had been elected president of the Spanish Club at her high school! She had been taking Spanish for three years now and was one of the top students in the program. She worked hard at her Spanish and had faithfully attended all the Spanish Club activities during her three years of study. She had a lot of great ideas about what she would do with the first Club party that was scheduled for two weeks away. "Would it be OK to have the party at our house?" she asked Mom and Dad. "Of course!" they agreed, and offered to help with any arrangements.

The day of the Spanish Club party arrived quickly and Trudy spent the entire day getting things ready. She had a CD of Spanish music to play when the kids began arriving. Mom had prepared taco chips and dip, and Dad had prepared a fruit drink that had *guava* in it. Trudy and her friend Karen had some games ready to play in Spanish. They even brought some song sheets from school to sing some of the fun songs they had learned in Spanish class. After the social activities, they were going to watch a Cantinflas movie.

The hour the party was scheduled to begin came and went, and only Karen and John, the boy from down the street, had arrived. Forty-five minutes later it became obvious that no one else was coming. None of the teachers showed up either! Trudy was sick with disappointment. What had she done wrong? She had announced the party several times in all the Spanish classes and a lot of kids said they were going. After Karen and John had gone home, she sobbed out her heart to her mother and vowed she would resign her position as Spanish Club President. She wasn't going to all that work again if her classmates, and even the teachers, couldn't support her.

CHAPTER SIXTEEN

BEYOND THE CLASSROOM

> When we use more than one of our senses, our learning is more complete. Usually the closer we are to actual experience, the more senses are involved. Learning increases as we move from words, to sound only, to sight only, to sight plus sound, to simulated experience, and to actual experience.
> --Edgar Dale

After you have spent several years teaching, you will become convinced that the 50 minutes per day you have with your students in the classroom doesn't come even close to the amount of exposure they need to become fluent. It has been estimated that a minimum of 600 hours is typically needed to become functional in a foreign language. Four hours a week times 25 weeks in a school year add up to about 100 hours per year. That means a student needs about six years of study to get the 600 hours. In addition, everyone knows that the hours we get in the classroom are not always fully effective, what with announcements, administrative matters, etc. It soon becomes obvious that if our students are to arrive at fluency, we have to get them many, many more hours of language use outside the classroom.

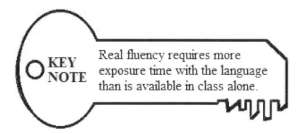

KEY NOTE
Real fluency requires more exposure time with the language than is available in class alone.

A second consideration of perhaps equal importance is the motivation factor. Students who are motivated and excitedly involved in learning the language will make greater and faster progress with the language. We need to supplement our work in the class with many motivating kinds of activities.

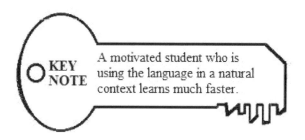

KEY NOTE
A motivated student who is using the language in a natural context learns much faster.

Besides the homework and lab hours we require of our students, there are other strategies we can use to increase their exposure to the language. If we can add a variety of natural and interesting activities to our classroom instruction, student learning will become intensified and focused. These two considerations lead us to the importance of additional programs outside the class.

THE SPANISH CLUB

A highly effective and motivating force beyond the classroom is an active Spanish club. Such an organization requires many hours of work and constant supervision, and the question must be asked: "Is the gain worth the pain?"

Is a Language Club Worth the Work? The experience of thousands of language teachers around the world indicates that the hours spent in the creation and direction of language clubs produce results that truly compensate for the time and effort required. Some of the benefits are:

- Increased language practice
- Reinforcement of what you are teaching in the class
- Use of the language in less stressful situations
- Greater motivation through more relevant use of the language
- More publicity for your program— hence higher enrollments
- Greater attention and increased respect by administrators and other teachers
- More opportunities for personal growth and development of individual students through participation
- More opportunities for development of leadership skills of individual students
- More opportunities for presentation of cultural information

Using Spanish in the Club. A decision that must be made from the start is how much of the Spanish club meetings and activities should be conducted in Spanish or English. While it is true that much of the organizational and administrative matters can be carried out better in the native language of the students, we are of the opinion that a good portion of each and every meeting and activity can and ought to be done in Spanish. In a business meeting at least a formal beginning (sort of like the "startup" [**BACA**] in the classroom) could be done in Spanish before switching over to English for more detailed and complicated matters.

Although some members will be limited in their use of Spanish, the characteristic that sets this group apart, one that they all share, is that they are learning Spanish. Of course the atmosphere should be totally relaxed and no one should be forced or ridiculed if they use English. Formal activities such as guest lectures, parties, drama nights, etc. can be done almost totally in Spanish.

Organizing the club. You as the Spanish teacher may well have to take the initiative in getting things rolling toward organizing the club, and then continuing in the lead role. Although some are of the opinion that the entire operation should be put into the hands of the students to allow them "to utilize their natural enthusiasm and allow them to follow their own interests," it has been our experience that this approach most often leads to disappointing failures and falling

short of expectations or potential. The notion of low-key, "staying in the background" works only when an extremely capable and reliable student leader (who appears only rarely) is available.

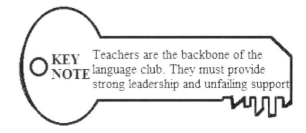

KEY NOTE Teachers are the backbone of the language club. They must provide strong leadership and unfailing support

Our recommendation would be that the teacher provide a type of "shadow leadership," that is, guiding, inspiring, and sometimes prodding, but allowing the student leaders get the spotlight and the credit.

1. School/Institution sanction. Most schools or institutions have specific regulations for clubs or organizations of an extra-curricular nature. You must, of course, learn what those regulations are to be able to qualify for whatever benefits might be available. Examples of benefits might be:

- Use of school facilities such as rooms for meetings, media equipment for showing videos, theater for talent nights and plays, equipment for sports activities, etc.
- Some schools have funds available for clubs that are officially sanctioned.
- Use of school name for official letters, postage, phone calls, etc.
- Authorization for a section in the yearbook.
- Permission and perhaps insurance coverage for field trips, use of buses, sponsoring a variety of activities such as dances, fund raising events, etc.

2. The role of the adviser. Official sanction from the institution usually requires that a member of the faculty function as a sponsor or adviser of the club. Your role as advisor must be very active. You might have to lead out in suggesting what types of activities can be most successful, appointing club officers (or at least serving as a "nominating committee" and setting up a slate of candidates you know will be hardworking and responsible), and generally making things happen. Certainly you will have to give strong support, talk up the club in your classes, recruit students from the school as a whole, attend the planning meetings, and attend every activity that you can.

3. Membership. Membership requirements have to be carefully spelled out from the beginning. They would include:

- Who can join? Just students in Spanish classes or anyone who wants to belong?
- Standards? Are you going to require certain grade point averages, minimal grades in Spanish classes?
- Sponsor? Is the club sponsor or adviser to be automatically one of the Spanish teachers or can it be a parent, a teacher of some other subject, a school administrator, or an advanced student?

We suggest that wherever possible, any one interested in joining be permitted to do so. This would allow you to use the talents of native speakers of Spanish who might not be taking classes at the time. It will also help with recruiting more students for your classes since many club members not studying Spanish will be motivated to take classes because of participation in club activities.

4. Officers (Organization of the Club). The most effective approach to selection of club officers seems to be to invite the Spanish students to apply to be considered for a position. The Spanish teachers can prepare an application form or the students can write a simple resume, perhaps even indicating which office they would like to serve in. The teachers then caucus to consider the applicants and choose those most likely to responsibly carry out their assignments or those most likely to benefit from the experience.

The usual kinds of club officers would be appropriate for the Spanish club:

- **President** — An effective approach is to have the office of President filled by the Vice-President from the preceding year. Thus a year of experience would have been gained and he/she has the knowledge to carry on efficiently.

SPANISH CLUB OFFICERS

- **Vice-President**—Following our suggestion from above, this person would have to have at least two years of study remaining, since he/she is also "president-elect." You may want to have a Second and Third Vice-President who can be given special assignments, and who can be possible last-minute President appointments in the not so rare possibility that the First Vice-President for some reason will not be able to assume the office of president the following year. Second and Third Vice-Presidents would also have to have two remaining years of school.
- **Secretary**—This is an important position, since this student usually takes minutes, records assignments, makes appointments, writes letters, and so on. The secretary also keeps the official lists of members up to date and handles the details of membership application.
- **Treasurer**—This officer should be separate from the Secretary (who has enough work). He/she receives dues and takes care of money earned through fund-raising activities. The treasurer can also be responsible for paying expenses and disbursing money for awards, gifts, and so on.
- **Historian**—The Historian is responsible for compiling the club history or scrapbook. He/she should write up accounts of club events, keep pictures of activities, collect newspaper articles about the club, and so on.
- **Committees**—The appointing of numerous committees will help spread the work around and involve the participation of more students—and when more students are involved greater success in the activities and events is ensured. You can have several standing committees such as:

- **Planning Committee.** (Usually includes the Pres., Vice-Pres., etc.) Meets to make plans for an entire year.
- **Activities Committee.** Responsible for setting up activities during the year, such as dances, picnics, speakers, movie night, drama night, etc.
- **Events Committee.** Responsible for school-wide events sponsored by the club, such as Foreign Language Week, Awards banquet, exchanges, etc.
- **Publicity Committee.** Responsible for creating and placing banners and posters, having announcements made on the school PA system, getting articles in newspapers (both school and community), and other stunts and gimmicks that will advertise, remind, and motivate students for each activity.
- **Service Projects Committee.** Responsible for finding and organizing service projects, such as repairing some thing in the school, Sub for Santa projects, cleaning up run-down areas, etc.

In addition, temporary committees would be appointed for each specific event such as decoration committee, music committee games committee, food committee, and clean-up committee.

5. Club meetings. Most of the year would involve two basic types of meetings: business or planning meetings for smaller, executive groups, and full club activity or event meetings. As mentioned the first type could have some part in Spanish, the second type could be almost entirely in Spanish. The club officers and standing committees could meet regularly, such as once a week or twice a month. The temporary committees would meet as often as necessary to prepare for the activity or event. Many teachers find that they can have at least two events or activities each month.

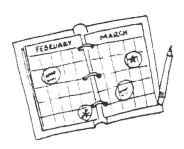

6. Possible Club activities. There is a wide variety of activities which could be sponsored by the Spanish Club. The teacher can make suggestions to the club officers, but they will undoubtedly come up with many creative ideas. Care needs to be exercised that the students planning the activities work closely with the teacher to make sure that what they are planning will be appropriate to school standards and regulations, and to keep them mindful that the underlying purpose for having activities is academic and not just an excuse for having a party. Here are some examples of activities the club could carry out:

- Guest speakers (Natives, parents or students who have visited Hispanic countries, officials from Hispanic countries, etc.)
- Game Night
- Film, videos
- Folk dance night
- Plays and skits night
- Club Picnic
- Night at Hispanic restaurant
- Spanish table at cafeteria (tertulia/cuchiparla)
- Dance sponsored by Club (Carnival)
- Sing-Along night

After many years of organizing and supervising innumerable club activities, we have a good idea of what the characteristics of a successful party are. We have prepared the following checklist that can be of great help to you as you guide the activities of your club.

HOW TO HAVE A SUCCESSFUL SPANISH CLUB PARTY
What are the characteristics of a good party?

- **Supervised and motivated by the teacher.** Even though it is organized, planned, and carried out by students, it is usually best that the teacher select and name the director/chairman/leader to assure that it is someone responsible who will do the work. The teacher must follow through and help with suggestions and advice.

- **Individual involvement.** If you want good attendance, you can best assure it if you have as many people involved as possible. These people will become motivated and will attend because of personal obligations. They also bring their friends. [Discourage the bringing of friends who do not speak Spanish.] And last, but not least, they help with the work. Form lots of committees and have as many on each committee as you can. [Publicity, program, games, music, food, clean up, transportation, etc.]

- **Lots of publicity.** The publicity must begin early. It should take several forms: posters, handouts in class, announcements by teacher and students, etc. There should be a final "blitz" the last few days before the party, and reminders the day of the party.

- **Convenient location and facilities.** Select a convenient and appropriate place for the party; perhaps in the school, in someone's home, a church, or club. Make sure you have enough room for activities, and the facilities you need to use, such as refrigerator to keep drinks cold, microwave to heat food, tape recorder or CD player for music, VCR for videos, etc. Make sure you have access to the room in time to decorate.

- **Atmosphere.** Decorate the room with a nice, festive, cultural look. Play background music in Spanish. Have signs reminding the students not to speak English at the party. Enforce or support the rule with fines, points, prizes for those who speak only Spanish, etc.

- **"Ice breakers" at beginning.** As students begin arriving, get them into the spirit of the party and get them using the language with "ice breaker" games such as ¿Quién soy? or Busca a tu cuate.

- **Formal, definite beginning of the party.** Just as in class, start out in Spanish, thank those who have helped, etc.

- **"Sing-along."** Sing some of the Spanish songs you have sung in class. Assign someone to bring along the song sheets, someone to play the guitar, or tapes and a tape or CD player, just as you do in class. Have someone teach a new song, but have a handout with the words already prepared.

- **Games in Spanish.** Have groups assigned to lead some fun games. Make sure they have all the materials needed [paper and pencils, lotería materials, concentración board, cards, name tags, prizes for winners, etc.]. Rotate every 15 to 20 minutes so everyone can play different games.

- **Main program.** The main part of the party could be one of many things: a speaker, slides, talent show, plays and skits, poetry, etc. Watching a video or dancing are not recommended because they take too long, not everyone is interested, and many people leave. If you do show a video or have a dance, do it at the end; those who want to watch it stay, and the others leave.

- **Food at the end of the party.** If you eat at the beginning, many students will eat and leave. Eat at the end. Have the students prepare authentic foods from Spanish countries, and have them teach the name and describe it to the group. One good idea is to have several different tables with food from different countries on each table, with a small card naming each dish and telling about it.

- **Special guests.** Invite important people that you want to impress. Parties can be good opportunities to show enthusiasm and progress to people such as school principals, department chairmen, school counselors, etc. Make them feel important and have them join in the festivities if they can. Occasionally you can have special parties for parents, but this usually can't be done in Spanish.

- **Cleanup committee.** Don't allow the teacher or director of the party to get stuck with all the work of cleaning up at the end. Make sure others are responsible to pick up, help wash dishes, take down decorations, sweep floors, and put away equipment.

Example of a Spanish Club party. The following is a model for a Spanish Club activity that was taken from an actual party held in the home of one of the authors of this textbook. Notice how the preceding checklist was carefully followed. Attendance was high because over 30 students were involved in the planning and activities. Virtually all the students (in Spanish of course) stated that it was one of the best parties they had ever attended. The person in charge of the *rompehielos* had the names prepared and put them on the students as they arrived, the person in charge of the *canción* had sheets with the words, a CD with the song on it, and arranged for the CD player, the person in charge of the *juego* arranged for the socks. The teacher arranged for the guest speaker and hung a Paraguayan flag outside her home.

EXAMPLE OF AN ACTUAL SPANISH CLUB PARTY

Advance planning and scheduling: In their yearly planning meeting the Club officers decided that the February activity would be a *Noche paraguaya* at the home of Señorita Sastre, one of the Spanish teachers. The date was selected and put on the calendar and cleared with Señorita Sastre.

First week of February: In their monthly executive meeting the Club officers assigned the activity committee to prepare the program and the publicity committee to post the announcement on the Club bulletin board, start announcing the event in Spanish classes, start preparing posters to put outside Spanish classrooms and have arrangements to make announcements over the school PA system the week of the activity. The president and vice-presidents were assigned to activate four *ad hoc* committees: program, refreshments, transportation and cleanup, asking specific club members to serve on the committees.

Second week of February: Señorita Sastre gave a class assignment to all students to do online research on the country of Paraguay, and bring to class a brief report with the following: a map of the country, a brief history, a picture of the flag, and two interesting facts that they had uncovered.

Third week of February: Señorita Sastre presented three culture capsules: *El arpa paraguaya, el mate,* and *el guaraní.* The song *Mi dicha lejana* was taught and sung by the class. The class learned how to play *Washingtón.* She passed out a recipe for making *chipas* and assigned them to try making them at home and promised extra credit to those who brought a dozen to the activity.

Fourth week of February: The publicity committee moved into action with posters and announcements. They also sent e-mails and text messages to all students reminding them of the activity. The refreshment committee found a store that sold *guaraná* and bought enough for the activity with club funds. The transportation committee took a few minutes in classes to arrange for car pools to take students to the activity The program committee prepared the following program. Señorita Sastre hung a Paraguayan flag on the front of her house, she had *ñandutí* and other realia displayed and the student in charge of the music had Paraguayan harp music playing as the students started to arrive.

NOCHE PARAGUAYA
El Club de Español de Podunk High School
27 de febrero

Lugar: Casa de la Srta. Sastre
Hora: 18:30
Rompehielos: ¿Quién soy?..Dora Smith
Bienvenida:..Margarita Nielson, Vice-presidente
Entrevista con una visitante especial............. Jenny Figueredo (de Asunción Paraguay)
Canción: Mi dicha lejana ....Alberto Zimmerman
Juego: Washingtón...Marco Martínez
Refrescos: Chipas y guaraná ....Estudiantes y comité de refrescos
Video: ....La misión

Gracias a todos los que han ayudado.
Favor de ayudar al comité de limpieza al final.

---

7. Sponsored school-wide events. The Club could sponsor or direct a number of traditional or yearly events, such as:

- Foreign Language week (Posters, displays, special assembly, articles in newspapers, etc.)
- Exchanges with other classes/schools (Yearly event with a nearby school.)
- Performing groups (Tuna, Singing Groups, folk dance groups, etc.)
- Fairs (A language fair for entire school with booths set up by language students in school cafeteria or gymnasium. Best in cooperation with other languages.)
- Spanish Assembly (An assembly for the entire school put on by the Spanish students, mostly in English, but with some numbers to show off Spanish skills.)
- Spanish Parent Night (An annual affair where parents are invited to attend [and to participate in] a program where you show off what the students have learned during the year.)
- Awards and Appreciation Banquet (At end of school year in a nice cafe or restaurant with awards, prizes, and certificates given to outstanding students, especially graduating seniors.)

8. Raising funds. The club can carry out a number of fund-raising activities to help with costs of: videos and books for the Spanish classes, field trips, parties and events, help with needy families and service projects, new equipment for the Spanish class, etc. Such activities might include:

- Club dues
- Full-length movie, charge admission (The Mission, A Disney film, etc.)
- Dance (Charge admission)
- Bake Sale
- Car Wash
- Sell Candy
- Magazine subscriptions
- Bingo Night
- Selling concessions at sports events

9. Publicity Measures. Your Club should take advantage of every measure possible to publicize the value of studying Spanish, the quality and usefulness of the Spanish classes offered at your school, and the Club activities and events. Some examples are:

- Using the exhibit cases
- Displays in hallways, library, cafeteria, etc.
- Have a permanent Spanish Club Bulletin Board, preferably in a hallway, or at least in one or all of the Spanish classrooms.
- Articles in school newspapers or local newspapers or on the school website.
- Announcements over school PA system

10. Service projects. Service projects can draw attention to your Club, build a close unity among the Club members, and more importantly, develop a caring, helping attitude in the students. Some possible service projects might be:

- School projects (Repairs, clean-up, painting, buying new equipment, etc.)
- Sub for Santa
- Add to library collections (Spanish, bilingual materials)
- Language information center (where anyone can find info., study abroad, AFS, etc.)
- Provide translation service (For persons who cannot speak English. Would be done by advanced students and reviewed by teachers in cases of important documents.)
- Tutoring (Advanced students work with beginning students, students who are confined to home, students who have been absent for long periods, etc.
- Visits to Spanish-speaking hospital patients, residents of retirement homes, etc.

11. Awards and Recognition Banquet.

Many schools have a traditional awards (or recognition or honors) banquet at the end of the school year in many areas such as English, Forensic or Drama department, Music Department, Sports teams, such as the Swimming team, etc.) For the same reasons you would want to do something similar with your Spanish students. Things that might be included are:

- Honoring outstanding (or graduating) students (awards or prizes of trophies, books, certificates, etc.)
- Recognition of greatest effort, greatest improvement, greatest dedication, greatest service, etc. (Some schools award the frijol de oro to these persons.)
- Appreciation to graduating Club officers for service.
- Recognition to other school or community persons who have contributed to the Spanish program.

In some cases, these awards and recognitions might be mentioned in an assembly of the entire school or even at a regional or district level.

12. Club Identity. It is important to have some visible signs of Club membership to help the members to develop a sense of identity and to publicize the achievements of the Club. Some examples are:

- Club sweaters or T-shirts ("¡El club de español - Número uno!", etc.)

- Club Motto (Siempre preparados, Siempre adelante, El idioma celestial, etc.)
- Club name (Sancho Panza, Los águilas, El círculo español, etc.)
- Club song (bird, color, flower, flag, logo/emblem, pin, etc.)
- Club magazine/Bulletin/Internet Site
- Club stationary (for official business, thank you notes, etc.)
- Club scrapbook or history
- Club bulletin board. Have a centrally located bulletin board where you can announce club activities, have cartoons and jokes in Spanish, and invite others to join.

13. Initiation. Some clubs find that a formal initiation builds a sense of belonging to the Club. Some suggestions are:

- Initiation night/ceremony
- Introduction (New member introduces self in Spanish or is introduced by an older member who becomes his mentor or "big brother or sister.")
- In a formal presentation give the new member his/her Club pin, a certificate of membership, a carnation, etc.

14. Partnership with other clubs. A partnership with a nearby school or with a school located in a Spanish-speaking country can be the source of some very rewarding activities. Some are:

- Skit night (Each school presents skits. Alternate meeting at each other's school every year.)
- "Friendly" Competition night ("Language bowl," "Trivia-Bowl," debates in Spanish, etc.)
- Talent night (Each school presents talent numbers.)
- Video or letter exchanges (these can easily be done online by creating a blog or wiki to which both schools have access).
- Travel and "home-stay" exchanges with the partner school in a foreign country.

Following is an example of a program that could be prepared for a skit night activity sponsored by the Spanish Club.

Noche de Teatro

Obras presentadas
por
Las clases de Español 3 y 4

1 de Abril
Podunk High School

7:30 - 9:30

In summary, these and many more activities can be carried out with an active and imaginative Spanish Club. True, it will require a great deal of time on the part of the teacher, but the rewards are great. These are often the things the students most remember years after leaving the school.

PENPALS / KEYPALS

A very rewarding out of class activity that you can involve your students in is to carry on a correspondence with penpals (via letters) or keypals (via email) in Spanish-speaking countries. Chat groups on the Internet are becoming popular, but we suggest caution in giving out personal information.

Getting names. If you have friends and acquaintances in Spanish-speaking countries you may find that they have family members who are interested in corresponding with your students. If not, then perhaps others at the schools where their children attend will be interested. There are also some organizations that set up such exchanges; you can find them by typing "international keypals" into an online search engine.

Helping write the letters. After giving out names of potential penpals or keypals that your students can write to, take a class hour and teach them how to write a letter or email message. Then, have them write the letters or messages as a class assignment. You can check them for correctness, and then have the students send them. As your students get replies, you can have them read them in class or post them on a class bulletin board or website. Make yourself available to individuals who want help in continuing a correspondence with their penpals or keypals.

INTENSIVE PROGRAMS AND LANGUAGE CAMPS

Intensive programs and language camps are a very effective way to motivate your students and maintain or improve their language skills during the summer. There are a number of established programs already available, or you can organize them on your own within your own school district.

Intensive programs. An intensive approach seems to be a fantastic way to learn. The basic concept is to spend several hours a day for a period of weeks or months with an almost exclusive concentration on and dedication to what is being learned. The results are almost immediate. With a foreign language, this approach permits an immersion in the language, instant and total use, and lends itself perfectly to interaction activities and simulations. Typically these types of programs will house and teach the students in facilities where they are isolated from normal daily activities in a hotel, a mountain lodge, a park, etc.

There are a number of intensive language programs across the country, notably the Foreign Service Institute (FSI) in Arlington, Virginia, which trains U.S. government personnel in many different foreign languages, the Defense Language Institute (DLI) at Monterey, California,

which trains military personnel, numerous Peace Corps training centers, and the Missionary Training Center (MTC) at Brigham Young University which is probably the largest (in terms of annual number of persons trained) language training center in the world.

The Berlitz schools are an example of a commercial organization that makes a profit from teaching languages in an intensive format. Numerous colleges and universities offer intensive language programs during regular semesters, especially in English as a Second Language (ESL), and many offer programs of this nature during the summer, notably Middlebury College in Vermont, where the students live in language houses and make a pledge to speak only the target language.

Very often private or public groups will organize short, intensive courses to give their personnel needed language skills. Examples are hospitals, police departments in areas of large Hispanic populations, large business firms which send their employees to other countries, and school systems where many children enter school not knowing English.

Language camps. While universities and private organizations can set up intensive programs fairly easily because they can control large segments of the students' time, it is very difficult to use this approach in public schools where the students are transported to school before and after classes and have other classes which will occupy most of their time. Public schools usually have to resort to language camps during months when school is not in session.

Many school districts have facilities in the country or mountains where they conduct special programs during the summer, such as nature and ecology studies. These facilities are ideal for language camps that can last from one to several weeks. Teachers can be drawn from the entire district and native speakers of Spanish can be brought in to provide opportunities for realistic practice. Classes can be taught and a wide variety of activities conducted that permit natural language use. Even the food can be culturally oriented. Evening activities can include movies and videos, plays and skits, talent shows, and conversation sessions.

There are a number of nationally organized language camps that students from any part of the country can attend. The Concordia Language Camps in Minnesota are the best known of this type. The U.S. Air Force Academy in Colorado sponsors the "Falcon Summer Foreign Language Camp" in June every year.

Retreats. A less ambitious approach to an intensive experience are "language retreats" which are usually conducted during the school year and consist of taking the students to an isolated facility for a full day of intensive activities or over night with two or three days of activities. These retreats can be best operated if two or more schools pool their teachers and resources.

PARTNERSHIP PROGRAMS

One of the most motivating out of class activities can be the establishing of an exchange or partner relationship with a school in a Spanish-speaking country. In these relationships both schools benefit from a number of activities that can be conducted.

Partner schools. Contact is made with a school in another country and a formal relationship is developed. Of course, this must be done on an official level, involving the directors or principals of both schools. Letters and pictures can be exchanged and in some cases, such as a school in a poor area of Latin America, some financial help can be provided by the students of the American schools by means of fund-raising activities. Surplus books can be collected and sent to the partner school.

Audio and video exchanges. If the partner school has equipment, classes can exchange audio and video recordings where individual students introduce themselves, and can include examples of their daily activities and special events. Again, the easiest way to do this is to make digital recordings and post them on a blog or wiki.

Teacher or student exchanges. Sometimes exchanges can be arranged between American teachers and teachers in a Spanish-speaking country. They exchange homes and teaching positions. This can also be done with individual students who would live in their exchange partner's home and attend their classes.

GETTING HELP

The enormous task of trying to incorporate even some of the things we have mentioned in this chapter cannot be fully completed unless you get help. Help can be found on both national and local levels.

Using National Resources

The federal government provides services that can be of great benefit to you. Besides giving grants for travel and study in foreign countries, which we will discuss in a later section of this chapter, there are also available:

• Funding for enrichment programs. Money is available for trying new programs, adding enrichment to classes, acquiring new technology, etc. You need to consult with school or district or state officials to find out what grants you can apply for. This kind of information is also included in the journals and newsletters of professional foreign language organizations.

• Programs for bring teaching assistants (aides) from foreign countries to help in U.S schools. Usually a school or university pays a small fee for participating in the program and provides board and room for the assistants, and sometimes pocket money. In exchange, the assistant works full time in the American school helping with classes and serving as a resource person. Two such groups that provide these services are the Institute of International Education and the AMITY Institute. (See *References* for more information.)

The *Instituto Cervantes* sponsored by the Spanish government to be of help to American schools that teach the language and culture of Spain. They make available teaching materials, national tests, etc.   (See **References** for more information.)

Using Community Resources

A very valuable resource, too often untapped by Spanish teachers, is the pool of Spanish speakers and persons interested in the language and Hispanic culture in the community where they are teaching. These people are often very supportive of the teaching of Spanish and willing to help in that process. As a teacher, you will want to identify these persons, learn what contributions they can make, and decide how you can best make use of them in your program

Finding them. The most obvious place to start will be with your own acquaintances. Friends or colleagues who speak the language may just be waiting for you to ask for help.

A second very rich source would be the parents, family, and friends of your students. Some teachers have the practice of handing out a resource list to their students at the beginning of a school year and asking them to list everyone they know who speak Spanish.   You could then prepare an information sheet to send out to those people asking if they are willing to help, what kinds of activities they would be interested in, and what days of the week and hours of the day they would be available.   You might also ask about talents (such as dancing or singing), realia they might have from Hispanic countries, slides and pictures, regional costumes, and other pertinent information such as address and telephone number.

Advanced students from other schools, from junior or community colleges, universities and other educational institutions can help with a number of activities ranging from helping with group activities in the class to serving as judges in foreign language fair competitions.

Don't neglect the other possibilities, such as Spanish-speaking personnel at the local hospitals, newspapers, police department, fire department, Mexican restaurants, etc. Is there someone in one of those organizations who could make presentations in your classes in Spanish? Is there a Hispanic club or booster group in your area?

Often some Hispanic country has a consulate near your school, and consular officials are often very happy to visit your school and support some of your functions. Why not ask the Mexican consul to make a presentation at one of your club events?

Asking them to help. Armed with your list of possible assistants from the community, you should plan activities, events, simulations, and even days where you would like help in classes, and then try to match people with activities. Call or email them early to check on availability and then send a letter or email spelling out the details of the activity, including the date and the hours. Call or email the day before as a reminder. It's a nice gesture to send a personal thank you note, or have the officers of the club do it on your club stationary.

Financial support. The community people we have been discussing can often be of help as you try to find money for different activities. Very often they can sponsor or even contribute to fund raising projects. If you are going to give awards and prizes for contests or honors night, sometimes these groups are willing to pay for the trophies or awards. If you have an activity that has a printed program, very often they are willing to pay for the program in exchange for a printed advertisement in the program.

Publicity. Try to establish contacts with local newspapers so you can have coverage of the events you are conducting. Radio stations are often willing to announce events and activities sponsored by educational institutions. Make sure that all your service projects are reported by the media in your community (newspapers, local radio and TV stations, online postings of events, etc.).

Finally, if you, the teacher, are personally involved in community affairs you will make many contacts which will allow you to promote your program. It will also make you aware of community needs where your students can make contributions, be it providing translation services, cleaning up parks, or visiting Hispanic patients in the hospital or retirement homes.

GETTING YOUR STUDENTS TO FOREIGN COUNTRIES

Nothing can rejuvenate or recharge your batteries better than frequently visiting Hispanic countries. You also need to keep up to date with changes, and in many cases become acquainted with areas you have never been before. There are several ways both you and your students can get to the foreign countries. We will treat teacher travel in depth in Chapter 18. Here we will discuss only ways to get your students foreign experience.

Scholarships and grants are often available from a number of sources: government, state, local, civic groups, national organizations, etc.

- There are many national "educational travel" groups that have a wide variety of travel experiences to foreign countries, ranging from strictly travel to "home-stays" with families in the foreign country. Most of these groups give teachers incentives to recruit students from their schools by giving them a free trip (they go along as chaperon) for each 6 to 8 students they recruit. If they recruit more, the teachers can take a spouse along or receive cash refunds. EF Educational Tours is perhaps the largest of these groups.

- Many U.S. institutions of higher learning and also special schools in the foreign countries have study programs ranging from one week to several months. These programs often include travel throughout the country.

- A number of summer work programs are available where students go abroad and work in hotels, restaurants, etc. and can earn money to pay expenses.

- Nationally sponsored exchange programs make it possible for students to live with families in a foreign country in exchange for taking a foreign student into their own home. Programs of this type include the Youth For Understanding and the American Field Service programs. Students in these types of programs usually stay in the foreign country for several months, attend school, travel with the family etc. Participation in a program of this type brings the student to a high level of language mastery.

- Many teachers organize their own tours for students from their schools. Mexico is a popular destination for these "home-grown" tours since it is so close and Mexican tourist agencies are eager to help. This approach is usually cheaper than the national groups, but requires a lot of work from the teachers and is difficult to set up unless you have some contacts. There are also some legal considerations such as travel and liability insurance which need to be taken care of. Some neighboring schools often combine to set up programs of this type.

CONCLUSION

Dedicated and conscientious language teachers will be constantly looking for out of class activities to supplement what they are doing in the class. It is often these activities that bring our students to an adequate mastery of the language, because with preparation and insistence on using the language, the students will put into actual practice, in real-life situations the skills they have been learning in the classroom. These activities can include language club sponsored activities, use of community personnel, and foreign travel experiences.

REFERENCES AND SUGGESTIONS FOR FURTHER READING

Amity Institute. *Amity Institute sponsors international educators to teach in US schools. Amity provides opportunities for global educators to share their knowledge with students, schools and communities. Amity Institute currently sponsors several programs in the field of international educational exchange.* http://www.amity.org/index.html

Figueroa, M. (1986). *Spanish resources and activities.* Lincolnwood, IL: National Textbook. Contains many suggestions on working with a Spanish Club. *Has interesting models for conducting Spanish Club meetings using parliamentary procedure, and a model constitution and bylaws for a Spanish Club.*

Instituto Cervantes. *An organization of the Spanish Government that promotes the study of Spanish throughout the world. There are centers in several large cities in the US.* http://cvc.cervantes.es/ensenanza/default.htm (click on *Materiales Didácticos*)

Paige, R. M., Cohen, A. D., Kappler, B., Chi, J. C., & Lassegard, J. P. (2006). *Maximizing study abroad: A student's guide to strategies for language and culture learning and use.* Minneapolis, MN: Center for Advanced Research on Language Acquisition. *An outstanding resource for students and teachers, this book is divided into sections on language learning strategies and culture learning strategies. It deals with such diverse topics as pre-departure preparation, adjusting to culture shock, homestays abroad, verbal and nonverbal cultural behavior, returning from study abroad, and much more. Contains several instruments for assessing students' language and culture learning strategies. Also available is an Instructor's Guide.*

Other Books by James S. Taylor (see Appendix C for information)

- *Me gusta cantar*
- *Me gusta jugar*
- *Me gusta actuar*
- *Me gusta comer*

STUDY ABROAD OPPORTUNITIES

American Field Service Intercultural Programs (AFS). This old and reliable organization has programs for one academic year, semester or trimester. AFS students live with a host family and attend a local secondary school as full-time students. Go to their website, watch the video and request information.

Youth for Understanding (YFU). One of the oldest and most reliable exchange programs for young people. Their organization includes over 50 countries and is of high quality. Visit their website: http://yfuusa.org/about-yfu.php

The Experiment in Inernational Living. This organization provides dynamic summer programs for high school students in 27 countries around the world. They stay with families that also have to commitment to take the student on travel adventures. Go to their website, watch a video and send for a catalog. http://www.experimentinternational.org/

Council on International Educational Exchange (CIEE) This organization sponsors High School Abroad programs, Summer High School Abroad programs, and Gap Year Abroad programs that allow U.S high school students and recent high school graduates to study abroad, to live with a native host family, work abroad, and/or volunteer. Visit their website and request information, especially for work abroad opportunities. http://www.ciee.org/hsabroad/high-school-study-abroad/index.html

EF Study Abroad. This for-profit organization has a wide variety of programs, including study abroad, international schools, and educational summer tours. It is especially attractive to teachers who go free if they recruit students. Go to their web site and check out all the different programs. http://www.ef.com/Default.aspx?bhcp=1

The Council on Standards for International Educational Travel (CSIET) is a not-for-profit organization committed to quality international educational travel and exchange for youth at the high school level. Its purpose is to identify reputable international youth exchange programs, to provide leadership and support to the exchange and educational communities so that youth are provided with meaningful and safe international exchange experiences, and to promote the importance and educational value of international youth exchange. Go to their site to check on reliability of programs you are not sure of. http://www.csiet.org/about/who-we-are.html

---

ACTIVITES FOR METHODS CLASSES

1. Attend a language club activity at your institution. Report to the class, discussing the successful aspects of the activity. What did you like? Was the language used? Was it motivating? What would you change?

2. Volunteer to help with a language club activity. Report your time spent as "horas de servicio."

3. Organize and carry out a class party, following the model for a party in this chapter. In class discuss the most successful outcomes of the party. What would you change?

4. Do you have friends in Spanish-speaking countries? Can they help you get names of persons who would like to be pen pals for your students. Begin to collect some pen pal lists. Share them with members of the methods class.

5. Find out about some language camps in your area. Volunteer to help with their program, or at least visit the camp. Report on your visit.

6. Watch a video of a Spanish Club activity: play night, party, dance night, etc. Hand in an informe with your comments.

7. Spend some time on the Internet looking for possible sources for penpals or keypals. Make a list and share it with your compañeros in the methods class.

8. Make arrangements to visit an intensive language program. Write up a list of the advantages and disadvantages of that type of program. Hand the list in to your methods teacher.

9. Find out if any schools in your local area have partnerships with schools in Hispanic countries. Talk to the administration and teachers in the school and write a report on how they feel about the program.

10. Visit the Amity Institute site on the WWW. Share what you learned with your classmates in the methods class. (The address is in the References section.)

11. Find someone who has been on an exchange program to a foreign country. Arrange for them to visit the class and talk about the experience.

CHAPTER SEVENTEEN

EVALUATING AND IMPROVING YOUR PROGRAM

YOUR OBJECTIVES FOR THIS CHAPTER ARE TO:

1. DISCUSS THE IMPORTANCE OF EVALUATING YOUR PROGRAM AND YOUR TEACHING.

2. IDENTIFY ASPECTS OF YOUR PROGRAM THAT SHOULD BE EVALUATED PERIODICALLY.

3. SUMMARIZE THE NATIONAL STANDARDS AND HOW YOU CAN USETHEM TO EVALUATE YOUR TOTAL PROGRAM.

4. DISCUSS THE PROBLEMS THAT COME FROM THE LACK OFARTICULATION AND HOW TO SOLVE THEM.

5. IDENTIFY WAYS YOU CAN GET HELP FOR YOUR PROGRAM FROM YOUR SCHOOL, DISTRICT, AND DIFFERENT PROFESSIONAL ORGANIZATIONS.

6. IDENTIFY GROUPS OUTSIDE YOUR SCHOOL THAT CAN GIVE YOU SUPPORT.

7. DESCRIBE WAYS TO RECRUIT STUDENTS FOR YOUR PROGRAM.

8. USE PUBLIC RELATIONS TO STRENGTHEN YOUR PROGRAM.

9. DESCRIBE WAYS OF WORKING WITH ADMINISTRATORS, ESPECIALLY PRINCIPALS, TO IMPROVE YOUR PROGRAM.

10. DESCRIBE WAYS OF WORKING WITH COUNSELORS AND USING THEIR HELP TO BUILD YOUR PROGRAM.

It was Friday afternoon, the last day of class, and a few students were still lounging around signing yearbooks and cleaning out lockers. Mr. M.Y. Firstyear walked wearily into the teacher's lounge and dropped into an easy chair. Mr. Stephenson, who taught English in the room next to his, smiled at him from across the room. "Well, we made it," exulted Stephenson, "How did you do this year?"

"Pretty good," answered Firstyear, "I really enjoyed teaching, and I don't think my students did so badly."

"Compared to what?" queried Stephenson.

Mr. Firstyear paused. "That's a good question. I would really like to have some way to tell how my students stack up compared to Spanish students in other schools, or in other areas."

~~~~

Stan Smedley, slumped into a chair with a sigh. He was worn out. Today had been especially rough, and none of his classes had responded to his satisfaction. The students were just going through the motions. No one had come to class prepared, they weren't interested in what he was presenting, and at the bell everyone had rushed out of the class like the room was on fire. They had shown a spark of interest when he let them sing, and had laughed at his "war stories," but it seemed like lately all they did was sing songs, tell stories, and play games. Stan was starting to be concerned about the enrollment in Spanish. When he had started teaching, more than half of the school student body was studying foreign languages. That year he had six classes of Spanish, with over 35 students in each class. But the next year the school offered some new classes in other subjects that competed with his, and this year he only had two first-year classes with 30 students, a second-year class with 20 students, and a third-year class with only 15. Mr. Whitbeck, the principal, had allowed him to carry the third-year class, and had counted his assignment as school audio visual coordinator as a class, but had warned Stan that if enrollment in Spanish continued to drop, he would have to teach a couple of basic math courses next year. Stan realized that most of his students were only taking one year of Spanish and the following year dropping Spanish to take one of the new classes such as computers or space science. How could he hope to compete with such popular classes?

~~~~

The 6th grade teacher called the class to order. "Students, today we have a special visitor. This is Mr. Joseph, the Spanish teacher from the junior high school. He has a very interesting activity he is going to conduct with you."

Mr. Joseph's big smile and warm personality won the students over immediately. "I know you are going to be registering for junior high in a couple of weeks," he began, "and I think it's really important that you study a foreign language. Some of you wonder if you can learn another language. Well, I have a very fun test I am going to let you take which will help us see if you have aptitude for foreign languages. The test doesn't really count toward anything, it just looks at aptitudes and characteristics that help people learn a language, and you can see if you have them. I'll come back in a couple of days and let you each know individually how you did."

Mr. Joseph was back in a few days and in a positive, skillful way praised all of the students on the results of the test and encouraged most of them to enroll for Spanish that fall as they entered junior high. Most of them did, and as usual Mr. Joseph had more students than he could accommodate.

CHAPTER SEVENTEEN

EVALUATING AND IMPROVING YOUR PROGRAM

> O wad some Power the giftie gie us
> To see ourselves as ithers see us!
> It wad frae mony a blunder free us,
> An' foolish notion.
> --Robert Burns

When a rocket is sent out to explore space, its speed, trajectory, and fuel supplies must be constantly evaluated to make sure it is still on course. If it is straying from the planned flight, then certain corrections must be made to make sure that the goal will eventually be reached. In teaching you need to dedicate time—perhaps at mid-year, but certainly at the end of the year—to take stock of how close you are coming to meeting your objectives. If your evaluations show that you are off course, you will need to make the adjustments necessary to get back on track. There are a number of strategies that will allow you to see how you are doing, and we will recommend certain people who can help you make adjustments.

This chapter will have three major focuses: 1) the evaluation of programs, especially in the light of national standards, 2) identifying the people who can help us make program adjustments and improvements, and 3) suggestions on how to build foreign language programs.

EVALUATING YOUR TOTAL PROGRAM

It may be that you are just one of many Spanish teachers at your institution, or maybe you are the only one. In any case, someone—perhaps you personally, another experienced teacher, or perhaps a committee—should make a careful appraisal of your school's total program to determine its quality. The following are some of the considerations that should be made.

- What percent of the population of your school is studying foreign languages? If it is less than 50%, a greater effort needs to be put out to make the entire student body more aware of the value of foreign language study.

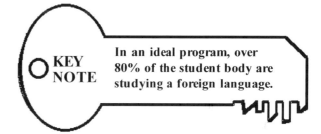

KEY NOTE

In an ideal program, over 80% of the student body are studying a foreign language.

- How many years of Spanish are offered in your school? If it is less than the optimal six years, and especially if it is less than the minimal four years, you will want redouble your efforts to work with the administration in increasing the number of years foreign languages are offered.

- What percent of your students drop out after one year of Spanish? After two? After three? If fewer than 50% of your students are continuing their foreign language study after one or two years, you will need to become more effective in your campaign to make them aware that fluency comes only with longer sequences. You must find ways to meet the competition of other courses, for example increasing the number of courses students in your school can take during a term or semester. Can you offer mini-courses like those we mentioned in Chapter 14?

You will also want to take a critical look at your own teaching. Are students leaving because of poor teaching? Is the textbook boring? Do you need to make the classes more relevant? Can you make them more interesting with greater use of technology, such as videos and computers? [We will have some specific suggestions about improving your *personal* teaching in Chapter 18.] There are a number of approaches you can use to evaluate your total program. Here are some of the most effective ones:

Comparison with a recognized program. Undoubtedly some language programs in your area have been singled out as exemplary. A telephone call to the state world language specialist could identify those programs and you could get enough information to make a careful comparison between the model program and your own. Better still, you could visit the model school yourself and confer with the teachers, soliciting suggestions on how to make your program better.

Checklist approach. There are a number of "checklists" where the characteristics of an effective foreign program are set out. We include the following as an example. Quite possibly many of the items do not apply to your specific situation, but it can be helpful to you in indicating the areas where changes might need to be made.

TOTAL PROGRAM CHECKLIST

☐ Does the *district* have a foreign language coordinator?
☐ Does the *school* have a foreign language coordinator, chairman, etc.?
☐ Does the school offer a sequence of at least six years of a foreign language? Even four?
☐ Is more than one foreign language offered in the school?
☐ Is over 80% of the total school population studying a foreign language?
☐ What percentage of the first year foreign language students continue on in second year? More than 50%?
☐ What percentage of junior high or middle school students continue studying in high school the language they began studying in junior high or middle school? Over 50%?
☐ Do the middle school foreign language students continue on in advanced classes in high school or do they start over?
☐ Does the school schedule allow elective classes such as foreign languages to compete?
☐ Do the middle school and high school foreign language teachers meet often to coordinate the curriculum?
☐ Is the same textbook series used within one school? Among the schools of the district?

Accreditation evaluations. On occasions, schools must undergo accreditation procedures and these too can be a source of feedback that can help us improve both the school program and our own teaching ability. Typically the accreditation process involves a self-evaluation by each of the subject area teachers in the school. Following guidelines provided by the accreditation agency, the teachers write up an evaluation to be used by the accreditation team when it visits the school. When the team is on site it looks at the areas surveyed in the self-evaluation form and makes suggestions. The team also observes the teachers, interviews the students, and looks at the quality of the program as a whole. These visits can be very valuable in helping you see how you compare with other schools, since the evaluation team has usually visited a number of other schools also.

EVALUATING YOUR SCHOOL'S INSTRUCTIONAL PROGRAM

While it may seem obvious, there should be very close coordination of instructional programs *within* a school. Surprisingly, some schools allow individual teachers complete freedom to determine objectives, decide on methods and approaches, select textbooks and materials, and plan their own curriculum and instructional activities. Thus one occasionally finds schools where two or more Spanish teachers are using different textbooks for the same level course (or not using a textbook at all), and are working completely independently (and indifferently) of each other. Needless to say, this causes real problems when students move from one level to another, and can lead to negative competition and contention. The most effective way to coordinate the instructional program within a school is to have one teacher designated as the "department chair" or FL coordinator. This person would be responsible for organizing frequent meetings for decision making, selecting a common textbook, cooperative planning by all foreign language teachers. Following is a checklist that might be used to evaluate the your school's instructional program.

SCHOOL INSTRUCTIONAL PROGRAM CHECKLIST

☐ Does the school have a long-term, articulated, and integrated sequential program?
☐ Are long-term, total course outlines prepared for each foreign language course?
☐ Does the school provide the materials, visual aids, and technological support that lead to learning?
☐ Is the textbook motivating, practical, and up-to-date?
☐ Is the textbook used as a tool, not a curriculum?
☐ Is a variety of print and non-print materials used, including authentic materials?
☐ Is the foreign language used exclusively in the classrooms and are the students encouraged to use it?
☐ Are the students taught the skills needed for communication and do they have skill-using activities during every class?
☐ Are listening comprehension activities with authentic language provided in every class period, such as audio recordings, videos, native speaker visitors, etc.?
☐ Are opportunities provided for communication in the foreign language in meaningful activities?
☐ Are most of the class activities student-centered?
☐ Is a wide variety of activities used?
☐ Do the classrooms allow a variety of seating arrangements to fit the types of activities conducted?
☐ Are the classrooms "cultural islands" reflecting Hispanic cultures?
☐ Is culture incorporated into every class hour and every activity possible?
☐ Do out-of-class assignments reflect course objectives?
☐ Do out-of-class assignments prepare students for in-class activities?
☐ Do tests and assessments reflect the way students are taught?
    ☐ Are listening comprehension tests given?
    ☐ Is there a variety of oral tests?
    ☐ Is oral proficiency evaluated in ways other than formal testing?
☐ Are all students able to be successful in some way?
☐ Do the students feel their teachers' love and concern for them?
☐ Do the students feel comfortable in taking risks?
☐ Do they have fun, enjoy the class?
☐ Are the students developing positive altitudes toward the language, Hispanic society, and cultural diversity?
☐ Is there an active, effective foreign language club?

Monitoring individual student progress. If you have carefully set up your objectives for each course you are teaching, you should be able to determine how close you come to meeting them. This can best be done by studying the numerous assessments that you will be giving the students during the year, including examinations.

Your students' progress (achievement) on regular classroom exams will tell you how well they are doing on specific materials, such as those contained in a single unit of study or a chapter in your textbook. If a majority of the students are scoring high on the tests, you can usually assume they are mastering the objectives (if the tests truly reflect the objectives). For example, if you are trying to develop listening comprehension and speaking ability, your chapter exams must not be strictly paper and pencil tests on grammar and vocabulary, but must include numerous listening and speaking tests. (See Chapter 12.)

Analyzing the results of different tests will help you determine if you have been effective in teaching some specific concept, for example, the past tense. If you have presented and practiced the past tense forms for some time, yet your students are not using them, something isn't working. If one approach does not produce results, you should try another, and another until you are confident that they have mastered the use of the past tense.

Proficiency Tests

Remember, too, that progress tests, even if they do measure communication skills, do not give you a completely accurate picture of the *total* progress of our students. For that, you have to make use of **proficiency tests.** This type of test allows you to look at the overall progress of your students in global terms. You may develop some proficiency tests to use in your own program, your school or district may develop such tests, or you may make use of some nationally standardized proficiency test. Following are some examples.

Standards-based Measurement of Proficiency tests (STAMP). Assessments like the Standards-based Measurement of Proficiency (STAMP) are quite effective in allowing teachers to evaluate their course's curriculum based on how students perform. With easy-to-read reports, STAMP can help you make adjustments in your classroom to improve student outcomes.

STAMP Features
- Available in Chinese, French, German, Italian, Japanese, and Spanish
- Available in reading, writing, and speaking
- Measures proficiency ranging from Novice-low to Intermediate-mid
- Age appropriate for grades 7 through 16

- Web-based
- Based on the ACTFL Proficiency Guidelines
- Textbook independent

Benefits for Teachers
- Provides validated, easy-to-use data
- Perfect for checking progress, placement, program and standards review, staff development, and instructional planning
- Access to longitudinal individual speaking and writing samples

Benefits for Students
- Engage in real-world language situations
- Emphasis on what students can do with the language
- Facilitates goal setting

Of course there is a fee for using the STAMP tests, but if you can find some way to get the money, they are well worth it. You can try out the tests free of charge by visiting their web site. Teachers may take a demo or practice test free of charge by visiting the following web site: http://avantassessment.com/products/about_stamp.html

The National Spanish Exam. The National Spanish Examinations are online, standardized assessment tools for Grades 6 -12, given voluntarily by teachers throughout the United States to measure proficiency and achievement of students who are studying Spanish as a second language. Since 2006, the National Spanish Examination has been administered in an online format through the Quia Corporation and is the first national world language exam administered online. The National Spanish Examinations are the most widely used tests of Spanish in the United States. In the spring of 2009, a total of 115,218 students participated in the online version of the exam. The National Spanish Examinations are recognized by many administrative and teaching associations and organizations at the local, state and national levels.

Students must be sponsored to take the exam in one of two ways. If the teachers are members of the American Association of Teachers of Spanish and Portuguese (AATSP) they can sponsor their students free of charge. If they are not they must pay a $75 fee. This fee allows that sponsor to order up to 50 tests for one level of the exam. If a sponsor has more than one level of students, then the sponsor will need to pay the $75 fee for each new level. In addition to the non-member national fee of $75, the sponsor must pay the national and chapter fees for the tests ordered. You can avoid paying the non-membership fees by paying regular AATSP dues.

NSE gives scholarships and rewards to students who have high scores on the exam. Visit the website to obtain more details. http://www.nationalspanishexam.org/

Advanced Placement Test. If you teach Spanish Advanced Placement classes, the success of your students on the AP exam will give you an indication of how you are doing in comparison with other schools in the nation. However, you should aware that it is difficult for non-native speakers of Spanish to get high on the AP tests because they are competing with heritage and native speakers. You should visit the AP Central website, maintained by the College Board. They have support boards, practice exams and many other resources to help your students prepare for the AP exam.

Portfolios (Linguafolios). A recent development in the area of assessment is the notion of self-evaluation. This approach was developed in the European Economic Union and focuses on the development of portfolios, with the evaluation of language proficiency referred to as *linguafolios*.

Basically, individuals prepare a portfolio on their experiences with language study and evaluates their skills. These portfolios can be maintained over periods of several years, and even though they are a self-evaluation it is amazing what an effect it has on the students' motivation and can be a valuable assessment tool for the teacher. To see examples of portfolios visit the web site: http://www.oapee.es/oapee/inicio/iniciativas/por tfolio.html

ARTICULATION

One area you must scrutinize very closely in your yearly evaluation is how well your program is articulated. We mentioned the importance of articulation in Chapter 14, and emphasized how essential it is that you coordinate your program with those of the other language teachers both within your school and with the schools that you feed into or feed into yours. We have discussed the desirability of providing sufficient years of language study to enable the students to progress into intermediate and advanced classes, but if the students are required to begin all over again every year or two, then any gains you have made may be lost.

Evaluating how well a program is articulated may require some sort of survey or follow up of the students as they move from one school to another. The following questions should be asked:

- What percent of the students graduating from middle school to junior high, from junior high to high school, from high school to college continue with language study?
- What percent of those who continue, move smoothly into the next level? What percent start over again? Why do they start over?
- What happens to the students as they enter college, do they start again in Spanish I, or do they enroll in intermediate or advanced classes?

Big dividends are waiting for enterprising teachers who make the effort to get acquainted with the language teachers in feeder schools, including elementary schools and colleges. Common goals can be discussed and programs can be coordinated. Some high school and junior high School teachers even trade places for a few days, teaching each other's classes, and learning to appreciate what their colleagues are trying to do. The following checklist will be of help to you in evaluating your program's articulation with other institutions.

PROGRAM ARTICULATION CHECKLIST

☐ Is there a district foreign language coordinator?
☐ Do the teachers at the different levels know each other?
☐ If there is a FLES program, is it coordinated with the next levels?
☐ Do the teachers at different levels meet frequently to coordinate the curriculum?
☐ Is the same textbook series used in the Junior and Senior High Schools?

HOW DO YOU GET HELP FOR YOUR PROGRAM?

The evaluation of your program is just the first step. If, as you examine it, you find that you are falling short in some areas, then you must take the second step: making changes. It should be evident that you can't complete the task alone and will need some help. That help can come in many ways and from a variety of sources. Teaching is not just an individual performance, it should be a team effort. Use your colleagues.

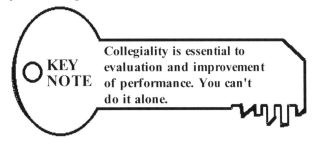

KEY NOTE — Collegiality is essential to evaluation and improvement of performance. You can't do it alone.

Let's look at some people who can help you in your search for excellence.

Entities Within Your School

Fellow teachers. There is usually a strong spirit of collegiality and mutual support among the members of the faculty of an educational institution. Fellow teachers can be one of your most fruitful sources of help. Even though they teach other subjects, their basic task is the same as yours—teaching students. Math, music, art, and English teachers can give you some positive suggestions on how to improve your total foreign language program. They too, worry about grading, motivating students, providing classroom atmosphere conducive to learning, etc. Talk to them about your problems and ask

questions. More often than not, they can help you find some solutions.

Discuss ways you can support each other's goals. Often you can help the math teacher by practicing some math skills in Spanish, or reinforce what the natural science or physics teachers are teaching by discussing in your Spanish class, in Spanish of course, the information they are presenting. Obviously the history and geography teachers can strengthen your Spanish students' learning of cultural information that you may be presenting in your class, and if any of the other faculty members speak Spanish, encourage them to use it occasionally in their classes.

The FL Department Chair. Large schools usually have a department chair for foreign languages. He or she is probably appointed by the principal but could be elected by the FL colleagues because of experience or formal training or leadership ability—in some school by turns. This person can improve your program by:

- coordinating the in-service teacher development aimed at establishing the basic school philosophy of teaching FLs (approach, method, and strategies)
- chairing the periodic department meetings
- establishing a uniform text program
- planning semester outlines of goals and objectives
- setting up and coordinating longer sequences
- implementing the requirements and suggestions of the state guide
- conducting brainstorming sessions to take care of in-school FL teaching problems

School administrators. Included among school administrators are principals, vice-principals, and assorted assistants. Each of these has the potential of contributing to your program.

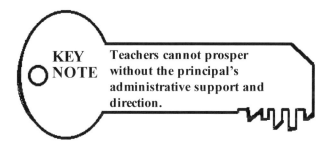

KEY NOTE   Teachers cannot prosper without the principal's administrative support and direction.

Usually the principal makes final decisions as to the number and levels of language courses that will be offered. The number of students to be enrolled in each class will be determined by the principal, and he or she is the person you have to convince that you need smaller class sizes to permit maximum interaction and practice. As you offer advanced courses, the principal will decide if you can carry a class with just a few students or if you have to combine classes. Decisions about budget for buying texts and materials, installing language laboratories, getting computer hardware and software, etc., are in his or her hands.

Establish a good relationship with the principal. Be willing to serve in school and community projects so that when the time comes to ask for support you will get a positive response. Don't forget to invite administrators to different activities; otherwise, your excellence and achievements may go unnoticed. We have included a "Guide" for working with principals in Appendix A at the end of the book that will be helpful in working with principals in organizing a model foreign language program.

Counselors. Counselors perform a very important mission: they are responsible for helping students plan their schedules, choose classes, and fill requirements. Thus they have a powerful influence on whether or not a student will study foreign languages, and are necessary to help FL teachers stop or avoid high drop-out problems. We have included a "Guide" to help you work with counselors in Appendix B at the end of the book.

You should make it a goal to establish a good relationship with school counselors by doing some of the following:

- Invite counselors to your department meetings when pertinent items are being discussed.
- Insist that FL students not be dropped from a course, or their program changed, without being interviewed by their FL teacher and FL chairman.
- Insist on being included in parent interviews where FL is a major topic in order to help the counselor as well as the FL program or FL teacher involved.
- Meet deadlines. If the counselor asks for grade sheets, enrollment numbers, or AP applications, be sure they are in on time.
- Assist counselors with the choice of college for your junior and senior students. Make sure you keep abreast of good foreign language programs at local and national colleges. Prospective foreign language majors will depend heavily on your advice, as well as that of the counselors. If possible arrange visits to FL classes at local universities. Career counseling is part of your job.
- Take over the advisement for Summer study, travel, exchange, and work programs for FL students. Let the counselors know that you are the resource person, and then collect materials. This should relieve the counselors of still another job.
- Assist counselors in evaluating and assigning credits from summer FL study programs or from foreign schools.
- Keep the foreign language students' guidance files up to date with any accomplishments and documents to help the student.
- Contact the counselor with the purpose of helping the FL student who is having difficulties early in the year, when something can still be done, rather than waiting until the matter is impossible to solve.
- Verbalize and write out your praise of the counselors.

Librarians and media-specialists. Usually these persons have a budget to spend each year for procuring books, magazines, and equipment for use in the school. You should make it one of your primary objectives to build a strong library collection of materials in Spanish and about Hispanic countries. This includes videos and computer software, music tapes and CD ROMs. Librarians seem to be forever complaining that teachers don't respond to their requests for input in selecting books and materials and they have to make decisions on their own. It stands to reason that if you as the Spanish teacher don't request materials in Spanish for your students to use, there won't be any.

Special education and subject-area specialists. These people have the responsibility to provide support to the regular teachers. Often they have foreign language skills and can adapt some of their activities to reinforce vocabulary or cultural information that you are teaching in the class. Make it a point to let them know what you are doing and ask if there is some way they can give your students additional practice.

Parents of your students. Parents can be very helpful because they are interested in the schools, the students, the curriculum, and the students' improvement. They can serve as teachers' aides in the classroom (sometimes for pay, usually *gratis*). They can be especially helpful if the foreign language program is in any danger of elimination in a budget crunch. Often the parents speak the target language and can help with activities that require language use.

Local Parent Teacher (Student) Associations (PTA). Your own PTA can help you strengthen your program with such things as fund raising campaigns, buying books for school libraries, and providing parent assistants and aides for classes. You as a Spanish teacher need to become acquainted with the officers of your local PTA and be aware of what assistance they can give. You need to tell them about the specific needs of your Spanish program and ask for their support and help.

Local school districts usually support professional activity of their teachers, and some even have a requirement of membership for teachers moving up their "career ladders" or moving ahead on the pay scale. Local school districts regularly sponsor in-service training for beginning teachers, and workshops for experienced teachers.

Larger school districts often have a **district FL supervisor (coordinator/specialist)** who was an outstanding foreign language teacher who had many years of experience and will be able to give you a good deal of help. This specialist usually coordinates the district curriculum, helps

with the hiring of new teachers, and helps with the improvement of in-service teachers with activities such as workshops, evaluation, use of technology, etc. The specialist's experience and general savvy can be of help to you with such things as:

- Goals, objectives, and methods and the associated unit planning—short term planning.
- Getting FL teachers involved on the long term planning committees: semester outlines and stream and level outlines for two, three, four, five, and six year programs.
- Textbook program adoption and subsequent coordination of the program in the district, something that requires orientation and committee organization, workshops for use of the new programs, preparation of picture files, use of video and computer programs that accompany the text, testing committees.
- Articulation between middle school or junior high school and senior high school—not to mention the elementary school or the college.
- Preparing and publishing a guidebook for the district.

City organizations usually exist in large cities such as Chicago, Los Angeles, and Atlanta. These groups sponsor local activities such as workshops and language fairs. Inter-school activities can be very motivating to your students and can give you some basis for comparison of your program with those of other schools.

District or regional alliances with local universities are sometimes organized to create a closer cooperation between the schools and colleges. Ways are also sought to allow the public schools take advantage of college facilities.

State School Boards or State Boards of Education also carry out programs for orientation, improvement of programs, and broadening of teaching skills. Most states have a **State Foreign (World) Language Coordinator (Specialist/Supervisor)** who can be of great help to teachers looking to design new programs, improve old ones, etc. These state specialists are usually responsible for establishing state guidelines for teacher certification, and the preparation of state curriculum guides for the language teachers of the state, state accreditation of schools, and general textbook adoption. Various committees are needed to accomplish those tasks and FL teachers form the committees. Volunteer to be named to those committees. The specialist would probably be very happy to respond to an invitation to evaluate your program.

Your state foreign language supervisor undoubtedly belongs to a national organization, the National Council of State Supervisors of Foreign Languages (NCSSFL) that meets each year to find ways to build programs and support the FL teachers of their state. As an organizational member of ACTFL, NCSSFL collaborates with ACTFL in an effort to promote FL study, provide resources to the teachers and conduct in-service activities at the state and local level.

The state supervisor usually conducts a variety of meetings, workshops, and other methods of passing on information from that yearly meeting to the language teachers of the state. They are especially active in informing teachers of grants, scholarships, and travel abroad opportunities.

Every state has a textbook adoption committee that is responsible to evaluate and approve textbooks for use in the state. The state board of education is also responsible for setting recertification standards and appointing teams to periodically evaluate school programs. These teams often consist of regular foreign language teachers combined with university professors. One of the best ways to have direct input in the selection of texts and materials which will be used in your own school's program is to volunteer to serve on state or district textbook committees.

University Teachers of FL Methods Courses.
How could you forget your favorite college teacher who is in a position to help with the latest methods, strategies, techniques, and even gimmicks to build your repertoire of teaching ideas? Often these university teachers are the supervisors and coordinators of the beginning courses at the university and they work with the teaching assistants and student instructors. Quite possibly they are also the college supervisors of student teachers. These university teachers comprise a great treasure trove of helps for all levels of teaching from the elementary schools

to the senior high schools and the colleges as well.

Program Help from Professional Foreign Language Associations

There are a number of professional organizations you should be acquainted with and actively participating in. We will mention only the most important, highlighting some of the ways they can help you with your *program*. It will be worth your time to look up each of them on the Internet and learn of the many services that they provide. In Chapter 18 we will suggest how some of these organizations can help you in your *personal teaching*.

State Foreign Language Associations All states have state foreign language associations. For example: the Utah Foreign Language Association (UFLA), the Foreign Language Association of Northern California (FLANC), the Arizona Foreign Language Teachers Association (AFLTA), etc. These organizations are composed of and directed by the foreign language teachers of the state, and provide such benefits as: yearly or bi-annual conventions, workshops for individual school districts, state testing programs, foreign study opportunities, monthly newsletters, financial grants for program innovations and excellence, etc.

Regional Conferences on Language Teaching.
Over the years there has been a movement to organize a network of regional Conferences on Teaching Foreign languages. This movement began with the Northeast Conference on Language Teaching and then gradually expanded to the rest of the country. Most recently organized were the **Southwest Conference on Language Teaching** and the **Northwest Conference on Language Teaching.** These organizations include several states grouped into an area, and make it easier for teachers to attend regional conferences.

As an example, the **Southwest Conference on Language Teaching** (said "Southwest COLT" for short) serves language educators in the states of Arizona, California, Colorado, Nevada, New Mexico, Oklahoma, Texas, and Utah. Its primary purpose is to hold an annual meeting each year in March or April to provide a forum to exchange ideas and help strengthen language teaching and learning in the region. The annual meeting moves to a new state in the region each year. The *Conference Reports* put the results of the oral presentations into the hands of members in a written form, along with other valuable information of interest to language teachers.

There are several salient national organizations that promote foreign language study and provide support and resources to language teachers. In this chapter we will point out the ways they can help you improve your program, and in Chapter 18 we will highlight the ways they can help you improve your personal skills.

The American Council on the Teaching of Foreign Languages (ACTFL) was created from the Modern Language Association in 1967. Prior to that time, there was no single entity representing teachers of all foreign languages at all educational levels. ACTFL (pronounced "act-full") was organized to fill that need, and is without doubt the most important national organization you could belong to. Some of the help that ACTFL gives your program is summarized here:

- Making students, school administrators, government officials, business and labor leaders, and the general public aware of the importance of second language learning.
- The establishment of the Joint National Committee for Lanaguages, an advocacy organization that seeks the support of the nations's leaders in efforts to promote foreign language study.
- In ACTFL's Annual Meeting, which is the country's major event in foreign language education, teachers can attend sessions about program improvement and can meet with some of the leaders of the most successful programs in the nation.
- Providing resources and materials to promote foreign language study and encouragement of longer sequences of language study.

Here is an example of an ACTFL promotion:

Sponsored by the American Council on the Teaching of Foreign Languages (ACTFL), Discover Languages is a national campaign for languages that builds on the momentum begun

during 2005: The Year of Languages. This initiative is a long-term effort to raise public awareness about the importance of learning languages and understanding cultures in the lives of all Americans. The key cornerstones of the campaign include public awareness, advocacy and policy; research and practice; and resources and collaboration. (www.DiscoverLanguages.org)

ACTFL has several publications, including *Foreign Language Annals*, a quarterly journal that publishes research studies, and the *Foreign Language Educator*, a magazine published six times a year that focuses on the latest practices, methods, and news related to foreign language teaching in the U.S. The most recent ACTFL publication, which began in December, 2009, is the ACTFL SmartBrief, a newsletter that summarizes and links language teachers to news articles pertinent to foreign language education. Read the following selections from the latest edition of this free newsletter (used by permission from ACTFL) and see how they could help you with some aspects of your program.

1) Budget concerns leave foreign language programs in jeopardy
Budget woes have Fairfax, VA officials questioning whether foreign language learning -- especially for younger students -- is needed. Marty Abbott, ACTFL's director of education, said the teaching of foreign languages in the U.S. is slowly gaining ground, and 16 states and Washington, D.C., require students to take foreign language courses to graduate. But while Fairfax officials say early foreign language programs are crucial to developing bilingual students, the recession leaves everything except

reading, writing and math on the chopping block. *The Washington Post* (11/17)

2) Close to $5 million is released for scholarships in language study
Nearly $5 million in scholarship money for students wishing to study foreign languages will soon be available under the Beatrice S. Demers Foreign Language Fellows Program, to be administered by the Rhode Island Foundation. Demers, who died in 2007, had been a professor of foreign languages for 30 years at the University of Rhode Island. According to Demers' wishes, the scholarships will be available to anyone wishing to learn a foreign language, but preference will be given to those who enroll at URI. *The Providence Journal* (11/14)

3) Foreign languages can offer study in adventure and romance
The process of learning a foreign language remains a powerful force in education, writes Edutopia contributing editor Owen Edwards in this blog post. Edwards credits his attempts at foreign language learning with helping him better appreciate his native language and suggests that educators encourage students to learn new languages by promoting the adventure and romance that comes with grasping another way of thinking and speaking. "Learn a language, and you learn a people," he writes. "Learn a people, and you learn about yourself." Edutopia.org (11/25)

4) Value of dual language program debated in Washington state district
Educators and parents in a Washington state school district are at odds over the merits of dual language courses for teaching English to students who speak Spanish. District officials recently eliminated dual language courses, citing low performance in the classroom and on standardized tests among dual language students. But some parents in the district, which is predominantly Latino, say the program helped their children retain ties to their native language and culture. *Yakima Herald-Republic* (11/17)

5) Columnist: Foreign language study should be required in Iowa
Foreign language study should be required for all students under Iowa's new core curriculum standards, argues Rekha Basu in this Des Moines Register column. By not compelling its students to learn a foreign language, Iowa is putting them at a disadvantage against/ students from other states, Basu writes, arguing that foreign language proficiency should be added as a 21st-century skill. *The Des Moines Register* (11/22)

6) February is Discover Languages month!
Buy your supplies now! Be ready to get your students, parents and colleagues involved in this monthlong event for foreign language learning! Visit the ACTFL online store at www.actfl.org to buy Discover Languages products!

There is no way we can overemphasize the importance of utilizing the resources of ACTFL. Their official web site is awesome. Visit it and inform yourself about all this national organization has to offer: www.actfl.org

National Language Resource Centers. The U.S. Department of Education sponsors 15 national language resource centers (http://nflrc.msu.edu/), which are housed at various universities around the country. Their mission is to improve and strengthen the nation's capacity to teach and learn foreign languages. Their areas of focus include testing, learning strategies, materials development and methodology, technology, professional development, and dissemination of information on commonly and less commonly taught languages. They provide latest news, grants, professional training programs, etc. Many resources centers send out free monthly electronic newsletters and sponsor Summer workshops for language teachers. Some of the better-known centers are the National Capital Language Resource Center (NCLRC) at Georgetown and George Washington University, the Center for Advanced Research on Language Acquisition (CARLA) at the University of Minnesota, and the Center for Language Education and Research (CLEAR) at Michigan State University. Check out their websites for valuable teaching resources and sign up for their monthly newsletters.

The Center for Applied Linguistics. The Center for Applied Linguistics (CAL) is a private nonprofit organization dedicated to the

study of language and culture and to the application of research on language and culture to educational and social concerns. As major language issues continue to be debated, the perspective of language experts remains essential to inform the dialogue. CAL's mission reflects an ongoing commitment to improving communication through better understanding of language and culture. The resources this center provides are incredible. Visit their website and spend some time looking for something that might help you.
www.CAL.org/earlylang/teaching/index

American Association of Teachers of Spanish and Portuguese (AATSP). This association can help you with the unique problems related to the teaching of Spanish. Perhaps the most important service that AATSP provides is the National Spanish Examination that we have previously mentioned. By administering this test to your students you can get a good picture of how they compare with other students at the same levels all across the nation. Awards are given to students with high scores in the examination.

Other services provided by AATSP include:

- The Annual Meeting, which has a variety of sessions relevant to Spanish teaching, is often held in Hispanic countries such as Spain and Mexico.
- A professional journal, Hispania, which includes material relevant to the classroom, articles about the Hispanic and Luso-Brazilian worlds, pedagogical issues, book reviews, linguistic problems as well as the traditional literary themes. Each issue contains valuable advertisements.
- The Sociedad Honoraria Hispánica which has chapters in eligible secondary schools and provides college and travel scholarships, certificates of excellence, the publication ¡Albricias! to which students submit creative writing efforts, and a variety of awards for both students and teachers.
- Cultural Units and materials that are loaned out to teachers for use in their classrooms.
- A Placement Bureau service to help Spanish teachers find jobs.
- ONCE, a service that provides names of students in Hispanic countries wishing to

maintain correspondence with American high school students of Spanish.
- Incentive materials for students, including medals, awards, and seals.
- Advocacy groups working in Washington to lobby for support for foreign language study.
- Opportunities for grass roots involvement through the organization of local chapters of AATSP.

Of Interest to FLES Teachers

The National Network for Early Language Learning (NNELL) is an educational community providing leadership in support of successful early language learning and teaching. Browse through the NNELL Web site to learn more about the organization and to gain access to valuable resources for educators, parents and policymakers advocating for K-8 programs of excellence in second language education. www.NNELL.org.

While you are in the mood for visiting web sites, check out these amazing sources that provide materials for FLES teachers:

- The Center for Applied Linguistics has a very valuable link for FL teachers from grades K-8. Go to their home page and in the search box type in the word *ñandutí*. There is very valuable information, resources and even lesson plans.

- **Mary Levine's FL Lesson Plans and Resources** is amazing! Go to the NNELL site to resources. You will connect from there. www.nnell.com.

- **Jim Becker's site.** Inside of Mary Levine's listing you will see Jim Becker's vast listings. www.nnell.com.

- **Anacleta's Spanish and World Language site.** Connect through Ana Lomba's site-resources. www.suenosdecolores.com.

- **Learn Spanish.** Resources and web links for learning Spanish. www.lingolex.com/spanish.htm

- **REACH.** Resources related to the Spanish language and to Hispanic cultures in the U.S. and in other Spanish-speaking nations. www.nflc.org/reach/mainintroen.htm
- **Santillana USA.** An International program with a strong following in Spain and Latin America. Program range is preK-12. A vast offering of colorful and age-appropriate materials, books and CD's. A new program for middle and upper grades is currently in development. Additionally, online resources "for teachers and parents" are available including FREE downloadable activities for your students. Company also offers assistance in grant writing at no charge and is located in Miami, Florida. www.santillanausa.com.

- **WLA.** World Language Advocates, centered in Miami, was founded by Trisha Conroy a mother who wanted her daughter to become bilingual. Visit her site to see what can be done with parental initiative. http://www.wlaflorida.com/about.html

Miscellaneous Organizations

Groups in Hispanic countries. Almost all the Spanish-speaking countries in the world maintain embassies and consulates in the United States that in turn sponsor various educational and informational programs and are affiliated with other agencies that feature aspects, concerns, and interests of these countries. For instance: the *Consejería de Educación* of the Spanish Embassy, the various consulate offices, Spanish-American Chambers of Commerce, Cultural Centers, etc. Most of these organizations and affiliates are very generous with booklets, pictures, posters, program notes, audio cassettes, video cassettes, overhead transparencies, and the like.

Recently the Ministerio de Cultura of Spain created the **Instituto Cervantes** (patterned after the Goethe Institute and the Alliance Française) that is interested in furthering with the study of Spanish language and culture around the world. In addition to scholarships for study in Spain, this institute makes materials such as music and videos available to teachers and administers a test of certification for teachers of Spanish. They have recently set up a program for Diplomas for Spanish Teachers and are currently setting up regional centers with consultants and materials to help the Spanish teachers in each region.

International Association of Language Laboratories (IALL) This group combines language teachers of all languages, language lab directors, educational technologists, computer specialists, software developers, and others in an organization which focuses on the use of technology. Its journal, the *IALL Journal of Language Learning Technologies*, can give much information about the use of technology in teaching languages.

CALICO. In the area of use of technology in the teaching of foreign language, **CALICO** (Computer Assisted Learning and Instruction Consortium), which had it birth at BYU, is perhaps the most important organization. It is a professional organization that serves a membership involved in both education and technology. **CALICO** has an emphasis on language teaching and learning but reaches out to all areas that employ the languages of the world to instruct and to learn. **CALICO** is a recognized international clearinghouse and leader in computer assisted learning and instruction. It is a premier global association dedicated to computer-assisted language learning (CALL). **CALICO** includes foreign language educators, programmers, technicians, web page designers, CALL developers, CALL practitioners, novice CALL users, second language acquisition researchers--anyone interested in exploring the use of technology for foreign language teaching and learning.

Membership Benefits include the ***CALICO Journal***, a thrice-yearly publication devoted to the dissemination of research in the use of technology in language learning. The ***CALICO journal***, annual conferences, special interest groups, and publishes a series of monographs on use of technology in language teaching.

BUILDING YOUR PROGRAM

In some states foreign languages are part of the "core" curriculum that is required of all students. In most states, however, foreign language study is an *elective* and consequently you as language teachers must constantly "sell your product," finding support wherever you can, continually building your program.

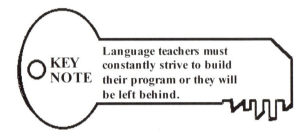

KEY NOTE   Language teachers must constantly strive to build their program or they will be left behind.

Not all language teachers have the same abilities, loyalties and preparation. Realizing that they are teaching one of the most important, potentially valuable subjects offered in our educational system, language teachers of outstanding quality will:

- Continually improve competence in language skills by all possible means, including periodic foreign residence.
- Keep abreast of development in the teaching of language and culture.
- Habitually convey a positive, enthusiastic attitude about teaching language and culture and about language learning.
- Have a genuine interest in young people, accept students where they are and help them progress to language proficiency and cultural appreciation.
- Be thoroughly dedicated to the language-teaching profession and establish good professional relationships with total staff.
- Understand thoroughly the basic philosophy of the text program used in the courses and develop it.
- Join and participate regularly in local, state, and national associations, especially those directly pertaining to language learning.
- Survey monthly the professional journals and new books (via at least the book reviews in the journals).
- Acquire additional formal preparation through in-service workshops and course work leading to higher degrees and professional certification.
- Test new programs and experimental ideas.

Recruiting Students

Good programs do not usually build themselves. Teachers must have a plan and take the right steps. Here are some tips received from practicing teachers

- Keep reminding that learning a language is a lengthy process. Compare the study of Spanish with building a house. In the first years you frame the house and lay the bricks. In the intermediate courses you move in the furniture. In the advanced courses you put in the piano, the jacuzzi, the big screen TV and other amenities. The more you can do with the language, the more you enjoy it.
- At parent teacher conferences, ask parents if their children are going to continue. Praise their progress and abilities and tell them about your advanced and AP classes and the importance that they continue in the sequence. Even in high school, parents have the greatest influence on what courses their children take.
- Talk about study abroad opportunities. Talk about how cool that experience can be and how important it is to continue with their study to be better prepared. Even if they don't go on one of those programs in High School, they can do it in college, but there shouldn't be a gap where they are not studying Spanish.
- Inform them that they can take advanced Spanish classes in place of Senior English classes (language arts elective).
- Tell them about scholarships that require additional language study. Find the names of scholarships and encourage your students to apply for them.
- Make it a habit to make constant "spot commercials," that is, remind them of the value of language study, the ways it is enriching their life, and how much they enjoy taking Spanish.

Examples of Successful Program Builders

We will present two examples here of teachers of other subjects who are successful program builders. Perhaps you can use some of these ideas in building your own program.

Music teachers. Music, like foreign languages in most schools, is an elective subject. The following anecdote will illustrate to what lengths some music teachers may go to build their programs:

This story is true; it happened to my first son, my second son, and then to my two daughters when each of them was in the sixth grade. Jim, my first son, was popular in his elementary school and was conscientious in his work. He wanted to be involved in school activities. One day at school he was approached by a young man, obviously a teacher, but unknown to Jim. He introduced himself as Mr. Taylor, said he was the music teacher from the junior high school, and asked Jim if he had ever taken music lessons. When Jim replied no, that he was more interested in other things, Mr. Taylor tactfully listened and allowed Jim to express his other interests, then said, "Let me see your hands." Jim held out his hands and allowed the teacher to examine them. "You have the hands of a cellist! I'm sure you could be a good cello player. Would you like to learn?" Jim nodded more out of politeness and astonishment than real desire. As he left, Mr. Taylor promised to make the arrangements. Jim saw Mr. Taylor several more times that day talking to other sixth graders, always looking carefully at their hands.

A few days later Jim announced at the dinner table, "Mom and Dad, I want to play the cello. Mr. Taylor, the music teacher at the junior high school, says I have the hands of a cello player. He's going to lend me a cello and give me free lessons on Tuesdays and Thursdays after school." Sure enough, the enterprising young music teacher followed up and had mini-courses after school for his selected musicians. Not a lot of progress was made in the next few weeks, but each experience was positive. The students who practiced were rewarded with a treat at the local ice cream parlor. They all performed in a recital at the end of the semester.

Needless to say, all those students enrolled in Mr. Taylor's music classes the following school year, as did the children from the other elementary schools feeding into the junior high school where Mr. Taylor had also been teaching mini-classes for violinists, flutists, clarinetists, and so on. His diligence and hours of extra work were now paying off. He had three large orchestra classes. Orchestra was fun. Students worked hard.

Then Mr. Taylor moved into the second phase of his plan. He visited each student's home and told the parents how well their children were doing. He then gave the parents the names of teachers or advanced students who could give private lessons for a minimal fee. We contacted a high school senior who had played the cello for a number of years. He came to our home once a week to give Jim lessons. The plan to give rewards to students for diligence also continued, i.e. compliments, M&M candies, competition (first chair, second chair, third chair), recitals, performances in the community, especially at Christmas time, in various towns, as well as centers for senior citizens, hospitals, and of course feeder schools. The students even enjoyed attending the teacher's performances.

Our home was filled with music; the whole family was thrilled. We were especially thrilled when Jim talked about Beethoven, Tchaikovsky, and Mozart. We watched him with great joy when he showed interest in concerts and types of music other than the ever-present rock. Jim went to concerts assigned or recommended, often with his mother and father. He played in church, later in a youth orchestra, finally in the state junior symphony orchestra. Jim still plays the cello, his children play musical instruments and there is music in their home

It didn't take much effort to convert our other children to good music. We now have a clarinetist, a violinist, two French horn players, a piano and saxophone player and several guitar players

Let's analyze a couple of aspects in this account to find applications to language teaching.

- The teacher didn't sit back waiting for students to come to him.
- He had very creative ways of recruiting students—"Let me see your hands."
- He didn't regret the many hours of outside work with no pay because it results in later payoffs.
- He took on all interested people.

Instead of hands, foreign language teachers could talk about other special qualities a young person might have, such as quick memorization and evidence of good memory. Foreign language teachers can and have made good use of foreign language aptitude tests, such as the MLAT and the *Pimsleur LAB* (See Chapter 12) to recruit students, giving the tests in all language arts classes in the feeder school and/or in the high school, using the results very positively, encouraging those with high scores to sign up for foreign languages, and encouraging those with lower scores to sign up anyway, indicating to them that interest in foreign language study is the most important consideration anyway—and trying out FL's is the only way to know really if a student is to be successful.

Another consideration for good recruitment is the ancestry of the students. Often you can determine it from their names. Looking at the school records, you can determine it for their mother's side, too. Encourage students with Spanish ancestry to sign up for Spanish. Sometimes students come from the foreign countries fairly recently and can be an excellent teacher's aide and be enrolled in the beginning class.

Do not restrict anyone because of difficulty in classes, even English classes. Our experience indicates that students can start at point zero in learning a foreign language, enjoying success and developing abilities in learning Spanish and building their self-esteem.

Drama teachers. Language teachers can also learn a basic concept from drama teachers. If drama students spent entire semesters practicing dramatic techniques but never put on a play, they would soon lose interest in what they were doing. Additionally, their parents would begin to wonder if they were accomplishing anything worthwhile. Thus, the drama teacher knows the value of "putting on the play." At the end of the weeks of study, work, and practice there is a "product" that can be seen and appreciated by the students and parents alike. The play is the culmination, the harvest, the visible evidence, the fruits of the labors.

Likewise, you must frequently come up with products of your work in the language class—some fruits of your labors that can give the students satisfaction and give the parents pride in their children's progress. Some "plays" that you can put on are these:

- Students can prepare skits as a culminating activity in the various units of work in the class; these are often appropriate for presentation to parents at a skit night, especially for holidays such as Christmas, Easter, and Halloween. Students also enjoy performing skits at school assemblies. (See the booklets on simulations, task performance activities, plays, games, and motivational materials for many specific ideas using skit-related possibilities.)

- Another excellent product presentation is in the competitions of foreign language fairs sponsored on a district or even regional level where several districts are involved. Here students can participate in speech contests, show-and-tell activities, poetry, drama presentations, conversational contests, oral interviews, culture bowl activities, and reading comprehension tests. (See Chapter 16, "Beyond the Classroom.") Students can participate in all of the activities of *Españolandia* such as money exchange, banks, post office, market, restaurants, *kioscos*, and the like.

Recruiting Ideas Summary. Let's summarize the ideas for recruiting students (the Foreign Language Teachers' version of the persuasive recruitment used by Mr. Taylor, who may have based his techniques on *Music Man* by Meredith Wilson):

1. Visit feeder schools every spring and invite students who will be coming to your school in the fall to enroll in your classes.
2. Recruit students in your own school.
3. Sponsor a dynamic Spanish club.
4. Give the students performance opportunities in the school for other students and for parents: assembly performance, plays, talent shows, talks, PTA presentations, presentations in Spanish at feeder schools, and so on.
5. Teach so well that your reputation is established and word gets around that Spanish classes are exciting and interesting.
6. Talk up foreign language teaching and study with counselors and administrators.

7. Find native speakers in the school who are participating in exchange programs such as American Field Service or in Youth for Understanding. Enlist them as teacher aides ("language squad").
8. Locate other teachers and administrators who can speak Spanish and have them talk to the students and parents. Persuade them to help in both class and Spanish club activities.
9. Feature foreign language (Spanish) in the school using the school newspaper, using the school display cases in the main hallways, arranging for the Mariachi band (that you perhaps organized) to play in the main foyer before or after school, celebrate the national foreign language week, sponsor interlingual dances and parties as a language club activity and invite club members to bring some friends, etc.
10. Have parents see performances in class and in school assemblies that show the culture of the Spanish-speaking countries.
11. Concentrate on effective articulation that builds Spanish in the "feeder" schools and in "successor" schools. Special second- and third-year student-tutors from the high school can help with beginning students in the elementary and junior high schools. Consider showing students how to tutor their parents and help the parents to learn Spanish.
12. Help students to participate in district, regional, state, and national foreign language fairs. (See Chapter 16, "Beyond the Classroom.")
13. Plan (with students) to have motivating summer or weekend camps, special clinics, retreats, and excursions (especially Spanish restaurants), etc.
14. Check the community for Spanish-American organizations and native Spanish speakers who can help with task performance activities and other simulations that nearly duplicate real activities that would happen in Spanish-speaking countries. (See the booklets on simulations, and on task performance activities, as well as Chapter 16 "Beyond the Classroom.")
15. Take advantage of the many opportunities to get your students to Spanish-speaking countries. Check the Study-Abroad programs or internship programs sponsored by many universities. (Some addresses are listed in the reference section of this Chapter.)

Public and School Staff Relations

Foreign language teachers are a part of a very complete instructional team composed of administrators, counselors, other language teachers, teachers of related subjects, and parents. We must nurture and care for our programs, always on the lookout for people who are sympathetic to our goals and who are in a position to give us support. Don't hesitate to use the arguments we developed in Chapter 2, "Are You Converted?"

What can the teacher do to retain a foreign language program if the administrator is on the verge of canceling the program? Find out the specific reasons why foreign language or your class in particular is in jeopardy.

1. Check your teaching.
   a. Are you teaching with enthusiasm?
   b. Do you enjoy speaking the foreign language and do you convey this happiness to your students?

2. Recruiting
   a. Have you maintained substantial enrollments in your classes?
   b. Do you actively "sell" your foreign language to your students and to the public—especially the parents? Do you involve parents in class and/or foreign language club activities?
   c. Do you actively recruit students within your school and from feeder schools?
   d. Do you help them "acquire" the language rather than just learn about the language? Does your class enable the students to experience the culture of the language and participate in listening, speaking, reading, and writing activities, and thereby serve as a source for recruiting students into real language courses?
3. Taking counter measures.
   a. As soon as you hear that your classes are going to be reduced, or your program eliminated, ask your supporting and loyal parents to go to the PTA president and ask him or her to go to the principal and ask

that the foreign language class(es) be continued. Get the parents and the PTA president to go to your local school board member and indicate the reasons why they want foreign language classes maintained in your school.

b. Contact your district coordinator (specialist or supervisor) as well as the state foreign language specialist and ask them to write letters to the principal in support of your foreign language classes.

This entire plan of action will reduce the practice of eliminating foreign language classes. But remember, the role of the teacher is very important. Realize that cutting out foreign language courses is a possibly convenient way to balance a tight budget, but for total education, it is not a good measure. There are other options much less drastic.

Using Publicity

You must constantly search for ways of putting your program into the spotlight at the school. Remember that other teachers are also committed to promoting their own programs and no one else is likely to give your program a boost if you don't take some initial action. Our keynote presents a well-known saying that is certainly true about educational programs:

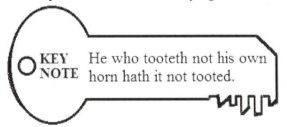

KEY NOTE   He who tooteth not his own horn hath it not tooted.

Celebrate Foreign Language Week

Many schools have found that a successful way to bring foreign language study to the attention of the students, parents, and for that matter to other teachers and school administrators, is to organize a celebration of National Foreign Language Week. The third week in February of every year has been officially designated by congress as National Foreign Language Week. There are national organizations that provide information and

suggestions to celebrate this period (see References).

Planning. Although commemorations of this type require much effort and time, the end results usually demonstrate their value. They must be coordinated with a number of groups in the school such as administrators, cooks, janitors, bus drivers, and other staff personnel—not to mention other teachers. You should do as much as possible to involve community people as well. This should be approached in terms of an annual, permanent or traditional celebration and as you develop programs and materials, they should be done carefully and with the idea of using them time after time. Foreign language teachers put aside the grammar, composition and testing in order to organize the "fun" activities for which academia leaves little time throughout the school year. Learning is not sacrificed; it simply assumes different forms. Through games, contests, guest speakers, performers, art, music, trivia, and international cuisine, students discover other cultures and learn to respect them as different, not wrong or inferior.

Total school involvement. During this week the foreign language classroom is extended to students who do not study foreign language. The faculty is encouraged to include foreign language and culture in their lesson plans for the week. Interdisciplinary assemblies and school-wide contests involve much of the student body. Different programs are run at the high school, middle school, and elementary levels, since some activities are better suited to a particular age or ability. Creativity is the key.

Case History of a Specific School

Following is a description of how Windsor Elementary School, in Orem, Utah, commemorates National Foreign Language Week.

Initial plans for the event are made in October. Foreign Language teachers hold a brainstorming session and also discuss and investigate available school funds, grant possibilities, and fund raising possibilities.

Starting in October they set up an agenda for each month so the planning and preparation is spread out and made achievable.

After the organizers **get clearance from the district office**, they do the following: prepare articles to be used in the newspaper, enlisting the help of media center personnel; set up an international banquet; check with local restaurants and other businesses for assistance, funding and advertising; and put the week's events on the school calendar early to avoid conflicts.

They choose a theme. Very early the foreign language teachers decide on a theme for Foreign Language Week. The theme is printed on a large colorful banner and hung in the front foyer. The art teacher supervises this and enlists the aid of other teachers. Various themes have included:

> *Languages unite the world*
> *We all smile in the same language*
> *It's a small world*
> *Welcome to the wonderful world of*
> *languages.*

Foreign Language Teachers survey their colleagues regarding their language and travel experience and choose five to highlight—one per day. They announce their plans for the week at faculty meeting and distribute an information sheet to all teachers.

One language is featured each day, and school announcements are given in the language of the day. Prior to the announcements, music from the designated country is played. Students practice words and expressions from the designated language—numbers, classroom items, "Hello," "How are you?", "Today is. . ." etc. [See coping card].

Each language is designated by a different color that is used on labels, word signs, pictures, and the like:

Mon.	German	green
Tues.	Chinese	red
Wed.	French	blue
Thur.	Russian	pink
Fri.	Spanish	yellow

Color coded labels are given to teach teacher to display in the classroom on the day featuring the corresponding language (desk, chalkboard, wall, light, paper, books, teacher, etc.)

Foreign language teachers plan the week's menu with the lunch supervisor several weeks in advance to have the menu for each day correspond as much as possible to the featured language. Tacos for Spanish day, chow mien for Chinese, soup for Russian, *Bratwurst* for German, etc. On the last day of the week in the year they feature flags and have a flag identification contest, they have the kitchen staff stick little flag picks in the dessert. The children have fun trying to identify the flags.

During the week displays are set up in the halls and foyers. Flags from the various countries are rented from the local university, and display cases hold items from various countries. On the walls are posters (travel-type) depicting foreign lands and colored balloons with the name of the color of the balloon in each of the foreign languages. Names of languages are written in bright butcher paper and displayed.

Signs with numbers, days of the week, and various phrases in the foreign languages—Hello, How are you? Fine. Good. Good morning. Good afternoon, Friend—also cover the walls. Pictures of children in native costumes are hung all around the cafeteria. Each of the rooms in the building are also labeled in the language of the day—office, library, rest rooms, cafeteria, etc. Each of these rooms is decorated with awnings from butcher paper in bright colors with scalloped edges.

The year the secretary's daughter was in Russia they decorated the outside of the office with minarets and hung a picture of the principal attired to look like Stalin.

An assembly is held which may vary from year to year, but basically consists of songs in foreign language sung by classes which want to participate, special guests such as dancers, singers, or musicians, fire dancers from Tonga, and a Maori stick game demonstrated by sixth graders. Everyone sings "Head, shoulders, knees and toes" in the various languages. A slide presentation depicts children from many countries. The school invites guests to the assembly, including the district supervisor, state school supervisor, Foreign Language supervisor, and others.

On one day, designated as costume day, faculty, students, lunch workers and staff wear clothing from other countries or make their own.

There is a prize for the class with the highest percentage of students in costume.

Each year a different contest is held, for example door decorating, contests involving identifying which language is being spoken, flag identification, poster contest (entries can be sent to a national contest).

Other activities have been used in various years. Once they held a treasure hunt (for a small candy bar, another goodie, trinket or gadget) with clues announced in the language of the day. Another year they invited family members or friends of students to individual classes to "show-and-tell" about their experiences in foreign countries, with displays of realia: food, clothing, toys, and the like. They encouraged teachers to teach their classes a song, game or dance in a foreign language. Most importantly, they had fun!

Since Foreign Language Week was first instituted, teachers and students have grown progressively more excited and receptive. The first year people said, "This is different," but were quite enthusiastic and cooperative. The second year they asked, "Are we having Foreign Language Week this year?" and were eager to participate. The third year people asked, "*When is Foreign Language week? I bought a skirt this summer to wear.*" They volunteered ideas and suggestions.

The first year planning and preparing for the event takes a great deal of work and time, but each year the task becomes easier because displays and ideas can be reused. All foreign language teachers can use the program and ideas described here to implant a successful foreign language week in their own school. Give it a try!

National Contests and Awards

Another idea for building programs is to make your students aware of national contests and awards. Students can be motivated by preparing for and participating in national contests and receiving awards. Such contests and awards are sponsored by the American Association of Teachers of Spanish and Portuguese (AATSP), the *Instituto Cervantes*, and the American Council on the Teaching of Foreign Languages (ACTFL). They vary in kind, extent, complication, and level, and must be searched out by referring to the newsletters and the journals published by these kinds of national organizations.

CONCLUSION

Success in teaching comes only as it does in other professions, we have to pay the price and keep working at it. We have to develop a pride in what we are doing and constantly work at improvement. In this chapter we have presented a variety of ways to build and improve programs. We have suggested a number of ways you can articulate and coordinate your program with other schools and institutions. If you sell your program to students, parents, counselors, and administrators, they in turn will sell it to others. You must be interested, cooperative, enthusiastic, confident, knowledgeable, and hard working. Know your facts on why foreign languages should be studied as long as possible—the two-year syndrome must be wiped out. Extremely effective is the foreign language teacher who believes in what he or she is doing and follows through. Is your personal philosophy of foreign languages well formulated? We fight for what we believe, and our task is to get everyone to believe what we believe—**that foreign languages are an integral part of every American's general education.** It's up to you to win everyone over with your good programs, your cooperation, and your positive attitude toward a working relationship. There are many marvelous and successful foreign language programs across the country. With dedication and hard work, yours can be one of them. We wish you great success in your efforts!

REFERENCES AND SUGGESTIONS FOR FURTHER READING

Jarvis, G. (Ed.). (1974). *ACTFL Review of FL Education* (ACTFL Review of Foreign Language Education, Vol. 6). Skokie, IL: National Textbook. (ERIC Document Reproduction Service No. ED162495) *See especially Ch. 3, "Public Awareness: How Can Associations and Institutions Use PR Skills?" by Anita Monsees, and Ch. 4, "Public Awareness: What can the Individual Teacher Do?" by Dona Reeves.*

Erickson, J., Haney, D., Semmer, M., & Theisen, T. (2008). You don't have to be an experienced lobbyist to make a difference. *The Language Educator, 3*(6), 57-59. *An example of how teachers successfully advocated for foreign language study in Colorado.*

Grittner, F. M. (Ed.). (1974). *Student motivation and the foreign language teacher: A guide for building the modern curriculum* (selected papers form the 1973 Central States Conference). Skokie, IL: National Textbook. (ERIC Document Reproduction Service No. ED134025) *See especially Ch. 4, "Making the Foreign Language Program Visible to the Public" by Gertrud Meyer, and Ch. 7, "Gaining Better Student Support for the Foreign Language Program" by Constance Knopp.*

Honig, L, J., & Brod, R. (1974). Foreign languages and careers. *Modern Language Journal, 58,* 157-185. DOI: 10.2307/325194 *Although now quite dated, much of the information on career possibilities for speakers of foreign languages is still relevant and quite useful.*

King, R., Riddle, E., & Taylor, D. H. (1994, March). *Windsor Elementary School celebrates Foreign Language Week.* Presentation at SWCOLT Annual Conference, Denver, CO.

Wilson, M., & Lacey, F. (1957) *The Music Man* [musical comedy]. As a promotion and hype, Professor Harold Hill said to Winthrop, "You have the perfect jaw for playing the cornet."

PROFESSIONAL ORGANIZATIONS OF INTEREST TO SPANISH TEACHERS

Note: We have included the URL of the professional organizations listed here to enable you to visit the sites and get in-depth details.

American Association of Teachers of Spanish and Portuguese (AATSP)
www.aatsp.org/

American Council on the Teaching of Foreign Languages (ACTFL) – Click on the "Advocacy" link under "Membership" for information and resources related to promoting language study. Also, the *Foreign Language Educator* magazine often contains articles on advocacy.   www.actfl.org/

The National Network for Early Language Learning (NNELL)
www.nnell.org/

Southwest Conference on the Teaching of Foreign Languages (SWCOLT)
www.swcolt.org/

Utah Foreign Language Association (UFLA)
http://organizations.weber.edu/ufla/

Modern Language Association (MLA)
www.mla.org/

PROMOTION OF SPANISH LANGUAGE AND CULTURE

Consejería de Educación
Embajada de España
www.educacion.es/exterior/usa/es/

Embassy of Spain
Cultural Office
www.spainculture.us/

Instituto Cervantes
www.cervantes.org/

World Language Specialist
Utah State Office of Education
http://www.schools.utah.gov/curr/for.lang/

Image Credits

p. 404: Brough, Peter. (2010, Nov. 26). School. *Open Clip Art Library.* Retrieved July 4, 2011 from http://www.openclipart.org/detail/98365/school-by-peterbrough. Public domain.

p. 409: American Council on the Teaching of Foreign Languages. (n.d.). *Discover Languages.* Retrieved July 4, 2011 from http://www.discoverlanguages.org/i4a/pages/index.cfm?pageid=4216. Used by permission.

ACTIVITIES FOR METHODS CLASSES

1. Working with your methods instructor, select a school district in your area, contact an official and evaluate their articulation: Is there a district foreign language coordinator? Do they have a district syllabus? Do they have district coordination meetings? Have they selected textbook series for the district? Etc. Report to your methods class.

2. Working with your methods instructor, select a college or university in your area, contact an official or teacher and evaluate their program of articulation with incoming students: How do they evaluate previous language study? Do they use a placement test? Do they give credit for beginning language classes if the students have had prior study in secondary schools? Can students get credit for college classes they skip? Etc. Report to your methods class.

3. Working with your methods instructor, select an elementary school or secondary school in your area, contact a teacher and evaluate their articulation with other schools: Do the elementary, junior high and senior high language teachers know each other? Do they coordinate their curriculum? Do they use the same textbook series? Do they meet frequently to coordinate programs? Do they ever make "teacher exchanges?" In large schools, is there a department chairman? Etc. Report to your methods class.

4. Divide the class into groups of five or six and pretend that each is an evaluation team charged with evaluating the program of a junior or senior high school. Have them prepare a list of the areas they would want to evaluate and how they would do it. Have each team report to the entire class.

5. Pretend that you have just finished your first year of teaching and want to evaluate your program. Develop a questionnaire you would give to your students. Consider the things you would want them to tell you. Discuss with your methods teacher.

6. Attend an activity or workshop sponsored by a professional organization. What were the objectives? Were they met? Write up a summary of the activity and hand in to your instructor.

7. Attend a professional presentation. Keep notes of what you learned. What things would you apply to your own classes? Hand in a report to your teacher summarizing what things you could apply in your own classes.

8. Find out if there are any local professional organizations in your area. What benefits can they offer you? Find out how you can join. Report to your methods professor.

9. Which national organizations are you interested in joining? Find an application for membership. How much will it cost? Do they have student memberships? Consider filling out and sending in the membership application. Report to your methods instructor.

10. Go to the library and find volumes of the professional journals mentioned in this chapter. Browse through the journals, learning what information is published in them and seeing the focus of the different sections. Find some interesting articles on foreign language teaching (not literature) and read them. Hand in short reports to your methods teacher.

ACTIVITIES FOR PRACTICING TEACHERS
BUILDING PROGRAMS

1. Visit FL (Spanish) classes in other schools and make a list of approaches, methods, strategies, and also attitudes that you could emulate to build your own FL program—also a list of the ones to avoid because of the negative effect.

2. Talk to other teachers in your school to find ways of making your classes so exciting that your program will grow and that students will be attracted.

3. Make a list of different activities as skit night, international dinners, cultural programs, slide or video shows of participants in program-building activities, and the like that you could conduct in your school.

4. Visit professional meetings and talk to the officers in order to make a list of possibilities to build programs and find out if the officers have memories of programs or if they have tried the ones in this chapter. Check on their plans for future programs or strategies.

5. Talk to music and drama teachers, and get more ideas on promoting courses.

6. Arrange an articulation meeting with the FL teachers in your feeder or successor schools. Discuss ways to improve articulation, using the suggestions in this chapter.

7. Interview officers of Spanish-American organizations in your community and discuss ways your students can help them meet their objectives, and what kinds of services they could provide to strengthen your school program.

8. Check with teachers at other schools to find out if they do activities such as FL week, celebrations, PTA involvement, student exchanges, Spanish club organizations, and the like in building programs and recruiting students.

9. Identify the significant people who can help you build programs that we have mentioned in this chapter, make an appointment and interview them about helping you build your program.

10. Arrange a special conference with administrators and counselors in your school and present the information in the Guides in the appendix.

11. Interview the state World Language Specialist about ideas for improving your program.

12. Visit the websites of the Spanish embassy and local consulates, the different organizations listed at the end of the chapter and ask for materials.

CHAPTER EIGHTEEN

EVALUATING AND IMPROVING YOURSELF AS A TEACHER

YOUR OBJECTIVES FOR THIS CHAPTER ARE TO:

1. EXPLORE WAYS OF ASSESSING YOUR PERSONAL TEACHING SKILLS AND EFFECTIVENESS.

2. IDENTIFY WAYS YOU CAN IMPROVE YOUR PERSONAL MASTERY OF THE FOREIGN LANGUAGE.

3. DETERMINE WHICH PROFESSIONAL ORGANIZATIONS CAN HELP YOU AS AN INDIVIDUAL AND EXPLAIN HOW TO JOIN THEM.

4. SUMMARIZE WHAT PROFESSIONAL ORGANIZATIONS OFFER YOU AS A TEACHER AND WHAT YOU MUST DO TO ACTIVELY PARTICIPATE IN THEIR PROGRAMS.

5. SUMMARIZE THE BENEFITS OF ATTENDING FOREIGN LANGUAGE CONFERENCES.

6. IDENTIFY WAYS YOU CAN PERSONALLY VISIT AND STUDY IN FOREIGN COUNTRIES AND WHAT TO DO WHEN YOU GET THERE THAT WILL HELP YOU IN YOUR TEACHING.

7. DESCRIBE WAYS TO AVOID OR CURE "BURNOUT" AND BECOME A MORE EFFECTIVE TEACHER.

Miss Tuffyd was understandably nervous about the interview. She really wanted to teach Spanish at Podunk High and if she were able to impress Mr. I. Hyrum Good, the job would be hers! She felt good about her command of the language and her ability as a teacher. She had gotten an excellent recommendation from her student teaching. She calmed the butterflies in her stomach and entered the room.

The first part of the interview went well, as Mr. Good talked about her background and her personal interests. Then he left her speechless with his next question, "Miss Tuffyd, what professional organizations are you a member of, or if you haven't joined any yet, which ones will you join as you begin to teach Spanish?" Her mind skipped back to all the job application forms she had filled out in the last few weeks and she recalled how each one of them had asked what academic or professional organizations she belonged to. She had, of course, had to leave that area blank. Perhaps she should have joined Sigma Delta Pi, the national Spanish honorary society, when she had been invited to join in her senior year, but it seemed like such a waste of money at the time. She also recalled how her methods teacher had urged them to get student membership in some language teachers' organization, but she couldn't recall the name right now. She felt her face redden as she replied, "No, Mr. Good, I don't presently belong to any professional organizations, and I can't remember the names of any that I would like to join." She could see that he was disappointed with her answer, and sensed that at that moment her feelings of success were slipping away.

~~~~

Mr. Washington had felt a sense of anticipation all week, and as he finished his written instructions for the substitute who would be taking his classes tomorrow, he could feel his mood lighten for the first time in weeks. He had been depressed about his teaching recently. His students seemed bored and uninterested, and he sensed that his own lack of enthusiasm about his program was passing on to them. He had realized at that time that the classic symptoms of "burn out" were setting in. It was then that he had decided to attend the regional language teachers' conference that was being held in the neighboring state, and had even volunteered to preside at one of the sessions. He had been pleasantly surprised when his principal informed him that the school and the district would be able to pay his registration plus the costs of his lodging and transportation. They must have thought that it was a valuable experience, because they were not only paying for the trip but also his substitute! Mr. Washington was sure that Dr. Gutierrez from State University would be at the conference and he could ask about using some of his tests to prepare his students for the AP test. He was really anticipating visiting the huge book exhibits he knew were going to be set up. He had gotten permission to adopt a new textbook series, and he wanted to spend several hours examining all the newest text programs. No doubt about it! With all the new ideas he was going to get from the sessions at the conference, with his new textbook, and with the supplementary materials he would order at the conference, he was going to shake off the "burn out" and renew his enthusiasm for teaching.

~~~~

Today Mrs. Wilson was embarrassed. The parents of one of her students were visiting the class, and they were native speakers of Spanish! At first Mrs. Wilson was tempted to teach the class in English because she didn't want them to notice her mistakes, but the students would have wondered why. All she could do was go on in her usual way, and then apologize later to the parents about her poor Spanish. Hopefully, they would be understanding when she explained that she had only taken classes at the university, and had never visited a foreign country.

CHAPTER EIGHTEEN

EVALUATING AND IMPROVING YOURSELF AS A TEACHER

> **Becoming a successful foreign language teacher is an ongoing, lifelong process, affording both satisfaction and excitement. The formal process begins at the university level as future teachers observe, practice, and then implement what they have learned. This process then continues while teaching. In a sense, it parallels the sprouting, growing, and maturing stages of life.**
> **--Taylor & Bateman**

This second of our chapters on "in-flight correction" focuses on your own personal preparation, qualities, and your effectiveness as a foreign language teacher. Assessment of an individual's performance is a delicate and complicated process. The education profession has wrestled with this problem for a number of years, usually trying to devise an instrument on which to base teacher salaries, promotions, or justification for dismissal. We are not so concerned here with those issues as we are on ways of discovering areas where improvement is needed. It seems logical to assume that if students are failing to learn, it may in some part be due to ineffective teaching. It also follows that if students are dropping out of programs, or a program is not building, that the teacher is probably at fault. Although sometimes hard on the ego and difficult to accept, the long-term benefits of a sincere and honest self-evaluation are well worth any embarrassment or personal anguish we might feel at the time.

EVALUATING AN INDIVIDUAL TEACHER

Once you have determined to take a long, hard look at your own teaching, you have a number of approaches available. Generally speaking, they will be in one of the following formats:

- Self-evaluation
- Evaluation by your Students
- Outside observer(s)
-

Self-evaluation has the disadvantage of being subjective and somewhat inaccurate. We do not always see ourselves in an objective light. However, self-evaluation is easy to do and has the advantage of being immediate. It can be conducted in a number of ways.

The very simple practice of taking a recording device into the classroom and recording what takes place in your classes can be very revealing. As you listen to what you have recorded you may be surprised at how little you use Spanish in the class, and perhaps that the students use even less. You might want to study ways you use the target language: Do you just ask questions? Do the students use Spanish only with you, the teacher? Do the students initiate conversation in the language? Do they use the language with each other? Do you waste a lot of time? Could you be better organized?

Using this same approach with a *video camera* can even be more revealing. You may learn that you spend most of your time at your desk, that you have some distracting nervous habits, that you favor some groups of students over others, and that some students never participate in class at all. We highly recommend the practice of periodically videoing your classes. As you watch the videos you will probably be in for some surprises, but you will readily see some areas where some adjustments can be made.

Student evaluations can be very helpful. Although students sometimes slant their comments according to their standing in the class and their relationship with the teacher, nevertheless they can help you discover what they see as the best aspects of the class and also the worst.

Student evaluations can answer four very important questions for you:

- What should you keep doing?
- What should you stop doing?
- What should you start doing?
- What should you do differently?

Many teachers regularly have their students evaluate their courses at the end of the term or year. These questionnaires should be completely anonymous and should include both questions that focus on specific areas and open-ended questions that allow the students to express their feelings about any aspect of the class. We have included a sample student questionnaire in the Appendix that can be adjusted to each teacher's particular situation.

Observer evaluations by someone from outside the class can give you a picture from someone in a neutral position. Input from school officials or from peers can be very helpful.

Most public schools require formal periodic evaluations of teaching effectiveness. They can be done by administrators or by peers who are also experienced teachers of the same subject. The objective of these evaluations is usually twofold; one to help the teacher improve, and two to provide a basis for advancement, recognition, or tenure. Unfortunately, these evaluation visits are sometimes done in such a confrontational or stressful manner that the teacher becomes defensive and is not receptive to making any changes. At the other extreme, many teachers who are notified in advance of the official visit prepare some marvelous lessons to parade before the evaluators which in no way resemble the usual classroom diet. Nevertheless, a competent and conscientious observer can usually see through any "window dressing" and give some valuable feedback that hopefully the teachers will use to improve their teaching.

A simple (unofficial or informal) invitation by one teacher to another, or by a teacher to an administrator to drop in and watch a class and then give positive suggestions for improvement is more likely to be acted upon than a formal, required observation.

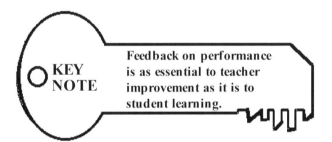

KEY NOTE Feedback on performance is as essential to teacher improvement as it is to student learning.

Checking Your Preparation for Teaching

Successful teaching is based on many factors: personality, rapport between teacher and students, classroom management, presentation and practice techniques, knowledge of and enthusiasm for the subject, etc. In addition, studies show that teachers who are confident in their use of the language are usually more effective. An evaluation of our personal mastery of Spanish can reveal areas where you need to improve. Sometimes simply using a checklist can give you valuable information. Consider the following:

PERSONAL PROFICIENCY AND PREPARATION CHECKLIST

☐ Do I understand the foreign language spoken at normal tempo at the Advanced or higher level according to the ACTFL Proficiency Guidelines?

☐ Do I speak the language intelligibly and with adequate command of vocabulary and syntax at the Advanced level or higher?

☐ Do I read the language with immediate comprehension and without translation at the Advanced level or higher?

☐ Do I write the language with clarity and reasonable correctness at the Advanced level or higher?

☐ Have I had experience with reading or through coursework that would help me improve my understanding of the language?

☐ Have I used the state curriculum guide (published periodically) or taken refresher courses at local universities that would further my understanding of the learner and the psychology of learning?

☐ Do I attend state workshops or university classes that would further my understanding (and that of my peers) of the evolving objectives of education in the state and in the nation and the place of foreign language learning in this context?

In addition to possessing the requisite subject knowledge and skills, language teachers must be able to teach them to students. The checklist continues.

☐ Can I demonstrate the ability to develop in the students a progressively increasing control of the four skills?

☐ Can I present the language as an essential element of the foreign culture, and show how this culture differs from that of the United States?

☐ Do I read newspapers and magazines, watch television, and keep up with events, new changes, prominent personalities in the Hispanic world?

☐ Can I present the foreign literature effectively as a vehicle for great ideas?

☐ Do I make judicious selection and use of methods, techniques, aids, and other equipment for language assessment?

☐ Do I correlate my teaching with the teaching of other subjects?

☐ Am I able to show that I can evaluate the progress and diagnose the deficiencies of student performance?

HOW DO WE GET HELP FOR PERSONAL IMPROVEMENT?

Having discovered some areas where things are not going well, you will be eager to take steps toward improvement. There are a number of people and groups which can be of help and support in this undertaking.

Peers and Colleagues

Developing a collegial relationship with fellow teachers can reap great rewards. Often their experience and preparation can help them see problems that you are unaware of. Sometimes teachers become so personally and emotionally involved that they cannot accept what others clearly see. This is especially true in regards to your personal relationships to your students.

Other teachers in your school may have experienced the same difficulties you are having and can share with you the steps that brought them success.

Professional Organizations

As a foreign language teacher, you will want to join forces with your thousands of colleagues throughout the country, or for that matter, throughout the world. You should be proud of your profession and should feel a part of a great team that is working together to achieve the same objectives. You will want to benefit from the strength and wisdom of that team as much as possible, at the same time contributing what you can from your own unique experience and talents. Nothing will help you do this better than becoming an active, participating member of some of the many professional organizations functioning throughout the country. We introduced the professional organizations that can help with your programs in Chapter 17. Here we will focus on what some of them can do for you personally. Let's start with the ones you will probably get acquainted with while still a student, move to those on a local level, and conclude with national and international organizations.

Student Academic and Honorary societies. If you are still in college, a number of general academic and honorary societies are available to university students and not only offer recognition of academic excellence, but also sponsor a number of activities which help the students grow both in scholarly and social skills. Organizations such as **Phi Kappa Phi** have been established to recognize and reward students who have excelled in their academic studies. These organizations regularly make scholarships available and sponsor lectures, workshops, cultural events, etc.

Subject-specific organizations such as **Sigma Delta Pi**, an international honorary society for students and teachers of Spanish, recognize and encourage excellence in the study of Spanish. Most colleges and universities have chapters of *Sigma Delta Pi* and as an upper division student you will probably be invited to join. We recommend that you do so because it will probably be your first step toward professionalism. Attendance at and participation in *Sigma Delta Pi* activities can contribute to your personal progress with the language and can increase your knowledge of Hispanic culture. Some typical activities might include:

- Lectures by distinguished professors
- Presentations by invited guests such as ambassadors, writers, musicians, etc.
- Publishing a student magazine, which could include your own writing
- Concerts of Hispanic music
- Dramatic productions (in Spanish)
- Movie or video nights
- Social events (Don Quixote's Birthday)

- Knowledge bowls (competitions)
- Informal sharing lunches

Obviously you can develop your own leadership skills by accepting responsibilities and assignments in the activities mentioned above.

General Teacher and Education-oriented Organizations. As you graduate from college and move out into the teaching profession, you will become acquainted with such organizations as the **National Education Association** (NEA) and its local subdivisions. The NEA originated as a strictly professional organization that encouraged adherence to strong ethical standards, but as teachers found it necessary to become increasingly active politically, and with the creation of teachers unions such as the American Federation of Teachers (AFT), NEA has gradually moved toward the posture of a union. NEA offers many benefits to its members, such as legal counseling and defense, lobbying on national and state levels, health and life insurance programs, etc.

Each state has a local version of these enormously powerful organizations, such as the Utah Education Association, the California Education Association, etc. These local organizations often become directly involved in negotiations of teachers with local districts in matters such as pay, insurance, teachers' rights and benefits, etc. They also offer free legal consultation to members who might need that kind of help.

Local school districts usually support professional activity of their teachers, and some even have a requirement of membership for teachers moving up their "career ladders" or moving ahead on the pay scale. Local school districts regularly sponsor in-service training for beginning teachers and workshops for experienced teachers. Larger school districts often have a district foreign language supervisor/coordinator who was usually an outstanding teacher with many years of experience and who will be able to give you a good deal of help. This supervisor usually coordinates the district curriculum, helps with the hiring of new teachers, and helps with the

428

improvement of in-service teachers with activities such as workshops, etc.

State School Boards or State Boards of Education also carry out programs for orientation, improvement, and broadening of teaching skills. Most states have a State World Languages Coordinator/Specialist who can be of great help to teachers looking to design new programs or improve old ones. These state specialists are usually responsible for establishing state guidelines for teacher certification, and the preparation of state curriculum guides for the language teachers of the state. You should become very well acquainted with the State Curriculum Guide and volunteer to serve on committees that prepare those documents.

Each state has a **State Foreign Language Association** (UFLA, FLANC, AFLTA, etc.) These organizations usually have a very low membership fee and it is very easy to get directly involved in activities. For example you should not hesitate to volunteer to make presentations of some ideas or techniques you have found to be successful at one of the State conferences.

Regional Conferences on Language Teaching. These conferences were organized to make it easier for teachers to attend multi-state conferences. As an example, the **Southwest Conference on Language Teaching** (SWCOLT) holds its annual meeting each year in March or April. The meeting moves to a new state in the region each year

National and International Organizations. We mentioned in Chapter 17 that the **American Council on the Teaching of Foreign Languages (ACTFL)** is the most important national organization for language teachers. ACTFL is dedicated to the improvement of teaching and learning of all languages at all levels of instruction. Contributions to your personal teaching provided by ACTFL include:

- The creation and administration of tests such as the ACTFL-ETS Oral Proficiency Interview (OPI), the Spanish PRAXIS tests, and others that are often used in job placement.

- The Annual ACTFL Meeting, which is the country's major event in foreign language education.
- Several publications, including *Foreign Language Annals* and the *Foreign Language Educator*, a quarterly journal that focuses on the latest practices, methods and research.

The ACTFL SmartBrief, a newsletter that summarizes and links language teachers to news articles pertinent to foreign language education can help teachers individually. Read the following selections from the latest edition of this free newsletter and see examples of how they could help in your efforts to improve your personal skills

1) Google launches tools that can be used to improve language skills
Google recently released a new dictionary that features definitions of words in English and 27 other languages and includes a feature that allows users to translate single words from English into other languages, and vice versa. It also provides access to International Phonetic Alphabet pronunciations. Google also launched a new Web search tool that allows users to search foreign language Web sites using English search terms. PC World (12/04)

2) ACTFL's National Language Teacher of the Year emphasizes common cultures
Lisa Lilley -- ACTFL National Language Teacher of the Year for 2010 -- brings culture into her high school Spanish classes through hands-on activities including role-playing games and lessons with foreign newspapers. "She wants them to have a passion for the language and culture," her Missouri district's foreign language facilitator said. "There's a difference between teachers who make you memorize and those who really make you think." Springfield News-Leader (Mo.) (12/03)

Since the foreign language you teach is Spanish, The American Association of Teachers of Spanish and Portuguese (AATSP) can give you help specific to Spanish in areas such as:

- The Annual Meeting, often held in Hispanic countries such as Spain and Mexico.

- *Hispania*, the professional journal which includes material relevant to the classroom, articles about the Hispanic and Luso-Brazilian worlds, pedagogical issues, book reviews, linguistic problems as well as the traditional literary themes. Each issue contains valuable advertisements.
- The loan of Cultural Units and materials for use by teachers in their classrooms.
- A Placement Bureau service to help Spanish teachers find jobs.
- Opportunities for participation in local chapters of AATSP.

Elementary School Teachers can get personal help from The National Network for Early Language Learning (NNELL), which is an educational community providing leadership in support of successful early language learning and teaching. The organization provides valuable resources for educators, parents and policymakers interested in FLES. You can go to their website and download their latest brochure.

Another organization that can help you is the **Instituto Cervantes** that is committed to furthering with the study of Spanish language and culture around the world. In addition to scholarships for study in Spain, this institute makes materials such as music and videos available to teachers and administers a test of certification for teachers of Spanish.

How Can You Be Active Professionally?

Sometimes teachers feel that they are too busy just teaching their classes to find time to participate in professional activities, but this should not be a deterrent. The benefits will far outnumber the difficulties you will encounter or the expenses you will incur.

- If you are a student, start now by joining student organizations and participating in their activities.
- If you are a teacher, commit yourself to always attend school and district professional activities, such as workshops, seminars, teaching presentations, etc.
- When you have begun teaching, join the local organizations. Become active. Run for office. Volunteer to participate on committees. Give presentations at annual meetings.

- Join the national organizations. Read the journals. Attend the conventions. Make a presentation on a national level.
- Make it a habit to read regularly the articles in the professional journals. You will find a wealth of materials, perhaps something with which you are personally having problems.

In all our years of teaching and working with teacher training programs, we have seen uncountable numbers of teachers become active professionally and without exception the results have been dramatic improvement of classroom teaching, and strengthening of programs. True, it does take time but it is time well spent.

PERSONAL IMPROVEMENT

Teachers come in all shapes and sizes. No two are alike. Some speak the language well but are weak in teaching experience; others are good teachers but still have a long way to go with their language skills. Yet they all share one point in common: the teachers are *the* major factor in bringing success to the classroom. When teachers don't do well, they often lay the blame on the textbook, the administration, or the students themselves. While it's true that in many cases failure may be partly ascribed to these areas, in the final analysis success rarely visits the classroom of a poorly-prepared teacher. First, you should take a long hard look in a mirror.

Do you work on improving your teaching?

The first year of teaching is always the hardest. You have to spend enormous amounts of time preparing lesson plans, preparing visual aids, developing ways to manage the classes, and others. This first year is usually pretty hard on your self-image too, because you have probably become painfully aware that you still have a long way to go in your personal preparation. You may have tried many activities that didn't work. Now you must find other possibilities to try. There are a number of ideas that will give you valuable help.

If you are teaching in an elementary or secondary school, you will want to explore the following possibilities:

1. Pre-service Activities. Don't stay away from the pre-teaching meetings and workshops scheduled by your school or district. They can be very valuable. They are usually held the week before the beginning of school, and can go a long way in preparing you to fit into the operation of your particular school, and merging your plans into the year-round schedule set up by the school.

2. In-service Workshops. During the school year there are a number of school workshop possibilities such as textbook selection, new textbook program, preparation for accreditation, departmental meetings, informal conversations with teachers, telephone conversations with teachers in other schools, consultation with the counselor(s), consultation with the principal(s), and even meetings with parents and students.

3. Career Ladder Programs. Generally this name is given to various approaches for teachers to obtain additional money for services rendered. Sometimes it is a kind of merit rating coupled with supplementary training opportunities and job or service possibilities. There are people who prefer to be teachers who do not want to be principals or other administrators or counselors, and therefore it is necessary to find ways to pay people more for teaching well. The problem is defining what "teaching well" means. Altruistically one assumes that teachers are interested in the improvement of instruction and expect that the rewards financially would follow with proper and adequate reporting.

Some of the competencies that various districts consider measurable and ratable and rewardable are these:

- Planning for instruction
- Delivery of instruction
- Evaluation of student progress
- Classroom management
- Professional leadership
- Communication skills

4. District Workshops. Each district sponsors several workshops a year. Some of these workshops have been mentioned already: textbook adoption workshops, new textbook orientation, curriculum guide development for the district, and implementation of curriculum

guides. Teachers are obligated to attend anyway so you can enjoy the in-service development.

5. Teacher Leaders. It is important to schools and districts to identify teacher leaders as part of the career ladder program or a similar program. Differentiating *status leaders* and *functional leader* is very important. Every teacher has the possibility of being a functional leader. *Status leaders* are usually appointed.

Beyond School and District

In addition to what you can learn from your own school and district, you can go beyond to other sources of help.

State workshops. Many of the tasks mentioned above have their origin in the state school responsibilities. Because the Federal Constitution does not mention Education, the full responsibilities rest with the state. You would be wise to volunteer to be part of various state committees, especially curriculum and textbook committees. Every state in the USA and most countries of the world have professional organizations or professional affiliates. Every FL teacher should seek out the state FL organization and attend the annual and sometimes semiannual meetings and read the newsletter or journal or meeting report(s). These meetings and periodicals are filled with helpful information and "how to" suggestions. You would do well to volunteer for committee assignments and run for organizational office: Secretary, vice president, or president (possibly in that order). Every meeting is a kind of workshop or source of helpful teaching information. The annual (or semiannual) meeting(s) are clinical in nature and usually in workshop format with at least one keynote address of a FL leader of national repute.

Regional Workshops. We have already mentioned the regional organizations. They have annual conferences and send out newsletters to advertise meeting times and reports of the conferences. Both the newsletter and the reports have very valuable articles, insights, suggestions, helps, and trends for you. As you get experience, you should conduct action research and give reports in those meetings as well as profit from the efforts of your colleagues.

National workshops and conferences. National organizations such as ACTFL typically hold pre- or post conference workshops in connection with their annual meetings. They may be half day or full day workshops. There are two main problems for teachers in getting involved with professional organizations. First, how do you afford them because each organization has annual dues (periodical is not extra), and second, how do you find the time and the travel money to go to all these meetings?

Here are some suggestions:

1. You have very rich relatives and you get money from them.
2. Your school or district subscribes for all the FL teachers and you receive the periodicals that are rapidly passed from FL teacher to FL teacher. The school or district pays for one of the group to go to nearby conventions.
3. As a member of the executive board, especially president, of your state FL association, you represent the whole organization and you give a summary report to the executive board and the board decides whether to offer an "outreach" program to the membership in a meeting for the whole state or in regions of the state, and you coach a few of your colleagues on the board to present the same workshop activities (you experienced at the national meeting) to the local membership. The State School Office, local universities, sometimes districts (combined), and even occasionally local industry might finance part, or all, of the "outreach" program.
4. You locate others who attended the meetings from other districts or nearby universities or even nearby states, and you sponsor an "outreach" program together for as many people as you can. The "Outreach" program is a mini-conference for which you would have to have a budget that can be reimbursed by the "paying audience." Some national and regional conferences (organizations) provide "Outreach" materials probably at cost for just such an arrangement.
5. The alliance or collaborative is another approach to solving the problems of staying up to date and building your repertoire of approaches, methods, procedures, techniques,

gimmicks, trends, ideas. The alliance idea is treated below in more detail.
6. You need to be alert to FL Conference announcements. There is almost always one or two nearby of the many that are held each year--that is, within 500 miles. Negotiate with your administrator to budget some money for a conference held within 500 to 800 miles; that money would be for travel and conference registration and lodging and possibly even two or three meals a day. Become an officer in the local FL organization and you may be able to represent the association at one of the conferences.
7. You need experience in workshops at conferences and in "outreach" programs to inoculate yourself against "burnout" or monotony and to stimulate your teaching enzymes or hormones to be at your very best all the time.

If after all these suggestions, you still can't attend conferences or workshops, audio recordings and videos of the presentations are often available online after the conference.. If you can't afford to join professional organizations, have your school or district librarian subscribe to the journals and you and other language teachers can read them in the library. They contain a wealth of practical information and ideas about language teaching.

Institutes at Colleges or Universities. These institutes came to the fore in the early 1960's under the National Defense Education Act (NDEA) and continue today, the late 1980's and the early 1990's, at least occasionally under the National Endowment for the Humanities. The money grants made it possible to offer participants excellent training (especially updating) plus a payment to the participants of a monthly stipend--thus rivaling a summer job.

Nowadays universities working with teacher education often sponsor summer institutes of their own for in-service teachers. These institutes can last anywhere from two weeks to two months. The university usually pays tuition and fees with scholarships, and, if the summer institute includes travel to a foreign country, it is often paid for by the program. These experiences can be refreshing, renewing and reinvigorating to teachers. Look for the universities to advertise or publicize these institutes. Sometimes foreign governments have special organizations to assist in providing in-service workshops.

Academic Alliances. These alliances are sometimes called faculty collaboratives. They use the original conception of the county medical society and bar association as their model. These associations were designed to bring colleagues in the same area together on a regular basis. These colleagues help keep each other up-to-date in their fields and take collective responsibility for the quality of the practice of the profession in their area. They accomplish this without spending much time or money. These alliances first started in the foreign languages with grants from the National Endowment for the Humanities, the Rockefeller Foundation, and the Exxon Education Foundation.

There are now hundreds of alliances involving thousands of educators. Groups are also forming in chemistry, English, geography, history and physics. Meeting monthly, bimonthly or quarterly, members help each other maintain the spirit of inquiry crucial to the healthy intellectual life of all faculty members regardless of the age of their students. Collaboratives also allow faculty already established in the profession to serve as mentors to their younger colleagues. "Outreach" programs are a natural part of alliance meetings. Activities at alliance meetings can also include:

1. Increasing the accountability of the FL teachers in the secondary schools through a good testing program in cooperation with colleges and university (in reasonable proximity).
2. Developing more intensive courses at the secondary level and more immersion courses at the elementary level. We must getting rid of the time differences—the "two years equals one" attitude.
3. Discussing problems in articulation on a professional basis with colleagues from the university and such issues as what should be covered in any term of a total program.
4. Inviting university drama groups, dance groups—especially folk dance groups, musical groups, panel discussion groups, symposia, to enrich the public secondary curriculum.

5. Improving attitudes toward experimentation and sharing results of action research.
6. Reviewing the journals for several organizations since no one subscribes to all periodicals that should be read.
7. Participating in, or listening to, panel discussions, allowing schoolteachers and college faculty to work as a team.
8. Visiting demonstration classes and each other's classes to collect ideas and to experience approaches.
9. Improving articulation through curriculum exchanges.
10. Reviewing conferences of general interest thus avoiding rising travel costs and shrinking budgets.

Have you had a methods class in language teaching? Do you read articles about new techniques and approaches? Are you always looking for new ideas and new materials you might use in your classes? Do you go back to methods courses or to summer courses or to programs leading to advanced degrees or even in-service workshops? A "no" answer to any of these questions should give you a strong signal that you need to take some sort of action leading to a better personal preparation.

The Benefits of Attending a Professional Conference

Let's take a few minutes and explore in depth the excitement, stimulation, relaxation, and satisfaction that come from attending one of these professional conference that we have so highly recommended. Most teachers find them so enjoyable that they eagerly look forward to them and consider them to be one of the highlights of the year.

Typically a conference will be set in a large city, usually in a large hotel or conference center. The professional organization is usually able to get significant discounts both with lodging and transportation, and with any luck, or heavy lobbying, your school administration will help you with the expenses. The conference itself usually lasts for about three days with anywhere from five to twenty "sessions" scheduled every two hours during most of the day. A "session" normally is a presentation, demonstration, or panel discussion made by one or more persons on a variety of subjects. The sessions are normally very well prepared and may report on research studies, results gained from using new approaches, or new materials or technology. Each session is usually accompanied by carefully prepared handouts and useful materials. You will find yourself furiously writing down ideas and new things you want to try in your classes as the speakers spark your interest or touch on a problem you have been having.

There are, of course, breaks for lunch and visits to the large exhibit halls where all the textbook and materials companies have splendid displays of their wares and where their salesmen ply you with refreshments and reasons why you should adopt their programs. Simply fill out their forms and you will be receiving complementary and examination copies for weeks afterward. You need to be careful or you may spend the entire year's budget on new videos, visual aids, or music that you "can't possibly get along without."

After sessions, during lunch, and in the exhibit halls you can spend hours talking and sharing with other teachers, presenters, nationally-renowned experts, officers of the organization, about anything and everything.

Special events will have been organized, such as a sumptuous luncheon organized by the Spanish Embassy, awards meetings where outstanding teachers and administrators are honored, a cheese and wine soiree offered by the Goethe Institute, a reception by one of the major textbook companies (complete with refreshments), or a cultural event sponsored by the Alliance Française. The host city also sponsors shopping tours and visits to tourist attractions.

Special interest groups meet together to discuss mutual problems, such as the FLES "swap-meet," the state foreign language coordinators group meeting, university supervisors of graduate assistants, or methods teachers.

Many conferences offer full-day or half-day workshops both before and after the official three days of the conference where teachers can get in-depth exposure and practice of such diverse things as OPI training, use of technology in the class, or how to use technology in teaching.

And believe us, we have mentioned only a few of the things that go on at a professional conference. Make it a habit to attend them. We promise that you will always return refreshed and with your head full of marvelous things you can use to improve both your own teaching performance and your program.

National Board Certification

When you have taught for at least three years, you are eligible to apply for certification by the National Board for Professional Teaching Standards. NBPTS is an independent, nonprofit organization founded in 1987 to create a system of advanced certification for teachers based on high and rigorous standards based on what teachers should know and be able to do. National Board certification complements, but does not replace, state licensing. While state licensing systems set entry-level standards for novice teachers, National Board certification establishes advanced standards for experienced teachers.

At the core of the National Board certification are standards that represent a consensus among teachers and other education experts about what accomplished teachers should know and be able to do. NBPTS Standards can be found at www.nbpts.org.

All National Board for assessments consist of two major parts: (1) four portfolio entries, and (2) six assessment center exercises. Portfolio entries are performance assessments of classroom teaching that include video, student work, and other teaching artifacts. Assessment center exercises ask candidates to respond to specific prompts including situations to which teachers must respond or explorations of pedagogical and content issues. The certification process is not cheap; the application fee is $2,500 with an additional $65 registration fee paid online at the NBPTS website. Often, however, scholarship or grant money is available from states to cover this cost.

National Board certification offers several advantages. Many states offer promotions or raises to National Board certified teachers; the state of Utah grants these teachers a Level 3 teaching license, the highest level license that the state offers. In addition, teachers who have participated in National Board certification have overwhelmingly stated it is the most powerful professional development experience of their careers. They say the experience changes them as professionals as they deepen their content knowledge and develop new approaches to working with their students.

YOUR RELATIONSHIP WITH YOUR STUDENTS

Here are some suggestions for improving your relationship with your students. You can provide variety in the teaching experience by meeting the needs and desires of your students. This goal is less obvious than one might think. The *scholastic needs* provide only the tip of a large iceberg. The sensitive teacher has observed that the students have *physical, emotional, psychological, and social needs* that are intimately related to their academic performance. We need to examine the "whole" student with regard to personal needs that affect learning in the classroom.

Physical needs include *hearing* the teacher, other students, audio recordings, and the details of pronunciation for auditory discrimination. The auditory quality of the varied performances and the various aids must be very important to the teacher. *Seeing* is equally important especially for the homemade materials we sometimes use. What about glare and darkness for the use of visual aids—even video broadcasts and transparency projection can be difficult to see. The highly touted picture files are not very effective if students can't see the pictures clearly. Sometimes we hold the pictures at a peculiar angle. What about *varying moods* of the students (and teacher)? at the end of the day, just before lunch time, just after lunch time, and after trying out for cheerleader, on game days, and on and on.

Emotional and Psychological Needs. All students need encouragements, acceptance, and praise. Students need to be treated as individual personalities with unique identities. All students need success. All students have their own rate of learning, their way of learning, and their own reasons for studying a foreign language. Probably the most important factor in motivating students is in their own goals and objectives.

Students respond more readily to reward than to punishment. It is better to comment positively on what the students have accomplished than to dwell on what they have failed to achieve. It is better to give an honest objective report of the facts concerning the students' performance than to attack their character and intentions.

Some students are timid; others are more gregarious and aggressive. Some students are talkative and others never have much to say.

Students learn at different rates, in different ways, and for different reasons because of different achievement patterns and motivational levels that are gradually acquired at home and at school. Some students are under achievers, and some are over achievers. Some students may apply themselves because they are "turned on" by the relevance of the subject to an area of extreme personal interest to them. Teachers may respond to these needs by individualizing their classes to provide for different rates of learning, different modes of learning, and different goals for learning.

Social Needs. Human beings live, work, and play in groups. A class at school is a group and it can be subdivided into smaller groups in which there is a need to be accepted by the group(s) and useful to it. The students feel that they are useful members when they give and take their appropriate share of the activities. Teachers need to establish a friendly, democratic atmosphere in which all students feel they belong and can participate. The teacher must encourage the development of tolerance and acceptance on the part of all students. Students who cannot produce as much in academic pursuits as their fellow students must be given opportunities to contribute in other ways to the class.

Since teachers who keep their eyes on the needs of the "whole" student will inevitably give that student a better chance to succeed in class, they will plan for much more variety and a good deal of individualization and, therefore, will help the students as great deal and help themselves by avoiding burnout.

IMPROVING YOUR PERSONAL LANGUAGE PROFICIENCY

How well prepared are you to teach your foreign language? Are you comfortable using it? Would you be embarrassed if a native were to visit your class and observe you teaching? Is your pronunciation good enough for your students to model? How about your cultural knowledge? Do you constantly read books about the countries where your language is spoken? Do you keep up on current events in those countries? Can you name the leaders of the countries, the important political and cultural leaders? How long has it been since you went back to renew your enthusiasm and get up to date?

It is not unusual for practicing foreign language teachers to realize that their own personal skills don't reach the levels expected by the profession. These minimally prepared teachers often have had only the number of courses required for a major or minor and have never had extensive experience using the language.

Another problem comes when teachers find themselves working only with beginning level classes, and they have to spend most of their time speaking with simple constructions and reduced vocabulary.

Other teachers find that they are losing their enthusiasm for their subject and approach their classes with apathy and very little interest. This feeling is referred to as "burnout," and can occur when the teacher spends several years teaching pretty much the same material in the same ways.

As you begin to teach language classes, you will find that your own use of the language improves. As you prepare lessons you will add many new words to your vocabulary. As you work *teaching* grammar concepts, and *practicing* them with your students, you will consciously correct mistakes that you personally have been making with those concepts. However, you will want your own progress to be much greater than that of your students.

Give specific focus on the specialized language of the classroom. When you first start teaching classes in the foreign language, you will realize that your vocabulary is quite weak in the specialized terms you will need to use in the classroom. How do you say such things as "to underline, to register, to 'flunk' a test, to 'sluff' or 'cut' class, to 'check a book out' of the library," to mention only a few? What words do we use in Spanish for "fees, scholarship, pencil sharpener, research," and others? Start a list of words you need and find out how to express them in Spanish. (See *Materiales para la clase* for a beginning list of these words and expressions.)

Another area where teachers are often weak is the use of command forms. You will constantly be giving directions to students to do things in class. You have to be able to command several people as a group or single individuals almost without thinking. At first you will have to work at it consciously, but by making lists of verbs (especially the irregular ones) and following a plan and practicing, you will use them perfectly. Playing games such as **Simon dice** or using Total Physical Response activities will give you good practice in this area.

You can take additional classes. If you live near a college or university you could enroll in classes in the evening or during the summer semester. If your basic command of the structure of the language is weak, you would want to take a grammar class which would allow you to practice and polish your own language use. Be careful that you take a practical course, not a theoretical course in grammar analysis. There needs to be ample time and opportunity to practice the structures you are reviewing until you can handle them easily. If you are a native speaker, and have learned the language unaware of the patterns, then you need to take a course that will help you be able to explain why and how the patterns are used. It doesn't help a student who asks why you say things a certain way, to be told "because it sounds right."

Perhaps you have never consciously worked on your own pronunciation. If you learned Spanish as a second language, you undoubtedly have areas where you can improve, where you can reduce your American accent and sound more authentic. Most colleges and universities have phonetics courses. Both natives and non-natives can profit from such a course that will alert them to the problems learners will have as they acquire a second set of pronunciation habits. Again, make sure that the class is practical.

It may be that you have had enough formal study of the grammar and phonology of the language and simply need more practice in hearing and speaking the language. In this case you need to take advanced conversation classes. Normally these classes are taught by native speakers, and are very small, and allow for a great deal of individual participation.

While literature classes and culture classes, that focus on fine arts, architecture, humanities and history, may not treat what you will usually teach in beginning and intermediate classes, they will give you additional practice with the language and a better background in "big C" culture.

There are a number of related areas that will give you a better background in "small c" culture. Classes in geography, current affairs, sociology, contemporary archeology, and the like will give you a greater understanding of the ways of life of the Spanish-speaking world.

There are many valuable education classes that will help you improve your skill as a teacher. Classes in the development of educational media, in the use of electronic equipment, in motivating students, in classroom management, and in similar courses all could be very valuable to you.

Arrange to get foreign country experience.

When you were a student at the university struggling to make ends meet, you probably could not afford to go the foreign countries where the language you were studying was spoken. However, once you are employed and have fewer educational expenses, you should begin to make plans to get abroad as often as you can. While it is true that it is difficult and sometimes expensive to spend some time in foreign residence, it is vital that every teacher get experience in a country where the language is used some way or another. If nothing else, you will have a certain amount of credibility in the eyes of your students. If you have "lived in Spain" then your statements about language use or about cultural traits will carry much more weight than if you have merely had classes. More importantly, foreign residence will increase your own confidence and self-image. If you know you can communicate in the language in real life then you will be confident that you can use it in the classroom.

How to get there. Some teachers are able to put aside some savings each year to pay for a visit to foreign countries every three or four years. Others find that the only way is by joining in with or setting up some type of study program for their students so that they are able to pay for their own expenses with program funds. There are three basic approaches you could pursue:

1. Personal travel
2. Student travel
3. Exchange programs

Teachers can avail themselves of the following options:

- Arranging an exchange with teachers in other countries.
- Sabbatical leaves or travel/study grants from your own school or district.
- Scholarships or travel stipends from government sources, such as the King Juan Carlos I scholarships awarded by Spain, the Fulbright exchange program, the National Endowment for the Humanities (NEH),
- There is a large number of study programs in foreign countries, sponsored both by American institutions and foreign schools, where teachers and advanced students can study in a "total immersion" environment. We have listed some of them in the *References* section and others can be found in professional journals.
- Many of the travel abroad programs regularly use language teachers as "tour leaders" in their programs. These teachers carry out duties to pay for the trip, or can even receive a salary.
- Most student educational travel abroad programs give teachers incentives to recruit students from their schools by giving them a free trip (they go along as chaperon) for each 6 to 8 students they recruit. If they recruit more, the teachers can take a spouse along or receive cash refunds. EF Educational Tours is perhaps the largest of these groups.
- Many teachers organize their own tours, especially to Mexico, which is close to the U.S. and take students from their own schools. This approach is usually cheaper than the national groups, but requires a lot of work from the teachers and is difficult to set up unless you have some contacts. There are also some legal considerations such as travel and liability insurance which need to be taken care of. Some neighboring schools often combine to set up programs of this type.

What to do when you get there. Once in the foreign country, you should have some specific plans to get the most out of the experience.

1. Task Performance Activities. Once you have arrived in the foreign country, you must set up a full program of activities that will allow you go use the language as much as possible. Live with a family or in a pension where no one speaks English. Avoid situations where English is used. Set up a schedule of things to do which you can prepare for, such as getting a haircut, visiting a beauty salon, buying certain items at a store. Find a native "resource" person (such as a member of the family you are staying with) who can help you with vocabulary and cultural information, or look words up in the dictionary or textbook. (Try going to a different store for each item rather than buying everything in one place. This takes more time but gives you a wider range of experiences and allows you more language use.)

2. Plan a number of activities every day that will take you into different aspects of life, such as eating in a cafe, going to a movie, watching TV, attending a wedding or funeral, going to a party, visiting a cemetery, attending mass or religious services, using a public telephone, attending university classes, going swimming in a public pool, walking in a park, visiting museums, visiting someone in a hospital, riding the busses or metro, visiting a factory, going to an amusement park, and so on. Go into different places to get information, such as a gas station and ask the price of gas, a car wash, and a lube job. Go to the post office and ask about mailing letters and packages. Find out what one has to do to get a driver's license, send a telegram, open a bank account, and so on.

3. Make it a point to "interview" several people each day, such as taxi drivers, lottery salesmen, policemen, hotel clerks, *porteros*, priests, salespersons, secretaries, military personnel, young children, and so on. Talk to teenagers and find out what the popular activities are, what the dating customs are, what they study in school, what their plans for a career are. If they will allow it, tape the interviews.

4. Make arrangements to visit schools and observe classes, taking notes of the words and expressions the teacher uses. Talk to teachers about their classes and students, talk about salaries and training, about goals and needs, and the like.

5. Make it point to get out of the city and visit a rural area and talk to the people there. Find out what they do for a living, what their education is like, what they do for diversion, and other possibilities.

6. Collect cultural materials. Look at everything with the eye of a teacher. Be constantly aware of what you can collect to take back to your classes to teach the culture.

What can you get for classroom decoration including pictures, flags, posters, post cards, maps, typical fabrics and calendars?

Remember the resource table in the back of your classroom? What can you get to put on it? Magazines, comic books, newspapers, children's storybooks, popular fiction books, history books, classics in translation, legends and fables, and text-books.

Realia are objects that reflect the culture of the people. Things you could take home for culture capsules are: dolls with regional costumes, clay figures, toys, shawls, ornamental knives, tickets, games, miniature furniture, greeting cards, typical clothing, cooking utensils, children's school supplies.

Don't forget the music! Buy records, sheet music, cassette tapes, song books. Take your tape recorder and tape music from the radio and TV.

Make sure you have **a good camera** which you are used to using and take lots of pictures. Don't take too many pictures of cathedrals and public buildings. Focus on people, types of stores, occupations, cars, children's games, weddings, busses, trains, gas stations, homes (rooms inside the homes) traffic signs, markets, and the like. Use video cameras for all of the above and more.

At-Home Activities for Fluency

There are a number of activities you can arrange at home to sharpen your skills. Consider the following:

Native friends. So you don't know anyone who is a native of the language? Then you will have to seek some friends and then arrange to spend time with them. This new friendship will allow you to practice the language in its normal use. Perhaps you can exchange hours with them if you can help with some skill they are trying to develop, such as English.

Movies, plays, cultural events. If not in your hometown, then seek out these events, showings, and happenings in the nearest larger city. Sometimes they are available on Spanish television channels or satellite or cable.

Video Programs. Your local video rental or retail outlet possibly has foreign video available. Of course you can check the nearest *Instituto Cervantes* library or catalog for extensive listings. The nearest large university's Spanish Department has a learning resource center with many videos of short learning cassettes as well as longer ones and full length movies.

Computer-assisted Instructional Programs are plentiful and can help you with all aspect of your language development. These are available from stores, libraries, *Instituto Cervantes*, Spanish Departments of universities, and other sources.

Audio Recordings are used for many language development programs for novice, intermediate and advanced speakers. These are available from stores, libraries, *Instituto Cervantes*, Spanish Departments of universities, and other sources.

Establish a reading program. Every language teacher should have a personal library of a variety of reading materials. You should spend some time each week, if not each day, reading and digesting new vocabulary words, observing grammatical patterns and expressions.

Books and magazines are available from stores, libraries, *Instituto Cervantes*, and the Spanish Department of nearby universities. Various agencies sponsor schools' obtaining free student and teacher magazines

Take some "retooling" classes at the university or the local community college or at a regional *Instituto Cervantes* or even in a Spanish-speaking country. Some of these are even sponsored by the government of the country.

COMBATING STRESS AND "BURNOUT"

Do you get up each morning with a heavy heart and physical discomfort in your stomach? Have you forgotten how it used to be when you went to school each day with such enthusiasm and anticipation that you could hardly wait for

class to start? Teachers often find themselves experiencing what is called "burnout," a condition in which you lose energy, creativity and enthusiasm about teaching often because of the incredible amount of stress in the profession. You no longer find yourself looking for new ways to teach and don't care much about what happens in the class, or the progress of your students. Experts feel that this is the result of years of "putting out" energy and work on the job without taking enough back in. Teachers need to feel that they are achieving, they need to feel appreciated, and they need to be rewarded for the contribution they are making. Diversion days and physical activity especially aerobic exercise must be included every day, or stress becomes insurmountable. If all these "reliefs" don't happen, then "burnout" takes place.

How to avoid "burnout." Teach differently each year. Do some interesting things, such as putting on plays, going on field trips, changing textbooks, and using complementary materials, taking students to Spain, Mexico, or Puerto Rico, getting an active language club going, and the like.

Work at developing warm and stimulating relationships with the faculty and staff of your school. Don't spend all your time talking to your colleagues about sports, health ailments, or family problems. Especially don't zero in on the trials and trauma created by disruptive or delinquent students. Talk about new ways of teaching, share some of the good things you have been reading, inquire about projects you know other teachers have been working on, ask and give advice on teaching problems. Why not visit other teachers' classes? What a novel idea! Everyone (especially the students) knows who the "great teachers" in your school are, arrange to watch them teach and find out why they are "great."

Running, walking, cycling, or swimming, along with active sports, such as tennis, basketball, racquetball, handball, and the like for sustained periods of time every day will do much to relieve stress and avoid burnout.

How to cure "burnout." Take a vacation to a foreign country and collect new materials. Exchange teaching positions with a teacher in a foreign country, or with a teacher on a different level: teach advanced classes, switch with the junior or senior high teacher or even with the local college teacher.

Go back to school and take some refresher courses, or attend a summer institute. Ask for a student teacher. Get a teacher's aide. Team-teach with another Spanish teacher. Do whatever it takes to put **vigor, vitality, and variety** into your teaching.

Variety is the lack of "sameness" and the presence of numerous different things. Human beings seek variety in their lives, for they loathe the monotony of routine and thrive in the stimulating arena of new and engaging experiences. The classroom must be such an arena if students are to learn and teachers are to survive.

The most obvious way to achieve variety in the classroom is to provide abundant learning activities. Every lesson plan should contain at least six different activities that should accomplish the following purposes:

1. to review recently learned material
2. to present new material
3. to practice the new material
4. to re-enter past material
5. to recombine old and new material
6. to evaluate

Review Chapters Six, Seven, Eight, Nine and Ten in this text, *Fundamentals of Language Teaching*, especially to put variety into the classes.

CONCLUSION

After our first few months of teaching and especially after the first year we must stop and ask the question, How am I doing? There are a number of yardsticks we can use to measure our progress. As we see that we fall short in some areas there are a wide number of sources for help, including many professional organizations that are marvelously equipped to help us succeed. Active membership and participation in these organizations can be tremendously rewarding in many ways. Get involved! Language teachers should take pride in their mastery of the foreign language and their understanding of the culture. Personal improvement in these areas should be a lifetime habit.

REFERENCES AND SUGGESTIONS FOR FURTHER READING

(FOR FULL INFORMATION ABOUT THE PROFESSIONAL ORGANIZATIONS, SEE THE REFERENCE SECTION IN CHAPTER 17)

Academic Alliances or School/College Faculty Collaboratives. The first of the series -- now numbering 19 in 1988 -- appeared in *Foreign Language Annals*, Vol. 18, No. 1, Feb., 1984, and continued through Vols. 19, 20, 21, etc.

American Council on the Teaching of Foreign Languages. (2002). Program standards for the preparation of foreign language teachers. Available at http://www.actfl.org/files/public/ACTFLNCATEStandardsRevised713.pdf

National Board for Professional Teaching Standards. www.nbpts.org

National Commission on Excellence in Education. (1983). *A nation at risk: The imperative for educational reform* (Report No. 065-000-00177). Washington, DC: US Government Printing Office.

FOREIGN RESIDENCE OR STUDY ABROAD OPPORTUNITIES FOR TEACHERS

National Endowment for the Humanities (NEH). This US Government organization provides travel and study grants for Spanish teachers. Visit their website for an overview of their *Endowment Programs*.   http://www.neh.gov/

Fulbright Teacher Exchange Program
http://www.fulbrightteacherexchange.org/

EF Study Abroad. This for-profit organization has a wide variety of programs, including study abroad, international schools, and educational summer tours. It is especially attractive to teachers who go free if they recruit students. Go to their website and check out all the different programs. http://www.ef.com/Default.aspx?bhcp=1

ACTIVITIES FOR METHODS CLASSES

1. Devise a plan for personal improvement of your Spanish proficiency. Discuss with your methods instructor and commit yourself to the plan. Keep track of your activities and progress. Make it a lifetime habit. Report your progress at the end of the semester. It could include one of the following, or something else you would like to do:

    a) Get copies of newspapers or magazines in Spanish, or find their websites. Read something every day, underlining new words and making notes of new expressions. Use the new words and expressions in Spanish conversations at least three to five times.

    b) Make a list of Spanish-speaking friends and make a pact with them to speak only Spanish. Meet at least once a week to talk about topics or information you have previously prepared.

    c) Find a computer program or grammar review book and review your use of Spanish structure. Determine areas where you are weak and practice until you are totally fluent in each area.

    d) Have an expert analyze your pronunciation and determine areas where your pronunciation is poor. Practice those sounds or problems until you are as close to native pronunciation as possible.

    e) [Natives] Study a typical Spanish textbook and look for grammatical concepts that you could not explain to students. Study those concepts until you understand them and prepare simple presentations that you could make in a class.

2. Subscribe to a magazine in Spanish, such as *Selecciones del Reader's Digest*. Make it a habit to read something every day, underlining new words and making notes of new expressions. Make it a point to use the new words and expressions every day. Report to methods professor.

3. Follow up on the suggestions in this chapter on how to get to a foreign country. Start saving your money and make plans to get there. Take advantage of internship or work programs for the summer. Debrief interns who worked in Spanish-speaking countries in the summer and see if you can do something similar. Talk it over with your methods instructor.

4. Find out as much as possible about scholarships and teacher exchange programs and send for more information and application forms. Report to your instructor.

5. Watch the video the *Global Classroom*, and explore the possibilities of taking a group of students on a travel program where you can travel free as a chaperon.

6. Prepare Task Performance Activities for yourself as well as your students to develop your language proficiency. Report to professor.

7. Determine ideas to improve your teaching by taking courses at local university—consider getting ideas for discipline, ideas to avoid stress—especially sport or aerobic courses, and ideas to get the three V's of burnout avoidance: *vitality* in teaching, *variety* in teaching and *vigor* in teaching and put the suggestions in this chapter to work. Report.

8. Form support groups and teams to work together on both the language development and teacher development.

9. Film a micro lesson or class you are teaching. Invite others to make suggestions for improvement.

10. Attend a professional presentation. Take notes of what was presented. Write up a report and comment on how you could use the information in improving your own teaching.

APPENDIX A

AN ADMINISTRATOR'S GUIDE TO DEVELOPING AN EFFECTIVE FOREIGN LANGUAGE PROGRAM

Administrators and Supervisors: Teachers cannot prosper without administrative support and direction. But even you need help in working with so many courses of study and especially an area so foreign as foreign languages! Foreign language instruction needs the specific attention, support, and direction from the district through a FL coordinator or a FL supervisor as well as the regular school administrators in order to insure that students gain the development to which they are entitled in a good foreign language program. The following guide has been prepared to give you that help.

Foreign language direction, supervision, and coordination. The following characteristics are *essential* for the development of a successful foreign language program:

1. There **must** be a **district** FL supervisor, or a FL teacher-leader who will be concerned and involved and active in the following aspects of cooperative FL teaching leadership:

    a. Clearly stated objectives in a carefully designed and developed district syllabus (semester outlines) based on the state course of study.
    b. A cooperatively designed and coordinated program of instruction encompassing several years of continuous foreign language learning.
    c. Workshops to provide materials and instructional aids of sufficient quality and quantity help teachers accomplish their objectives.
    d. An excellent testing program including proficiency testing in the four major areas (listening comprehension, speaking, reading and writing), placement testing, aptitude testing, culture testing, and the like.
    e. Adoption of a uniform text and approach.
    f. District articulation, allowing for a smooth transition between elementary school and middle school, middle school and high school, and high school and college.
    g. Availability of university or "concurrent enrollment" courses when the high schools cannot offer sufficiently advanced courses.
    h. Teacher inter-visitation and exchange within the district for varying lengths of time from one period to a week, and in some cases a whole semester or even a whole year—especially middle school or junior high school teachers exchanging with high school teachers. Among other things, this will enable teachers of various levels to understand the problems their colleagues face in the other levels. In the absence of such a program, junior high school teachers may not be aware of what the foundation they are laying should allow students in the higher levels to do, and high school teachers may not be aware of what it takes to teach junior high school students the foreign language.
    i. Provision of model programs with excellent demonstration teachers within the districts for their colleagues to emulate.
    j. In-service workshops, providing for teachers to update their awareness of how people learn languages and what methods and strategies best achieve that goal.
    k. Personal involvement of the FL supervisor or FL department chair in the interview process of hiring candidates for a position as a language teacher and a voice in the hiring, dismissal, and salary increases of language teachers.

    Nota bene: Many of the challenges that schools presently face would be solved if we would implement these ideas.

2. A school principal who actively supports foreign language teachers in their assignments and who will work with the district FL coordinator.

3. A staff of professionally competent, enthusiastic FL teachers with a competent FL department head who will work with the district FL coordinator.

4. Students who are aware of the value of foreign language learning and who have resolved to put forth the effort required to learn another language.

Developing a successful foreign language program. Administrators need to do the following:

1. Consult with language experts to determine what is desirable and possible for the school.

2. Select languages that reflect as much as possible the interests of the community and for which competent, enthusiastic teachers are available.

3. Make election of language study possible for all students, not just the college bound. Language instruction should be part of the official core of general education courses in the secondary school. Offer more than the minimum number of years required for college entrance. Four to six years is the optimum. Expend every effort to keep students in the stream of a foreign language course for four to six years.

4. Provide foreign language instruction for all students at the earliest possible grade level. It is suggested that any one or all three of the following plans is followed.

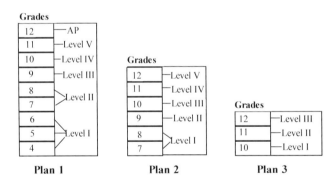

| | Plan 1 | Plan 2 | Plan 3 |

If foreign language instruction is adopted in elementary school, it is suggested that this articulated Plan 1 be followed. Under this plan, the students' interests remain high because they are able to experience progress and success as they advance from one level to another in a well-coordinated program. Ultimately they are offered Advanced Placement for which they may receive college credit for their efforts. This makes possible a smooth transition into university more advanced courses.

If the school district is unable to provide a well-articulated program in foreign language beginning in the elementary school, Plan 2 is suggested. If foreign language instruction is initiated in the junior high school, there are certain advantages over starting at a later time. A well-coordinated six-year program can be offered. Students who begin at this age will have minimal interference from their native language. Most universities offer credit at a reduced fee to students who score high on college achievement or AP tests. Students who have completed five levels of secondary school work should easily qualify for this advantage. In most cases, they should be able to complete university-level courses in high school.

Plan 3—a Level 1, 2, 3 sequence in high school—would serve a district which could provide no more than this *minimum*. Students under this plan should be encouraged to continue their foreign language study in the college or university since the three years of study is barely more than the minimal college entrance requirement. This points to a need for careful articulation between the high school and the university.

A Level 1, 2, 3 sequence in high school can provide an opportunity for students who have studied a foreign language somewhere else in junior high school to add another language in their program at the high school level.

5. Employ only well-trained FL teachers whose major interest is language teaching and who are motivated toward perfecting their own fluency and acquiring new techniques of language instruction.

6. Select new teaching materials on the basis of teaching goals continually agreed upon by district and school committees and in consultation with available resource people.

7. Involve FL teachers in all decisions concerning selection of language, scope, and sequence texts and materials.

8. Provide a district coordinator or supervisor who has a competent foreign language background and who is directly responsible for supervision and promotion of the program. If budgets do not allow for a full-time supervisor, an experienced, competent FL teacher in the district can be given the responsibility of assisting beginning teachers.

9. To the extent possible, avoid excessively large language classes, ideally not exceeding a maximum of twenty-five students at the secondary level. Fifteen to twenty would be better, allowing the teacher to give one-on-one attention to the development of students' speaking skills in the language.

10. A class schedule of seven or more periods provides the best opportunity for the maximum number of students to study a foreign language.

Other Important Administrative Questions. In developing a foreign language program, administrators should ask such questions as:

1. Is the curriculum flexible enough and are there sufficient periods in the school day to allow students to enroll in foreign language classes without difficulty in scheduling?

2. Has provision been made for continuity of instruction from its beginning through grade 12 so that students may develop *real* proficiency in the language, including plans for long sequences, allowing students the opportunity to study at least three years, preferably six, and helping teachers and students to avoid the dropout problem?

3. Is the program well-articulated and coordinated between levels in any given school and/or between elementary and junior high, between junior high and senior high, and between senior high schools and college?

4. Is a variety of assessment techniques and instruments used, such as surveys, case studies, interviews, contests, publications, reporting, and observation?

5. Are the preparation and skills of the FL teaching staff adequate to meet the objectives of the program?

6. Does the school system promote in-service training, evening courses, summer institutes, and travel abroad, as well as opportunities to attend and participate in regional and national FL conferences, and provide compensation for teachers engaging in such activities?

7. Is adequate supervision given the program to insure appropriate and effective instruction?

8. Are parents apprised of the developing foreign language program?

9. Have sufficient space, materials, and equipment—computers, audio-visual equipment, foreign language periodicals, books, realia, and the like—been provided for teachers to create a varied and stimulating program and to accommodate individual differences?

10. Are provisions made for assessment and implementation of new developments and materials in the field of foreign languages as well as for overcoming existing weakness and resistance to change?

Relationships with the teacher. The administrators have the responsibility of assuring teachers a situation that will provide the highest professional growth. Teachers work most effectively when they have:

1. Time to keep informed about the latest research, programs, and new materials in their field.
2. Time to work individually with students.
3. Time to prepare suitable classroom and laboratory materials.
4. Time to visit other schools with similar programs.
5. Time to participate in study groups and workshops.
6. Time to develop extracurricular activities such as language clubs and plays.
7. Time and financial assistance to attend professional meetings.
8. A budget for purchase of audiovisual materials, films, slides, foreign language newspapers and magazines.
9. Encouragement to participate in summer workshops, language institutions, and to travel to countries and areas where the language they teach is spoken.

Importance of foreign language study. Political and technological developments in the last few decades have necessitated a complete modification in foreign language instruction in all facets of language learning with emphasis on oral communication. Countries and people are now only hours distant by travel, not weeks or months. Politically, peoples are clamoring for independence, higher living standards, and are looking to world powers for information and help. These developments have thrust on citizens of the United States exacting responsibilities that cannot be met until lines of communication are established. In order to correct the language deficiency in our society, it is now necessary for the American school system to achieve a great deal more in foreign language instruction than ever before attempted. If our nation is to rise to the challenge of fostering intercultural understanding including effective use of communication skills, foreign language instruction must be offered to this nation's youth. Americans can no longer insist that other people learn English in order that communication can take place.

The following facts should be considered when setting up programs for FL study.

1. Language study helps students to become more articulate, broadens students' cultural and intellectual horizons, and increases respect and tolerance for ideas, values, and achievements of a foreign culture.

2. Many colleges and universities have instituted, restored, and increased their requirements in foreign language, both for admission and for graduation.

3. All students should have the opportunity to elect foreign language study and to continue it as long as their interest and ability permit.

4. Students should begin language learning at an early age. The advantages of an earlier start are greater ease in learning and the chance to develop near-native proficiency in speaking. However, students can start at any age and enjoy certain advantages.

5. Students entering the secondary schools from an elementary school foreign language program should be given the opportunity to continue in the same language through at least a four-year sequence without interruption.

6. It is important to identify students who are exceptionally capable in language learning in order to give them the time to become linguists or other language specialists.

7. Since students may eventually become our national leaders, they need a high level of foreign language competency and should be encouraged to study foreign languages.

8. Students who are native speakers of a foreign language taught in schools do not benefit from the usual beginning courses designed for English-speaking students. Such students should, therefore, be encouraged to take foreign language classes designed for their special needs.

9. The particular foreign language which a student studies in school is a matter of individual motivation based on such considerations as which languages are available, family preference, community background, vocational interest, travel opportunities, and the like.

10. Administrators should neither suggest nor imply that one foreign language is easier to learn than another, or that one language has greater social acceptance or appeal.

11. Students should not be permitted to "shop" the language department if they initially experience problems—generally students should stay with the language they started. Too much is lost if students keep starting over.

12. The administrator is encouraged to consult with the foreign language teachers on all matters concerning the foreign language program.

Source: *Utah Administrators' Conference on Foreign Language Programs*, held at Brigham Young University, directed by Dr. James S. Taylor

APPENDIX B

A COUNSELOR'S GUIDE TO SUPPORTING AN EFFECTIVE FOREIGN LANGUAGE PROGRAM

The Counselor's Role in Supporting Foreign Language Programs. The counselor is in a crucial position to help a Foreign Language program grow and develop. Too often the counselors are not aware of all the ramifications of FL studies and the many possibilities for application intrinsically and extrinsically. The following will be of help to you:

Importance of foreign language study. Political and technological developments in the last few decades have necessitated a complete modification in foreign language instruction in all facets of language learning with emphasis on oral communication. Countries and people are now only hours distant by travel, not weeks or months. Politically, peoples are clamoring for independence, higher living standards, and are looking to world powers for information and help. These developments have thrust on citizens of the United States exacting responsibilities that cannot be met until lines of communication are established. In order to correct the language deficiency in our society, it is now necessary for the American school system to achieve a great deal more in foreign language instruction than ever before attempted. If our nation is to rise to the challenge of fostering intercultural understanding including effective use of communication skills, foreign language instruction must be offered to this nation's youth. Americans can no longer insist that other people learn English in order that communication can take place.

The following facts should be considered when counseling students about FL study:

1. Language study helps students to become more articulate, broadens students' cultural and intellectual horizons, and increases respect and tolerance for ideas, values, and achievements of a foreign culture.

2. Many colleges and universities have instituted, restored, and increased their requirements in foreign language, both for admission and for degrees.

3. All students should have the opportunity to elect foreign language study and to continue it as long as their interest and ability permit. Even students with physical or learning disabilities should not automatically be excluded from foreign language classes. Recent research has shown that most students classified with disabilities can succeed in learning a foreign language.

4. Students should begin language learning at an early age. The advantages of an earlier start are greater ease in learning and the chance to develop near-native proficiency in speaking. However, students can start at any age and enjoy certain advantages.

5. Students entering the secondary schools from an elementary school foreign language program should be given the opportunity to continue in the same language through at least a four-year sequence without interruption.

6. It is important to identify students who are exceptionally capable in language learning in order to give them the time to become linguists or other language specialists.

7. Since students may eventually become our national leaders, they need a high level of foreign language competency and should be encouraged to study foreign languages.

8. Students who are native speakers or "heritage speakers" of a foreign language taught in schools do not benefit from the usual beginning courses designed for English-speaking students. Such students should, therefore, be encouraged to take foreign language classes designed for their special needs. If there is a sufficient number of these students, the school should consider creating separate classes for them. Research shows that learning literacy skills in their native language can actually improve these students' academic work in English as well.

9. The particular foreign language which a student studies in school is a matter of individual motivation based on such considerations as which languages are available, family preference, community background, vocational interest, travel opportunities, and the like.

10. Counselors should be careful not to suggest or imply that one foreign language is easier to learn than another, or that one language has greater social acceptance or appeal.

11. Students should not be permitted to "shop" the language department if they initially experience problems—generally students should stay with the language they started. Too much is lost if students keep starting over.

12. Counselors should consult with the foreign language teachers on all matters concerning the foreign language program.

APPENDIX C

BOOKLETS FOR SPANISH TEACHERS
By James S. Taylor and Others

Materiales para animar la clase de español (Techniques and materials for teaching the class in Spanish, "Features of the week", using humor in the classroom, traditional poetry and verses, a collection of "warm-ups" with numerous models, and Jaime Sastre's source list for finding materials .)

Me gusta jugar (A collection of motivating games for practicing Spanish skills.)

Me gusta cantar (A revision of *Canciones, cultura y gramática*. Techniques for using songs in the Spanish class, many examples of a variety of songs and how to teach them, and an extensive list of songs to practice grammatical and cultural concepts and where to find them. Also includes visual aid examples.)

Me gusta conversar (A revision of *Simulaciones y actividades de conversación para la clase de español*, including many Task Performance Activities [TPA].)

Me gusta actuar (A revision of *Obras teatrales para la clase de español*. A collection of three levels of short and humorous skits and plays for Spanish classes.)

Dynamic Activities for Practicing Spanish Grammar (An extensive collection of dynamic, interactive, oral practice activities for almost every grammatical concept in the Spanish language. Includes practice models and visuals.)

Me gusta comer (A booklet with suggestions and techniques for including the cuisine of Hispanic countries in the Spanish class. Includes simple recipes that can be prepared by teachers and students.)

Me gusta celebrar (A booklet with ideas and materials that can be used in activities in celebrating holidays and special festive days in the Spanish class, such *as Día de las brujas, Día de dar gracias, Navidad, 5 de mayo*, etc. Includes vocabulary lists and visuals for teaching, games and activities.)

Dilo con sabor (A program for helping individuals at all levels make their Spanish more colorful and interesting.)

Me gusta hablar español. (An approach to teaching Spanish to children, with materials and sample lesson plans.)

cultura, Cultura y kultura (Samples of different types of cultural concepts ["small c," "Big C," and big "K" cultures] which can be taught in a Spanish class, with techniques for teaching them, a collection of over 100 culture capsules, and a list of over 1,000 more.)